MW01134506

COMPLEX LITIGATION AND ITS ALTERNATIVES

SECOND EDITION

JAY TIDMARSH
Judge James J. Clynes, Jr., Professor of Law
Notre Dame Law School

ROGER H. TRANGSRUD
James F. Humphreys Professor of Complex
Litigation and Civil Procedure
The George Washington University Law School

CONCEPTS AND INSIGHTS SERIES®

444 Cedar Street, Suite 700
St. Paul, MN 55101
1-877-888-1330

Printed in the United States of America

ISBN: 978-1-59941-065-4

To Mom and in memory of Dad

— J.T.

To Darryl and Cindy

— R.H.T.

PREFACE

When we wrote the first edition of this *Concepts and Insights* book fifteen years ago, we entitled it *Complex Litigation: Problems in Advanced Civil Procedure*. Complex litigation presented a "problem" because the adjudicatory system that had been established for ordinary litigation often broke down under the demands of mass injury and redress. In studying complex litigation, students were simultaneously engaging in a critique of the ordinary processes of litigation, and being asked whether the ordinary system should be reformed to accommodate the needs of the "big case."

Much has changed in this field in the past decade and a half. To reflect those changes, we have also changed the title of the book. The fundamental problem that this book addresses—how should society respond to problems of mass injury?—remains the same. But the answer that the legal system has provided has changed somewhat in recent years. Litigation still remains a principal vehicle for resolving mass disputes, but the techniques that courts can use have shifted as the result of changes in both statutory law and judicial precedent. The real growth in recent years, however, has come from competitors to private litigation: arbitration, regulatory and criminal actions by governments, and even compensation funds sponsored by potential defendants.

In this new edition, we maintain a focus on the litigation process, whose framework is necessary for understanding alternatives to litigation. Initially, the principal challenges for most mass disputes are whether, when, and how to aggregate related cases in a single courtroom, so the book opens with chapters devoted to aggregation techniques. Traditionally, once the claim and party structure is established, a case proceeds through the pretrial process and perhaps to trial and a remedial phase. Because complex cases might also wend along this path, all these topics are also covered in this edition.

Increasingly, however, mass disputes exit the litigation system by means of settlements that establish structures resembling administrative compensation schemes. And many disputes never enter the litigation system at all, as corporations require consumers to forego group litigation in return for individual arbitration or agree to mass settlement structures before individual litigation commences. Because of the rise of these approaches, this new edition devotes more attention to settlement, arbitration, and other alternatives to private litigation.

In addition to a somewhat shifted focus, this edition also tries a new approach to conveying the material. Our prior edition was all text, a traditional treatise meant principally for students. This edition is something of a hybrid between a casebook, a student treatise, and a research tool for lawyers and judges. While we still maintain the textual focus, we also include occasional problems and questions so that students can test their comprehension of the material. For professors who are interested, we also have available a set of edited cases that can be taught in conjunction with this book, thus dispensing with the need for a traditional casebook. For practitioners, judges, and scholars, we include footnotes providing cases and other sources as a starting point for research. We also included some practical pointers, especially when they illustrated a larger theme. In balancing readability against thoroughness, however, we found it necessary to omit many cases, as well as wonderful practical and scholarly literature, that have shaped our thinking.

Complex litigation is an ever-evolving field. We captured major developments as recent as January, 2018. Inevitably, however, the law will continue to change.

We thank those who were instrumental in bringing this manuscript to press. Ryan Pfeiffer, Tessa Boury, and Staci Herr of Foundation Press were patient editors. Our research assistants, Stacey (Wagner) Callaghan, Stephen Cord, Ran Xu, and David Spicer were excellent. Lu Ann Nate provided invaluable assistance in helping to prepare the manuscript and proofreading.

Our goal has been to create a text that introduces law students and lay readers to the difficulties posed by mass litigation, while maintaining the sophistication necessary for judges, practitioners, and scholars. We welcome your comments.

Notre Dame, Indiana
Washington, D.C.
February, 2018

SUMMARY OF CONTENTS

PART 4. THE REMEDIAL PHASE

TABLE OF CONTENTS

COMPLEX LITIGATION AND ITS ALTERNATIVES

SECOND EDITION

INTRODUCTION: THE PROBLEM(S) OF COMPLEX LITIGATION

If you have picked up this book to learn something about complex litigation, you might reasonably expect the book to begin with a definition of "complex litigation." Unfortunately, you are going to be disappointed. Although judges, lawyers, and scholars all agree that "complex civil litigation" exists, there is no commonly agreed meaning of the term.

Instead of providing a formal (and probably contentious) definition, we begin with the easier task of identifying the problems that complex litigation poses—a subject on which there is widespread agreement. To do so, we first step back to consider the structure of American civil litigation.

The American Civil-Justice System

The American civil-justice system operates on a number of foundational principles and assumptions. Many of them are not unique to American legal culture. For instance, nearly all legal systems aim for the fair, accurate, efficient, and final resolution of disputes, and seek to respect the dignity of the participants in the process. They seek to achieve these goals by ensuring that reason has a principal role to play in determining the law and the facts, and in applying the law to the facts. But the way in which the American system gives effect to these universal impulses is in a number of regards distinct. Let us highlight five principles and assumptions that underlie the American approach and that bear directly on the problem of complex litigation.

First, American litigation is decentralized: power over lawsuits is shared broadly rather than concentrated. Among the major features of this dispersion of power are:

- *Adversarialism*. American procedure is adversarial—the most adversarial in the world. In the classic adversarial model, a person is represented by a lawyer of her choosing. The lawyer presents evidence and shapes arguments tailored to the client's legal situation. We sometimes call this the "day in court" ideal: every person is entitled to her day in court, and to make basic decisions such as whether to sue, when to sue, where to sue, with whom to sue, against whom to bring suit, and which claims or defenses to assert. An adversarial system places significant responsibility on the litigants and their lawyers to shape and push the case forward to conclusion—tasks often performed by the judge in other legal systems. The judge, on the other hand, is expected to remain passive (until the parties ask the court to act) and neutral.

- *Federalism*. Rather than employing a single system of courts, the American system uses a dual system—state and federal—to adjudicate disputes. Of the two, the federal system is far smaller; its jurisdiction to hear cases is limited and often overlaps with that of the state courts. Within each court system, more than one court is often able to hear a case. A plaintiff often has a choice of courts within which to file a case, thus diffusing adjudicatory power between the state and federal governments and among the states.
- *Jury trial*. Although judges will declare the law in all cases and will also determine the facts in some cases, in many trials a jury of lay people listens to the evidence and determine the facts. A judge cannot disturb the jury's factual determinations as long as they are within the range of reason.

Second, parties may assert as many claims or defenses as they have in a single lawsuit; parties are not limited to picking only one claim or defense. Relatedly, additional plaintiffs and defendants can be joined together in a single suit as long as it is efficient to do so. The liberal joinder of claims, defenses, and parties can be roughly captured by the word "transactionalism": the ability to resolve all disputes that arise out of a set of related factual events or occurrences in one lawsuit.

Third, the system is "trans-substantive": the same procedural rules apply regardless of the nature of the dispute. This approach is the opposite of common-law procedure, in which the procedural rules used to resolve one legal theory might not apply to another theory. Today one set of rules fits all claims.

Fourth, the goal of litigation is to resolve the case "on the merits." That may seem an obvious assumption—as well as the goal of every civil-justice system. But "on the merits" has a particular meaning in the American context. In days of yore, the common law insisted on strict enforcement of its substantive and procedural rules; it rarely bent its rules to achieve a fair result in an individual case. The modern system has the opposite orientation: procedural rules are never supposed to get in the way of deciding the merits of each dispute. Toward that end, the system does not expect the *pleadings* that commence the case to say very much, instead relying on a *disclosure-and-discovery* process that allows the parties to get all the information they need to make their strongest arguments and to make fully informed decisions about whether to settle. The "on the merits" orientation has also led to the creation of procedural rules that give judges broad discretion to shape the dispute-resolution process to the needs of a particular case. In short, procedural rules—the rules by which disputes are resolved—are seen as the "handmaid of justice" rather than a roadblock to the accurate enforcement of the parties' rights and obligations.

Finally, litigation should be efficient, in the sense that the total costs of the litigation process should be kept to their lowest level. Costs in litigation come principally in two forms. The first and most obvious cost is the direct cost of litigation: the lawyers' fees, the costs of discovery, the costs of judicial time, and so on. The second is the cost of error. When a claim is decided incorrectly, it is not only a cost to the losing party but also a cost to society: people are less likely to engage in risky but socially beneficial behavior if they cannot trust the judicial system to vindicate their conduct. Direct costs and error costs are often inversely related: the more that the court and parties invest in litigation, the less likely it is that the court's decision will be erroneous; and vice versa. In social-welfare terms, the broad goal is to minimize the cost of harms caused by the actors' conduct, the cost of preventing those harms, and transaction costs such as litigation costs.[1] Often, although not always, achieving this goal means keeping the combination of the direct costs of litigation and error costs from litigation at their minimum. In colloquial terms, the outputs of the legal system should be reasonably accurate but also reasonably cheap.

Different sources of legal authority give shape to these foundational principles. The United States Constitution—in particular, Article III, which establishes the scope of federal "judicial Power"; the Due Process Clauses of the Fifth and Fourteenth Amendments; and the Seventh Amendment's right to civil jury trial—is a critical starting point. But federal and state statutes, federal and state procedural codes (the Federal Rules of Civil Procedure and their state-court counterparts), and common-law rulemaking put most of the flesh on the constitutional skeleton.

As lawmakers and rulemakers fill in the details of the American system, they face an inevitable problem: It is impossible to meet every goal in full. To take an extreme example, a very cheap way to resolve disputes is to flip a coin; but the coin flip's wonderful efficiency runs afoul of the goal of accurate decision-making (as well as the due-process requirement of reasoned adjudication). The details of the American civil-justice system represent a compromise among competing policies. But these policy choices tell only part of

---

1 *See* GUIDO CALABRESI, THE COSTS OF ACCIDENTS (1970).

the story. The American system is a product of historical practice as much as conscious design.

The Problem of Complex Litigation

Certain types of cases expose the cracks, gaps, or tensions in a civil-justice system designed in accordance with these assumptions. These cases have at least one of the following characteristics:

- *A large number of potential parties and claims.* In some cases a large number of potential plaintiffs and defendants, who can assert an array of claims and defenses, exist. Think, for instance, of a mass injury such as an airplane crash or exposure to asbestos, or the broad harm that can be caused by fraudulent statements made in connection with the purchase or sale of securities in publicly traded companies. The transactional assumption would often allow these claims to be brought together. But with an adversarial approach, each plaintiff controls his or her own case, including such important decisions as who to join with, who to sue, what claims to bring, and where to sue. If litigation decisions are left to each individual, the dispersion of judicial authority and the lawyers' jockeying for legal advantage will result in the cases being diffused geographically, and sometimes temporally, across multiple federal and state courts; as a result, the same issues would be litigated time and again, resulting in significant inefficiencies and conflicting judgments. In other cases—those in which individual recoveries are small—leaving litigation decisions to each individual may mean that no one will sue, and wrongdoers can get away with inflicting harm that may be small in the individual instance but massive in the aggregate.

- *A large quantity of information and issues.* Some cases involve vast quantities of information, often technical in nature. For example, a single antitrust or patent case may involve millions of pages of documents and electronic communications. A mass tort may involve thousands of pages of medical records per victim. Under our "on the merits" orientation, the parties are entitled to discover this information, as long as it is relevant and non-privileged. The difficulties presented by massive quantities of information are principally three-fold. The first is the difficulty of gathering information in a cost-effective manner. The second is the problem of comprehending information—both for the lawyers who must digest all the information they receive and for the factfinder, whether judge or jury. Third, large quantities of information produce large numbers of factual and legal issues, which are often very knotty to resolve.

- *Difficulty in providing effective redress.* Delivering the right remedy to each victim lies at the heart of any litigation system. In some cases, determining the precise remedy is challenging. For instance, when a large number of victims exist, determining the correct remedy can be cost-prohibitive, especially when the harm suffered by any individual is small. Similarly, in school-desegregation or employment-discrimination cases, a proper remedy requires alterations in institutions and cultures that are often resistant, if not impervious, to structural change. American courts are not generally seen as political actors, but institutional-reform litigation can thrust them uncomfortably into this new role.

Cases that present at least one of these characteristics are usually regarded as "complex." Many complex cases possess two or even all three of these features. For instance, large numbers of parties and claims often mean large quantities of information and difficulties in providing individualized redress.

Many of the causes of complexity in litigation lie beyond the litigation system. Among them are the rise of a mass-consumer society in which a single corporate decision can harm myriad individuals; an expansive system of legal rights; and a culture in which litigants are willing to use the court system to challenge behavior they deem unlawful. To some extent, however, the structure of the American litigation system is itself a cause of complexity. The transactional principle tends to make the aggregation of large numbers of parties and claims in one case possible; the desire to resolve each case on its individual merits leads to a disclosure-and-discovery system in which it is possible to seek massive quantities of information; and due process and the goal of resolving disputes on their merits lead to a commitment to provide individually tailored relief.

Imperfect Solutions

Various solutions can address some of the difficulties that complex cases pose. Parties can be forced to litigate together in a single forum, rather than in disparate forums across the country. The ability to discover information or assert multiple claims can be curtailed. Rather than lay jurors, factfinders possessing fewer comprehension difficulties can be employed.

But these solutions present their own problems, not the least of which is the friction they create with foundational principles. Forcing parties into a single lawsuit runs afoul of the adversarial ideal, and perhaps federalism concerns as well. Trying a patent-infringement claim to a group of expert engineers may run afoul of the right to a jury trial of one's peers. Problems in providing a remedy can be solved by determining the total harm caused and then giving every plaintiff an equal amount of money (or even more radically, giving the money to a worthy charity); but this approach belies the goal of deciding each case on its merits.

Some difficulties that complex cases pose are intractable, defying any solution. For instance, a lawsuit cannot change the cultural attitudes on which a successful remedy might depend. Nor can a lawsuit change the basic structure of the American mass-production economy.

Complex litigation, therefore, requires tradeoffs and a frank recognition that perfect justice is not possible. Because courts cannot achieve fully all the goals of the civil-justice system, the question is how much courts can, or should, give on one foundational principle or another. Engaging in these necessary tradeoffs, however, brings concerns for equality of treatment to center stage. Can we countenance a two-tiered system of justice—one for the ordinary litigant (who retains control of the case and obtains an individually styled remedy) and one for the victim of a mass wrong?

Procedure and Outcome

Behind this question lies an important point about the nature of procedural rules. Process affects outcome. In one sense, this is obvious. If you put the frosting into the cake batter before baking, you get a different result than if you put the frosting onto the cake after the batter has baked. Procedural rules are the same. When you choose one set of procedures to resolve a case (say, rules that give the parties very little right to discover relevant information), you are likely to get an outcome different from the one you would get with a different set of procedures (say, rules that allow broad access to relevant information). For now, it is not important to know which rules are "better" in some global sense; it is enough to appreciate that certain procedural choices are likely to have certain predictable influences on outcome. We will occasionally describe experimental or other data about the ways in which some procedural choices that seem responsive to the problems of complex litigation can also be expected to influence the outcome in favor of one party or the other. Procedural rules are not outcome-neutral, and you should pay close attention to the consequences of procedural choices in complex litigation.

The relationship between procedure and outcome has another dimension. People who are pragmatic—as many successful judges and lawyers are—care a lot about arriving at a good substantive outcome. One way to get a good outcome is to manipulate procedural rules. But how we act can sometimes be as important as the outcome of our actions. You might want a particular outcome (say, an A on a final exam), but you would not undertake a certain procedure (say, hacking into your professor's computer) to attain that result. Procedural rules have value independent of the outcomes that they produce—such as ensuring the right to participate in decisions affecting litigants' lives, enhancing litigants' autonomy and dignity, advancing equality, and limiting governmental power. In finding the best way to resolve a particular problem in a complex case, judges and lawyers should certainly focus on attaining a good substantive outcome for affected parties. When that outcome requires changes in traditional procedural rules, they should also be attentive to the sacrifice of procedural values that such a change would entail.

A Final Question

Complex litigation also poses another large question: Should we use courts to resolve large social disputes? Writing sixty years ago, just as the phenomenon of complex litigation was first emerging, Professor Lon Fuller argued that certain types of cases—those that he labeled "polycentric"—could not be resolved through adjudication.[2] Adjudication requires the parties to be able to participate in the decision-making process through reasoned proofs and arguments; and for polycentric disputes, it is impossible for all the persons affected by the case to participate in this fashion. For these cases, Fuller argued, the only legitimate ways to resolve the cases were through either the political process or contract.

In an equally famous article written twenty years later, Professor Abram Chayes challenged Fuller's analysis.[3] By then courts had accumulated significant experience in desegregation and other litigation involving major institutions. As Chayes showed, courts were in fact resolving polycentric disputes. To do so, however, judges had abandoned the traditional adversarial model in favor of a "public law" approach in which the judge exercised more control over

---

[2] Lon L. Fuller, *The Forms and Limits of Adjudication*, 92 HARV. L. REV. 353 (1978). Although the article was widely known and cited, Professor Fuller never completed it. The article was ultimately published in unfinished form after his death.

[3] Abram Chayes, *The Role of the Judge in Public Law Litigation*, 89 HARV. L. REV. 1281 (1976).

the case, especially during the remedial phase. Chayes defended the legitimacy of this move.

Although neither used the word "complex," Fuller's "polycentric" litigation and Chayes's "public law" litigation describe major aspects of the phenomenon that we today call "complex litigation." Their interlocking critiques of each other's position still define the field and the problems that complex litigation poses today. Many of the purported solutions to complex litigation have required the abandonment of the passive, reactive judge of adversarial theory—and have turned the judge into a far more powerful political actor, exactly as Professor Chayes described. Whether the solution is to employ a non-traditional litigation device such as a class action or a non-litigation device such as a compensation plan run by a defendant, novel techniques have replaced traditional individualized adjudication, exactly as Professor Fuller predicted. Whether the development of these alternatives to traditional adjudication are positive or disconcerting is the most fundamental question in complex civil litigation.

The Roadmap for This Book

At this point we turn from the broad outlines of complex litigation to the specific ways in which the problem of complexity manifests itself, the various legal doctrines that can help (or hinder) a court in addressing complexity, and the potential alternatives to litigation. The first part of the book explores the first problem of complex litigation: the difficulties presented by a large number of parties. It explores the legal mechanisms by which a court can "aggregate" related claims, as well as the important limits on a court's ability to do so. Because it fits well thematically at this point, the first part also examines alternatives to adjudication—some of which (like settlement class actions) operate as adjuncts to the judicial system and some of which (like arbitration) operate outside of the judicial system.

The second and third parts of the book examine the second problem: the existence of vast quantities of information. It details the ways in which a court deals with problems of vast information first during the pretrial and then during the trial phase of a case.

Part Four turns to the third manifestation of complexity: the problem of determining and implementing remedies. It also explores a topic that often drives complex litigation as a practical matter: attorney's fees.

As you study specific doctrines, you should bear in mind that complex litigation is something of a seamless web: end-of-the-day matters such as trial management or remedial difficulties often influence theoretically antecedent issues about whether (and how) to aggregate claims and structure the pretrial process. Thus, although we begin with the logically primary question of the ways in which courts can aggregate claims, you should reserve judgment on the wisdom of a particular aggregation technique until you see the ways in which courts address the pretrial, trial, and remedial problems that aggregated cases can present *and* the viability of alternatives to litigation.

Moreover, as you encounter new procedural doctrines or techniques, you should always ask what values or goals a particular doctrine or technique advances, as well as the values or goals it retards. You should ask whether the particular doctrine or technique that is being used to resolve some manifestation of complexity creates unjustified inequalities among similarly situated litigants; whether it vests too much power in a government official (the judge); and whether, given the legal doctrines and techniques on offer, the world of politics or contract would be a better (or worse) place to resolve the dispute.

Part 1

AGGREGATING CASES

This Part assumes that the conduct of a defendant (or group of defendants) has caused harm to a large number of people. The questions that it considers are:

- Whether the dispute between the plaintiffs and defendants should be resolved in one lawsuit (or at least a limited number of lawsuits);
- If so, what procedural techniques might accomplish this type of resolution; and
- What limits exist on our ability to use these techniques to aggregate related claims and cases.

"Aggregation" has a more precise definition that we come to at the end of Chapter One, but for now let's use the word to describe any process that allows a single court to resolve all the claims of one or more plaintiffs against one or more defendants. Aggregation can be voluntary (the plaintiffs can agree to aggregate their cases) or involuntary (in the sense that one or more plaintiffs are required, by virtue of rules of procedure, to litigate their claims either with other plaintiffs with whom they have not voluntarily joined or in a forum not of their choosing).

Aggregation of either type has benefits and drawbacks. Involuntary aggregation also generates a set of unique additional concerns. Chapter One examines the general benefits and costs of aggregation and also introduces vocabulary that cuts across all aggregation techniques. With this foundation we examine the particulars of aggregation doctrine. Chapters Two through Five consider the principal approaches to aggregation: joinder, consolidation, stays, and preclusion. Chapter Six turns to the most powerful device to prevent repetitive relitigation: class actions. Chapter Seven examines bankruptcy, as well as other litigation and non-litigation options to resolve mass disputes. Finally, Chapter Eight considers the choice-of-law difficulties that aggregation can cause—difficulties that both affect the ability of courts to aggregate cases and spill forward to create pretrial, trial, and remedial problems that the remaining parts of this book consider.

Chapter 1

SOME VOCABULARY AND BASIC PRINCIPLES

Before we consider the specifics of aggregation, this Chapter stops to explain some basic concepts and terms of art that are central to the discussion in the following chapters. The Chapter begins with the arguments for and against aggregating a large-scale dispute into a limited number of lawsuits. Arguments about using specific aggregation methods often return to these fundamental benefits and costs. As a result, before examining particular devices, a good grasp of the arguments that drive the doctrine is essential.

Still with the goal of providing the fundamental framework for understanding the law of aggregation, the Chapter next discusses in general terms the jurisdictional and other limits that make aggregation difficult. It closes with a more precise definition of aggregation, and an overview of the types of techniques that courts have used to reduce the repetitive litigation of related cases. This overview also provides a roadmap for the chapters that follow.

A. Benefits of Aggregation

Aggregation has five major benefits.

1. Cost Internalization

The first benefit is *cost internalization*, or *deterrence*. From an economic point of view, the law should force wrongdoers to pay for ("internalize") all the harm that they cause. Facing full cost internalization for their wrongs, rational economic actors have an incentive to take the proper amount of care when deciding how to act. For example, assume that a credit-card company that takes no care overcharges each of 1,000 customers by $1,000, for a total of $1 million in damage to the cardholders (and $1 million in wrongful profit to the company). Assume further that if the defendant had taken $100,000 in care, no overcharges would have resulted. It is socially optimal for the defendant to take care; an expense of $100,000 saves harm of $1 million. Further assume that, due to the costliness of litigation, only five customers will sue. In this scenario, the company has no reason to take care. It is cheaper to pay $5,000 in damages than to take $100,000 in care, even though society is worse off. Aggregating the cardholders' claims, so that the company faces a realistic threat of a $1 million judgment, acts to deter its wrongdoing.

The deterrence argument has special salience in *negative-value* or *small-stakes* cases: cases in which the value of the individual recovery is smaller than the costs of bringing a case. Suppose that the same credit-card company cheats 1 million customers out of $1 apiece; had it taken precautions costing $100,000, it could have avoided all harm. This a textbook example of a negative-value case. Few people (and none who are economically rational) will go to court for $1; certainly no lawyer will take such a case. In a world without aggregation devices, the credit-card company has reason to cheat each customer out of $1 rather than to spend $100,000 in precautions. In a world with such devices, however, the prospect of a $1 million judgment is likely to induce the company to invest $100,000 in precautions, thus avoiding a social loss.

As we will see, this negative-value rationale, which is a species of the cost-internalization rationale, has dominated American thought about certain aggregations devices—particularly class actions—for twenty years. Note that the connection between cost internalization and aggregation is not airtight. Other mechanisms, such as a $1 million fine leveled against the credit-card company by a regulatory agency, provide the same deterrence, even though they may not provide compensation to the victims. Under the cost-internalization rationale, aggregation has only instrumental value; if other mechanisms provide better deterrence at a cheaper price, they should be preferred. Compensation to victims is beside the point.

2. Lowering Transaction Costs

Aggregation can lower transaction costs, in particular the costs of litigating cases. Transaction costs are inevitable, but as the Introduction discussed, a good rule of thumb is to keep litigation costs as low as possible in order to reduce their distorting effect on socially useful conduct.[4] And aggregation can do exactly that. Aggregation can reduce costly repetitive litigation of issues common to all or most of the aggregated claims. By banding claims together, aggregation achieves economies of scale, with the costs of litigation now spread across the group. No rational person will spend $50,000 to recover a $1 claim, but if the $50,000 in litigation expenses can be spread across one million claimants, spending a nickel to make a dollar makes sense. There are also benefits to the defendant, which need not pay the expenses and fees associated with being haled into court and proving the same matters time after time. And the savings in time and labor for the courts and the justice system can also be

---

[4] *See supra* note 1 and accompanying text.

substantial: a single judge can dispense justice in thousands of cases that might otherwise have clogged the dockets of numerous courts.

Lowering transaction costs can feed back into the cost-internalization rationale. Claims that were expensive to litigate separately become more economical to bring, thus enhancing the likelihood of litigation and the deterrent effect on wrongdoers. But the two rationales exist uneasily with each other, at least in the negative-value context. No rational plaintiff with a negative-value claim will bring a lawsuit; therefore, absent aggregation, there are no litigation expenses. By lowering litigation costs per claim, aggregation creates litigation (and litigation costs) where otherwise there would have been none. But recall that litigation expenses are not the only transaction costs in the litigation system. Error costs arise when the legal system fails to enforce rights accurately. Failing to compensate the million credit-card customers for their $1 losses is an error cost of this type: cardholders might engage in fewer credit-card transactions than are socially optimal if the legal system does not provide redress for the credit-card company's misbehavior. In short, while aggregation may create certain transaction costs in negative-value cases, it reduces others.

Whether a given aggregation technique increases or decreases transaction costs is a context-specific question that cannot be answered definitively as a matter of theory. In the cases in which aggregation reduces transaction costs, the reduction is an argument in favor of using an aggregation technique.

3. Equalizing Investment Incentives

When many plaintiffs have related claims, traditional one-on-one litigation has a free-rider problem that discourages optimal investment in litigation by plaintiffs. Assume that a defendant's conduct injures 1,000 victims, each in the amount of $10,000 (thus, the total damage is $10 million). The plaintiffs' cases are essentially identical. Each plaintiff has a 40% chance of winning, but could increase the odds of winning to 90% by investing an extra $50,000 in the case. The rational plaintiff will not spend $50,000, when the payoff for doing so is to raise the value of her claim by only $5,000 (from $4,000 to $9,000). Now, if the plaintiff could spread the additional $50,000 in expenses across the other 999 victims, then the expenditure would be worthwhile; the plaintiff would pay 1/1,000 of the total investment ($50), and get a $5,000 return on the investment. In the American system, however, one plaintiff cannot generally force other potential plaintiffs to contribute to a mutually beneficial litigation expenditure. And some potential plaintiffs may stay on the sidelines, hoping to free-ride off of the expenditures of the remaining plaintiffs. Therefore, as long as the cases remain separate, no plaintiff will spend the money to improve the odds of winning.

The situation is different for the defendant. Suppose that the defendant could spend $100,000 more on the litigation and reduce the plaintiff's chance of winning $10,000 from 40% to 10%. It might seem irrational for the defendant to spend $100,000 just to save $3,000, but it isn't. Facing an expected liability of $4 million (a 40% chance of losing $10 million) without the $100,000 investment but only $1 million (a 10% chance of losing $10 million) with the investment, the defendant's expenditure is justified.

The consequence of differential investment incentives in individual litigation is to skew outcomes in favor of defendants, who have an incentive to invest heavily in outcome-influencing litigation expenses, and against individual victims, who do not. An evident solution to the problem is to equalize the incentives on both sides. One way to do so is to aggregate all the plaintiffs' claims, so that the stakes for both sides (and thus their incentives to invest in litigation) are the same.

4. Buying "Global Peace"

Aggregating all related claims allows one proceeding to end the controversy in one fell swoop, thus avoiding the costs of relitigating common matters time and again. Bringing an early end to a dispute that would otherwise be dispersed across various state and federal jurisdictions has obvious advantages for victims. But it also can benefit defendants. Markets dislike risk, including the risks posed by mass lawsuits. Thus, a corporation facing such litigation can have a difficult time attracting investment or engaging in new initiatives. If the cases can be settled or otherwise resolved in a single proceeding, the company's legal exposure has a finite and known limit. For this reason, American corporations have sometimes seen their market values rise once they announce a *global settlement* (so named not because the case has an international dimension, although it may, but because the resolution of the case is comprehensive, or at least nearly so).

A global resolution of claims can be especially valuable in cases involving *temporal dispersion* of claims. "Temporal dispersion" arises when different plaintiffs suffer harms at different times, so that they will bring their claims at different times. The problem is particularly acute with respect to mass torts involving exposure to a defendant's product; such cases can be spread out over twenty to fifty years. Waiting to aggregate until the claims have almost run their course fails to achieve the economies of aggregation, and may leave those who file later with claims of limited value because the defendant may have exhausted its assets or declared bankruptcy after paying earlier claims. Aggregating earlier in the litigation cycle means that a global resolution will necessarily determine the rights of *future plaintiffs*—a term of art meant to refer to those plaintiffs who have not yet filed suit. A subset of this group is known as the *future future plaintiffs*—a term of art referring to those potential plaintiffs who have not yet suffered an injury (and indeed, may not have yet been exposed to the defendant's deleterious product).[5] Trying to treat those already injured and those whose injuries lie in an uncertain future fairly among themselves can be one of the challenging dimensions of global peace, but such fairness is nearly impossible to achieve in the absence of a comprehensive resolution of claims.

5. Ensuring the Fair Treatment of Alleged Victims

That consideration leads to a final argument often made in favor of aggregation: the ability to deliver an adequate and fair remedy to alleged victims of a defendant's misconduct. One critical task of a civil-justice system, unlike the criminal or regulatory alternatives, is to provide appropriate compensation to the victims of harm. Included within this rationale is the idea of fairness: similarly situated plaintiffs are more likely to be treated equitably among themselves when they are aggregated than when they are separated into a series of individual lawsuits. A known deficiency of individual litigation is horizontal inequity: awards for people with similar injuries are highly variable from state to state, between the state and federal judicial systems, and even from jury to jury in the same courthouse.

Another problem is temporal inequity, which comes in two flavors. The first is unfairness to future plaintiffs. Suppose that the defendant has limited assets of $5 million, and that its actions have hurt 1,000 victims in the amount of $10,000 apiece. With individual litigation, the first 500 victims to sue will receive full compensation, and the next 500 will receive nothing. Therefore, early-filing plaintiffs can deprive later-filing plaintiffs of any realistic remedy. Second, and conversely, suppose that the first plaintiff gets an injunction requiring the defendant to do X. A second plaintiff prefers an injunction requiring the defendant to do Y, and a third plaintiff prefers Z. It may not be possible—or at least it may be prohibitively expensive—for the defendant to meet obligations X, Y, and Z simultaneously. But American law binds neither the second nor the third plaintiff to the result (X) achieved in the first case; they can still seek their own remedy. If a court allows the later-filed cases to proceed, later-filing plaintiffs can either deprive the first plaintiff of a hard-fought victory or whipsaw the defendant by forcing it to do Y or Z in addition to X.

---

[5] The other subset of future plaintiffs is the *present future plaintiffs*: persons who have suffered an injury but have not yet filed suit.

As appealing as achieving equity among victims appears, grounding it in a theory of justice is difficult. Fair and equitable treatment of similarly situated victims is not a principle of general application in American law, which typically allows each victim to pursue an individual remedy. Nor is such a theory easy to tease out of the major Western discussions of justice, none of which is concerned with the unique problems of interpersonal fairness with which modern aggregation deals. Aristotle's analysis of corrective justice did not consider the possible inability of a wrongdoer to compensate every victim fully or the variability in victims' awards due to horizontal or temporal dispersion. Kant's categorical imperative—to treat others as ends, not merely as means—maps onto some aspects of the interpersonal obligations arguably due to fellow victims; but the principle is too far removed from the reality of modern complex litigation to provide practical guidance. Likewise, neither the Millian harm principle—that my right to act ends when I harm you—nor the Millian utility principle—to achieve the greatest good for the greatest number—has anything to say about whether the law should smooth out the variability in value of similar claims. The Rawlsian veil of ignorance provides no clear basis for handling the problem of variability in values.

Likewise, not all variability in claims due to horizontal or temporal dispersion is unjustified: different courts may apply different law, or law may evolve over time. On the assumption that horizontal and temporal inequity is a matter about which we should be concerned, however, aggregation can usefully bring all the interested claimants into one case, thus allowing a single court to smooth out the variability in awards or to hammer out competing interests into a single injunction. Put differently, aggregation can create a type of remedial equity that individual litigation cannot.

B. Drawbacks of Aggregation

Criticisms of aggregation techniques are varied and nuanced. Here we focus on the main arguments, again introducing important vocabulary and concepts that bear on the discussion of specific aggregation techniques in later chapters. Like the arguments favoring aggregation, the arguments against aggregation range from economics to justice to politics.

1. Overdeterring Behavior

As we have just seen, one of the stated benefits of aggregation is their capacity to achieve a full measure of deterrence for illegal behavior. The contrary argument is that aggregation can also overdeter. A simple but limited example arises under some consumer and other statutes that impose statutory-minimum damages (say,

$100), even though the actual harm suffered by any victim is far less. If we aggregate the claims of a million consumers, we have suddenly created a $100 million case—an amount far in excess of actual harm and probably a level of deterrence far in excess of that which the legislature intended.

A more serious overdeterrence concern arises because of the size of an aggregated suit. Because they cannot take the chance that an adverse judgment will impose a very substantial liability on the balance sheet, many companies will settle large-scale cases—even when, they claim, the cases lack merit and their behavior is lawful. Back in the early 1970s, Professor Handler described the class action, which is one aggregation technique, as a form of "legalized blackmail."[6] A quarter of a century later, Judge Posner observed (also in the context of a class action) that aggregation can "forc[e] . . . defendants to stake their companies on the outcome of a single jury trial, or be forced by fear of the risk of bankruptcy to settle even if they have no legal liability."[7]

The overdeterrence criticism is important, but don't overplay it. When a law provides for a compensatory remedy and the victims receive fair value on their claims, the overdeterrence argument is not a concern. A large award does not necessarily imply overdeterrence. People who contend that aggregation abets "legalized blackmail" are often making one of two distinct arguments: first, the threat of such mass litigation deters companies from engaging in legal behavior; or second, aggregation skews the chance of recovery toward plaintiffs, thus forcing defendants to settle claims at inflated prices. The first argument concerns overdeterrence; the second argument concerns excessive transaction costs (specifically error costs).

2. Increasing Transaction Costs

Although a touted strength of aggregation is its capacity to reduce the costs of litigation, aggregation can have the opposite effect. In negative-value cases, there are no litigation expenses in the absence of aggregation because no one would file a claim whose value is less than the cost of its prosecution. (Of course, the absence of enforcement, while saving on direct litigation costs, creates error costs.) Moreover, a defendant facing massive, aggregated litigation may ratchet up its investment in litigation expenditures to match the higher expected value of an aggregated proceeding. Finally, some forms of aggregation impose unique costs not found in ordinary litigation. For instance, in many American class actions, class

---

[6] Milton Handler, *The Shift from Substantive to Procedural Innovations in Antitrust Suits—The Twenty-Third Annual Antitrust Review*, 71 COLUM. L. REV. 1 (1971).

[7] *In re* Rhone-Poulenc Rorer, Inc., 51 F.3d 1293 (7th Cir. 1995).

members must be allowed to *opt out* of (or leave) the class action. To give effect to this right, class members must receive notice of the right. Providing such notice can be expensive.

Aggregation can also increase certain error costs. We just mentioned the blackmail concern: the fear of massive liability may force defendants to pay more to buy global peace than the (arguably frivolous) cases are worth. As we also emphasized, the size of an aggregated settlement isn't by itself the issue; the concern is that aggregation forces the defendant to pay a *peace premium*, over and above the sum total of the individual claims, just to make the aggregated proceeding go away.

Whether a peace premium is a real problem is uncertain at a number of levels. The first level is whether the problem of excessive settlements even exists. Some data show that aggregation is hardly a get-rich-quick scheme, at least for the average plaintiff. One study of securities-fraud class actions revealed that, over the past ten years, the average settlement award amounted to only 2–3% of the estimated damage.[8] A different study showed that, in absolute dollars, the median damage award in American state-court class actions was $350 per class member; in federal court the amount was $517.[9] Moreover, a peace premium (if it exists) may not be a result of error, but rather the claimants' bargaining power to obtain appropriate value for their claims and also to extract some of the savings that the defendant realizes from avoiding the relitigation of common issues. Likewise, a common criticism of aggregation, which we discuss in the following section, is the incentive of those who are in charge of the aggregated proceeding (especially the lawyers) to sell out the claims of the group for dimes on the dollar. If this criticism is true, the real problem of aggregation is not excessively high settlements but excessively low settlements.

The excessive-settlement, or blackmail, rationale also assumes that the value that individual litigation assigns to claims is the true value of those claims, so that any upward distortion that aggregation creates in that value is an error cost. The data on the accuracy of this assumption are mixed. Two experiments have suggested that aggregating cases tends to increase the likelihood that plaintiffs will prevail in the lawsuit but to depress the per-plaintiff award.[10] One

---

8 *See* Cornerstone Research, Securities Class Action Settlements: 2015 Review and Analysis fig. 7 (undated).

9 Thomas E. Willging & Shannon R. Wheatman, *Attorney Choice of Forum in Class Action Litigation: What Difference Does It Make?*, 81 NOTRE DAME L. REV. 591, 639 tbl. 15 (2006).

10 See Irwin A. Horowitz & Kenneth S. Bordens, *The Consolidation of Plaintiffs: The Effects of Number of Plaintiffs on Jurors' Liability Decisions, Damage Awards, and Cognitive Processing of Evidence*, 85 J. APPLIED PSYCHOL. 909 (2000); Irwin A. Horowitz & Kenneth S. Bordens, *The Effects of Outlier Presence, Plaintiff*

explanation for the first result is the nature of human intuition: a factfinder who sees more injuries is likelier to infer that the defendant must have done something wrong. A second explanation is informational overload: the presence of more plaintiffs makes it difficult to absorb the facts of each cases, so the factfinder employs simplifying strategies. Information loading may also explain the second result: factfinders may have difficulty distinguishing among claims and therefore blend cases. The study also found other effects of case aggregation on litigation outcomes. For instance, the existence of an "outlier" case, in which one plaintiff has a claim far stronger than those of other plaintiffs, makes litigation outcomes more variable, with more verdicts for defendants.

These two experiments suggest that, insofar as error costs are concerned, aggregation works at cross-purposes: although aggregation generally increases the odds that plaintiffs will prevail, the average award per plaintiff declines. Whether the two effects cancel each other out is not something that the present data tell us.

In any event, aggregating claims is not the only input affecting case value; so does the timing of aggregation. According to the *maturity thesis* first proposed by Professor McGovern,[11] claims that are temporally dispersed follow a predictable pattern: in the early cases, defendants (who usually have better initial access to evidence) win; as the plaintiffs' bar gets more information and learns how to try the cases better, they achieve breakthrough victories; and finally, as the defendants adjust to these new strategies, the cases reach a level of maturity in which outcomes become more predictable and claims can be valued with greater confidence. If this thesis is true, *when* related claims are aggregated can matter as much as *whether* they are. Aggregate too early, and the defendant benefits; aggregate soon after breakthrough victories, and the plaintiffs benefit. Aggregate once the claims are fully mature, and the legal system suffers some inefficiencies due to repetitive litigation (albeit with better data about the true settlement value of the claims yet to be resolved).

The reality is that the procedures used in a case change the value of a claim. There exists no ideal process that perfectly values every claim. Different processes result in different case values. Claiming that the value achieved in an aggregated proceeding is an error, while the value achieved in individual litigation is correct, reflects a bias in favor of individual litigation. If we start from the

---

Population Size, and Aggregation of Plaintiffs on Simulated Civil Jury Decisions, 12 LAW & HUM. BEHAV. 209 (1988).

[11] *See* Francis E. McGovern, *An Analysis of Mass Torts for Judges*, 73 TEX. L. REV. 1821 (1995).

perspective of aggregation, it is individual litigation that erroneously values claims.

In the end, whether aggregation saves more in transaction costs (principally due to a reduction in relitigation of common issues and in certain error costs) is an empirical question for which existing data provide an inadequate answer, especially across the broad array of potential aggregation techniques. But the concern is an important one to keep in mind as we consider the application of specific techniques in specific scenarios.

3. Creating Agency Costs

Agency costs can arise whenever you have someone else (your agent) look after your interests. Agency costs have long been a concern in corporate behavior: the stockholders want the officers and directors of a company to look after their interests, but officers and directors also have private interests (in large salaries, for example) that may diverge from those of the stockholders (who may prefer smaller salaries). Whenever the ownership of assets is divided from their day-to-day control, the risk exists that the agents who control the assets may use the assets to pursue their own interests to the detriment of the interests of the owners. The agency-cost problem becomes more acute when the principal has limited interest in or ability to monitor the work of the agent.

Scholars have noted the parallels between stockholders and claimants swept up in aggregate litigation.[12] Like stockholders, these claimants turn over day-to-day management and control of their claims to agents: the lawyers and plaintiffs who lead the charge on behalf of the entire group. In theory, these agents work to realize the maximal value for each claimant's claim. In reality, the criticism runs, these agents look after their own interests, using the claims of others to the extent that the claims help them to achieve their own goals (say a higher attorney's fee or a better settlement of their own claims) and sacrificing the claims of others when it is expedient to do so. For example, if the true value of a claim (net of costs) is $100, and the lawyer negotiates its settlement for $30 in return for a hefty attorney's fee, then the agency cost is $70. (Note that, as long as the fee is less than $70, the defendant is happy to be complicit in this arrangement.)

The agency-cost criticism sounds as if it is inconsistent with the first criticism—that aggregate litigation overdeters defendants. Although tension exists between the two critiques, they can co-exist:

---

[12] For an important early article on agency costs in class actions, see Jonathan R. Macey & Geoffrey P. Miller, *The Plaintiffs' Attorney's Role in Class Action and Derivative Litigation: Economic Analysis and Recommendations for Reform*, 58 U. CHI. L. REV. 1 (1991).

if agency costs are high enough, then defendants could be paying too much *and* victims could be receiving too little. The victims' lawyers could be making out like bandits.

The risk of agency costs is a real one. Lawyers who represent a group of claimants often have the single largest stake in the case. For instance, assume that a million credit-card customers have each been duped out of $1. The lawyer representing them in an aggregated proceeding has invested 1,000 hours in the case (with a fair hourly rate being $300 per hour) and has also fronted $50,000 in expenses out of pocket. The lawyer has far more at stake in the case than any victim. When the defendant floats an offer of $400,000 to settle the case and the alternative is to try the case to an uncertain outcome, you can see the pressure that the lawyer is under to agree to the settlement and to persuade the victims to accept it. This settlement might result in only $50,000 for the victims (or five cents on the dollar), but the victims have very little incentive to complain because they wouldn't sue otherwise and five cents is better than nothing. It also isn't worth the effort to complain over ninety-five cents. An unscrupulous lawyer knows that, and may cash out a good deal for himself or herself while hanging the clients out to dry.

Unfortunately, the standard fee arrangements under which lawyers are paid do nothing to lessen the conflict between lawyers and clients. If the lawyer is paid an hourly rate as a fee, the lawyer has an incentive to spend more hours on the case than are reasonably justified. If the lawyer receives a contingency fee, the lawyer often has an incentive to underwork a case. Assume, for instance, that counsel can work 200 hours and achieve a settlement of $300,000. If counsel puts another 200 hours into the case, the value of the settlement will increase to $450,000; and another 200 hours will increase the settlement to $500,000. Finally, assume that the lawyer will either be paid $300 per hour (the going market rate) or a contingency fee of twenty percent of the recovery. If the lawyer charges by the hour, the lawyer will work 600 hours, even though the victims would have preferred that the lawyer stop at 400 hours (because the lawyer's fees for the last 200 hours worked ($60,000) exceed the additional value added to the victims' claims ($50,000), thus costing the victims $10,000). On the other hand, under a contingency fee, the lawyer will want to stop working at 200 hours, because the next 200 hours spent on the case will garner an additional fee of only $30,000 (twenty percent of the additional $150,000 that the second 200 hours earns); $30,000 amounts to an hourly rate of $150, half of the hourly fee that the lawyer could make doing other legal work. Neither the hourly nor the contingency arrangement induces the lawyer to spend the amount of time on the case that is optimal from society's viewpoint: 400 hours.

This hypothetical is stylized, but the concern that it raises is a general one. Although the disparity in incentive between counsel and client exists in any case, the problem is exacerbated in large-scale litigation because of the size of the attorney's stake in the case, the lack of incentive for most victims to monitor the lawyer's behavior, and the victims' lack of legal sophistication.

These realities have led some critics of some aggregation devices to argue that aggregation fosters collusion between victims' lawyers and defendants. Collusion arises when a defendant "bribes" the plaintiff's lawyer by agreeing to pay a generous amount in attorneys' fees in return for the lawyer's agreement to recommend acceptance of an inadequate settlement. Collusion is an extreme form of the general agency-cost problem. It may be a particular risk in cases involving repeat players, where a limited number of plaintiffs' law firms and defense firms capture much of the legal-services market for complex cases and repeatedly interact with each other in a "you scratch my back and I'll scratch yours" manner.

Although not precisely collusion, another manifestation of the same problem arises when different lawyers jockey to represent the victims. For instance, it is not unusual for different lawyers to file class actions on behalf of the same victims for the same conduct. In these cases defendants might conduct a *reverse auction*, pitting counsel in the different actions against each other. They may offer the counsel in the first class action $300,000 to settle, then go to the counsel in the second case and dangle an offer of $275,000. The lawyer in the second case stands to gain nothing in fees if the first case settles, so is under some pressure to agree. The defendant can then go back to the first counsel and drop the offer to $250,000; now the first counsel faces the prospect of no fees if the second case settles for $275,000. The defendant can keep this process going until eventually it gets a bargain-basement price.

There are famous examples of class actions and other aggregated proceedings in which the only people who seem to come out well are the lawyers. The poster child for poorly served clients is Dexter Kamilewicz. In *Hoffman v. BancBoston Mortgage Corp.*, an Alabama state-court class action alleged that a bank incorrectly calculated the amount of escrow surplus for 715,000 mortgagors. The case settled, with each class member becoming entitled to a refund of any escrow surplus held by the bank, less a deduction for attorneys' fees and expenses. The class attorneys received somewhere between $8.5 million and $14 million in fees. Mr. Kamilewicz, one of the class members, opened his monthly bank statement to discover that he had received a $2.91 refund, but that his account had been charged

$91.33 to pay for fees and costs. The class action left Mr. Kamilewicz worse off.[13]

Although stories of collusion and rapacious counsel are rampant among critics of American aggregation, the strongest version of the criticism is overdrawn. Many lawyers try to be faithful agents of their clients, not to line their own pockets. A disparity between what a victim receives and what the lawyer receives is inevitable when the number of victims is large. When viewed as a percentage of recovery, attorneys' fees in class actions typically run between twenty and thirty percent, which is less than the thirty-three to forty percent contingency fee common in individual litigation.

4. Ethical Concerns

Although the problem of the faithless lawyer is often cast in terms of agency costs, another lens through which to view the issue is legal ethics. In the American system, lawyers are ethically obligated to represent each client with competence and vigor. To ensure that each client receives a lawyer's single-minded devotion, a lawyer is required to avoid the simultaneous representation of clients with conflicting interests. When representing a group, however, a lawyer represents victims with similar but not necessarily identical interests. For instance, one client might want an immediate settlement, and another might demand that the defendant be held responsible at trial. Some might want cash now, and others might trade cash today for reforms of the defendant's practices that are valuable in the long run.

American rules of legal ethics were designed for traditional one-on-one litigation. They are inadequate to address the demands placed on lawyers for groups. Some courts and commentators have called for replacing traditional ethical requirements with more realistic ethical rules. One idea is to develop a "communitarian ethic," based on achieving the good of the group. Another idea is to develop a "communicatarian ethic," based on public articulation and defense of the choices made on behalf of the group. Perhaps enhanced democratic participation by members of the group—with the lawyer following majority or supermajority will—could work. Yet another idea is to reconceive the lawyer's "client" as the group, rather than the individual members within the group. All approaches come to the same point: achieving the common good. Of course, "the common good" is a phrase that conceals as much as it reveals. Does it mean that counsel should aim to achieve "the greatest good for the greatest number"—with all the moral freight that this Millian approach entails? Or are there some limits (perhaps based in Aristotelian or

---

13 The history of the case is recounted in *Kamilewicz v. Bank of Boston Corp.*, 92 F.3d 506 (7th Cir. 1996).

Kantian principles) on what the lawyer can do to individuals like Dexter Kamilewicz when pursuing the common good?

The real-world laboratory of moral theory that aggregation provides arises from the fact that lawyers for groups—even selfless lawyers unconcerned about their own bottom lines—cannot perfectly represent the interests of each member of the aggregate.

5. Depriving Individuals of Their "Day in Court"

A fifth criticism of aggregation is its departure from the traditional form of litigation. The traditional American form is sometimes described by the catchphrase "day in court"; all persons with a legal complaint are entitled to submit evidence and argument in support of their claims, while all persons accused of wrongdoing are entitled to rebut those claims with proofs and arguments of their own. In particular, plaintiffs control choices such as whether, when, with whom, against whom, and in which court to bring suit.

As a practical matter, a litigant's "day in court" is more an ideal than a reality. Most people with legitimate claims cannot afford a lawyer to prosecute them. Even when they can, clients usually have little contact with their lawyers, and they exercise little control over the course of litigation. And in the federal system, ninety-nine percent of cases end short of trial. Nevertheless, even though the civil-justice system often falls short, the "day in court" ideal describes the type of justice that the American system strives to deliver.

Behind the "day in court" ideal lies the concept of autonomy: individuals have a right to control important decisions in their lives and their property, of which a legal claim is one species. The ideal also draws on, and is closely linked to, an adversarial approach to litigation. To an extent, the "day in court" ideal also finds reflection in constitutional rights: the Due Process Clauses of the Fifth and Fourteenth Amendments have been read to guarantee litigants both the opportunity to be heard and certain adversarial protections—as well as the right not to be bound by a lawsuit's judgment unless the individual is joined personally in the suit.[14]

Aggregation devices turn this ideal on its head. Individual victims do not make most of the critical litigation decisions. They often do not choose the lawyer who represents them or the rest of the group; in fact, they likely will never meet their lawyer, who knows nothing about their individual circumstances. As we will see, in some

---

[14] *See* Mullane v. Cent. Hanover Bank & Trust Co., 339 U.S. 306 (1950) (right to "notice and opportunity for hearing"); Mathews v. Eldridge, 424 U.S. 319 (1976) (right to adversarial procedures unless their benefits exceed their costs); Martin v. Wilks, 490 U.S. 755 (1989) (right not to be bound to a judgment unless made a party). These due-process guarantees are not absolute. *See, e.g.*, Taylor v. Sturgell, 553 U.S. 880 (2008) (describing six circumstances in which a judgment can bind a nonparty).

situations individuals can lose their right to an individual day in court when their legal interests are adequately represented by others.

Even if the group (and the group's lawyer) perfectly represents the interests of the individuals within the group, there is a felt loss of individual freedom. In effect, the government (through its courts and judicial procedures) hands a person's lawsuit over to strangers and forces the person to accept the outcome that these strangers achieve. Such an infringement on freedom requires justification.

6. Changing the Political Dynamics in Society

In the United States the judiciary is often described as the "least dangerous branch." On this view, courts are neutral dispensers of justice, untainted by the political considerations that dominate the legislative and executive branches. Judges decide individual cases; they lack the institutional competence to make judgments about the best interests of society as a whole. Their relative lack of democratic accountability makes them poor agents of popular will.

This view of the judiciary is, of course, controversial. In the eyes of some, judges are no less political than other officials, and individual adjudication is no less influenced by political factors than legislative or executive decisions. Some believe that judges make decisions as good (or at least as equally responsive to popular will) as those made by elected officials. But among those who argue that judges should not "legislate from the bench," aggregation can be problematic because judges appear to be stepping into the middle of large political and social controversies.

It is important to disaggregate this criticism. Many complex cases are "structural reform" cases that integrate public education, reform prisons, or challenge discrimination in the workplace. In theory, a lawsuit brought by a single student, prisoner, or employee could achieve the same result. Therefore, some criticism of aggregation in structural-reform cases is a disguise for the argument that judges lack the authority to reform governmental or corporate institutions. To take an example, Thurgood Marshall filed *Brown v. Board of Education* as a class action. The controversy over the legitimacy of school desegregation had nothing to do with the fact that the case was a class action; the issue was whether the terms of the Equal Protection Clause allowed courts to engage in such social restructuring.

On the other hand, sometimes criticism about the institutional legitimacy of aggregation is not a mask for disagreement with the substantive law. Aggregation allows judges to wield more power. When hearing a single case claiming injuries from a defective product, a judge exercises a modest power over the manufacturer. When hearing a consolidated action composed of ten thousand such victims, a judge's decisions may bankrupt a company that is the lifeblood of a community. In theory, ten thousand separate lawsuits have the same potential; but at least the power would be dispersed among many judges and juries, and no single judge could be accused of playing God by making decisions whose economic, social, and political consequences are too large to ignore.

As we saw, aggregation can achieve different outcomes from individual litigation. Some scholars argue that these outcome-influencing effects warp the substantive law, so that aggregation changes the operation of the substantive law. This alleged shift in the law occurs outside of the usual avenues through which law is changed in a democracy. According to this critique, some aggregation techniques—especially those not adopted through the legislative process—are anti-democratic.

In the mix of political considerations is federalism. For reasons that we will see, federal courts possess certain advantages for handling large-scale litigation. As a result, federal courts handle much of this litigation, even when state law is the source of the parties' rights. As a result, aggregation has shifted some power to the federal system—a reality that those who believe in the power of state courts to determine the rights of their citizens find disconcerting.

Another political criticism also has salience. The regulatory effect of aggregation—which generally creates greater deterrence than individual litigation—is undeniable. Plaintiffs' lawyers act as private attorneys general to achieve wide-scale enforcement of the law. As a rule, however, regulatory enforcement is the province of government—in particular, executive or administrative institutions with the capacity to weigh the political, economic, and social ramifications of different levels and methods of enforcement. Individual lawsuits can interfere with efforts to achieve the right level of enforcement, but typically only at the margins. An aggregated proceeding, however, has a far greater potential to upset nuanced regulatory approaches. This "regulation by litigation" arises in the judicial branch, whose judges and (in some cases) juries possess little institutional competence to weigh and balance the range of regulatory concerns beyond the strictly legal.

C. Limits on Aggregation

The foregoing summary of the benefits and drawbacks of aggregation operates at a general level. Before we explore aggregation devices and alternatives that indirectly achieve aggregation, it is also important to understand jurisdictional and venue rules that limit a court's capacity to aggregate related litigation, even when the benefits of doing so outweigh the costs.

"Jurisdiction" refers to a court's power to enter a judgment that binds the parties. There are two kinds of jurisdiction: subject-matter and territorial. You have probably encountered these concepts in Civil Procedure. At this point, we sketch only the outlines of jurisdiction and venue as a refresher. We explore on how jurisdictional and venue rules can thwart aggregation, and how they might be altered to encourage more aggregation, in succeeding chapters.

1. Subject-Matter Jurisdiction

Subject-matter jurisdiction involves the court's power to adjudicate claims of the type asserted by the plaintiff. State courts are often said to be courts of *general jurisdiction*: they have the power to render a judgment in all lawsuits other than those excluded by the United States Constitution or Congress. In contrast, federal courts are said to be courts of *limited jurisdiction*: they are able to hear only certain types of disputes. State courts typically have *concurrent jurisdiction* with federal courts; unless federal subject-matter jurisdiction is exclusive, a plaintiff can choose to bring a case that lies within federal jurisdiction in a state court instead. In this situation, and with a few important exceptions, the defendant has the option to remove the case from state to federal court (*removal jurisdiction*).

As we will see, federal courts enjoy certain institutional advantages in complex cases. Because federal jurisdiction is limited, however, those advantages are unavailable when a federal court cannot hear a dispute. Therefore, it is critically important to understand the limits on federal subject-matter jurisdiction.

Limits arise principally from two sources: the Constitution and Congress. Article III of the United States Constitution allows federal courts to hear only nine categories of cases or controversies. It also gives Congress the power to establish federal courts other than the United States Supreme Court—a power that has long been interpreted to allow Congress further to define and limit the scope of the subject-matter jurisdiction of the federal district courts and courts of appeals. Unless a federal district court has both constitutional and statutory jurisdiction over the subject matter, it cannot validly adjudicate the case. The case must be filed in state court or perhaps in a foreign court.

Principal forms of federal subject-matter jurisdiction include cases "arising under" the United States Constitution, federal laws, or federal treaties (*federal-question jurisdiction*);[15] cases between citizens of different states or between citizens of a U.S. state and a foreign country or its citizens (*diversity jurisdiction*);[16] and suits in which the United States is a party. In addition, as long as one claim lies within the federal court's jurisdiction, other related claims can sometimes be brought as part of the federal case, even though these claims would not have created federal jurisdiction on their own (*supplemental jurisdiction*).[17]

As a rule, the statutory grants of federal jurisdiction are far narrower than the constitutional grants. For instance, with federal-question jurisdiction, the Constitution requires only that an issue of federal law form an "original ingredient" of a case, even if the issue is not disputed by the parties or if the issue arises in a defense.[18] But under 28 U.S.C. § 1331, the statute that grants federal-question jurisdiction in most cases, the issue of federal law must be a component of the plaintiff's original claim against the defendant; this requirement is called the "well pleaded complaint rule."[19]

Likewise, with diversity jurisdiction the Constitution requires only *minimal diversity*: in other words, one plaintiff must have citizenship different from one defendant, even if other plaintiffs or defendants have the same citizenship as those on the opposing side.[20] But 28 U.S.C. § 1332(a), the statute that grants diversity jurisdiction in most cases, requires *complete diversity*: in other words, no plaintiff may have the same citizenship as any defendant.[21] With diversity jurisdiction, Congress has also imposed a *matter-in-controversy* (or *amount-in-controversy*) requirement, under which the dispute must exceed a certain value in order for a federal court to hear the case.

---

15 Although other, more specific grants of federal-question jurisdiction exist, the default statute is 28 U.S.C. § 1331.

16 Although some other jurisdictional statutes are also premised on diversity of citizenship, the default statute is 28 U.S.C. § 1332(a).

17 The statute detailing supplemental jurisdiction and its limits is 28 U.S.C. § 1367.

18 *See* Osborn v. Bank of U.S., 22 U.S. (9 Wheat.) 738 (1824).

19 *See* Louisville & Nashville R.R. v. Mottley, 211 U.S. 149 (1908).

20 *See* State Farm Fire & Cas. Co. v. Tashire, 386 U.S. 523 (1967).

21 *See* Strawbridge v. Curtiss, 7 U.S. (3 Cranch) 267 (1806). On occasion, Congress has granted federal courts jurisdiction on a "minimal diversity" basis. We will discuss two of these instances—28 U.S.C. § 1335 (interpleader) and 28 U.S.C. § 1332(d) (class actions)—in later chapters. A third instance is 28 U.S.C. § 1369, which is known as the Multiparty, Multiforum Trial Jurisdiction Act of 2002. Section 1369 has a very limited scope; it grants jurisdiction when the case "arises from a single accident" and "at least seventy-five people have died in the accident at a discrete location." Even when the requisite minimal diversity exists in such a situation, the court must decline jurisdiction when "the substantial majority of all plaintiffs" and "the primary defendants" all reside in the same state. For one of the rare cases to invoke jurisdiction under the Act, see Passa v. Derderian, 308 F. Supp. 2d 43 (D.R.I. 2004) (nightclub fire that killed 100 people and injured 200).

For most diversity cases, that amount is presently set at $75,000, so a federal diversity case must exceed that amount by at least one penny. The traditional rule is also that each plaintiff must meet the amount in controversy; it is not enough that other plaintiffs do or that, when all the plaintiffs' claims are added together, the amount in controversy is met.

Like the well-pleaded-complaint rule and the rule of complete diversity, the rule against aggregation of different parties' claims to meet the amount in controversy is not constitutionally required. The Constitution contains no amount-in-controversy limit.

Other jurisdictional limits also exist in certain situations. A part of Article III's "case or controversy" requirement, the doctrine of *standing* demands that a complaining party must suffer an injury that is attributable to the defendant's conduct and redressable in court.[22] The Eleventh Amendment comes into play when states and state officials are sued.[23] Both doctrines are fraught with interpretive difficulties that lie beyond this book; but they are important matters to navigate, especially in "public law" litigation.

For now, it is important to see how the doctrine of subject-matter jurisdiction limits the ability of parties or judges to aggregate litigation. Suppose that a citizen of New Jersey designs and manufactures a product in New Jersey that injures hundreds of individuals across the country. Each plaintiff has the right, under what is often referred to as the "master of the complaint rule," to choose which claims to assert, which defendants to join, and in which court to file the case. If the claim is based on state law (i.e., no federal question), then plaintiffs who are citizens of New Jersey cannot file their cases in federal court. Plaintiffs from other states, like Montana or Oregon, may file in federal court or may instead file in state court—although in some instances the defendant may be able to remove the case to federal court. As we will see, it is difficult to aggregate cases that lie in different court systems (federal court and state court, or in the courts of different states). Especially in light of plaintiffs' ability to manipulate subject-matter jurisdiction by asserting (or failing to assert) certain claims against certain parties to obtain a favorable forum, the limits of subject-matter jurisdiction

---

[22] Lujan v. Defenders of Wildlife, 504 U.S. 555 (1992).

[23] There are ways to work around the Eleventh Amendment's barrier to federal jurisdiction in cases seeking injunctive relief (principally by suing a state official in his or her personal capacity); in rarer circumstances, states can also be sued for damages. *See Ex parte* Young, 209 U.S. 123 (1908); Seminole Tribe of Fla. v. Florida, 517 U.S. 44 (1996); Tennessee v. Lane, 541 U.S. 509 (2004). The penumbra of state sovereign immunity of which the Eleventh Amendment is a piece may deprive even state courts of jurisdiction to entertain claims seeking damages from a state. *See* Alden v. Maine, 527 U.S. 706 (1999).

substantially influence the ability to aggregate related cases in a single forum.

2. Venue

The same is true of venue. Venue determines which courts within a system of courts are appropriate to hear a case. For instance, there are ninety-four federal district courts spread across the country. Some districts encompass an entire state; there is, for instance, only one federal district for the entire state of Alaska. Some states have two, three, or even four federal districts within their boundaries; New York and California, for instance, are divided into four federal districts. When a case lies within the subject-matter jurisdiction of the federal courts, rules of venue determine which of the ninety-four districts may hear the dispute.

The United States Code contains specific venue rules for different types of claims. There is also a default venue provision when no specific provision applies: 28 U.S.C. § 1391. Under § 1391, the district in which a substantial part of the events occurred is a proper venue, as is the district in which any defendant "resides" (if all defendants reside in the same state).[24] In the hypothetical of the New Jersey manufacturer whose product causes injury nationwide, the federal court for the District of Alaska is a proper venue for a plaintiff whose injury occurred in Anchorage; meanwhile, a plaintiff injured in Miami could properly sue in the federal court for the Southern District of Florida. The federal court for the District of New Jersey would be a proper venue for both cases, but there is no requirement that plaintiffs file in that court when another district court is also a proper venue. Thus, venue rules can spread related cases across numerous federal districts.

3. Territorial Jurisdiction

Territorial jurisdiction concerns the court's power over the parties themselves, as opposed to the subject matter of the lawsuit. Territorial jurisdiction is distinct from subject-matter jurisdiction, and a court must possess both forms of jurisdiction. For territorial jurisdiction, a rule or statute must authorize the court to assert jurisdiction over the parties, and then that assertion must comply with the United States Constitution—in particular, the Due Process Clause. Territorial jurisdiction can be broken into three types: *in rem* (jurisdiction asserted directly over property rather than over the person who allegedly owns or possesses the property, where the

---

[24] American citizens "reside" in the state in which they are a citizen. Foreign citizens may be sued in any district. Corporations and other legal entities reside in the state in which they maintain their principal place of business (when they sue as plaintiffs), and in any district in which they are subject to the court's personal jurisdiction (when they are sued as defendants).

lawsuit involves a dispute over the rights of all persons in the property), *quasi in rem* (jurisdiction asserted over property, where the lawsuit may or may not involve a dispute concerning the property and in any event settles only the rights of the parties—as opposed to the rights of all persons—in the property), and *in personam* (jurisdiction over a natural person or legal entity, where the lawsuit seeks a judgment that binds the parties to comply with the judgment's terms). Although the first two forms of territorial jurisdiction raise important ideas that we encounter later, they are rarely implicated in a complex case, so it is best to defer their consideration for now.

The Constitution authorizes numerous forms of *in personam* (or personal) jurisdiction. The first and simplest is consent: The parties agree to submit to the jurisdiction of the court. As a rule, consent exists for plaintiffs, who, in filing the case in a particular court, are deemed to have consented to its authority to enter a judgment binding them. But a defendant can also consent. Closely related to consent is waiver: A party can lose the right to claim that the court lacks power over it by failing to preserve the argument or by litigating the case on its merits (thus suggesting that the party has submitted to the authority of the court).

Second, natural persons are subject to the jurisdiction of the courts of a state within which they are physically present at the time that they are served.

The third form of personal jurisdiction recognized under the Constitution is *general jurisdiction*.[25] A natural person is always subject to jurisdiction in the courts of a state in which he or she is a citizen, even when the lawsuit has nothing to do with that state. For instance, if a citizen of Maine negligently gets into a car accident while on vacation in California, the injured plaintiff can sue the defendant in Maine, even though the lawsuit itself is based on events that occurred entirely in California.

In contrast, the fourth and final form of personal jurisdiction—*specific jurisdiction*—depends entirely on the lawsuit-related contacts between the parties (especially the defendant) and the forum state. In the prior example, a California court would have jurisdiction over the Maine defendant for a lawsuit relating to the accident, even if the Maine defendant had never been in California before the accident and was in the state for only a few hours. The reason is that the defendant is said to have "minimum contacts with [California] such that the maintenance of the suit does not offend

---

[25] Note that the term "general jurisdiction" has one meaning in the law of subject-matter jurisdiction and another, very different meaning in the law of personal jurisdiction.

traditional notions of fair play and substantial justice."[26] Determining when the parties' (especially the defendants') contacts with a state are sufficient to satisfy this test is a fact-intensive inquiry behind which lies a number of sometimes inconsistent Supreme Court opinions. Although the doctrine of specific jurisdiction remains in flux today, the basic analysis seems to contain two steps, at least for jurisdiction over a defendant: first, determining whether the defendant "purposefully avail[ed] itself of the privilege of conducting activities within the forum State"; and second, determining whether it would be unreasonable or unfair to subject the defendant to that court's authority, in light of the burden to the defendant as well as the interests of the plaintiff, the forum state, and other states.[27]

As a rule, federal courts follow the territorial-jurisdiction rules (and are limited by the same constitutional constraints) as a state court in the same district as the federal court sits. But there are some exceptions, including the occasional availability in federal court of "nationwide service of process": the ability of a federal court to exercise jurisdiction over a defendant with case-specific contacts with the United States as a whole, even if the defendant has no contacts with the state in which the federal court is located.[28]

In multiparty cases, territorial jurisdiction can pose problems for the aggregation of related claims. It may be difficult or impossible to find a single forum in which all defendants are subject to personal jurisdiction for all claims, thus forcing the dispersion of related cases across multiple forums. For example, in *Bristol-Myers Squibb Co. v. Superior Court of California*,[29] more than 600 plaintiffs who consumed a prescription drug sued in California state court. Many of the plaintiffs had no connection to California, but the defendant had sold more than 187 million pills in California and made more than

---

26 Int'l Shoe Co. v. Wash., 326 U.S. 310 (1945) (internal quotation marks omitted).

27 *See* World-Wide Volkswagen Corp. v. Woodson, 444 U.S. 286 (1980).

28 Although the Supreme Court has never addressed the issue, lower courts generally view nationwide service of process as constitutional as long as the defendant has minimum contacts with the United States as a whole. *See* Mwani v. Bin Laden, 417 F.3d 1 (D.C. Cir. 2005); *but see* NGS Am., Inc. v. Jefferson, 218 F.3d 519 (6th Cir. 2000) (requiring some connection between the defendant and the forum state). When a court has territorial jurisdiction over a defendant because one claim asserted against that defendant permits nationwide service of process, but other claims against that defendant rely on ordinary rules of personal jurisdiction, a nice question arises: may a court that has no jurisdiction over a defendant except through nationwide service of process exercise territorial jurisdiction over the defendant with respect to the remaining claims? The Supreme Court has not addressed this issue, but many lower courts have adopted a doctrine of *pendent personal jurisdiction* to authorize jurisdiction over all claims, at least when all the claims arise from a common nucleus of operative fact. *See* Picot v. Weston, 780 F.3d 1206 (9th Cir. 2015).

29 582 U.S. ___, 137 S. Ct. 1773 (2017).

$900 million in California sales. Nonetheless, the United States Supreme Court held that the California activities of the defendant were not related to the claims of the non-California plaintiffs, so that a California state court lacked the authority to adjudicate the claims of non-California plaintiffs.

Moreover, as we will see, plaintiffs sometimes become involved in lawsuits on an involuntary basis. These plaintiffs also require some due-process protection to prevent the overreaching of a court with which they have no connection. The boundaries that personal jurisdiction places on the power to adjudicate the claims of all plaintiffs and all defendants in one forum limit the utility of some of the best aggregation tools presently available.

D. Four Strategies to Avoid Repetitive Litigation

Until now, we have talked about "aggregation" as if it were a single magical device that allowed all related litigation to be brought before a single court. In fact, there are a host of different aggregation devices, and these different devices implicate the benefits and drawbacks of aggregation to greater or lesser degrees.

The following chapters get into the details of specific aggregation devices. In considering the specific devices, you might find helpful the following summary of the four general approaches that courts can use to deal with the problem of repetitive litigation:

- *Joinder.* Joinder devices allow one or more of the persons interested in a lawsuit to add additional claims or parties. For instance, suppose that one hundred people are injured in a train wreck caused by a brake failure, and each has grounds to file an action against the railroad and the manufacturer of the brakes. Joinder rules determine whether all the plaintiffs can join together and whether they can sue both defendants in a single case.

- *Consolidation and Transfer.* Sometimes parties choose not to (or cannot) join all claims involving all parties in one case. Therefore, separate lawsuits arise. For instance, perhaps Passenger #1 in the train wreck decides to bring one lawsuit against the railroad and a second lawsuit against the manufacturer of the brakes. Passenger #2 decides to bring her own lawsuit in the same court, but she sues both the railroad and the manufacturer in one case. Passenger #3 also sues both defendants, but in a different court. Consolidation doctrines determine when a court may consolidate separate cases filed in the same court. Transfer doctrines determine when cases filed in different courts may be brought together into a single court. Consolidated or transferred cases remain technically separate; the parties do not join other cases. But consolidation and transfer allow a court to treat separate cases as parts of a larger entity.

- *Injunctions and Stays.* An indirect method to achieve a common resolution of related claims involves injunctions or stays. With an injunction, the court in which Passenger #1 has filed suit may issue an injunction ordering the remaining passengers not to file suit in any forum other than the one in which Passenger #1's case is pending. This injunction does not in itself lead to aggregation of all the cases; Passengers #2 through #100 could decline to file suit anywhere. But the effect of an injunction is to limit the number of courts in which cases are pending. A stay is a form of an injunction, but usually is entered by a court to keep itself from proceeding with a case. Assume that Passenger #2 files her case in a different court and that Passenger #1's court has not issued an injunction. The court hearing Passenger #2's case can issue a stay, declining to proceed with the case (either forever or at least until Passenger #1's case is over). Neither injunctions nor stays bring cases before a single court, as do joinder and consolidation. Indirectly, however, they can have this effect: if Passenger #2 wants her claim adjudicated now, the only option to avoid a properly issued injunction or stay is to file the claim in the court hearing the claim of Passenger #1.

- *Preclusion.* Preclusion is another indirect method to resolve common issues. With preclusion, some or all of the determinations from Passenger #1's case are applied to later cases. Relitigation of the claims or issues determined in Passenger #1's case is thus avoided. Preclusion does not force other parties to join Passenger #1's case, but if their rights may be determined by the case, they have an incentive to do so. Even if they do not join, efficiencies are achieved because an issue is decided once, rather than repetitively in lawsuit after lawsuit.

The American civil system adopts each of these approaches to some extent, but substantial obstacles with the latter two methods make joinder and consolidation the principal strategies in many situations. (The exception is the class action, which straddles the line between a joinder and a preclusion device.)

At this point, it is probably worth making a distinction between the direct aggregation devices (joinder and consolidation mechanisms) and the indirect aggregation devices (injunctions, stays, and preclusion). As a rule, the term "aggregation" refers to the process of bringing together actual or potential lawsuits into a larger collective; thus, the direct aggregation devices of joinder and consolidation, as well as class actions, are usually considered to be the card-carrying aggregation devices. Injunctions, stays, and preclusion (except for the class action, to the extent that it is a preclusion rather than a joinder device) are not regarded as aggregation methods because at best they can encourage, rather than require, the collection of related lawsuits into a single proceeding.

Even if they are not aggregation devices in the ordinary vernacular, however, injunctions, stays, and preclusion remain thematically important to the question of aggregation because sometimes joinder, consolidation, and transfer techniques are not available—especially when cases are lodged in different court systems or when there are significant numbers of "future plaintiffs." Injunctions, stays, and preclusion are the only remaining tactics to reduce repetitive litigation.

We now turn to the details of specific devices.

Chapter 2

JOINDER

In our system of adversarial justice, plaintiffs possess the "venue privilege" and are "masters of the complaint." These phrases essentially mean that each plaintiff is entitled to determine whether to file suit, in which court to file suit, which claims to assert in that court, whether to join with other plaintiffs in the suit, and which defendant(s) to sue. Rules of subject-matter jurisdiction, territorial jurisdiction, and venue frame, to some degree, the selection of court, claims, and parties.

Rules of joinder also frame these questions. Rules of *claim joinder* help to determine which claims a plaintiff may assert against a defendant, as well as which claims a defendant may assert back against a plaintiff. Rules of *party joinder* help to determine which parties may be brought together in one case. In the federal system, rules of joinder are found mostly in the Federal Rules of Civil Procedure. These rules cannot alter or expand jurisdiction and venue.[30] Therefore, even if a Federal Rule permits the joinder of a claim or party, that joinder must also be permissible under the statutes and constitutional provisions that establish subject-matter jurisdiction, territorial jurisdiction, and venue.

This Chapter examines, first, the rules of claim joinder and, second, the more intricate rules of party joinder. These rules apply in cases of all sizes, from simple car accidents to massive antitrust conspiracies. The focus in the Chapter is the manner in which joinder rules assist (or limit) the aggregation of complex litigation in a single forum.

Before we begin, a note on the procedure of joinder: joinder occurs in the *pleadings*, in particular in the complaint and the answer. If two plaintiffs want to bring three claims against four defendants, they include all the parties in the caption of the complaint and assert all the claims in the body of the complaint. If one or more of the parties believes that joinder is improper, the usual recourse is to file a motion seeking dismissal or severance of the offending claims or parties.

A. Claim Joinder

The simple rule of claim joinder is "bring 'em if you got 'em." In other words, under the combination of Federal Rules of Civil Procedure 8(d) and 18(a), a party asserting a claim may join with that

---

[30] *See* FED. R. CIV. P. 82.

claim any other legal theories or claims that the party has against that defendant—whether or not the theories are inconsistent with each other or the claims are unrelated to each other.[31] For instance, if a plaintiff wants to assert both a negligence and a strict-liability theory arising out of an injury, no problem. Allege them both, even if they rely on inconsistent legal theories. Likewise, if the plaintiff has a negligence claim and a completely unrelated breach-of-contract claim against a defendant, allege them both. For each such theory or claim the court must have jurisdiction over the subject matter and the defendant(s), and venue must be proper; these independent doctrines may limit the plaintiff's ability to join claims. But as far as the rules of claim joinder are concerned, there are no limits.

Two principles underlie this approach. The first is to prevent the pleadings from becoming a game full of traps of the unwary; recall that the modern American civil-justice system is oriented toward resolving disputes on their substantive merits rather than on procedural technicalities. The other is efficiency: it is better to resolve theories and claims in one forum rather than in two or more. Efficiency gains are most evident when the two theories or claims are related: why relitigate overlapping factual or legal propositions when they can be resolved once and for all in one case? Obviously, this principle is not as much in play when the two claims are unrelated, but even then a court hearing both cases may be able to forge a single settlement (and has the power to sever the claims under Rule 42(b) in the event that efficiency is not achieved by joint handling).

The same basic rule and principles guide the pleading of defenses: each defendant may assert all defenses having merit, regardless of their consistency.

Although Rules 8 and 18 permit joinder of claims on a capacious scale, it is important to remember that each plaintiff is master of that plaintiff's complaint. A plaintiff is free to assert only some of the theories or claims that are available. In many instances, the doctrine of preclusion will bar a plaintiff from asserting claims arising out of the same transaction, and perhaps bar the relitigation of certain issues, in a later case;[32] so a plaintiff has an incentive to bring related claims in the first lawsuit. But a plaintiff willing to pay the preclusion price is free to plead less rather than more.

The defendant has some ability to alter the claim structure that the plaintiff has established for the case. Most notably, a defendant against whom a plaintiff has asserted a claim may assert against

[31] We assume that each of the theories or claims asserted have merit. If they do not, a court may in some instances impose sanctions under Rule 11 of the Federal Rules of Civil Procedure, 28 U.S.C. 1927, or its inherent power.

[32] We discuss the law of preclusion in more detail in Chapter Five.

that plaintiff any claims that the defendant has. These claims are usually referred to as *counterclaims.* Rule 13(a) states that, with only a couple of exceptions, a defendant "must state" any counterclaim that "arises out of the transaction or occurrence that is the subject matter of the opposing party's claim." It is generally understood that a defendant who fails to assert such a *compulsory counterclaim* loses the right to assert it in a future case. Under Rule 13(b) a defendant may also assert a *permissive counterclaim*—a counterclaim that does not arise out the same transaction or occurrence—but suffers no penalty by choosing not to do so.

Under Rule 13(g) a defendant can also assert a *crossclaim* against a co-party (in other words a co-defendant), and under Rule 14(a) can assert a *third-party* (or *impleader*) *claim* against a person who may be liable to the defendant if the defendant is liable to the plaintiff. (Impleading a third-party defendant is a matter of party joinder, rather than claim joinder, but it is worth mentioning now so that you can understand the scope of the defendant's ability to alter the plaintiff's claim structure.) There are no claim-preclusive consequences—though possible issue-preclusive consequences—if a defendant chooses not to file a crossclaim or third-party claim.[33]

A court has territorial jurisdiction over plaintiffs against whom any counterclaim is asserted; and counterclaims do not affect or destroy venue. Crossclaims and third-party claims also do not affect venue; but there must be territorial jurisdiction over a crossclaim defendant or third-party defendant. Subject-matter jurisdiction is more complicated. Under the doctrine of supplemental jurisdiction, a federal court has jurisdiction over a compulsory counterclaim even if the court would not have had jurisdiction over the counterclaim had it been brought independently. The same is true of crossclaims and third-party claims. For permissive counterclaims, however, a federal court cannot hear the case unless the court would have had subject-matter jurisdiction over the counterclaim had it been brought as an independent action.

Although jurisdictional rules sometimes limit claim joinder and preclusive consequences also bear on the claim structure, the rules of claim joinder are fairly straightforward: as a general matter, parties can assert any legal theories or claims that they have.[34] Insofar as we are worried about the ability to aggregate all aspects of a complex

---

[33] When a defendant asserts a proper crossclaim or third-party claim, Rule 18(a) then allows the defendant to tack on any other claims—related or unrelated—that the defendant has against that party. *See* Lehman v. Revolution Portfolio LLC, 166 F.3d 389 (1st Cir. 1999).

[34] The Federal Rules of Civil Procedure, read literally, have a couple of minor gaps that prevent the assertion of some claims, but these gaps are not worthy of extended discussion—in part because many courts have interpreted the Rules in a way that fills them in. *See, e.g.*, Luyster v. Textron, Inc., 266 F.R.D. 54 (S.D.N.Y. 2010).

case, claim joinder creates no substantial roadblock. On the other hand, you can see how the capaciousness of the claim-joinder rules can complicate a case, as many theories and claims can be packed into one lawsuit.[35] That complexity does not create aggregation problems, but it makes more challenging the tasks of developing the facts and narrowing the issues during pretrial and trial—concerns that we take up in Parts Two and Three.

B. Party Joinder

Party joinder expands a case beyond a single plaintiff and a single defendant. Basic design questions for any civil-justice system are whether, and under what conditions, multiple parties should be permitted to join or be joined in a case. Three fundamental models of party joinder exist. The first, *voluntary* (or *permissive*) *joinder*, allows the parties (principally, but not necessarily exclusively, the plaintiffs) to determine the party structure. The second, *involuntary joinder*, requires the joinder of specified parties even if other parties would prefer a different structure. The third, *intervention*, allows the parties to establish the initial party structure, but then affords those left out of the case an opportunity to enter the case.

The distinctions among these models are somewhat artificial, and they are not mutually exclusive. In fact, the American civil-justice system employs all three approaches. Even when joinder is permissible under the rules of party-joinder, however, the party autonomy that lies at the core of the joinder rules—together with the doctrines of subject-matter jurisdiction, territorial jurisdiction, and venue—imposes limits on the aggregation of all related parties in one lawsuit. As you steep yourself in the details of party joinder and jurisdiction, constantly keep in mind the big-picture issue that underlies the technicalities: To what extent do these rules and doctrines aid (or conversely thwart) the single-forum resolution of related cases?

1. Voluntary Joinder

a. Rule 20

The principal voluntary-joinder rule is Federal Rule of Civil Procedure 20, which governs the joinder of both plaintiffs and defendants. Rule 20(a)(1) states that "[p]ersons may join in one action as plaintiffs" when two elements are met: The plaintiffs "assert any right to relief jointly, severally, or in the alternative with respect to or arising out of the same transaction, occurrence, or series of

---

35 For an old but good example of the ways in which the combination of counterclaims, crossclaims, and third-party claims can hijack a simple case and turn it into a complex affair, see *LASA per L'Industria del Marmo Società per Azioni of Lasa, It. v. Alexander*, 414 F.2d 143 (6th Cir. 1969).

transactions or occurrences," and "any question of law or fact common to all plaintiffs will arise in the action." Rule 20(a)(2) states the counterpart for joining defendants: "Persons . . . may be joined in one action as defendants" when "any right to relief is asserted against them jointly, severally, or in the alternative with respect to or arising out of the same transaction, occurrence, or series of transactions or occurrences," and "any question of law or fact common to all defendants will arise in the action."

Rule 20 authorizes joinder of both plaintiffs and defendants to the full scope of a transaction. In this sense, it is consistent with, and indeed one of the foundations for, the modern American preference to organize litigation around the transactional unit—the group of factual events that give rise to the plaintiffs' claims.[36]

The critical word in Rule 20 is "may": Rule 20 joinder is permissive, both in the sense that plaintiffs with related claims may, but are not required to, join together; and in the sense that the plaintiff(s) may, but are not required to, join all defendants. Each putative plaintiff has a choice whether to join with others whose claims arise from the same transaction; the plaintiffs who band together choose which of the possible defendants they will include in the lawsuit. Rule 20 does not require that plaintiffs join together, or that they join all defendants. Instead, Rule 20 relies on a model of consent: no person can be made a plaintiff against his or her will, and no person can be made a defendant against the will of the plaintiffs. This permissive approach to joinder is highly consistent with an adversarial system and with the "master of the complaint" rule that is one of our adversarial system's manifestations.

Two other important terms in Rule 20 are "transaction or occurrence, or series of transactions or occurrences" and "common." Perhaps the most famous case interpreting this language is *Mosley v. General Motors Corp.*,[37] which involved the joinder of plaintiffs. In *Mosley*, ten employees brought suit against their employer and union, alleging racial and gender discrimination in hiring, promotion, and terms of employment. The ten plaintiffs sued both individually and as representatives of a class of similarly situated employees. They worked in different plants, held different jobs, and had been discriminated against in different ways (some based on race and others on gender; some in hiring decisions and others in promotion or other workplace decisions). Without deciding whether the case could be maintained as a class action on behalf of all affected employees, the district court held that the joinder of the ten named

---

36 *See supra* p. 2.

37 497 F.2d 1330 (8th Cir. 1974).

plaintiffs did not satisfy Rule 20. As a result, it severed the case into ten separate lawsuits.

The Eighth Circuit reversed, holding that the district court had abused its discretion. The court began with Rule 20's "transaction or occurrence" test, describing it as flexible. "The purpose of the rule is to promote trial convenience and expedite the final determination of disputes, thereby preventing multiple lawsuits. . . . Single trials generally tend to lessen the delay, expense and inconvenience to all concerned." Therefore, a court should interpret "transaction or occurrence" so that "reasonably related claims for relief by or against different parties [can] be tried in a single proceeding." Applying these principles to the complaint, the key fact was the plaintiffs' allegation that each plaintiff's injury arose from the same company-wide policy of racial discrimination. (The court never addressed the allegations of gender discrimination, or whether they also arose from the same policy.) Even though this policy had different individual manifestations, the critical core fact of a company-wide policy was the wellspring of all the claims, thus satisfying the "transaction of occurrence" test.

The Eighth Circuit then held that the complaint's allegations satisfied Rule 20's "commonality" requirement. Rule 20 "does not require that all questions of law and fact raised by the dispute be common," nor does it "establish any qualitative or quantitative test of commonality." The company-wide discriminatory policy was "basic to each plaintiff's recovery. The fact that each plaintiff may have suffered different effects from the alleged discrimination is immaterial."

Having been cited more than 3,200 times, *Mosley* is famous for its expansive reading of Rule 20(a) and for its case-by-case approach to the Rule's application. Most courts have agreed with *Mosley*'s casting of the "transaction or occurrence" language in efficiency terms and with its supposition that efficiency is generally achieved with fewer, larger lawsuits rather than more, smaller lawsuits. Although strongly supported by the language of Rule 20(a), *Mosley*'s holding that a single common question of law or fact is adequate to satisfy the "common question" requirement is also noteworthy; it is impossible to imagine a complaint meeting the "transaction or occurrence" prong that fails the "common question" prong.

Despite its influence, *Mosley* is best viewed as a case on one end of the Rule 20 spectrum rather than as the ultimate word on its meaning. Other cases have required a somewhat tighter connection among the putative plaintiffs' claims in order to satisfy Rule 20.[38]

[38] For a case disagreeing with *Mosley* on comparable allegations, see Grayson v. K-Mart Corp., 849 F. Supp. 785 (N.D. Ga. 1994). *See also* Acevedo v. Allsup's

The United States Supreme Court's narrower interpretation of a similar commonality requirement in the federal class-action rule (Rule 23(a)(2)) also suggests the need for caution.[39] In addition, courts are sensitive to fairness concerns that temper the efficiency approach to Rule 20. In particular, courts recognize that the joinder of numerous parties can sometimes create jury confusion or other difficulties that impinge on the accurate resolution of the case.[40] The concern is most salient for the joinder of defendants; when possible, plaintiffs can be expected to choose a structure that maximizes the prejudice against the defendants. In *Desert Empire Bank v. Insurance Co. of North America,* the court of appeals stated that the critical issue for Rule 20 joinder of defendants is whether joinder "comport[s] with the principles of fundamental fairness."[41] Other cases, however, suggest that there is no difference in the plaintiff-joinder and defendant-joinder contexts, and the determining factors in both contexts are trial convenience, the plaintiff's need for complete relief, and the elimination of multiple lawsuits.[42]

The lines drawn around Rule 20 sometimes appear driven more by concerns for efficient case management than by a close parsing of Rule 20's language.[43] For instance, one judge allowed the joinder of drug patients independently harmed by deceptive trade practices to file a joint complaint, as long as they all resided in the same judicial district (but not if they resided in different districts).[44] Another court allowed plaintiffs who had received a medical device to join together in one products-liability action as long as they sued the same

---

Convenience Stores, Inc., 600 F.3d 516 (5th Cir. 2010) (denying joinder of 800 employees, working in different stores, who were allegedly underpaid); Boschert v. Pfizer, Inc., No. 4:08–CV–1712 CAS, 2009 WL 1383183 (E.D. Pa. May 14, 2009) (rejecting the joinder of four plaintiffs who alleged defective-design claims against a drug manufacturer when the "the prescriptions were provided through different health care providers, . . . the drug was taken at different times for various durations[, the plaintiffs'] alleged symptoms are not the same and their medical histories appear to have varied greatly"). For a case rejecting *Mosley* under a state's party-joinder rule, see Miss. Life Ins. Co. v. Baker, 905 So.2d 1179 (Miss. 2005).

39 *See* Wal-Mart Stores, Inc. v. Dukes, 564 U.S. 338 (2011) (discussed *infra* notes 308, 332–334, 408–412, 442, 899–901 and accompanying text).

40 For a case raising, but ultimately rejecting, such concerns with respect to the joinder of eighteen plaintiffs, see *Alexander v. Fulton Cty.*, 207 F.3d 1303 (11th Cir. 2000).

41 623 F.2d 1371, 1375 (9th Cir. 1980). *See also* Intercom Research Assoc., Ltd. v. Dresser Indus., Inc., 696 F.2d 53 (7th Cir. 1982).

42 League to Save Lake Tahoe v. Tahoe Reg'l Planning Agency, 558 F.2d 914 (9th Cir. 1977).

43 *Cf.* Robin J. Effron, *The Shadow Rules of Joinder*, 100 GEO. L.J. 759 (2012) (describing the policies that drive the interpretation of Rule 20 and create seeming variability in outcomes).

44 *In re* Avandia Mktg., Sales Practices & Prod. Liab. Litig., No. 07–md–01871, 2008 WL 2078917 (E.D. Pa. May 14, 2008).

manufacturer and had the device implanted at the medical facility.[45] A different court facing medical-device litigation set the joinder limit at plaintiffs who lived in the same state and were represented by the same lawyer.[46]

> *Problem 1*
>
> A drug that was used to treat symptoms in menopausal women was alleged to cause breast cancer. Fifty-seven women who took the drug sued the fourteen manufacturers of the drug, alleging both a products-liability theory and a theory that the manufacturers conducted a nationwide marketing campaign that understated the risks of the drug. Different plaintiffs took different manufacturers' drugs, and different treating physicians prescribed the drug for each plaintiff.
>
> Were the plaintiffs and defendants properly joined in one case? *See In re* Prempro Prods. Liab. Litig., 591 F.3d 613 (8th Cir. 2010).

Whatever its outer limits, Rule 20 has sometimes been used to join thousands of plaintiffs and hundreds of defendants in one case.

i. Strategic Considerations in Rule 20 Joinder

Rule 20 gives plaintiffs the power to achieve the joinder of related claims in many cases. In a moment, we turn to the limits on Rule 20 joinder, but before we do, it is worth spending a little time on the reasons why plaintiffs might not be interested exercising the power to achieve a socially optimal level of joinder. Begin with the proposition that procedural rules affect outcomes. Although the outcome effects of many procedural rules have never been studied, there are experimental data on the effect of joinder on case outcomes. In brief, these data suggest that, as more plaintiffs are joined, the likelihood of victory for the plaintiffs increases. But as more plaintiffs are added, the damages awarded per case tend to fall. Moreover, as more plaintiffs are added, the jury tends to focus more on outlier cases; although more plaintiffs generally make a recovery more likely, the results are unpredictable when the outlier cases are weak.[47]

---

[45] *In re* Orthopedic Bone Screw Prods. Liab. Litig., MDL 1014, 1995 WL 428683 (E.D. Pa. 1995).

[46] *In re* Norplant Contraceptive Prods. Liab. Litig., 168 F.R.D. 579 (E.D. Tex. 1996).

[47] The studies are cited *supra* note 10. One of the studies noted that the maximum plaintiff-favoring "joinder effect" occurred when four plaintiffs were joined; the effect diminished when ten plaintiffs joined together. One possible reason was information overload; the mock jurors in the experiment may have been unable to distinguish individuals as the numbers rose, and instead blended or averaged the cases.

A more recent empirical study explored the effect of joining multiple defendants, each of whom had allegedly infringed the plaintiff's patent. Although the defendants' infringements were independent of each other, one court routinely allowed the cases

These data confirm an old intuition of many trial lawyers: try your good cases separately, but your "dogs" together. If you represent a plaintiff with a strong case, you might be very reluctant to join it with other, weaker cases. On the other hand, if you represent a plaintiff with a weak case, you might be very eager to achieve broad joinder—perhaps even more joinder than is socially optimal.

There are other reasons why a lawyer may not wish to achieve a socially optimal level of joinder. For instance, in thinking through the chances for success on a claim, a lawyer will also undoubtedly think about which court system—state or federal—gives the best chance of recovery, not which court system holds out the best prospect for socially optimal aggregation. And lawyers who are more attentive to their fees than the best interests of their clients (think agency costs!) might establish a party structure that maximizes the per-hour recovery of the lawyer, even if a different structure would have minimized the overall costs to the clients, the defendant, and the court.

The strategic considerations inherent in joining parties reflect a more general proposition about procedural rules: litigants consider the private benefits that they gain from their actions, not the overall social benefits.[48] With this insight in mind, we can explore some of the limits of the voluntary-joinder approach.

ii. Limitations on Rule 20 Joinder

Recall that we are seeking procedural tools that will achieve an optimal level of aggregation. Rule 20 sounds like it could do the job; it allows joinder of plaintiffs and defendants to the full scope of the transaction, as long as it is efficient to do so. But a number of features of voluntary joinder prevent it from achieving its potential.

The most significant limit on voluntary joinder lies in the word "voluntary." Each plaintiff must consent to join the case, and they must then agree on the group of defendants that they wish to sue. A plaintiff cannot use Rule 20 to force the involuntary joinder of other plaintiffs; a defendant cannot use Rule 20 to force the joinder of

---

to be joined under Rule 20. The study suggested that the joinder of multiple defendants was driven mostly by strategic considerations such as reducing plaintiff-side costs, increasing defense costs, and generating prejudice against the defendants. *See* David O. Taylor, *Patent Misjoinder*, 88 N.Y.U. L. REV. 652 (2013). It should be noted that Congress recently enacted a specific provision for the joinder of patent defendants, preventing joinder of defendants "based solely on allegations that [each alleged infringer] infringed the patent." 35 U.S.C. § 299(b).

48 *See generally* Steven Shavell, *The Fundamental Divergence Between the Private and the Social Motive to Use the Legal System*, 26 J. LEGAL STUD. 575 (1997) (arguing that litigants often make privately beneficial decisions that are not socially justified because the litigants consider only the benefits they garner and the costs they incur, while they ignore the benefits of the lawsuit that they do not capture and the costs that their behavior imposes on others).

additional plaintiffs or defendants;[49] and the court cannot use Rule 20 as a source of *sua sponte* ("on its own initiative") power to force the joinder of either plaintiffs or defendants.[50] Plaintiffs will typically join together only when they see some tactical advantage in doing so—in other words, only when they perceive that the outcome of a joined suit will be more favorable (due to higher recoveries or lower costs) than the outcomes of separate suits. In resolving the tensions among the procedural goals of autonomy, transactionalism, and efficiency, Rule 20 ultimately sides with autonomy.

A second limit of Rule 20's voluntary-joinder approach arises in mass disputes that are geographically or temporally dispersed. It may be impossible, or at least prohibitively costly, to identify all the plaintiffs with potential claims, contact them, and obtain the consent necessary to join them as parties. As long as voluntary joinder is the default approach to mass litigation, dispersion of claims is inevitable.

Third, doctrines of jurisdiction impede socially beneficial joinder even when the parties want it. Start with territorial jurisdiction. Under the theory of consent, a court has personal jurisdiction over each plaintiff who voluntarily joins a case.[51] But there must also be a basis of jurisdiction over each defendant joined in the case. The basis does not need to be the same for each defendant; it might be general jurisdiction for one, and specific jurisdiction for another. But some basis must exist. The mere fact that other defendants are subject to a court's jurisdiction is insufficient. Also insufficient is the fact that Rule 20 authorizes joinder, or the fact that it would be efficient to join all related defendants. The doctrine of territorial jurisdiction developed long before the phenomenon of modern mass disputes, and it has so far proven impervious to concerns for optimal aggregation.

Subject-matter jurisdiction presents a more complex picture. To simplify the discussion, we focus only on the two main fonts of federal jurisdiction: federal-question jurisdiction under 28 U.S.C. § 1331 and diversity jurisdiction under 28 U.S.C. § 1332. The same concept applies to subject-matter jurisdiction as to territorial jurisdiction: each claim that each plaintiff asserts against each defendant requires a basis of jurisdiction; if a federal court lacks authority to adjudicate certain claims against certain parties, those claims and

[49] As we discussed *supra* note 33 and accompanying text, a defendant can use Rule 14 to add third-party defendants who might be liable to the original defendant if the original defendant is liable to the plaintiff.

[50] *See* Lyne v. Arthur Anderson & Co., No. 91 C 1885, 1991 WL 247576 (N.D. Ill. Nov. 12, 1991); Pan Am. World Airways, Inc. v. U.S. Dist. Ct. for the Cent. Dist. of Cal., 523 F.2d 1073 (9th Cir. 1975).

[51] *See supra* Chapter 1.C.3. *Cf.* Adam v. Saenger, 303 U.S. 59 (1938) (holding that a plaintiff who files a complaint also consents to the court's jurisdiction over counterclaims).

parties (and sometimes the entire case) must be dismissed from federal court.

Applying this principle can get tricky. If the complaint alleges a violation of federal law pertinent to all plaintiffs and all defendants, 28 U.S.C. § 1331 gives a federal court subject-matter jurisdiction over the entire controversy. So far, so good. But things get harder when the claims are based in whole or part on a source other than federal law.

As discussed above, diversity jurisdiction under § 1332(a) requires complete diversity and an amount in controversy (presently set at $75,000) that each claim must exceed.[52] Thus, if plaintiffs from Maine and Massachusetts want to sue defendants from Michigan and Wisconsin on state-law claims that are worth $100,000 apiece, the case could be filed in federal court. But if dispute also involves a defendant from Maine, the case could be filed only in state court—unless the claim against the Maine defendant involved a federal question for which § 1331 provides a jurisdictional basis.

When some of the claims by some of the plaintiffs against some of the defendants lie within a federal court's federal-question or diversity jurisdiction and others do not, supplemental jurisdiction under 28 U.S.C. § 1367 comes into play. First, assume that at least one claim by one plaintiff against one defendant arises under federal law, while other claims against other defendants arise under state law. Under 28 U.S.C. § 1367(a), a federal court would have jurisdiction over all claims by and against all parties as long as all the claims "are so related . . . that they form part of the same case or controversy under Article III of the United States Constitution." The proper test for constitutional relatedness varies; for some types of claims, it is "logical relationship,"[53] for some "common nucleus of operative fact,"[54] and for some the Supreme Court yet to develop a test. Courts and commentators have generally argued that all the tests come down to the same point: § 1367(a) authorizes a federal court to hear all claims arising out of the same transaction or occurrence as long as at least one of those claims involves a federal question.

Now assume that all the claims arise out from the court's diversity jurisdiction, but only some of those claims meet the terms of § 1332(a). Consider two scenarios. In the first, plaintiffs from Maine and Massachusetts (each with a claim for $100,000) join defendants from Massachusetts, Michigan, and Wisconsin. In the second, the same plaintiffs sue only the defendants from Michigan

---

52 *See supra* notes 20–21 and accompanying text.

53 Moore v. N.Y. Cotton Exch., 270 U.S. 593 (1926).

54 United Mine Workers of Am. v. Gibbs, 383 U.S. 715 (1966).

and Wisconsin, but the Massachusetts plaintiff has a claim for only $50,000.

Both scenarios invoke § 1367(b), which comes into play when the claims creating federal jurisdiction are based solely on diversity of citizenship. Due to a curious omission in the statutory language, § 1367(b) fails to specify the jurisdictional consequences for either scenario. The literal language of § 1367(b) suggests that jurisdiction exists in both situations as long as the plaintiffs' claims meet the terms of § 1367(a). But the Supreme Court has held otherwise, at least in part: § 1367(b) provides no jurisdiction in the first scenario (because it contravenes the time-honored rule of complete diversity), but it permits jurisdiction in the second (because complete diversity is maintained).[55]

These rules of supplemental jurisdiction, which we summarize only in brief, often make it impossible to assert all the claims of all the plaintiffs against all the defendants in a single federal court. Unless the complaint invokes in part a federal question, the common citizenship of just one plaintiff and one defendant destroys federal jurisdiction. That failure is not the end of the matter; such a case could still be filed in state court. For reasons that we explore in later chapters, however, federal courts possess institutional advantages with regard to aggregation, so relegating a case to state court is unlikely to achieve optimal aggregation.[56]

A fourth limit on voluntary joinder's ability to achieve optimal aggregation arises from the intersection of the "master of the complaint" rule with jurisdictional and venue doctrines. Even when the limits of subject-matter and territorial jurisdiction do not prevent the joinder of all related claims and parties, these doctrines give plaintiffs who wish not to participate in an aggregated resolution of

---

[55] Exxon Mobil Corp. v. Allapattah, 545 U.S. 546 (2005). *Allapattah* itself involved the application of 28 U.S.C. § 1367(b) to claims joined under Rule 23, the federal class-action rule. We take up the intersection of Rule 23 and § 1367(b) *infra* note 458 and accompanying text. A companion case to *Allapattah*, *Ortega v. Star-Kist Foods, Inc.*, raised the Rule 20 issue discussed in the text. The Court's logic applied equally in the Rule 20 and Rule 23 contexts.

[56] As for venue, little needs to be said. When defendants are resident in different states, 28 U.S.C. § 1391(b)(1) is not applicable: this section provides venue in the federal district in which any defendant resides, but only if all defendants reside in the same state. While § 1391(c) expands the definition of residence for corporations in a way that sometimes keeps this provision in play for mass disputes involving only corporate defendants, § 1391(b)(1) cannot serve as the basis for venue in cases that include individual defendants from different states. Nonetheless, other venue provisions (likely § 1391(b)(2) and at a minimum the catch-all § 1391(b)(3)) may still provide venue in at least one federal district. Thus, venue alone is unlikely to trip up a mass joinder effected under Rule 20, although it may limit the number of appropriate venues.

a mass dispute ample tools to attain that objective.[57] The simplest technique is to forswear any federal-question claims, join a non-diverse plaintiff or defendant (or limit the relief sought in the complaint to no more than $75,000), and then sue in state court. Although federal courts have removal jurisdiction over many state-court lawsuits that could originally have been filed in federal court, such a case could not have been filed in federal court originally.[58] If enough plaintiffs take this tack, related cases that might have been filed in a single proceeding end up dispersed across the state and federal courts.

There are very few countermeasures to thwart disaggregation tactics. Some defendants who have wanted a lawsuit to be heard in federal court have argued that the claims against some of the non-diverse plaintiffs or defendants who were joined in state court lack merit; they remove the case to federal court, ask the court to eliminate the meritless claims, and assert jurisdiction over the remainder. Other defendants have claimed that the non-diverse plaintiffs or defendants were not properly joined in state court; again, on removal they have asked the federal court to dismiss the misjoined parties and assume jurisdiction over the remainder of the case.[59]

> *Question 1*
>
> Although the voluntary-joinder approach under Rule 20 is unlikely on its own to achieve the aggregation of related cases, keep in mind what we learned in the Introduction and Chapter One: procedural rules often involve a mix of values, and the aggregation of related claims has costs as well as benefits. Does Rule 20 strike the right balance among procedural values, in light of the benefits and costs of aggregation?

The first of these arguments is often referred to as "fraudulent joinder" or "improper joinder." It requires the defendant seeking removal to show that the jurisdictional facts (such as the citizenship of the parties) are fraudulently stated; that

[57] Of course, the simplest technique of all is to withhold consent, thus preventing joinder under Rule 20. As Chapter Three discusses, however, cases that are separately filed in federal court can often be consolidated in a single federal court. A plaintiff who wants to avoid consolidation in federal court must therefore put federal jurisdiction out of reach.

[58] 28 U.S.C. § 1441(a). Another technique to avoid federal jurisdiction is to file a diversity-based case in a court of a state of which one of the defendants is a citizen. *Id.*, § 1441(b)(2). As long as a non-diverse defendant or a home-state defendant remains in the case for more than one year, the case is generally not removable even if the non-diverse or home-state defendant is subsequently dropped from the case. *But see id.* § 1446(b)(3) (allowing removal when the plaintiff "has acted in bad faith in order to prevent a defendant from removing the action").

[59] When a plaintiff limits the amount in controversy to $75,000 or less, 28 U.S.C. § 1446(c)(2)–(3) govern whether the case is removable. In general, a good-faith allegation limiting the amount to less than the amount in controversy controls, but the statute specifies some exceptions.

the complaint has no merit under state law with respect to only the non-diverse parties; or that the claims asserted by or against the non-diverse parties have no connection to the case against the diverse parties.[60] The second doctrine is often referred to as "fraudulent misjoinder" or "procedural misjoinder." It requires a showing that the state-law equivalent to Rule 20 would not allow the joinder of the diverse parties with the non-diverse parties whose presence in the lawsuit thwarts complete diversity.[61] With both doctrines, the burden of proving improper joinder is high. Neither doctrine is a satisfactory means to overcome a plaintiff's conscious decision to seek a disaggregated resolution of his or her claim in state court when the claims asserted by or against non-diverse parties are legitimate.

b. Interpleader

Although a doctrine of limited scope, interpleader presents an interesting contrast to Rule 20 joinder and suggests a way in which a voluntary-joinder rule could be constructed to aid the process of aggregating related suits. The problem to which interpleader is responsive is a simple one. Suppose that one person possesses a piece of property or an asset (say, a car), and each of five other people has a non-frivolous claim to ownership of the car. (To make matters simple, assume as well that the person in possession of the property claims no ownership interest.) In such a situation, each claimant to the car might sue the person in possession of the car to get it. Each potential owner has little reason to join the other claimants, because their interest in the car may prove superior. In a lawsuit against only the possessor, however, each person is sure to gain the car, because the disinterested possessor by definition has no claim to ownership. If the first claimant prevails in her lawsuit, the possessor is in an untenable position. Because none of the other claimants was party in the first case, none is bound by its outcome; therefore, the possessor would not be able to use the prior judgment establishing the first clamant as the owner as a defense in later cases. If the possessor hands over the car, he risks later suits by other claimants for conversion. Moreover, the first claimant might be subject to further litigation if any of the other four claimants sue her. This pattern might repeat itself as even more claimants bring suit.

Enter the doctrine of interpleader, first developed in the olden days of equity. Equity allowed the person holding the property (called

60 *See, e.g.*, Wilson v. Republic Iron & Steel Co., 297 U.S. 92 (1921); Cuevas v. BAC Home Loans Servicing, LP, 648 F.3d 242 (5th Cir. 2011).

61 The seminal case is *Tapscott v. MS Dealer Service Corp.*, 77 F.3d 1353 (11th Cir. 1996), *abrogated on other grounds by* Cohen v. Office Depot, Inc., 204 F.3d 1069 (11th Cir. 2000). Some courts and scholars have criticized the doctrine for its unpredictability and complexity. *See* 14B CHARLES ALAN WRIGHT ET AL., FEDERAL PRACTICE AND PROCEDURE § 3723 (4th ed. 2009).

the stakeholder) to join and sue all the claimants preemptively. This suit established the ownership interests in the property for all claimants, thus avoiding the costs of a multiplicity of suits and the possible injustice of the stakeholder being liable multiple times. To accomplish this result, the person who would have been the defendant in the underlying actions (the stakeholder) turned the tables and became the plaintiff in the new suit.[62] As part of the interpleader proceeding, the court in equity could also issue an injunction preventing the prosecution of cases against the stakeholder in other courts.

For our purposes, two critical features of interpleader merit mention. The first is the incentive to join all interested parties. Setting the party structure remains in the hands of the stakeholder, who is free to join as many (or as few) of the claimants as he wishes. Because anyone left out of the suit could sue the stakeholder in other litigation, however, the stakeholder is likely to join all interested parties. The second critical feature is equity's power to enjoin separate actions. Although Chapter Four explores anti-suit injunctions in more detail, you can already appreciate the value (in aggregation terms) of interpleader's one-two punch: both a power to join all interested parties in one case and a power to prevent parties from escaping the net by bringing actions elsewhere.

In modern litigation, there are two types in interpleader. One is called *rule interpleader* and the other *statutory interpleader*. Rule interpleader is the more direct descendant from equity practice. Rule 22(a)(1) of the Federal Rules of Civil Procedure provides: "Persons with claims that may expose a plaintiff to double or multiple liability may be joined as defendants and required to interplead." The critical phrase—"double or multiple liability"—has been construed narrowly, in accordance with the original purpose of interpleader. There must exist a *res* or some other defined asset against which multiple inconsistent claims exist. Rule 22 does not cover situations in which a defendant (say, a manufacturer of a defective product) might be liable to two or more plaintiffs for their separate injuries.

Rule interpleader is subject to the usual rules of jurisdiction and venue. Except in the unusual situation in which the claims to the property raise a federal question, state law will determine the parties' rights. Thus, the plaintiff-stakeholder(s) and the defendant-

---

[62] One limit of interpleader was its unavailability when the stakeholder claimed an interest in the property. This restriction was eventually relaxed to permit suits "in the nature of interpleader." For ease of reference, we refer to both traditional interpleader and suits "in the nature of interpleader" by the single term "interpleader." Another limit is the requirement that the "stakeholder must have a good faith belief that there are or may be colorable competing claims to the stake." Michelman v. Lincoln Nat'l Life Ins. Co., 685 F.3d 887 (9th Cir. 2012).

claimant(s) must be completely diverse, and the amount in controversy must exceed $75,000. The federal court must be able to exercise territorial jurisdiction over each defendant. The usual challenges of asserting jurisdiction over out-of-state defendants may make it impossible for complete joinder to be accomplished and (because a court's injunctive power can run only against those over whom it has jurisdiction) for repetitive lawsuits to be prevented. Venue also does not bend for rule interpleader, although, under 28 U.S.C. § 1391(b)(2), venue is almost surely available in the district in which the property is located.[63]

Statutory interpleader is a far more powerful tool, and therefore used with greater frequency. 28 U.S.C. § 1335(a) grants original jurisdiction to the federal district courts to entertain "actions of interpleader or in the nature of interpleader" when a stakeholder has "in his or its custody or possession money or property of the value or amount of $500 or more." 28 U.S.C. § 1335 states two additional jurisdictional requirements: First, "[t]wo or more adverse claimants, of diverse citizenship, . . . are claiming or may claim to be entitled to such money or property"; and second, the plaintiff has either "deposited such money or property . . . into the registry of the court, there to abide the judgment of the court" or has given a satisfactory bond to the court. Thus, statutory interpleader extends federal subject-matter jurisdiction to the constitutional maximum of minimal diversity;[64] it also slashes the amount-in-controversy requirement to a trivial $500. Except in the rare case in which all adverse claimants are from a single state, § 1335 effectively overcomes one of the great obstacles to single-forum aggregation—federal subject-matter jurisdiction.

Statutory interpleader also overcomes other hurdles to single-forum aggregation. 28 U.S.C. § 2361 provides that a court "may issue its process for all claimants"; service may be accomplished in "the respective districts where the claimants reside or may be found." In plain English, the limitations of state-law territorial jurisdiction are wiped away, and nationwide service of process is permitted. 28 U.S.C. § 1397 authorizes venue in a § 1335 action in "the judicial district in which one or more claimants reside." As a result, there is no difficulty in situating the entire controversy in a single venue.

---

[63] Of course, intangible property can raise interesting issues under § 1391(b)(2), as can property that does not lie within U.S. borders. *See* Atcom Support LP v. Maria, C.A. No. 15–28–RGA–MPT, 2016 WL 4118914 (D. Del. Aug. 1, 2016).

[64] In *State Farm Fire & Casualty Co. v. Tashire*, 386 U.S. 523 (1967), the Supreme Court held that Article III of the Constitution required only minimal, as opposed to complete, diversity; thus, the minimal-diversity requirement of § 1335 was constitutional.

Statutory interpleader also has a final useful power: 28 U.S.C. § 2361 authorizes a court invoking jurisdiction under § 1335 to issue an order that "restrains [all claimants] from instituting or prosecuting any proceeding in any State or United States court affecting the property, instrument or obligation involved in the interpleader action until further order of the court."

Statutory interpleader seems to constitute a how-to manual of aggregation: a method to join all interested nonparties (combined with a realistic incentive to do so); subject-matter jurisdiction, territorial jurisdiction, and venue rules so generous that only truly single-state or truly international disputes escape its reach; and anti-suit injunctive power.

Despite its impressive scope as an aggregation device, statutory interpleader is not a silver bullet for aggregation problems; like every device, it has limitations. The primary limitation derives from interpleader's requirement that the dispute concern property—a *res*. Most complex disputes do not involve skirmishes over a *res*; they involve personal liability of individuals or corporations. If the underlying claims against the interpleader plaintiff seek an injunction requiring the interpleader plaintiff to take (or refrain from taking) some action, the analogy to a *res* stretches too thin. Hence, interpleader has never been perceived as a joinder option in cases seeking injunctive relief. Even when the claims seek money, typically the defendant's assets are only indirectly relevant to the suit; they will be called upon to satisfy the judgments of the claimants, but no claimant has a claim against any specific asset. To date, courts have not relaxed the traditional touchstone of interpleader: the *res*.

If interpleader is to work as a more generally useful device to aggregate cases, therefore, something in a defendant's possession must be analogized to a *res* in which claimants have a legal interest. For monetary claims, one creative idea arises when the value of the asserted claims exceeds the amount of the interpleader plaintiff's assets. In other words, the interpleader plaintiff has limited funds with which to satisfy the claimants; not all claims can be paid in full. The interpleader plaintiff risks insolvency, and claimants who file too late risk receiving nothing (while the early-filing claimants get full recoveries). Even though no claimant has a claim to ownership of any specific portion of the interpleader plaintiff's assets, might the plaintiff's limited funds be analogized to a *res*?

So far, no federal court has stretched the language of § 1335 (requiring claims assertable against a stakeholder's "money or property") to include limited-fund cases. Nor is such an argument likely to prevail. First, using interpleader in this fashion is historically inapt. The reason that stakeholders sought, and equity granted, interpleader relief was the risk of multiple liability; when the stakeholder has sufficient assets to pay all claims, or even when the stakeholder's limited funds mean that the early filers get all the assets, no multiple-liability concerns arise. Second, using interpleader in these situations (and especially in limited-fund cases) effectively substitutes interpleader for bankruptcy, without providing to creditors the protections of the bankruptcy code. A third obstacle is the maxim, occasionally recited in interpleader suits, that those who seek equity must have "clean hands."[65] Given that the stakeholder plaintiff often is facing multiple suits due to its alleged wrongdoing, its hands are unclean within the meaning of the maxim.

None of these arguments absolutely precludes the limited-fund-as-*res* argument, but practical considerations also make the argument problematic. For instance, one of the jurisdictional prerequisites of § 1335 is the deposit of the *res* into the court (or, in the alternative, the posting of a bond). Rule interpleader has a comparable requirement. When the "*res*" amounts to the sum total of the stakeholder's assets, depositing the *res* into the court is usually impossible. And a bond (which may cost 10% or more of the face value of the assets) is likely to be so expensive that it might cripple ongoing operations. Furthermore, in limited-fund cases, most stakeholders have no incentive to obtain a bond, or to use interpleader, for a simple reason: At the end of the day, they have nothing left for themselves. In contrast, bankruptcy holds out some hope that a debtor will emerge as a going concern after reorganization, with some of its capital preserved. With interpleader, the defendant is essentially forced to liquidate; and defendants rarely have an incentive to do so voluntarily.

Another pragmatic difficulty is one that we have encountered before: identifying all potential claimants in instances in which they are geographically or temporally dispersed. Unless all claimants can be identified and joined, there is a risk of additional lawsuits after completion of the interpleader action.

The stubborn requirement of a *res* poses one last difficulty for a broad use of interpleader. As the Supreme Court made clear in *State Farm Fire & Casualty Co. v. Tashire*, interpleader "cannot be used to solve all of the vexing problems of multiparty litigation arising out of a mass tort" and is not designed to be an "all-purpose 'bill of peace.' "[66] In *Tashire*, a truck-bus collision in California killed two passengers

---

[65] *See* Farmers Irrigating Ditch & Reservoir Co. v. Kane, 845 F.2d 229, 232 (10th Cir. 1988) ("It is the general rule that a party seeking interpleader must be free from blame in causing the controversy, and where he stands as a wrongdoer with respect to the subject matter of the suit or any of the claimants, he cannot have relief by interpleader.").

[66] 386 U.S. at 535, 537.

and injured thirty-three. The owner of the truck held a $20,000 insurance policy, which was grossly inadequate to cover the victims' damages. Victims began to sue the owner of the truck, the bus line, and the two drivers in various federal and state courts. The drivers of the vehicles and the truck owner were citizens of Oregon, so the truck owner's insurer paid the $20,000 policy into the United States District Court for the District of Oregon, and commenced a § 1335 interpleader action against the victims, the bus line, and both drivers. The federal court then invoked its § 2361 power to enjoin prosecution of all other lawsuits against the truck owner. When the bus company asked that the injunction be expanded to prevent the prosecution of suits against the company or its driver in any forum other than the District of Oregon, the district court obliged.

The Supreme Court held that the injunction in favor of the bus company and its driver was broader than necessary to protect and determine the ultimate ownership of the *res* (the truck owner's insurance proceeds). The Court rejected the notion that the fortuity of a limited insurance policy could "sweep[ ] dozens of lawsuits out of the various state and federal courts" at the behest of a single defendant with a limited interest in the case. It also refused to read the interpleader statute in a way that would deprive litigants their "substantial rights" to "choose the forum in which to establish their claims." To allow a $20,000 insurance policy to shape the litigation would allow "the tail . . . to wag the dog." The Court contrasted this situation with a case in which "the fund [in the interpleader plaintiff's possession] itself is the target of the claimants. It marks the outer limits of the controversy."

Tashire shows that, even when it is more economical and convenient to force all the claims into a single federal forum, economy and convenience are rarely sufficient reasons, by themselves, to overcome plaintiffs' adversarial right to locate their suits in forums of their choosing. Statutory

Problem 2

A restaurant sold oysters that sickened 349 patrons. It had already settled 105 cases for $347,000. Another 105 cases had been filed, and 139 patrons had not yet sued. The restaurant carried insurance policies with remaining limits of $1,552,000. The insurers deposited this amount into court and brought a suit in interpleader against the remaining claimants and the restaurant. The court enjoined existing and potential claimants from suing in other courts. The restaurant was marginally solvent at best—and perhaps insolvent. The insurers asked the trial court enjoin patrons from suing the restaurant in other courts until the present interpleader suit was resolved. What result? *See* Aetna Cas. & Sur. Co. v. Ahrens, 415 F. Supp. 1235 (S.D. Tex. 1975).

interpleader has all the bells and whistles of a useful aggregation device: broad rules of subject-matter jurisdiction, personal jurisdiction, and venue that make it possible for one court to determine conclusively the entire dispute; joinder authority placed in the hands of a party with an incentive to effect broad joinder; and a power to issue anti-suit-injunctions that keep claimants from escaping the aggregated proceeding. At present, however, interpleader remains a limited tool, useful principally in insurance-coverage litigation that arises around the fringes of large-scale disputes. Given the perceived need for strong aggregation devices, interpleader's fixation on the existence of a *res* seems archaic to some observers. To others, however, it acts as an important check on excessive aggregation.

2. Required Joinder

A different approach is mandatory, or required, joinder. Under this concept, the law specifies the parties that must be joined in a particular dispute. Even in a system oriented toward voluntary joinder, some mandatory joinder might be adopted—in particular, for unique circumstances in which leaving the joinder decisions in the hands of the litigants is inadvisable. Federal Rule of Civil Procedure 19 reflects this insight. The issue for us is whether the need for optimal aggregation might be one of those situations.

Derived from equity practice, Rule 19 was not originally developed with the needs of complex litigation in mind. Rule 19 requires the joinder of certain nonparties if their joinder is feasible. Equity's term for such nonparties was "necessary parties," and although the present Rule 19 no longer uses the term, the old label persists. Who exactly is a "necessary party"—or put differently, exactly when can we justify the joinder of nonparties against their will or the will of the plaintiff? Once we identify such persons, a second issue arises. What happens when it becomes impossible to join a required party due to some barrier, such as a lack of subject-matter jurisdiction, a lack of territorial jurisdiction, a lack of venue, or an immunity to suit? By definition, the party is required. Should the court dismiss the case? Should it muddle along and adjudicate the case on a less than complete basis? Or should it have the power to remove the barrier to suit through creative interpretation of jurisdiction, venue, or immunity rules?

Rule 19 attempts to answer these questions. Rule 19(a) defines who a *required person* (or necessary party) is. Rule 19(b) describes how a court is to respond when a required person cannot be joined—in particular, whether the case must be dismissed in the required person's absence.

a. Rule 19(a): Required Persons

Rule 19(a) lists three types of required persons:

- A nonparty in whose absence "the court cannot accord complete relief among existing parties" (Rule 19(a)(1)(A));
- A nonparty who "claims an interest relating to the subject of the action and is so situated that disposing of the action in the [nonparty's] absence may . . . as a practical matter impair or impede the [nonparty's] ability to protect the interest" (Rule 19(a)(1)(B)(i));
- A nonparty who "claims an interest relating to the subject of the action and is so situated that disposing of the action in the [nonparty's] absence may . . . leave an existing party subject to a substantial risk of incurring double, multiple, or otherwise inconsistent obligations because of the interest" (Rule 19(a)(1)(B)(ii)).[67]

At the risk of simplification, Rule 19(a)(1)(A) protects the interests of existing plaintiffs in achieving a complete remedy by forcing the joinder of nonparties that might undo the remedy. Rule 19(a)(1)(B)(ii) protects the interests of present defendants by forcing the joinder of nonparties whose separate suits might force the defendant to provide too much remedy to a group of claimants. And Rule 19(a)(1)(B)(i) protects the interests of nonparties by forcing their joinder when the existing case will significantly impair their ability to obtain a remedy in subsequent litigation.

Recast in this light, Rule 19's required joinder rejects the view that joinder should occur merely because aggregation is efficient. It seems more consistent with a view that required joinder should be limited to situations of "remedial inequity." Either the plaintiff or the nonparty will get less remedy than is fair, or the defendant will provide more remedy than is fair.

Cases have also interpreted Rule 19(a) in a way that is narrower than an efficiency rationale would dictate, but in a way that is consistent with the concerns for remedial equity. For instance, in *Temple v. Synthes Corp.*,[68] the plaintiff filed one suit in federal court against the manufacturer of a medical device and another in state case against the doctor who performed the operation and the hospital

---

[67] Note the similarity of this language with that of Rule 22 interpleader. Like Rule 22, the language has not been understood to mean that the prospect of a defendant being liable to some plaintiffs but not to others creates "double, multiple, or inconsistent obligations."

[68] 498 U.S. 5 (1990).

in which the operation occurred. The plaintiff could have filed the entire case in federal court; complete diversity of citizenship and the requisite matter in controversy were present. But the plaintiff did not wish to do so, and the doctor and hospital could not remove the state case to federal court since it had been filed in their home state. The manufacturer filed a motion to dismiss the federal case, arguing that the doctor and hospital were required parties. The district court ordered the plaintiff to join the state-court defendants or face dismissal, reasoning that it had jurisdiction over the claims and that judicial economy would be served by joinder. When the plaintiff did not comply, the district court dismissed the case against the manufacturer.

The Supreme Court overturned the dismissal in a *per curiam* opinion. "It has long been the rule," the Court said, "that it is not necessary for all joint tortfeasors to be named as defendants in a single lawsuit"; the various defendants were merely "permissive parties." Although the Court recognized that there existed a "public interest in limiting multiple litigation," this consideration was not sufficient to alter Rule 19(a)'s requirements.

Similarly, in *Eldredge v. Carpenters 46 Northern California Counties Joint Apprenticeship and Training Committee*,[69] two plaintiffs brought a sex discrimination case against a joint labor-management committee that ran a training program for tradespeople. To be admitted to the program, an applicant must have been hired by an employer and then placed on the applicant registry through a union hiring hall. Women were significantly underrepresented in the program.

Since it trained applicants hired by employers and vetted by local unions, the defendant claimed that the 4,500 employers and 60 union locals involved in the hiring process were required persons. The district court ordered their joinder. When the plaintiffs found it impossible to do so, the district court held that the absent employers and unions were necessary for complete relief and the case could not proceed without them. It dismissed the case.

The court of appeals reversed. Although it recognized that the employers had an interest in the fate of the training program, it did not believe that their absence left the remaining parties with incomplete relief. If the program itself discriminated, relief against it was appropriate—even if the relief did not eradicate the root cause of the discrimination by employers and unions.

Arguably, *Eldredge* got the Rule 19(a) analysis wrong. To a large extent, the training program's purported discrimination resulted

[69] 662 F.2d 534 (9th Cir. 1982).

from discrimination engaged in by employers and unions. If employers continued to discriminate in their hiring practices after *Eldredge*, then one of two propositions appears to be true. First, the training program would still take applicants on the same basis as before the lawsuit, meaning that, under Rule 19(a)(1)(A), the employers needed to be part of the case in order for the plaintiffs to get complete relief. Second, the program would train apprentices on a non-discriminatory basis, forcing employers to choose between altering their hiring practices and foregoing training for their new employees. Under the second possibility, the nonparty employers' interests in in hiring a well-trained work force of their choosing would be practically impaired, thus bringing Rule 19(a)(1)(B)(i) into play. So aren't the employers required persons?

Not if Rule 19(a) is understood in accordance with the principle of remedial inequity. Failing to join the employers did not give the plaintiffs less relief than they were entitled to. Nor did it make the training program subject to double or inconsistent obligations. Finally, the nonparty employers and unions did not enjoy a legal right to discriminate: their state-law contractual rights with the training program were subsidiary to the federal requirement of non-discrimination. Hence, the lawsuit did not threaten the legitimate interests of the employers and unions.

Rule 19 has never been used to achieve joinder of related cases in mass litigation.[70] One reason is Rule 19(d)'s exemption of Rule 23 class actions from the ambit of Rule 19. Another reason is the consequence of reading Rule 19(a) broadly: the potential dismissal of claims under Rule 19(b). Courts seem to interpret Rule 19(a) with this consequence in mind. For instance, we know of no cases in which Rule 19 has been used to join significant numbers of additional plaintiffs against an insolvent defendant (on the Rule 19(a)(1)(B)(i) theory that the defendant's limited assets would be exhausted before the additional plaintiffs could reduce their claims to judgment). Nor has Rule 19 been much invoked in "public law litigation," in which large numbers of constituencies may be interested in the reform of a government institution—even though such joinder could in theory be required under Rule 19(a)(1)(B)(i) (because those not joined may have their interests impaired by the reform) or under Rules 19(a)(1)(A) and 19(a)(1)(B)(ii) (because some of the constituencies may bring later litigation challenging the reform, thus denying the original plaintiffs complete relief and possibly subjecting the institution to inconsistent obligations).

---

70 *Cf.* Pan Am. World Airways, Inc. v. U.S. Dist. Court for the Cent. Dist. of Cal., 523 F.2d 1073 (9th Cir. 1975) (Rule 19(a) could not serve as basis for district court to provide notice to nonparties of the pendency of a related lawsuit arising from a major aviation disaster).

b. *Rule 19(b): "Indispensable" Parties*

If a person is required to be joined under Rule 19(a), the court must assess whether it has jurisdiction and venue over the reformulated case, as well as jurisdiction over the required person. If no obstacles are present, the person is joined and the case proceeds. If the addition of the required person would destroy subject-matter jurisdiction or venue, if the court lacks personal jurisdiction over the required person, or the person enjoys immunity from suit, the case cannot proceed with the required party.[71] So the question is what the court should do: proceed without the required person or dismiss the case.

Rule 19(b) instructs a court to determine whether "in equity and good conscience" the case can proceed. The Rule lists four factors that guide the "equity and good conscience" determination:

- The extent of prejudice to the parties or nonparty if joinder is not effected;
- The possibility that the prejudice might be lessened by creative shaping of the relief;
- The adequacy of a judgment rendered in the nonparty's absence; and
- The availability of an adequate remedy to the plaintiff if the case is dismissed.[72]

When a court determines it is better to dismiss the case rather than to let it proceed without the required person, the person used to be labeled an "indispensable party." After stylistic revisions to Rule 19 in 2007, this label was dropped, but the phrase continues to be used in common legal parlance. It is important to realize that not all required persons incapable of being joined are indispensable. Only those required persons whose absence demands dismissal of the lawsuit merit the label. Although courts resist dismissing the case if possible, dismissal due to absence of a required person occurs in some instances.

---

[71] There is a very small exception to this statement: When a Rule 19(a) person is served within 100 miles of the courthouse, a federal court can assert personal jurisdiction. *See* FED. R. CIV. P. 4(k)(1)(B).

[72] In *Provident Tradesmens Bank & Trust Co. v. Patterson*, 390 U.S. 102 (1968), the Court cast these four factors into four interests served by the indispensable-party rule: the plaintiff's interest in the forum, the defendant's interest in avoiding excessive relief, the nonparty's interest in the outcome of the case, and the interest of the court and public in "complete, consistent, and efficient settlement of controversies." In some ways, this functional analysis seems preferable, but it likely leads to the same outcome as the stated Rule 19(b) factors.

An excellent case demonstrating the operation of Rules 19(a) and 19(b) is *Republic of the Philippines v. Pimentel*.[73] In *Pimentel* victims of human-rights abuses during the regime of Ferdinand Marcos, the Philippine dictator, won a recovery of nearly $2 billion. As they tried to collect the award, they discovered approximately $35 million in a brokerage account that Marcos had opened. But the victims were not the only claimants against this money. Another person who alleged that Marcos had stolen valuable assets from him also claimed ownership, as did various entities of the Philippine government.

The brokerage house commenced an interpleader suit against the various claimants. The entities of the Philippine government asserted their immunity from suit in an American court. They also moved to dismiss the case because they were required persons in whose absence the case could not, in equity and good conscience, proceed. The lower courts agreed that the entities were required persons but allowed the case to proceed in their absence.

The Supreme Court reversed, holding that the governmental entities were required parties and that, in light of their immunity from suit, the proper solution was to dismiss the case. The parties conceded, and the Court accepted, that the entities of the Philippine government were required to be joined under Rule 19(a) because their interest in the $35 million brokerage account would be impaired in their absence—in other words, the case presented a Rule 19(a)(1)(B)(i) problem. Perhaps. Another way to analyze the facts is that, as nonparties to the interpleader proceeding, the Phillippine entities would not be bound by the result of the proceeding. Thus, they were still free to sue the brokerage house for converting their assets. On this view, the case presented a Rule 19(a)(1)(B)(ii) problem for the brokerage house, which may have been subject to double liability. Either way (and it is not unusual for absent parties to fit within more than one Rule 19(a) category), the entities of the Philippine government needed to be joined in the case.

Due to their immunity from suit, however, joinder was impossible. Thus, Rule 19(b) came into play. As the Court observed, the application of Rule 19(b) sometimes reveals that "[r]equired persons may turn out not to be required for the action to proceed after all." But in *Pimentel* dismissal was necessary. Applying the four "equity and good conscience" factors, the Court held that the interests of the governmental entities were entitled to comity, the potential prejudice to these interests was great, and there was no way to lessen the prejudice. Even though dismissal significantly prejudiced both the victims and the brokerage house, and even though "plaintiffs will

---

[73] 553 U.S. 851 (2008).

be left without a forum for definitive resolution of their claims[,] . . . that result is contemplated under the doctrine of foreign sovereign immunity." Applying a de novo standard of review, the Court ordered dismissal of the case.

Pimentel shows how Rule 19 may frustrate the aggregation of related cases. Indeed, the potential for dismissal under Rule 19(b) creates a perverse litigation dynamic. The plaintiff has little reason to call attention to the nonjoinder of Rule 19 required persons because, if they cannot be joined, their absence may result in dismissal of the plaintiff's case. The defendant has an incentive to press the argument for joinder only when the required persons cannot be joined and might be regarded by the court as indispensable, thus requiring dismissal of the case.

An obvious solution to this problem is to create aggregation-friendly interpretations of subject-matter jurisdiction, territorial jurisdiction, venue, or other impediments to optimal joinder. Those changes, together with a broader reading of Rule 19(a) to encompass persons whose related claims could be efficiently handled together, would assist in aggregating (albeit involuntarily) claimants. Such changes, however, would require congressional action. At present, Federal Rule 82 makes clear that the Federal Rules cannot expand jurisdiction or venue, 28 U.S.C. § 2072(b) makes clear that the Federal Rules cannot affect substantive rights like sovereign immunity, and 28 U.S.C. § 1367(b) makes clear that, in diversity cases, no supplemental jurisdiction exists over the claims of Rule 19 parties.

Simply put, structural limitations make it exceedingly difficult to use Rule 19 as a tool for optimal aggregation. On the other hand, Rule 19 is a potential cause of some mischief in the pursuit of such aggregation.

3. Intervention

Intervention is something of a hybrid—a midpoint between voluntary and required joinder. The idea of intervention is to permit a nonparty who has interests in ongoing litigation, but has not been joined by the existing parties, to join (or intervene in) the case.

In its way, intervention is a form of voluntary joinder. There is no requirement that a person intervene, and no preclusion of that person's claim if he or she chooses not to intervene.[74] On the other hand, intervention shifts to putative intervenors some measure of the plaintiff's autonomy to shape the litigation as the plaintiff wishes. Intervention is arguably justified by the transactional preference to

---

74 *See* Martin v. Wilks, 490 U.S. 755 (1989).

adjudicate all aspects of a set of related events in a single case. Efficiency also supports intervention, but only when intervention reduces repetitive litigation and does not inject so many new parties or issues into the case that any gains from eliminating duplicative litigation are wiped out.[75]

In the federal system, Rule 24 strikes the balance among these competing concerns. Rule 24 distinguishes between two types of intervention: intervention of right (Rule 24(a)) and permissive intervention (Rule 24(b)).

a. Intervention of Right

As its name implies, intervention of right grants to the putative intervenor a right to intervene; he or she is able to enter the case as a party with full rights of participation, even when the existing parties oppose intervention and even when the court thinks that intervention is undesirable. Intervention of right can arise under either Rule 24(a)(1) or Rule 24(a)(2). Rule 24(a)(1) authorizes intervention of right when a "timely" request for intervention has been made and when, in addition, a statute authorizes intervention. This provision is rarely invoked; there are few such statutes, and those that exist tend to permit intervention in language remarkably similar to Rule 24(a)(2).

Thus, whether intervention of right is possible is usually a matter of Rule 24(a)(2). Rule 24(a)(2) authorizes intervention when a "timely" application has been made and when, in addition, the putative intervenor "claims an interest relating to the property or transaction that is the subject of the action, and is so situated that disposing of the action may as a practical matter impair or impede the movant's ability to protect its interest, unless existing parties adequately represent that interest." Courts usually parse Rule 24(a)(2) into four elements:

- Timeliness;
- A protectable interest;
- An impairment of that interest; and
- A lack of adequate representation.

[75] *See* Smuck v. Hobson, 408 F.2d 175 (D.C. Cir. 1969) ("The decision whether intervention of right is warranted thus involves an accommodation between two potentially conflicting goals: to achieve judicial economies of scale by resolving related issues in a single lawsuit, and to prevent the single lawsuit from becoming fruitlessly complex or unending.").

For the most part, each element has been read in a flexible way in order to achieve (in the words of one famous formulation) as much joinder "as is compatible with efficiency and due process."[76]

To begin with the bookends, neither timeliness nor adequacy of representation poses a significant hurdle to intervention of right. Timeliness depends on a host of factors, such as the length of the delay before seeking to intervene, the reason for the delay, and the prejudice to the various participants created by intervention or non-intervention.[77] Depending on the reason for intervention, a party may intervene even after trial or on appeal; if the putative intervenor is interested in asserting claims that might affect the trial process, however, intervention must occur sufficiently in advance of trial that no prejudice will result to the parties.

As for adequacy of representation, *Trbovich v. United Mine Workers of America* noted that the requirement is fulfilled when the putative intervenor shows that representation of the intervenor's interest " 'may be' inadequate; and the burden of making that showing should be treated as minimal."[78] In *Trbovich*, a disgruntled union member sought to intervene in a case brought by the government to obtain a new election of union officers. Even though both the government and the union member had a similar goal, the Court held that representation by the government was inadequate; the government was required by statute to serve the public interest, not the union member's private interests. A putative intervenor seeking to represent his or her specific interests generally has little difficulty identifying sufficient factual, legal, or strategic differences from existing parties to clear the "minimal" inadequacy threshold.[79]

The remaining two issues—interest and impairment—present greater challenges for putative intervenors. Exactly what should count as an "interest" for purposes of Rule 24(a)(2) has been the subject of disagreement, both in the Supreme Court and elsewhere. In one case, the Supreme Court took a stringent line, holding that the target of an IRS investigation did not have a "significantly protectable interest" in his corporation's records when the IRS subpoenaed the records as part of its investigation.[80] On the other

---

76 *See* Nuesse v. Camp, 385 F.2d 694 (D.C. Cir. 1967) (speaking specifically of the "protectable interest" element).

77 *See* 7C CHARLES A. WRIGHT ET AL., FEDERAL PRACTICE AND PROCEDURE § 1916 (3d ed. 2007).

78 404 U.S. 528 (1972).

79 For a case failing to find that the burden had been met in the context of environmental litigation commenced by the government, see United States v. Hooker Chems. & Plastics Corp., 749 F.2d 968 (2d Cir. 1984). *See also* Edwards v. City of Houston, 78 F.3d 983 (5th Cir. 1996) (describing presumption of adequacy in governmental litigation).

80 *See* Donaldson v. United States, 400 U.S. 517 (1971).

hand, the Court permitted the intervention of California at the remedial phase of an antitrust case brought by the United States; California's interest was its desire to ensure a competitive marketplace for its citizens.[81]

The same disagreements manifest themselves in the decisions of the lower courts. The generous view of "interest" is the dominant one. For instance, employees who were alleged victims of racial discrimination were found to have a sufficient interest to intervene as plaintiffs in a case brought by similarly situated employees;[82] students who were hopeful to gain admission to college or law school under an affirmative-action program were found to have an interest to intervene as defendants in litigation that seeking to end the program;[83] and chambers of commerce and municipalities concerned about the deleterious economic consequences of an environmental suit against a major industry were found to possess a sufficient interest to intervene as defendants.[84]

Cases often focus on whether broad joinder comports with the concerns of efficiency and due process. Most courts read Rule 24(a)(2) liberally in large "atypical cases."[85] As is often true of legal tests that involve a measure of discretion, cases to the contrary can also be found.[86] The "interest" test is elastic.

The same general orientation toward intervention, with the same cautionary countertrend, exists for the "impairment" element. As an initial matter, finding an impairment creates a theoretical challenge. Because a nonparty who fails to intervene is not typically bound by the judgment and is free to bring a separate lawsuit, denial of the putative intervenor's application does not impair or impede the putative intervenor's legal rights. Courts have answered this challenge by seizing on Rule 24(a)(2)'s phrase "as a practical matter"; even if the outcome of a case does not *legally* affect the putative intervenor's interests, the case might *practically* impinge on those interests. One practical constraint, often relied on by parties seeking to intervene, is the *stare decisis* effect of the case: the court's ruling on questions of law or evidentiary admissibility in the first case

---

81 *See* Cascade Nat. Gas Corp. v. El Paso Nat. Gas Co., 386 U.S. 129 (1967).

82 *See* Cook v. Boorstin, 763 F.2d 1462 (D.C. Cir. 1985).

83 *See* Grutter v. Bollinger, 188 F.3d 394 (6th Cir. 1999).

84 *See* United States v. Reserve Mining Co., 56 F.R.D. 408 (D. Minn. 1972). The judge allowed numerous states and environmental groups to intervene as plaintiffs.

85 *See Nuesse*, 385 F.2d at 700.

86 *See, e.g.*, Coalition to Defend Affirmative Action v. Granholm, 501 F.3d 775 (6th Cir. 2007) (organizations that had worked to enact a state constitutional amendment did not have a "substantial legal interest" that justified intervention of right in a lawsuit challenging the amendment). *Cf.* Susan Bandes, *The Idea of a Case*, 42 STAN. L. REV. 227 (1990) (finding that federal courts employ at least six different tests to determine an "interest").

might establish unfavorable precedents that would guide the court in a subsequent case filed by the putative intervenor.[87] Another recognized constraint exists when the first lawsuit might establish a remedy that would have a negative, subsequently uncorrectable effect on the putative intervenor's economic or other interests.[88]

Starting from the premise that all four of the stated Rule 24 (a)(2) factors are directed toward a single purpose of achieving the broadest joinder consistent with efficiency and due process, some courts have suggested that the four factors should be interpreted with flexibility; as long as efficiency and fairness are served, a weak showing on one factor can be overcome by a strong showing on other factors.[89] Other opinions have suggested that strict adherence to each of the four factors is required,[90] or else have suggested that efficiency and due process are not the only relevant considerations in making an intervention determination. Perhaps the best example of this latter line of thinking is *Bethune Plaza, Inc. v. Lumpkin*,[91] in which the court of appeals took a narrower view of *stare decisis* as an impairment factor. *Bethune* held that only the *stare decisis* effect of an *appellate* decision can constitute an impairment, but even then no impairment exists if *amicus curiae* participation is adequate. In reaching this conclusion, the court of appeals rejected the notion that broad representation of various interests and perspectives is an unadulterated good: "Permitting intervention liberally raises the costs of litigation and makes settlement harder, which may well discourage the initial suit and effectively block the real plaintiff from vindicating its own rights. To allow [putative intervenors] to intervene as of right would turn the court into a forum for competing interest groups, submerging the ability of the original parties to settle their own dispute (or have the court resolve it expeditiously)."[92]

---

87 Atlantis Dev. Corp. v. United States, 379 F.2d 818 (5th Cir. 1967); *Cook*, 763 F.2d at 1470; *but see* Bethune Plaza, Inc. v. Lumpkin, 863 F.2d 525 (7th Cir. 1988) (holding that a potential *stare decisis* effect did not support intervention in the district court, but might justify intervention on appeal). *See also* FDIC v. Jennings, 816 F.2d 1488, 1492 (10th Cir. 1987) (*stare decisis* effect not enough to justify intervention when plaintiff's and putative intervenor's theories of liability differed, intervenor would inject new issues into trial, and intervention would make a complicated suit less manageable).

88 *Reserve Mining*, 56 F.R.D. at 414; *Edwards*, 78 F.3d at 1005–06.

89 *See, e.g.*, Kleissler v. United States Forest Serv., 157 F.3d 964 (3d Cir. 1998); Daggett v. Comm'n on Governmental Ethics & Election Practices, 172 F.3d 104 (1st Cir. 1999).

90 *See Kleissler*, 157 F.3d at 975 (Becker, J., concurring).

91 863 F.2d 525 (7th Cir. 1988).

92 *Id.* at 531–33. *See also* FDIC v. Jennings, 816 F.2d 1488 (10th Cir. 1987) (stare-decisis effect not enough to justify intervention when plaintiff's and putative intervenor's theories of liability differed, intervenor would inject new issues into trial, and intervention would make a complicated suit less manageable).

Bethune Plaza highlights the inherent tensions in our modern procedural goals—in particular, the tensions between transactionalism and efficiency on the one hand and adversarialism and autonomy on the other. Some have argued that the broad view of joinder is particularly appropriate in "public law litigation," which involves myriad interests that the traditional two-party structure of adversarial litigation cannot adequately capture.[93] Whether adversarial litigation is capable of accommodating and determining such a range of interests is a matter about which others have expressed skepticism.[94]

> *Problem 3*
>
> An animal-rights organization sued a state official to enjoin the state from authorizing certain trapping activities that allegedly violated the Endangered Species Act. An association of trappers now seeks to intervene on the side of the defendant, claiming that its members would suffer decreased income from trapping, increased expenses in replacing certain traps, and decreased recreational opportunities. The plaintiff claims that everyone, including the putative intervenor, had an interest in complying with federal law. Should intervention be allowed? *See* Animal Prot. Inst. v. Merriam, 242 F.R.D. 524 (D. Minn. 2006).

The relationship between Rule 24(a)(2) and Rule 19(a)(1)(B)(i) has been long noticed. Given the nearly identical "interest" and "impairment" language in the two provisions, an interesting question is whether every person who applies to intervene is a required person, thus making intervention irrelevant. The standard reply is that the different purposes of the two rules—one to force into a case those whose absence would create such unfairness that it might be better to dismiss the case rather than let it continue and the other to let into the case a nonparty who wants to contribute something to the case's resolution—should lead to different interpretations of the similar language. As one court observed:

> [T]he fact that the two rules are entwined does not imply that an "interest" for the purpose of one is precisely the same as for the other. The occasions upon which a petitioner should be allowed to intervene under Rule 24 are not necessarily limited to those situations when the trial court should compel him to become a party under Rule 19.[95]

Aside from the limits imposed by Rule 24, other structural limits also prevent intervention from being a cure-all for aggregation difficulties. The first issue, once again, is the voluntary nature of

---

93 *See* Chayes, *supra* note 3.

94 *See* Fuller, *supra* note 2.

95 *See Smuck*, 408 F.2d at 178.

intervention; a putative intervenor who wants to observe from the sidelines, or file his or her lawsuit elsewhere, is free to do so. For this reason, intervention is most common in public-law cases involving requests for injunctive relief against government programs; here, the initial lawsuit might well determine the shape of the program, so organizations and individuals with an interest in the program want to have a place at the table as the lawsuit goes forward. But in cases seeking damages, a potential plaintiff who wishes to proceed separately (on the view that individual litigation better serves his or her interests) is unlikely to seek intervention. In situations in which cases are temporally dispersed, intervention becomes even more challenging, as those who do not yet have an injury may not have either the knowledge or the incentive to intervene.

Second, the troika of subject-matter jurisdiction, territorial jurisdiction, and venue impose some—albeit fewer—limits on the ability to aggregate cases through intervention. Territorial jurisdiction and venue are not problematic; an application to intervene amounts to the putative intervenor's consent to have the court exercise jurisdiction over him or her. Venue is determined by the shape of the original lawsuit; intervention cannot affect or defeat it.[96]

Subject-matter jurisdiction, however, remains an issue. If the putative intervenor's claim contains a basis for federal jurisdiction (whether federal question or diversity), there is no problem. When the claim asserted by or against the putative intervenor has no independent basis of federal jurisdiction, the issue is more complicated. If the plaintiff's original claim is based at least in part on a federal question or other non-diversity ground, then a federal court has supplemental jurisdiction over claims asserted by means of intervention of right under 28 U.S.C. § 1367(a), but there would be no jurisdiction over claims asserted through permissive intervention. If the sole basis of federal jurisdiction over the plaintiff's original claims is diversity, however, then 28 U.S.C. § 1367(b) makes clear that there is no subject-matter jurisdiction over any claims in intervention, whether of right or permissive.[97]

---

[96] *See* WRIGHT ET AL., *supra* note 77, § 1918 ("The intervenor cannot question venue.").

[97] Prior to the passage of § 1367 in 1990, federal courts had supplemental (then called ancillary) jurisdiction over all claims seeking intervention of right when no independent basis of jurisdiction existed. Section 1367(b) changed that rule when claim of intervention of right, over which there was no independent basis of jurisdiction, was sought in a diversity case.

A second jurisdictional difficulty may be standing.[98] A person seeking to intervene of right must possess standing.[99] The impact of this requirement on aggregation is, however, likely to be small. Requiring standing will have some effect in public-law litigation—in particular, on the ability of public-interest organizations to bring their specific concerns before a court. But when courts seek to use intervention to aggregate related cases, putative intervenors who have a valid claim and are asking to intervene in the present case presumably possess standing.

That said, it should be evident that intervention is not a doctrine likely to aid significantly in aggregating related claims. If potential plaintiffs with related claims wish to pursue their claims together, they will likely agree to join their claims under Rule 20. If one or more of the plaintiffs refuses to join with others, then the others could in theory use Rule 24 to force their way into the case. But it seems more likely that they will pursue their own litigation rather than join with hostile co-parties; other doctrines, which we explore in the next chapter, may then lead to combining the cases. As with Rule 20, the weakness of Rule 24 is its incentive structure. When a lawsuit will effectively bar or limit his or her rights, a putative intervenor has an incentive to intervene, and Rule 24 provides the necessary tool. When no such restriction exists and a putative intervenor is capable of enforcing his or her rights in separate litigation, there is usually much less incentive—and more important, no obligation—to intervene.

Nor can a broader assertion of judicial power overcome these limits. No court has claimed a *sua sponte* power to order a nonparty to intervene in a case.

In short, intervention of right tells a now-familiar story: private incentives, as well as structural constraints in joinder rules, jurisdictional statutes, and the Constitution, often thwart the aggregation of related claims even when such aggregation would be regarded as socially optimal.

b. Permissive Intervention

Rule 24(b) authorizes permissive intervention under a fairly loose standard: "the court may permit anyone to intervene" as long as a statute grants such a right or the putative intervenor "has a claim or defense that shares with the main action a common question of law or fact." The key to permissive intervention is Rule 24(b)'s use of the word "may": the trial judge has broad discretion to deny the

---

[98] *See supra* note 22 and accompanying text.

[99] *See* Town of Chester v. Laroe Estates, Inc., 581 U.S. ___, 137 S. Ct. 1645 (2017).

application to intervene or to limit the permissive intervenor's participation to something less than the full rights accorded the other parties in the case. Because of the limits of permissive intervention, intervention of right is the preferred avenue for most putative intervenors, as well as the one that is more thematically important in terms of the ability of the parties and the court to structure a lawsuit that includes nonparties.[100]

C. An Assessment of Joinder

Joinder is the principal procedural mechanism by which courts are able to adjudicate related disputes in a single forum. The joinder rules are structured to permit joinder on a liberal scale. The federal system and the systems of most state courts stand ready to determine all claims by or against all parties whose lawsuits arise out of the same "transaction or occurrence." This phrase has been consistently interpreted to permit joinder when joint treatment is efficient. Thus, the joinder rules are capacious enough to allow much of the aggregation needed in complex litigation.

But this potential for aggregation is not fully realized, for two reasons. First, even though the system *permits* broad joinder, it does not *require* such joinder. The joinder system also values litigant (especially plaintiff) autonomy highly. For the most part, the parties (especially plaintiffs) determine the party structure. Leaving such structural issues in the hands of the parties is an approach highly consonant with the adversarial model of American litigation. But adversaries are likely to be motivated not by the social interest in the fair and efficient resolution of mass disputes but by their private interests in achieving the best outcome. In some instances, social and the private interests will converge, and optimal aggregation will occur. In most instances, it will not. And courts possess virtually no *sua sponte* power to override adversarial jousting and fill in the gaps of party joinder to achieve optimal aggregation.

Second, joining everyone in one case is not always realistic. Claims might be geographically dispersed. In this situation, doctrines of jurisdiction (both subject-matter and territorial) and venue—which were not developed, and have generally not been interpreted, with the needs of complex litigation in mind—might make aggregation in one forum impossible. It would in theory be possible to loosen those rules; for instance, Congress could abolish the "well pleaded complaint" rule for federal-question jurisdiction, move to "minimal diversity" and lower (or no) amount-in-controversy requirements for diversity jurisdiction, expand territorial

---

[100] For a short examination of Rule 24(b) permissive intervention and other doctrines of limited participation such as *amicus curiae*, see JAY TIDMARSH & ROGER H. TRANGSRUD, MODERN COMPLEX LITIGATION 117, 120–21 (2d ed. 2010).

jurisdiction to nationwide service of process for complex cases,[101] and create generous rules of venue. But Congress has not done so, and seems unlikely to do so as a general matter in the near future. Even loosened jurisdiction and venue rules, however, can do nothing about claims that are temporally dispersed, because those that have not yet received injuries cannot yet join the case. The problem of these "future plaintiffs" is particularly acute in certain mass torts involving exposure to substances whose alleged health effects are manifested years later.

Although the law of joinder is limited in its capacity to achieve joinder, it remains a principal vehicle for aggregating related cases. The following chapters examine other methods by which American courts respond to the problem of repetitive litigation. Keep in mind that the combination of techniques to achieve aggregation, not any technique judged in isolation, determines the effectiveness of the response to mass disputes.

> *Question 2*
>
> Aggregation—even optimal aggregation—can frustrate litigant autonomy to structure a case in a litigant's best interests. Decisions about whether to aggregate and when to aggregate can also influence outcomes for litigants. Are the benefits of optimal aggregation worth the costs? Does this type of cost-benefit analysis ignore values that are not easily captured in such a balance?

One of these alternative methods is the class action. The federal class-action rule, Rule 23, is included among the joinder rules in the Federal Rules of Civil Procedure. Rule 23 is often described as a joinder rule. In many ways, however, it is best seen as a preclusion device, so we defer its consideration until we have examined preclusion as a tool to achieve consolidation. Because of the potential impact of class actions on the aggregation of related cases, it is especially important to reserve judgment on the efficacy of the joinder rules that we have examined to date until you study Rule 23.

---

101 Congress's constitutional authority to enact a nationwide service-of-process statute for claims based on state law is uncertain, although the American Law Institute believes that the power exists. *See* COMPLEX LITIGATION: STATUTORY RECOMMENDATIONS AND ANALYSIS 155 (AM. L. INST. 1994) ("The power of Congress to supply a federal national-contacts long-arm statute for use in complex cases seems clear."). The Institute has recommended enactment of a nationwide service-of-process statute for all complex cases, whether grounded in federal or state law, *see id.* § 3.08.

Chapter 3

CONSOLIDATION, TRANSFER, AND REMOVAL

A different strategy for aggregating related claims is to allow plaintiffs to file their cases in any forums they choose, and then to gather the cases into a single forum for resolution. Various mechanisms to achieve the consolidation of cases are available. Most were not designed with the needs of mass aggregation in mind, although one device—the multidistrict-litigation statute—was intended specifically for this purpose. Each method has limits that we examine as we proceed through the Chapter. One noteworthy limit of general applicability is worth mentioning at the outset: All consolidation devices work only with regard cases that have been filed. If effective, consolidation may present a solution to the problem of geographical dispersion of related cases. Consolidation also works less well when jurisdictional dispersion—the spreading of cases across state and federal courts—is in play. And none can address the problem of temporal dispersion; courts cannot act with respect to cases that have not been filed by the time that the consolidated proceeding ends.

The Chapter begins with the simplest form of consolidation: the consolidation of cases that have been filed in the same court. It then moves to the transfer of cases pending in different districts within the same court system, and finally to the transfer of a case from one court system (federal or state) to the other (state of federal).

A. Consolidation Within a District

Assume that two plaintiffs have both filed a case for injuries suffered at the hands of a defendant who has manufactured an allegedly defective product that each plaintiff used. Both plaintiffs file their cases in the same federal district court. For simplicity's sake, assume as well that this court possesses subject-matter jurisdiction over the claims in both cases, territorial jurisdiction over the defendant, and venue. Finally, assume that neither plaintiff wants to join with the other under Rule 20(a).

This hypothetical brings squarely into play the court's power to consolidate cases properly before it. In the federal system, the basic rule permitting consolidation is Federal Rule of Civil Procedure 42(a), which states that a court "may . . . join for hearing or trial any or all matters at issue in the actions" or "consolidate the actions" as long as the "actions before the court involve a common question of law or fact."[102]

The "common question" requirement is the only necessary condition for consolidation; the consolidated cases need not arise out of the same transaction or occurrence, as required for joinder under Rule 20(a). Rule 42(a)'s use of the word "may" suggests that the court retains broad discretion to consolidate cases—for pretrial purposes, trial purposes, or both—in appropriate circumstances.[103]

Because a single common question of law or fact is not a high threshold, the critical issue is usually whether consolidation is appropriate. For instance, suppose that two cases both alleging injury from the same fraudulent securities misrepresentation are filed in the same district. Should they be consolidated? Almost all of us would say "yes." Now suppose that the two victims of asbestos exposure, who worked for the same company but during different time periods and in different occupations, file separate suits in the same court. Should these cases be consolidated? A lot of us would say yes, but with less certainty. What if the two plaintiffs worked for different companies? Or what if there were two thousand, instead of two, plaintiffs? Now we get into grayer areas—but of course these are the areas that often matter in bringing together related cases in mass disputes.

As a general matter, courts have tended to answer these questions by asking whether consolidation would promote judicial economy. Increasingly, however, courts are recognizing that economy is not the only issue, and "[c]onsiderations of convenience and economy must yield to a paramount concern for a fair and impartial trial."[104] Relevant concerns in determining economy and fairness include "the specific risks of prejudice and possible confusion" if separate cases are consolidated, "the risk of inconsistent adjudications of common factual and legal issues" if the cases are not consolidated, "the burden on parties," "the length of time required to conclude multiple suits as against a single suit," and "the relative expense" of the consolidated and non-consolidated alternatives.[105]

---

102 Prior to the creation of Rule 42, federal courts had held that they had inherent power, both in law and equity, to consolidate cases in the same district. Johnson v. Manhattan Ry. Co., 289 U.S. 479 (1933).

103 *See* Johnson v. Celotex Corp., 899 F.2d 1281 (2d Cir. 1990) ("The trial court has broad discretion to determine whether consolidation is appropriate.").

104 *See id.* at 1285.

105 *See* Hendrix v. Raybestos-Manhattan, Inc., 776 F.2d 1492 (11th Cir. 1985). *Hendrix* was a case involving consolidation of cases claiming injuries from exposure to asbestos in the workplace. In this context, *Hendrix*, *Johnson*, and other cases have cashed out these general considerations into a specific set of criteria to determine consolidation: (1) the existence of a common worksite, (2) similarity of plaintiff occupations, (3) similarity in time of exposure, (4) types of diseases suffered by plaintiffs, (5) whether plaintiffs were living or deceased, (6) status of discovery in each

Thus, the appropriateness of consolidation cannot be answered without some sense of the pretrial and trial techniques that could be employed to resolve a large consolidated action—matters that we take up in Parts Two and Three.

The case law on consolidation is mixed. For instance, in *Katz v. Realty Equities Corp. of New York*,[106] the court found no abuse of discretion in the consolidation for pretrial purposes of twelve securities actions that arose out of a series of transactions allegedly designed to defraud the public. In *Johnson v. Celotex Corp.*,[107] the cases of two asbestos workers who worked at the same jobsite, who suffered from asbestosis, and who were represented by the same lawyer were consolidated for trial—even though their exposures occurred during different time periods, the plaintiffs had different occupations, and one plaintiff had died of his exposure while the other remained alive. In *Consorti v. Armstrong World Indus., Inc.*,[108] the court of appeals approved the trial consolidation of four cases brought by plaintiffs suffering from mesothelioma against various asbestos defendants. The court stated that "[c]onsolidation is a valuable and important tool of judicial administration. This is especially true when the courts are overwhelmed with huge numbers of cases which involve substantially the same questions of fact .... [C]onsolidation is also capable of producing, with efficiency and greatly reduced expense for all parties, a fairer, more rational and evenhanded delivery of justice." Although the court acknowledged that "[t]he obligation of the courts to deliver justice is paramount, and it may not be scrapped for the benefit of cheaper and more rapid dispositions," it noted that "the judiciary ... must be open to discarding habits that have outlived their usefulness, and must bend under the pressures of modern life to find greater efficiency in accomplishing its mission."

On the other hand, *Malcolm v. National Gypsum Co.*[109] reversed as an abuse of discretion the trial consolidation of 48 asbestos cases involving plaintiffs injured in various New York powerhouses. The court thought that, due to different worksites, occupations of plaintiffs, times of exposure, and types of diseases, the district court had gone "too far in the interests of expediency and [sacrificed] basic fairness in the process." Specifically, the court mentioned the possibility of jury confusion. While Rule 42(a) was "designed to

---

case, (7) whether the same counsel represented the parties in each case, and (8) the types of cancer suffered by plaintiffs.

[106] 521 F.2d 1354 (2d Cir. 1975).

[107] 899 F.2d 1281 (2d Cir. 1990).

[108] 72 F.3d 1003 (2d Cir. 1995), *vacated and remanded on other grounds sub nom.* Consorti v. Owens-Corning Fiberglas Corp., 518 U.S. 1031 (1996).

[109] 995 F.2d 346 (2d Cir. 1993).

achieve efficiency," the court cautioned that it was not intended to "compromis[e] a litigant's right under the Seventh Amendment to a jury trial." Likewise, in *In re Repetitive Stress Injury Litigation*,[110] the court granted writs of mandamus against the pretrial consolidation of forty-four cases against defendants that made or distributed products allegedly causing an array of repetitive stress injuries. The only commonalities among the cases were at a high level of generality, a fact which led the court to observe that "[t]he systemic urge to aggregate litigation must not be allowed to trump our dedication to individual justice."

It is difficult to draw definite lessons from the array of cases. No easy distinction reconciles them. It is tempting to say that consolidation should be used primarily in negative-value securities litigation like *Katz*, in which it makes little economic sense to bring individual suits and the argument for individualized justice is therefore the weakest. But consolidation was allowed in large-stakes tort cases like *Johnson and Consorti*. It is also tempting to suggest that consolidation should be easier in "mature" litigation in which the lack of novel issues should make joint treatment especially efficient. But *Malcolm* suggests that maturity is not dispositive, and the lack of maturity in *Katz* was not an insuperable barrier. It is further tempting to suggest that consolidation is possible as long as the plaintiffs consent to consolidation, but the plaintiffs consented to consolidation in *Malcolm* and *Repetitive Stress Injuries*. Another distinction—that pretrial consolidations should be easier to obtain than trial consolidations—does not account for *Repetitive Stress Injuries*, which refused to permit even pretrial consolidation. The number of cases is a final possible distinction: two, four, or twelve actions can be consolidated, but forty-four or forty-eight cannot. But this reconciliation suggests that consolidation fails at the moment when it is most needed—when hundreds of cases threaten to create inefficiency or unequal treatment of similarly situated parties.

Thus, even the "simple" case of intra-district consolidation raises hard questions of the proper balance of efficiency, litigant autonomy, jury trial, judicial discretion, transactionalism, and (to the extent that consolidation is easier in some types of cases than others) trans-substantivity.

A separate issue of intradistrict consolidation arises when related cases are filed in the same district, but in different divisions of that district. In this situation, transfer of all cases to one division is the necessary first step; consolidation is the second. Rule 42(a) does not seem to authorize intradivision transfer, but 28 U.S.C. § 1404(a), which we consider in more detail in the following section, does.

---

110 11 F.3d 368 (2d Cir. 1993).

Essentially the same considerations of efficiency and fairness apply under both Rule 42(a) and § 1404;[111] but the need to proceed in two steps can slow down the process of consolidation—and frustrate single-forum consolidation if some of the cases cannot be moved among divisions or if one case successfully obtains transfer away from the remainder of the consolidated cases.

In many ways, the arguments over the breadth of consolidation should seem familiar. They are not unlike the arguments over the breadth of voluntary joinder under Rule 20(a). True, Rule 20(a) has not only a "common question of law or fact" requirement but also a "transaction or occurrence" requirement; thus, the breadth of Rule 42(a) consolidation is arguably broader. And Rule 42(a) has the advantage that a judge has the *sua sponte* power to consolidate cases; the judge is not beholden to the joinder choices of the plaintiffs.[112] But the two powers work in tandem. Plaintiffs attain a certain degree of joinder under Rule 20(a). To the extent that the plaintiffs' choices dictate that they file separate cases in the same district and division, the court can then tie the cases together under Rule 42(a).[113] Given the common orientation of Rules 20(a) and 42(a) to allow as much aggregation as efficiency and fairness dictate, the considerations that govern the application of two Rules are, unsurprisingly, overlapping.

> *Question 1*
>
> One pedagogical difficulty with studying each aggregation method separately is understanding how the methods interact. Does the operation of Rule 42(a) make you think better of the voluntary-joinder approach of Rule 20(a)?

B. Transfer Between Districts

Transfer moves a case from the docket of a court in one district of a court system to the docket of another court within that same system. The party moving to transfer usually perceives some advantage from transfer—perhaps easier access to witnesses or evidence, convenience for the moving party, inconvenience to other parties, or securing a better judge or jury pool. Not all of these are noble reasons, nor are they all reasons that courts accept as legitimate. Therefore, whatever the private motivations, a party seeking transfer couches the motion in terms of efficiency, convenience, and fairness.

---

111 *See In re* Radmax, Ltd., 720 F.3d 285 (5th Cir. 2013).

112 Devlin v. Transp. Commc'ns Int'l Union, 175 F.3d 121 (2d Cir. 1999).

113 It is important to note that consolidation does not merge the consolidated cases into a single case. Each case retains its individual identity, and a judgment must ultimately be rendered in each one. *See* Johnson v. Manhattan Ry. Co., 289 U.S. 479 (1933).

Even a simple one-claim, two-party case can be transferred. Our concern, however, is whether transfers can aid single-forum aggregation when cases are dispersed over several courts within a single court system. Thus far, state courts have not developed interstate transfer mechanisms,[114] nor are there transnational transfer mechanisms. Most states allow transfer from the courts of one county to the courts of another, but that transfer process works only when a single state's court system contains all the related litigation. The only functional transfer mechanisms for litigation dispersed across state lines exist on the federal-court level, a fact that is sometimes cited as an advantage of the federal system as a forum for multi-party litigation.

Federal courts enjoy a number of specialized mechanisms to transfer cases in specific circumstances,[115] but only two transfer statutes have general applicability to multi-party litigation: 28 U.S.C. § 1404 and 28 U.S.C. § 1407. A third mechanism—inherent judicial power—is today more theoretical than real.

1. Section 1404 Transfers

The first general transfer provision is 28 U.S.C. § 1404. Enacted in 1948 and superseding the doctrine of *forum non conveniens*,[116] § 1404 permits one federal court to transfer a case "to any other district or division where it might have been brought or to any district or division to which all parties have consented." The standard for transfer is "[f]or the convenience of parties and witnesses, in the interest of justice." Although one of the parties usually moves for a § 1404(a) transfer, the judge has a *sua sponte* power to order transfer.[117] Once the case is transferred, the transferor court has nothing more to do with the case; the transferee court handles the case to its conclusion.

In explicating the § 1404(a) standard, courts have considered a wide array of efficiency and fairness considerations, including the location of major events and evidence, the interest in a speedy trial,

---

[114] The Uniform Laws Commission proposed the Uniform Transfer of Litigation Act, patterned on 28 U.S.C. § 1404 (the federal venue-transfer statute), in 1991. The Act would allow transfer from the courts of one adopting state to the courts of another adopting state. No state, however, has ever enacted the proposed Act.

[115] *See, e.g.*, 28 U.S.C. § 1406 (permitting court to transfer improperly venued case to a proper venue); 28 U.S.C. § 1412 (permitting bankruptcy case to be transferred "in the interest of justice or for the convenience of the parties").

[116] For a discussion of *forum non conveniens*, which remains a relevant doctrine when transfer is not possible (i.e., when a party wishes to move a case from a court of one state to the court of another state or from a court of one nation to a court of another nation), see *infra* notes 190–191, 195 and accompanying text.

[117] *See* 15 CHARLES ALAN WRIGHT ET AL., FEDERAL PRACTICE AND PROCEDURE § 3844 (4th ed. 2013).

and the single resolution of related cases;[118] they have then balanced these factors against countervailing considerations, including the plaintiff's interest in his or her chosen forum.[119] The district court has broad discretion in weighing factors and deciding whether or not to transfer the case.

> *Problem 1*
>
> A product-liability mass tort has resulted in the filing of cases in federal and state courts across the country. Some of the cases involved plaintiffs exposed to the product in Manhattan; these cases have been filed in the United States District Court for the Southern District of New York. Other cases involved plaintiffs exposed to the product in Brooklyn; these cases were filed in the United States District Court for the Eastern District of New York. The distance between the courthouses is less than two miles. A single judge (from the Eastern District) has already been appointed to oversee both sets of cases. Would a § 1404 transfer of the Southern District cases to the Eastern District be appropriate? *See In re* Joint E. & S. Dists. Asbestos Litig., 769 F. Supp. 85 (E. & S.D.N.Y. 1991).

Section 1404(a) is not specifically designed for complex litigation, but it has occasionally been used with success to bring related cases dispersed across federal forums before a single court. Section 1404(a) has some noteworthy aggregation-friendly features, including a standard flexible enough to achieve optimal multi-party aggregation and a *sua sponte* judicial power to override the adversarial gamesmanship that sometimes keeps cases apart.

In addition, § 1404(a) can sometimes aid aggregation in consumer disputes. An increasingly common feature of many consumer contracts is a forum-selection clause: the parties agree by contract to litigate their disputes in a venue specified in the contract. Although these are usually adhesion contracts, courts have enforced forum-selection clauses as long as they are not unconscionable or unduly unfair.[120] Despite the clause, plaintiffs sometimes file their cases in other forums. The Supreme Court has held that, barring exceptional circumstances, a federal court in which the case was filed should use § 1404(a) to transfer the case to the federal district court designated in the forum-selection clause.[121] Thus, when

---

[118] For a discussion of some of the most common considerations, see *id.* §§ 3847–54.

[119] A plaintiff may seek a transfer, *see* Ferens v. John Deere Co., 494 U.S. 516 (1990); in this case, the plaintiff's venue preference is not a relevant consideration. In most cases, however, either a defendant or the court *sua sponte* initiates the transfer request, so respecting the plaintiff's choice of venue has significant, although not dispositive, weight.

[120] For a case enforcing a forum-selection clause under admiralty law, see Carnival Cruise Lines, Inc. v. Shute, 499 U.S. 585 (1991).

[121] Atl. Marine Constr. Co. v. U.S. Dist. Court for the W. Dis. of Tex., 571 U.S. 49 (2013). When the forum-selection clause points to a state court or foreign tribunal,

a group of consumers have a common dispute regarding the contract, and when all the contracts select the same federal forum, § 1404(a) aids consolidation.

For several reasons, however, § 1404(a) is not a generally useful solution to the problem of aggregation. The first problem is § 1404(a)'s requirement that the case can be transferred only to a district "where it might have been brought" or a district "to which all parties have consented." In *Hoffman v. Blaski*,[122] the Supreme Court held that the phrase "where it might have been brought" meant that a case could be transferred only to a district in which venue would have been proper when the case was filed. *Hoffman* further held that the defendant's willingness to consent to the transfer to an improper venue was irrelevant. The phrase "to which all parties have consented" was added in 2011 specifically to overrule this latter holding in *Hoffman*. Unless all parties consent to a transfer to an improper venue (and it seems unlikely that every party in every case will do so), however, *Hoffman*'s first limit remains, and the cases can be transferred only to a federal district court that had venue over each and every case. As we have seen, venue rules often make it impossible to locate all cases in a particular forum, so finding a single proper venue for all the cases in a large multi-party dispute is unlikely.

A second, related problem is that a court cannot transfer a case to a district that lacks territorial jurisdiction over the defendant. This rule, most famously stated by Learned Hand in *Foster-Milburn Co. v. Knight*,[123] has never been expressly endorsed by the Supreme Court. In light of *Hoffman*, however, it seems likely that the Court would do so.[124]

Third, § 1404(a) requires that the transfer motion be made in the court from which transfer is sought (the "transferor court"). Making such motions is not a great burden when only a few cases are subject to transfer. With widely dispersed litigation, however, the burden of filing hundreds of transfer motions is significant, and successful aggregation depends on the willingness of dozens of federal judges, acting independently, all to agree about the convenience and justice of coordinated handling in a single forum (the "transferee court").

---

the federal court should use the doctrine of *forum non conveniens* to dismiss the case. *See infra* note 214 and accompanying text.

[122] 363 U.S. 335 (1960).

[123] 181 F.2d 949 (2d Cir. 1950).

[124] *See* WRIGHT ET AL., *supra* note 117, § 3845. After a 1988 amendment to § 1391 brought venue over corporate defendants into closer alignment with territorial jurisdiction, this problem is less acute, but it remains an occasional impediment.

Fourth, § 1404(a) can transfer only cases filed in federal court. Cases filed in state court, as well as those that have not been filed at the time of the transfer, are not subject to § 1404.

Fifth, when some parties have agreed to a forum-selection clause and others have not, the strong possibility exists that the case may fracture into pieces—unless the forum selected in the clause is one to which the entire case can be transferred or one to which all parties consent.[125]

From an aggregation perspective, § 1404(a) has one especially useful feature: the court's *sua sponte* power to transfer, which can overcome aggregation-dispersing strategic choices by the parties. Nonetheless, § 1404(a) does not overcome significant structural impediments to aggregation (i.e., territorial jurisdiction and venue), and it lacks a single decision-maker to make aggregation decisions.

2. Section 1407 (Multidistrict) Transfers

28 U.S.C. § 1407, the multidistrict-litigation (MDL) statute, was created in 1968, largely in response to the filing of dispersed antitrust actions. The statute establishes the Judicial Panel on Multidistrict Litigation, which comprises seven federal judges. According to § 1407(a), whenever "civil actions involving one or more common questions of fact are pending in different districts," the Panel may transfer the cases "to any district for coordinated or consolidated pretrial proceedings." Section 1407(a) also provides a standard that guides the Panel's decision: "[t]ransfers . . . will be for the convenience of the parties and witnesses and will promote the just and efficient conduct of such actions." The statute also authorizes the Panel to sever any claim and remand it to the original forum.[126]

According to § 1407(c), the Panel can act either *sua sponte* (by issuing a "show cause order") or on the motion of a party. Under rules of procedure that the Panel has developed, the Panel can also transfer related actions (usually called "tag-along actions") that are filed after the initial group of cases has been transferred.[127]

---

[125] *See In re* Howmedica Osteonics Corp., 867 F.3d 390 (3d Cir. 2017) (applying a four-step framework and determining that claims against some defendants should be transferred from the forum required by the forum-selection clause for another defendant).

[126] An important limit on MDL transfer arises in cases removed from state court under the "mass action" provision of 28 U.S.C. § 1332(d)(11). For further details on mass actions, see *infra* notes 163, 165, 169–168 and accompanying text. Mass actions may be transferred to an MDL court only if a majority of the plaintiffs agree to the transfer, the cases are part of a certified class action, or the plaintiffs request class certification. *See* 28 U.S.C. § 1332(d)(11)(C).

[127] *See* Rules of Procedure of the Judicial Panel on Multidistrict Litigation 1.1(h), 7.1, 7.2.

Although the Panel orders transfer, it does not itself handle the consolidated cases; instead, it designates a judge in a federal district court (the "transferee court") to handle an MDL case. The transferee court is responsible for all further pretrial proceedings in the MDL. The transferee judge presides over common discovery, which is done once in the transferee court rather than multiple times in each transferor court. The transferee judge renders a single consistent ruling on pretrial matters—including case-dispositive or claim-dispositive motions.

The MDL transferee judge has one significant limitation on his or her power. The MDL statute permits consolidation only for pretrial purposes. Indeed, 28 U.S.C. § 1407(a) requires, "at or before the conclusion of . . . pretrial proceedings," that the Panel remand the consolidated cases back to their transferor forums "unless [they] shall have been previously terminated." For a number of years, transferee judges skirted this requirement by "self-transferring": using § 1404(a) to transfer the MDL cases to the MDL judge's own court for trial as well as pretrial purposes.[128] In *Lexecon Inc. v. Milberg Weiss Bershad Hynes & Lerach*,[129] however, the Court held that an MDL transferee judge has no power to self-transfer; the language of § 1407 contemplates that MDL cases should return to their original forums once pretrial proceedings conclude. Congress has considered legislation to overturn *Lexecon* and give the Judicial Panel (not the transferee judge) the power to transfer cases for trial purposes as well. Such a power would make a greater inroad into the plaintiff's right to control the litigation than the present MDL statute, and so far Congress has left the present system intact.[130]

When the transferee judge believes that the MDL proceedings have accomplished their purpose, the judge advises the Panel that the cases are ready for remand back to the transferor forum. (The Panel can remand even without a recommendation from the MDL judge, but it rarely does so.) When remand occurs, the transferee court's pretrial rulings travel back to the transferor forum, and are afforded deference by the transferor court under the law-of-the-case doctrine. Some hairy, and largely unresolved, issues can arise when the MDL transferee court enters a ruling that would be

---

128 Self-transfer worked only when the transferee court was a court to which a § 1404(a) transfer could be made.

129 523 U.S. 26 (1998).

130 The parties can waive any venue objections and allow the transferee judge to hear the case, but this "*Lexecon* waiver" must be clear and unambiguous. *See In re* Depuy Orthopaedics, Inc., 870 F.3d 345 (5th Cir. 2017) (holding that consent to try two bellwether cases before the MDL judge did not waive venue objections for the trial of other cases, but that mandamus should not be granted because the objecting party could appeal at the conclusion of the proceeding).

impermissible under the law of the transferor circuit.[131] These issues remain unresolved in large part because, like most federal litigation, MDL cases are almost always resolved during the pretrial process, whether by settlement or summary judgment. The remand required by *Lexecon* is more theoretical than real in most MDL proceedings.

When facing a transfer decision, the Judicial Panel on Multidistrict Litigation has two tasks. The first is to decide whether the proposed transfer meets the standard of § 1407(a). If the answer to the first inquiry is "yes," the second issue is to designate the judge to whom the cases should be transferred. Unlike § 1404, § 1407 does not limit transfer of cases only to a district with original venue over the case or to a venue to which the parties consent; in theory, any federal judge and any federal district court can serve as host for an MDL proceeding.

On the first question, the statutory factors—"actions involving one or more common questions of fact," "convenience of the witnesses and the parties" and "promot[ing] the just and efficient conduct of" the consolidated cases—echo the § 1404(a) factors and are no less vague. One way to get a better sense of what they mean is to read decisions of the Judicial Panel. Unfortunately, virtually all of the Panel's opinions are boilerplate, briefly reciting the nature of the litigation in one paragraph and then concluding in the next paragraph that the statutory factors are (or are not) met.[132] A handful of opinions are longer and more revealing, but it is difficult to know if the reasoning of those opinions carries over to the boilerplate decisions, which rarely cite prior Panel opinions.

A few general observations about the Panel's opinions can be made. The "common questions" requirement has not proven to be a significant hurdle in most circumstances, although a few Panel

---

[131] *Compare* Kalama v. Matson Navigation Co., 875 F.3d 297 (6th Cir. 2017) (holding that transferor circuit has jurisdiction to hear appeal from claims dismissed in an MDL transferee court located in a different circuit, after the Judicial Panel remands the non-dismissed claims to the transferor court and the transferor court enters judgment on the non-dismissed claims), *and In re* Briscoe, 448 F.3d 201 (3d Cir. 2006) (stating that an appeal from an MDL transferee judge's decision would be taken in the transferor court's circuit if the case was remanded), *with In re* Food Lion, Inc., Fair Labor Standards Act "Effective Scheduling" Litig., 73 F.3d 528 (4th Cir. 1996) (ordering the Judicial Panel to re-transfer a remanded case to the transferee forum, so that the MDL judge's dispositive summary-judgment ruling on one claim could be appealed and determined under the law of the transferee circuit).

[132] As proof of the formulaic nature of Panel decisions, you can look at the following cases, all decided in the same year, all involving different legal theories, and all using virtually identical language: *In re* Land Rover LR3 Tire Wear Prods. Liab. Litig., 598 F. Supp. 2d 1384 (J.P.M.L. 2009) (products liability); *In re* Wachovia Corp. Pick-A-Payment Mortg. Mktg. & Sales Practices Litig., 598 F. Supp. 2d 1383 (J.P.M.L. 2009) (consumer fraud and deceptive sales practices); *In re* Regions Morgan Keegan Sec., Derivative & Emp. Ret. Income (ERISA) Litig., 598 F. Supp. 2d 1379 (J.P.M.L. 2009) (securities fraud and ERISA liability); and *In re* Aftermarket Auto. Lighting Prods. Antitrust Litig., 598 F. Supp. 2d 1366 (J.P.M.L. 2009) (antitrust).

decisions have suggested that the common factual questions must predominate over individual ones for MDL transfer to be appropriate. The "convenience" requirement is an important one, but this issue is often passed over quickly in the Panel's transfer opinions, with the Panel often citing the elimination of duplicative litigation, the reduction of repetitive discovery costs, and the conservation of the parties' resources as the critical convenience factors when consolidating cases—or the lack of these elements when denying consolidation. The convenience that matters is convenience in the aggregate; individual inconvenience can be tolerated as long as overall convenience is achieved. The "just and efficient conduct" requirement, which to some extent sweeps both of the prior elements within its ambit, is the central issue in most transfer decisions. The Panel has never assayed a complete list of the factors it considers in making its determination of justice and efficiency. Among the factors the Panel frequently recites are:

- The significance and importance of common issues of fact.
- Whether, and to what extent, consolidation will reduce costs, especially discovery costs, and conserve the resources of the parties, their lawyers, and the federal judicial system.
- The number and location of cases. Although the Panel has consolidated as few as two cases, MDL transfer is more likely when there are more cases and when they are geographically dispersed.
- The number of lawyers and, relatedly, the ability of the lawyers to create informal networks to coordinate and share information. Informal cooperation reduces the need for an MDL proceeding.
- The age and progress of the cases. The Panel is less likely to order transfer when cases are at vastly different stages of litigation, especially when some are nearing trial. The Panel was traditionally reluctant to consolidate cases that were still in their immaturity, but it has shown more willingness to do so in more recent years.
- The position of the parties regarding transfer. When most parties agree to transfer, transfer becomes more likely.
- Multiple requests for preliminary or permanent injunctive relief. The Panel is more likely to order transfer when the injunctions requested in individual

cases would subject the defendant to inconsistent standards.

- The existence of overlapping class actions. MDL transfer avoids the problem of dueling classes.[133]

Conversely, the Panel professes never to be influenced by choice-of-law concerns.[134] The Panel's blinders do not mean that choice-of-law considerations are absent from MDL proceedings. Quite the contrary, as we will see later.[135] But the Panel refuses to get caught up in them.

A final factor that seems to influence the Panel has been the availability of other aggregation mechanisms. For reasons that we will explore in detail in Chapter Six, one of the best aggregation devices is the class action. But class actions have been more difficult to obtain as a result of decisions over the past twenty years. To some extent, the Panel has stepped into the void, using the MDL process to effect the aggregation of cases that, twenty years ago, it would have been far more reluctant to do.[136]

Once the Panel decides that MDL consolidation is appropriate, it must then select the transferee judge. Often, the plaintiffs and principal defendants agree about the need for MDL consolidation, but they fight tooth and nail over where the case should be consolidated. As we see in Part II, a judge presiding over an aggregated proceeding has broad powers, and different judges use those powers in different ways. Different pretrial procedures can result in different outcomes. So getting the "right" judge is crucial for all participants.

Several factors can influence the Panel's selection of a judge. The first, and necessary, condition is willingness. Some judges love the challenge of MDL cases; others can do without their headaches. Relatedly, the Panel considers the judge's success in handling big litigation, including prior MDLs. Experience with the type of case being consolidated also matters, although on rare occasion the Panel picks a judge with no prior background in the litigation. The number of cases pending before different judges may have some bearing, but the judge with the most cases does not necessarily get the nod. Other

---

[133] For a fuller discussion of factors influencing the Panel, written by its then-Chair, see John G. Heyburn II, *A View from the Panel: Part of the Solution*, 82 TUL. L. REV. 2225 (2008).

[134] *In re* Gen. Motors Class E Stock Buyout Sec. Litig., 696 F. Supp. 1546 (J.P.M.L. 1988).

[135] *See infra* text following note 597.

[136] See Richard L. Marcus, *Cure-All for an Era of Dispersed Litigation? Toward a Maximalist Use of the Multidistrict Litigation Panel's Transfer Power*, 82 TUL. L. REV. 2245 (2008).

factors, like the location of relevant events, witnesses, parties, and evidence, can also matter.[137]

The importance of the MDL process in modern complex litigation can hardly be overstated. Especially as other aggregation mechanisms such class actions have faltered, use of the MDL process to bring federal cases together has grown. As of this writing, the federal courts have approximately 339,000 pending civil cases. Of that number, about 124,000 (or 36.5 percent of all federal civil actions) are presently part of an MDL proceeding. A total of 227 MDL dockets, spread across 183 transferee judges in 51 federal districts, are open. The largest MDL docket presently contains more than 20,000 cases.[138]

The MDL process has become one of the dominant features in modern federal litigation. It is easy to see why. The MDL process possesses advantages that other joinder or consolidation methods do not. In the first instance, there are no limits on the forum to which the cases can be transferred. The Panel is not limited just to districts that have territorial jurisdiction over all the defendants or venue over the entire case.[139]

Second, strategic behavior by the parties is no barrier. The Panel has a *sua sponte* power to order transfer; it need not await a motion by the parties.

Third, the MDL statute provides a central decision-maker to transfer related litigation. Motions for transfer need not be filed in multiple forums. Transfer of later-filed cases is possible.

Fourth, the standards under which transfer occurs are flexibly stated, so the Panel has the discretion to ensure that only the cases truly meriting aggregation receive it.

Fifth, the judges on the Judicial Panel are well-versed in complex litigation, and they tend to choose as transferee judges others of similar skill. Thus, the parties are likely to appear before a

---

[137] *See* Daniel A. Richards, Note. *An Analysis of the Judicial Panel on Multidistrict Litigation's Selection of Transferee District and Judge*, 78 FORDHAM L. REV. 311 (2009) (analyzing the factors that the Panel cites in selecting a transferee forum and judge).

[138] As of April 2018, sixteen MDL proceedings carried no active cases and ten contained only one active case. Roughly 31% of MDL proceedings contained ten or fewer actions; 44% contained between eleven and one hundred. Although accounting for only 8% of the total number of MDL proceedings, nineteen MDLs contained more than 1,000 cases; these MDLs accounted for more than 84% of all transferred actions.

[139] *See In re* Aviation Prods. Liab. Litig., 347 F. Supp. 1401 (J.P.M.L. 1972) ("Transfer of civil actions pursuant to 28 U.S.C. § 1407 is for pretrial purposes only and the fact that all parties are not amenable to suit in a particular district does not prevent transfer to that district for pretrial proceedings where the prerequisites of Section 1407 are otherwise satisfied.").

sophisticated judge. A single judge also creates consistency and uniformity with respect to pretrial rulings.

Until now, we have painted a fairly rosy picture of the MDL process. In fact, MDL transfers are not a panacea for all the ills of multi-party, multi-forum litigation. They raise numerous practical and theoretical problems. The first is the common difficulty of all federal consolidation and transfer mechanisms: the MDL statute can consolidate only those cases already filed in federal district courts. Cases are filed in state courts, as well as cases that are not ripe to be filed, lie beyond the consolidating power of the Panel.

A second problem is endemic to all devices that affect a plaintiff's forum choice: MDL transfer violates the plaintiffs' adversarial ability to control the litigation. Of course, § 1407 does so in a less severe way than other devices, since the transfer is only for "pretrial proceedings." Nonetheless, most MDL proceedings end during the pretrial process, whether through settlement or dismissal. Because the Panel considers the overall benefits and costs of aggregation in making a transfer decision, transfer can occur even when it imposes large costs on individuals caught up within the process.

Third, and relatedly, concentrating cases tends to concentrate legal representation. We explore this issue in detail in Chapter Ten, but it will not surprise you that a transferee judge who receives MDL cases soon appoints a small group of lawyers to represent all the plaintiffs. The MDL world is a specialized practice, and certain plaintiffs' firms tend to dominate multidistrict litigation. Not only does this concentration deprive individual litigants of their chosen lawyers and of the fine-grain knowledge of individual circumstances that the litigants' own lawyers would know, but it also creates a risk that repeat-player plaintiffs' firms will look after their long-term interests as MDL players rather than the immediate interests of the plaintiffs in this MDL, thus raising the specter of agency costs.[140]

Fourth, because the transferee judge possesses a plethora of pretrial powers that might affect the outcome of the litigation, the choice of the transferee judge might well determine the outcome of hundreds or thousands of related suits. One study presented a hypothetical mass disaster to a group of federal judges, and asked how they would resolve the litigation. Different judges chose different techniques, some of which would likely have led to dismissal and others to multi-million-dollar settlements.[141] This issue can be especially problematic when cases are immature. An MDL transfer

---

[140] *See* Elizabeth Chamblee Burch, *Monopolies in Multidistrict Litigation*, 70 VAND. L. REV. 67 (2017).

[141] *See* E. Donald Elliott, *Managerial Judging and the Evolution of Procedure*, 53 U. CHI. L. REV. 306 (1986).

that occurs early in the litigation cycle can deprive plaintiffs of the opportunity to perfect their cases through trial and error.

Fifth, an MDL pretrial proceeding can take longer to complete than the pretrial phase in any single individual suit, even though the total time for handling all cases goes down. The delay can be especially troublesome for individual cases in which discovery was already winding up.

A sixth criticism is the very flexibility of the MDL standards that seemed to have been one of its strengths. A decision to consolidate cases in an MDL proceeding is one of the most critical in the litigation, but the Panel's discretion is only loosely constrained. Nor is the precedent that the Panel has developed in its opinions an especially transparent or useful check on its authority. Lawyers and academics might hope for better guidance on, and a more intellectually honest appraisal of, the reasons behind such consequential litigation decisions.

Finally, some commentators have argued that MDL transfer orders bring weak cases out of the woodwork. Because most transferee judges forge a settlement, lawyers with cases whose merits were too thin to press independently sometimes rush into federal court—and then let the tag-along process sweep the cases into the MDL proceeding, freeride on the discovery, and bide their time to get a share of the anticipated recovery.

Some of the problems of multidistrict litigation are reflected in the Panel's treatment of asbestos litigation. In 1977, when 103 cases were pending in the federal courts, the Panel issued a show-cause order proposing to "multidistrict" federal asbestos litigation. It backed off in light of the

Problem 2

A large internet service provider suffered a security breach that exposed private information of at least 500 million users. Within a month, five actions had been filed in three federal courts (Northern District of California, Southern District of California, and Southern District of Illinois). A plaintiff who filed in the Northern District of California moved for § 1407 consolidation in the Northern District of California, the district in which the service provider was also headquartered. Subsequent to the filing of the motion, fourteen more cases had been filed in various federal districts. Among the common questions were the service provider's security measures, the nature of its investigation into the breach, and reasons for its supposed delay in notifying users of the breach. Damages may be a more individualized issue. All parties supported centralization in the Northern District of California. Is consolidation appropriate? *See In re* Yahoo! Inc. Customer Data Sec. Breach Litig., 223 F. Supp. 3d 1353 (J.P.M.L. 2016).

unanimous opposition of plaintiffs and defendants.[142] Over the course of the next fourteen years, as the number of federal asbestos cases sky-rocketed, the Panel refused to multidistrict asbestos litigation on four more occasions. Finally, in 1991, faced with more than 26,000 pending federal asbestos cases, the Panel consolidated the cases in a single transferee forum over the continuing opposition of many (but not all) parties.[143] The Panel's 1991 decision is one of its lengthiest and most thorough, analyzing both the failures of individual litigation and the need for the consolidated handling of the asbestos controversy.

By 1991, however, very little additional pretrial work needed to be done in asbestos cases; almost all the relevant information had been discovered over the course of thousands of state and federal lawsuits. The MDL transfer generated a large number of individual settlements, as well as a failed effort to craft a global settlement,[144] but such consolidation seemed to stretch the purpose of multidistrict litigation. Over the course of almost twenty years, 180,000 federal asbestos cases were dumped into the MDL, where they mostly languished without resolution (even outlasting the transferee judge presiding over the litigation). Not until 2009 did a new transferee judge begin to dispose of the docket with an aggressive combination of settlement, dismissal, and remand.

A different object lesson arose in the breast-implant litigation of the 1990s. After a couple of significant successes in individual trials, breast-implant products-liability cases suddenly blossomed across the country. Despite the immaturity of the litigation, and perhaps still smarting from its failure to respond more aggressively in the asbestos litigation, the Panel consolidated the first 78 cases quickly;[145] more than 10,000 tag-along cases ultimately followed. The transferee judge, in coordination with state-court judges and a bankruptcy court, engineered a series of settlements that ran to billions of dollars for thousands of claimants. Although resolving so many cases so quickly seems a notable success for an MDL proceeding that was active for only a few years, the early victories by plaintiffs in individual actions ultimately appeared to have been something of an anomaly, and even today the long-term health effects of leaking breast implants are, except for some rare diseases, a matter of scientific and medical debate. The *Silicone Gel* MDL, driven

---

142 *In re* Asbestos & Asbestos Insulation Materials Prods. Liab. Litig., 431 F. Supp. 906 (J.P.M.L. 1977).

143 *In re* Asbestos Prods. Liab. Litig. (No. VI), 771 F. Supp. 415 (J.P.M.L. 1991).

144 *See* Amchem Prods., Inc. v. Windsor, 521 U.S. 591 (1997). We will examine the *Amchem* settlement and its flaws *infra* notes 355–361, 415–416, 487 and accompanying text.

145 *See In re* Silicone Gel Breast Implants Prods. Liab. Litig., 793 F. Supp. 1098 (J.P.M.L. 1992).

by the desire to avoid another asbestos catastrophe rather than by science, arguably got too far ahead of the game.

Of course, a couple of anecdotes from massive MDLs should not condemn a process that has done considerable work in multi-party, multi-forum lawsuits, both large and small, for fifty years. Moreover, many of the criticisms of the MDL process are not unique; we encounter them with other aggregation techniques. Because MDL aggregation is the first broadly effective aggregation device that we have seen, however, appreciating the negative dimensions of MDL consolidations counterbalances any unbridled enthusiasm about the positive features of the device.

3. Other Possible Transfer Authorities

In addition to §§ 1404(a) and 1407(a) transfers, courts have occasionally entertained other authorities to transfer cases between districts. Before settling on § 1404(a) as the authority to transfer cases in *In re Joint Eastern and Southern Districts Asbestos Litigation*,[146] Judge Weinstein opined the § 1404 might not "exhaust[ ] the power of courts within the same circuit to consolidate cases pending in different districts for trial." He raised the possibility that either Rule 42 or a court's inherent power, perhaps bolstered by the All Writs Act,[147] might serve as a basis allow interdistrict transfers in "mega-mass tort cases pending before the courts in different districts in the same circuit."

Thus far, such claims of additional power are more theoretical than real. Like all Federal Rules of Civil Procedure, Rule 42 cannot affect or extend the ordinary rules of venue.[148] The statutory powers and limits of §§ 1404 and 1407 seem to occupy the transfer field, leaving little room for vaguely specified inherent powers.[149] Moreover, the Supreme Court has not construed the All Writs Act broadly to respond to related difficulties posed by multi-party, multi-forum litigation.[150] In any event, Judge Weinstein confined his tantalizing suggestion to the consolidation of cases within a single federal district.

---

146 769 F. Supp. 85 (E. & S.D.N.Y. 1991).

147 28 U.S.C. § 1651.

148 FED. R. CIV. P. 82. Other cases have rejected the use of Rule 42 to effect interdistrict consolidation. *See* Town of Warwick v. N.J. Dep't of Envtl. Prot., 647 F. Supp. 1322 (S.D.N.Y. 1986).

149 *Cf.* Dietz v. Bouldin, 579 U.S. ___, 136 S. Ct. 1885 (2016) (holding that a court's inherent power must be a "reasonable response to the problems and needs confronting the court's fair administration of justice" and "cannot be contrary to any express grant of or limitation on the district court's power contained in a rule or statute") (internal quotation marks omitted).

150 We discuss the All Writs Act, and the Court's interpretation of it, in greater detail *infra* notes 170–173, 231–251 and accompanying text.

C. Transfer Between Federal and State Courts

The consolidation and transfer devices that we have considered so far in this Chapter make possible the aggregation of cases filed in federal court. As we have seen, the limited subject-matter jurisdiction of the federal courts make it likely that related cases will be spread across state and federal forums. The final issue to consider is whether any devices allow transfer of cases from federal court to state court, or conversely, state court to federal court.

1. Federal-to-State Transfer

Because no state-to-state transfer mechanism presently exists,[151] a federal-to-state transfer device would likely defeat single-forum aggregation unless cases filed in various state courts could also be consolidated in one state court. At one point, the American Law Institute proposed a court, modeled after the Judicial Panel on Multidistrict Litigation, with the authority to move cases from federal to a single state court and also to move all state cases into the same state forum.[152] Of course, such an authority would not achieve single-forum consolidation in the unusual settings in which federal jurisdiction over some of the claims is exclusive.

At present, however, discussion regarding a federal-to-state transfer is a moot point. No such authority exists. In the next chapter, we will briefly examine some doctrines under which a federal court might stay a case in favor of related state proceedings;[153] beyond those doctrines, which are of very limited scope and rarely apply in the multi-party context, no general federal-to-state transfer device exists. Indeed, a general federal-to-state transfer mechanism would run counter to the usual view that federal courts have a "virtually unflagging obligation . . . to exercise the jurisdiction given them."[154] The lack of such a device is a reason why federal courts are often viewed as a better forum for multi-party litigation.

2. State-to-Federal Transfer: Removal

It is possible to transfer a case from state to federal court through removal. Barring the availability of one of the specialized removal provisions in the United States Code, removal must occur under 28 U.S.C. § 1441. A number of limits accompany removal. The most important is the need for federal-subject-matter jurisdiction: a party cannot properly remove a case to federal court when the case

---

151 *See supra* note 114 and accompanying text.

152 *See* COMPLEX LITIGATION, *supra* note 101, ch. 4.

153 *See infra* Chapter 4.B.4.i.

154 Colo. River Water Conservation Dist. v. United States, 424 U.S. 800 (1976).

lacks subject-matter jurisdiction.[155] A plaintiff who immunizes a case to federal jurisdiction—say, by declining to plead federal-question theories and then suing only non-diverse defendants on state-law theories—has little fear of litigating in federal court. Securing a state forum may require the plaintiff to give up some legal theories and claims against some parties, but plaintiffs whose objective is to litigate in state court can often realize this goal.

Another limit on removal is consent. If a defendant is happy enough to be in state court, the defendant does nothing; unless a notice of removal is filed within thirty days of the time when a case first becomes removable, the defendant loses the right to remove. In a multi-defendant case, the usual rule is that all the defendants (or at least all those who have been served at the time that the notice of removal is filed) must join in the notice; if any defendant declines, removal is not proper.[156] Under § 1441 courts do not possess a *sua sponte* power to move cases into the federal system against the will of one or more defendants.

Other limits also exist. Among the most significant is the "forum defendant" rule, which bars removal of a diversity case from state court if the case is filed in a court of a state in which a defendant is a citizen.[157] Another limit on removal is the "year and a day" rule: when a case remains in state court for more than one year, and then becomes removable on the basis of diversity jurisdiction because the non-diverse parties have dropped out of the case, it cannot be removed unless it can be shown that the plaintiff's decision to join (and then drop) the non-diverse parties was a result of "bad faith."[158]

Some jurisdictional statutes of importance to complex litigation ease these removal limits. In Chapter One, we described two jurisdictional statutes—28 U.S.C. § 1332(d) (class actions) and 28 U.S.C. § 1369 (multi-party, multi-forum litigation)—that rely on the principle of minimal diversity, thus making it more difficult for a plaintiff to structure the litigation to avoid removal.[159] The class-action statute is especially noteworthy for two of its provisions. If a

---

155 *See* 28 U.S.C. § 1441(a) ("[A]ny civil action brought in a State court of which the district courts of the United States have original jurisdiction, may be removed by the defendant or the defendants . . . .").

156 *See* 28 U.S.C. §§ 1441 (a), 1446(b)(2)(A). Section 1446(b)(2) also lays out the removal process when defendants are served at different times.

157 *Id.* § 1441(b)(2).

158 *Id.* § 1446(c).

159 In Chapter Two, we examined a third minimal-diversity statute: 28 U.S.C. § 1335 (statutory interpleader). As we saw, the plaintiff in interpleader would usually be the defendant in the underlying actions. Hence, the plaintiff in interpleader already has an incentive to file the case in federal court in order to take advantage of the unique features of federal authority (such as nationwide service of process, generous venue, and anti-suit injunctions). In theory, however, a state-court interpleader action could be removed to federal court under the jurisdiction provided by § 1335.

class action meeting the terms of § 1332(d) is filed in state court, special removal provisions ease the removal of the class action to federal court.[160] First, the "year and a day" rule does not apply: a state-court case is removable within thirty days of the date on which the plaintiff seeks to certify a class action in state court, even if that the case has been ongoing in state court for more than one year.[161] Second, as long as any defendant seeks removal, the case is removed; defendants need not unanimously consent.[162]

Section 1332(d) provides jurisdiction in another situation: mass actions. Rather than employing class actions, plaintiffs' lawyers sometimes use the state-law equivalent of Rule 20(a) to join large numbers of plaintiffs in one mass state-court case. Traditionally, unless complete diversity existed over a mass action (and plaintiffs' lawyers usually ensured that it did not), removal jurisdiction was lacking. In 2005, however, Congress provided minimal-diversity removal jurisdiction over "mass actions." Mass actions are defined as civil actions involving 100 or more claimants who "are proposed to be tried jointly on the ground that the plaintiffs' claims involve common questions of law or fact."[163]

This jurisdiction is limited in a number of ways. First, it exists only over those claims that exceed the amount in controversy (presently set at more than $75,000).[164] Second, a mass action cannot be removed when a defendant's motion to consolidate gathers up 100 or more cases; rather, only the plaintiffs' voluntary decision to handle 100 or more cases jointly for trial triggers removal.[165] Removal is also barred when all the cases result from an "event or occurrence" in the state (or a contiguous state) in which the case is filed,[166] and when

[160] We examine the jurisdictional requirements of § 1332(d) *infra* notes 459–481 and accompanying text. For now, we assume that the state-court class action met the jurisdictional requirements of § 1332(d) and could have been filed in federal court.

[161] 28 U.S.C. § 1453(b).

[162] *Id.*

[163] 28 U.S.C. § 1332(d)(11)(B)(i). Even if each case is filed separately, a proposal by the plaintiffs to try 100 or more cases jointly triggers this provision. Whether particular requests in state court for consolidated handling—for instance, motions to consolidate cases for pretrial purposes—implicitly contain a proposal for joint trial is an issue that has been much litigated. *See, e.g.*, Corber v. Xanodyne Pharms., Inc., 771 F.3d 1218 (9th Cir 2014) (en banc); Atwell v. Boston Sci. Corp., 740 F.3d 1160 (8th Cir. 2013).

[164] 28 U.S.C. § 1332(d)(11)(B)(i). Although the matter is not free from doubt, it appears that removal is possible only when, in total, the value of the mass-action cases exceeds $5 million. For further exploration of some of the complexities of the amount-in-controversy requirement, see *Lowery v. Ala. Power Co.*, 483 F.3d 1184 (11th Cir. 2007).

[165] 28 U.S.C. § 1332(d)(11)(B)(ii)(II). Left unstated in this exclusion is whether *sua sponte* judicial consolidation can trigger removal.

[166] *Id.* § 1332(d)(11)(B)(ii)(I); *see* Abraham v. St. Croix Renaissance Grp., L.L.L.P., 719 F.3d 270 (3d Cir. 2013) (holding that pollution released into the environment over ten years was a single "event or occurrence").

cases are brought on behalf of the public pursuant to a statute authorizing such an action.[167]

The mass-action provision was enacted in 2005 as a part of the Class Action Fairness Act. Courts are still sorting through the meaning of its provisions. Gamesmanship on both sides abounds. One obvious trick for a plaintiffs' lawyer seeking to avoid mass-action removal is to file a series of 99-plaintiff lawsuits in the same court. For instance, in *Anderson v. Bayer Corp.*,[168] a plaintiffs' firm brought five products-liability actions composed of plaintiffs who had taken an allegedly defective drug. Each case had at least one plaintiff who was not diverse from the defendant. The firm limited each case to 99 plaintiffs, although a counting error resulted in 100 plaintiffs in one case. The defendant removed all five cases on the theory that the suits were one mass action of nearly 500 plaintiffs.

The court of appeals held that the case involving 100 plaintiffs was properly removed, but the cases with 99 or fewer plaintiffs were not. The court of appeals focused on the language of the mass-action provision, including its exclusion of jurisdiction when trial consolidation resulted from a defense motion, in concluding that the plaintiffs' structure of the action controlled removal. If plaintiffs structured each case with 99 plaintiffs, removal of the group of cases was forbidden.

Even when removal is available, it solves only half of the aggregation problem. Usually a state-court case is removed to the federal district that encompasses the same geographical area as the state court. If state-court litigation of related cases is widely dispersed, successful removal still leaves cases spread across many federal forums. Another technique—typically § 1404(a) transfer or MDL consolidation under § 1407(a)—supplies the necessary second step for single-forum aggregation. But not always. In a curious, aggregating-frustrating caveat, Congress refused to permit the Judicial Panel on Multidistrict Litigation to transfer a mass action under § 1332(d) to an MDL proceeding "unless a majority of the plaintiffs in the action request transfer pursuant to section 1407."[169]

Aside from the barrier that limited federal subject-matter jurisdiction erects, removal suffers from other flaws with which you are now familiar. One is its case-by-case approach; there is no centralized removal authority. A defendant faced with 1,000 state-

---

[167] 28 U.S.C. § 1332(d)(11)(B)(ii)(III). Courts have needed to discern whether *parens patriae* or similar actions by state attorneys general seeking recovery on behalf of their citizens are effectively a mass action of 100 or more plaintiffs. The majority view is no. *See* Nevada v. Bank of Am. Corp., 672 F.3d 661 (9th Cir. 2012); *but see* Louisiana *ex rel.* Caldwell v. Allstate Ins. Co., 536 F.3d 418 (5th Cir. 2008) (yes).

[168] 610 F.3d 390 (7th Cir. 2010).

[169] 28 U.S.C. § 1332(d)(11)(C)(i).

court actions must file a notice of removal in each one, and then it must take the second step of obtaining single-forum federal aggregation. Individualized removal is expensive, especially if the plaintiffs contest the legitimacy of the removal and seek remand.

Another flaw is the lack of *sua sponte* judicial power to order removal of state-court actions. Removal requires consent, sometimes of one, and usually of all, defendants. Defendants desirous of single-forum aggregation in federal court have the incentive to seek removal. But defendants who are content with a state forum can thwart efficient aggregation.

For a time, federal courts found a way to work around these two flaws: the All Writs Act.[170] The All Writs Act, which has been around since the earliest days of our republic, provides: "The Supreme Court and all courts established by Act of Congress may issue all writs necessary or appropriate in aid of their respective jurisdictions and agreeable to the usages and principles of law." The rather vague powers granted by the Act seem to have little to do with removal, but federal judges handling massive multi-party litigation sometimes found that related state-court litigation was threatening their ability to resolve a federal case. Many of these cases involved situations in which the federal-court litigation had settled (or was nearing a settlement), and the state-court litigation frustrated the federal court's ability to implement the settlement. To parry the threat, defendants removed the offending state-court cases and then sought their transfer to the federal judge handling the federal settlement. The claimed source of this removal power, which judges sometimes suggested that they could invoke *sua sponte*, was the All Writs Act. By invoking this removal authority, which was not grounded in § 1441, courts were able to override the limits on removal such as the "year and a day" rule, the forum-defendant rule, and the requirement that all defendants must consent.

The practice of "All Writs removal" ended abruptly in *Syngenta Crop Protection, Inc. v. Henson*.[171] In *Syngenta* plaintiffs had filed toxic-tort claims relating to use of an insecticide in a state court in Louisiana. A related federal case pending in the United States District Court for the Southern District of Alabama resulted in a settlement. The Louisiana plaintiffs intervened in the federal case and were allowed to participate in the settlement on the condition that they dismissed their state-court claims. When they returned to state court, however, they claimed that the settlement required them to dismiss only some of their claims. When they sought to continue the litigation, the defendant, understandably chagrined, first

---

170 28 U.S.C. § 1651(a).

171 537 U.S. 28 (2002).

removed the case to federal court and then obtained its transfer to the Southern District of Alabama. The federal judge, equally chagrined, dismissed the Louisiana plaintiffs' case.

The Supreme Court held that the All Writs Act did not authorize this practice. It acknowledged that "Act authorizes a federal court 'to issue such commands . . . as may be necessary or appropriate to effectuate and prevent the frustration of orders it has previously issued in its exercise of jurisdiction otherwise obtained.' "[172] But it concluded that more specific legislative authorities superseded the general powers of the Act. In this case, Congress had carefully delineated the removal powers of the federal courts. Thus, the defendants "may not, by resorting to the All Writs Act, avoid complying with the statutory requirements for removal." The Court also noted that the All Writs Act was not itself a grant of federal jurisdiction, so that it could not supply a jurisdictional authority to obtain removal under § 1441.[173]

The American Law Institute has proposed legislation that would overcome these difficulties. Its idea, part of which we encountered while discussing MDL proceedings, was to create a "Complex Litigation Panel," modeled after the Judicial Panel on Multidistrict Litigation, to aggregate multi-party, multi-forum litigation in a single court. The proposal gave the Panel the power to remove state-court cases to the federal court selected for aggregating the litigation. It could also "reverse-remove" federal cases to state court if it believed that a state court was the proper forum for aggregation. The Panel could move cases from one federal court to another (like the present Judicial Panel) or from one state court to another.[174]

> *Question 2*
>
> Does the ALI's proposal to create a Complex Litigation Panel with broad powers of removal and transfer, thrill you? Or chill you?

3. Cooperation

Given the dual system of state and federal courts, the limits on federal-court subject-matter jurisdiction, and plaintiffs' adversarial right to be masters of their complaints, it is almost inevitable that, in a large multi-party, multi-forum case, consolidation of all related cases in one forum will be impossible. An alternative to aggregation

---

172 *Id.* at 32 (quoting United States v. N.Y. Tel. Co., 434 U.S. 159 (1977)).

173 In another holding, the Court rejected the argument that the All Writs Act, joined together with a federal court's ancillary jurisdiction to enforce a settlement, provided a removal authority.

174 *See* COMPLEX LITIGATION, *supra* note 101. For good measure, the Panel was also invested with the power to issue anti-suit injunctions, a subject we consider in the next chapter. *See infra* note 251.

is cooperation and coordination of cases between courts. Cooperation works best when fewer judges are involved: for instance, when the federal cases are consolidated before a single transferee judge (typically through the MDL process) and a limited number of state courts host the vast majority of the state-court claims. Proximity between the federal and relevant state courts is also useful. A good working relationship among the judges and clear delineation of responsibilities are also keys to success. Among the concerns with cooperation are that one judge (usually the federal judge) will dominate the proceedings and, relatedly, that insufficient attention is paid to federalism and litigant-choice factors.

Whatever the concerns with state-federal coordination of cases, judicial cooperation has enjoyed some notable successes. Some commentators have analyzed a number of instances of cooperation, both successful and not, and developed best practices.[175]

D. An Assessment of Consolidation

As with joinder, the story of consolidation is a mixed bag. Some opportunities for aggregation exist, but so do limits. Common themes emerge across both joinder and consolidation: whether a *sua sponte* power to aggregate exists; whether a centralized body, as opposed to different parties and judges making individualized decisions, makes the aggregation decision; whether aggregation in a single forum is possible in light of jurisdictional and venue restrictions; whether the problem of temporal dispersion of claims and the aggregation of future plaintiffs is possible; and whether our present structure properly balances litigant autonomy, efficiency, and fairness.

We are about to turn to indirect ways to achieve aggregation: stays, injunctions, and preclusion. As we will see, these techniques can aid in the aggregation of related cases in some circumstances. For the most part, however, the joinder and consolidation doctrines that we have encountered provide the best available mechanisms for single-forum aggregation. (The one major exception, which we reserve until you see all other alternatives, is the class action.) No doctrine does a perfect job of aggregation, but the combination of joinder and consolidation techniques puts us on the road to the broad aggregation of related claims.

As we have explored these techniques, always with an eye toward whether each might be the Holy Grail of aggregation and why it falls short, we have also raised (sometimes gently) criticisms about whether aggregation is worth pursuing. As you now look back across

---

[175] *See* JAMES G. APPLE ET AL., FED. JUDICIAL CTR. & NAT'L CTR. FOR STATE COURTS, MANUAL FOR COOPERATION BETWEEN STATE AND FEDERAL COURTS (1997); William W Schwarzer et al., *Judicial Federalism in Action: Coordination of Litigation in State and Federal Courts*, 78 VA. L. REV. 1689 (1992).

joinder and consolidation, you should be able to evaluate both the benefits and the costs of single-forum aggregation. You should also be able to begin to form an opinion about whether our legal system should continue down the road of building even better aggregation mechanisms, get off the road and let individuals control their own party structures and forums, or stay pat.

Chapter 4

STAYS AND INJUNCTIONS

The terms "stay" and "injunction" are, in many contexts, interchangeable. Here we have a specific meaning for each word. A "stay" is a decision by a court not to proceed with a case pending before it. A stay stops the case in the court issuing the stay. The stay may be temporary, or the court may make it permanent by dismissing the case. The intended effect of a stay is to force the plaintiff to proceed with the case in another forum, although whether the plaintiff does so is the plaintiff's choice. On the other hand, an "injunction" is an order (usually directed to a litigant or potential litigant) not to proceed with an action in a forum other than the court issuing the injunction. An injunction issued against litigation elsewhere has the effect of forcing the plaintiff to file the case in the court issuing the injunction, if the plaintiff chooses to proceed at all.

Generally stays or injunctions are issued at the behest of a party, but courts have some *sua sponte* power to issue them as well. The traditional standards for issuing stays and injunctions were narrow. The standards were not calibrated with the needs of modern aggregation in mind.

As a modern aggregation mechanism, stays are usually inferior to injunctions because they require each judge in each forum to make a decision to stay the litigation in favor of a single other forum. And like most joinder and consolidation mechanisms, stays work only in cases that have been filed. Anti-suit injunctions more directly accomplish the goal; a single decision-maker can sweep cases out of all other forums, effectively funneling the litigation to the remaining forum. Moreover, anti-suit injunctions can in theory reach nonparties; they present the first realistic solution to remedy the problem of the future plaintiff that we have encountered.

This Chapter examines the traditional limits on stays and injunctions, as well as the ways in which the devices have been (or could be) recalibrated to assist the aggregation of complex litigation. It begins with a brief study of *in rem* litigation before moving to *in personam* litigation filed in different federal, state, and foreign courts.

A. *In Rem* Litigation

In rem litigation involves a dispute over a *res*—typically real estate but perhaps personal property like money, stock, insurance proceeds, or the like. The litigation typically determines ownership in the *res*, although *in rem* proceedings have broader uses in admiralty. When ownership interests in a *res* spread across juridical boundaries, so that related litigation might arise in different courts, the multi-party, multi-forum dispersion problem that we have been studying can arise.

Few complex cases involve *in rem* disputes over the ownership of specific assets; the one exception, perhaps, is bankruptcy, in which the debtor's estate is considered a *res* that must be distributed among creditors.[176] Nevertheless, studying how the law uses stays and injunctions in *in rem* litigation provides some important background for, as well as interesting contrasts to, the more typical problem of *in personam* litigation.

In American law, a longstanding "principle, applicable to both federal and state courts, is . . . that the court first assuming jurisdiction over the property may maintain and exercise that jurisdiction to the exclusion of the other."[177] This principle is logical. If two courts assert jurisdiction over a *res*, the possibility exists that one court will decide that Claimant A owns the property, while the other will find that Claimant B is the owner. We have seen how the need for a binding, comprehensive determination of ownership interests motivated the development of one branch of Rule 19 required-person joinder, as well as the doctrine of interpleader.

The same concern for clarity and finality in property rights led to the development of an anti-suit injunctive power, so that the first court to properly assert territorial jurisdiction over a *res* enjoys the power to enjoin all other later-filed proceedings.[178] If that first court is a federal court, the federal court can enjoin proceedings affecting the *res* in all other federal and state courts.[179] If the first court is a

---

[176] We examine bankruptcy *infra* Chapter 7.A.1.

[177] Penn Gen. Cas. Co. v. Pa. *ex rel.* Schnader, 294 U.S. 189 (1935); *see* Mandeville v. Canterbury, 318 U.S. 47 (1943) (holding that, when two cases "are *in rem* or *quasi in rem*, so that the court or its officer must have possession or control of the property . . . to proceed with the cause and to grant the relief sought, the court first acquiring jurisdiction or assuming control of such property is entitled to maintain and exercise its jurisdiction to the exclusion of the other"). This principle assumes that the first court can properly exercise jurisdiction over the *res*. *Cf.* Fall v. Eastin, 215 U.S. 1 (1909) (holding that a divorce decree in a state in which real property is not located is not entitled to full faith and credit in the state in which the property is located, when the decree was used to try to preclude litigation in the latter state regarding the ownership of the property).

[178] As a general rule, a court that encompasses the place where the *res* is physically located is the only court that can properly assert jurisdiction over the *res*. Intangible property presents somewhat greater challenges. *Cf.* Shaffer v. Heitner, 433 U.S. 186 (1977) (holding that, in a *quasi in rem* proceeding against stock owned by an alleged wrongdoer, a court could exercise jurisdiction over stock only if it could exercise jurisdiction over the owner).

[179] *See* Kline v. Burke Constr. Co., 260 U.S. 226 (1922) ("The rule . . . that the court first acquiring jurisdiction shall proceed without interference from a court of the other jurisdiction is a rule of right and of law based upon necessity . . . ."). Perhaps the

state court, it can enjoin all federal proceedings.[180] The same rule appears to hold for one state court enjoining another, although the cases are harder to find.[181]

Anti-suit injunctions involving foreign litigation follow the same path. An American court will stay its hand when a foreign court first acquires jurisdiction over a *res*.[182] Conversely, an American court may issue an injunction when it first acquires jurisdiction.[183] Whether a foreign court will respect the injunction is another matter.

B. *In Personam* Litigation

In personam litigation comprises the vast bulk of multi-party, multi-forum litigation. In an effort to lay out the complicated doctrines regarding stays and injunctions clearly, we proceed through four situations (stays and injunctions between one federal court and another federal court, between state courts, between an American court and a foreign court, and between federal and state courts). The last situation is the trickiest and often the most critical in complex litigation. Once again, we will see that federal courts enjoy an advantage over state courts as a forum for aggregation.

1. Stays and Injunctions Between Federal Courts

A federal court has no general power to enjoin *in personam* litigation pending in other federal districts merely because it is related to a case pending in the district. There are a couple of exceptions to this rule. First, a federal court in a statutory-interpleader[184] or bankruptcy[185] proceeding has the power to enjoin related litigation pending in other federal courts. Second, a federal court has a limited power with respect to duplicative *in personam*

---

most noteworthy anti-suit injunction is the automatic stay in bankruptcy; when a bankruptcy petition is filed, 11 U.S.C. § 362 automatically suspends all proceedings in all federal and state courts against the debtor. *See also id.* § 105 (authorizing a court sitting in bankruptcy to issue any injunction "necessary or appropriate to carry out the provisions" of the Bankruptcy Code).

180 Princess Lida of Thurn & Taxis v. Thompson, 305 U.S. 456 (1939).

181 *See, e.g.*, Cloverleaf Enters., Inc. v. Centaur Rosecroft, LLC, 815 N.E.2d 513 (Ind. App. 2004).

182 Dailey v. Nat'l Hockey League, 987 F.2d 172 (3d Cir. 1993); *cf.* SEC v. Banner Fund Int'l, 211 F.3d 602 (D.C. Cir. 2000) (affirming a refusal to stay American litigation that was filed before litigation in Belize that was arguably *in rem*).

183 China Trade and Dev. Corp. v. M.V. Choong Yong, 837 F.2d 33, 36 (2d Cir. 1987) ("When a proceeding is *in rem*, and res judicata alone will not protect the jurisdiction of the first court, an anti-suit injunction may be appropriate.").

184 *See* 28 U.S.C. § 2361. Recall that this injunctive power has limits; a court can only enjoin litigation affecting the property that is subject to interpleader. *See supra* note 66 and accompanying text. A comparable anti-suit injunctive power seems to exist for rule interpleader as well.

185 *See supra* note 179.

litigation when cases pending in two or more districts involve essentially the same parties and claims.

The starting point for this latter power is *Kerotest Manufacturing Co. v. C-O-Two Fire Equipment Co.*[186] In *Kerotest*, a patent owner brought an action against a company that bought component parts alleged to infringe the patent. The company then brought an action against the patent owner, seeking both a declaration of the patent's invalidity and an injunction against prosecution of the first lawsuit. The district court in the second case initially stayed its own proceedings, but eventually reversed course and enjoined the patent owner from proceeding in the first court. The Supreme Court held that "[w]ise judicial administration, giving regard to conservation of judicial resources and comprehensive disposition of litigation," should have led the second court to stay itself until completion of the first case.

In the patent area, a nice body of law, replete with a rule—the first-filed case wins, with the judge in the second forum dismissing the later-filed case or the judge in the first forum enjoining the parties from proceeding elsewhere—and exceptions, has sprung up around the *Kerotest* doctrine.[187] But the *Kerotest* stay has not enjoyed broad use in complex litigation. *Kerotest* involved essentially the same parties and claims in both proceedings, and courts have tended to confine *Kerotest* to that circumstance.[188] Moreover, *Kerotest* recognized that transfers under 28 U.S.C. § 1404 could also address duplicative litigation, thus diminishing the need to seek a stay, dismissal, or anti-suit injunction. In light of the transfer provisions in 28 U.S.C. §§ 1404 and 1407, the *Kerotest* stay has become a fairly esoteric aspect of federal-court practice.

It is fair to say that federal courts have yet to develop a dismissal, stay, and anti-suit injunction authority sensitive to the needs of modern complex litigation. On the other hand, given § 1404 and especially § 1407, the need for such an authority is limited.

---

186 342 U.S. 180 (1952).

187 Curtis v. Citibank, N.A., 226 F.3d 133, 138–39 (2d Cir. 2000); William Gluckin & Co. v. Int'l Playtex Corp., 407 F.2d 177 (2d Cir. 1969). For a case applying the doctrine in a non-patent context, see Kohn Law Group, Inc. v. Auto Parts Mfg. Miss., Inc., 787 F.3d 1237 (9th Cir. 2015).

188 For cases suggesting in dicta that courts could use *Kerotest* stays and anti-suit injunctions to prevent related, duplicative litigation on a broader scale, see Schauss v. Metals Depository Corp., 757 F.2d 649 (5th Cir. 1985) (suggesting an anti-suit injunctive power that could be employed against nonparties); Asset Allocation & Mgmt. Co. v. W. Emp'rs Ins. Co., 892 F.2d 566 (7th Cir. 1989) (Posner, J.) (arguing that the power to prevent duplicative litigation "is not a traditional equitable power that the courts are exercising in these cases but a new power asserted in order to facilitate the economical management of complex litigation" and that the power "is to be exercised with due regard for the balance of convenience in litigating the parties' disputes in one forum rather than another").

Perhaps a doctrine could be crafted to fill in some of the gaps that these statutes possess, but such a doctrine would surely be subject to the criticism that courts should not exceed the limits of the aggregation powers that Congress has specified.

2. Stays and Injunctions Between State Courts

Some states have rules, equivalent to the *Kerotest* doctrine, that permit a state court to issue an anti-suit injunction against other courts within the same state, or to stay its hand in favor of another court within the state. In addition, some states have designated a particular court as a "complex litigation court" or have created a special "complex litigation docket" to coordinate related cases arising in the same county or state. Other states have created intrastate equivalents to the Judicial Panels on Multidistrict Litigation in order to coordinate or transfer litigation within the courts of the state.

More difficult issues arise with regard to related cases pending in the courts of two different states. Here, three distinct doctrines come into play. First, akin to a *Kerotest* stay, a number of state courts will dismiss or stay their own proceedings when an identical case is proceeding in another forum. Most of these cases involve stays that run in favor of a first-filed federal proceeding involving the same parties and same issues, but there is no reason in principle why the same result should not hold with regard to comparable litigation in another state's court.[189]

Second, courts in most states apply the doctrine of *forum non conveniens*. In general terms, *forum non conveniens* permits a court to stay or dismiss an action that when another forum is more convenient. Faced with a stay or dismissal, the plaintiff will presumably refile the case in the more convenient forum. The factors that a court considers in deciding whether to stay or dismiss on *forum non conveniens* grounds vary from state to state, but they usually are divided into public-interest factors (such as having local controversies determined in a court familiar with the relevant law) and private-interest factors (such as the convenience to the parties and witnesses, and respect for the plaintiff's choice of forum).[190] Because invocation of the doctrine results in a stay or dismissal of

---

[189] *See* Dura Pharms., Inc. v. Scandipharm, Inc., 713 A.2d 925 (Del. Ch. 1998) (staying Delaware action in favor of first-filed Alabama action); LA. CODE CIV. PROC. art. 532 (permitting Louisiana courts to stay proceedings when litigation "on the same transaction or occurrence, between the same parties in the same capacities" is "pending in a court of another state or of the United States").

[190] The development of the *forum non conveniens* doctrine has been heavily influenced by *Gulf Oil Co. v. Gilbert*, 330 U.S. 501, 508 (1947), which suggested four public-interest and four private-interest factors. *See also* TEX. CIV. PRAC. & REM. CODE § 71.051 (listing six statutory factors). *Gilbert* was decided the year before 28 U.S.C. § 1404 was enacted. As a result, at the federal level § 1404 displaced *forum non conveniens* when the case could be transferred to a more convenient federal forum.

litigation on grounds unrelated to the merits of the case, state courts often regard *forum non conveniens* motions with disfavor.

As its name implies, *forum non conveniens* is principally calibrated to deal with issues of convenience, not with issues of complex litigation. One state court indicated in dicta that the presence of "multiple parties" and "complex litigation" were two circumstances in which the general reluctance to dismiss an action on *forum non conveniens* grounds might be overcome.[191] Nonetheless, the doctrine is not tailored to the needs of complex litigation. Moreover, a party seeking to consolidate cases in a single forum bears the heavy burden of filing a *forum non conveniens* motion in every case in every other state court, and then must hope that all other state courts agree to stay or dismiss their cases. Like its less draconian cousin, 29 U.S.C. § 1404, *forum non conveniens* suffers from the lack of a centralized decision-maker.

Third, and most controversially, some state courts issue anti-suit injunctions against parties to prevent them from proceeding in the courts of other states. These injunctions are hard to obtain, for they upend the comity among the courts of our fifty states.[192] *Golden Rule Insurance Co. v. Harper*[193] states a fairly standard position:

> An anti-suit injunction is appropriate in four instances: 1) to address a threat to the court's jurisdiction; 2) to prevent the evasion of important public policy; 3) to prevent a multiplicity of suits; or 4) to protect a party from vexatious or harassing litigation. The party seeking the injunction must show that "a clear equity demands" the injunction. A single parallel proceeding in a foreign forum, however, does not constitute a multiplicity nor does it, in itself[,] create a clear equity justifying an anti-suit injunction. [Internal quotation marks omitted.]

Even when an anti-suit injunction is issued, other state courts may not heed it. A common reason for non-enforcement is the enjoining court's lack of territorial jurisdiction over the person(s) enjoined. Even if jurisdiction exists, a court is not required to give

---

191 Sabino v. Ruffolo, 562 A.2d 1134 (Conn. App. Ct. 1989).

192 *See* Advanced Bionics Corp. v. Medtronic, Inc., 59 P.3d 231 (Cal. 2002) (refusing to authorize an anti-suit injunction against a later-filed action involving the same subject matter unless "an exceptional circumstance . . . outweighs the threat to judicial restraint and comity principles"); Ackerman v. Ackerman, 631 N.Y.S.2d 657, 657 (1995) ("The rule of comity forbids our courts from enjoining an action in a sister State unless it is clearly shown that the suit sought to be enjoined was brought in bad faith, motivated by fraud or an intent to harass the party seeking an injunction, or if its purpose was to evade the law of the domicile of the parties.") (internal quotation marks omitted).

193 925 S.W.2d 649 (Tex. 1996).

full faith and credit to the antisuit injunctions of other states, and will do so only when comity dictates.[194]

In a now-familiar refrain, the doctrines available to state courts to prevent related litigation in multiple state courts fitfully address the problem of multi-party, multi-forum litigation. The inefficacy of these devices in most situations highlights the advantage that federal courts, with their powers of transfer under § 1404 and § 1407, possess with respect to the aggregation of related actions.

3. Stays and Injunctions in Transnational Litigation

The same techniques—stays or dismissals in favor of foreign litigation and anti-suit injunctions against foreign litigation—apply in the context of transnational litigation. First, under *forum non conveniens*, a federal or state court can dismiss or stay a case in favor of litigation in a foreign forum when *forum non conveniens* factors suggest that the foreign litigation is more convenient.[195] Second, some American courts have developed a tailored approach, akin to the *Kerotest* stay, that stays or dismisses American litigation in favor of duplicative litigation that is first filed in a foreign court.[196]

Third, American courts claim the power to issue anti-suit injunctions that bar parties from pursuing litigation in foreign courts. The classic case is *Laker Airways Ltd. v. Sabena, Belgian World Airlines*.[197] Laker, a British corporation brought an antitrust suit in an American federal court against foreign airlines. The airlines then filed claims, which would have been counterclaims in the American suit, against Laker in a British court. The real purpose of the British suit was to obtain an injunction barring Laker from

---

[194] Mahan v. Gunther, 663 N.E.2d 1139 (Ill. App. Ct. 1996); *see* Baker v. Gen. Motors Corp., 522 U.S. 222, 236 (1998) (stating that, under the principle of full faith and credit, "antisuit injunctions regarding litigation elsewhere, even if compatible with due process as a direction constraining parties to the decree, in fact have not controlled the second court's actions regarding litigation in that court").

[195] The principal case is *Piper Aircraft Co. v. Reyno*, 454 U.S. 235 (1981), in which a products-liability suit against an American airplane manufacturer was dismissed when the plane crash occurred in Scotland and all the victims were citizens of the United Kingdom. Although *forum non conveniens* has essentially disappeared in domestic federal-court-to-federal-court litigation due to the rise of § 1404, *see supra* note 190, it still retains its importance and bite in transnational litigation. For a critical appraisal of the doctrine in this context, see Maggie Gardner, *Retiring* Forum Non Conveniens, 92 N.Y.U. L. REV. 390 (2017).

[196] See Philips Elecs., N.V. v. N.H. Ins. Co., 692 N.E.2d 1268 (Ill. App. Ct. 1998) (upholding a stay of two claims in favor of related British litigation and a denial of a stay with respect to two less related claims); Caspian Invs., Ltd. v. Vicom Holdings, Ltd., 770 F. Supp. 880 (S.D.N.Y. 1991) (stating that the factors in granting a stay or dismissal in favor of foreign litigation "include the similarity of parties and issues involved, promotion of judicial efficiency, adequacy of relief available in the alternative forum, considerations of fairness to all parties and possible prejudice to any of them, and the temporal sequence of filing for each action").

[197] 731 F.2d 909 (D.C. Cir. 1984).

prosecuting its American suit. The British court issued the injunction. Laker then obtained an injunction from the federal court barring the defendants from prosecuting the British suit. The British injunction and American counterinjunction created an international dilemma that subsided only when the House of Lords vacated the British injunction. In *Laker* the court of appeals affirmed the district court's issuance of the counterinjunction, but indicated that anti-suit injunctions should be issued only in rare circumstances due to concerns for international comity. It stated that "duplication of parties and issues alone is not sufficient to justify issuance of an antisuit injunction."

State courts also become entangled with foreign litigation, and they express comparable reluctance to enjoin foreign proceedings.[198]

4. Stays and Injunctions Between State and Federal Courts

In considering the uses of stays (including dismissals) and injunctions in the state-federal context, it is useful to break down the discussion into four component parts: stays by federal courts in favor of state-court litigation; stays by state courts in favor of federal-court litigation; injunctions by state courts against federal-court litigation; and injunctions by federal courts against state-court litigation. As you will see, federal courts again enjoy an advantage in their ability to issue aggregation-friendly injunctions.

a. Federal-Court Stays in Favor of State-Court Litigation

A loose collection of doctrines permits, and sometimes requires, federal courts to stay their own proceedings in favor of litigation or administrative proceedings ongoing in a state. They doctrines have no underlying consistency in theme and were for the most part conceived without the problem of multi-party, multi-forum litigation in view.

Many of the doctrines fall within the judicially created concept of "abstention." Abstention doctrines have tended to develop out of a tension between the general statutory command to exercise jurisdiction over cases of a particular type and the belief that the courts of the other system are better situated to handle this specific case. The touchstone for most abstention doctrines is federalism, specifically the respect due to the constitutional integrity and independence of states and their judicial systems. As a result, the fit between complex cases and abstention is poor, and the federalism

---

[198] *See* Gannon v. Payne, 706 S.W.2d 304 (Tex. 1986); *but see* Owens-Corning Fiberglas Corp. v. Baker, 838 S.W.2d 838 (Tex. App. 1992) (affirming the issuance of an "anti-anti-suit injunction" against defendants that had asked Canadian courts to enjoin Canadian plaintiffs from filing cases in Texas courts).

concerns that motivate abstention are as likely to thwart as to assist optimal aggregation.

Abstention is also one of the most discussed and controversial aspects of federal jurisdiction. Here we sail quickly over deep waters, sketching only the basics of abstention and its relationship to complex litigation.[199]

There are at least three, and perhaps as many as six, forms of federal abstention. The three "card-carrying" forms of abstention are *Pullman*[200] abstention, *Burford*[201] abstention, and *Younger*[202] abstention. The other three doctrines, which the Supreme Court has never called abstention doctrines but nonetheless act much the same, are *Colorado River*[203] abstention, *Thibodaux*[204] abstention, and certification of state-law issues to the highest court of a state.

Five of the six forms of abstention have little relevance to the aggregation of multi-party, multi-forum disputes. To begin, *Thibodaux* abstention is moribund. Later decisions have so cabined in *Burford* abstention that it too is on life support, although it occasionally pops up in the context of state receivership proceedings or other litigation that can be regarded as complex.[205] Certication of an unclear question of state law might arise in a complex federal case, but such certification practice does nothing to aid aggregation of related cases in a single forum. Likewise, *Pullman* abstention, which allows federal courts to abstain when a state court's ruling on an unclear question of state law might obviate the need for a federal court to decide a constitutional issue that might create friction with important state policies, does not aid aggregation unless similar litigation is ongoing in state court. *Younger* abstention requires a federal court to abstain in most instances from deciding a federal lawsuit alleging that an ongoing state criminal or civil-enforcement proceeding violates federal law. Some multi-party, multi-forum cases

---

199 For more detailed treatment (and two distinct views of abstention), see RICHARD H. FALLON, JR. ET AL., HART & WECHSLER'S THE FEDERAL COURTS AND THE FEDERAL SYSTEM (6th ed. 2009); MARTIN H. REDISH, FEDERAL JURISDICTION (2d ed. 1990) [hereinafter HART & WECHSLER]. Bibliographies on the abstention literature can be found in 17A CHARLES ALAN WRIGHT ET AL., FEDERAL PRACTICE AND PROCEDURE § 4241 (3d ed. 2007), and 17B CHARLES ALAN WRIGHT ET AL., FEDERAL PRACTICE AND PROCEDURE § 4252 (3d ed. 2007).

200 R.R. Comm'n v. Pullman Co., 312 U.S. 496 (1941).

201 Burford v. Sun Oil Co., 319 U.S. 315 (1943).

202 Younger v. Harris, 401 U.S. 37 (1971).

203 Colo. River Water Conservation Dist. v. United States, 424 U.S. 800 (1976).

204 La. Power & Light Co. v. City of Thibodaux, 360 U.S. 25 (1959).

205 Gonzalez v. Media Elements, Inc., 946 F.2d 157 (1st Cir. 1991) (*Burford* abstention in favor of state insolvency proceeding proper); *cf. In re* Joint E. & S. Dists. Asbestos Litig., 78 F.3d 764 (2d Cir. 1996) (*Burford* abstention to permit state courts to calculate certain set-off rights under settlement involving the trust of an insolvent debtor improper).

involve state criminal proceedings, and issue-preclusive effects can spill over into the civil proceedings if the state criminal trial results in a conviction. But *Younger* abstention is not targeted at that issue, so it is unlikely to be of use in most complex federal litigation.[206]

That leaves *Colorado River* abstention, which states that, as a matter of "wise judicial administration," a federal court should sometimes abstain in favor of a parallel state proceeding. Three principles shape a federal court's decision. First, there is a strong presumption against *Colorado River* abstention; as the Court in *Colorado River* said, federal courts have "the virtually unflagging obligation . . . to exercise the jurisdiction given them." Thus, "the circumstances permitting the dismissal of a federal suit due to the presence of a concurrent state proceeding for reasons of wise judicial administration are . . . limited . . . ."

Second, "exceptional" circumstances allow abstention. Six factors are central: (1) the principle, which we have encountered, that the court first assuming jurisdiction over property may exercise that jurisdiction to the exclusion of other courts; (2) the inconvenience of the federal forum; (3) the desirability of avoiding piecemeal litigation; (4) the order in which jurisdiction was obtained by the concurrent forums; (5) the source of governing law, whether state or federal; and (6) the adequacy of the state-court proceeding to protect the litigants' rights.[207] No single factor is determinative, but "the balance [is] heavily weighted in favor of the exercise of jurisdiction."[208]

Third, two critical variables in deciding whether *Colorado River* abstention is appropriate are whether Congress intended to avoid duplicative litigation and whether the state proceeding is a superior mechanism to resolve the dispute. For instance, in *Colorado River*, which involved a dispute among the United States and more than 1,000 persons regarding water rights, the Court's decision to require abstention was influenced by a federal statute that contained a "clear federal policy" to avoid piecemeal adjudication of water rights and by

---

[206] *See* Sprint Commc'ns, Inc. v. Jacobs, 571 U.S. 69 (2013) (refusing to apply *Younger* abstention when a related action was pending in state court; stating that, "even in the presence of parallel state proceedings, abstention from the exercise of federal jurisdiction is the 'exception, not the rule.' "). Federal courts sometimes stay civil proceedings until a federal criminal investigation is complete. They do so not as a matter of *Younger* abstention, which applies only to a federal suit challenging the validity of a state prosecution, but as a matter of sensible case management. *See* MANUAL FOR COMPLEX LITIGATION, FOURTH § 20.2 (2004).

[207] This list derives from *Colorado River* and a subsequent decision, *Moses H. Cone Mem'l Hosp. v. Mercury Constr. Corp.*, 460 U.S. 1 (1983). Lower courts have not treated it as exhaustive. *See* Caminiti & Iatarola v. Behnke Warehousing, Inc., 962 F.2d 698 (7th Cir. 1992) (adding the relative progress of state and federal proceedings, the presence or absence of concurrent jurisdiction, the availability of removal, and the strength of the federal claim).

[208] *Moses H. Cone*, 460 U.S. at 16.

the Court's belief that adjudication of water rights was "appropriate for comprehensive treatment in the forums having the greatest experience and expertise, assisted by state administrative officers acting under the state courts." In contrast, the Supreme Court found abstention inappropriate in *Moses H. Cone Memorial Hospital v. Mercury Construction Corp.*, a case in which no statutory policy of avoiding piecemeal litigation was present, the state court had no institutional superiority in deciding the contractual and statutory issues in the case, and serious doubts existed about whether the state court could provide relief equivalent to the relief available in federal court.

Two other restrictions limit *Colorado River*'s utility as an aggregation mechanism. First, it is generally thought that a case involving claims lying exclusively within federal jurisdiction should not be stayed in favor of related state litigation.[209] Second, *Colorado River* abstention is not generally thought to be available unless the parties and claims in the federal case are included among the parties and claims in the state case.[210]

Colorado River abstention is useful in insurance-coverage litigation,[211] and has also been invoked to dismiss a case in favor of a state class action that was capable of resolving all the issues in the federal suit.[212] Whether these uses are consistent with the stringency of *Colorado River* abstention is debatable, but at a minimum the high degree of parallelism that must exist between the state and federal cases makes *Colorado River* abstention a limited aggregation tool in complex litigation. Unless a single comprehensive action has been filed in one state court, the case for *Colorado River* abstention is very weak. And in the typical multi-party, multi-forum context of geographical and jurisdictional dispersion, no single state court hosts all the related litigation.

---

[209] *See* 17A WRIGHT ET AL., *supra* note 199, § 4247.

[210] *See* Great Am. Ins. Co. v. Gross, 468 F.3d 199, 208 (4th Cir. 2006) ("[W]e have strictly construed the requirement of parallel federal and state suits, requiring that the parties involved be almost identical."); *but see In re* Chi. Flood Litig., 819 F. Supp. 762, 764 (N.D. Ill. 1993) (stating in dicta that *Colorado River* abstention can be appropriate when the defendants in state and federal court are the same and the state and federal plaintiffs "share equivalent litigation interests"; abstention nonetheless denied because the federal actions could be expeditiously resolved and tort issues were neither novel nor complex).

[211] *See, e.g.*, Lumbermens Mut. Cas. Co. v. Conn. Bank & Trust Co., 806 F.2d 411 (2d Cir. 1986) ("The critical factor . . . is the desirability of avoiding piecemeal litigation and the possibility of two interpretations of the same policy language in different courts, leaving the insured possibly with insufficient coverage from the insurers . . . ."); Ins. Co. of Pa. v. Syntex Corp., 964 F.2d 829 (8th Cir. 1992) (dismissing federal declaratory-judgment action by insurer in favor of more comprehensive insurance-coverage litigation in state court).

[212] Allison v. Sec. Benefit Life Ins. Co., 980 F.2d 1213 (8th Cir. 1992) (alternate holding).

A final doctrine that might push a case from federal court to state court is *forum non conveniens*. Although use of the doctrine has been much curtailed in federal court after the advent of 28 U.S.C. § 1404, it can still be used to dismiss a federal case not only in favor of a foreign court but also "perhaps in rare instances where a state or territorial court serves litigational convenience best."[213] "Rare" is the right word. Except occasionally in the bankruptcy context and more recently in the context of enforcing forum-selection clauses,[214] courts do not invoke the *forum non conveniens* factors to stay federal litigation in favor of state proceedings; the doctrine does little to aid the aggregation of dispersed federal cases before a single state court. In any event, it is not clear that this doctrine varies much from the results that could be achieved with *Colorado River* abstention.

Aside from judicially crafted abstention doctrines, Congress occasionally either requires or permits federal courts to abstain from the exercise of their jurisdiction.[215] Of the statutory abstention doctrines, the ones of greatest relevance to complex litigation are mandatory and discretionary doctrines relating to federal jurisdiction over class actions. We consider them in more detail in Chapter Six;[216] for now, it is enough to note that they come into play principally when the class action centers on parties and disputes from a single state, for which a state court would be an appropriate forum for resolution of all claims.

Judges enjoy a *sua sponte* power to invoke these doctrines, but like many other doctrines that we have considered, no single, centralized federal authority determines whether abstention or *forum non conveniens* dismissal is proper when related litigation is spread across numerous federal courts. A party wishing to push federal litigation over to a state court in which the litigation could be consolidated needs to move for a stay in each federal action, or else to consolidate all the actions through the MDL process and then try to convince the transferee judge to stay all the consolidated federal cases.

---

[213] Sinochem Int'l Co. v. Malaysia Int'l Shipping Corp., 549 U.S. 422 (2007).

[214] *See* Atl. Marine Constr. Co. v. U.S. Dist. Court for the W. Dist. of Tex., 571 U.S. 49 (2013) (stating that "the appropriate way to enforce a forum-selection clause pointing to a state or foreign forum is through the doctrine of *forum non conveniens*)."

[215] *See, e.g.*, 28 U.S.C. §§ 1332(d)(3) (discretionary abstention in certain class actions), 1332(d)(4) (mandatory abstention in certain class actions), 1334(c)(1) (discretionary abstention in cases arising under bankruptcy jurisdiction), 1334(c)(1) (mandatory abstention in cases arising under bankruptcy jurisdiction), 1367(c) (discretionary abstention for claims asserted under the federal court's supplemental jurisdiction).

[216] *See infra* notes 466–478 and accompanying text.

b. State-Court Stays in Favor of Federal-Court Litigation

State-court stays or dismissals in favor of federal-court litigation—in effect, "reverse abstention"—are less traveled ground. Such abstention is complicated by the Supremacy Clause, under which state courts must hear cases arising under federal law unless they have a neutral, non-discriminatory reason for refusing to hear the federal claim that lies within their concurrent jurisdiction. For instance, in *Howlett v. Rose*,[217] the Supreme Court held that a state court must hear a § 1983 claim against a state official when the state court would have entertained a state-law tort claim against the same official for the same injury; the state's refusal to hear the federal claim was not "a neutral state rule regarding the administration of the courts."[218]

Prior to *Howlett*, some state courts adopted something akin to reverse-*Pullman* or reverse-*Burford* abstention when a decision on a federal issue might obviate the need to decide a difficult issue of state constitutional law or when state-court review of a difficult issue of federal law threatened federal policy.[219]

In addition, a number of states stay or dismiss cases under a rule of comity that operates like reverse-*Colorado River* abstention: the state court stays its hand when a similar case is already pending in federal court, regardless of whether the claims arise under state or federal law.[220] The power to stay has been applied to claims brought under both state and federal law. The factors used to determine whether abstention in favor of an earlier-filed federal case

---

[217] 496 U.S. 356 (1990).

[218] *See also* Testa v. Katt, 330 U.S. 386 (1947) (requiring a state court to hear a case involving a federal price-gouging statute); *cf.* Haywood v. Drown, 556 U.S. 729 (2009) (holding that states cannot refuse to entertain federal civil-rights claims against certain government officials when it held its courts open to similar lawsuits against other officials); *but see* Douglas v. N.Y., New Haven & Hartford R.R., 279 U.S. 377 (1929) (allowing a state court to decline jurisdiction of a case arising under federal law when it had a "valid excuse").

[219] *See, e.g.*, Gnutti v. Heintz, 539 A.2d 118 (Conn. 1988) (requiring state courts to abstain from hearing Medicaid disability suits until federal administrative and judicial avenues are exhausted)

[220] *See, e.g.*, Eways v. Governor's Island, 391 S.E.2d 182 (N.C. 1990) (affirming dismissal of a case based on state law when a federal court sitting in bankruptcy was the first court to acquire jurisdiction); Barnes v. Peat, Marwick, Mitchell & Co., 344 N.Y.S.2d 645 (N.Y. App. Div. 1973) (stay issued in case alleging violation of federal and state securities law); Farmland Irrigation Co. v. Dopplmaier, 308 P.2d 732 (Cal. 1957) (denial of a stay in favor of related federal patent litigation was within the trial court's discretion). In most states this power is judge-made; in North Carolina it is statutory. *See* N.C. GEN. STAT. § 1–75.12(a) ("If, in any action pending in any court of this State, the judge shall find that it would work substantial injustice for the action to be tried in a court of this State, the judge on motion of any party may enter an order to stay further proceedings in the action in this State."); *cf.* 2009 CONN. PRACTICE BOOK § 23–14 ("The judge to whom complex litigation cases have been assigned may stay any or all further proceedings in the cases . . . .").

should occur vary. For instance, California considers six factors: whether multiple litigation is designed to harass an adverse party; the avoidance of unseemly conflicts with the federal court; whether the rights of the parties can best be determined by the state court or the federal court; the availability of witnesses; the stage to which the proceedings in federal court have advanced; and whether the federal action is pending in a California federal court as opposed to another federal court.[221] North Carolina courts consider eight: the nature of the case; convenience of the witnesses; the availability of compulsory process to produce witnesses; the relative ease of access to sources of proof; the applicable law; the burden of litigating matters not of local concern; the desirability of litigating matters of local concern in local courts; and convenience and access to another forum.[222]

On the other hand, New York's rule is more stringent rule, permitting abstention only when the parties, the causes of action, and the requested relief are identical, or when the first-filed federal action will necessarily determine the issues in the state case.[223] In a similar vein, Texas requires a stay in cases between the same parties unless there is fraud, sinister motive, inattention, or delay in filing and prosecuting the federal suit.[224]

Courts also differ on whether a stay in favor of a federal action is a duty or a matter of discretion; whether a stay can be issued in favor of a case in a federal court of another state; and whether the proper remedy is a stay or a dismissal.

> *Question*
>
> When state courts use reverse-*Burford*, reverse-*Pullman*, and reverse-*Colorado River* abstention to stay claims arising under federal law, are they employing "neutral state rule[s] regarding the administration of the courts" within the meaning of *Howlett*?

An alternative ground for achieving a stay or dismissal is *forum non conveniens*. As long as the doctrine is not exercised in a manner discriminatory to the assertion of federal rights in state

221 *Farmland Irrigation*, 308 P.2d 732; Thomson v. Cont'l Ins. Co., 427 P.2d 765 (Cal. 1967); Caiafa Prof'l Law Corp. v. State Farm Fire & Cas. Co., 19 Cal. Rptr. 2d 138 (Cal. Ct. App. 1993).

222 Home Indem. Co. v. Hoechst-Celanese Corp., 393 S.E.2d 118 (N.C. Ct. App. 1990); *but see* Park E. Sales, LLC v. Clark-Langley, Inc., 651 S.E.2d 235 (N.C. Ct. App. 2007) (affirming a refusal to stay a state proceeding in favor of a federal bankruptcy proceeding solely on the ground that the issues, while overlapping, were not identical).

223 Allied Props., LLC v. 236 Cannon Realty LLC, 769 N.Y.S.2d 880 (N.Y. App. Div. 2004); Guilden v. Baldwin Secs. Corp., 592 N.Y.S.2d 725 (N.Y. App. Div. 1993). Florida too seems to require an identity of parties and issues; its courts will also refuse a stay if the federal docket is too congested. City of Miami Beach v. Miami Beach Fraternal Order of Police, 619 So.2d 447 (Fla. Dist. Ct. App. 1993); Koehlke Components, Inc. v. S.E. Connectors, Inc., 456 So.2d 554 (Fla. Dist. Ct. App. 1984).

224 Alpine Gulf, Inc. v. Valentino, 563 S.W.2d 358 (Tex. App. 1978).

court, the Supreme Court has recognized *forum non conveniens* as a neutral reason for dismissing a state-court federal claim.[225] After dismissal, the action can then presumably be filed in either another state court or in federal court; but *forum non conveniens* cannot guarantee that the alternate forum will be a federal court, thus limiting the doctrine's use in multi-party, multi-forum litigation.

State-court stays or dismissals introduce complications in the pursuit of single-forum aggregation. Assuming that the best forum for aggregation is a federal forum, abstention-like or *forum non conveniens* doctrines can aid aggregation as long as all the plaintiffs refile their stayed or dismissed actions in federal court. But the doctrines are often complex, and do not guarantee that a stay or dismissal will issue merely because aggregation in a federal forum would be better in terms of efficiency and fairness. In addition, in what is now a much-repeated refrain, these doctrines lack a central decision-maker who can act to dismiss or stay all the state cases in favor of federal proceedings. A party with the incentive to aggregate related cases must go state-by-state, and then courtroom-by-courtroom within each state, to secure stays and dismissals. Without a guarantee of success, the task is often not worth its price.

c. *State-Court Injunctions Against Federal-Court Litigation*

An anti-suit injunction is the mirror image of a stay: a single court orders the parties not to proceed elsewhere, rather than asking each judge before whom a case is pending to stay or dismiss the pending case. In this sense, anti-suit injunctions hold far more promise as a means to aggregate related cases.

But that fact does not mean that a court always has the power to issue such an injunction. Indeed, to cut to the chase, a state court has no power to enjoin an *in personam* federal action. None. The Supreme Court has long followed Justice Story's view that "the State Courts cannot injoin proceedings in the Courts of the United States."[226] In spite of a passing later suggestion that states might have such power,[227] the Supreme Court again rejected any state-court power to enjoin federal *in personam* proceedings in *Donovan v. City of Dallas*.[228]

It is difficult to imagine a more compelling case for an anti-suit injunction than *Donovan*. Plaintiffs lost a class action in state court. More than one hundred plaintiffs, some of whom had been plaintiffs

---

[225] Missouri *ex rel.* S. Ry. Co. v. Mayfield, 340 U.S. 1 (1950).

[226] 2 JOSEPH STORY, COMMENTARIES ON EQUITY JURISPRUDENCE 186 (1836); *see* Farr v. Thomson, 78 U.S. (11 Wall.) 139 (1871).

[227] *See* Balt. & Ohio R.R. v. Kepner, 314 U.S. 44 (1941).

[228] 377 U.S. 408 (1964).

in the state action, then brought suit in federal court on the same claims. The state court issued an injunction requiring the plaintiffs to dismiss the federal case. They refused. On certiorari from the court's order of contempt, the Supreme Court held that the state injunction was invalid, noting that Congress "has in no way relaxed the old and well-established judicially declared rule that state courts are completely without power to restrain federal-court proceedings, in *in personam* actions . . . ."

General Atomic Co. v. Felter[229] strengthened *Donovan. Felter* arose out of a contract dispute that spawned litigation around the country, including in federal court. A New Mexico state court hearing one aspect of this litigation enjoined General Atomic from filing a case in any other court or a claim before any arbitral panel. General Atomic had not yet done so, but it wanted to file a third-party complaint in a federal lawsuit. The Supreme Court held the injunction invalid because General Atomic's "opportunity [in federal court] to fairly litigate the various claims arising from this complex action would be substantially prejudiced if the injunction were allowed to stand." Then-Justice Rehnquist dissented. He argued that, because federal courts can enjoin state proceedings when necessary to protect their jurisdiction or judgments (we will see why shortly), "a state court must have a similar power to forbid the initiation of vexatious litigation in federal court."

Because the *Donovan-Felter* bar does not seem to be a rule of constitutional dimension, Congress could overturn it.[230] Until Congress acts, however, *Donovan* and *Felter* provide yet another reason why state courts are less than ideal forums for hosting complex litigation—especially in light of the (albeit limited) power that federal courts enjoy to enjoin the inefficient relitigation of issues in state court. We turn to that issue now.

d. *Federal-Court Injunctions Against State-Court Litigation*

Unlike state courts, federal courts enjoy an anti-suit injunctive power. But the power is limited, once again due to the concerns for federalism and respect for the sovereignty of states and their judicial systems. The law is complex, and we focus only on the ability of a federal court to use this power to aid in the aggregation of related actions in a single (federal) forum.

---

[229] 434 U.S. 12 (1977).

[230] *Cf.* STUDY OF THE DIVISION OF JURISDICTION BETWEEN STATE AND FEDERAL COURTS § 1373 (AM. L. INST. 1969) (recommending that Congress allow state courts to enjoin *in personam* federal actions when "warranted" by equitable principles and "the injunction is necessary to protect against vexatious and harassing relitigation of matters determined by an existing judgment of the State court in a civil action").

Discussion of the federal anti-suit injunctive power necessarily begins with two statutes. The first statute is 28 U.S.C. § 2283, the Anti-Injunction Act. This Act prohibits a federal court from "grant[ing] an injunction to stay proceedings in a State court except as expressly authorized by Act of Congress, or where necessary in aid of its jurisdiction, or to protect or effectuate its judgments."[231] A cornerstone of our federal system, the purpose of § 2283 "is to prevent needless friction between state and federal courts."[232] When Congress expressly authorizes federal courts to issue anti-suit injunctions, as it has in such contexts as bankruptcy,[233] statutory interpleader,[234] and § 1983 actions,[235] then a federal court both has a clear source of power to issue an anti-suit injunction and meets the first exception of § 2283. These statutory powers to issue anti-suit injunctions can be useful in avoiding repetitive litigation of related claims, but each is confined to its particular circumstances (bankruptcy, interpleader, and civil-rights claims against state actors). None of these statutes provides an all-purpose authority to aggregate cases in a federal forum.

That reality brings into focus the second statute, 28 U.S.C. § 1651. The All Writs Act, which we first encountered in the context of removal,[236] provides federal courts with the power to "issue all writs necessary or appropriate in aid of their respective jurisdictions and agreeable to the usages and principles of law." If the All Writs Act provided a source of power for federal courts to enjoin state-court proceedings that affected a federal case, then parties to a case in federal court could obtain an injunction barring plaintiffs from proceeding in state court. If the federal cases could then be consolidated (likely through MDL transfers), single-forum consolidation lies within reach. Nor would the Anti-Injunction Act be a hindrance. The closeness of the All Writs language (granting a power to issue orders when "necessary or appropriate in aid of their respective jurisdictions") and the Anti-Injunction Act language (excepting from the anti-suit injunction provision those injunctions "where necessary in aid of [a federal court's] jurisdiction") suggests

---

231 Although the Anti-Injunction Act lists only three exceptions, a fourth also exists: an anti-suit injunction can be issued at the behest of the United States. *See* Leiter Minerals, Inc. v. United States, 352 U.S. 220 (1957). When no state action is pending when the injunction issues, the Act does not apply. Dombrowski v. Pfister, 380 U.S. 479 (1965); *cf.* Standard Microsystems Corp. v. Tex. Instruments, Inc., 916 F.2d 58 (2d Cir. 1990) (Act applies even if the motion for an anti-suit injunction in federal court preceded the filing of the state action, as long as the motion had not yet been granted).

232 Mitchum v. Foster, 407 U.S. 225 (1972) (internal quotation marks omitted).

233 11 U.S.C. §§ 105(a), 362.

234 28 U.S.C. § 2361.

235 *See Mitchum*, 407 U.S. at 242–43.

236 *See supra* notes 170–173 and accompanying text.

that an injunction granted under the All Writs Act would also meet the terms of the Anti-Injunction Act.[237]

From the viewpoint of aggregation, one of the difficulties with this argument is that "necessary in aid of jurisdiction" exception to § 2283 has been construed very narrowly. The leading case is *Atlantic Coast Line Railroad Co. v. Brotherhood of Locomotive Engineers*,[238] which held that both the exception, as well as the third "protect or effectuate its judgments" exception, "imply that some federal injunctive relief may be necessary to prevent a state court from so interfering with a federal court's consideration or disposition of a case as to seriously impair the federal court's flexibility and authority to decide that case."[239] This restrictive language is not conducive to a broad federal anti-suit power that might rein in state-court litigation related to a federal case.

Indeed, in *Kline v. Burke Construction Co.*,[240] the Court, interpreting the All Writs Act, held that, "where the action first brought is *in personam* and seeks only a personal judgment, another action for the same cause in another jurisdiction is not precluded." Likewise, in *Vendo Co. v. Lektro-Vend Corp.*,[241] the plurality opinion noted that "[w]e have never viewed parallel *in personam* actions as interfering with the jurisdiction of either court."

That said, federal courts have enjoined state-court proceedings in unique situations. The seminal case is *In re Corrugated Container Antitrust Litigation*,[242] in which defendants agreed to settle a multidistricted class action alleging violations of federal antitrust law. Before the settlement was finalized, however, disgruntled members of the class filed a new class action in South Carolina state court, alleging violations of South Carolina's antitrust laws. This action threatened to upset the federal settlement, for the defendants had little reason to settle the federal suit if it faced additional liability in state court. The district court enjoined the class members from continuing their South Carolina proceeding.

On appeal, the Fifth Circuit appeared to assume that the district court possessed the power to issue the anti-suit injunction; it skipped

---

237 An injunction issued pursuant to the All Writs Act would also presumably meet the first exception to the Anti-Injunction Act: an "Act of Congress" that authorized an injunction.

238 398 U.S. 281 (1970).

239 The leading case on the third (or "relitigation") exception is *Chick Kam Choo v. Exxon Corp.*, 486 U.S. 140 (1988), which suggests that the exception does not come into play until a state proceeding threatens to undo the preclusive effect of a federal judgment.

240 260 U.S. 226 (1922).

241 433 U.S. 623 (1977) (plurality opinion).

242 659 F.2d 1332 (5th Cir. 1981).

straight to the injunction's consistency with the Anti-Injunction Act. Under the facts of the case, the court of appeals thought that an injunction was necessary to preserve the jurisdiction over the probable settlement; while the settlement fund was not yet reduced to a *res*, the court was within its power to stabilize the situation until the propriety of the settlement was determined.

The scope of a court's authority to issue an anti-suit injunction was more clearly presented in a factually similar case, *In re Baldwin-United Corp.*[243] *Baldwin-United* involved more than 100 securities-fraud actions consolidated in an MDL proceeding. Eighteen of the twenty-six defendants in the lawsuits eventually agreed to settle. Believing that the proposed settlements were inadequate, the attorneys general of various states began investigations with an eye toward commencing *parens patriae* lawsuits on behalf of their citizens. The district court issued an injunction preventing the attorney general of New York and other attorneys general receiving notice of the injunction from commencing a case in any state or federal court. The injunction in *Baldwin-United* was broader than *Corrugated Container*'s injunction in two respects: it operated against persons who were not parties in the MDL proceeding, and it extended the injunction to benefit not only the eighteen defendants that settled but also the eight that did not.

The Second Circuit affirmed the injunction. Drawing on the principle that the first court to obtain jurisdiction of a *res* can enjoin other courts from proceeding,[244] the court of appeals thought that an injunction was necessary to preserve the court's jurisdiction over a potential settlement that was "so far advanced that it was the virtual equivalent of a *res* over which the district court required full control." Since the attorneys general were merely seeking relief on behalf of citizens who were already class members, the court of appeals was untroubled by the their nonparty status. Extending the injunction to non-settling defendants was a closer question in the court's mind, but it thought the action justified—at least until the situation regarding the scope of the settlement came to rest. The court of appeals located the authority for both halves of the anti-suit injunction in the All Writs Act: "An important feature of the All-Writs Act is its grant of authority to preserve the court's ability to reach or enforce its decision in a case over which it has proper jurisdiction."

But this principle has clear limits. In *Retirement Systems of Alabama v. J.P. Morgan Chase & Co.*,[245] the same court of appeals reversed a district court's decision to enjoin a state-court action from

---

243 770 F.2d 328 (2d Cir. 1985).

244 *See supra* note 177 and accompanying text.

245 386 F.3d 419 (2d Cir. 2004).

proceeding to trial until the related federal multidistrict litigation had been tried, holding that Anti-Injunction Act barred the anti-suit injunction. Unlike *Baldwin-United*, *Retirement Systems* involved no prospective settlement fund that might be analogized to a *res*, nor did it threaten the ability of the federal court to try the case on the date that it had proposed. Settlement discussions that held out some prospect of a settlement were an insufficient basis on which to base an injunction; something more equivalent a *res* was needed to escape the prohibition of § 2283.

Another effort to read the Anti-Injunction Act narrowly in order to enjoin multi-forum litigation foundered in *Smith v. Bayer Corp.*[246] In *Smith*, a West Virginia plaintiff filed a class action, brought on behalf of similarly situated West Virginians, alleging breach-of-warranty claims against a pharmaceutical company. Their case was removed to federal court, and transferred to an MDL proceeding in Minnesota. The transferee judge denied the motion to certify a class under Federal Rule of Civil Procedure 23.

Back in West Virginia, two other plaintiffs filed a similar class action in West Virginia state court. Their case was not removable to federal court due to the presence of non-diverse defendants. When the plaintiffs moved to certify their case as a class action, the pharmaceutical company asked the MDL judge to enjoin the state court from hearing the motion for class certification. The MDL judge did so, and the court of appeals affirmed.

The Supreme Court reversed. Without pausing to consider the source of the MDL court's underlying power to issue the injunction, the Court held that Anti-Injunction Act prohibited an injunction for two reasons. First, the Court rejected the view of the lower courts that the federal injunction fit within the terms of the third, "protect or effectuate its judgments" exception to the Act because the issues to be decided in the West Virginia class-certification motion were not identical to those decided in the Rule 23 motion. Although the text of West Virginia's class-action rule was essentially identical to that of Rule 23, the West Virginia Supreme Court had interpreted its rule differently—and more favorably to class certification. Therefore, "[t]he federal court's resolution of one issue does not preclude the state court's determination of another. It then goes without saying that the federal court may not issue an injunction." The Court emphasized that the exceptions to § 2283 are to be construed narrowly, and that doubts about enjoining a state-court proceeding "should be resolved in favor of permitting the state courts to proceed."

Second, the Court noted that the MDL court's ruling bound only the parties to the transferred case. The reason is the usual rule,

---

[246] 564 U.S. 299 (2011).

explored in more depth in the next chapter, that only parties are bound by a court's judgment. Because the MDL court decided that no class of West Virginia plaintiffs existed, the plaintiffs in West Virginia state court remained strangers to the federal litigation. As nonparties to the MDL proceeding, they could not be bound by its decision on class certification, and were free to pursue their own motion for class certification under state law. The court recognized that this ruling could lead to relitigation of the class-certification issue; as soon as a court denied class certification, another member of the class could step forward in some other court to try again. The answer to this dilemma lay in principles of *stare decisis* and comity, as well as removal to federal court if available—not an anti-suit injunction.

Prior to *Smith v. Bayer Corp.*, the Third Circuit had observed that "u]nder an appropriate set of facts, a federal court entertaining complex litigation, especially when it involves a substantial class of persons from multiple states, or represents a consolidation of cases from multiple districts, may appropriately enjoin state court proceedings in order to protect its jurisdiction."[247] The Eleventh Circuit also recognized a " 'complex multi-state litigation' exception . . . enables a district court to enjoin a state court proceeding in aid of its jurisdiction when it has retained jurisdiction over complex, *in personam* lawsuits."[248] It is not clear that a "complex multi-state litigation" exception survives the logic of *Smith v. Bayer Corp.* Nor is it clear that *Corrugated Container* and *Baldwin-United* remain good law.[249]

> *Problem*
>
> A federal court handling a mass tort certified a class action and approved a settlement. Due to the nature of the class action, no class members could opt out of the settlement. One part of the settlement was an order requiring all class members covered by the settlement not to file any further suits involving the tort at issue. A plaintiff covered by the settlement nonetheless filed suit in state court. The federal court held the plaintiff and her lawyer in contempt. Did the court's order contravene the Anti-Injunction Act? *See* Juris v. Inamed Corp., 685 F.3d 1294 (11th Cir. 2012).

Even when the power to issue an anti-suit injunction exists and the Anti-Injunction Act would not prohibit such an order, some courts have noted another problem with these injunctions when they are issued against nonparties: territorial jurisdiction. Some nonparties might lie beyond the

247 *In re* Diet Drugs, 282 F.3d 220 (3d Cir. 2002).

248 *In re* Bayshore Ford Trucks Sales, Inc., 471 F.3d 1233 (11th Cir. 2006).

249 *See* Adkins v. Nestle Purina PetCare Co., 779 F.3d 481 (7th Cir. 2015) (reversing an anti-suit injunction against a related state-court class action even after a federal class action reached a tentative settlement).

reach of service of process. A court's power to issue an order that binds a nonparty over whom a court otherwise lacks jurisdiction is debatable. Once again, the strongest argument arises when the lawsuit has produced something, like a settlement fund, that might be analogized to a *res*. In the end, however, such a fund does not itself create *in rem* jurisdiction, so the analogy may not hold.[250]

Therefore, despite its potentially broad sweep and the presence of a centralized decision-maker, federal courts' anti-suit injunctive power is significantly constrained in ways that make it useful for optimal aggregation only over a limited range of cases. Put differently, the concern for optimal aggregation is not the concern of the All Writs Act and the Anti-Injunction Act. Although commentators have occasionally called for a more expansive power,[251] a general anti-suit injunctive power designed to achieve aggregation of cases pending in state and federal courts does not presently exist.

C. An Assessment of Stays and Injunctions

In some situations, stays, dismissals, and injunctions aid the aggregation of multi-party, multi-forum litigation. Those circumstances are limited at present; for the most part, stays, dismissals, and injunctions are best seen as a supplement to other aggregation powers, useful (if at all) to fill gaps that other mechanisms fail to reach. Nonetheless, both because they can be useful in a few instances and because they are a necessary component of any broad reform package to achieve greater aggregation, this collection of doctrines regarding stays, dismissals, and injunctions is an important component in any discussion about multi-party, multi-forum aggregation. Understanding these doctrines is also essential for appreciating what the present limits on aggregation are and why they exist.

---

250 *See In re* Gen. Motors Corp. Pick-Up Truck Fuel Tank Prods. Liab. Litig., 134 F.3d 133 (3d Cir. 1998) (holding that lack of personal jurisdiction over plaintiffs prevented an MDL court from issuing an injunction that barred a state-court settlement after an MDL court refused to approve a nearly identical settlement); *but see In re* Bridgestone/Firestone, Inc. Tires Prods. Liab. Litig., 333 F.3d 763 (7th Cir. 2003) (holding that territorial jurisdiction posed no bar to an anti-suit injunction when, among other reasons, one claim alleged a violation of RICO, a federal statute for which nationwide service of process existed).

251 As part of its series of reforms intended to permit greater aggregation of multi-party, multi-forum litigation, *see supra* notes 152 & 174 and accompanying text, the American Law Institute recommended that a single court to which related state and federal cases had been transferred by its proposed Complex Litigation Panel have the power to "enjoin transactionally related proceedings" in other courts when these cases "substantially impair[ ] or interfere[ ] with the consolidated actions" and the injunction "would promote the just, efficient, and fair resolution of the actions before" the court. COMPLEX LITIGATION, *supra* note 101, § 5.04.

Once again, the scope of the aggregation doctrines available to American courts falls short of the needs of optimal aggregation. The Anti-Injunction Act reminds us, however, that optimal aggregation is neither the only relevant value, nor perhaps the most important. Maintaining a proper respect for the dignity and independence of state, federal, and foreign courts is a vital aspect of any aggregation doctrine.

Chapter 5

PRECLUSION

Your Civil Procedure course probably exposed you to the law of preclusion. The two main forms of preclusion are claim preclusion ("res judicata") and issue preclusion ("collateral estoppel"). Another form of preclusion, the preclusion of unasserted compulsory counterclaims, is related to, but distinct from, the two basic forms. For the most part, preclusion and related doctrines have developed through the common law, rather than through statutes.

The basic idea of preclusion is to use a final judgment on the merits in one case to bar, or preclude, relitigation of the same or similar claims or issues in later cases.[252] Claim preclusion bars a party from litigating in later suits claims that either were, or should have been, brought in the first case. Issue preclusion bars a party from relitigating in later cases factual or legal issues that were litigated, determined, and essential to the judgment in the first case.

Claim preclusion appears to have some potential to achieve, at least indirectly, the goal of single-forum aggregation. If a judgment for the defendant in the first case precluded later plaintiffs from bringing claims arising out of the same event, then preclusion would act as a powerful inducement to later plaintiffs to join the first case. Issue preclusion is less useful as an aggregation device. If a judgment from one case precludes relitigation of issues decided in that case in later cases, later cases involving distinct issues can still be filed. But issue preclusion at least curtails the costly relitigation of identical issues in subsequent cases.

Like the anti-suit injunction, preclusion is also a technique with potential to address the problem of temporal dispersion. If the claims of future plaintiffs can be determined (or at least the issues presented in those cases narrowed) by a present lawsuit, then expansive future litigation can be eliminated or reduced to manageable size.

Standing against a broad use of preclusion law to eliminate claims or costly relitigation of issues is the fundamental "day-in-court" principle upon which the American system of party joinder is built. As the Supreme Court held in *Hansberry v. Lee*, "[i]t is a principle of general application in Anglo-American jurisprudence

---

[252] As a general matter, each jurisdiction (state and federal) creates its own rules of preclusion. A useful guide to the law of preclusion and the circumstances in which a court must give preclusive effect to a judgment rendered in another jurisdiction is DAVID L. SHAPIRO, CIVIL PROCEDURE: PRECLUSION IN CIVIL ACTIONS (2001).

that one is not bound by a judgment *in personam* in a litigation in which he is not designated as a party or to which he has not been made a party by service of process."[253] The Court has continued to hew to this principle. In *Martin v. Wilks*,[254] the Court explained that "[t]his rule is part of our 'deep-rooted historic tradition that everyone should have his own day in court.' A judgment or decree among parties to a lawsuit resolves issues as among them, but it does not conclude the rights of strangers to those proceedings."

To sort out how these concerns balance against each other in the context of multi-party, multi-forum litigation, the following material is broken into two sections: first, a section on the use and limits of claim preclusion; and second, a section on the use and limits of issue preclusion.

A. Claim Preclusion

The hornbook statement of claim preclusion is this: A valid final judgment on the merits precludes, in a subsequent action between the same parties, any claim that was or should have been brought in the first case.[255] To start with the idea of a "claim that was or should have been brought," most American jurisdictions give a transactional definition to the word "claim." Any legal theories that are related in time, space, or motivation are part of the same transaction and hence part of the same claim.[256] The real bite of this broad transactional definition arises from the fact that claim preclusion bars not only the claims that the plaintiff originally filed in the first case, but also the claims that the plaintiff *should* have filed. Given the liberality of claim joinder,[257] a plaintiff must present all transactionally related claims in the first case on pain of losing them forever.[258]

In addition, claim preclusion requires a "judgment" that is "valid," "final," and "on the merits," as well as the "same parties." The *judgment* requirement dramatically limits the effectiveness of claim preclusion. Most cases, including most multi-party, multi-forum cases, settle; and in most of these cases, the case is dismissed and no judgment is entered, thus depriving the proceeding of any preclusive

---

253 311 U.S. 32 (1940).

254 490 U.S. 755 (1989).

255 *See, e.g.*, Federated Dept. Stores, Inc. v. Moitie, 452 U.S. 394 (1981).

256 RESTATEMENT (SECOND) OF JUDGMENTS § 24 (AM. L. INST. 1982). A few jurisdictions use more restrictive definitions of "claim."

257 *See supra* Chapter 2.A.

258 This rule applies regardless of whether the plaintiff wins or loses the first case. If the plaintiff wins, all the plaintiff's claims are "merged" into the judgment; the plaintiff cannot try to obtain more by bringing a second case invoking a new legal theory. If the plaintiff loses, all the claims are "barred" by the judgment; again, the plaintiff cannot seek relief in a second case by invoking a new ground for recovery.

effect in future litigation.[259] The other characteristics of a judgment (validity, finality, and merit-based) can limit a judgment's preclusive effect as well, but not in ways that raise unique issues for multi-party, multi-forum litigation. *Validity* depends on whether the court issuing the judgment had jurisdiction over the subject matter and the parties, and the party against whom preclusion is sought had notice of the first action. Depending on the law of the relevant jurisdiction, *finality* requires either a final determination of legal rights in the trial court or a final determination after appeal. And the *on the merits* requirement, which is slippery around its borders, generally means that the judgment must relate to the substantive merits of the case rather than to a preliminary procedural matter such as a lack of jurisdiction or a failure to meet the statute of limitations.[260] Although there are no unique "complex litigation" spins on these characteristics of a judgment, each could, in appropriate circumstances, limit the ability to use a judgment in one case to prevent the litigation of claims in a later case.

By far the most substantial limitation on a broad use of claim preclusion in complex litigation, however, is the *same parties* requirement. With a few exceptions, "same parties" means what it says: Claim preclusion can be used only in later litigation between exactly the same parties that had been involved in the first case. Complex litigation, however, rarely involves repetitive litigation by the same parties; it involves litigation by new parties in new forums.

There are exceptions to (or perhaps expansions of) the "same parties" requirement. According to the Supreme Court's decision in *Taylor v. Sturgell*,[261] the classic exceptions are six in number:

- A person who agrees to be bound by the determination of issues in an action between others is so bound;
- A pre-existing "substantive legal relationship" between a party to the judgment and the person sought to be bound—including succeeding owners of property, bailor and bailee, and assignor and assignee—binds the latter.

---

[259] An exception to this statement is the consent decree, in which the court incorporates the parties' settlement into a final judgment. Consent decrees have long been used in institutional-reform and environmental litigation.

[260] *Cf.* Semtek Int'l Inc. v. Lockheed Martin Corp., 531 U.S. 497 (2001) (discussing preclusive effect to be given in state court when federal court in a prior action dismissed the case on statute-of-limitations grounds). The term "on the merits" is somewhat misleading, and has been abandoned by the *Restatement (Second) of Judgments*. The reason is that certain judgments that do not determine the merits of a dispute—for instance, judgments dismissing a case for failure to state a claim or for willful discovery violations—are entitled to claim-preclusive effect. Nonetheless, the phrase "on the merits" remains in general usage in the case law.

[261] 553 U.S. 880 (2008).

- A person who assumes control over a party's litigation is bound "[b]ecause such a person has had 'the opportunity to present proofs and argument,'" and thus "has already 'had his day in court' even though he was not a formal party to the litigation";
- A "proxy"—a person who acts "as the designated representative of a person who was a party to the prior adjudication"—brings the later litigation;
- "[I]n certain limited circumstances," such as "properly conducted class actions[ ] and suits brought by trustees, guardians, and fiduciaries," a nonparty "may be bound by a judgment because she was 'adequately represented by someone with the same interests who [wa]s a party' to the suit."
- "[I]n certain circumstances a special statutory scheme," such as bankruptcy, probate, and proceedings that may be brought only on behalf of the public, "may 'expressly foreclos[e] successive litigation by nonlitigants . . . if the scheme is otherwise consistent with due process.'"

Two of these circumstances—class actions and bankruptcy—are of general significance to multi-party, multi-forum litigation, and the following two chapters consider them in more depth. Otherwise, the exceptions are of limited utility in preventing the relitigation of related claims across multiple forums. One or another of the exceptions may snare a case or two, but none is broadly helpful.

Two Supreme Court decisions reinforce the limited utility of preclusion in complex litigation. The first case is *Martin v. Wilks*; the second is *Taylor v. Sturgell*. In *Martin*, a group of African-American firefighters sued the City of Birmingham for racial discrimination. No white firefighters intervened in the case to protect their interests in employment and promotion. The case resulted in a consent decree that arguably disadvantaged white firefighters. A group of white firefighters filed an objection to the decree and sought to intervene to contest the decree. The district court rejected their objection on the merits and application to intervene as untimely. The consent decree was entered.

When the decree led the city to designate five African-American firefighters as eligible for a promotion, a group of white firefighters challenged the consent decree as illegal and void. In a 5–4 decision, the Supreme Court held that the white firefighters were not bound to the prior consent decree and were free to challenge it. The rationale for the majority's decision was somewhat unclear. On one reading, it is a constitutional decision: in particular, there were due-process problems with binding a nonparty to a prior judgment, so the white firefighters were free to contest the consent decree. On another reading, the case was merely an interpretation of the joinder provisions in the Federal Rules of Civil Procedure, which contemplated joinder (including intervention under Federal Rule 24) rather than preclusion as the proper mechanism for binding a person to a judgment.[262]

A strong dissent argued that permitting the subsequent action to go forward, when the plaintiffs in the second action knew of the prior action, might deprive the parties in the first case of their legal rights and upset a court's ability to achieve resolve a massive dispute without fear of a rear-guard collateral attack: "in complex litigation this Court has squarely held that a sideline-sitter may be bound as firmly as an actual party if he had adequate notice and a fair opportunity to intervene and if the judicial interest in finality is sufficiently strong."

Congress overruled the outcome of *Martin v. Wilks* the following year, so that a Title VII consent decree now binds nonparties who had "actual notice" of the adverse effect of the proposed decree on their interests and "a reasonable opportunity to present objections."[263] But *Martin v. Wilks* is still good law in other contexts. At one point, the American Law Institute proposed to build off of the Title VII approach. Under this idea, a court could issue an order permitting nonparties within the court's jurisdiction to intervene. Whether they did so or not, the judgment (favorable or unfavorable) would preclude nonparties with respect to common claims or issues should they ever file future litigation.[264] The ALI argued that this "notice and opportunity to intervene" approach was consistent with the Due Process Clause, and would be a useful partial solution to dealing with the relitigation created by the existence of future plaintiffs. Thus far, no court or legislature has accepted the ALI's invitation to create a "notice and opportunity to intervene" exception to the usual bar against nonparty preclusion.

Taylor v. Sturgell involves a different attempt to use claim preclusion to avoid repetitive litigation. Before *Taylor v. Sturgell*, a few courts had developed the doctrine of "virtual representation." Its

---

[262] In a subsequent case arising out of state court, the Court viewed *Martin* as resting on Due Process grounds. Richards v. Jefferson Cty., 517 U.S. 793 (1996). *Cf.* S. Cent. Bell Tel. Co. v. Alabama, 526 U.S. 160 (1999) (holding that a judgment cannot bind nonparties; citing *Richards* but not *Martin v. Wilks*).

[263] 42 U.S.C. § 2000e–2(n)(1)(B); *see* Briscoe v. City of New Haven, 654 F.3d 200 (2d Cir. 2011) (statute did not preclude a nonparty from challenging a Title VII consent decree when no formal fairness hearing was held before approval of the decree, so no "reasonable opportunity to present objections" existed).

[264] *See* COMPLEX LITIGATION, *supra* note 101, § 5.05.

basic concept was to bind a person to a prior judgment as long as the person's interests had been adequately represented by another person in the prior litigation. The doctrine's touchstone was adequate representation; a party in the first case needed to have had an interest closely enough aligned with a nonparty in the first case that it was both fair and efficient to saddle the nonparty with the outcome obtained in the first case. Among those courts that adopted the theory (and not all did), the requirements for adequate representation varied. In whatever its precise form, virtual representation was principally useful in cases in which the first judgment was adverse to the interests of the person sought to be bound in the second case. Thus, future plaintiffs could find their claims determined by an action to which they were not a party.

Taylor v. Sturgell presented near-perfect facts to test the concept. Aviation enthusiasts wanted to obtain government documents relating to a 1930s-era aircraft to help restore a plane. The plane's owner sought the records through the Freedom of Information Act, but the government denied the request. The owner challenged the denial in federal court in Wyoming. In a case that made its way to the Tenth Circuit, the denial was upheld. A month later, the executive director of an antique-aircraft association, who knew the owner and wanted to help with the restoration, filed a request for the same records. The request was again denied, and the director brought suit in a federal court in the District of Columbia. On appeal, the D.C. Circuit held that the director was bound by the prior Tenth Circuit decision because the owner had "virtually represented" the director's interests in the prior litigation. As proof of the closeness of the representation, the court of appeals noted the identity of interest, the adequacy of the representation in the prior case (the director's lawyer was the same as the owner's lawyer), the closeness of the relationship between the parties, and the tactical maneuvering in the two cases.

The Supreme Court reversed. It began with the traditional due-process requirement that only parties can be bound by a judgment. The Court acknowledged the six exceptions to that rule, but showed no appetite for expanding the list to include a seventh exception for "virtual representation." To do so, the Court held, would be to expand the exception for "adequate representation" beyond its present limits to create, in effect, a "common-law kind of class action"—thus binding people even when the party in the first lawsuit lacked a proper alignment of interests or an understanding of his or her responsibilities as a representative. The Court also pointed out that such a doctrine "might spark wide-ranging, time-consuming, and expensive discovery . . . under a standard that provides no firm guidance." The law of preclusion, however, "is intended to reduce the burden of litigation on courts and parties; thus, " 'crisp rules with sharp corners' are preferable to a round-about doctrine of opaque standards."[265]

Taylor v. Sturgell was not a complex case, but its reasoning leaves little room to argue that a "virtual representation" doctrine can tamp down repetitive litigation of claims by multiple parties in multiple forums.

Therefore, the present shape of claim preclusion holds out very limited promise as a means to avoid repetitive litigation of claims, especially claims asserted by future plaintiffs. Both the "notice and opportunity to intervene" and "virtual representation" approaches could breach this barrier, but legislative action is likely required. Even then, the constitutionality of either approach hinges on how strictly the Supreme Court adheres to the Due Process Clause's general demand that a judgment does not bind nonparties.

B. Issue Preclusion

As its name implies, issue preclusion seeks not to preclude entire claims in future litigation, but to preclude the re-litigation of certain factual or legal issues.[266] In complex cases, this preclusion may be enough. If a judgment in one case determines factual issues that are relevant to a host of related cases, and if the judgment can conclusively establish these common issues for other cases, then the later cases can focus entirely on any remaining non-common issues. The question is whether issue preclusion can deliver on this promise.

The hornbook statement of issue preclusion is this: A valid, final judgment bars a party's relitigation, in a subsequent case, of identical legal or factual issues that were litigated, actually determined, and essential to the final judgment of the first case.[267] Some of the requirements of issue preclusion—such as "judgment," "validity," and "finality"—are the same for claim and issue preclusion. Otherwise, the two doctrines diverge. Most critically, issue preclusion applies only to issues, not claims. Furthermore, the elements of an "identity of the issues," the issue's litigation and actual determination, and its necessity to the judgment have no counterpart in the law of claim preclusion. Also gone, at least in most jurisdictions, is claim preclusion's requirement that the first case and

---

[265] The Court remanded the case to determine if the director might be regarded as an agent or proxy of the owner, thus permitting preclusion on one of the standard exceptions.

[266] Since claim and issue preclusion are distinct, one doctrine may apply even if the other does not. In particular, issue preclusion may bar litigation of certain factual issues in later litigation even if claim preclusion does not bar litigation of the entire claim.

[267] *See* RESTATEMENT, *supra* note 256, § 27.

later cases involve the same parties; in most jurisdictions, it is enough if the party sought to be bound in the second case was a party to the first judgment, even if the other party was not.

To begin with the requirement of *identity of issues*, the issue decided in the first case must be substantially the same as the issue presented in the second case. For instance, if Maine uses a different standard to determine negligence than North Carolina, then the finding of negligence from a judgment rendered under Maine' law is generally not entitled to preclusive effect in an action in North Carolina. Similarly, differences in the burdens of proof may keep a fact found in one case from translating over to a second case. Finally, the issue may be so fact-intensive that preclusion is not possible. A finding that exposure to a toxic substance caused the first plaintiff's cancer cannot be preclusive of the whether exposure to that substance caused a second plaintiff's cancer.[268]

The requirement that the identical issue have been *litigated and actually determined* can also create difficulties. Unlike claim preclusion, which extends preclusive effect both to claims that were litigated and to claims that should have been litigated, issue preclusion applies only to issues that were litigated and decided. In many complex cases, different lawyers will emphasize and try different issues. If the toxic-tort case proceeds only on a strict products liability theory and the second case proceeds on negligence and warranty theories, the facts of negligence and warranty were neither litigated nor decided in the first case. The first judgment cannot preclude litigation of these issues in the second case.

But bringing multiple theories in the first litigation creates its own difficulties. Many cases are tried to juries, and the jury usually renders a general verdict that makes it impossible to know exactly what the jury decided. For instance, in a toxic-tort case, assume that the plaintiff in the first action tries both negligence and strict-liability theories to the jury. The jury returns a verdict for the plaintiff. In a second action, a new plaintiff sues the same defendant, but only for negligence. The second plaintiff cannot use the first judgment to bar the defendant from relitigating the issue of negligence because it is not clear that the jury in the first case decided that the defendant was negligent. It might instead have decided that the defendant was strictly liable.

---

[268] As long as it meets the other requirements for issue preclusion, the first action might be preclusive on the general issue whether the defendant's substance is capable of causing the type of cancer from which the first plaintiff suffered; later plaintiffs might be able to prevent the defendant from arguing that its substance could not cause such a cancer. But to use the first judgment to preclude the defendant's ability to argue that the second plaintiff is not suffering from the relevant cancer or that the second plaintiff's exposure did not cause the cancer is a bridge too far.

The requirement that an issue be *essential* to the judgment adds yet another roadblock to issue preclusion. An issue is "essential" only when the judgment in the first case could not stand without that issue having been determined as it was. Assume that both negligence and strict-liability theories are pursued in the first action, and a jury renders a special verdict finding that the defendant was both negligent and strictly liable. The jury's finding of negligence is not preclusive in the second case, because the finding was not essential; the defendant would still have lost the case on the strict-liability theory regardless of the outcome on the negligence issue.[269] When the first lawsuit ends in a general verdict, finding an issue that was both determined and essential to the judgment is often difficult, thus limiting the utility of issue preclusion to prevent relitigation of common issues in related cases.[270]

Assuming that all these shoals of issue preclusion can be navigated, a final difficulty looms: the requirement that issue preclusion runs only against a party to the first action. Until recently, issue preclusion existed only between the "same parties"—with "same parties" having the same meaning as it has for claim preclusion.[271] This requirement was usually referred to as *mutuality of preclusion*: a person could not take advantage of an issue determined in a prior case unless that person would have been bound by the opposite finding. Since parties are the only persons usually bound by a judgment, the mutuality rule meant that only parties to the prior judgment or their privies could use the prior judgment in a second case. If one plaintiff sued and won the first case, a second plaintiff could not use any of the issues—even those that were litigated, determined, and essential to the judgment—in the second case. Obviously, the mutuality rule severely limits the utility of issue preclusion in multi-party, multi-forum litigation.

All is not lost. The great majority of American jurisdictions, including the federal courts, have now abandoned the mutuality rule, and permit non-mutual issue preclusion in certain circumstances. One circumstances is known as *defensive issue preclusion*, which applies when a plaintiff successively sues defendants. For instance, assume that a plaintiff was allegedly injured by exposure to a substance at work; two defendants made the substance, and the

---

[269] In some jurisdiction, the existence of a decision based on alternative grounds is preclusive on the issues necessary to both grounds; thus, both the issue of the defendant's negligence and its strict liability would be preclusive in the second action. Most jurisdictions still adhere to the traditional approach, and accord no preclusive effect on either ground.

[270] For a case showing the difficulty of using a general jury verdict to preclude the manufacturer from contesting liability in future cases, see Hardy v. Johns-Manville Sales Corp., 681 F.2d 334 (5th Cir. 1982).

[271] *See supra* note 261 and accompanying text.

plaintiff used them both. In the first case, the plaintiff sues only the first manufacturer. In a special verdict, the jury determines that the defendant was negligent, but that the plaintiff's disease was not caused by the substance to which he was exposed. Therefore, the judge enters judgment against the plaintiff.[272] Now, in a second case the plaintiff sues the second manufacturer, again claiming injury due to exposure.

Under the mutuality rule, the second manufacturer could not take advantage of the finding about a lack of causal connection because it had not been a party in the first lawsuit. But allowing the plaintiff two bites at the apple is unseemly; not only might inconsistent verdicts result, but the plaintiff has an incentive not to effect the broadest joinder possible in the first case. This result serves neither fairness nor efficiency.

Under the doctrine of defensive issue preclusion, however, a new defendant in later litigation can defend itself by using a litigated, determined, and essential finding from a prior case against a party (usually a plaintiff) to the prior case.[273] Defensive issue preclusion, however, is only occasionally useful in complex litigation. Repeated litigation of common issues by one plaintiff against multiple defendants sometimes occurs, and defensive issue preclusion is useful to prevent this behavior. But the real challenge in most complex cases is repeated litigation of common issues by multiple plaintiffs against a defendant (or defendants). Defensive issue preclusion does not address this situation.

The second inroad on the old mutuality rule, *offensive issue preclusion*, is more useful, but also more controversial. Under this doctrine, new plaintiffs can use the factual findings from a prior case against a party (usually a defendant) to that case. For instance, suppose that the plaintiff in the first case sues a defendant due to injuries suffered in a workplace exposure to a defendant's chemical. The theory of recovery is negligence, and the defendant disputes negligence, the capacity of the substance to cause injuries of the type from which the plaintiff suffered, and the causal connection between the exposure and the plaintiff's injury. The plaintiff wins a general verdict. A new plaintiff, also suffering from the same injury, now brings a new lawsuit against the same defendant, claiming that the

---

[272] Note how the special verdict removes any doubt about whether the causal issue was both determined and essential to the judgment. Had there been only a general verdict, it would have been impossible to know what the jury actually determined; had a special verdict determined both that the defendant was negligent and that the substance did not cause the plaintiff's injury, then the finding of a lack of causation would not have been essential to the judgment.

[273] The Supreme Court has adopted defensive issue preclusion as a part of the federal law of preclusion. Blonder-Tongue Labs., Inc. v. Univ. of Ill. Found., 402 U.S. 313 (1971).

substance also caused her injuries. We know that the jury in the first case must have determined that the defendant was negligent, that the substance was capable of causing the type of injury from which both plaintiffs suffered, and that the first plaintiff was so injured; otherwise, the verdict could not stand. All three determinations were also essential to support the judgment.

In the second case, the new plaintiff does not care about the third finding, but can she take advantage of the first two? If so, a great deal of repetitive litigation in the second case could be eliminated. If many others are claiming or could in the future claim the same injury, then the first lawsuit will eliminate even more repetitive evidence in later lawsuits. Indeed, there is no need to aggregate these suits, because the first case will have already determined the common issues; each lawsuit can then focus on case-specific questions like the causal connection between each new plaintiff's exposure and injury, as well as the amount of damages. Best of all, offensive issue preclusion is not limited in its application to cases that have been filed. In temporally dispersed litigation, future plaintiffs who file in later years can still use the findings.

The promise of offensive issue preclusion sounds wonderful, but there are also problems. A principal concern is that the doctrine gives plaintiffs an incentive to wait and see, rather than to join together. The reason is that plaintiffs cannot be bound by a judgment in favor of the defendant, but can take advantage of a judgment in favor of the prior plaintiff; hence, a rational plaintiff might prefer not to join the first case. It also seems unfair to preclude a defendant who has won a number of verdicts, only to suffer an eventual loss; it should be allowed to continue to contest an issue on which reasonable juries have differed.[274] Other grounds for unfairness can also exist: for instance, the defendant may not have had an incentive to litigate the issue in the first case vigorously (maybe the first plaintiff's damages were only $1,000) or may not have had the procedural opportunities in the first case that give us confidence in the quality of judgment (maybe the first case was in small-claims court).

For these reasons, courts have accepted offensive issue preclusion with caution. The seminal case under the federal law of preclusion is *Parklane Hosiery, Inc. v. Shore*,[275] in which a corporate defendant had been found liable for securities-fraud violations in an enforcement action commenced by the Securities and Exchange Commission. Subsequently, stockholders in the company brought a class action, and proposed to use the judgment in the SEC case to

---

[274] Recall Professor McGovern's maturity thesis: that defendants often win the first few cases before a plaintiff finally achieves a breakthrough victory. *See supra* note 11 and accompanying text.

[275] 439 U.S. 322 (1979).

estop the defendant from contending that it had not violated the securities laws. If successful, this use of preclusion would have streamlined the second litigation enormously. But the defendant objected, claiming that preclusion was unfair.

The Supreme Court allowed the use of offensive issue preclusion in federal court. Recognizing the doctrine's potential dangers, the Court gave district courts discretion in deciding when to apply it, and identified four circumstances in which that discretion should generally disfavor use of the doctrine: when the plaintiff seeking to preclude the defendant had the opportunity to join the prior case but did not; when the defendant did not have the same incentive in the first case to contest the issue; when there have been prior inconsistent judgments, with some favoring the defendant; and when the defendant did not have procedural opportunities or safeguards available in the first case that were available in the second. Applying those factors in the case before it, the Court found that the stockholders could not have joined the SEC enforcement action, the defendant had every incentive to contest the issue of securities fraud in the SEC suit, no prior inconsistent judgments existed, and no procedural opportunities were available in the second action that were unavailable in the first.[276] Therefore, it approved of the use of offensive issue preclusion.

In many complex cases, however, one or more of these four limits will trip up the effort to use offensive issue preclusion. For instance, *Hardy v. Johns-Manville Sales Corp.*[277] involved an attempt to use a prior judgment to keep an asbestos defendant from contesting certain issues regarding the dangers of asbestos and its liability. The plaintiffs pointed to a prior case (*Borel*) in which the defendant had lost a judgment for $68,000. As is typical with immature litigation, approximately half of the 70-odd asbestos cases that had been tried after *Borel* had resulted in judgment for the defendant. At the time of *Borel* the defendant was facing no other asbestos litigation; by the time of *Hardy*, the defendant was facing thousands of asbestos claims, many seeking millions of dollars. The district court allowed the fifty-eight plaintiffs in *Hardy* to use the *Borel* judgment offensively against the defendant.

The court of appeals reversed. It held that the prior inconsistent verdicts, as well as the defendant's relatively weak incentive to litigate liability in *Borel* because the catastrophic crush of litigation

---

[276] The SEC action had been bench-tried, and the stockholders' case was to be tried to a jury. That difference in procedural opportunity did not, however, matter to the Court. It thought that "the presence or absence of a jury as factfinder is basically neutral."

[277] 681 F.2d 334 (5th Cir. 1982).

that ultimately followed from this single loss was unforeseeable at the time, made offensive issue preclusion improper.

Parklane Hosiery's two other limitations—lack of procedural opportunities in the first case and refusal to join the first case—can also derail offensive issue preclusion in complex litigation. Lack of procedural opportunities is rarely invoked as a reason to reject the preclusive effect of a prior judgment, but some cases exist.[278] The "refusal to join" circumstance is perhaps the least well-developed of the *Parklane Hosiery* exceptions. The cases invoking the limitation tend to involve multidistrict litigation in which some plaintiffs were clearly taking a "wait and see" attitude, but even here preclusion is sometimes permitted.[279] This limitation would almost surely not apply to plaintiffs who were not injured at the time of the first case, who were unaware of the case, or who were unable, for jurisdictional or other reasons, to join the case.

Both defensive and offensive issue preclusion are limited in an extremely important way: they can be applied only against a person that was party to prior litigation. Thus far, most courts been unwilling to abolish this limitation on the use of issue preclusion against nonparties. One reason is the bedrock principle that a person cannot be bound by an adverse judgment unless that person is a party to the case. This principle affirms the autonomy and individual control over litigation. As we have seen, our party joinder and preclusion systems are constructed around the view that all litigants are entitled to their day in court.

There have been a few older cases that extended issue preclusion to plaintiffs who were not parties in a prior proceeding,[280] but it is

---

[278] *See, e.g.*, Snider v. Consol. Coal Co., 973 F.2d 555 (7th Cir. 1992) (no issue preclusion what evidence was excluded in the first case but was important to the defense in the second case); Ala. *ex rel* Siegelman v. U.S. Envtl. Prot. Agency, 911 F.2d 499 (11th Cir. 1990) (no issue preclusion when a party joined only on certain claims in the first case and was not required to litigate the issues in play in the later case).

[279] *Compare In re* Air Crash Disaster at Stapleton Int'l Airport, Denver, Colo., on Nov. 15, 1987, 720 F. Supp. 1505 (D. Colo. 1989), *rev'd on other grounds*, 964 F.2d 1059 (10th Cir. 1992) ("We find that in cases not consolidated for trial, justice, fairness and equity weigh against permitting 'wait and see' plaintiffs to assert non-mutual offensive collateral estoppel."), *with In re* Air Crash at Detroit Metro. Airport, Detroit, Mich., on Aug. 16, 1987, 776 F. Supp. 316 (E.D. Mich. 1991) (permitting issue preclusion in favor of "wait and see" plaintiffs when the plaintiffs would have been unable to participate in the trial even had they filed suit earlier).

[280] For example, in *Lynch v. Merrell-National Laboratories*, 646 F. Supp. 856 (D. Mass. 1986), *aff'd on other grounds*, 830 F.2d 1190 (1st Cir. 1987), a judge held that a plaintiff was precluded from proving causation in a case involving Bendectin exposure because a jury in a related multidistrict case had found that no causal connection between Bendectin and the plaintiff's type of injury existed. The plaintiff in *Lynch* had expressly opted out of the MDL trial in favor of a remand of his case to the transferor forum. The court of appeals expressed skepticism about the district court's preclusion theory, and found another ground on which to affirm the judgment. Similarly, in *Hardy*, 681 F.2d 334, the district court extended the preclusive effect of

difficult to imagine how these cases survive the Supreme Court's more recent decisions in cases such as *Martin v. Wilks* and *Taylor v. Sturgell*. Thus, issue preclusion can help complex litigation run more efficiently in some instances, but it is not a silver bullet that provides for a single resolution of issues that overlap in related litigation—and it never will be unless we sacrifice our basic commitment to bind people to outcomes only when they participate as parties in shaping that outcome.

C. An Assessment of Preclusion

Historically, the law of preclusion has mediated the tension between finality and a full and fair opportunity to litigate claims and issues. Complex litigation poses new challenges for the best way to strike this balance. Nor does using preclusion to achieve a single resolution of common issues avoid the policy battles that we encountered with joinder, consolidation, stays, and injunctions. The same fundamental questions remain. For instance, when is it appropriate to deprive an individual of his or her day in court, or of the right to control the presentation of his or her case? When should concerns for efficiency lead us to apply preclusion principles as a means to achieve aggregation? Should expansive preclusion rules apply only to complex cases, and (given the outcome-affecting potential of such rules) what justifies changing these rules in complex but not ordinary cases?

Our study of preclusion brings to an end our initial examination of the ways in which the American legal system has thought to deal with multi-party, multi-forum litigation. The next two chapters cycle back to other devices—such as class actions and bankruptcy—that pick up elements of these methods. As we will see, these devices are powerful, but limited both in their scope and in their capacity to channel dispersed litigation into a single resolution. Perhaps the ultimate lesson of these chapters is that no single mechanism is perfect in all situations. Successfully aggregating claims and preventing repetitive litigation of common issues may require the creative use of multiple approaches, rather than any single doctrine or method.

---

the judgment in *Borel* to fourteen asbestos defendants not involved in *Borel*. The court of appeals reversed, although in dicta it noted that issue preclusion might apply to a defendant that had participated in the trial of a prior case and then settled precisely to avoid the preclusive effect of a judgment entered against other defendants.

Chapter 6

CLASS ACTIONS

The class action is the most controversial procedural device in the United States. Even ordinary folk who wouldn't know Rule 24 intervention from Rule 22 interpleader have heard about class actions. A lot of misinformation about class actions floats around. We will try to cut through these misimpressions to give a clear view of benefits of and problems with class actions.

To begin with a few basic concepts, class actions bring together into one case the claims of a group of people (the *class*). The class is represented by a single person or small group of people (the *class representative(s)*), who conduct the class action on behalf of its members. As a rule, a lawyer (*class counsel*) works to present the class's case. The members of the class do not need to do anything to become part of the class.

A judge will decide whether to *certify* a class; if the class is certified, then the members are part of the class, even if they do not know about the case. In some instances, as we will see, class members can *opt out* of the class action. If they cannot or do not opt out, however, a judgment in a properly conducted class action binds the class members as well as the class representatives. You might want to read that last sentence again: the class action's preclusive effect on the claims of class members is the crux of why class actions are both so powerful and so controversial. A single certification decision by a single judge can create a single process to resolve the claims of thousands or even millions of potential plaintiffs.

If you are wondering how this preclusive effect squares with the principles that you learned in the last chapter—that only parties to a case can be bound by a judgment in that case—recall *Taylor v. Sturgell*: properly conducted class actions are an exception to the due-process requirement that judgments bind only parties.[281] Sometimes class actions are described as a rule of joinder: the members of the class join the lawsuit, and as parties to the case are bound to the judgment. Indeed, the federal class-action rule, Rule 23, can be found in the middle of the joinder rules. But the "joinder" of class members is surely a legal fiction. It is probably better to view class actions as an exception to the ordinary rules of preclusion—an exception that, as we will see shortly, affects the shape of Rule 23.[282]

---

[281] *See supra* note 261 and accompanying text.

[282] It is important to note that the preclusive effect of a judgment is limited only to those claims that class members share in common and are asserted in the class

This Chapter opens with a brief overview of class actions: a bit of their history and the basic structure of Rule 23. It then turns to an intensive look at each of the requirements of Rule 23. Next, the Chapter examines how class actions negotiate some of the usual limits on single-forum aggregation, especially subject-matter and territorial jurisdiction. Finally, the Chapter explores how class actions can be used not to litigate the claims of a class but rather to settle a controversy without litigation. This "settlement class action" holds out promise, but also raises concerns, as a way to handle the difficult problem of future plaintiffs.

A. An Overview of Class Actions

The earliest lawsuit that we might today regard as a class action arose in 1199, when an English churchman sued his entire parish for tithes that he thought were due him.[283] Similar actions by or against groups to enforce communal rights or obligations occurred throughout medieval and early modern times with little discussion about their propriety. As such communal rights and obligations disappeared, the modern class action emerged as a part of English equity practice. A person claiming a legal right feared that various suits filed at various times by various parties might challenge that right. To prevent multiple suits and possibly inconsistent awards of relief, the defendant filed a "bill of peace" in equity, asking the chancellor to resolve all the related cases and to bind persons in the "multitude," whether or not they were parties in an ongoing case.

In his treatise on equity, Justice Story advocated for the American adoption of the bill of peace.[284] In 1842, Federal Equity Rule 48 authorized class actions when (1) the parties were "very numerous, and cannot, without manifest inconvenience and oppressive delays in the suit, be all brought before" the court, and (2) "sufficient parties" were present "to represent all the adverse interests of the plaintiffs and the defendants in the suit." Rule 48

---

action. If a class member has a unique individual claim against the defendant, the judgment in the class action does not bar the individual claim. *See* Cooper v. Fed. Reserve Bank of Richmond, 467 U.S. 867 (1984) (discussed further *infra* notes 492–493 and accompanying text).

[283] The case is *Master Martin v. Parishioners of Nuthampstead*, a report of which can be found in SELECT CASES FROM THE ECCLESIASTICAL COURTS OF THE PROVINCE OF CANTERBURY c. 1200–1301 (Norma Adams & Charles Donohue eds., Selden Soc'y No. 95, 1981).

[284] *See* 2 JOSEPH STORY, COMMENTARIES ON EQUITY JURISPRUDENCE AS ADMINISTERED IN ENGLAND AND AMERICA ch. XXII (1836); *see also* West v. Randall, 29 F. Cas. 718 (No. 17,424) (C.C.D.R.I. 1820) (Story, J.) (stating that "the court may be enabled to make a complete decree between the parties, may prevent future litigation by taking away the necessity of a multiplicity of suits, and may make it perfectly certain, that no injustice shall be done, either to the parties before the court, or to others, who are interested by a decree, that may be grounded upon a partial view only of the real merits").

applied only to cases seeking equitable relief; there were no class actions for damages. Rule 38 of the 1912 Equity Rules shifted the criteria somewhat, permitting class actions when "the question was one of common or general interest to many persons constituting a class so numerous as to make it impracticable to bring them all before the court."

With some significant additional changes, Equity Rule 38 became Rule 23 of the Federal Rules of Civil Procedure in 1938. For the first time, albeit in narrow circumstances, a class action could seek damages. Creating the first general-purpose class actions for damages and making class-wide civil-rights injunctions easier to obtain, a substantial amendment in 1966 molded Rule 23 into nearly its present shape. Additional amendments in 1998 and 2003, plus a textual restyling in 2007, completed the task.[285]

Perhaps the most significant case to shape the contours of the present Rule 23, as well as similar class-action rules in state courts,[286] is *Hansberry v. Lee*.[287] In the 1920s, fearing that it might become integrated as the African-American population expanded, a white neighborhood on the south side of Chicago adopted a strategy that was spreading across the country: the racially restrictive covenant. In these covenants each property owner pledged not to sell or rent the property to an African-American. The covenant ran with the land, so that it bound future owners as well as the present ones. The *Hansberry* covenant had one catch: it became effective only after the owners of ninety-five percent of the frontage in the neighborhood had signed. The neighborhood association's campaign to collect signatures went on for months.[288]

In 1932, an African-American physician rented one of the properties subject to the covenant. A nearby property owner (and wife of the man responsible for the campaign to collect signatures) brought suit to enforce the covenant against the property owner. The suit, *Burke v. Kleiman*,[289] was brought in Illinois state court as a class action on behalf of all signatory property owners. Critical to the success of the case was the validity of the covenant—in particular, whether the owners of the requisite ninety-five percent of the frontage had signed. The parties stipulated to the fact that the

285 As of this writing, the Advisory Committee for the Civil Rules has proposed a number of changes to Rule 23 that may take effect within a few years. Legislation presently pending in Congress also proposes changes to some aspects of class-action practice, especially in class actions seeking recovery for personal injury.

286 Every state except Mississippi and Virginia has a class-action rule. Even Virginia sometimes allows class-like relief as a judicial matter.

287 311 U.S. 32 (1940).

288 The campaign was supported, and likely bankrolled, by the University of Chicago, whose campus lay to the east of the neighborhood.

289 189 N.E. 372 (Ill. 1934).

owners of ninety-five percent of the frontage had signed. On this basis, the trial court issued enjoined the rental to the physician, and the award was upheld on appeal. The case said nothing specifically about whether a class action was proper, but under Illinois law of the day, a common interest sufficed for class treatment.

Fast forward to 1938, when a number of property owners subject to the covenant sold their homes to white purchasers who were front men that immediately turned around and sold the properties to African-Americans. (Ironically, the man who had secured the covenants' signatures, and whose wife brought the prior case, engineered the sales after falling out with the neighborhood association.) A white property owner again brought a class action in Illinois state court seeking to kick the new owners out of their homes. The defendants[290] principally argued that racially restrictive covenants were illegal and unconstitutional, but they also tried to prove that owners of ninety-five percent of the frontage had never signed, thus rendering the covenants ineffective. The plaintiffs argued that restrictive covenants were legal. They also argued that the *Burke* class action had determined the covenants' validity; and because the defendants' predecessors in interests (that is, the owners in 1932 of the properties the defendants purchased) were members of the class, they were bound by that finding.

The Illinois courts found for the plaintiffs. They refused to examine the defendants' evidence that less than ninety-five percentage of the frontage had signed because the defendants were bound by the decree in *Burke*. On certiorari, the United States Supreme Court ducked the constitutionality of racially restrictive covenants.[291] Instead, it held that the Illinois courts had violated the due-process rights of the defendants by binding them to *Burke*'s finding that the covenants were valid. It remanded the case to give the defendants a chance to contest the covenants' validity.

On one level, the Court might be faulted for ducking the critical constitutional question, but on another, its reasoning went to the very heart of class actions—and in the process laid the foundation for modern class-action law. The Court began its analysis with the "principle of general application in Anglo-American jurisprudence that one is not bound by a judgment *in personam* in a litigation in which he is not designated as a party or to which he has not been made a party by service of process." This principle was grounded in

---

[290] The defendants were the African-American property owners, Carl and Nannie Hansberry and Harry Herbert Pace; Pace's company, which financed the sales; and several white property owners who either had facilitated or were threatening to facilitate sales to African-Americans.

[291] The Court held restrictive covenants unconstitutional eight years later, in a case argued by a young Thurgood Marshall. Shelley v. Kraemer, 334 U.S. 1 (1948).

the Due Process Clause, meaning that state courts as well as federal courts are required to respect it. The Court then acknowledged that the general principle contains "a recognized exception that, to an extent not precisely defined by judicial opinion, the judgment in a 'class' or 'representative' suit, to which some members of the class are parties, may bind members of the class or those represented who were not made parties to it." The Due Process Clause is satisfied as long as the class members "are in fact adequately represented by parties who are present, or where they actually participate in the conduct of the litigation in which members of the class are present as parties, . . . or where the interest of the members of the class, some of whom are present as parties, is joint, or where for any other reason the relationship between the parties present and those who are absent is such as legally to entitle the former to stand in judgment for the latter."

Of these possible ways for class-action preclusion to satisfy the Due Process Clause, the critical one in most instances is *adequate representation*. The next question is exactly what "adequate" representation means. In *Hansberry* the Court held that the defendants had not been adequately represented in *Burke* because the class had an internal conflict of interest between those who wanted the covenant enforced and those who did not (remember that the covenant ran with the land, so that future owners such as the African-American defendants in *Hansberry* were in the class). The class representative could not adequately represent the interests both of those who wanted the covenant enforced and those, like the defendants in *Hansberry*, "whose substantial interest is in resisting performance." As the Court said of the 1933 class action, "[s]uch a selection of representatives for purposes of litigation, whose substantial interests are not necessarily or even probably the same as those whom they are deemed to represent, does not afford that protection to absent parties which due process requires."

The Court particularly mentioned the fear that such a conflict "would afford [opportunities] for the fraudulent and collusive sacrifice of the rights of absent parties." That concern was raised on the facts of *Hansberry*, in which some evidence at the *Hansberry* trial suggested that the owners only fifty-four percent of the frontage had signed the covenants, and that the *Burke* suit was a collusive effort to render the covenant enforceable. The Supreme Court cited this figure in rendering the facts of the case, noting that *Burke*'s finding that the covenant was in force rested on a stipulation that was false—and perhaps even fraudulently or collusively agreed to by the lawyers in *Burke*.[292] Concern for collusion between the class counsel and the

---

[292] In fact, the evidence suggesting the 54 percent figure was deeply flawed, and it is possible that, depending on the resolution of a few factual disputes regarding

opposing counsel has framed concerns for class actions ever since *Hansberry*.

Hansberry also acknowledged that class actions traditionally required both a large number of parties and common interests among class members. And it is from *Hansberry*'s tripartite framework—numerous parties, common questions, and adequacy of representation—that the present Rule 23 has been built.

The present Rule 23 came into effect in 1966. For now, focus on Rules 23(a), 23(b), and 23(g). Rule 23(a) states the necessary conditions for *all* class actions. In addition to meeting each of the Rule 23(a) requirements, class actions must meet one additional requirement of Rule 23(b).[293] In essence, Rule 23(a) ensures two things: that a class action will be economical and efficient and that the class representatives will adequately represent the class members' interests. In addition, Rule 23(g) describes the factors that a court must consider when choosing class counsel who will adequately represent the class.

Rule 23(b) shows that large numbers, common interests, and adequate representation are insufficient for a class action: there must be another reason why a case deserves class treatment. Rule 23(b)(1) provides two such reasons that more or less replicate circumstances in which traditional equity would have entertained a class action. Rule 23(b)(2) was new in 1966, and reflected, in part, experience with civil-rights litigation in the wake of *Brown v. Board of Education*.[294] It permitted class actions when injunctive or declaratory relief was appropriate for the class as a whole. Rule 23(b)(3), also new in 1966, allowed class actions when common issues among class members predominated and a class action was superior to other means for resolving the dispute.

---

signatures, 95 percent of the frontage had in fact signed and that the covenant was valid. But the plaintiffs in *Hansberry* stood on the preclusive effect of *Burke* and did not refute the defendants' evidence that only 54 percent of the frontage had signed. For further discussion of this issue, as well as the back story of the *Hansberry* litigation, see Jay Tidmarsh, *The Story of* Hansberry*: The Foundation for Modern Class Actions*, *in* CIVIL PROCEDURE STORIES 217 (Kevin M. Clermont ed. 2004). One interesting side note: Carl and Nannie Hansberry were the parents of Lorraine Hansberry, who was eight when her family moved into the white neighborhood. Lorraine Hansberry would go on to write *A Raisin in the Sun*, an award-winning play about an African-American family in Chicago contemplating a move into an all-white neighborhood.

[293] A class action can, but need not, meet more than one of the Rule 23(b) requirements. In addition, some claims or class members may meet one Rule 23(b) requirement, while others may meet another.

[294] 347 U.S. 483 (1954). For an examination of the difficulties in enforcing *Brown* that led to Rule 23(b)(2), see David Marcus, *Flawed but Noble: Desegregation Litigation and Its Implications for the Modern Class Action*, 63 FLA. L. REV. 657 (2011).

As we explain shortly, Rules 23(b)(1)(A) and 23(b)(2) are in nearly all circumstances available only when injunctive relief is involved. Rule 23(b)(1)(B) sometimes allows monetary relief, but the terms under which it permits money judgments are narrow. The only class action that generally allows monetary relief—and therefore the class action that stirs the most controversy—is the Rule 23(b)(3) class action.

The adventuresome nature of the Rule 23(b)(3) class action is reflected in a structural feature that is essential to understanding the modern class action. Unlike the other Rule 23(b) class actions, Rule 23(b)(3) gives class members a right to opt out of a class action.[295] For this reason, the three class actions found in Rule 23(b)(1) and 23(b)(2) are described as *mandatory*: class members cannot remove themselves from the class.[296] The Rule 23(b)(3) class action, on the other hand, is usually referred to as an *opt-out class action*. Class members who opt out leave from the class, and any judgment in the class action does not bind them. Opt-outs are free to pursue litigation on their own.

The default position in an opt-out class action like Rule 23(b)(3) is "remain": unless a person takes the affirmative step of opting out, the person remains in the class and is bound by the outcome. This default position can be contrasted with the opt-in approach—found in the Federal Labor Standards Act and in some foreign countries—that class members must take affirmative steps to join the class in order to be bound.[297]

Of course, a right to opt out is fairly meaningless unless class members know of their right. Hence, Rule 23(c)(2)(B) describes in some detail the notice that must be provided to class members in an opt-out class action. Rule 23(c)(2)(B) requires that the notice must be "the best notice that is practicable under the circumstances,

---

[295] *See* FED. R. CIV. P. 23(c)(2)(B)(v).

[296] As a matter of discretion, courts in rare cases have allowed class members to opt out of (b)(1) or (b)(2) class actions. *See* Eubanks v. Billington, 110 F.3d 87 (D.C. Cir. 1997); Cty. of Suffolk v. Long Island Lighting Co., 907 F.2d 1295 (2d Cir. 1990); *but see* Thomas v. Albright, 139 F.3d 227 (D.C. Cir. 1998) (district court abused its discretion in permitting plaintiffs to opt out). The Supreme Court has never ruled on whether this is an acceptable practice.

[297] For the opt-in approach of the FLSA, see 29 U.S.C. § 216(b). The original 1938 version of Rule 23 also had a form of class action, known as the "spurious class action," that was effectively an opt-in approach. For an argument to adopt an opt-in approach to Rule 23, see Scott Dodson, *An Opt-In Option for Class Actions*, 115 MICH. L. REV. 171 (2016). *See also* Kern v. Siemens Corp., 393 F.3d 120 (2d Cir. 2004) (reversing district court's decision that it had the equitable authority to certify an opt-in class action).

including individual notice to all class members who can be identified through reasonable means."[298]

One of the dynamics of class-action litigation over the decades since 1966 has been the attempt by class counsel to expand the scope of mandatory class actions. One reason is the sometimes considerable expense of giving notice, an expense which class counsel typically bears. Other reasons include the greater preclusive effect of a mandatory class action (an effect sometimes desired by defendants wishing to settle an array of claims) or the chance to obtain a greater fee if no class members can opt out to pursue their own claims (an outcome often desired by class counsel).

Before we plunge into the details of Rule 23, let us mention five other matters of general import. First, although most class actions involve a class representative bringing claims as plaintiff against a defendant (or defendants), a class action brought by a plaintiff against a class of defendants is possible (albeit unusual). One difficulty of defendant class actions is finding a defendant both competent and willing to accept the responsibility of representing others. If the class is certified under Rule 23(b)(3), another problem is the ability of defendant class members to opt out. In any event, our principal concern is finding means to aggregate a large number of related claims, so our focus lies on plaintiff class actions.

Second, it is possible to break a single class into subclasses. Rule 23(c)(5) permits this division, and states that each subclass is considered its own class. Each subclass must have its own representative bound by an obligation of adequate representation to the subclass; the subclass representative is also a representative of the class as a whole. "Subclassing," as this process is known, may be a way to ensure even tighter connections among the interests of certain subsets of class members when they are in some tension with the interests of other class members; but in the end, each class representative bears an obligation to represent the entire class's interests as well. Therefore, if each subclass has unacceptable conflicts of interest with other subclasses, the internal conflicts do not permit certification of the class. For instance, the conflicts of interest and adequate-representation problem described in *Hansberry* could not have been swept away if *Burke* had established two subclasses, one wanting enforcement of the covenant and one opposing it. The internal conflict was too great to allow both groups into one class.

---

[298] Notice may also be given to members of mandatory class actions if appropriate. FED. R. CIV. P. 23(c)(1). In addition, in all class actions, class members must receive notice of any proposed settlement, so that they might either object to the settlement or, if still permitted in a (b)(3) class action either by Rule 23(c)(2) or by the judge under Rule 23(e)(4), opt out.

Third, Rule 23(c)(4) makes it possible to maintain a class action "with respect to particular issues." The meaning of this provision is uncertain. One view is that a class action can be certified as long as the requirements of Rules 23(a) and 23(b) are met with respect just to the issues certified; the other view is that the entire case must be capable of certification, even though certification is sought only on some of the issues in the case. The former view could lead to much greater use of class actions, as class actions effectively become a device for obtaining preclusion on the certified common issues which individual class members could then use in subsequent individual or aggregate litigation.[299]

Fourth, a court does not have *sua sponte* power to order class certification. The process to certify a class begins with a pleading that nominates a class representative and alleges compliance with the relevant provisions of Rule 23. Rule 23(c)(1)(A) requires the court to decide the matter at "an early practicable time." Typically a court will order a motion for class certification to be filed by a particular date. Before that date, parties are able to conduct discovery regarding the elements of Rules 23(a) and 23(b).[300] If the court grants class certification, its order must *define* (or describe who is in) the class and *appoint* class counsel.[301] If the class is a (b)(3) opt-out class, it must also direct that notice of the case and the right to opt out be given to potential class members. A class-certification decision is subject to later revision.[302] Indeed, a court can, either *sua sponte* or on motion, decide that class treatment is improper and *decertify* the class.[303]

Finally, although the final-judgment rule of 28 U.S.C. § 1291 does not generally permit appeal of a district's court's decisions until the final judgment in the case is entered, Rule 23(f) creates an exception for a class-certification order. The party aggrieved by the class-certification order may, within fourteen days of the order, petition the court of appeals to review the class-certification decision.

---

299 For a proposal for how to make broader use of issue classes, see Elizabeth Chamblee Burch, *Constructing Issue Class Actions*, 101 VA. L. REV. 1855 (2015). Legislation presently pending in Congress would require courts to adopt the latter, narrower view of issue classes.

300 A court may compel the party seeking class certification to bear the cost of discovery bearing on the motion, at least when the discovery required is extensive and expensive to produce, *see* Boeynaems v. LA Fitness Int'l, LLC, 285 F.R.D. 331 (E.D. Pa. 2012), although such an order is rare.

301 *See* FED. R. CIV. P. 23(c)(1)(B).

302 *See* FED. R. CIV. P. 23(c)(1)(C).

303 In one of the most striking examples of the decertification power, a plaintiff won $32 million for a certified class at trial, but after trial the court chose to decertify the class—and entered judgment only for the class representative's $134 recovery. *See* Mazzei v. The Money Store, 829 F.3d 260 (2d Cir. 2016) (affirming the decertification order).

Entertaining such an appeal lies within the discretion of the court of appeals. Nonetheless, it is common for courts of appeals to grant such petitions because of the outcome-influencing effect of a certification order on the course of the lawsuit. If the class is not certified, the case may no longer be economically feasible, while if the class is certified, the pressure on the defendant to settle may be so great that the case will end without appellate review of the certification order.[304]

Like all aggregation devices, class actions are not perfect. Although their preclusive effect may resolve a large number of claims in one suit, including (as *Hansberry* implies) the claims of future plaintiffs, adequately representing these plaintiffs presents a challenge (as *Hansberry* shows). The other requirements of Rule 23 also impose barriers to aggregation. If the class seeks money, complete aggregation is typically not possible: class members may opt out and litigate individually. Moreover, there is no *sua sponte* power to create a class action; judges must wait for a plaintiff to propose a class action, and the class is limited by the scope of the class that the class representative proposes. And Rule 23 contains no power of anti-suit injunction. Finally, class actions pose some unique issues regarding personal jurisdiction—explored in Section C of this Chapter—that can make aggregation of claims trickier. On the positive side, however, class actions also have unique rules of subject-matter jurisdiction—also explored in Section C—that make aggregation in federal court simpler.

Class aggregation also raises all the concerns for aggregation that we described in Chapter One, including agency costs, the pressure to settle meritless claims to avoid a catastrophic liability, the resolution of immature claims, the loss of autonomy and the individual's right to a day in court, and the grant of great power to a single court to affect the future of large institutions and millions of individuals. On the other hand, if conducted in a way that minimizes these costs, class actions promise great benefits, such as deterrence (especially in negative-value claims), streamlined costs, equalized incentives to litigate, and fair and equitable treatment of similarly situated victims of widespread harm.

With the skeleton of class actions now framed, we turn to a detailed examination of the elements of Rule 23. As we examine the minute and sometimes arcane specifics of Rule 23, understand what is ultimately at stake: as each element becomes harder to satisfy, the

---

[304] *See* Blair v. Equifax Check Services, Inc., 181 F.3d 832 (7th Cir. 1999) (listing three factors relevant to a court of appeal's decision to permit an appeal: whether the decision not to certify sounds the "death knell" for the litigation, whether the decision to certify puts "considerable pressure on the defendant to settle," and whether "an appeal may facilitate the development of the law"); *In re* Brewer, 863 F.3d 861 (D.C. Cir. 2017) (applying three comparable factors).

utility of class actions as an aggregation device declines; as each element is interpreted more generously, the utility expands. When class actions become easier to maintain, the need for the other aggregation devices that we have explored decreases; when they become harder to maintain, the pressure on other aggregation devices to take up the slack increases.

B. The Elements of Rule 23

The party seeking class certification must meet each element of Rules 23(a) and 23(g), as well as at least one element of Rule 23(b). This party also bears the burden of proving each element.[305] In this section we examine the elements of Rule 23(a), Rule 23(g), and Rule 23(b) in turn.

Before we begin, one important matter merits discussion: how deep into a complaint's allegations may a court peer in deciding a class-certification motion? If a court must accept the allegations at face value, then every well-pleaded class action must be certified—a clearly untenable view. On the other hand, if class members must prove the merits of each class member's case in order to prove entitlement to membership in the class, then class certification will do nothing to reduce costs and streamline litigation. The Supreme Court has staked out a middle ground, stating in *General Telephone of the Southwest v. Falcon* that a class action "may only be certified if the trial court is satisfied, after a rigorous analysis, that the prerequisites of Rule 23(a) have been satisfied."[306] The content of a "rigorous analysis" has varied among courts and over time. Parties opposing class certification have generally pushed for a more aggressive understanding of this phrase, demanding that the proponent of class certification provide a great deal of proof about the underlying merits of the claim in order to evaluate whether the plaintiffs' case presents common questions and meets typicality, adequacy, predominance, and 23(b) concerns. Parties pressing for certification have rejected the notion that a class-certification motion is in effect a mini-trial of the case in chief.

The Supreme Court has not wavered from the requirement of a "rigorous analysis." In some cases, it has pressed hard on the evidentiary basis for the putative class's claims. In *Falcon*, the Court noted that "the class determination generally involves considerations that are enmeshed in the factual and legal issues comprising the

---

[305] *See, e.g.*, Oplchenski v. Parfums Givenchy, Inc., 254 F.R.D. 489 (N.D. Ill. 2008).

[306] 457 U.S. 147 (1982). This statement seemed to conflict with language from a prior decision, in which the Court had stated that a class-certification motion should not turn into "a preliminary inquiry into the merits of a suit." Eisen v. Carlisle & Jacquelin, 417 U.S. 156 (1974).

plaintiff's cause of action."[307] In *Wal-Mart Stores, Inc. v. Dukes*,[308] the Court noted that "Rule 23 does not set forth a mere pleading standard" and that "[f]requently . . . 'rigorous analysis' will entail some overlap with the merits of the plaintiff's underlying claim. That cannot be helped." On the other hand, in *Amgen Inc. v. Connecticut Retirement Plans & Trust Funds*,[309] the Court stated that "Rule 23 grants courts no license to engage in free-ranging merits inquiries at the certification stage. Merits questions may be considered to the extent—but only to the extent—that they are relevant to determining whether the Rule 23 prerequisites for class certification are satisfied."

1. The Rule 23(a) Prerequisites

Rule 23(a) contains four enumerated criteria, as well as two criteria that are derived from the Rule's introductory text:

- The first, unnamed criterion is the requirement of a "class": a seemingly obvious and simple requirement that is actually rather complex.
- The second, unnamed criterion is the requirement that the person(s) representing the class be members of the class.
- The third criterion is Rule 23(a)(1)'s demand that the class be "so numerous that joinder of all members is impracticable" (the "numerosity" requirement).
- Fourth is Rule 23(a)(2)'s requirement that "there are questions of law or fact common to the class" (the commonality" requirement).
- Fifth, Rule 23(a)(3) requires that "the claims or defenses of the representative parties are typical of the claims or defenses of the class" (the "typicality" requirement).
- Sixth, Rule 23(a)(4) demands that "the representative parties will fairly and adequately protect the interests of the class" (the "adequacy" requirement).

These six criteria interlink, all with an eye toward ensuring that a class action is fair and efficient, and that the absent class members will receive adequate representation of their claims. Although we study each criterion separately, the criteria are not independent of

---

[307] 457 U.S. at 160 (*quoting* Coopers & Lybrand v. Livesay, 437 U.S. 463 (1978) (internal quotation marks omitted)).

[308] 564 U.S. 338 (2011).

[309] 568 U.S. 455 (2013).

each other. Each layer bolsters Rule 23's fundamental concerns with the fairness, efficiency, and adequacy of class actions.

a. A Defined "Class": Herein of "Ascertainability"

Rule 23(a) permits a class action to be brought by "one or more members of a class." At the most basic level, a class action cannot exist without a "class." Rule 23(c)(1)(B) further confirms the need for a class by requiring a court that certifies a class to "define the class and the class claims."

From the viewpoint of optimal aggregation, a proper class definition is important. Because judges cannot create class actions *sua sponte*, aggregation through the class mechanism depends on a class representative stepping forward. The scope of the class definition created by counsel therefore determines the extent of the aggregation that the class action can achieve. Class counsel has an incentive to craft a class that will survive the gauntlet of requirements in Rules 23(a) and 23(b); if a class is too large and sweeps together disparate claims, for instance, it might run afoul of commonality, typicality, or adequacy concerns. Beyond that, counsel will craft a class that promises the greatest private gain for the class or the greatest fees for counsel, not a class of socially optimal size. A court's power to trim or expand a class definition can alter this dynamic to some extent, but courts are generally at the mercy of counsel in defining the amount of aggregation that a class action can achieve.[310]

Being clear about who is, and who is not, in a class is significant for a number of other reasons. Unless the boundaries of a class are definite, it may be difficult to assess whether the class meets the numerosity and commonality requirements, or whether the class representative meets the typicality and adequacy requirements. Moreover, if the class is a (b)(3) opt-out class, class members must receive notice—including *individual* notice when possible—of their opt-out right. Targeting the notice to the right group of people is difficult and potentially expensive when the scope of the class is uncertain. The same concern arises when a class action settles. In order for class members to weigh in on the settlement, Rule 23(e)(1) requires notice of the settlement be directed to class members; once again, effective notice becomes very difficult when the scope of the class is uncertain. A clear sense of the boundaries of a class is also important for distributing any remedy. It matters as well for future litigation. Judgments in class actions bind the members of the class, but not nonparties. If an individual files a subsequent suit, the court

---

[310] For an examination of this problem and a proposed solution, see David Betson and Jay Tidmarsh, *Optimal Class Size, Opt-Out Rights, and "Indivisible" Remedies*, 79 GEO. WASH. L. REV. 542 (2011).

in the second case must be able to determine whether this person was, or was not, a member of a class whose claims are precluded.

A fair amount of law has risen up around the requirement of a defined class. One strand of the doctrine states that classes—in particular, (b)(3) classes—whose membership is not knowable cannot be certified. For instance, in *Rice v. City of Philadelphia*,[311] a plaintiff who was challenging lengthy pretrial detentions in Philadelphia brought a class action on behalf of all people "who are, who have been, or who will be illegally detained." The complaint sought both injunctive relief, for which a (b)(2) class was the appropriate vehicle, and damages, for which a (b)(3) class was the appropriate vehicle. The court certified the (b)(2) injunctive class. But it held that the class definition was too broad and amorphous for the damages (b)(3) class, both because the claims of some of the past detainees had expired and because it was impossible to determine damages for those who had not yet been detained.[312]

In a similar vein, classes that are defined in relation to class members' state of mind are disfavored.[313]

A different strand concerns the "fail-safe" doctrine, which bars certification of a class defined in terms of the merits of the class members' claims. For instance, in *Randleman v. Fidelity National Title Insurance Co.*,[314] the class was defined as those victims of the defendant's practices who were "entitled to relief." As the court noted, this definition effectively shielded class members from the preclusive effect of an adverse judgment: "Either the class members win or, by virtue of losing, they are not in the class and, therefore, not bound by the judgment."[315]

An especially controversial strand of the "class" requirement has come to be known by the term "ascertainability." Flowing from the strands that we have just described is a general principle that a class must be defined with reference to objective criteria. No courts dispute the principle at this level of generality. Some courts, however, have particularized this requirement, demanding that a class must be

---

311 66 F.R.D. 17 (E.D. Pa. 1974).

312 *See also* Brecher v. Republic of Arg., 806 F.3d 22 (2d Cir. 2015) (holding that a class defined as all owners of beneficial interests in a bond series, without reference to the time owned, was too indefinite). *Brecher* gave as an example of inadequate definition a class of "those wearing blue shirts": this definition "has no limitation on time or context, and the ever-changing composition of the membership would make determining the identity of those wearing blue shirts impossible."

313 *See* Simer v. Rios, 661 F.2d 655 (7th Cir. 1981); DeBremaecker v. Short, 433 F.2d 733 (5th Cir. 1970).

314 646 F.3d 347 (6th Cir. 2011).

315 *See also* Messner v. Northshore Univ. Health Sys., 669 F.3d 802 (7th Cir. 2012) (describing a "fail-safe" class as "one that is defined so that whether a person qualifies as a member depends on whether the person has a valid claim").

defined so that its membership is "currently and readily ascertainable based on objective criteria."[316] When class membership requires extensive and individualized factfinding, it fails to meet this requirement. Put differently, unless there is a "reliable and administratively feasible" way to determine who is, and who is not, in the class, a class cannot be certified.[317]

A requirement that the identity of class members be readily ascertainable from objective sources could limit the scope of Rule 23 substantially. Take the Third Circuit's decision in *Carrera v. Bayer Corp.* In *Carrera* plaintiffs proposed to bring a class action on behalf of Florida consumers who had bought a weight-loss supplement that allegedly made false claims about health benefits. The court reversed the district court's decision to certify the class because it was not readily ascertainable who was in the class. Many purchasers had no receipts to prove their purchase, nor did the defendant (which distributed the supplement through drug stores) know who had bought its product. The plaintiffs argued that the identity of class members could be obtained through affidavits from class members or from the records of drug stores for purchasers who used customer-loyalty cards, and that experienced claims administrators could devise methods to weed out most false claims. The court of appeals rejected these alternatives; affidavits could be falsified and were therefore not objective, it was uncertain how many purchasers had loyalty cards, and claims administrators cannot screen out all fraudulent claims.

Carrera and similar cases have defended this "administrative-feasibility" variant of the "ascertainability" concept by arguing that it ensures efficiency in the management of the class action; that it protects absent class members, who are more likely to receive notice of the case (and then to choose how best to protect their interests, perhaps by opting out); and that greater clarity in the scope of the class helps defendants by making clearer the preclusive effect of a final judgment. The second of these policy arguments suggests that "administrative feasibility" is an especially important requirement in (b)(3) opt-out class actions; and *Carrera* hinted, without quite holding, that its ascertainability doctrine might be limited to (b)(3) cases.

Cases like *Carrera* set off a firestorm in courts of appeals around the country. In the immediate aftermath, some courts of appeals sounded sympathetic to the *Carrera* approach.[318] But the doctrine

---

[316] *See* Marcus v. BMW of N. Am., LLC, 687 F.3d 583 (3d Cir. 2012).

[317] *See* Carrera v. Bayer Corp., 727 F.3d 300 (3d Cir. 2013).

[318] *See* EQT Prod. Co. v. Adair, 764 F.3d 347 (4th Cir. 2014) ("A class cannot be certified unless a court can readily identify the class members in reference to objective criteria.").

also had detractors, who pointed out that this approach would make many small-stakes or negative-value class actions impossible to bring and would therefore allow defendants to escape responsibility for unlawful conduct. Others pointed out that demanding a high level of objective proof of class membership created a requirement found nowhere in the text of Rule 23; that Rule 23(b)(3) already contained sufficient mechanisms to prevent truly inefficient class litigation; and that subjective proof such as an affidavit was sufficient to create a triable issue of fact in an individual case, so it was unclear why it was insufficient in a class action.

As a result of these criticisms, more recent cases have tended to reject, or at least put the brakes on, the strong ascertainability approach of *Carrera*. In a more recent case, the Third Circuit itself softened the requirement, which it described as "narrow," "not relevant in every case[,] and . . . independent from the other requirements of Rule 23."[319] In point-by-point refutations of the logic of *Carrera*, the Second, Sixth, Seventh, and Ninth Circuits have rejected the very existence of the Third Circuit's ascertainability approach, arguing instead that proof of class membership is a matter that can be dealt with under Rule 23(b)(3).[320] The Eighth Circuit has expressed similar skepticism, acknowledging the traditional principles of adequate class definition and clear ascertainability without accepting the "heightened standard" of the Third Circuit.[321]

The ascertainability issue remains one of the present hot-button issues in class-action practice. The stronger the requirement, the smaller the number of class actions that will be certified. The advisory committee that amends the Federal Rules of Civil Procedure examined the question, but decided not to wade into the debate by rule amendment. The House of Representatives has passed a bill that would require class actions seeking monetary relief to be "defined with reference to objective criteria" and to demonstrate "a reliable and administratively feasible mechanism" for determining "whether putative class members fall within the class definition" and "for distributing directly to a substantial majority of class members any monetary relief secured for the class."[322] This language parrots much of the language of *Carrera*, although whether it would be interpreted as in the heightened fashion of *Carrera* or in the less restrictive

---

[319] Byrd v. Aaron's Inc., 784 F.3d 154 (3d Cir. 2015).

[320] *See In re* Petrobas Sec., 862 F.3d 250 (2d Cir. 2017); Briseno v. ConAgra Foods, Inc., 844 F.3d 1121 (9th Cir. 2017); Mullins v. Direct Digital, LLC, 795 F.3d 654 (7th Cir. 2015); Rikos v. Procter & Gamble Co., 799 F.3d 497 (6th Cir. 2015) (following *Mullins*).

[321] *See* Sandusky Wellness Ctr., LLC v. Medtox Sci., Inc., 821 F.3d 992 (8th Cir. 2016).

[322] H.R. 985, 115th Cong. (2017).

fashion of *Byrd* is impossible to know as of today. As of this writing, the bill is languishing in the Senate with low prospects of passage.

Finally, a poor class definition sometimes generates other problems that are the immediate cause of a court's refusal to certify a class. For example, in *Rahman v. Chertoff*,[323] the court cited a litany of problems with the class definition in a (b)(2) class action claiming that citizens on watch lists experienced unconstitutional screening procedures when they re-entered the country: "the classes grow or shrink with the plaintiffs' contentions as the case progresses"; "[e]ven in retrospect the court will not know who is in tghe class and who is not"; and "it is impossible to tell whether all the named plaintiffs are (or will be at the end of the case) members of the classes they purport to represent." Rather than finding the class definition too imprecise, *Rahman* found that the class representative failed to meet Rule 23(a)(3)'s typicality requirement.

> *Problem 1*
>
> A class action alleges that a brand-name cooking oil falsely claimed that the oil was "100% natural." The class is defined as "[a]ll persons who reside in [eleven states] who have purchased [the oil] within the applicable statute of limitations periods established by the laws of their state of residence." Is this definition sufficiently definite? *See* Briseno v. ConAgra Foods, Inc., 844 F.3d 1121 (9th Cir. 2017).

b. Membership in the Class

A second implied requirement of Rule 23(a)—that the class representative must be a member of the class—derives from Rule 23(a)'s introductory language that "[o]ne or more members of a class may sue or be sued." This requirement also has roots in the Article III requirement of standing, and in the real-party-in-interest requirement of Rule 17(a).[324] The requirement has led a number of

[323] 530 F.3d 622 (7th Cir. 2008).

[324] The class representative(s) must have Article III standing in order to bring an action on behalf of class members. A separate issue, so far unanswered by the Supreme Court, is whether each member of the class must have standing. The issue has arisen most frequently in the context of a class member's lack of standing to object to a settlement provision that did not adversely affect the class member. *See, e.g.*, Huyer v. Van de Voorde, 847 F.3d 983 (8th Cir. 2017) (dismissing objection due to lack of standing). In other contexts, an arguable lack of standing has not necessarily defeated certification. *See In re* Cmty. Bank of N. Va. Mortg. Lending Practices Litig., 795 F.3d 380 (3d Cir. 2015) ("[O]nly named plaintiffs, and not unnamed class members, need to establish standing."); Parko v. Shell Oil Co., 739 F.3d 1083 (7th Cir. 2014) (declining to decide whether each class member had standing when the defendant claimed that many class members had suffered no injury and determining standing would require the district court to hold individualized trials just to rule on class certification). Defendants sometimes argue that class members who have suffered no injury lack Article III standing. A court's usual approach to this argument is to examine the class definition to determine whether it appears that class members have suffered harm. "[T]his approach does not contemplate scrutinizing or weighing

courts to hold that a union or other cooperative association seeking to represent its members cannot serve as a representative for the class due to its inability to obtain a remedy for itself.[325]

c. Rule 23(a)(1): Numerosity

Each of the four numbered elements of Rule 23(a) has spawned an interpretive body of case law that imposes significant constraints on the use of class actions. Of the four, the numerosity requirement of Rule 23(a)(1) usually presents the least serious obstacle. Rule 23(a)(1) requires that the class to be "so numerous that joinder of all members is impracticable." Although the dictionary definition of "impracticable" is "impossible," it has long been understood that in Rule 23(a)(1) the word means "difficult" or "impractical."

Rule 23(a)(1) imposes "no strict numerical test for determining impracticability of joinder."[326] Nonetheless, some rough numerical guidelines exist. Below a certain point—around 15 to 20 putative class members—joinder through other devices is practicable, and Rule 23(a)(1)'s numerosity requirement bars class certification.[327] Above a certain point—100 or more putative class members—most courts find the numerosity requirement to be *per se* satisfied.[328]

In the middle lies the uncertain ground in which policy analysis helps to determine the answer. When resolving a difficult issue of numerosity, courts resort either to the policies underlying class actions (such as the prevention of litigation hardship or

---

any evidence of absent class members' standing or lack of standing during the Rule 23 [certification] stage." *In re* Deepwater Horizon, 739 F.3d 790 (5th Cir. 2014). In a recent concurrence, however, Chief Justice Roberts noted that class members who had no injury raised standing issues. *See* Tyson Foods, Inc. v. Bouaphakeo, 577 U.S. ___, 136 S. Ct. 1036 (2016). *Cf. In re* Tobacco II Cases, 207 P.3d 20 (Cal. 2009) (holding that, under state law, only class representatives needed to meet standing requirements). Aside from standing, a lack of harm suffered by some class members, or even a great difference in the type of harm suffered by class members, may bear on other issues such as the (a)(3) typicality of the class representative's claim or the (a)(4) adequacy of the class representative's representation.

[325] *See, e.g.*, Farmers Co-op. Oil Co. v. Socony-Vacuum Oil Co., 133 F.2d 101 (8th Cir. 1942) (co-op cannot represent individual farmers in an antitrust suit); Wilhite v. S. Cent. Bell Tel. & Tel. Co., 426 F. Supp. 61 (E.D. La. 1976) (union can represent its members when seeking injunctive relief for discrimination in employment, but not for monetary relief). Rule 23.2 ameliorates some of the problems that the class-membership requirement creates in suits by or against unincorporated associations.

[326] *In re* Am. Med. Sys., Inc., 75 F.3d 1069 (6th Cir. 1996).

[327] *See* Gen. Tel. Co. of the Nw. v. EEOC, 446 U.S. 318, 330 (1980); Novella v. Westchester Cty., 661 F.3d 128 (2d Cir. 2011).

[328] A figure of 100 class members is conservative. The Second Circuit has suggested that the presumptive minimum for meeting the numerosity requirement is forty. *Novella*, 661 F.3d at 144. One of the reasons that a party opposing certification may argue for a heightened ascertainability standard or for standing for each class member is to reduce the number of class members to a level below the numerosity threshold. *See Parko*, 739 F.3d at 1084–85.

inconvenience)[329] or to multi-factor tests (such as consideration of judicial economy, geographic dispersion of class members, resources of class members and their ability to commence individual suits, and requests for injunctive relief).[330]

Except in close cases, the numerosity issue is usually conceded.

d. *Rule 23(a)(2): Commonality*

Rule 23(a)(2) requires that "there are questions of law or fact common to the class." If the claims of the class members (including those of the class representatives) fail to present common questions of law or fact, the risk that the class representatives will not adequately represent all class members is high. It is also hard to see how a class action will achieve significant gains in efficiency.

The hard question is how much commonality among the claims of class members is required. Must the class member have most questions in common, or only a few? Is one question sufficient? Rule 23(a)(2) is silent. The only textual hint is in Rule 23(b)(3), which permits an opt-out class action to be maintained when common questions "predominate" over individual ones. This language implies that the (a)(2) requirement can be satisfied when common questions do not predominate (whatever "predominate" means).

Traditionally, Rule 23(a)(2)'s commonality requirement rarely presented a stumbling block to class certification. Even a single common question was usually thought to be sufficient; the more exacting inquiries of typicality (Rule 23(a)(3)) and adequacy (Rule 23(a)(4)) did most of the heavy lifting to screen out cases unsuitable for class treatment. As one well-known Fifth Circuit case observed, "[t]he threshold of 'commonality' is not high."[331]

That view of commonality changed after the Supreme Court's decision in *Wal-Mart Stores, Inc. v. Dukes*.[332] In *Wal-Mart* the plaintiffs alleged that Wal-Mart had engaged in pervasive gender discrimination in its pay and promotion practices. The plaintiffs sought to represent a class of all women who were working for the company or who had worked for the company during the relevant time period—an estimated 1.5 million women. Wal-Mart had not adopted any national policy of gender discrimination; to the contrary, its corporate policy was to devolve pay and promotion decisions to each region and even each store. The class plaintiffs' theory was that

---

329 *See In re* Drexel Burnham Lambert Group, Inc., 960 F.2d 285 (2d Cir. 1992); Boggs v. Divested Atomic Corp., 141 F.R.D. 59 (S.D. Ohio 1991).

330 *See In re* Modafinil Antitrust Litig., 837 F.3d 238 (3d Cir. 2016); Robidoux v. Celani, 987 F.2d 931 (2d Cir. 1993).

331 Jenkins v. Raymark Indus., Inc., 782 F.2d 468 (5th Cir. 1986).

332 564 U.S. 338 (2011).

providing this discretion to lower-level managers, when combined with the company's male-dominated corporate culture, caused disparate treatment of women.

The litigation history of *Wal-Mart* is complex. To simplify the case to the elements necessary to understand the Supreme Court's decision, the plaintiffs had obtained certification for a (b)(2) class with respect to declaratory and injunctive relief against Wal-Mart's pay and promotion practices as well as backpay. Whether Rule 23(b)(2) could be used to obtain monetary relief like backpay was one issue before the Court; we examine the Court's decision on that point later in this section.[333] Before resolving that issue, the Court addressed whether a class seeking injunctive relief could stand in light of the commonality requirement of Rule 23(a)(2).

The Court divided 5–4 on the question. Writing for the majority, Justice Scalia held that the class failed to clear the commonality bar. For commonality, the critical issue was *not* whether the class members' claims raised a common question but whether adjudication could provide a common *answer*—in other words, whether "determination of [a question's] truth or falsity will resolve an issue that is central to the validity of each one of the claims in one stroke." As a first step, "[c]ommonality requires the plaintiff to demonstrate that the class members 'have suffered the same injury.' " But that step alone is insufficient, for people with very different work histories might both claim to have suffered a gender-discrimination injury under Title VII. In addition, the claims of class members "must depend upon a common contention." Moreover, this common contention "must be of such a nature that it is capable of class-wide resolution." Thus, Rule 23(a)(2) demands that a class action be able to "generate common answers apt to drive the resolution of the litigation."[334] Or, as the Court opined more colloquially, Rule 23(a)(2) requires "some glue holding" the claims of class members together.

Turning to the plaintiffs' complaint, the Court saw no glue. Not every member of the class had been harmed by the practice of giving local managers discretion with respect to wages and promotions. Wal-Mart had no company-wide testing procedures or evaluation practices that might have created company-wide gender biases in employment decisions. Indeed, Wal-Mart's corporate policies specifically forbade gender discrimination. Its policy of devolving discretion to lower-level managers, together with an allegedly male-dominated corporate culture, may have affected some women in the

---

[333] *See infra* notes 408–412 and accompanying text.

[334] The quoted language in the text came originally from a law-review article written by the late Professor Richard Nagareda, whose work heavily influenced the majority in *Wal-Mart. See* Richard A. Nagareda, *Class Certification in the Age of Aggregate Proof*, 84 N.Y.U. L. REV. 97 (2009).

class. But the plaintiffs' expert could not say how many women had experienced such discrimination. The majority thought it "unbelievable" that every manager would exercise discretion in a gender-biased fashion. Moreover, local variations in the work force might explain some of the pay differentials among male and female workers; the Court rejected company-wide evidence that Wal-Mart paid women less because that evidence would not necessarily explain pay differentials in each local market. The majority also dismissed anecdotal evidence of hundreds of instances of gender discrimination because they did not show that each member in the 1.5 million-member class had suffered similarly. Therefore, in the absence of "convincing proof of a companywide discriminatory pay and promotion policy," the majority concluded, the plaintiffs had "not established the existence of any common question."

The dissent disagreed, arguing that a "common question" meant only that certain common matters needed to be in dispute and that the majority's focus on the dissimilarities among class members had impermissibly snuck the "predominance of common questions" requirement for (b)(3) classes into Rule 23(a)(2).

The plaintiffs in *Wal-Mart* overreached in seeking to certify a nationwide class action in which the claims of class members had a high degree of variability. Certainly, after *Wal-Mart*, it is difficult to certify a single class action in which different acts of different people injure different plaintiffs in different ways, even when all the injuries have a common core (say, the sale of a similar product such as asbestos). But, as we will see, mega-class actions were already running afoul of other requirements in Rule 23. Thus far, *Wal-Mart*'s strengthening of the (a)(2) commonality requirement has not seemed to constrain class-action practice unduly.

e. Rule 23(a)(3): Typicality

The Rule 23(a)(3) requirement—that "the claims or defenses of the representative parties are typical of the claims or defenses of the class"—begins the turn from the concern for the efficiency of the class mechanism to the concern for the adequacy of the class representative. Commonality is also concerned to a degree with adequacy; without common questions uniting the class, it is hard to see how the class representative can adequately represent the interests of the entire group. But efficiency is the primary focus of Rule 23(a)(2): without common questions, it is difficult to see how bundling the claims of a numerous class into one case will achieve efficiency. Typicality too has an efficiency focus: if the claim of the representative is not comparable to the claims of the rest of the class, then the different evidence necessary to prove the different claims reduces the efficiency of the class proceeding. But disparate claims also raises the specter of constitutionally inadequate representation: if the claims of the representative diverge from those of the class, the representative may be more concerned with successfully presenting his or her own case at the expense of proving the cases of the rest of the class.

Courts do not require that the legal claims and relevant evidence of the class representative identically match the claims and evidence of the class.[335] If they did, very few class actions could ever be certified. The hard question of Rule 23(a)(3) is how much variance between the class representative's case and those of the class members is permissible.

At one end of the spectrum is the case in which all legal issues and relevant evidence are identical but for some minor variations. For instance, a cell-phone carrier may have overcharged its customers for data usage. The only variance among the customers' cases is the amount of data that each customer used, and that amount is readily determined from the carrier's computerized billing records. Such a case would likely pass over the typicality bar.

At the other end of the spectrum is *General Telephone of the Southwest v. Falcon*.[336] A Mexican-American employee, Falcon, alleged that his employer had discriminated against him by failing to give him a promotion. He then filed a class action on behalf of all Mexican-Americans who had been the victims of the company's discriminatory behavior—whether in an initial decision not to hire or in a decision not to promote. The district court ruled that the company had not discriminated against Falcon in hiring him, but it had intentionally discriminated in failing to promote him. With regard to the claims of the class, the converse was true: the company did not generally discriminate in its promotion practices, but it did discriminate in its hiring practices. The district court awarded Falcon and those disappointed Mexican-American job applicants who could be located a backpay remedy.

The court of appeals upheld the decision. It specifically rejected the defendant's argument that Falcon, whose claim of individual discrimination varied from the claims of other class members, could not serve as class representative. Using an "across-the-board" theory, it held any victim of employment discrimination could represent all other victims discriminated against on the same racial or ethnic basis.

---

[335] *See* Baby Neal *ex rel.* Kanter v. Casey, 43 F.3d 48 (3d Cir. 1994) ("[N]either [commonality nor typicality] mandates that all putative class members share identical claims.").

[336] 457 U.S. 147 (1982).

The Supreme Court reversed. To be a class representative, Falcon needed to " 'possess the same interest and suffer the same injury' as the class members." But the more anecdotal evidence of intentional discrimination necessary to prove Falcon's claim of individual discrimination in promotion was significantly different from the statistical evidence used by Falcon to prove the class's claim of discrimination in hiring and promotion.

The Court's opinion was opaque in one critical way: it was unclear whether its holding was based on an absence of Rule 23(a)(2) commonality, a failure of Rule 23(a)(3) typicality, or a lack of Rule 23(a)(4) adequacy of representation. Indeed, the Court seemed to regard the matter as somewhat beside the point, stating in its well-known footnote 13:

> The commonality and typicality requirements of Rule 23(a) tend to merge. Both serve as guideposts for determining whether . . . maintenance of a class action is economical and whether the named plaintiff's claim and the class claims are so interrelated that the interests of the class members will be fairly and adequately protected in their absence. Those requirements therefore also tend to merge with the adequacy-of-representation requirement, although the latter requirement also raises concerns about the competency of class counsel and conflicts of interest.

Falcon correctly perceived the interrelationship among the elements of Rules 23(a)(2), –(a)(3), and –(a)(4). Each element is a piece of an interlocking inquiry into the efficiency of the class proceeding and *Hansberry*'s demand for constitutionally adequate class representation. Ultimately, attending to those big-picture issues remains as critical to success in obtaining or resisting class certification as satisfying the more specialized inquiries of the Rule 23(a) subparts.

Nonetheless, courts will usually analyze commonality and typicality as distinct elements.[337] *Falcon* is generally perceived as a typicality case. Courts often use its takeaway line—that the class representative must "possess the same interest and suffer the same injury" as the class members—as a starting point for their (a)(3) typicality analysis. But that starting point conceals as much as it reveals.[338] Among the common fact patterns that raise typicality concerns are:

---

[337] *See, e.g.*, *Baby Neal*, 43 F.3d 48 (noting that, although they "tend to merge . . ., commonality and typicality are distinct requirements under Rule 23").

[338] The Supreme Court has used the same phrase in *Falcon* as the jumping-off point for its analysis of (a)(2) commonality, *see* Wal-Mart Stores, Inc. v. Dukes, 564

- A class representative, injured by one of the defendant's products, who seeks to represent class members who were harmed by comparable but distinct products;[339]
- A class representative who knew facts of which other class members were unaware, where such knowledge is relevant to recovery;[340]
- A class representative, injured by one defendant, who seeks to represent class members who were harmed by the identical conduct of different defendants;[341]
- A class representative whose length of exposure to a toxic substance varies from those of the lengths of exposure of class members;[342]
- A class representative who is subject to unique defenses not generally assertable against the rest of the class;[343]
- A class representative whose only available relief (say, an injunction) is not the same as the relief that class members can claim (say, damages).[344]

As these examples show, the typicality inquiry requires a court to dive into specific claims, defenses, and evidence. For almost any

---

U.S. 338 (2011), and (a)(4) adequacy, *see* Amchem Prods., Inc. v. Windsor, 521 U.S. 591 (1997).

339 *See, e.g., In re* Am. Med. Sys., Inc., 75 F.3d 1069 (6th Cir. 1996) (decertifying class in part due to typicality concerns).

340 *See, e.g., In re* HealthSouth Corp. Sec. Litig., 213 F.R.D. 447 (N.D. Ala. 2003) (no typicality).

341 *See, e.g.*, La Mar v. H & B Novelty & Loan Co., 489 F.2d 461 (9th Cir. 1973) (no typicality); *cf.* Easter v. Am. W. Fin., 381 F.3d 948 (9th Cir. 2004) (class representative lacked standing to represent class members injured by other defendants).

342 *See, e.g.*, Ball v. Union Carbide Corp., 385 F.3d 713 (6th Cir. 2004) (no typicality; also no commonality); *In re* Methyl Tertiary Butyl Ether ("MTBE") Prods. Liab. Litig., 209 F.R.D. 323 (S.D.N.Y. 2006) (no typicality when pollution of each well involved unique factual issues).

343 *See, e.g., HealthSouth*, 213 F.R.D. 447 (N.D. Ala. 2003) (no typicality); *cf.* Beck v. Maximus, Inc., 457 F.3d 291 (3d Cir. 2006) (stating that "unique defenses bear on both the typicality and adequacy of a class representative"); CE Design Ltd. v. King Architectural Metals, Inc., 637 F.3d 721 (7th Cir. 2011) (same).

344 *See, e.g., MTBE*, 209 F.R.D. 323 (no typicality; also no adequacy). *See also* Broussard v. Meineke Disc. Muffler Shops, Inc., 155 F.3d 331 (4th Cir. 2001) (holding that no typicality exists when "each putative class member's claim for lost profits damages was inherently individualized and thus not easily amenable to class treatment"); *but see* Smilow v. Sw. Bell Mobile Sys., Inc., 323 F.3d 32 (1st Cir. 2003) (holding that individualized damages calculations do not defeat class certification). *Cf. In re* Payment Card Interchange Fee & Merch. Disc. Antitrust Litig., 827 F.3d 223 (2d Cir. 2016) (treating differing interests of class members in either injunctive or damages relief as a matter of inadequacy under Rule 23(a)(4)).

case finding typicality, there is a legally and factually similar case finding a lack of typicality. Principles of universal application are hard to come by. What courts ultimately look for, however, is an alignment of interests between the representative and the class, so that "in pursuing his own claims, the named plaintiff will also advance the interests of the class members."[345] Thus, even if a class representative is self-interested rather than altruistic, his or her actions will advance the interests of all.

f. Rule 23(a)(4): Adequacy of the Class Representative

Rule 23(a)(4)'s requirement—that "the representative parties will fairly and adequately protect the interests of the class"—completes the turn toward addressing the due-process concern for adequate representation. As the prior subsection showed, typicality handles one piece of the adequacy inquiry. The (a)(4) inquiry tends to focus on more particularized issues.

The first is the physical and mental capacity of the class representative. A court generally expects the class representative to be able to make decisions on behalf of the class to the same extent as a litigant in an individual suit. Physical or mental infirmities that hinder the representative's ability to carry out his or her responsibilities suggest a lack of adequacy.[346] Of course, such an incapacity is not an absolute barrier; a patient in a mental institution can serve as representative for others in the institution when challenging the institution's conditions, or a gravely ill person can represent others made gravely ill by the defendant's conduct.[347] In most situations, class counsel chooses class representatives with care, so the issue of infirmity rarely arises.

A second concern is knowledge. Parties opposing class certification usually depose the putative class representative, in the process eliciting evidence that the representative is not intimately familiar with the litigation or with the responsibilities of a class representative. They then use this lack of knowledge to argue that the person is not an adequate representative. Courts are usually unimpressed with this tactic; they do not expect the class representative to have a law degree. A representative with basic knowledge of the nature of the case and a willingness to work with

---

[345] *See American Medical*, 75 F.3d 1069; *accord* Just Film, Inc. v Buono, 847 F.3d 1108 (9th Cir. 2017).

[346] *See id.* (questioning whether a person with a history of psychological problems could serve as class representative).

[347] *See* Wyatt *ex rel.* Rawlins v. Poundstone, 169 F.R.D. 155 (M.D. Ala. 1995) (finding that two mentally disabled patients were adequate representatives of a class of disabled patients at state institutions).

class counsel to provide input at relevant points in the litigation will clear this hurdle.[348]

Third, the court may examine the class representative's resources and incentives to litigate. That said, courts have long rejected the argument that a person with only a slight financial interest in the litigation could not serve as class representative because the person lacked the incentive to press the case vigorously. A class representative's large financial stake is sometimes cited as a positive feature, but a small stake is rarely disabling.[349] The one exception is in the context of certain securities-fraud litigation. In an attempt to cut back on what it perceived to be frivolous securities class actions brought by "professional" class representatives with minuscule financial holdings in the target defendants, Congress passed the Private Securities Litigation Reform Act of 1995, which requires, among other things, that the shareholder with the largest financial stake in the outcome of the litigation should be the presumptive class representative.[350]

A greater concern is the honesty and trustworthiness of the representative. A lack of conscientiousness in handling prior fiduciary obligations, demonstrated neglect in positions of trust, serious criminal misconduct, or a lack of candor are black marks against a class representative.[351]

Counsel and commentators occasionally argue that the personal characteristics of the class representative do not matter much, because the class action is really under the control of class counsel; as long as counsel is an adequate and vigorous advocate, the foibles of the class representative will not affect the course of the litigation. This idea is sometimes referred to as the "figurehead" theory: the

---

348 *See* Black v. Rhone-Poulenc, Inc., 173 F.R.D. 156 (S.D. W. Va. 1996) (requiring, as part of a class-certification order, that class counsel explain again the responsibilities of a class representative to the named representatives and apprise the class representatives of all filings in the case); Peil v. Nat'l Semiconductor Corp., 86 F.R.D. 357 (E.D. Pa. 1980) (noting that requiring a class representative to have "first-hand knowledge" of the complex facts of the case "would render the class action device an impotent tool"); *cf.* Rattray v. Woodbury Cty., 614 F.3d 831 (8th Cir. 2010) (holding representative inadequate in part because of a delay in amending the complaint to request a class action and then a further delay in filing the motion for class certification).

349 *See* Dolgow v. Anderson, 43 F.R.D. 472 (E.D.N.Y. 1968).

350 *See* 15 U.S.C. §§ 77z–1(a)(3)(8)(iii), 78u–4(a)(3)(B)(iii).

351 *See* Kaplan v. Pomerantz, 132 F.R.D. 504 (N.D. Ill. 1990) (decertifying a class when the class representative gave false deposition testimony). Ethical propriety and dishonesty do not necessarily doom a class representative. *See* CE Design Ltd. V. King Architectural Metals, Inc., 637 F.3d 721 (7th Cir. 2011) (holding that representative was not adequate in part due to possibly untruthful testimony, but noting that defendants should not "try to derail legitimate class actions by conjuring up trivial credibility problems"); Robert H. Klonoff, *The Judiciary's Flawed Application of Rule 23's "Adequacy of Representation" Requirement*, 2004 MICH. ST. L. REV. 671.

class representative is nothing more than a figurehead for the class, so the only important concern is the quality of class counsel.[352] Whatever its merits, courts reject the argument out of hand.[353]

The final adequacy concern is generally the most significant: conflicts of interest either between the class representatives and the class members or among the class members. When conflicts exist, certifying a class action becomes problematic if not impossible. Strictness with respect to conflicts is inevitable in the wake of *Hansberry*, which found a deficiency of constitutional dimension in the differing interests of the class members who wanted a racially restrictive covenant enforced and those who wanted the covenant's legal and factual validity attacked.

One type of conflict that everyone agrees is unacceptable is a defendant's membership in the class; any class definition must be written carefully to exclude the defendants. Another clearly unacceptable conflict is collusion between the representative and the defendant. A defendant cannot bribe the representative with, say, a million dollars in return for the representative's neglect of the class's claims. That much is obvious. The difficulty lies in ferreting out collusion on often ambiguous facts. For instance, is a defendant's offer to settle the representative's claim on terms somewhat more favorable than those extended to class members a bribe, a recognition of the relative strength of the representative's case, or a deserved recompense for the time and labor of assuming the sometimes difficult job of class representative?[354]

The Supreme Court's most detailed exploration of the relationship between Rule 23(a)(4)'s adequacy requirement and

---

[352] *See* Jean Wegman Burns, *Decorative Figureheads: Eliminating Class Representatives in Class Actions*, 42 HASTINGS L.J. 165 (1990) (contending that named class plaintiffs have no legal authority and serve no useful purpose); *cf.* Macey & Miller, *supra* note 12 (arguing that discovery into the characteristics of the named plaintiffs should be prohibited since they are mere figureheads).

[353] *See In re* Am. Med. Sys., Inc., 75 F.3d 1069 (6th Cir. 1996); *see also* Unger v. Amedisys Inc., 401 F.3d 316 (5th Cir. 2005) ("Class representatives must satisfy the court that they, and not counsel, are directing the litigation.").

[354] *See* Shane Grp., Inc. v. Blue Cross Blue Shield of Mich., 825 F.3d 299 (6th Cir. 2016) (noting concerns with a settlement that provided $10,000 incentive awards for individuals and $50,000 for organizations that served as class representatives); Radcliffe v. Hernandez, 818 F.3d 537 (9th Cir. 2016) (noting that "incentive awards for serving as class representatives are often appropriate," but cautioning that "they should be scrutinized carefully, because if such members of the class are provided with special incentives in the settlement agreement, they may be more concerned with maximizing those incentives than with judging the adequacy of the settlement as it applies to the class members at large") (internal quotation marks omitted); Rodriguez v. West Publ'g Corp., 563 F.3d 948 (9th Cir. 2009) (disapproving settlement with large incentive awards that "created an unacceptable level of disconnect between the interests of the contracting class representatives and class counsel, on the one hand, and members of the class on the other": noting that "[w]e expect those interests to be congruent").

conflicts within a class is *Amchem Products, Inc. v. Windsor.*[355] *Amchem* involved a settlement class action that sought to resolve the claims of thousands of asbestos claimants who had not yet filed suit. Some of those claimants were already suffering an asbestos-related injury; others had not yet suffered an injury. Of this latter group, some were likely to suffer injury in the near future, others would suffer injury in the more distant future, and still others would escape any injury. It was impossible to tell which individuals fell into which category. Some of *Amchem*'s class representatives had existing asbestos injuries, and some did not. The settlement created a schedule that provided a specific range of payments permissible for each type of asbestos injury. Aside from a limited number of exceptional cases each year, all the presently injured and those that manifested injuries in the future were to receive a settlement within the stated range.

The Supreme Court held that the settlement structure created irreconcilable conflicts of interest among class members. First, those claimants who were already injured had an interest in large immediate awards; those yet to be injured had an interest in preserving the bulk of settlement funds for later, when their injuries manifested themselves. Second, the present claimants had no need to be concerned with the effects of inflation on the scheduled damages; in contrast, future claimants had an interest in seeing damage awards rise over time to account for inflationary effects and ensure real-dollar consistency among temporally dispersed awards. On both of these matters (and on some minor matters as well), the settlement favored the presently injured over the future plaintiffs. *Amchem* held that these internal conflicts were sufficient to doom the class under Rule 23(a)(4).

Amchem suggested possible solutions to avoid these conflicts of interest: to bring separate class actions on behalf of each set of interests, or to form separate subclasses out of each set of interests. But the Court gave no guidance about the circumstances in which the conflicts are so great that separate classes or subclasses, whose use make class aggregation more cumbersome and less efficient, need to be employed.

One of the challenges posed by *Hansberry* and *Amchem* is to determine the point at which conflicts among class members are so significant that Rule 23(a)(4) is implicated. In *Hansberry* the conflict was on a legal matter; but in *Amchem* the conflict between early- and late-filing victims was more practical. Both cases sound as though

---

[355] 521 U.S. 591 (1997). We examine other aspects of *Amchem infra* notes 415–416, 487 and accompanying text).

the Court has zero tolerance for intra-class conflicts; any conflict, legal or practical, defeats class certification.

But rarely are the interests of all class members so perfectly aligned that each class member has precisely the same practical incentives and legal interests as every other class member. For instance, some class members may prefer to settle and others to litigate; some class members may prefer more injunctive relief, and others more money; some class members may have a stronger claim on one theory and some may have a stronger theory on another.[356] Given that intra-class conflicts are almost inevitable,[357] a zero-tolerance policy for conflicts dooms most class actions.

Courts and commentators have struggled to distinguish permissible from intolerable conflicts. One court of appeals stated that "the existence of minor conflicts alone will not defeat a party's claim to class certification: the conflict must be a 'fundamental' one going to the specific issues in controversy. A fundamental conflict exists where some party members claim to have been harmed by the same conduct that benefitted other members of the class."[358] This analysis explains *Hansberry*, but is less congruent with the conflicts found to have been class-defeating in *Amchem*.

---

[356] *See In re* Payment Card Interchange Fee & Merch. Disc. Antitrust Litig., 827 F.3d 223 (2d Cir. 2016) (holding that interests of some class members in obtaining an injunction and of other in obtaining damages created a conflict that made the representation of both types of members in one class inadequate under Rule 23(a)(4)).

[357] For a more extended proof of the point, see Jay Tidmarsh, *Rethinking Adequacy of Representation*, 87 TEX. L. REV. 1137 (2009). *See also* Charles Silver & Lynn Baker, *I Cut, You Choose: The Role of Plaintiffs' Counsel in Allocating Settlement Proceeds*, 84 VA. L. REV. 1465 (1998). ("Conflicts of interest and associated tradeoffs among plaintiffs are an unavoidable part of all group lawsuits and all group settlements.").

[358] Valley Drug Co. v. Geneva Pharms., Inc., 350 F.3d 1181 (11th Cir. 2003).

One way to think through conflicts of interest within a class is to reason forward from the nature of the class action. If we view class actions as nothing more than an aggregation of individual claims, then intra-class conflicts will arise whenever a litigation strategy or use of a particular piece of evidence enhances the recovery for some class members but retards the recovery of other class members (or at least fails to advance the recoveries of those class members as much as an alternate litigation strategy or evidence). Put differently, if the class representative must act to maximize the value of each class member's claim, then conflicts abound and adequacy can be a substantial hurdle. Any claim, fact, or litigation strategy that advances the value of some members' claims but reduces the value of other members' claims creates an impermissible conflict. On this aggregation-of-individuals account of class actions, protection of the individual within the aggregate trumps efficiency and general welfare; a class representative who cannot protect that autonomy is inadequate.

Problem 2

A class action alleges that ten related medical devices manufactured by the defendant are defective. The cause of the malfunctions vary from device to device. One class representative had issues with the first two models of the device, before receiving a third that was satisfactory. The representative had memory issues and a lack of common sense, resulting in his total disability. Along with three other representatives added later, he sought to represent a class of at least 15,000 other persons across the country who also received one or more of these devices. Does this class action meet the requirements of Rule 23(a)? *See In re* Am. Med. Sys., Inc., 75 F.3d 1069 (6th Cir. 1996).

A different view of class actions also changes the concept of disqualifying conflicts of interest. Some scholars have argued that a class action should be viewed not as an amalgam of individual claims but rather as its own collective entity—not unlike a corporation—with an ultimate goal of maximizing the value of the claims of the class as a whole. On this view, intra-class conflicts are not problematic as long as the class action is designed to achieve the greatest good for the greatest number. Collusion remains a conflict, for it harms the interests of the class as a whole. But mere disagreements about litigation strategy do not raise adequacy concerns if the class representative takes the action that adds the most value to the totality of the class. This collectivist viewpoint is most compelling—and conversely, the aggregation-of-individuals account is least attractive—in negative-value cases, in which the alternative to class litigation is often no litigation (and no recovery) at all. Given that society's interests in deterrence are advanced by such negative-value litigation, the conflicts of interest necessary to derail a class action on adequacy grounds must be substantial.[359]

Other accounts of adequacy and the permissible level of intra-class conflict are possible. One idea is to tolerate conflicts that make class members no worse off than they would have been in individual litigation. This approach does not require class representatives to maximize the values of all individual members' claims, but it also prevents the sacrifice of some class members' interests on the altar of the greatest good for the greatest number.[360]

Whatever the theoretical merits of these views, cases such as *Hansberry*, *Wal-Mart*, *Falcon*, and *Amchem* signal the Supreme Court's present commitment to viewing class actions as a vehicle for aggregation of individual claims. As such, the class action is a device approached with some suspicion, and the "inherent tension between representative suits and the day-in-court ideal" must be closely monitored and carefully managed.[361]

Some literature has focused on mechanisms to enhance the alignment of interests within a class. Following the literature on corporations—which similarly create a legal structure in which ownership of an asset is divorced from its day-to-day control, thus creating a substantial risk of agency costs—the class-action literature has analyzed three different strategies described in short as loyalty, voice, and exit. Loyalty strategies try to create incentives for class representatives and counsel to pay attention to the interests of those they represent. Voice strategies try to give the class members more control over the conduct of the class action, especially at critical moments such as settlement. Exit strategies allow class members to leave the class.[362]

Ensuring an alignment of the interests of class representatives and class members and an alignment among class members (the critical functions of Rules 23(a)(2), –(a)(3), and –(a)(4)) is a loyalty strategy. An example of the exit strategy arises in (b)(3) classes, which contain an opt-out right. A fair question is whether adopting both approaches is a belt-and-suspenders affair: if class members are

---

[359] For an analysis of the two class-action models—as the aggregation of individuals or as a distinct collective entity—see David L. Shapiro, *Class Actions: The Class as Party and Client*, 73 NOTRE DAME L. REV. 913 (1998).

[360] *See* Tidmarsh, *supra* note 357. This approach works best in conjunction with additional protections to ensure faithful representation. *See* JAY TIDMARSH, CLASS ACTIONS: FIVE PRINCIPLES TO PROMOTE FAIRNESS AND EFFICIENCY (2013).

[361] *See* Ortiz v. Fibreboard Corp., 527 U.S. 815 (1999).

[362] For a general discussion of these strategies, see John C. Coffee, Jr., *Class Action Accountability: Reconciling Exit, Voice, and Loyalty in Representative Litigation*, 100 COLUM. L. REV. 370 (2000).

allowed to opt out of a class action, is there even any need to worry about the adequacy of their representation? If they don't like what they see in the class representative, they can just leave the case. Of course, this argument does not work in (b)(1) and (b)(2) class actions, which contain no opt-out right. Nor is it realistic to think that class members will know enough about the claims of other class members or the motivations of class representative(s) to exercise their opt-out rights with the full information on which the exit strategy is premised. Some check on the loyalty (or adequacy) of the class representative is also necessary.

A final point: The adequacy of the class representative is an ongoing concern. Even if a representative is adequate at the time of certification, later events may change that assessment and require selection of a different representative or decertification of the class.

Rule 23(a)(4) has existed more or less in its present form since 1966. The text of the Rule speaks only to the adequacy of the class representative. For many years, however, courts also recognized that Rule 23(a)(4) also served a second, equally important function: as a check on the adequacy of class counsel. Concern for counsel's adequacy was supported not by the text of Rule 23(a)(4), which never mentions class counsel, but rather by the stubborn reality that class counsel effectively controls the course of class litigation. If the representation of the class's interests is to be truly adequate, counsel must also be up to the job.[363]

In 2003, an amendment that added Rules 23(g) and 23(h) finally made explicit the requirement of adequacy of class counsel. We turn to that issue now.

2. The Rule 23(g) Prerequisite

In the absence of a statute to the contrary, Rule 23(g) requires the court to appoint class counsel.[364] Rule 23(g)(4) states the fundamental responsibility of class counsel: "Class counsel must fairly and adequately represent the interests of the class." Rule 23(g)(1) provides a list of factors that must enter into the court's appointment decision: counsel's prior work to pursue the claims brought by the class, counsel's experience in class-action and complex-litigation practice, counsel's knowledge of the applicable

---

[363] The Supreme Court acknowledged the role of Rule 23(a)(4) in assessing the adequacy of class counsel in Falcon's famous footnote 13, in which it stated that Rule 23(a)(4) "raises concerns about the competency of class counsel." Gen. Tel. of the Sw. v. Falcon, 457 U.S. 147 (1982).

[364] The principal exception to this rule is the Private Securities Litigation Reform Act, which contemplates that the lead plaintiff—typically the class member with the largest amount at stake in the case, *see supra* note 350 and accompanying text—select class counsel. *See In re* Cendant Corp. Litig., 264 F.3d 201 (3d Cir. 2001).

law, and counsel's financial resources. The court may also consider any other relevant matters bearing on adequacy and may use the appointment as the opportunity to set the fee structure for class counsel.

Although the lawyer who initially files the class action and does the work to argue for class certification often has a leg up, more than one lawyer or law firm can—and often does—apply to be class counsel.[365] In such a case, Rule 23(g)(2) requires the court to appoint the "adequate applicant" who is "best able to represent the interests of the class." For a period of time, especially in securities-fraud litigation, some courts used an auction method to appoint class counsel. In essence, the court solicited bids, compared fee structures (which often varied wildly among competing firms, from simple percentages of recovery to sliding scales based on factors such as the length of the litigation and the size of the recovery). After winnowing out any inadequate firms, the court chose the fee structure that, in its judgment, gave the most value to the class.[366] The auction method never spread far beyond securities litigation, and for all practical purposes ended as a result of a devastatingly critical Third Circuit decision.[367]

We return to many of the specific issues involved in selecting class counsel in later chapters. Chapter Ten examines in more detail the power of a trial court to appoint counsel for an aggregated group, whether in an MDL proceeding or a class action. We will learn more at that point about the kinds of counsel structure that courts can employ in a class action. Chapter Ten also examines some of the unique ethical issues that a lawyer representing a group of litigants, including a class, faces. Chapters Sixteen and Eighteen discuss attorneys' fees in greater detail. We will learn more at that point about how different fee structures give counsel different incentives for representing the class.

Nevertheless, because the adequacy-of-counsel issue raises some specific concerns and has connections to the adequacy-of-class-representative issue, a brief examination of the unique issue of class counsel is best undertaken now. The principal concern regarding class counsel is agency cost: the fear that counsel will not act as a faithful agent of the class, but use the class's claims to enrich

---

[365] *See, e.g.*, *In re* Cardinal Health, Inc. ERISA Litig., 225 F.R.D. 852 (S.D. Ohio 2005).

[366] The seminal case adopting the auction method was *In re Oracle Securities Litigation*, 132 F.R.D. 538 (N.D. Cal. 1990).

[367] *See Cendant Corp.*, 264 F.3d 201. *Cendant* left open a small window for the auction process, but very few cases can fit through it.

themselves.[368] Even if we reject the "figurehead theory,"[369] the importance of class counsel in securing a result for the class is evident. And the tension between the interests of counsel and the interests of the class is equally evident. Class counsel, who often fronts the cost of notice and other large litigation expenses, usually has far more at stake in the outcome of the litigation than any class member. Moreover, class counsel is often unaware of the particular circumstances of many class members. The pressure on counsel to look out for his or her own interests—especially the interest in recovering fronted expenses and in receiving a fee that can easily range into seven or eight figures in large class actions—can be enormous. The same is true of public-interest lawyers, whose devotion to a cause can make it difficult to represent the interests of class members when they do not align with that cause.

Available checks on counsel's self-interested behavior are limited. In negative-value or small-value class actions, class members have little incentive to monitor the work of counsel closely. The defendant has some incentive to ensure that the counsel adequately represents the class; otherwise, the outcome achieved may not have preclusive effect in future litigation, and the defendant will be exposed to additional litigation. But once the threshold of bare adequacy is crossed, the defendant prefers to face a mediocre, rather than a talented, adversary.[370] And the court is constrained in its ability to monitor the work of class counsel. It needs to remain neutral, not to act as co-counsel prosecuting the class's claims or to second-guess counsel's every litigation decision. Nor do a court's limited resources allow it to engage in day-to-day supervision of class counsel's activities.

Against this backdrop, the law on adequacy of counsel divides, as with class representatives, into two categories: first, particular concerns about the qualities or characteristics of particular lawyers that raise adequacy concerns, and second, conflicts of interest. In the former category, reputation and experience (both in class-action practice and with the particular substantive field of law at issue in the case) are significant, as is putative counsel's financial wherewithal. Deficiencies in experience, knowledge, or funding make

---

368 *Cf. In re* Walgreen Co. Stockholder Litig., 832 F.3d 718, 724 (7th Cir. 2016) ("The type of class action illustrated by this case—the class action that yields fees for class counsel and nothing for the class—is no better than a racket. It must end.").

369 *See supra* note 352 and accompanying text.

370 A study that examined ten years of reported class-certification opinions, found that, in more than twenty percent of the cases, the defendant did not contest adequacy of counsel, and the court took that concession as proof of adequacy. *See* Klonoff, *supra* note 351.

an appointment an uphill climb.[371] A lack of zealous advocacy, either in the present class action or in other cases that come to the court's attention, works to putative counsel's detriment.[372] Ethical misconduct in other litigation is another concern that might derail an application for class counsel.[373]

As with class representatives, conflicts of interest, not the unsavory characteristics of class counsel, tend to be the Waterloo for many applicants. Conflicts of interest within a class—the types of conflicts that lead a court to deny certification under Rule 23(a)(4)—make it ethically difficult for class counsel to represent the class adequately. But such internal class conflicts are usually ferreted out under Rule 23(a)(4), leaving to Rule 23(g) the task of addressing a more limited set of conflicts: the conflicts between the interests of the class and the interests of class counsel.

For instance, a lawyer who is a member of a class, or who has a close personal relationship with the class representative, is generally disqualified from serving as class counsel.[374] Likewise, the simultaneous representation of another class whose membership overlaps with the present class action can also create an impermissible conflict when both classes are seeking recovery from the same pool of assets.[375] This inability to represent multiple classes is one reason why we do not see more use of smaller, discrete,

---

[371] *See Cardinal Health*, 225 F.R.D. 552 (choosing the firm with the most extensive experience in the subject matter of the litigation, rather than other firms with more extensive class-action experience); *cf.* Myrick v. WellPoint, Inc., 764 F.3d 662 (7th Cir. 2014) (noting in dicta that "plaintiffs and their counsel must be prepared to meet [the expenses that a class action entails] or be deemed inadequate representatives").

[372] *See* Gomez v. St. Vincent Health, Inc., 649 F.3d 583 (7th Cir. 2011); Dubin v. Miller, 132 F.R.D. 269 (D. Colo. 1990).

[373] *See* Eubank v. Pella Corp., 753 F.3d 718 (7th Cir. 2014) (holding that class counsel was inadequate when he tried to settle case before his law license was suspended for misappropriating assets at a prior law firm); Creative Montessori Learning Ctr. v. Ashford Gear LLC, 662 F.3d 913 (7th Cir. 2011) (noting that counsel's deceitful misconduct in obtaining the names of potential class representatives gave the court "no basis for confidence that [class counsel] would prosecute the case in the interest of the class, of which they are the fiduciaries, . . . rather than just in their interest as lawyers who if successful will obtain a share of any judgment or settlement as compensation for their efforts"); *Cardinal Health*, 225 F.R.D. 552 (declining to appoint one firm as class counsel in part due to firm's questionable litigation tactics in a prior class action).

[374] *See Eubank*, 753 F.3d 718 (class counsel was inadequate when class representative was son-in-law); Zylstra v. Safeway Stores, Inc., 578 F.2d 102 (5th Cir. 1978) ("[A] attorneys who are partners or spouses of named plaintiffs, or who themselves are members of the class of plaintiffs . . . should not be permitted to serve as counsel for the class.").

[375] *See Cardinal Health*, 225 F.R.D. 552; Kurczi v. Eli Lilly & Co., 160 F.R.D. 667 (N.D. Ohio 1995); *cf.* Seijas v. Republic of Arg., 606 F.3d 53 (2d Cir. 2010) (noting that representation of eight classes, as well as non-class litigants, competing for the same assets did not create an impermissible conflict at the liability phase of the litigation; reserving judgment on adequacy if the cases proceeded to a damages phase).

separate classes that might avoid some of the Rule 23(a) problems in mega-classes like *Wal-Mart* or *Falcon*. Counsel who can represent only one of a number of smaller classes ends up with a limited recovery.[376]

A related conflict of interest can arise when class counsel also represents individual litigants in related litigation. For instance, in the asbestos class settlement that came before the Supreme Court in *Amchem Products, Inc. v. Windsor*,[377] the class consisted of persons who had not yet filed asbestos lawsuits. The proposed class counsel—two lawyers from two of the largest plaintiffs' asbestos firms—already represented many clients who had filed suit, as well as some who were about to file suit. Class counsel settled their "inventory" of claims (both those previously filed and those not yet filed) on terms that were more generous than those that the class members received. This arrangement led to bitter recriminations claims that the defendants had bought out class counsel: in return for higher payments on their own cases (for which they received a substantial contingency fee), counsel sold out the interests of other future plaintiffs. The district court rejected this argument after hearing from legal-ethics experts on both sides. The Third Circuit and the Supreme Court declined to address the issue, deciding the case on other Rule 23 grounds.[378] But the odor of collusion hung over the case throughout the appellate process.

A related concern is whether class counsel can continue to represent the class when some members object to a settlement that class counsel has reached. When other class members support the settlement, a conflict of interest within the class emerges. Depriving the class of its advocate at the moment that this conflict emerges jeopardizes class settlements. More generally, it cannot be expected

---

376 A related question, on which there is little legal guidance, is whether separate counsel must be appointed for subclasses created under Rule 23(c)(5). As a rule, one counsel proposes to represent each subclass. *See, e.g., In re* Telectronics Pacing Sys., Inc., Accufix Atrial "J" Leads Prods. Liab. Litig., 172 F.R.D. 271 (S.D. Ohio 1997). When subclasses are created on grounds unrelated to differences among class members that might put them into opposition, a single counsel might be able to represent all subclasses. But in *Amchem Products, Inc. v. Windsor*, 521 U.S. 591 (1997), the Supreme Court also suggested (in dicta) that separate classes or subclasses might be used to avoid some of the conflicts of interest among class members that the single large class posed. If subclasses were to be used in this situation, it is difficult to see how one counsel could represent the admittedly conflicting interests of various subclasses.

377 521 U.S. 591. For further discussion of *Amchem*, *see supra* notes 355–361 and accompanying text, *infra* notes 415–416, 487 and accompanying text.

378 *See* Georgine v. Amchem Prods., Inc., *rev'd on other grounds*, 83 F.3d 610 (3d Cir. 1996), *aff'd sub nom*. Amchem Prods., Inc. v. Windsor, 521 U.S. 591 (1997). The indictment of class counsel's behavior is rendered most directly in an article by a legal-ethics experts who testified against approval of the settlement. *See* Susan P. Koniak, *Feasting While the Widow Weeps:* Georgine v. Amchem Prods., Inc., 80 CORNELL L. REV. 523 (1995).

that class counsel will operate with the same single-minded loyalty to the interests of each class member as a lawyer in a traditional one-on-one relationship should exhibit toward an individual client.[379] But how best to conform lawyers' traditional ethical obligations to the needs of class actions without providing a license to class counsel to do whatever counsel wishes—with all the agency-cost problems that such an approach entails—remains an open question.

As with the adequacy of class representatives, class counsel must meet the adequacy bar at all times during the litigation. Many adequacy concerns do not arise until discovery is underway or, even more likely, until the settlement is announced. A court is free to reexamine the vigor of counsel's representation and the potential for conflicts at any time. That said, very few class actions stumble on the adequacy-of-counsel requirement.[380]

Problem 3

Class counsel for a mass tort consisted of lawyers from several law firms. When a settlement was reached, some class members objected. The settlement also split class counsel; some firms supported the settlement, and some wished to represent the objecting class members to stop the settlement. The lawyers who represented the class want to ban the lawyers who represent the objectors due to their former representation of class members who now support the settlement. Are the lawyers representing the class now inadequate because of the conflict within the class? *See In re* "Agent Orange" Prod. Liab. Litig., 800 F.2d 14 (2d Cir. 1986).

3. The Final Element: Satisfying One Rule 23(b) Requirement

Establishing the requirements of Rules 23(a) and 23(g) should mean that a class action will achieve efficiencies and will adequately represent the interests of the class members. In and of themselves, however, these reasons have always been deemed insufficient for class treatment. Some additional reason is also needed to overcome our system's preference to allow each litigant to proceed independently with his or her lawsuit.

Rule 23(b) supplies that additional reason. Rule 23(b) lists four different class actions: the (b)(1)(A), the (b)(1)(B), the (b)(2), and the (b)(3) class action. Each presents a scenario that makes a class action

---

[379] *See In re* Corn Derivatives Antitrust Litig., 748 F.2d 157 (3d Cir. 1984) (Adams, J., concurring) (arguing that "courts cannot mechanically transpose to class actions the rules developed in the traditional lawyer-client setting context" and that "a resolution of such issues would appear to call for a balancing process").

[380] *See* Klonoff, *supra* note 351 (finding that, out of 687 cases discussing adequacy of class counsel, only 31 cases held that counsel was inadequate).

necessary, or at least compelling. It is possible that a case may involve more than one scenario, and in such instances a court may certify the class—or different parts of the class—under different provisions. To take a simple example, a case may request both an injunction and damages. Assuming that the Rule 23(a) and Rule 23(g) elements are met, a court could certify the injunctive claim under Rule 23(b)(2) and the damages claim under Rule 23(b)(3).

Class-action practitioners often refer to class actions by their designations under Rule 23(b)—saying, for instance, "I'll be taking depositions in a (b)(3) class action next week." Practitioners also well understand the pertinent differences among these class actions: most critically, that (b)(3) class actions are generally the vehicle for obtaining monetary relief and that (b)(3) classes are the only class actions to afford an opt-out right to class members.

One final thought before we proceed. A majority of Rule 23 class actions seem to be certified under Rule 23(b)(3). We say "seem to" because the only data—from a survey done in four federal district courts more than twenty years ago—put the percentage of (b)(3) class actions at sixty-one percent.[381] That sample size is small, and changes in the law since that time have made (b)(3) class actions more difficult to certify. Whatever the exact percentage of (b)(3) class actions, nearly all of the controversy about class actions arises from Rule 23(b)(3) cases, in no small part because Rule 23(b)(3) is the most capacious of the class actions and because it is only class action in which monetary recovery is generally available.

a. The "Inconsistent Standards" Class Action: Rule 23(b)(1)(A)

Rule 23 (b)(1)(A) permits a class action when independent suits by class plaintiffs would create a risk of "inconsistent or varying adjudications" that might establish "inconsistent standards of conduct" for the defendant. The risk of separate suits by class members who seek injunctive relief generally applicable to the class fits within this provision. In such a situation, different injunctions might order the defendant to do different things, and the defendant might be unable to comply with all the orders; hence, bringing the plaintiffs together in a single suit is necessary to prevent injustice either to the whipsawed defendant or to later filing claimants who cannot obtain the award they prefer because the defendant is already committed to a different course of action.

It is settled law that the risk of inconsistent damage awards—in which some plaintiffs might lose, some might win a modest

---

[381] THOMAS E. WILLGING ET AL., FED. JUDICIAL CTR., EMPIRICAL STUDY OF CLASS ACTIONS IN FOUR FEDERAL DISTRICT COURTS (1996). Twenty-nine percent were (b)(2) class actions, and the remaining ten percent were split evenly between (b)(1)(A) and (b)(1)(B) class actions.

amount, and some might win large judgments—does not generate "inconsistent standards of conduct" and therefore is not covered by the Rule. Ordering a defendant to pay differing amounts of damages to similarly situated plaintiffs does not whipsaw the defendant; it is perfectly feasible for the defendant to pay one claimant and not pay another.[382] Although this linguistic interpretation might be questioned,[383] courts have shown no interest in doing so. Rule 23(b)(1)(A) devolved from equity practice, and has, as a practical matter, been invoked almost entirely in cases seeking injunctive or declaratory relief.

Plaintiffs' attorneys have shown some creativity in avoiding this limit. For instance, in *In re Merck & Co., Inc., Securities, Derivative & "ERISA" Litigation*,[384] the class sought damages due to alleged breaches of fiduciary responsibility by the administrators of various retirement plans. The court noted that the case would determine whether the administrators acted properly and therefore would establish their standard of conduct going forward. Individual lawsuits created a risk either that the same conduct might be judged legal (or illegal)—thus putting the plan administrators in a bind about how to act—or that the first decision in the first case would establish the administrators' course of conduct—thus denying later-filing plaintiffs effective relief.[385]

In the same vein, some states have recognized that a defendant owes an obligation of medical monitoring to those persons exposed to a defendant's harmful product but not yet injured by it. One way to provide a remedy for a monitoring claim is to award plaintiffs a sum of money to seek appropriate medical testing. Some class plaintiffs, however, have argued the defendant should create a monitoring program—a form of relief that the district court would establish by injunction. In *In re Teletronics Pacing Systems, Inc. Accufix Atrial "J" Leads Products Liability Litigation*,[386] the court took the next analytical step: because individual cases might require the defendant to establish monitoring programs that would clash with each other, certifying a Rule 23(b)(1)(A) class of victims entitled to medical monitoring was appropriate.

---

382 *See, e.g.*, *In re* Dennis Greenman Sec. Litig., 829 F.2d 1539 (11th Cir. 1987).

383 *See* Note, *Class Certification in Mass Accident Cases under Rule 23(b)(1)(A)*, 96 HARV. L. REV. 1143 (1983); *see also In re* Merck & Co., Inc., Sec., Derivative & "ERISA" Litig., MDL No. 1658 (SRC), 2009 WL 331426 (D.N.J. Feb. 10, 2009) (noting that "the proposition that certification under this subsection is inappropriate when the primary relief sought is money damages . . . inserts a requirement into 23(b)(1)(A) that is not present").

384 MDL No. 1658 (SRC), 2009 WL 331426 (D.N.J. Feb. 10, 2009).

385 *See In re* Ikon Office Solutions, Inc., 191 F.R.D. 457 (E.D. Pa. 2000).

386 172 F.R.D. 271 (S.D. Ohio 1997).

Because an award of money to seek private medical testing would appear to be an adequate remedy at law, and because the evidence of conflicting monitoring programs was speculative, the result in *Telectronics* is debatable.[387] If the result is good law, *Telectronics* achieves something rather extraordinary: it brings into a single, non-opt-out class action the claims of persons with no present injuries (i.e., "future claimants"). Once all future claims are joined, the parties might then be able to craft a settlement of the future tort claims (as well as the monitoring claims), obviating a great deal of future litigation.[388]

The fundamental point of the (b)(1)(A) class action is to protect a defendant from the injustice of trying to comply with class members' demands for inconsistent remedies. The analogy is to Rule 19 (a)(1)(B)(ii), which requires the joinder of persons to protect a defendant from "a substantial risk of incurring double, multiple, or otherwise inconsistent obligations."[389] The rationale behind Rule 23(b)(1)(A) is much the same, but here the interested parties are so numerous that individual joinder is impracticable. Unlike Rule 19(a)(1)(B)(ii), however, each affected party need not be joined in order to protect the party's interests.[390] That work is done by the class representative.

At the same time, if different plaintiffs have different interests that might lead them to seek different relief from the defendant, the conflict of interest among class members in a (b)(1)(A) class is patent. Whether a single class representative is capable of adequately representing these interests is not a matter on which courts have focused. Put differently, whether any class properly certifiable under

---

[387] For a case disagreeing with *Telectronics*, see O'Connor v. Boeing N. Am., Inc., 180 F.R.D. 359 (C.D. Cal. 1997). *See also* Zinser v. Accufix Research Inst., Inc., 253 F.3d 1180 (9th Cir.), *amended*, 273 F.3d 1266 (9th Cir. 2001) (using Rule 23(b)(1)(A) is inappropriate when plaintiffs sought creation of a monitoring fund, rather than a monitoring program). For a court reaching the result in *Telectronics* under Rule 23(b)(2), see *Day v. NLO, Inc.*, 144 F.R.D. 330 (S.D. Ohio 1992); *but see* Barnes v. Am. Tobacco Co., 161 F.3d 127 (3d Cir. 1998) (holding that the individual issues were too great to certify a (b)(2) medical-monitoring class).

[388] Indeed, *Teletronics* ultimately settled all future claims under Rule 23(b)(1)(B) (*not* Rule 23(b)(1)(A)), but the court of appeals ordered the class decertified. *In re* Telectronics Pacing Liab. Litig., 221 F.3d 870 (6th Cir. 2000). For a fuller exploration of whether it is possible to settle the cases of future claimants by means of a class action, see *supra* notes 355–361 and accompanying text, *infra* notes 396–401, 483–490 and accompanying text.

[389] *See supra* Chapter 2.B.2.1. Rule 19(a)(1)(B)(ii)'s concern for "double or multiple" obligations finds an echo in another joinder device—Rule 22 interpleader—which permits mandatory joinder when a defendant faces "double or multiple liability."

[390] Indeed, Rule 19(d) renders Rule 19 inapplicable when Rule 23 can be invoked.

Rule 23(b)(1)(A) can also slip through Rule 23(a)(4)'s zero-tolerance policy for conflicts of interest internal to the class is an open question.

Arguably the (b)(1)(A) class action tilts too far in the direction of avoiding unfairness to defendants, in the process tolerating conflicts that should be fatal to class certification. One solution is to tailor the class narrowly, so that it comprises only those persons whose interests are aligned in obtaining the same relief from the defendant.[391] Presumably other classes or subclasses could then be crafted to represent the interests of those who prefer the defendant to act in a different manner. But this solution also makes the class mechanism more unwieldy and expensive. Another solution, which we have already explored, is to craft an understanding of adequate representation that tolerates some internal class conflicts.[392]

b. *The "Impaired Interest" Class Action: Rule 23(b)(1)(B)*

Like Rule 23(b)(1)(A), Rule 23(b)(1)(B) concerns itself with the untoward effects that separate lawsuits by class members create. Unlike the (b)(1)(A) class, the focus of the (b)(1)(B) class is not on the untoward consequences to the *defendant*, but rather on the untoward consequences that individual suits by putative class members would have on the rights of *other putative class members*. Thus, the (b)(1)(B) mandatory class action seeks to prevent the risk of individual actions "that, as a practical matter, would be dispositive of the interests of the other members not parties to the individual adjudications or would substantially impair or impede their ability to protect their interests." When this scenario arises, the idea is to gather all the interested plaintiffs into a single class, and then to find an appropriate, complete, and equitable solution to the controversy.

As the counterpart to Rule 23(b)(1)(A) is Rule 19(a)(1)(B)(ii), the counterpart to Rule 23(b)(1)(B) is Rule 19(a)(1)(B)(i). Both are concerned with absent parties whose interests might be fundamentally compromised by other parties' lawsuits. Both are designed to protect the interests of these absent claimants by bringing all related claimants together in one suit. With Rule 23(b)(1)(B), however, the number of absent parties is so great that their individual joinder is impracticable.

Parallels also exist between Rule 23(b)(1)(B) and Rule 24(a)(2), which permits a person with potentially impaired interests to intervene in a case. As we saw earlier, impairment for Rule 19(a)(1)(B)(i) purposes and impairment for Rule 24(a)(2) purposes

---

[391] The text of Rule 23(b)(1)(A), however, does not demand such a unity of interest within the class; it contemplates that individual adjudications involving members of the certified class would create inconsistent standards of conduct for the defendant, thus suggesting that the class members have varying interests.

[392] *See supra* notes 358–362 and accompanying text.

are not the same thing.[393] The same is true for Rules 23(b)(1)(B) and 24(a)(2): the impairment language gets a different, more restrictive meaning under Rule 23. In particular, the *stare decisis* impairment that is often regarded as sufficient when intervention is sought under Rule 24(a)(2) is not regarded as a sufficient reason to invoke Rule 23(b)(1)(B).[394]

As with Rule 23(b)(1)(A), the reason for class treatment in this situation is the concern for fairness: here, the equitable treatment of similarly situated class members, especially those class members who might not obtain an adequate remedy because they could not file suit or reduce their claim to judgment before other class members obtained judgment in their cases. For instance, Rule 23(b)(1)(B) has been employed to resolve injunctive claims that seek to restructure an institution, given that restructuring has an effect on the interests of other class members who also have a relationship with the institution.

Rule 23(b)(1)(B) has similarly been used when a suit seeks to require a company to pay a particular shareholder a dividend that would, as a practical matter, establish similar shareholders' rights to a dividend. Claims concerning the management or distribution of trust funds, or other forms of property in which numerous claimants have beneficial or joint ownership interests, also can be certified under Rule 23(b)(1)(B). For example, if a suit might require a court to replace a trustee if the trustee has shown to breach his or her fiduciary duty, that remedy affects the interests of all the beneficiaries of the trust, so a (b)(1)(B) class is appropriate.[395]

As these examples show, some Rule 23(b)(1)(B) class actions involve injunctive relief, but others involve damages. Of the three mandatory class actions, Rule 23(b)(1)(B) is the only form in which class members as a general matter might receive an award of damages.

Perhaps the most frequently discussed use of Rule 23(b)(1)(B) has been its use in the context of a "limited fund"—in other words, a fund of money that is insufficient to pay fully all the claims against that fund. Like interpleader, litigation by individual class members might result in the full satisfaction of the early-filed claims, and modest or no satisfaction of the later-filed claims. But the defendant has little incentive to join all the claimants, since he or she is probably indifferent about the fund's distribution among potential claimants. The question is whether, when the claimants against the

---

393 *See supra* note 95 and accompanying text.

394 *See In re* Dennis Greenman Sec. Litig., 829 F.2d 1539 (11th Cir. 1987).

395 *See In re* Merck & Co., Inc., Sec., Derivative & "ERISA" Litig., MDL No. 1658 (SRC), 2009 WL 331426 (D.N.J. Feb. 10, 2009).

fund are numerous enough, Rule 23(b)(1)(B) might countenance a class of all the early-filing and late-filing claimants.

When the fund is a well-defined asset, like an insurance policy, Rule 23(b)(1)(B) seems perfectly suited to the problem. But what if the "fund" is the defendant's assets, and the argument is that the class members' legitimate claims against the fund might exceed those assets? In this circumstance, early-filing claimants would receive full value on their claims, and later-filing claimants would receive pennies on the dollar or nothing from a now-insolvent defendant. But who has early claims and who has late claims often rests on fortuitous circumstances. It seems only fair to bring all claimants into one suit and then to accomplish an equitable distribution of assets for all class members.

Creative plaintiffs' lawyers pushed this argument in a number of high-profile mass-tort cases. Certification under Rule 23(b)(1)(B) promised a number of benefits: no class notice upon certification, thus making the class less expensive than a (b)(3) class; no opt-outs, thus resolving the dispute in one fell swoop; and a rationale on which present and future claimants could all be joined in one suit, thus addressing the geographical and temporal dispersion of claims that so frustrates many of the aggregation mechanisms that we have examined. The question is whether Rule 23(b)(1)(B) can be interpreted to reach these limited-fund cases.

In *Ortiz v. Fibreboard Corp.*,[396] the Supreme Court answered "rarely." The facts of *Ortiz* are complicated. Fibreboard, an asbestos manufacturer, struck a deal designed to resolve all future claims by means of a Rule 23(b)(1)(B) class, employing a limited-fund theory. Fibreboard had limited assets; at the time of the settlement, the company's balance sheet was about $235 million, plus $10 million in available insurance proceeds. But Fibreboard also had a valuable potential asset. Two of Fibreboard's old insurance carriers had written insurance policies during the 1950s that arguably made the insurers responsible to indemnify Fibreboard in unlimited amounts for Fibreboard's asbestos claims that arose from exposure to Fibreboard's asbestos before 1959. (Asbestos litigation did not take off until the late 1960s, so these insurers were unaware of the scope of their coverage.) Fibreboard was responsible for paying claims based on post-1959 exposure; other than the $10 million in available proceeds, it had exhausted all post-1959 insurance assets.

At a certain point, the two insurers refused to continue to indemnify Fibreboard, arguing that their obligations under the pre-1959 policies were not unlimited and had long since been met.

---

[396] 527 U.S. 815 (1999). We look at other aspects of *Ortiz infra* notes 441, 488–490 and accompanying text.

Fibreboard sued its insurers in California state court. Fibreboard won at the trial level, and the insurers appealed.

Just days before the appellate court in California was to release its decision—a decision that would leave Fibreboard either with access to the vast assets of two major insurance companies to settle claims of pre-1959 asbestos exposure or with virtually no assets to settle any asbestos cases—Fibreboard, the insurers, and lawyers who had represented plaintiffs in prior litigation against Fibreboard reached a settlement for $1.535 billion with respect to all future asbestos claims that might be asserted against Fibreboard.[397] Of that amount, the insurers contributed $1.525 billion and Fibreboard contributed $10 million. Thus, the settlement left untouched both Fibreboard's remaining assets of $235 million and the insurance companies' remaining assets, which totaled in the billions of dollars.

Simplifying the details somewhat, the settlement provided for a trust to pay victims based on a range of factors, including the type of disease, age, income, and responsibility of other asbestos defendants. The historical values paid by Fibreboard in similar prior cases also guided the settlement trust's administrator. A victim dissatisfied with the trust's award could proceed to mediation, arbitration, a settlement conference with a federal judge, and (if still not satisfied) trial. At trial, Fibreboard's exposure was capped at $500,000 (on the theory that Fibreboard had never paid more than this amount in any prior asbestos case), and punitive damages were not allowed. Unlike the *Amchem* settlement, on which the *Fibreboard* settlement attempted to improve, awards for later-filing claimants could rise with inflation because awards were pegged in part to historical awards, which could rise over time.

The settlement had one catch. The insurers agreed to settle only if the settlement ended their indemnity obligations and gave them "global peace." That demand meant that the settlement needed to sweep in all future plaintiffs on a mandatory basis—something that was impossible under a Rule 23(b)(3) class action. Hence, the plaintiffs filed a case seeking certification of a mandatory class action under Rule 23(b)(1)(B). The theory of the settling parties was that the $1.535 billion settlement kitty was a limited fund, which might

---

[397] In a side agreement that was worth about $1 billion, the insurers also agreed to compensate plaintiffs who had previously settled with or won verdicts against Fibreboard. To "pay" these claims, Fibreboard had used a blend of up-front cash and an assignment to the plaintiffs of its indemnity rights against the insurers. These plaintiffs therefore had a vested interest in Fibreboard's success in the California insurance-coverage litigation. The insurers also agreed to provide Fibreboard with $475 million to settle any presently pending litigation.

be depleted by early-filing claimants unless all claimants were brought before the court.[398]

The trial court certified the class and approved the settlement. The court of appeals affirmed, but the Supreme Court vacated the decision in light of its decision in *Amchem Products, Inc. v. Windsor*. On remand, the court of appeals again affirmed.

The Supreme Court reversed. It recognized that Rule 23(b)(1)(B) is an appropriate vehicle to resolve a limited-fund scenario. But it also required that Rule 23 should hew closely to equity's traditional understanding of a limited fund. In particular, in order to come within the terms of Rule 23(b)(1)(B), a limited fund must satisfy three criteria: the fund, set at its maximum, must be inadequate to satisfy the "aggregated liquidated claims"; the whole of the fund must be devoted to the payment of these claims; and the claimants with common theories of recovery must be treated equitably among themselves.

Leaving open the broader question whether a limited-fund theory could ever be used to aggregate tort claims under Rule 23(b)(1)(B), the Court held that the *Ortiz* settlement failed to fulfill these criteria in two ways. First, the fund from which compensation was to be provided was not set at its maximum, but was instead established at an amount agreed upon by the parties.[399] The Court suggested two different ways of showing the existence of a limited fund: either that the value of the asbestos claims assertable against Fibreboard exceeded the available assets of the insurers and Fibreboard, thus rendering them insolvent; or that the insurance policies had limits which the assertable asbestos claims exceeded. Although recognizing that the method was not traditional, the Court suggested that a limited fund might be shown through a third approach: showing that the assertable claims exceeded the amount of insurance companies' assets, discounted by the risk of Fibreboard losing the insurance-coverage litigation.[400] The *Ortiz* settlement amount of $1.535 billion was not derived through any of these methods. It did not throw into the kitty all the available assets of the insurers and Fibreboard, nor had the parties shown that this figure reflected an appropriate discounting of the insurers' total assets in

---

[398] Whether the case could be certified under Rule 23(b)(1)(B) was debatable at the time of the settlement. As a result, the parties also negotiated a back-up settlement agreement, under which the insurers would provide Fibreboard with a lump sum of $2 billion in return for a complete release of the insurers' obligations to indemnify Fibreboard for any present or future claim.

[399] The Court also noted that the tort claims were unliquidated, which made Fibreboard's future liability uncertain. But it did not base its holding on this fact.

[400] As an example, if the insurers' combined assets were $10 million, and Fibreboard had a sixty percent chance of prevailing on the coverage dispute, the fund would be $6 million.

light of the possibility that they might win the insurance-coverage litigation.[401]

The second stumbling block in the *Ortiz* settlement was its failure to meet the third element of a (b)(1)(B) limited fund: the equitable treatment of those with a claim against the fund. The Court specifically noted two deficiencies. First, the class definition included within the class only those with no pending claims against Fibreboard. The claims of all those who had previously settled with Fibreboard but had not yet been fully paid, as well as all those who had pending claims against Fibreboard, settled separately through a somewhat different mechanism and under somewhat different terms. Second, the class members who had been exposed to Fibreboard's asbestos during the time that the insurance policies were in effect (up to 1957 for one policy and up to 1959 for the other) had claims that were far more valuable than those whose exposure occurred after 1959. Post-1959 claimants could look only to Fibreboard' modest assets for satisfaction. Within the class, therefore, were people with inconsistent interests; the pre-1959 claimants and their differing legal position required separate representation and perhaps separate classes or subclasses. The settlement, however, made no distinctions among class members in terms of representation, and it provided no greater settlement amounts to those exposed before 1959. The Court noted that this (b)(1)(B) concern overlapped with the (a)(4) adequacy problem detected in *Amchem*, and it implied that it would have reversed the case on (a)(4) grounds had it been necessary to reach the issue.

Ortiz does not abolish the limited-fund theory, but the square corners that litigants must turn to invoke the theory reduces the utility of Rule 23(b)(1)(B) in most situations.

Problem 4

Plaintiffs sought claims for compensatory and punitive damages, arguing that the Constitution imposes a limit of the total amount of punitive damages that a defendant could be expected to pay for the same conduct. Because the victims had claims for punitive damages that exceeded this limit, they sought to certify a (b)(1)(B) class action of all victims—but only with respect to their claim for punitive damages. Does Rule 23(b)(1)(B) permit certification of a class on a theory of "limited punishment"? *See In re* Simon II Litig., 407 F.3d 125 (2d Cir. 2005).

401 The Court also noted that the settlement preserved for Fiberboard virtually all of its $235 million in corporate assets. While it did not base its holding on this fact, the Court observed that "it hardly appears that such a regime is the best that can be provided for class members."

One of the notable features of the (b)(1)(B) class action is frequent conflicts of interests among class members. For instance, *Ortiz* states that the (b)(1)(B) class might proceed on a limited-fund theory when (among other requirements) the claimants are treated equitably among themselves; thus, Rule 23(b)(1)(B) achieves a type of justice that individual litigation cannot. True enough, but the interests of the early-filing claimants, who would receive full recoveries without the class action, differ markedly from the interests of the late-filing claimants, who receive no recovery unless the class action is certified. Assuring fair treatment does not make the conflict go away; it just makes us feel better about putting conflicting interests together in one class.

A fair question is whether a limited-fund (b)(1)(B) class action—even one that meets the demand of *Ortiz* to treat similarly situated class members equitably—passes muster under *Hansberry*'s understanding of due process. Or perhaps due process, which is a flexible concept, tolerates a certain amount of internal class conflict when a class action is used to achieve equity among class members—which was certainly not what was going on in *Hansberry*.

Even if limited-fund class actions survive the conflict-of-interest hurdle, they face other problems. Principal among them is their consistency with the Bankruptcy Code, which sets in place specific substantive and procedural protections for creditors when a debtor is insolvent. At least in those limited-fund class actions in which the size of the fund is determined by the full assets of the defendant, a (b)(1)(B) class action looks like an attempt to distribute the assets to a select group of creditors in derogation of the statutory process for orderly distribution of a debtor's assets.

A final point about the (b)(1)(B) class action: as we saw in Chapter Four, courts sometimes enjoy a power to issue anti-suit injunctions. In *In re Federal Skywalk Cases*,[402] the Eighth Circuit reversed the certification of a (b)(1)(B) mass-tort class action on the theory that the mandatory nature of a (b)(1)(B) class action effectively prevented class members from bringing suit elsewhere. In addition, the court of appeals noted that the "substantial effect" of the certification order was to enjoin victims of the mass tort, including those who had previously commenced litigation in state court, from proceeding with their claims elsewhere. With respect to those victims who had filed in state court, the court of appeals held that the injunction implicit in a (b)(1)(B) class action fit within none of the exceptions to the Anti-Injunction Act, and therefore was barred by the Act. As a result, the certification order was vacated.

---

[402] 680 F.2d 1175 (8th Cir. 1982).

Federal Skywalk can be criticized for its questionable assumptions, especially that a mandatory class action contains an implicit anti-suit injunction. Whatever the merits of that argument on the facts of the case, a number of opinions—almost all of which are now thirty years old—have held that the Anti-Injunction Act prevents certification of a limited-fund (b)(1)(B) class action.[403]

The (b)(1)(B) class action remains an aggregation mechanism of uncertain scope. One thing is clear: it is not likely to serve as a broadly useful tool for aggregating related claims.

c. *The Injunctive Class Action: Rule 23(b)(2)*

Also a mandatory class action, Rule 23(b)(2) requires class certification when "the party opposing the class has acted or refused to act on grounds that apply generally to the class, so that final injunctive relief or corresponding declaratory relief is appropriate respecting the class as a whole." The (b)(2) class action is usually described as the injunctive class action, and has been used to certify class actions in a host of circumstances requiring injunctive relief, such as civil-rights, government-benefits, and employment-discrimination litigation. It had also seen occasional use in areas such as medical monitoring claims.[404] Its two essential elements—"generally applicable" conduct and a request for final injunctive or declaratory relief—are straightforward.

Nonetheless, Rule 23(b)(2) has posed a few interpretive difficulties. One is its relationship with Rule 23(b)(1)(A), which also is designed principally to handle claims for injunctive relief. Whether both forms of class action are necessary, or whether Rule 23(b)(2) is redundant of Rule 23(b)(1)(A), is a nice question. The redundancy between the Rules seems intentional. The predecessor to Rule 23(b)(1)(A) permitted class certification when a class sought "joint" or "common" relief. In the wake of *Brown v. Board of Education* and other early civil-rights litigation, some courts had shown themselves reluctant to interpret Rule 23 to authorize civil-rights class actions. Rule 23(b)(2) was written to make crystal clear that class actions were proper in the then-emerging civil-rights litigation, in which litigants usually sought injunctive relief.

---

[403] *See, e.g., In re* Temple, 851 F.3d 1269 (11th Cir. 1987).

[404] The medical-monitoring experience is checkered. *Compare* Cook v. Rockwell Int'l Corp., 151 F.R.D. 378 (D. Colo. 1993) (certifying medical monitoring class), *with* Cook v. Rockwell Int'l Corp., 181 F.R.D. 473 (D. Colo. 1998) (decertifying same class). Recent cases have been decidedly opposed to this use of Rule 23(b)(2). *See, e.g.*, Gates v. Rohm & Haas Co., 655 F.3d 255 (3d Cir. 2011) (affirming the denial of a (b)(2) medical-monitoring class when the need for individual proof of causation and medical necessity deprived the class of its necessary cohesion); *In re* St. Jude Med., Inc., Silzone Heart Valve Prods. Liab. Litig., 425 F.3d 1116 (8th Cir. 2005) (same).

A second question is whether the claims of the class members must be "cohesive"—in other words, whether the legal and factual issues common to the class are of a sufficiently tight-knit quality that the class will be efficient to manage and try. Such a requirement of cohesion may sound a lot like the "predominance" and "superiority" requirements of Rule 23(b)(3)—and it is.[405] You might reasonably object to reading these requirements into a different provision of Rule 23(b).

But some courts have pointed either to the language or to the structural features of Rule 23(b)(2) to justify a requirement of cohesion. For instance, the need for the injunctive remedy to "apply generally" to "the class as a whole" arguably demands a comparably high degree of similarity among the claims of class members; therefore, claims of class members that pose "diverse legal and factual issues preclude class certification" under Rule 23(b)(2).[406] Without using the word "cohesion," other courts have pointed out that the inability of class members to opt out requires that there be "few conflicting interests among class members," and that the defendant's conduct must have harmed class members in essentially the same way.[407] The idea of a cohesion requirement also received a boost from *Wal-Mart Stores, Inc. v. Dukes*, in which the Supreme Court noted that "[t]he key to the (b)(2) class is the indivisible nature of the injunctive or declaratory remedy warranted—the notion that the conduct is such that it can be enjoined or declared unlawful only as to all of the class members or as to none of them."[408]

Wal-Mart made this observation while resolving yet another interpretive issue of Rule 23(b)(2): whether a (b)(2) class can be used to award money. Recall that *Wal-Mart* involved a class of female workers alleging gender discrimination in pay and promotion practices. The class sought backpay in addition to injunctive relief. Nothing in the text of Rule 23(b)(2) suggests that the Rule can be used for anything other than injunctive or declaratory relief. But a slight window was left open by the Advisory Committee's Note to the 1966 amendment that created Rule 23(b)(2). The Note stated that Rule 23(b)(2) "does not extend to cases in which the appropriate final

---

[405] Indeed, some courts adopting the cohesion requirement have suggested that cohesion is more stringent than the predominance and superiority requirements. *See* Barnes v. Am. Tobacco Co., 161 F.3d 127 (3d Cir. 1998).

[406] *See St. Jude*, 425 F.3d 1116; *Gates*, 655 F.3d 255 (3d Cir. 2011) (same).

[407] *See* Casa Orlando Apartments, Ltd. v. Fed. Nat'l Mortg. Ass'n, 624 F.3d 185 (5th Cir. 2010)

[408] 564 U.S.338 (2011) (internal quotation marks omitted). The Court went on to note that the "case-specific inquiry into whether class issues predominate or whether class action is a superior method of adjudicating the dispute" was unnecessary when a class seeks an "indivisible injunction." The Third Circuit used this language to bolster its argument for a (b)(2) cohesion requirement. *See Gates*, 655 F.3d 255.

relief relates exclusively or predominantly to money damages." Implicit in (although not logically required by) this statement is the converse proposition: that Rule 23(b)(2) can be used to aggregate claims for damages as long as these claims do not predominate over the injunctive claims.

For many years, lower courts accepted this implication, certifying (b)(2) classes as long as the monetary relief was merely "incidental to" (as opposed to "predominating over") the injunctive relief.[409] The only issue dividing the lower courts was where to place this line. A fair characterization of the cases is that, over time, courts allowed more and more monetary relief to be awardable in a (b)(2) class.[410] The significance of this trend, of course, was to make it impossible for class members with "incidental" monetary claims to opt those claims out of class treatment. The lack of an opt-out right also reduced the expense of providing notice and increased the amount of aggregation that could be achieved in cases seeking both injunctive and monetary claims.

In *Allison v. Citgo Petroleum Corp.*,[411] the Fifth Circuit took a different tack, arguing that "incidental" monetary relief was awardable in a (b)(2) class only when the damages flowed directly from the injunctive relief, were awarded to the group as a whole, and were easy to calculate using objective standards. *Allison* sent shock waves through other courts, some of which tightened up on their use of Rule 23(b)(2) to award damages and some of which rejected the constraints of *Allison*.

In a portion of the opinion that was unanimous, *Wal-Mart* resolved the circuit split by returning to the text of Rule 23(b)(2). Rule 23(b)(2) awards indivisible relief, which money is not. When individualized relief like money is at stake, class members have a due-process right to opt out and proceed individually; to deprive them of that right through in a mandatory (b)(2) class would raise constitutional concerns that the narrower interpretation of Rule 23(b)(2) avoided. The contrary implication in the Advisory Committee's Note, the Court decided, "does not in our view suffice to establish a disposition that has no basis in the Rule's text, and that does obvious violence to the Rule's structural features."

The Court's bright line opposing the award of monetary relief in a (b)(2) class action left even *Allison*, which has been until then the

---

409 The seminal case was *Wetzel v. Liberty Mutual Insurance Co.*, 508 F.2d 239 (3d Cir. 1975).

410 This expansion occurred largely before the "cohesion" requirement became a staple in the Rule 23(b)(2) jurisprudence of some courts; it is unlikely that claims for damages, which typically require proof of individual circumstance, would be regarded as cohesive.

411 151 F.3d 402 (5th Cir. 1998).

narrowest understanding of "incidental damages," on thin ice. After citing *Allison*, the Court declined to decide "whether there are any forms of 'incidental' monetary relief that are consistent with the interpretation of Rule 23(b)(2) we have announced and that comply with the Due Process Clause." Because the plaintiffs could not meet the *Allison* standard, the Court left to another day the issue of whether it is possible under any circumstances—even the highly restrictive circumstances of *Allison*—to certify a (b)(2) class for claims that seek monetary relief.[412]

At this point, we turn to the final class-action form: the opt-out class action of Rule 23(b)(3). Before we do, however, it is worth recalling a point that we made earlier. As we have gotten into the weeds of Rules 23(a), 23(g), and 23(b), we have encountered a lot of jargon and technical doctrines. It is easy to get caught up in those details, as class-action practitioners will. But recall what is behind all the technicality and what has motivated all the interpretive creativity that has shaped the law of Rule 23. Class actions can be potent aggregation devices and powerful enforcers of the law. They also pose risks, from agency costs to loss of litigant autonomy to large judgments for modest harms. To step back even further, beyond the world of class actions lie other aggregation mechanisms, which raise their own difficulties—one of which that, in general, they are far less effective than class actions in preventing repetitive relitigation. Every technical doctrine that makes class certification more difficult has an effect on the legal system's ability to achieve broad aggregation, and puts more pressure on other aggregation devices, each with its own costs, to fill the void left by the absence of a class action.

> *Problem 5*
>
> Plaintiffs sought certification of a (b)(2) class action on a claim of contract interpretation. Depending on the outcome of that claim, some class members were also entitled to receive money. With respect to those class members, certification of a separate Rule 23(b)(3) class was also sought. Can the contract-interpretation claims be certified under Rule 23(b)(2)? *See* Gooch v. Life Investors Ins. Co. of Am., 672 F.3d 402 (6th Cir. 2012).

In the end, most of us want a civil-justice system that provides the most benefit at the lowest reasonable cost. Of course, this goal does not tell us how much values like adequate deterrence or individual autonomy are worth, and we are likely to disagree when

[412] Judge Posner has held that monetary relief can be awarded in a (b)(2) class when it is formulaic and easily calculable by a computer program; the case involved adjustments made to retirement accounts that flowed from a declaratory judgment determining the rights of plan participants. *See* Johnson v. Meriter Health Servs. Emp. Ret. Plan, 702 F.3d 364 (7th Cir. 2012).

we weigh these values against each other. This is the big picture that you should keep in mind even amid the fine details of Rule 23.

d. *The Opt-Out Class Action: Rule 23(b)(3)*

The final form of class action provides for class certification when two elements are satisfied: "the questions of law or fact common to class members predominate over any questions affecting only individual members," and "a class action is superior to other available methods for fairly and efficiently adjudicating the controversy." To explicate these elements of "predominance" and "superiority," Rule 23(b)(3) lists four factors:

- "(A) the class members' interests in individually controlling the prosecution or defense of separate actions;
- "(B) the extent and nature of any litigation concerning the controversy already begun by or against class members;
- "(C) the desirability or undesirability of concentrating the litigation of the claims in the particular forum; and
- "(D) the likely difficulties in managing a class action."

Most of these factors address the "superiority" question. Only (A) and (B) have arguable bearing on the "predominance" issue.[413]

Thus, in a (b)(3) class, the class members are united principally by the efficiency that class treatment promises in relation to individual or other forms of aggregate litigation. The drafters of the 1966 amendment to Rule 23 thought that this efficiency was a sufficient basis for class treatment. Their choice has been debated in the crucible of litigation and academic commentary ever since.

The principal reason for the controversy surrounding the (b)(3) class is a simple fact: it is the only class action likely to result in the recovery of money. And money is at the heart of what makes class actions both powerful and controversial. Given that many people never sue—especially in negative-value cases but even in cases of large value—a class action seeking monetary recovery on behalf of an entire class of victims creates a more realistic threat of full enforcement than individual suits. In negative-value cases, it also creates litigation where, by definition, none would have existed

---

[413] In theory, a court could determine compliance with Rule 23(b)(3) by examining "predominance" and "superiority" but not the four (A)–(D) factors. Or a court could analyze compliance by applying only the four factors. Or a court could use a "belt and suspenders" approach and analyze both the "predominance" and "superiority" elements and the four factors. All of these approaches can be found in different judicial opinions.

otherwise. In positive-value cases, it removes from each individual the right to control his or her litigation. The threat of a substantial damage award can lead defendants to settle cases—possibly even cases that lack substantial merit—rather than roll the dice at trial. A large pot of money also creates the concern that class counsel will look after its own financial interests rather than the interests of the class, and that the interests of some class members may receive greater weight than the interests of others in pursuing claims and distributing relief.

In short, both the hopes and the fears of aggregating large numbers of claims in a single proceeding are on full display in the (b)(3) class action.

These hopes and fears—especially the fears—have shaped the interpretation of Rule 23(b)(3). To begin, the "predominance" element has an evident connection to the "commonality" element of Rule 23(a)(2). While Rule 23(a)(2) requires common questions of law or fact, Rule 23(b)(3) requires that these questions predominate. After *Wal-Mart Stores, Inc. v. Dukes*,[414] the (a)(2) common questions must provide common answers that drive the litigation forward. So what more does "predominance" add to the picture?

This is an important question, asked by (among others) Justice Ginsburg in her *Wal-Mart* dissent. The Supreme Court has addressed Rule 23(b)(3)'s predominance requirement only three times, once before *Wal-Mart* and twice since. In *Amchem Products, Inc. v. Windsor*,[415] a settlement tried to resolve the claims of asbestos victims who had not yet filed suit, including many who had not yet been injured. The class was certified as a (b)(3) opt-out class action. More than 80,000 class members opted out.[416] Many who remained attacked the settlement on fairness grounds and also challenged certification of the class on numerous grounds.

As we previously saw, *Amchem* overturned class certification in part because of the conflicting interests among class members made their representation in a single class inadequate under Rule 23(a)(4). Before it reached the (a)(4) ground, however, the Court noted an even more fundamental flaw: the questions common to the class did not predominate. Certainly some common questions existed: for instance, whether asbestos was a defective product, what asbestos companies knew of the dangers of asbestos (and when they knew it),

---

[414] 564 U.S. 338 (2011). For a discussion of *Wal-Mart*'s (a)(2) holding, see *supra* notes 332–334 and accompanying text).

[415] 521 U.S. 591 (1997) (also discussed *supra* notes 355–361, *infra* note 487 and accompanying text).

[416] The number of opt-outs reached almost 250,000, but the district court determined that many of these opt-outs had not been exercised by the class members personally, and were therefore ineffective.

and the disease processes that asbestos could trigger. The district court also relied on two other commonalities: the members' shared experience of asbestos exposure and their common interest in receiving prompt and fair recoveries with a minimum of expense. The settling parties also argued that the fairness of the settlement was a predominating question.

The Court began by rejecting the argument that common interests regarding settlement count in the "predominance" analysis; rather, predominance requires examination of "the legal and factual inquiries that qualify each class member's case as a genuine controversy, questions that preexist any settlement." With regard to those factual and legal questions, the Court noted that the shared experience of asbestos exposure may have satisfied the (a)(2) commonality requirement, but the (b)(3) predominance requirement "is far more demanding." The Court pointed to "the greater number of questions peculiar to the several categories of class members, and to individuals within each category, and the significance of those uncommon questions" to argue that "any overarching dispute about the health consequences of asbestos exposure cannot satisfy the Rule 23(b)(3) predominance standard." Quoting from the court of appeals' decision, the Court then went on to mention specific factual variations that defeated predominance, including different exposures to asbestos for different lengths of time, different injuries, different smoking histories, and different medical expenses and future medical needs. It then noted how "[d]ifferences in state law . . . compound these disparities." In the end, the Court thought that the class was simply too "sprawling"—it later also used the phrase "unselfconscious and amorphous"—to meet the (b)(3) requirement.

In the process of discussing Rule 23, *Amchem* also expressed some doubt about the utility of Rule 23(b)(3) as a vehicle for aggregating mass torts. Although the Court did not entirely prohibit (b)(3) certification in "cases in which individual damages run high," it indicated that the principal reason for (b)(3) classes is the negative-value case. In tort cases like those in *Amchem*, each plaintiff had a significant interest in making and controlling critical litigation decisions.

The Court's second significant examination of Rule 23(b)(3)'s predominance requirement was *Amgen Inc. v. Connecticut Retirement Plans & Trust Funds*,[417] a securities-fraud class action seeking monetary recovery. A typical requirement for any fraud claim is proof of reliance: the allegedly defrauded victim must rely on the defendant's fraudulent, material misrepresentations. Because reliance is an individual issue, it appears to work against class

[417] 568 U.S. 455 (2013).

certification. In a prior decision, *Basic Inc. v. Levinson*,[418] however, a plurality of the Supreme Court had erected a presumption: that the price of a security in an open, efficient market reflects all publicly available information concerning the security, so that reliance on a material misrepresentation regarding a security could be presumed. In effect, this presumption eliminated proof of individual reliance, and replaced it with proof of a class-wide nature, including the existence of a public misrepresentation and the efficiency of the market. Without the presumption, many (b)(3) class actions for securities fraud would be difficult to maintain; and without a class action, many small-stakes securities investors would have little to no incentive to prosecute their claims for securities fraud.

In *Amgen*, the defendant argued that, in order to obtain class certification, the plaintiffs were required to prove that the misrepresentations were material. Its argument was that only material misrepresentations affected the price of the stock; therefore, to obtain the *Basic* presumption, materiality needed to be shown. A majority of the Court disagreed, noting that "the office of a Rule 23(b)(3) certification ruling is not to adjudicate the case; rather, it is to select the 'metho[d]' best suited to adjudication of the controversy 'fairly and efficiently.' " Thus, "the focus of Rule 23(b)(3) is on the predominance of common *questions*."

The issue of materiality, the Court held, was common to the class; if the misrepresentations were material, then the class was one step closer to winning its case; if the misrepresentations were immaterial, then the class lost the case. Because "materiality" was an objective rather than subjective inquiry, the relevant evidence regarding materiality was common to the class.

Amgen is principally a case about how rigorously a court must analyze the complaint's allegations to rule on class certification. The answer is not too rigorously, as long as any answer that the case yields is one that applies class-wide and thus advances the resolution of the case. In the process of resolving this issue, *Amgen* also had important things to say about the scope of Rule 23(b)(3)'s predominance requirement; but it was not a detailed discussion of what makes, or breaks, predominance.

The same is true of the third (b)(3) case, *Comcast Corp. v. Behrend*.[419] *Comcast* involved antitrust allegations against a cable company. The plaintiffs argued that (b)(3) certification was appropriate on four separate claims. To demonstrate that the class questions predominated, the plaintiffs provided an expert witness who created a regression model through which damages due to the

---

[418] 485 U.S. 224 (1988).

[419] 569 U.S. 27 (2013).

four alleged violations could be measured on a class-wide basis. The district court certified the class on only one of the four antitrust theories, and the court of appeals affirmed.

The Supreme Court reversed. After describing the "rigorous analysis" conducted for the Rule 23(a) requirements,[420] the Court noted that "[t]he same analytical principles govern Rule 23(b). If anything, Rule 23(b)(3)'s predominance criterion is even more demanding than Rule 23(a)." Looking into the plaintiffs' theory, the court found a mismatch between the theory of class-wide liability (limited to one allegation only) and the damages model (which assumed four violations of the law). Because "a model purporting to serve as evidence of damages in this class action must measure only those damages attributable to that theory," the plaintiffs failed to demonstrate that damages were measurable on a class-wide basis for the only viable class-wide legal theory. Thus, an apparent commonality on which the district court based its predominance holding did not exist. The majority's decision was narrow. It did not hold that the plaintiffs could never meet the predominance element, only that, "[w]ithout presenting another methodology, respondents cannot show Rule 23(b)(3) predominance: Questions of individual damage calculations will inevitably overwhelm questions common to the class." This statement raises an important question: whether an adequate means of proving class-wide damages is essential to (b)(3) certification, or whether a (b)(3) class can be certified on the strength of predominant liability issues alone.[421]

The Supreme Court has had far less—in fact, next to nothing—to say about the second (b)(3) element: superiority.[422] On the plain reading of the language, a plaintiff must demonstrate that all other methods of aggregation that we have considered in this book—joinder mechanisms; consolidation, transfer (in particular MDL treatment); anti-suit injunctions; and preclusion—will not adjudicate the controversy as fairly and efficiently as a class action. All the strengths and weaknesses that we have examined for each device

---

[420] On the need for rigorous analysis of the Rule 23(a) elements, see *supra* notes 306–309 and accompanying text.

[421] The methodology of the plaintiffs' expert was controversial, and the defendant argued that the opinion was inadmissible. When the Supreme Court granted certiorari in *Comcast*, it framed the question presented in a manner suggesting that it wished to decide the standard of reliability for expert testimony on class-certification motions. Given *Comcast*'s resolution of the case, this issue remains an open, and important, question.

[422] The Court's only discussion of superiority occurred in *Amchem Products, Inc. v. Windsor*, 521 U.S. 591 (1997). There the Court made a single reference to superiority in the particular context of a settlement class action. *See infra* note 487 and accompanying text.

bear on the question of certification under Rule 23(b)(3); if any mechanism is better, (b)(3) certification must be denied.

But superiority has often been understood to mean both more and less than the text suggests. On the one hand, some courts compare a class action not only to other litigation alternatives, but also to non-litigation alternatives, such as arbitration or a private compensation scheme run by the defendant. Other courts, seizing on Rule 23(b)(3)'s requirement that a class action be a superior means for "adjudicating the controversy," permit comparison only to other litigation alternatives.[423]

Of course, conducting a comparison of costs and benefits (whether just to litigation alternatives or to a broader array of ways to resolve the dispute) is difficult, if not impossible, due to the lack of certainty about the building blocks from which an accurate comparison can be constructed: likelihood of outcome, amount of recovery under various alternatives, litigation expenses, and so on. As a result, some courts have substituted for a true superiority analysis an analysis of the four factors in Rule 23(b)(3)(A)-(D), with a special emphasis on the final factor of manageability.

Courts adopting this approach often come to conflicting results on the same patterns of facts. For instance, some courts ignore the size of the potential recovery in deciding whether individual class members have an interest in individual control of their litigation (the Rule 23(b)(3)(A) factor); others limit class actions to cases in which the individual recovery would be small—but even here they often disagree about how small a "small" recovery should be. Some courts consider the wealth of class members (and thus their ability to afford individual litigation); others do not. Some courts consider the variability in the size of potential awards as a relevant consideration; others do not.[424]

In most courts that examine superiority through the lens of the (A)-(D) factors, the ultimate determination whether a class action is superior devolves into the question whether a class action is manageable.[425] "Manageability," of course, is quite a different inquiry

---

423 *Compare In re* ConAgra Peanut Butter Prods. Liab. Litig., 251 F.R.D. 689 (N.D. Ga. 2008) (finding a refund program superior to class treatment), *with In re* Hannaford Bros. Co. Customer Data Sec. Breach Litig., 293 F.R.D. 21 (D. Me. 2013) (finding comparison to a private program precluded by the text of Rule 23(b)(3)).

424 For a critique of the ways in which courts have inconsistently applied the factors bearing on superiority, see Christine P. Bartholomew, *The Failed Superiority Experiment*, 69 VAND. L. REV. 1295 (2016).

425 *See* Six (6) Mexican Workers v. Ariz. Citrus Growers, 904 F.2d 1301 (9th Cir. 1990) (upholding certification after examining only issues of manageability); *cf.* Newton v. Merrill Lynch, Pierce, Fenner & Smith, Inc., 259 F.3d 154, 191 (3d Cir. 2001) (stating that a class action must be the "best" method for resolving the dispute, but in fact analyzing superiority almost exclusively in terms of the class action's

than superiority; a class action can be manageable even if it is not the best means for resolving a case.

Courts have tended to blend the predominance and superiority requirements into some presumptive rules:

- Issues of individual reliance usually bar certification.[426]
- A class action involving the application of numerous and varying state laws usually fails on (b)(3) grounds.[427]
- A mass-tort case that is immature is not suitable for (b)(3) certification.[428]
- A case in which the size of the potential liability might present a "bet the company" catastrophe for the defendant raises red flags that make (b)(3) certification unlikely.[429]
- Individualized defenses that can be asserted against class members may result in a denial of certification, but not in all circumstances.[430]
- Differing damages calculations for class members do not, merely because of that fact, take the case beyond the bounds of Rule 23(b)(3), especially when damages

---

manageability); Romero v. Producers Dairy Foods, Inc., 235 F.R.D. 474, 491 (E.D. Cal. 2006) ("Whether a case is manageable as a class action can be an overriding consideration in determining superiority.") (internal quotation marks omitted).

426 *See* Castano v. Am. Tobacco Co., 84 F.3d 734 (5th Cir. 1996) ("[A] fraud action cannot be certified when individual reliance will be an issue."); *but see* Klay v. Humana, Inc., 382 F.3d 1241 (11th Cir. 2004) (upholding certification when reliance was evident and could be proven by common evidence).

427 *See Castano*, 84 F.3d 734; *Klay*, 382 F.3d 1241. But "[v]ariations in state law do not necessarily preclude a 23(b)(3) action," especially when some class members "possess slightly differing remedies based on state statute or common law" but "sufficient common issues to warrant a class action" exist. *See* Hanlon v. Chrysler Corp., 150 F.3d 1011 (9th Cir. 1998); *accord, In re* Hyundai & Kia Fuel Econ. Litig., 881 F.3d 679 (9th Cir. 2018); Sullivan v. DB Invs., Inc., 667 F.3d 273 (3d Cir. 2011) (en banc) ("[V]ariations in the rights and remedies available to injured class members under the various laws of the fifty states [do] not defeat commonality and predominance.") (internal quotation marks omitted; alteration in original).

428 *See Castano*, 84 F.3d 734; *Newton*, 259 F.3d 154; *cf.* Pella Corp. v. Saltzman, 606 F.3d 391 (7th Cir. 2010) (noting the "the risk of error in having complex issues that have enormous consequences decided by one trier of fact rather than letting a consensus emerge from multiple trials").

429 *See* Szabo v. Bridgeport Machs., Inc., 249 F.3d 672 (7th Cir. 2001); *In re* Rhone-Poulenc Rorer, Inc., 51 F.3d 1293 (7th Cir. 1995).

430 *Compare* Lusardi v. Lechner, 855 F.2d 1062 (3d Cir. 1988) (questioning whether (b)(3) certification is proper given individual defenses), *with* Smilow v. Sw. Bell Mobile Sys., Inc., 323 F.3d 32 (1st Cir. 2003) ("Courts traditionally have been reluctant to deny class action status under Rule 23(b)(3) simply because affirmative defenses may be available against individual members.").

are easily calculable; but great difficulties in individual proof of damages, when joined with other individual issues, can trip up class certification.[431]

- Statutory damages that far exceed actual damages (say, a statutory damages of $100 per violation in a case involving one million credit-card customers whose actual damages are perhaps only pennies) may lead some courts to deny certification under Rule 23(b)(3).[432]

In addition, a number of courts examine the ascertainability issue, which we previously examined as an aspect of the Rule 23(a) prerequisites,[433] as a matter of manageability and superiority.

These default rules combine to make certain types of cases very difficult to bring. Mass-tort class actions, already on life support after *Amchem*'s skeptical attitude, will almost never pass through the gauntlet of default rules. RICO claims, which often require proof of individual reliance, are also difficult to certify. Nationwide class actions involving state-law claims are highly suspect. On the other hand, smaller class actions involving states whose laws are identical may pass muster. Likewise, securities-fraud, antitrust, and consumer-protection cases, which involve small losses for most victims, may still be susceptible to (b)(3) treatment.[434]

---

431 *Compare* McLaughlin v. Am. Tobacco Co., 522 F.3d 215 (2d Cir. 2008) (rejecting class certification in part because plaintiffs' method for calculating damages on a class-wide basis was impermissible), *abrogated on other grounds by* Bridge v. Phx. Bond & Indem. Co., 553 U.S. 639 (2008), *with Smilow*, 323 F.3d 32 ("The individuation of damages in consumer class actions is rarely determinative under Rule 23(b)(3).").

432 *Compare* Bateman v. Am. Multi-Cinema, Inc., 623 F.3d 708 (9th Cir. 2010) (holding that such a class action, involving $29 million to $290 million in statutory damages and little actual damage, can be certified), *with* Ratner v. Chem. Bank N.Y. Trust Co., 54 F.R.D. 412 (S.D.N.Y. 1972) (denying certification of a statutory-damages class due to a lack of superiority).

433 *See supra* Chapter 6.B.1.a.

434 This is not to say that such cases are automatically certifiable. *See In re* Hydrogen Peroxide Antitrust Litig., 552 F.3d 305 (3d Cir. 2008) (vacating class certification in antitrust case); *In re* Initial Pub. Offerings Sec. Litig., 471 F.3d 24 (2d Cir. 2006), *clarified on reh'g*, 483 F.3d 70 (2d Cir. 2007) (vacating class certification in securities-fraud case).

Still, it is important to note the attitudinal shift about (b)(3) class actions. Nearly every major Supreme Court decision has failed to support a (b)(3) class (whether rejecting certification on a Rule 23(a) ground or a Rule 23(b)(3) ground). Benchmark decisions in the lower courts have, during the past twenty-odd years, almost uniformly been negative about the adventurous use of Rule 23(b)(3) to recover damages on behalf of large numbers of victims.[435] For reasons that we explain in more detail in Chapter Seven, consumer-protection class actions are increasingly rare due to the presence of pre-dispute arbitration agreements. The field of operation for Rule 23(b)(3) is shrinking.[436] Rule 23(b)(3) is far from a dead letter, but any portrait of Rule 23(b)(3) as a behemoth running amok is surely overdrawn.

Problem 6

Consumers alleged that their cell-phone carrier charged them for incoming calls in violation of their service agreements. They sought to represent a class of similar consumers for state-law breach-of-contract and consumer-protection claims. Individual damages varied, but the plaintiffs' expert said that he could develop a computer program to determine which consumers were subject to overcharges and the amount of the overcharges. The consumer-protection claim allowed for the assertion of either actual or a minimum amount of statutory damages. The defendant claimed that variations in damage calculations predominated over common issues. Should a (b)(3) class be certified? *See* Smilow v. Sw. Bell Mobile Sys., Inc., 323 F.3d 32 (1st Cir. 2003).

The consequence of that fact is that courts and lawyers must look elsewhere when they believe that mass litigation requires aggregate treatment. A principal cause of the rise in size and influence of the MDL process has been the decline of the (b)(3) class action. Most other aggregation mechanisms have substantial limits—including a near-universal inability to handle the problem of future plaintiffs. None of the devices builds in the protections of the (b)(3) class for the victims swept into an aggregate proceeding: an assurance of fair and efficient treatment, an assurance of adequate representation, or the right to opt out.[437] Shrinking the scope of (b)(3) class actions also shrinks the scope of protections in aggregate litigation.

---

[435] Among the landmark decisions, which we have cited in prior notes, are *Rhone-Poulenc*, *Castano*, *Initial Public Offerings*, and *Hydrogen Peroxide*.

[436] *See* Robert H. Klonoff, *The Decline of Class Actions*, 90 WASH. U. L. REV. 729 (2013) ("The class action device, once considered a 'revolutionary' vehicle for achieving mass justice, has fallen into disfavor.")

[437] There have been efforts to import some of the class-action protections into other aggregate litigation. *See, e.g.*, PRINCIPLES OF AGGREGATE LITIGATION (AM. L. INST. 2010).

The prior paragraph is not intended to argue that Rule 23(b)(3) must be used more broadly. Class actions, especially (b)(3) class actions, raise serious questions even as they promise substantial benefits. Among the considerations that you should evaluate, as you think about the role that Rule 23(b)(3) should play in a system of aggregate litigation, is the basic question of superiority. Limiting the scope of Rule 23 will not make the problem of aggregate litigation go away; it limits the availability of one option for addressing the problem. Limits on Rule 23 increase reliance on other aggregation methods that may, or may not, be better ways to handle the dispute.

C. Jurisdictional Issues Regarding Class Actions

Until now, we have assumed that a federal court has both territorial and subject-matter jurisdiction over a class action. In this section, we see how considerations of territorial jurisdiction limit both state and federal courts, and how rules of subject-matter jurisdiction constrain the federal courts.

1. Territorial Jurisdiction

Neither Rule 23 nor any federal statute provides a general territorial-jurisdiction rule for class action. Two types of concerns arise. The first is jurisdiction over absent class members. The second is jurisdiction over defendants.

a. Territorial Jurisdiction over Plaintiffs

A unique territorial-jurisdiction question created by class actions is the scope of the court's jurisdiction over plaintiffs—in particular, over absent class members with no minimum contacts or connections with the class-action forum. This question of jurisdiction over plaintiffs is unique to class actions. With permissive joinder rules such as Rule 20 or Rule 24, the voluntary action of a plaintiff in entering a case creates consent to the court's jurisdiction over that plaintiff. With class actions, however, only a blithe lover of legal fictions could conclude that absent class members have consented to the forum's jurisdiction. Given that the forum court will determine the rights of class members, it does not seem unreasonable to expect some connection between class members and the forum. Without this connection, a judgment determining a class member's claims would be invalid as to that class member, just as a judgment entered against a defendant over whom the court has no jurisdiction is invalid with respect to that defendant.

This question will not arise in every case. If a class action filed in a state or federal court in California includes only citizens of California, then the connection between the class members and the court is evident. But many class actions include class members from states other than the forum state. Under what circumstances can a court in the forum state exercise jurisdiction over their claims?

The Supreme Court addressed this issue in *Phillips Petroleum Co. v. Shutts*,[438] a case that has cast its long shadow over the law of class actions ever since. *Shutts* involved a Kansas state-court class that was certified under an opt-out rule equivalent to Rule 23(b)(3). The defendant in *Shutts* had allegedly failed to make appropriate royalty payments to 33,000 owners of natural-gas leases. The class was nationwide in scope; only about 1,000 of the class members were citizens of Kansas. Approximately 5,000 class members either opted out of the class or were otherwise excluded from it, meaning that most of the remaining 28,000 members were citizens of other states (principally Oklahoma, Texas, and Louisiana). Most of these "absent class members" (a term of art referring to class members not citizens of the forum state) had no contacts with Kansas.

The defendant contended that the Kansas state court could not constitutionally exercise jurisdiction over the non-resident class members unless they affirmatively consented to the court's jurisdiction by opting into the case. The United States Supreme Court rejected the idea that absent class members must consent to jurisdiction by opting into the class. Instead, the Court held that providing an opt-out right (accompanied by constitutionally adequate notice advising them of this right) satisfied due process. The Court thought that the contexts of territorial jurisdiction over defendants and territorial jurisdiction over plaintiffs were sufficiently distinct to justify an opt-out rule for class members. Unlike a defendant, who faced the power of a state's judicial system alone, class members were constitutionally entitled to adequate representation at all times. Moreover, the class members had no obligation to defend or prosecute the case with their own resources or to incur expenses in a distant forum. The district court was also obliged to watch over the class members' interests and not to approve unreasonable settlements. Because the Kansas class-action rule afforded these procedural protections for absent class members, the Supreme Court held that the Kansas court had properly exercised jurisdiction over all absent class members.

Shutts is an 800-pound gorilla in the law of aggregation. The reason is not so much what *Shutts* holds on its facts of the case. Holding that an opt-out right is constitutionally required in a class action that already afforded an opt-out right is no great matter. As we have seen, however, not all class actions have opt-out rights; (b)(1)(A), (b)(1)(B), and (b)(2) class actions are mandatory. None of the other techniques that we explored to aggregate litigation—such

---

[438] 472 U.S. 797 (1985).

as MDL treatment, anti-suit injunctions, or preclusion—has an opt-out right. If *Shutts* means that all aggregation devices must afford an opt-out right to plaintiffs that have no minimum contacts with the forum, then mandatory nationwide class actions or other mandatory aggregations are a thing of the past. Aside from the expense that the requisite notice would entail, an opt-out right in (b)(1) and (b)(2) cases would almost certainly mean that some class members will opt out and commence litigation in other forums—even though the (b)(1) and (b)(2) class actions were designed to avoid the evils of multiple litigation. The mandatory class action's potential for single-forum aggregation would vanish. The same story could be told about other aggregation mechanisms.[439]

Shutts recognized the concern, but studiously avoided an answer. In its famous footnote 3, the Court stated that its "holding today is limited to those class actions which seek to bind known plaintiffs concerning claims wholly or predominately for money judgments. We intimate no view concerning other types of class actions, such as those seeking equitable relief."

The Supreme Court twice granted certiorari to decide whether the Due Process Clause requires an opt-out right in mandatory class actions. Each time the Court dismissed the writ as improvidently granted.[440] *Ortiz v. Fibreboard Corp.*[441] also presented the issue. Recall that *Ortiz* held that the case did not meet the conditions for certification under Rule 23(b)(1)(B). In the process, it made a cryptic and perhaps telling reference to *Shutts*, noting that "[t]he inherent tension between representative suits and the day-in-court ideal is only magnified if applied to damage claims gathered in a mandatory class." The Court also made reference to *Shutts* in its (b)(2) analysis in *Wal-Mart Stores, Inc. v. Dukes*,[442] arguing that one reason no monetary relief could be awarded in a (b)(2) class action was the

[439] For instance, the Third Circuit has held that a court cannot issue an anti-suit injunction preventing plaintiffs over whom it has no territorial jurisdiction from commencing litigation elsewhere. *Shutts* served as the backbone for its argument. *See In re* Gen. Motors Corp. Pick-Up Truck Fuel Tank Prods. Liab. Litig., 134 F.3d 133 (3d Cir. 1998); *but see In re* Bridgestone/Firestone, Inc., Tires Prods. Liab. Litig., 333 F.3d 763 (7th Cir. 2003) (arguing that *Shutts* did not apply to an anti-suit injunction in a case involving violations of RICO, which permits nationwide service of process). On the other hand, MDL transferee courts have generally found that *Shutts* does not bar their assertion of power over the claims of plaintiffs whose cases are transferred to a transferee court. *See* Howard v. Sulzer Orthopedics, Inc., 382 F. App'x 436 (6th Cir. 2010).

[440] Ticor Title Ins. Co. v. Brown, 511 U.S. 117 (1994); Adams v. Robertson, 520 U.S. 83 (1997). It also ducked the *Shutts* issue in an anti-suit injunction case. *See* Smith v. Bayer Corp., 564 U.S. 299 (2011).

[441] 527 U.S. 815 (1999) (discussed *supra* notes 396–401 and accompanying text, *infra* notes 488–490 and accompanying text).

[442] 564 U.S. 338 (2010) (discussed *supra* notes 308, 332–334, 408–412 and accompanying text).

"serious possibility" that such an award would run afoul of the opt-out right that *Shutts* required. Thus, the shadow of *Shutts* loomed over *Ortiz* and *Wal-Mart*, leading the Court to construe Rules 23(b)(1)(B) and 23(b)(2) narrowly to avoid constitutional concerns.

Lower courts have taken a number of stabs at dealing with the *Shutts* problem. The usual reading of footnote 3 is that *Shutts* requires no opt-out right in mandatory class actions seeking only injunctive relief, thus avoiding the need to provide notice and an opt-out right for injunctive class actions.[443] With respect to monetary relief requested in a mandatory class action, a number of responses to *Shutts* have been assayed. One approach has been to argue that the *Shutts* applies only to state-court class actions, on the theory that federal courts possess jurisdiction over class members as long as they have minimum contacts with the United States as a whole.[444] That approach seems inconsistent with *Ortiz* and *Wal-Mart*, both of which were filed in federal court.

Courts also tried to circumvent *Shutts* by holding that the opt-out requirement did not apply to mandatory class actions in which claims for injunctive relief predominated over claims for monetary relief, but that rationale has been overtaken by *Wal-Mart*, which denied certification of mandatory (b)(2) classes for all (or nearly all) claims seeking monetary relief.[445] A different tack is to argue that objectors who appeared in the district court to contest the merits of the settlement, and not just the court's jurisdiction, consented to the court's jurisdiction over them.[446]

Shutts contains another ambiguity. The class members in *Shutts* for whom an opt-out right was constitutionally required had no minimum contacts with Kansas. It was uncertain whether *Shutts* required that an opt-out right be extended only to out-of-state citizens with no minimum contacts with the forum, or whether the

---

443 *Cf. In re* Integra Realty Res., Inc., 354 F.3d 1246 (10th Cir. 2004) (not applying *Shutts* in a (b)(1)(B) defendant class action because recovery of fraudulently transferred money did not seek monetary relief).

444 *See id.* (noting that the scope of *Shutts* "remains open as to class actions in *federal* court"); Ahearn v. Fibreboard Corp., Civ. A. No. 6:93cv526, 1995 U.S. Dist. LEXIS 11523 (E.D. Tex. July 27, 1995); 7AA CHARLES A. WRIGHT ET AL., FEDERAL PRACTICE AND PROCEDURE § 1789.1 (3d ed. 2005) (raising issue); *but see* Arthur R. Miller & David Crump, *Jurisdiction and Choice of Law in Multistate Class Actions After* Phillips Petroleum v. Shutts, 96 YALE L.J. 1 (1986) (arguing that *Shutts* applies in federal court). If *Shutts* did not apply in federal court, federal court possesses yet another advantage over state courts as an aggregation forum.

445 White v. Nat'l Football League, 822 F. Supp. 1389 (D. Minn. 1993), *aff'd* 41 F.3d 402 (8th Cir. 1994).

446 White v. Nat'l Football League, 41 F.3d 402 (8th Cir. 1994); *cf. In re* Real Estate Title & Settlement Servs. Antitrust Litig., 869 F.2d 760 (3d Cir. 1989) (holding that court did not have jurisdiction over a class member whose appearance contested only jurisdiction).

opt-out right also extended to claims for monetary relief brought by those over whom Kansas had minimum contacts. If opt-out rights must be afforded to all class members, then the ability to craft single-state mandatory class actions for monetary recovery in states that interpret their class-action rule more liberally than *Ortiz* and *Wal-Mart* interpret Rule 23 is hampered. Although the tenor of *Shutts* and the Court's later discussions in *Ortiz* and *Wal-Mart* seem to suggest that no opt-out right need be afforded to class members possessing minimum contacts with the forum, there is enough loose language in *Shutts* to support the latter view.[447]

Shutts contains a final ambiguity. In *Shutts*, all class members were known and received individual notice of their right to opt out. In some cases, individual notice to all class members is impossible. Whether *Shutts* precludes a court from exercising jurisdiction over class members who neither have minimum contacts with the forum nor receive actual notice of their right to opt out is unclear. Thus far, however, courts have not been impressed by the argument.[448]

> *Problem 7*
>
> A court certifies a limited-fund class action case meeting the three criteria of *Ortiz v. Fibreboard Corp.* under Rule 23(b)(1)(B). The fund is deposited into the court, and the court will be required to distribute the money to class members, some of whom have no contacts with the forum federal court. Does *Shutts* require that the class members be given a right to opt out? *See* Juris v. Inamed Corp., 685 F.3d 1294 (11th Cir. 2012).

It is a slight—but only a slight—exaggeration to say that the fate of mandatory class actions—and perhaps all mandatory aggregation—hinges on the uncertain scope of *Shutts*. If *Shutts* affects only state courts, then federal courts enjoy a significant aggregation advantage. If it affects only state-law claims, then asserting federal-question claims is the key to mandatory aggregation. If *Shutts* requires that an opt-out right be extended to all plaintiffs swept up in any form of mandatory aggregation, then mandatory aggregation is impossible in widely dispersed litigation. Whatever the ultimate answer on the scope of *Shutts*, its holding has twice led the Supreme Court to interpret the scope of mandatory class actions narrowly. Because the shape of the

---

447 *Compare* Grimes v. Vitalink Commc'ns Corp., 17 F.3d 1553 (3d Cir. 1994) (stating that a court can "bind absent class members who had sufficient minimum contacts with the forum" even in the absence of an opt-out provision), *with* Patricia A. Solomon, Note, *Are Mandatory Class Actions Constitutional?*, 72 NOTRE DAME L. REV. 1627 (1997) (suggesting that opt-out rights must be afforded to all members of an opt-out class).

448 *See In re* "Agent Orange" Prod. Liab. Litig. MDL No. 381, 818 F.2d 145 (2d Cir. 1987) (holding that *Shutts* does not require individual notice); *In re* "Agent Orange" Prod. Liab. Litig., 996 F.2d 1425 (2d Cir. 1993) (same).

class action has a spillover effect on the rest of the law of aggregation, *Shutts* casts a long shadow indeed.

b. Territorial Jurisdiction over Defendants

The usual rules of territorial jurisdiction over defendants apply to defendants in class actions.[449] Class actions, whether filed in state or federal court, require a standard basis of jurisdiction—general, specific, presence, or consent—over each defendant. Federal class actions do not establish nationwide service of process, unless the underlying theory of liability (say, a RICO or Sherman Act violation) permits it. Thus, a class action's capacity to attain a single resolution of all disputes against all defendants is subject to the same constraints as other forms of aggregate litigation.

But a few twists on this principle exist. For instance, suppose that the defendant's activities with respect to the claims of the named representatives establishes specific jurisdiction over the defendant for those claims. But the class action is nationwide, and the activities of the defendant in the forum state have no connection to the claims of some of the class members. Recall the United States Supreme Court's decision in *Bristol-Myers Squibb Co. v. Superior Court of California*,[450] in which a non-class mass tort in state court joined together the claims of more than 600 people who alleged injuries from the defendant's prescription drug, Plavix. The defendant engaged in plenty of activity in the forum state (California): it employed 160 people in research and development and 250 sales representatives in the state, sold 187 million Plavix pills, and made $900 million in sales within the state. Nonetheless, with respect to the lawsuits of the plaintiffs who had not purchased or been prescribed Plavix in California, a California court could not exercise personal jurisdiction over the defendant.

Carried over to the nationwide class-action context, *Bristol-Myers Squibb* could signal a problem. Even if there exists jurisdiction over the defendant with respect to the claims of class members whose claims involve forum-related minimum contacts, does jurisdiction exist over the defendant with respect to class members' claims that are unrelated to the forum? Before *Bristol-Myers Squibb*, courts usually held that personal jurisdiction was determined with reference to the claims of the named representatives, and exercised a kind of "pendent personal jurisdiction" over the claims of class members. In her dissent in *Bristol-Myers Squibb*, Justice Sotomayor noted that the decision did not "confront the question whether its opinion here would also apply to a class action in which a plaintiff

---

449 For a summary of these rules, see *supra* Chapter 1.C.3.

450 582 U.S. ___, 137 S. Ct. 1773 (2017) (discussed *supra* note 29 and accompanying text).

injured in the forum State seeks to represent a nationwide class of plaintiffs, not all of whom were injured there." The opinions in the early post-*Bristol-Myers Squibb* world have split, with some cases confining *Bristol-Myers Squibb* to non-class mass torts and a somewhat larger number arguing that the decision applies equally to mass torts and class actions.[451] Following up on a line in the *Bristol-Myers Squibb* majority opinion that the decision may not apply in federal court,[452] one district court has held it can exercise personal jurisdiction over a defendant with respect to the claims of out-of-state class members when (a) the defendant had waived its jurisdictional objection for other out-of-state class members, (b) the case presented one federal-question claim, (c) litigation in the forum state imposed no burden on the defendant, and (d) judicial economy was advanced.[453]

The final word has yet to be written on this potentially important limit on nationwide class actions. Plaintiffs can sidestep the problem by suing in a state that can assert jurisdiction over the defendant (for example, the state of the defendant's citizenship or the state in which the defendant engaged in the activity causing nationwide injury). But this solution may not achieve single-forum aggregation if multiple defendants are involved.

2. Subject-Matter Jurisdiction

For cases arising under federal-question jurisdiction, the rules of subject-matter jurisdiction are the same regardless of whether the case involves a single plaintiff or a class action. As long as a claim arising under federal law appears on the face of the well-pleaded class complaint, subject-matter jurisdiction is present.[454]

---

[451] *Compare In re* Chinese-Manufactured Drywall Prods. Liab. Litig., MDL No. 09–2047, 2017 WL 5971622 (E.D. La. Nov. 30, 2017) (finding personal jurisdiction over the defendant in each set of MDL cases, but also noting that the rules regarding class actions are different from those regarding mass actions because of the additional due-process protections applied to class actions), *with In re* Dental Supplies Antitrust Litig., 16 Civ. 696 (BMC)(GRB), 2017 WL 4217115 (E.D.N.Y. Sept. 20, 2017) ("The constitutional requirements of due process does not wax and wane when the complaint is individual or on behalf of a class. Personal jurisdiction in class actions must comport with due process just the same as any other case.").

[452] *See Bristol-Myers Squibb*, 137 S. Ct. at 1783–84 ("[S]ince our decision concerns the due process limits on the exercise of specific jurisdiction by a State, we leave open the question whether the Fifth Amendment imposes the same restrictions on the exercise of personal jurisdiction by a federal court.").

[453] *See* Sloan v. Gen. Motors LLC, No. 16–CV–07244, 2018 WL 784049 (N.D. Cal. Feb. 7, 2018).

[454] *Cf.* Blevins v. Aksut, 849 F.3d 1016 (11th Cir. 2017) (holding that the mandatory declination of jurisdiction contained in the § 1332(d), discussed *infra* notes 467–476 and accompanying text, applied to only diversity class actions and did not affect class actions asserting a federal question).

For diversity cases, however, the situation is more complicated. Recall the traditional doctrine that each plaintiff must be of diverse citizenship from each defendant, and that each plaintiff must have the requisite amount in controversy (presently, more than $75,000). Applied to class actions, this doctrine raises two critical questions: whether each class representative and each member of a class must be of diverse citizenship from any defendant, and whether each class representative and each member of the class must have more than $75,000 at stake. The answers to these questions have varied over the years.

To begin, in *Supreme Tribe of Ben-Hur v. Cauble*,[455] the Supreme Court held that diversity of citizenship was determined by comparing the citizenship of the class representatives to the citizenship of the parties opposing the class. The citizenship of unnamed class members was ignored; even if some class members had the same citizenship as some of the opposing parties, jurisdiction under § 1332 existed. This holding constitutes a modest breach of the rule of complete diversity.

On the amount-in-controversy point, however, the traditional rule did not bend. In *Snyder v. Harris*,[456] none of the 4,000 class members had a claim meeting the requisite amount in controversy, but together the class's claims exceeded $1.2 million. Following the usual rule that plaintiffs cannot aggregate jurisdictionally insufficient individual claims, *Snyder* held that subject-matter jurisdiction was lacking. Four years later, in *Zahn v. International Paper Co.*,[457] the Court addressed the situation in which some, but not all, class members had claims that met the amount-in-controversy requirement. *Zahn* held that the claim of each class member needed to be jurisdictionally sufficient; the claims of class members with insufficient claims could not be tacked onto the claims of class members with sufficient claims.

The upshot of *Ben-Hur* and *Zahn* was that the incomplete diversity of class members was ignored for purposes of § 1332, but the inadequacy of the amount of a class member's claims was not. These rules might not have been entirely consistent, but there they were. These rules gave plaintiffs room for tactical maneuvering; a plaintiff who wanted a federal forum could find a diverse class representative, while one who wanted a state forum could name a non-diverse representative. Because the amount-in-controversy requirement was a tougher hurdle, small-stakes class actions based on state law almost always fell into the state courts.

---

455 255 U.S. 356 (1921).

456 394 U.S. 332 (1969).

457 414 U.S. 291 (1973).

The passage of 28 U.S.C. § 1367 in 1990, combined with the Supreme Court's interpretation of § 1367 in *Exxon Mobil Corp. v. Allapattah Services, Inc.*,[458] overruled the result in *Zahn*. Federal jurisdiction now existed over the claims of class members with jurisdictionally insufficient claims as long as other class members had jurisdictionally sufficient claims.

For all practical purposes, *Allapattah* was a dead letter when it was decided. Earlier in 2005, responding to the perception that state-court class actions were yielding unfairly generous awards injuring American business interests, Congress enacted the Class Action Fairness Act of 2005 ("CAFA").[459] CAFA's jurisdictional provisions gave federal courts considerably more original and removal jurisdiction over class actions. It created a new § 1332(d), which is the most complex jurisdictional grant ever enacted. CAFA is premised on minimal, rather than complete, diversity: if any member of a putative class action has different citizenship from any defendant, the diversity requirement is met.[460] Likewise, CAFA altered the amount-in-controversy requirement from a per-plaintiff amount to an aggregate class amount of more than $5 million.[461]

CAFA also created removal provisions that make it easier for a class action filed in state court to be removed to federal court.[462] CAFA permitted a single defendant to remove the case (the usual rule being that all defendants must join in a petition for removal). It allowed a class action to be removed even when the case had been filed in the home state of a defendant (the usual rule being that such cases are not removable). And it allowed a case to be removed even if

---

[458] 545 U.S. 546 (2005).

[459] Pub. L. No. 109–2, 119 Stat. 4 (2005).

[460] 28 U.S.C. § 1332(d)(2)(A)-(C). CAFA defined a "class action" to be "any civil action filed under rule 23 of the Federal Rules of Civil Procedure or similar State statute or rule of judicial procedure authorizing an action to be brought by 1 or more representative persons as a class action." *Id.* § 1332(d)(1)(B); *see* Williams v. Emp'rs Mut. Cas. Co., 845 F.3d 891 (8th Cir. 2017) (holding that case was removable under CAFA when it was a representative action comparable to a class action, even though the plaintiff did not seek certification under the state's class-action rule). Under this definition, subject-matter jurisdiction attaches when the plaintiff seeks class certification. On the theory that jurisdiction is measured at the time that the case is brought into federal court, federal courts have therefore retained jurisdiction over cases removed to federal court even when the court ultimately denies class certification. *See* Cunningham Charter Corp. v. Learjet, Inc., 592 F.3d 805 (7th Cir. 2010).

[461] *Id.* § 1332(d)(2); *see* Hammond v. Stamps.com, Inc., 844 F.3d 909 (10th Cir. 2016) (holding that, to meet the amount-in-controversy requirement, it is necessary to show only that "a fact finder *might* legally conclude that damages exceed the statutory amount") (internal quotation marks omitted).

[462] CAFA also provided for the removal of non-class "mass actions," in which one hundred or more individuals propose to try their cases jointly. *See* 28 U.S.C. § 1332(d)(11). For further discussion of jurisdiction over mass actions, see *supra* notes 163, 165, 169–168 and accompanying text.

the plaintiffs first sought class treatment more than a year after filing the case in state court (the usual rule being that changes in party structure that first establish diversity jurisdiction more than one year after a case is filed in state court cannot serve as a basis for removal).

At the same time, CAFA imposes important limits on federal jurisdiction. Among the cases exempt from CAFA's provisions are:

- Diversity-based class actions with fewer than 100 members.[463]
- Diversity-based class actions against state officials or government entities when the federal court could probably not grant relief in any event.[464]
- Diversity-based class actions involving shareholder claims against a corporation's management or certain state-law claims alleging securities fraud.[465]

The most important exceptions to CAFA, however, are three provisions known as the "home-state exception," the "local-controversy" exception, and the "discretionary-jurisdiction exception." The first two exceptions are mandatory; the third, as its name implies, is a matter of judicial discretion. Taken as a group, the provisions try to respect federalism concerns by ensuring that class actions focused principally on a single state are heard in state court. The ways in which that basic intuition are worked out make the exceptions very complicated in practice.

All three exceptions involve some factual determinations, a fact that raises the issue of the burden of proof. The courts of appeals have generally held that the party invoking federal jurisdiction bears the burden of proving any facts relevant to jurisdiction, while the party seeking to invoke an exception to jurisdiction (such as the home-state exception, the local-controversy exception, or the discretionary-jurisdiction exception) has the burden of proving the exception.[466] Burden-of-proof issues tend to arise when a case is removed from state court, meaning that typically the defendant(s) seeking removal must prove minimal diversity and the amount in controversy, while the plaintiffs seeking remand must prove the factual elements of the relevant exception(s).

---

463 28 U.S.C. § 1332(d)(5)(B).

464 *Id.* § 1332(d)(5)(A).

465 *Id.* § 1332(d)(9). Federal jurisdiction over state-law securities-fraud class actions is already covered in other provisions of the United States Code.

466 *See, e.g.*, Serrano v. 180 Connect, Inc., 478 F.3d 1018 (9th Cir. 2007); Evans v. Walter Indus., Inc., 449 F.3d 1159 (11th Cir. 2006).

The home-state exception requires a federal court to decline jurisdiction when "two-thirds or more of the members of all proposed plaintiff classes in the aggregate, and the primary defendants, are citizens of the State in which the action was originally filed."[467] The goal of letting state courts adjudicate a controversy concentrated in that state is evident. But the text also contains two ambiguities. First, unless the exact size of a class and exact number of in-state class members are known, how can a court make the two-thirds calculation? Second, what makes a defendant "primary"?

On the first point, plaintiffs seeking to remain in state court can often avoid precise calculations by defining the class to include members of only one state. Otherwise, they must provide proof—perhaps using surveys or examinations of records such as addresses—of the size of the class and its citizenship.[468] On the second point, the exception requires *all* the primary defendants to be from the same state as two-thirds of the plaintiffs.[469] As for the meaning of a "primary defendant," one court of appeals has defined the phrase as "a chief defendant or chief class of defendants."[470] (You are forgiven if you find the phrase "chief defendant" no clearer than "primary defendant.") Another court of appeals has stated, perhaps more helpfully, that primary defendants are determined by a number of factors, such as whether the defendants "are directly liable to the proposed class, as opposed to being vicariously or secondarily liable based upon theories of contribution or indemnification," whether the defendants are a "real target" of the lawsuit, and whether the defendants have "potential exposure to a significant portion of the class and would sustain a substantial loss as compared to other defendants if found liable."[471]

The local-controversy exception applies to class actions in which more than two-thirds of the class are citizens of the state in which the case is filed, at least one defendant from whom "significant relief" is sought and whose "alleged conduct forms a significant basis for the claims asserted" is a citizen from the same state, and the "principal injuries resulting from the alleged conduct or any related conduct of each defendant were incurred in the State in which the action was

---

467 *Id.* § 1332(d)(4)(B).

468 *See In re* Hannaford Bros. Co. Customer Data Sec. Breach Litig., 564 F.3d 75 (1st Cir. 2009) (holding that a single-state class action fit within the home-state exception even though the case was related to class actions in the same MDL that were multi-state in nature); Dennison v. Carolina Payday Loans, Inc., 549 F.3d 941 (4th Cir. 2008) (recognizing that single-state class actions fit within the exception).

469 *See* Watson v. City of Allen, 821 F.3d 624 (5th Cir. 2016).

470 *Id.*

471 *See* Vodenichar v. Halcon Energy Props., Inc., 733 F.3d 497 (3d Cir. 2013).

originally filed."[472] The thrust of this provision is to keep disputes whose conduct, injuries, and parties are concentrated in a single state in the courts of that state. Once again, however, ambiguities arise:

- In calculating the number of in-state class members in relation to the size of the class, citizenship at the time of filing, not at the time of injury matters. Courts have split over whether proof of residence creates a presumption of citizenship that can be rebutted only by specific contrary evidence.[473]
- "Significant relief" seems to be a matter of the amount requested, as well as whether available monetary and injunctive relief is sought against the in-state defendant.[474]
- "Significant basis" requires a comparison of the conduct of the in-state defendant(s) with that of any out-of-state defendants, and then asks if "[t]he local defendant's alleged conduct [is] an *important* ground for the asserted claims in view of the alleged conduct of all the Defendants." (Again, we let you judge whether "important ground" clarifies "significant basis.")[475]
- "Principal injuries" can be confined only to those injuries that arose in-state, even if the defendant's "related conduct" injured people in other states.[476]

---

[472] 28 U.S.C. § 1332(d)(4)(A). A final requirement for declination of jurisdiction is that no class action asserting essentially the same allegations against any of the defendants has been filed in the prior three years. *See* Dutcher v. Matheson, 840 F.3d 1183 (10th Cir. 2016) (holding that a prior similar case that was filed as a class action defeated this requirement, even though certification had been denied).

[473] *See* Mason v. Lockwood, Andrews & Newman, P.C., 842 F.3d 383 (6th Cir. 2016) (holding that residence is presumptive evidence of citizenship; collecting cases); Preston v. Tenet Healthsystem Mem'l Med. Ctr., Inc., 485 F.3d 793 (5th Cir. 2007) (holding that proof of address on the date of the injury did not establish proof of citizenship on the date that the case was filed, so that no "credible estimate" could be made about whether the two-thirds-plus-one element had been proven). *See also* Hollinger v. Home State Mut. Ins. Co., 654 F.3d 564 (5th Cir. 2011) ("The evidentiary standard for establishing citizenship and domicile at this preliminary stage must be practical and reasonable.").

[474] *See* Benko v. Quality Loan Serv. Corp., 789 F.3d 1111 (9th Cir. 2015); *cf.* Coleman v. Estes Express Lines, Inc., 631 F.3d 1010 (9th Cir. 2011) (stating relief is not significant when it would be "small change" in relation to the total relief sought).

[475] *See* Kaufman v. Allstate N.J. Ins. Co., 561 F.3d 144 (3d Cir. 2009); *accord*, *Mason*, 842 F.3d at 395–96.

[476] *See Kaufman*, 561 F.3d at 158 (reading "conduct or related conduct" in the disjunctive, so that the defendant's in-state conduct can be considered independently as a basis to deny federal jurisdiction).

The third exception to CAFA's jurisdiction is more flexible; it is not mandatory, and the lawsuit's focus on a single state is less concentrated. It applies when more than one-third but less than two-thirds of a class are citizens of the state in which the case is filed and the "primary defendants" are from the same state.[477] Assuming that these elements are established (using the same methods for determining citizenship and defining "primary defendants" already discussed), then a court may decline jurisdiction "in the interests of justice and looking at the totality of the circumstances." The statute directs courts to implement this open-ended standard by considering six factors:

- whether the claims "involve matters of national or interstate interest";
- whether the "laws of the State in which the action was originally filed" or of another state will apply to the claims;
- "whether the class action has been pleaded in a manner that seeks to avoid Federal jurisdiction";
- whether the forum has "a distinct nexus with the class members, the alleged harm, or the defendants";
- whether the number of forum-state class members "in all proposed plaintiff classes in the aggregate is substantially larger than the number of citizens from any other State," with the remaining class members "dispersed among a substantial number of States"; and
- whether, during the prior three years, one or more similar class actions had been filed.[478]

Although CAFA has had the effect of expanding federal jurisdiction, plaintiffs who wish to avoid federal court still have some opportunities to do so. One principal method is to create a class action containing only members from a single state and then to sue at least one important defendant from that same state.[479] You might also

[477] 28 U.S.C. § 1332(d)(3).

[478] For a case applying each factor, and ultimately holding that jurisdiction should be declined, see Preston v. Tenet Healthsystem Mem'l Med. Ctr., Inc., 485 F.3d 804 (5th Cir. 2007).

[479] For diversity purposes, a corporation has citizenship both in the state of its incorporation and in the state of its principal place of business. 28 U.S.C. § 1332(c)(1). Some corporations have tried to use their dual citizenship to defeat the single-state class-action strategy. For instance, if the defendant is incorporated in Georgia with its principal place of business in Florida, it might argue that its Florida citizenship immunizes it from remand to state court when sued by a class of Georgia-only citizens. Thus far, courts have not been impressed with this logic. Because the corporation is also indisputably a citizen of Georgia, so the discretionary and mandatory provisions

have thought about another time-honored trick of plaintiffs seeking to avoid federal diversity jurisdiction: limit the amount in controversy to $5,000,000 or less. That one won't work, at least if a legitimate argument exists that the value of the class action exceeds $5,000,000. In *Standard Fire Insurance Co. v. Knowles*,[480] the plaintiff filed a class action in state court, stipulating that they were limiting the class's claims for relief to $5,000,000. Whether the case might exceed that amount was a close question, but the defendant removed the case to federal court under CAFA, and provided (debatable) evidence that the case was worth just a bit north of the required amount. Based on the stipulation, the district court remanded the case, but the Supreme Court held thgat, until the case was certified as a class action, the named plaintiff had no authority to represent the putative class members and therefore no authority to limit the amount of their claims. Therefore, at the time that the case was filed (which is the point at which federal subject-matter jurisdiction is usually measured), the stipulation did not bind the class members and was not yet effective. The federal court had subject-matter jurisdiction—a result that furthered CAFA's goal of ensuring "[f]ederal court consideration of interstate cases of national importance."[481]

> *Problem 8*
>
> An Oklahoma citizen files a class action in Oklahoma state court against an Oklahoma defendant, alleging that the defendant violated an Oklahoma statute requiring certain interest payments for oil and gas leases. All the leases concern land located in Oklahoma. About 48% of the class members were from Oklahoma, with 21% from Texas and the remainder spread across the country. The defendant removed the case to federal court, and the plaintiff moved for remand. What ruling? *See* Speed v. JMA Energy Co., 872 F.3d 1122 (10th Cir. 2017).

D. Settlement Class Actions

Up to this point, we have assumed that the plaintiff has filed a class action in order to litigate the class's claims. Unsurprisingly, many class actions settle after some period of litigation; indeed, as we have seen, one of the concerns about class actions is their potential to force *in terrorem* settlements. Beginning in the 1980s, however, some litigants found a new use for class actions: as a convenient vehicle for settling a broad dispute and obtaining "global peace." Under this approach, a plaintiff's lawyer (or group of lawyers)

---

of §§ 1332(d)(3) and –(d)(4) still apply. *See* Life of the S. Ins. Co. v. Carzell, 851 F.3d 1341 (11th Cir. 2017).

480 568 U.S. 588 (2013).

481 568 U.S. at 595 (internal quotation marks omitted).

and one or more defendants negotiate a global settlement of all claims arising from allegedly wrongful behavior. The defendant agrees to the settlement on the condition that the case is certified as a class action. Without class certification, the settlement collapses. The settlement often contains other conditions, such as the defendant's reservation of a right to withdraw from the settlement if too many class members opt out of the case and an agreement on the amount of the class counsel's fee (or at least an agreement from the defendant not to oppose whatever fee the class counsel requests).[482]

These "settlement class actions" hold certain benefits but also raise great concerns. On the positive side, they can be used to resolve a great number of claims quickly. A multitude of claims can be resolved without the expense of litigation, and a class settlement can provide an equality of treatment for like claimants that individual settlements probably will not. Of particular benefit, settlement class actions can resolve the claims of "future future" plaintiffs—something that a traditional litigated class action, which requires class members to have presently viable claims in order to meet standing requirements—cannot do.[483] The only way to address the claims of "future future" plaintiffs is through settlement, and a settlement class action can accomplish this result.

But there are also enormous risks with the device. Because they do not propose to litigate the case, the plaintiffs lack the leverage to exact a premium in return for settling. This problem is especially acute in immature litigation, in which the values of the claims are uncertain.[484] Another concern is that the lawyers who negotiate for the class are looking for a quick payout in return for little work and therefore are willing either to collude with the defendant or to sell out the best interests of the class.[485] In the case of "future future" plaintiffs, the difficulty of monitoring the work of the lawyers is especially acute: because the class members do not yet have litigable

---

[482] We examine different aspects of the mechanics of class-action settlements in Chapters 16, 17, and 18. The focus of this section is whether it is permissible to use Rule 23 as a mechanism to pre-negotiate and settle a mass dispute without attempting to litigate the dispute.

[483] It remains uncertain whether future plaintiffs have standing in a settlement class action. The argument was pressed in *Amchem Products, Inc. v. Windsor*, 521 U.S. 591 (1997). The Supreme Court rejected the class action on other grounds, but noted that "Rule 23's requirements must be interpreted in keeping with Article III constraints." It repeated the admonition in *Ortiz v. Fibreboard Corp.*, 527 U.S. 815 (1999).

[484] Conversely, proponents argue that settlement class actions are particularly appropriate for mature litigation, when the average values of cases are well-known and the savings from preventing the relitigation of common issues are manifest.

[485] Keep in mind that, at the time that the negotiations occur, the lawyer negotiating for the class has not yet been appointed class counsel, and therefore bears no fiduciary responsibility to the putative class. *See In re* Bluetooth Headset Prods. Liab. Litig., 654 F.3d 935 (9th Cir. 2011).

claims, they have little incentive to pay attention to the case. Another problem with "future future" plaintiffs is the difficulty of giving constitutionally effective notice to class members who are by definition unknown.[486]

As we have seen, the Supreme Court twice overturned the certification of settlement class actions intended to resolve the claims of future plaintiffs: in *Amchem Products, Inc. v. Windsor*[487] and in *Ortiz v. Fibreboard Corp.*[488] Neither case rejected outright the use of settlement class actions for either present or future claims. But the logic and outcomes of the cases suggest that the proper judicial stance toward settlement class actions is wariness. In *Amchem*, for instance, the settling parties argued that some of the requirements for class certification could be relaxed, and others interpreted in light of the class's common interest in obtaining a fair settlement. The Court agreed that "[s]ettlement is relevant to a class certification." In particular, faced with "a request for settlement-only class certification, a district court need not inquire whether the case, if tried, would present intractable management problems." On the other hand, "other specifications of the Rule—those designed to protect absentees by blocking unwarranted or overbroad class definitions—demand undiluted, even heightened, attention in the settlement context." The reason for this heightened attention is that "a court asked to certify a settlement class will lack the opportunity, present when a case is litigated, to adjust the class, informed by the proceedings as they unfold."

Amchem went on to emphasize that the text of Rule 23 "limits judicial inventiveness" and that "[t]he safeguards provided by the Rule 23(a) and (b) class-qualifying criteria . . . are not impractical impediments—checks shorn of utility—in the settlement-class context." It also required that the common interests that shape a class predate the settlement; thus, a common interest in a fair settlement could not be used to satisfy the criteria of Rules 23(a) and 23(b). As *Amchem* and *Ortiz* show, meeting the requirements of Rule 23 is especially tricky when a class action seeks to settle future claims, due to the potential for intra-class conflicts of interest that a settlement generates.

Despite the caution with which settlement class actions must be crafted to address constitutional concerns and the language of Rule

---

486 *Amchem* also questioned whether notice effective under the Due Process Clause and Rule 23 could be provided "to legions so unselfconscious and amorphous" as a class of future asbestos plaintiffs. 521 U.S. at 628.

487 For a further discussion of *Amchem*, see *supra* notes 355–361, 415–416, 487 and accompanying text).

488 527 U.S. 815 (1999) (further discussed *supra* notes 396–401, 441 and accompanying text).

23, they are used, especially to settle the claims of plaintiffs with present (rather than future) injuries.[489] For instance, a settlement class action resolved claims arising from the BP oil spill in the Gulf of Mexico. The court of appeals in that case imposed an important limit on the settlement class action: all class members have suffered some colorable injury. While the court noted that a defendant could certainly settle individual claims that have no legal merit, a "class settlement is not a private agreement between the parties. It is a creature of Rule 23, which authorizes its use to resolve the legal claims of a class 'only with the court's approval.' " Because "the goal of global peace does not trump Article III or federal law[, courts] do not have the authority to create a cause of action (and their corresponding subject-matter jurisdiction over it) and then give peace with regard to that cause of action."[490]

Rule 23 was not written with the settlement class action (or the problem of "future future" plaintiffs) in mind, so any settlement class action must be shoehorned into the traditional elements of Rule 23. The Advisory Committee on the Civil Rules has twice explored the idea of creating a distinct Rule 23(b)(4) with standards for settlement class actions, but on both occasions it has opted not to push the idea through the rulemaking process.

The settlement class action turns existing doctrine to a new purpose: the class action becomes a form of alternative dispute resolution for mass disputes. The settlement class action is less a "complex litigation" device than a "complex ADR" device, with an affinity to other ADR devices described in Chapter Seven.

E. Preclusion, Full Faith and Credit, and Collateral Attack

Class actions involve a trade-off: a class judgment binds class members, but class members receive a guarantee of adequate representation in return. If the representation is inadequate, then the class judgment has no preclusive effect, and the class members are free to litigate their claims elsewhere. The exact scope of a class judgment's preclusive effect raises a number of questions that establish unique rules of preclusion in the class-action context.

1. The Scope of Claim Preclusion

Although a properly constituted class action binds class members to the judgment, a separate question is exactly how broad

[489] *See, e.g.*, *In re* Am. Int'l Grp., Inc. Sec. Litig., 689 F.3d 229 (2d Cir. 2012) (vacating the denial of class certification in a securities-fraud settlement class action and remanding for further proceedings); Sullivan v. DB Invs., Inc., 667 F.3d 273 (3d Cir. 2011) (en banc) (affirming an antitrust settlement class action).

[490] *In re* Deepwater Horizon, 732 F.3d 326 (5th Cir. 2013).

this preclusive effect is. Under the usual rules for claim preclusion, a judgment binds a plaintiff with respect not only to the claims that were brought but also to the claims that "should have been brought"—with this last phrase typically meaning all other claims arising out of the same transaction or occurrence.[491] In the class-action context, however, this definition poses some problems. Suppose that a class member has suffered an injury. One of the two legal bases for recovery is common to the class. The other basis, arising from the same facts, is unique to the class member. If the case is certified as a class action on the class-wide theory of recovery and judgment is entered against the class, is the class member precluded from asserting the individual theory in later litigation?

Cooper v. Federal Reserve Bank of Richmond[492] held that the answer was no. In *Cooper* employees claimed that they had been the victims of racial discrimination. Four employees brought claims as representatives of a class of similarly situated African-American workers. Included as class members were five employees known as the Baxter petitioners. The Baxter petitioners were afforded a right to opt out, but they did not do so.

At trial, the district court found that the employer had engaged in a pattern or practice of racial discrimination by failing to provide promotion and assignment opportunities for African-American employees in pay grades 4 and 5. The court also concluded that there was insufficient evidence of such a pattern or practice for employees in other pay grades. At this point, the Baxter petitioners, who held jobs in higher pay grades, sought to intervene to press their claims that, even though there may not have been a pattern or practice to deny promotions in their pay grade, they had been individually discriminated against with respect to promotion. The court denied intervention, saying that the petitioners could file their own suit. When they did so, the employer moved to dismiss the case on preclusion grounds. On interlocutory review, the court of appeals held that the Baxter petitioners' claims were precluded.

The Supreme Court reversed. It stressed that a pattern-or-practice claim relies on different standards and different evidence than a claim of individual discrimination. A pattern-or-practice claim may fail even when a few individual instances of discrimination exist. Therefore, the failure of the pattern-or-practice case for employees in higher pay grades proved nothing about whether the Baxter plaintiffs had been the victims of individual discrimination. The preclusive scope of the class judgment was limited: it "bars the class members from bringing another class action against the [employer]

---

[491] *See supra* notes 255–258 and accompanying text.

[492] 467 U.S. 867 (1984).

alleging a pattern or practice of discrimination for the relevant time period and (2) precludes the class members in any other litigation with the Bank from relitigating the question whether the Bank engaged in a pattern and practice of discrimination against black employees during the relevant time period." Critically, "[t]he judgment is not, however, dispositive of the individual claims the Baxter petitioners have alleged in their separate action."

The employer argued that this result was inconsistent with the purpose of Rule 23, which was to resolve mass controversies expeditiously. But the Court stated that "the converse is true. The class-action device was intended to establish a procedure for the adjudication of common questions of law or fact. If the Bank's theory were adopted, it would be tantamount to requiring that every member of the class be permitted to intervene to litigate the merits of his individual claim." Indeed, the Court said, Rule 23's "purposes might well be defeated by an attempt to decide a host of individual claims before any common question relating to liability has been resolved adversely to the defendant."

Cooper's holding should be kept in perspective. If a class action could have been certified for two claims but the class representative brought only one, the judgment on the first claim would be preclusive on the claim that was not brought. But that fact also raises new questions. For instance, suppose that a class action asserts only one of two possible claims. In subsequent litigation, may a class member respond to a defense of claim preclusion by showing that a class action on the second claim could not have been certified? In this setting, the shoes are on the other feet: the defendant argues that a claim could have been certified, and the class member argues that it could not have been.

The question is usually avoided because most class actions settle. The settlement agreement typically requires class members to release all claims against the defendant, even those that are individual in nature. Indeed, *Cooper* is one of the Supreme Court's least cited class-action decisions, and many of its implications for preclusion remain to be worked out.[493] As a case involving federal

---

[493] *Compare* Cameron v. Tomes, 99 F.2d 14 (1st Cir. 1993) (noting that "[c]ases on *res judicata,* ample in many areas, are fairly sparse where preclusion of distinctive individual claims is urged based upon an earlier class action judgment" and holding that a prisoner's claims of unconstitutional confinement were unique to his situation and therefore not barred by prior institutional-reform suit challenging the prison's conditions), *with* Rasheed v. Aiken, 1 F.3d 1244, 1993 WL 299358 (7th Cir. 1993) (Table) (holding that claims of a sect of Muslim prisoners were barred by a consent decree in a prior class action that focused on the general conditions of worship for Muslims prisoners; noting that the plaintiff had an opportunity to object to the class settlement and did not).

claims and the federal law of preclusion, *Cooper* also does not determine the preclusive effect of a class judgment in state court.[494]

2. Adequacy Redux

Cooper bears on a related preclusion problem. Imagine that class members can assert two (or more) claims, including one claim for which class treatment is appropriate and another claim for which class treatment is either inappropriate or highly debatable. Perhaps, for instance, one fraud-based claim does not require proof of individual reliance, while a related claim does. As we have seen, the issues of individual proof make class certification for the latter claim is unlikely, if not impossible. As a result, class counsel rationally decides to bring only the first, easily certifiable claim.

Some courts have held that, by abandoning class members' valuable claims, class counsel has proven to be inadequate, and thus denied class certification on this basis. In *McClain v. Lufkin Industries, Inc.*,[495] class counsel pleaded only injunctive claims in order to obtain class certification under Rule 23(b)(2); counsel failed to plead class members' claims for compensatory and punitive damages, which would have required separate and more uncertain certification under Rule 23(b)(3). The court of appeals held that, by failing to pursue class members' monetary claims, the class representatives proved themselves inadequate, thus defeating class certification on (a)(4) grounds. Likewise, in *Bowden v. Phillips Petroleum Co.*,[496] a state court held flatly that "class representatives who split the claims of the class are per se inadequate."

This simplistic approach lacks necessary analytical depth. As *Cooper* suggests, individual claims, which are not certifiable on a class-wide basis, are not subject to preclusion. It cannot be a sign of inadequate representation not to plead such claims, given that the class members are no worse off; they still retain the right to press these claims on an individual basis. Moreover, *Cooper* likely prevents preclusion from attaching to class-wide claims that cannot be certified due to the limits of Rules 23(a) and –(b). Finally, it may well be a rational decision for class counsel not to pursue every possible class claim. The cost and difficulties of certifying or proving some claims may outweigh their expected value to class members. Moreover, the result of cases like *McClain* or *Bowden* may make it

---

494 For instance, Texas uses a different approach, holding that class members are precluded "from asserting claims in subsequent individual litigation which arose from the same transaction or subject matter and either could have been or were litigated in the prior suit." Bowden v. Phillips Petroleum Co., 247 S.W.3d 690 (Tex. 2008); *see also* Thompson v. Am. Tobacco Co., 189 F.R.D. 544 (D. Minn. 1999) (suggesting that the same rule might apply in Minnesota).

495 519 F.3d 264 (5th Cir. 2008).

496 247 S.W.3d at 697.

impossible for class members to recover on any claims. Especially with negative-value claims, this is likely a worse outcome for class members than obtaining recovery on some, albeit not all, claims.

As always, a more reliable guide to adequacy is to ask whether class counsel's actions make the class members worse off than they would be if their claims were litigated individually.[497]

3. Collateral Attack

The constitutional demand of adequate representation creates another preclusion quandary. If the class representative loses the case, or even wins it for a paltry sum, class members might understandably believe that they were inadequately represented. If they then file their own lawsuits, the issue of adequacy might end up being litigated over and over. And if any plaintiffs prevail on their claim of inadequacy, their cases are resurrected. The class action may not provide the global peace that it promises.

This process of claiming in the second case that the first judgment is invalid due to inadequate representation is usually known as *collateral attack. Hansberry v. Lee*[498] involved exactly such an attack. But in *Hansberry* the trial court in the first class action never stopped to certify the case as a class action, nor to determine whether the requirements of a class action had been established. Most important, the court made no finding that the class representative in the first case was adequate (a failure made excusable because adequacy was not an element of Illinois class-action law until *Hansberry* itself made adequacy a constitutional requirement).

After *Hansberry*, a court is almost always going to make a finding that the class representation is adequate.[499] So the modern question becomes whether that finding of adequacy is binding on class members when they try to attack the judgment collaterally. If it is, class members are barred as a matter of issue preclusion from challenging the claim-preclusive effect of the class judgment. If it is not, then class judgments can be challenged in later cases.

This intellectual puzzle of issue preclusion wrapped inside claim preclusion has weighty policies on each side. On the side of giving issue-preclusive effect to a finding of adequacy (and thus limiting collateral attacks to rare cases like *Hansberry*) are concerns for the finality of judgments, the need for global peace, and the elimination

---

[497] *See supra* note 360 and accompanying text.

[498] 311 U.S. 32 (1940) (discussed *supra* notes 287–292 and accompanying text).

[499] *But see* Hesse v. Sprint Corp., 598 F.3d 581 (9th Cir. 2010) (permitting collateral attack on a state-court class settlement when state court made no findings of adequate representation).

of expensive relitigation. On the side of not affording issue-preclusive effect is the need to enforce the due-process right to adequate representation, discourage collusive behavior, minimize other agency costs, and respect the individual class member's right to a "day in court."

Given the weight of the arguments on each side, it is perhaps unsurprising that different courts have come out to opposite conclusions on the question. A leading case is *Epstein v. MCA, Inc.*,[500] which involved securities fraud under both federal and Delaware law. Plaintiffs commenced a class action in federal court, which had exclusive jurisdiction over some of the federal claims. Other plaintiffs filed a class action in Delaware state court, asserting claims under Delaware state law. The state claims appeared to be considerably weaker than the federal claims. The defendant struck a deal with class counsel in the state-court action on terms favorable to the defendant. (Indeed, what may have been going on was a reverse auction, in which the defendant played the two sets of class counsel against each other to get the best deal.) The Delaware state court found the settlement fair (even though it could not have awarded damages for the federal violations at trial), and also found the representation by the class representative and class counsel in the state proceeding adequate. The federal plaintiffs argued that they were not bound by the Delaware judgment due to inadequate representation. *Epstein* held that, as long as the state court found that the representation was adequate, the class members who did not opt out were bound by that finding and were therefore barred from claiming inadequate representation as a means to attack the Delaware judgment collaterally.

In contract, *Stephenson v. Dow Chemical Co.*[501] involved plaintiffs who were members of a toxic-tort class action that settled in 1984. The settlement called for the settlement fund to remain open only until 1994; at the time of settlement, the scientific evidence suggested that all injuries would manifest by that point. The settlement also released the claims of all "future plaintiffs" in the class. After the settlement fund closed, two of the "future plaintiffs" filed individual suits, claiming that their injuries first manifested themselves after the 1994 cutoff. They argued that the judgment approving the settlement did not bind them because they were inadequately represented. Relying on the logic of *Amchem*[502] and

---

500 179 F.3d 641 (9th Cir. 1999).

501 273 F.3d 249 (2d Cir. 2001), *aff'd in part by an equally divided Court and vacated in part*, 539 U.S. 111 (2003).

502 Amchem Prods., Inc. v. Windsor, 521 U.S. 591 (1997) (discussed *supra* notes 355–361, 415–416, 487 and accompanying text).

Ortiz,[503] the court of appeals held that future plaintiffs whose claims first arose after the termination of the settlement fund received inadequate representation, so that the plaintiffs were free to attack the judgment collaterally.

The split between *Epstein* and *Stephenson* played out in other cases and in a raft of scholarly commentary. The Supreme Court granted certiorari in *Stephenson* to resolve the issue. It affirmed the Second Circuit's decision on an unrelated point of removal jurisdiction, but on the critical issue of collateral attack, it split four to four, with Justice Stevens not participating.

The Court has not returned to the matter. One reason has been the strong swing of momentum in favor of the *Epstein* approach, which is highly restrictive of collateral attacks. Even the Second Circuit subsequently limited *Stephenson* to its facts, holding that it applied only in the unique context of future plaintiffs; in ordinary litigation involving present class claimants, the Second Circuit has now prohibited collateral attacks.[504] In 2010, the American Law Institute also came out against a broad right of collateral attack.[505]

Although the issue seems to have come to rest for now, the closeness of the question in *Stephenson*, *Hansberry*'s allowance of collateral attack, and stray dicta in opinions such as *Shutts*[506] keep alive the prospect that no class judgment is safe from later challenge by disgruntled class members. One way to tamp down the problem (even if it remains theoretically alive) is to ensure that class settlements are substantively fair; it was the lopsided nature of *Epstein*'s settlement and the blindness to the interests of *Stephenson*'s future class members that drove the collateral attacks in both cases.

4. Full Faith and Credit and Transnational Class Actions: Resolving Claims Beyond a Court's Boundaries

Epstein implicitly involved another significant class-action question: whether a court can approve a settlement of class claims that lie beyond its jurisdiction. As a general rule, a court need not give full faith and credit to a judgment when the prior court did not have jurisdiction to render the judgment.[507] In *Epstein*, the state court that approved the settlement and release of the class members'

---

[503] Ortiz v. Fibreboard Corp., 527 U.S. 815 (1999) (discussed *supra* notes 396–401, 441, 488–490 and accompanying text).

[504] *See* Wal-Mart Stores, Inc. v. Visa U.S.A., Inc., 396 F.3d 96 (2d Cir. 2005).

[505] *See* PRINCIPLES OF AGGREGATE LITIGATION, *supra* note 437, § 2.07(a).

[506] Phillips Petroleum Co. v. Shutts, 472 U.S. 797 (1985) ("[T]he Due Process Clause of course requires that the named plaintiff at all times adequately represent the interests of the absent class members.").

[507] *See, e.g.*, Durfee v. Duke, 375 U.S. 106 (1963).

federal claims had no jurisdiction to resolve some of the federal claims, which lay within the exclusive jurisdiction of the federal court. Why, then, should the federal court have given any credit to the state-court judgment, at least to the extent that it released these federal claims?

The short answer is because the Supreme Court said so. In *Matsushita Electric Industrial Co. v. Epstein*,[508] a prior iteration of the same dispute that returned to the Ninth Circuit in *Epstein*, the Supreme Court held that the Delaware judgment approving the state-court settlement of the federal claims had preclusive effect in federal court as a matter of the Full Faith and Credit Act.[509] In arriving at this conclusion, the Supreme Court applied a standard full-faith-and-credit principle: that the court determining whether to enforce a judgment (here, the federal court in *Epstein*) must give the same preclusive effect to the judgment as the court that rendered the judgment (here, the Delaware state court). Delaware had a general rule that it did not give preclusive effect to a judgment releasing claims over which it had no jurisdiction, but its rule with respect to class actions was the opposite. Therefore, the federal court was bound to give preclusive effect to the judgment approving the settlement.

It is important to note the limits of this holding. If the court approving the settlement would not preclude the later assertion of the settled claims that lay beyond its jurisdiction, then the second court is free, as a matter of full faith and credit, to entertain those claims. This result is akin to collateral attack, because the judgment in the class action does not buy peace from further litigation—although the lever to achieve that result is not the Due Process Clause's guarantee of adequate representation but rather the scope of full-faith-and-credit doctrine.

A different issue arises when a class action includes citizens of foreign countries. In recent years, the Supreme Court has drastically curtailed the extraterritorial effect of federal law,[510] but in some cases foreign citizens are still swept up in American class actions. Although many countries (numbering around forty at the time of this writing) have adopted some form of class action in recent years, some of these countries, as well as other countries in the world, may not afford American class judgments preclusive effect due to their deep skepticism about American-style class actions, discovery, and jury trials.

---

508 516 U.S. 367 (1996).

509 28 U.S.C. § 1738.

510 *See* RJR Nabisco, Inc. v. European Cmty., 579 U.S. ___, 136 S. Ct. 2090 (2016); Kiobel v. Royal Dutch Petroleum Co., 569 U.S. 108 (2013).

In *In re Vivendi Universal, S.A. Securities Litigation*,[511] the district court held that class members from countries that would not give preclusive effect to an American class action should be excluded from membership in the class. After conducting a searching inquiry into the class-action and preclusion law of various European countries, the court in *Vivendi* included English and French citizens as class members but excluded Austrian and German citizens. The result can be criticized,[512] and the fate of foreign-citizen preclusion in transnational class actions is a matter that is likely to be debated in future years. Because foreign class actions have been so rare until recently, American courts have not yet staked out a position on the converse proposition: the preclusive effect that a foreign class judgment deserves. With the rise of such class actions, however, this issue is likely to emerge in the near future.[513]

F. Settling as a Tactic to Moot the Class Action

Defendants often wish to avoid a class action. As we have seen, they often try to resist certification by arguing that a class action fails to meet one or more of the requirements of Rule 23 or a similar state-court rule. A different tactic to avoid class certification is to try to settle the claim of the class representative before the class-certification motion is decided. Without a class representative, the class action falls apart.

Buying off the class representative occurs with some frequency, especially when the offer also includes a reasonable fee for the putative class counsel. Because no class action yet exists, these settlements lie beyond the purview of the judge, who must approve any settlement once the class is certified.[514]

When the class representative declines to settle, however, some defendants have switched gears: they make a formal Rule 68 offer. Under a Rule 68 offer, the defendant agrees to allow the entry of judgment against it in the amount of the offer. If the plaintiff accepts, the case ends; if the plaintiff declines, the plaintiff must pay the

---

[511] 242 F.R.D. 76 (S.D.N.Y. 2007).

[512] *See* Zachary Clopton, *Transnational Class Actions in the Shadow of Preclusion*, 90 IND. L.J. 1387 (2015); Linda Sandstrom Simard & Jay Tidmarsh, *Foreign Citizens in Transnational Class Actions*, 97 CORNELL L. REV. 87 (2011).

[513] *Cf.* Midbrook Flowerbulbs Holland B.V. v. Holland Am. Bulb Farms, Inc., 874 F.3d 604 (9th Cir. 2017) (recognizing a Dutch judgment under state law even though Dutch procedure limited discovery into relevant materials). *Midbrook* was not a class action, but is interesting in part because the Netherlands has recently enacted, and appears to be using successfully, a form of collective relief akin to a settlement class action. *See Wet collectieve afwikkeling massaschade*, Stb. 2005, p. 340. On the emergence of class actions in other countries, see Deborah R. Hensler, *The Globalization of Class Actions: An Overview*, 622 ANNALS AM. ACAD. POL. & SOC. SCI. 7 (2009).

[514] FED. R. CIV. P. 23(e).

defendant's costs incurred after the offer unless the final judgment exceeds the offer. The twist that class-action defendants add is to make a full-value offer. For instance, if the class representative's claim is worth $2,000, the defendant will offer $2,000 (plus, assuming that the claim involves fee shifting, a reasonable fee for the putative class counsel).

In non-class-action situations, defendants have little incentive to make full-value offers. In the class-action context, however, there is method to the madness. Most certifiable class actions are small-stakes or negative-value claims. Victims have no incentive to file a claim on their own. If the class representative accepts the offer, the defendant avoids a potentially large settlement or judgment for the class as a whole. If the class representative declines the offer, the defendant then argues that the case is moot: because the defendant has offered the plaintiff all the relief that the plaintiff could have obtained at judgment, no justiciable dispute exists.

Some courts of appeals accepted this argument, holding that the putative class representative's case was moot even though the class representative never accepted the offer and therefore received nothing for the claim. Others rejected the tactic, holding that the failure of the defendant to accede to the plaintiff's demand for class certification meant that the Rule 68 offer had not provided the plaintiff with all the relief requested, so a justiciable dispute still existed.

The Supreme Court waded into the controversy twice. In the first case, it avoided the question about the validity of the gambit because the plaintiff had conceded that the Rule 68 offer mooted the case; four Justices in dissent made no bones about their view that, absent such a concession, federal courts should not bless the tactic.[515] In the second case, the Supreme Court faced the issue directly, and held that an unaccepted Rule 68 offer (or other settlement offer) did not render a consumer's complaint moot.[516] Over a dissent by three Justices, the Court held that a rejected settlement offer "had no continuing efficacy." As a result, the putative class representative's claim was not moot. "While a class lacks independent status until certified," the Court concluded, "a would-be class representative with a live claim of her own must be accorded a fair opportunity to show that certification is warranted."

Nonetheless, a defendant can still make an offer to a putative class representative. If the representative accepts, the class action collapses. When the offer is for the full amount of the class representative's claim, putative class counsel is caught in an ethical

---

515 Genesis Healthcare Corp. v. Symczyk, 569 U.S. 66 (2013).

516 Campbell-Ewald Co. v. Gomez, 577 U.S. ___, 136 S. Ct. 663 (2016).

bind. What are counsel's obligations to the one client he or she has—the putative representative—in relation to counsel's obligations toward those counsel seeks to represent? To what extent can putative counsel consider the fees that a class action portends when making a recommendation to the class representative about accepting a full-value offer? Ethical rules designed for one-client settings provide little guidance.

G. Conclusion

This Chapter has been long—the longest in the book. We will return again to class actions in Chapter Sixteen, where we examine the process by which courts approve class settlements under a "fair, reasonable, and adequate" standard. For now, as we have reminded you from time to time as we waded through the weeds of class-action practice, the reason for our deep engagement with Rule 23 is that class actions lie at the center of the law of aggregation in America. Lying at the center does not mean that the class action solves every problem of aggregation or that it is always available as an aggregation technique. As this Chapter has shown, neither of these propositions is true. The class action lies at the center of the debate because it remains the most generally effective aggregation device. Its terms and limits create the form around which all other aggregation mechanisms mold themselves. If the class action's form shrinks, as it has done in recent years, other devices necessarily expand to fill the void. Should the class action broaden in scope in the future, other devices will become less relevant.

Moreover, class actions contain a wealth of doctrines and ideas that might affect the shape of these other devices. For instance, *Shutts* puts all mandatory aggregation devices under a constitutional cloud. Similarly, MDL cases contain no requirement that the lawyers put in charge of the MDL plaintiffs adequately represent the plaintiffs. Should there be such a requirement? In most forms of aggregation other than the class action, the court has no role in approving a settlement, meaning that a greater risk of collusive, sell-out, or just plain inadequate mass settlements exists. Should court approval of all mass settlements be required? And should the standard be "fair, reasonable, and adequate," as it is for class actions?

These and many comparable questions arise in the shadow of Rule 23 and its state-law counterparts. To craft any workable solutions to aggregation, you must work your way through the law of class actions: what class actions are and what they should be.

Chapter 7

ALTERNATIVE APPROACHES TO RESOLVE MASS LITIGATION

Until now, we have focused on the use of private lawsuits to respond to mass alleged injuries. In a strong regulatory state, the problem of mass injury is often dealt with through up-front regulation or post-injury governmental administrative or criminal proceedings. In a country with a more *laissez faire* attitude toward regulation, such as the United States, post-injury regulation through private litigation is more the norm.

But the choice of response to mass injuries is not an either-or situation. In recent years, other countries have moved toward more litigation-centered processes for mass disputes; for instance, many countries now authorize class actions in certain circumstances. Conversely, in the United States, potential litigants or interested regulatory agencies have adopted other processes—criminal, administrative, and private—that seek to resolve disputes outside of the traditional private-litigation setting.

Most of these processes remain in their infancy. Whether they will ultimately overtake private litigation as the principal forms for resolving mass disputes is uncertain. But lawyers who operate in the mass-dispute arena must be aware of the range of alternative dispute-resolution (ADR) processes that might affect or be brought to bear on a mass dispute.

This Chapter begins with non-traditional litigation processes to resolve mass disputes. It then moves to administrative processes and private means of dispute resolution. As we will see, some of these processes can, in proper circumstances, aid the resolution of mass disputes; others are at best an adjunct to or even detrimental to private enforcement of rights in a mass-injury environment.

A. Other Litigation Processes

Aside from private litigation, three processes rely principally on the court system to resolve mass disputes: bankruptcy, *parens patriae* actions, and criminal prosecutions. Of the three, the *parens patriae* action has the most venerable lineage, but the bankruptcy proceeding has the broadest array of tools to achieve single-forum aggregation. Criminal prosecutions lag far behind in terms of usage and utility as a form of mass-dispute resolution.

1. Bankruptcy

Although the field of bankruptcy is centuries old, using bankruptcy as a tool to aggregate related litigation is a relatively recent development. In 1982, Johns-Manville, then the world's largest manufacturer of asbestos, filed for Chapter 11 bankruptcy. The filing sent shock waves through the legal community. Part of the shock resulted from the fact that Johns-Manville was still solvent. The other part resulted from the way in which Johns-Manville proposed to use bankruptcy: to consolidate both present *and future* asbestos claims in one forum, to create a mechanism to pay present and future claims, and to emerge from the Chapter 11 reorganization intact, healthy, and litigation-free.

Bankruptcy is a highly technical field; here we can provide only a basic overview, geared specifically to its use in complex litigation. We focus first on the substantive law of bankruptcy, then on some of bankruptcy's jurisdictional and procedural features. With this basic understanding, we explore some of the difficulties that remain in mapping bankruptcy law onto the needs of single-forum aggregation.

a. Substance

To begin with the most basic proposition, bankruptcy provides a means by which a person (called the debtor) can get out from under his or her debts. The Bankruptcy Code, presently found in Title 11 of the United States Code, states the terms under which the debtor can obtain this relief. Under the Code, the bankruptcy court collects a debtor's assets (called the bankruptcy estate) and then distributes the estate to those of the debtor's creditors that file claims against the estate. The Code specifies the priorities for distribution of the estate. Because a debtor usually has insufficient assets to meet all its debts, this priority system often means that some creditors receive full payment and others receive partial or no payment.

After the assets are distributed, the debtor receives a "discharge," which wipes away the debts and allows the debtor a "fresh start" free of financial obligations that the debtor had incurred up to the time of the bankruptcy. The Bankruptcy Code allows the debtor to exclude certain assets from the estate, and it does not discharge certain types of debt. It also provides a power by which the bankruptcy court can void preferential transfers that the debtor made to creditors or others in the months leading up to the bankruptcy.

The process of collecting the debtor's assets, voiding preferential transfers, and distributing the assets is often complex, and in many cases the court appoints a bankruptcy trustee to accomplish these tasks. In some cases, the court allows a debtor corporation to continue to operate the business; the debtor is known as a "debtor in possession." In other cases, the court appoints the trustee or another person to run the business. In either event, once the debtor enters bankruptcy, the corporation is run to maximize its value for the creditors. The bankruptcy estate is seen in the law as a separate legal entity—a *res* over which the bankruptcy court can exercise jurisdiction.

In some instances, a debtor seeks the protection of the bankruptcy court and files a voluntary petition. In other cases, the debtor's creditors file an involuntary petition. Contrary to popular belief, a debtor need not be insolvent to enter bankruptcy. Sometimes bankruptcy is necessary to deal with the severe cash-flow problems of a solvent debtor.

Because bankruptcy discharges legal claims against the debtor, a defendant facing thousands of lawsuits can find bankruptcy useful. But bankruptcy is often seen as a last resort, for a debtor may lose control of the business after filing a bankruptcy petition.

Although any person or entity can use bankruptcy, we focus on corporate bankruptcies because corporations are usually the defendants in mass disputes. Corporations can take advantage of a unique form of bankruptcy. For most debtors, the outcome of bankruptcy is distribution of all assets to creditors; these are usually referred to as Chapter 7 liquidations. But Chapter 7 does not provide for discharge of a corporation's debts, so a corporation that wishes to continue operating as a business must resort instead to Chapter 11, which provides for corporate reorganization in bankruptcy. (One quick point: Chapter 11 should not be confused with Title 11, which contains the entire Bankruptcy Code (including Chapter 11).) A Chapter 11 reorganization allows the corporation to pay its debts, obtain a discharge, and emerge after discharge as a going concern.

Reorganization is also more important from the standpoint of complex litigation. If a corporation liquidates under Chapter 7 and goes out of business, it is indifferent about how the claims asserted against it are paid. Assume that the corporation has $100 million in assets, is facing judgments in 100 cases for $1 million (i.e., $100 million), is presently litigating 1,000 additional claims that seek $1 million apiece (i.e., $1 billion in present claims), and expects that 2,000 more people are likely to assert $1 million claims in the future (i.e., $2 billion in future claims). If the corporation liquidates, it doesn't care whether its assets go to pay the claims already reduced to judgment or whether those with present or future claims also receive a share of the assets.

In particular, it seems likely that the 2,000 future claimants will be out of luck. Because they do not yet have claims to assert, they do not meet the ordinary definition of a creditor. By the time that they have claims, the corporation will have liquidated and they will be without an effective remedy. Chapter 7 liquidations do nothing to avoid the unfairness caused by the temporal dispersion of claims—an unfairness that has been a primary motivation in our search for better aggregation tools. If the corporation reorganizes, however, the situation is different. It has little incentive to go through bankruptcy if it still faces the prospect of 2,000 new suits after discharge. If the reorganization process can figure out a way to handle not only the present claims but also the future claims, then Chapter 11 holds out significant promise as a way to aggregate—and resolve—related claims against a debtor.

The basic goal of a Chapter 11 reorganization is to construct a reorganization plan that simultaneously satisfies the needs of creditors and the goal of the corporation to remain a financially viable concern after bankruptcy. The Bankruptcy Code allows a debtor to submit a plan for accomplishing these aims. Creditors and other interested parties can submit competing plans.

The Bankruptcy Code requires the bankruptcy court to organize creditors and other interested parties into classes of claims and classes of interests. A distinction exists between impaired and unimpaired creditors; unimpaired creditors are fully paid under the plan, while impaired creditors receive less than full value. As a general rule, each class of impaired creditors must vote to accept a reorganization plan before it becomes effective. (Unimpaired creditors are not entitled to vote.) A class of claims accepts the plan when a majority in number and two-thirds in dollar amount vote in favor of the plan. In addition, the plan must receive approval from all classes of interests (most typically shareholders in the corporation), but here approval requires a favorable vote of those holding two-thirds in dollar amount.[517] The classes' consent is not alone sufficient to result in the plan's approval; the classes' approval is just one of sixteen statutory findings that a bankruptcy court must make before approving the plan.[518] For the most part, however, a plan that meets all classes' approval is likely to satisfy the remaining statutory factors.

---

517 11 U.S.C. § 1126.

518 *See id.* § 1129(a). Another factor is that at least one class of impaired creditors must approve the plan. Some debtors have sought to game the system by creating a class of creditors whose interests are only minimally or insignificantly impaired as a means of garnering support from one class of creditors. Such "artificial impairment" violates the spirit and perhaps the letter of the law, and it can in some instances raise due-process concerns. *See In re* Combustion Eng'g, Inc., 391 F.3d 190 (3d Cir. 2004) (vacating an order confirming a reorganization plan that had created two trusts to pay two classes of similarly situated asbestos victims, one of which was treated far better than the other).

In limited circumstances, a bankruptcy court can also accept a plan when one or more classes of claims or interests reject it. To do so, the court invokes Chapter 11's "cramdown" provision—so named because the court crams the plan down the throats of unwilling classes. The plan must still meet all statutory factors other than approval of all classes. The court must then determine that the plan is "fair and equitable."[519] The phrase has a particular meaning in this context. Essentially, a plan is "fair and equitable" when each person in each class of secured claims that did not approve the plan receives full value, and each person in each class of unsecured claims or interests that did not approve the plan either (1) receives the full allowed value of their claims or (2) receives less than the full amount but no class of claims or interests that are "junior" (in terms of payment priority) to the disapproving class receives anything of value. This last provision is known as the "absolute-priority rule." As a general matter, secured claims take priority over unsecured claims, which in turn take priority over shareholders and other interests. Therefore, it is impossible to cram down a plan that gives secured creditors less than full value or that give shareholders any value if unsecured claims are less than fully compensated.

It is common in Chapter 11 proceedings for creditors to organize a committee that works to hammer out a plan with the debtor and the trustee. The committee often includes representatives from each class of creditors and interests. Negotiations occur against the backdrop of the debtor's plan and the limit on the court's cramdown power that the absolute-priority rule imposes.

A critical variable in the success or failure of a reorganization plan is the composition of the classes of claims and interests. In theory, a bankruptcy court can stack the deck in favor of or against a plan by putting into the same class various combinations of persons that support or oppose the plan. The Bankruptcy Code imposes some limits on a bankruptcy court's power to classify claims; a plan cannot place "a claim or interest in a particular class unless such claim or interest is substantially similar to the other claims or interests of such class."[520] Nonetheless, classification of claims "can be a creative process (and an important one too if the debtor needs an affirmative vote of a non-insider-impaired creditor class to set up a cram-down of an objecting creditor class under section 1129(b))."[521] Debtors' plans often try to gerrymander classes to secure the most favorable voting

---

519 11 U.S.C. § 1129(b)(2).

520 *Id.* § 1122(a).

521 *See* STAN BERNSTEIN, BUSINESS BANKRUPTCY ESSENTIALS 94 (AM. BAR ASS'N 2009).

treatment. The limits of creativity in the classification process remain uncertain.

Another critical variable is the allowance and estimation of claims that have not yet been reduced to judgment. Assume that, in our hypothetical, the only unsecured creditors are the present and future plaintiffs (in other words, the 100 plaintiffs holding $1 million judgments against the debtor, the 1,000 with present but unresolved claims, and the 2,000 with future claims). It is easy to know the value of the claims of the first 100 because they have been reduced to judgment. But what about the remainder? Must the bankruptcy court determine whether each of the 3,000 present and future claimants has a viable claim and how much it is worth? Recall that a court cannot approve a plan without determining that half in number and two-thirds in value of those with legitimate claims have voted in favor of the plan. The court cannot wait for each case to come to judgment before holding the vote; the process would take too long and defeat the goal of getting the debtor back on its feet quickly.

Collecting assets, voiding preferences, crafting classes of claims and interests, fostering negotiations with creditors' committees, allowing and estimating claims, conducting votes, approving or cramming down plans—these are just some of the large legal challenges that bankruptcy courts face. But the jurisdictional reach and procedural powers of a bankruptcy court make bankruptcy, whatever its complexities and limitations, an attractive aggregation tool in certain circumstances.

b. Jurisdiction and Procedure

As we have seen, an ideal aggregation mechanism possesses certain features: (1) a single court system with subject-matter jurisdiction over all claims asserted by and against the relevant parties and potential parties; (2) if jurisdiction is not exclusive, a mechanism for removal of claims from other courts; (3) a transfer mechanism to allow all the cases to be consolidated for pretrial and trial in the aggregating forum; (4) territorial jurisdiction over all parties and potential parties in the aggregating court; (5) the aggregating court's power to stay proceedings in other courts; and (6) a mechanism for joining (or precluding) the claims of potential parties who cannot or do not wish to assert their claims at the present time.

Measured against these criteria, bankruptcy is the most powerful aggregation tool that we have encountered.

i. Subject-Matter Jurisdiction

The federal district courts have "original and exclusive jurisdiction of all cases under title 11,"[522] as well as "original but not exclusive jurisdiction of all civil proceedings arising under title 11, or arising in or related to cases under title 11."[523] This language makes a distinction among (1) a "case," which is the process triggered when a bankruptcy petition is filed; (2) a "civil proceeding," which is a controversy that is resolved in the context of settling the debtor's affairs; and (3) a "related to" case, which (in general terms) is a case that might affect the debtor's estate. Although the court has exclusive jurisdiction only with respect to the "case" itself, the concurrent jurisdiction over "civil proceedings" and "related to" cases provides one court system—the federal system—that can hear the claims by or against all parties.

There are a couple of flies in the ointment. One is an unresolved constitutional concern about the breadth of "related to" jurisdiction.[524] Another is abstention. In some instances a bankruptcy court may, "in the interest of justice, or in the interest of comity with State courts or respect for State law, . . . abstain[ ] from hearing a particular proceeding arising under title 11 or arising in or related to a case under title 11."[525] In other instances a district court must abstain, upon timely motion, in "a proceeding based upon a State law claim or State law cause of action, related to a case under title 11 but not arising under title 11, with respect to which an action could not have been commenced in a court of the United States absent jurisdiction under [§ 1334]" if the "action is commenced, and can be timely adjudicated, in a State forum of appropriate jurisdiction."[526] Mandatory abstention has one important limitation: the liquidation or estimation of personal-injury and wrongful-death claims "shall not be subject to the mandatory abstention provisions of section 1334(c)(2)."[527]

ii. Removal

Because federal jurisdiction is not exclusive for civil proceedings and "related to" cases, some mechanism for removal of these cases is necessary for global aggregation to occur. In most circumstances, any "party" has the right to remove "any claim or cause of action in a civil

---

522 28 U.S.C. § 1334(a).

523 *Id.* § 1334(b).

524 *See* HART & WECHSLER, *supra* note 199, at 765–68 (describing constitutional issues).

525 28 U.S.C. § 1334(c)(1); *In re* Legates, 381 B.R. 111 (Bankr. D. Del. 2008) (listing twelve factors to consider when invoking discretionary abstention).

526 28 U.S.C. § 1334(c)(2).

527 *Id.* § 157(b)(4).

action . . . to the district court for the district where such civil action is pending, if such district court has jurisdiction of such claim or cause of action under section 1334 of [Title 28]."[528] The district court, however, "may remand such [removed] claim or cause of action on any equitable ground."[529]

Because removal occurs to the federal district encompassing the state court from which the case was removed, a venue-transfer mechanism for aggregating related proceedings in one federal forum is still required.

iii. Venue and Transfer

Venue over a bankruptcy case lies either in the district of the debtor's domicile, residence, principal place of business, or principal location of assets, or in the district in which certain related bankruptcy proceedings are pending.[530] With minor exceptions, proceedings and "related to" cases also "may be commenced" in the district court in which the bankruptcy case has been filed.[531] So far, so good: the bankruptcy case, as well as civil proceedings and "related to" cases, can be venued in a single forum.

As far as a mechanism to transfer removed cases from the district to which they have been removed to the district in which the bankruptcy case is pending, bankruptcy has two distinct transfer provisions. First, "[a] district court may transfer a case or proceeding under title 11 to a district court for another district, in the interest of justice or for the convenience of the parties."[532] Second, "personal injury tort and wrongful death claims" must be tried either "in the district court in which the bankruptcy case is pending, or in the district court in the district in which the claim arose, as determined by the district court in which the bankruptcy case is pending."[533] While judges typically transfer tort cases to forums other than the forum in which the bankruptcy case is pending, they can consolidate tort cases in the bankruptcy forum.

---

[528] *Id.* § 1452(a).

[529] *Id.* § 1452(b).

[530] *Id.* § 1408.

[531] *Id.* § 1409(a). Some cases hold that, despite the use of the word "may," § 1409(a) requires that proceedings and "related to" cases be filed in the district in which the bankruptcy case is pending. The better reading of § 1409 and related provisions, however, is that proceedings and "related to" cases can be commenced in any federal district in which venue exists. *See* Brock v. Am. Messenger Serv., Inc., 65 B.R. 670 (D.N.H. 1986).

[532] 28 U.S.C. § 1412. A split in authority exists over whether § 1412 or § 1404 governs the transfer of "related to" cases. *See* Dunlap v. Friedman's, Inc., 331 B.R. 674 (S.D. W. Va. 2005). The issue matters because § 1412 transfers are not encumbered by § 1404's requirement that transfer can occur only to a district in which venue was initially proper or to which the parties consent.

[533] 28 U.S.C. § 157(b)(5).

Both transfer mechanisms allow the transfer of a case for all purposes, including trial. Nonetheless, proceedings and "related to" cases can often be brought in multiple venues. Except for tort claims, no mechanism, akin to § 1407, provides for transfer of all cases and proceedings to a single forum. Venue-transfer provisions are perhaps the weakest link in bankruptcy's use to aggregate claims—although some courts in large bankruptcies have used the venue provisions to centralize all cases in one forum.[534]

iv. Territorial Jurisdiction

Bankruptcy courts have their own rules of procedure, which often mimic the Federal Rules of Civil Procedure. One rule that is significantly different, however, is Bankruptcy Rule 7004(d), which is entitled "Nationwide Service of Process." It states in full: "The summons and complaint and all other process except a subpoena may be served anywhere in the United States." Thus, district courts sitting in bankruptcy enjoy nationwide service of process.

v. Staying Related Litigation

Some of the deficiencies in subject-matter jurisdiction, removal, and venue can be cured if the bankruptcy court has the power to stay cases in other forums. The primary source for a stay in bankruptcy is the "automatic stay" provision, 11 U.S.C. § 362. Section 362 is long and intricate; here we highlight basic principles. Under § 362, filing a bankruptcy petition automatically—in other words, without the need for a court order—"operates as a stay, applicable to all entities, of . . . the commencement or continuation . . . of a judicial, administrative, or other action or proceeding against the debtor that was or could have been commenced before the commencement of the case under this title." Section 362 also stays various actions that are designed to jump a particular creditor ahead of the queue and disadvantage other creditors and the bankruptcy estate. Note that the stay does not make distinctions among the bankruptcy case, civil proceedings, and "related to" cases; any actions and proceedings that might affect the debtor's estate must halt.

The automatic stay of § 362 has some limits. Section 362(b) does not stay a variety of claims, although few of these claims are likely to arise in complex litigation. Moreover, a party can petition the bankruptcy court for relief from the automatic stay. The standard ground for granting such relief is that a party in interest in the bankruptcy case lacks "adequate protection"—in other words, the party's interest in specific property is likely to become less valuable

---

[534] *See* A.H. Robins Co. v. Piccinin, 788 F.2d 994 (4th Cir. 1986); Shared Network Users Grp., Inc. v. WorldCom Techs., Inc., 309 B.R. 446 (E.D. Pa. 2004).

during the pendency of the bankruptcy case.[535] Litigants with unsecured claims typically cannot take advantage of this limit.

Next, the automatic stay operates only on proceedings that affect the debtor's estate. Actions against parties other than the debtor do not typically come within the stay. Even should a stay run to third parties, the stay is not permanent; it expires, at the latest, at the end of the bankruptcy case. The case against the debtor having ended, the cases against third parties can now proceed—unless the bankruptcy proceeding achieves a global settlement of all claims against all parties.

Finally, the automatic stay affects only those claims that were or could have been brought on the date of the bankruptcy petition. It does not affect proceedings or cases that first arise after the petition was filed. With post-petition cases, the stay is important only in the sense that it prevents any effort to enforce a judgment against the debtor.[536]

A secondary source of power to enter a stay is 11 U.S.C. § 105, which authorizes a court to "issue any order, process, or judgment that is necessary or appropriate to carry out the provisions of this title." This grant suggests a quasi-All Writs Act power that can smooth over the limitations of § 362, but § 105 is not quite as broad as it sounds. A § 105 stay is available only when "a policy embraced in some other part of the Bankruptcy Code justifies it."[537]

vi. Joining or Precluding Nonparties

The automatic stay prevents prosecution of presently filed claims and claims that could have been brought before the petition's filing. Thus, the stay solves a part of the "future plaintiff" problem—in particular, the problem of the "present futures" (those with matured claims that have not yet filed). But the stay does not run against "future futures" (those whose claims have not yet matured). Furthermore, a stay, although necessary, is a weak tool; barring statute-of-limitations issues, nonparties can wait out the bankruptcy case and file after the stay has dissolved. What is really needed is a way either to join nonparties mandatorily or to preclude their claims if they fail to join.

---

535 11 U.S.C. § 362(d)(1).

536 *See* Bellini Imports, Ltd. v. Mason & Dixon Lines, Inc., 944 F.2d 199 (4th Cir. 1991).

537 *See* DOUGLAS G. BAIRD, THE ELEMENTS OF BANKRUPTCY 9 (rev. ed. 1993); *In re* Joint E. & S. Dists. Asbestos Litig., 982 F.2d 721 (2d Cir. 1992) ("[E]quitable considerations . . . [are] not a license to courts to invent remedies that overstep statutory limitations.").

The Bankruptcy Code adopts the preclusive method: discharge of the debtor's debts.[538] A tool of great power, the discharge "voids any judgment at any time obtained, to the extent that such judgment is a determination of the personal liability of the debtor with respect to any debt discharged," and it also "operates as an injunction against the commencement or continuation of an action, the employment of process, or an act, to collect, recover, or offset any such act as a personal liability of the debtor."[539] Therefore, a person who, as of the date of the filing of the petition for bankruptcy, has a claim against the debtor must assert the claim in the bankruptcy proceeding—or else the claim is forever barred.[540]

The preclusive effect of a discharge has qualifications and limitations. First, a debt cannot be discharged unless the debt was listed or placed on a schedule of liabilities in such a way that the creditor had an opportunity to file a timely proof of claim.[541] Next, the court can discharge only debts accrued up to a specified time during the bankruptcy proceedings.[542] When long latency periods create "future future" plaintiffs, a defendant has little reason to invoke the powerful aggregative potential of bankruptcy to receive a discharge of present claims, only to face a new onslaught of claims thereafter. Third, the bankruptcy discharge is effective only against the debtor, not against other defendants (unless they too file for bankruptcy). The discharge cannot resolve all aspects of a multi-defendant controversy.

vii. Other Provisions

Two other provisions merit mention. First, most activity in bankruptcy cases occurs before bankruptcy judges, who are Article I appointees. The requirement that federal cases be adjudicated by Article III judges limits the powers of bankruptcy judges, and has led to a curious division of responsibility in which district judges are authorized to (and almost always do) refer to bankruptcy judges most "core proceedings," but cannot refer to bankruptcy judges "non-core proceedings" and tort actions that are core proceedings.[543] We will not wade into the swampy distinctions between "core" and "non-core" proceedings or address the constitutional issues engendered by this division of responsibility—except to note that important issues remain unresolved. Our point is that bankruptcy acts as an imperfect

---

538 There are important types of debts that cannot be discharged in bankruptcy, but we do not explore them here. *See* 11 U.S.C. § 523.

539 *Id.* §§ 524(a)(1), –(a)(2).

540 *See* Martin v. Wilks, 490 U.S. 755 (1989) (noting that bankruptcy is an exception to the usual rule that a court can preclude only parties' claims).

541 11 U.S.C. § 523(a)(3).

542 For the cut-off dates, see *id.* §§ 502(f), 727(b), 1141(d).

543 *See* 28 U.S.C. § 157.

aggregator. Some proceedings are likely to be conducted by the district judge and some by the bankruptcy judge, with the district judge acting in effect as an appellate court over the bankruptcy judge. A district judge can avoid this split by declining to refer a case to the bankruptcy court or by withdrawing an order of reference. Given the intricacies of bankruptcy law, however, district judges are loathe to exercise this power even in complex cases.

Second, the Seventh Amendment, which guarantees the right to jury trial in certain civil actions, casts a large shadow over bankruptcy law. Bankruptcy was equitable in nature, so juries were not employed. Therefore, the essential functions of the bankruptcy court—collecting the debtor's assets, allowing claims against the estate, and distributing assets—do not involve jury trial. But many of the civil proceedings and "related to" cases over which the district court has jurisdiction carry a right to jury trial. There is considerable debate about how far the jury-trial right carries into bankruptcy proceedings and whether Article I bankruptcy judges can conduct jury trials.[544]

c. *Accommodating Bankruptcy to the Needs of Mass Litigation*

Although bankruptcy is the most comprehensive device for the aggregation of related cases in a single forum, it has important limits that we have just explored. In some cases, courts have attempted to fashion mechanisms that work around these limits, thus increasing the aggregative potential of bankruptcy. This section focuses on a few of these measures.

i. The Estimation Process

Because many major bankruptcies are corporate reorganizations, and because such bankruptcies are unlikely to compensate every class of creditors in full, courts must usually seek each class's approval of the reorganization plan. Class approval requires a majority in number and two-thirds in value of all claims to vote for the plan. When plaintiffs have claims of different size, this requirement imposes an obstacle. In theory, to know if a plan has been approved, the court must first try each case to determine its merit and value, and then weight the vote of each plaintiff with a meritorious claim according to that plaintiff's percentage of the total recovery. To do so, however, would be a herculean, if not impossible, task when hundreds or thousands of claims are involved. Bankruptcy's potential to reduce costs in relation to one-on-one litigation would vanish.

---

544 *See* Granfinanciera, S.A. v. Nordberg, 492 U.S. 33 (1989); BAIRD, *supra* note 537, at 20–22.

In the *Dalkon Shield* bankruptcy, the district court solved this problem by estimating a $1 value for each claim—in effect, assuming that every plaintiff's claim was of identical merit and value. The court of appeals affirmed, in part because any other method would have led to "intolerable delay" in the reorganization process and in part because any error was harmless in light of the fact that the voting claimants overwhelmingly (to the tune of 94%) supported the reorganization plan.[545]

Estimating the value of claims matters for other reasons as well. Before a court can approve a reorganization plan, it must find that the holders of claims within each class of impaired creditors will receive at least as much under the reorganization plan as under a liquidation of the corporation's assets.[546] Again, the court must have some sense of the value of the plaintiffs' claims to make this finding. In the same *Dalkon Shield* litigation, the court of appeals affirmed the trial court's estimate of the plaintiffs' claims, which was based on estimates provided by plaintiffs, defendants, creditors, and other interested groups. These estimates varied by a factor of ten, and the court chose a number near the midpoint. A database of claimants that a court-appointed special master created formed the basis for all the estimates.

As you might expect, the difficulty of estimation and voting is compounded when future plaintiffs are involved.[547]

ii. Using the Bankruptcy Forum to Aggregate Claims Against Other Defendants

Although bankruptcy can work well as a means to concentrate claims against the debtor in one forum, one of the problems of bankruptcy as an aggregation tool is its inability to concentrate the claims against defendants other than the debtor in the bankruptcy forum. This limitation means that bankruptcy adds yet another forum with which complex litigation must be coordinated. For instance, in the silicone-gel breast-implant litigation in the 1990s, federal claims were concentrated in an MDL proceeding in the Northern District of Alabama, while the bankruptcy proceedings against one of the principal actors went forward in the Eastern District of Michigan. The two judges worked to coordinate proceedings with each other and with state courts handling similar litigation, but such coordination may not always be possible or effective. Moreover, the looming discharge of one major player in

---

545 *See In re* A.H. Robins Co., 880 F.2d 694 (4th Cir. 1989).

546 *See* 11 U.S.C. § 1129(a)(7)(A).

547 *See In re* Combustion Eng'g, Inc., 391 F.3d 190 (3d Cir. 2004) (discussing voting issues with certain claims); *In re* Quigley Co., 346 B.R. 647 (Bankr. S.D.N.Y. 2006) (diluting the votes of certain claimants).

mass litigation puts pressure on remaining plaintiffs and defendants in other cases.

In some instances, non-debtor defendants have attempted an end run around this limitation and achieved a partial aggregation of all claims in the bankruptcy forum. One path has traveled through the bankruptcy court's "related to" jurisdiction. Non-debtors who are co-defendants of a debtor have argued that the lawsuits against them are related to the debtor's bankruptcy case because, should the plaintiffs prevail against them, they would be able to assert claims for indemnity and contribution against the debtor. Thus, the lawsuits against the co-defendants might affect the administration of the bankruptcy estate, and all the claims should be heard in one forum. Non-debtor defendants who have made this argument have typically invoked removal jurisdiction (if the cases filed against them are in state court) or venue-transfer provisions (if the cases filed against them are in federal court) to invoke the protection of the bankruptcy court.

With a couple of exceptions, however, courts have rejected this move. Illustrative is *In re Federal-Mogul Global, Inc.*[548] Asbestos victims alleged that exposure to asbestos fibers in friction products, including automotive brakes, had caused their illnesses. One of the defendants went into bankruptcy. At that point, plaintiffs severed or dismissed their cases against the debtor and proceeded against the remaining defendants, which included the major American automakers. The automakers removed the state-court cases, and on their motion, the district court invoked 28 U.S.C. § 157(b)(5) to provisionally transfer all the cases to the bankruptcy forum. In support of their request for transfer, the automakers argued that no credible scientific evidence supported the claim that friction products could cause asbestos-related injuries or deaths, so that a single, consolidated lawsuit could determine, once and for all, that expert testimony to the contrary was inadmissible and that friction-product claims throughout the country were baseless.

The district court held that it lacked "related to" jurisdiction over the non-debtor claims and remanded the cases to state court. The basis for its decision was *Pacor, Inc. v. Higgins,*[549] which held that "related to" jurisdiction existed only when "the outcome of [the] proceeding [against a non-debtor] could conceivably have any effect on the estate being administered in bankruptcy." *Pacor* interpreted the word "conceivably" narrowly; it did not grant jurisdiction over the automakers' cases because the effect on the debtor's estate would

548 300 F.3d 368 (3d Cir. 2002).

549 743 F.2d 984 (3d Cir. 1984), *overruled in part on other grounds*, Things Remembered, Inc. v. Petrarca, 516 U.S. 124 (1995).

arise only from a separate lawsuit for indemnity or contribution. On appeal, the remand order was affirmed.

Pacor's interpretation of "related to" jurisdiction has received near-universal acceptance in other courts and has in large measure been endorsed by the Supreme Court.[550] On occasion, a court sitting in bankruptcy has taken a somewhat broader view and swept lawsuits against non-debtors into the bankruptcy proceedings. The best-known instance was *In re Dow Corning Corp.*,[551] in which the principal manufacturer of allegedly defective silicone-gel breast implants was a joint venture of two major corporations. The joint venture declared bankruptcy, and the district court held that it had "related to" jurisdiction over the claims asserted against the two parent corporations, which were not only co-defendants but also shareholders. The court of appeals in *Dow Corning* stated that prospect of indemnity and contribution actions between the debtor and the co-defendants, especially in the context of a mass tort, created a sufficient threat to the debtor's reorganization plan to invoke "related to" jurisdiction. But later courts, including *Federal-Mogul*, have tended to limit *Dow Corning* to the unique situation of a joint-venture debtor and closely affiliated non-debtors.

A second path to bring non-debtors within the protection of the bankruptcy proceeding arises when a debtor and non-debtor settle potential indemnity or contribution claims between themselves. The paradigm is a payment of money by a non-debtor to the debtor; the debtor releases all claims against the non-debtor and in return agrees to use the money to settle or otherwise resolve plaintiffs' claims against the non-debtor that arise out of the transaction or occurrence giving rise to the indemnity or contribution claims. The non-debtor agrees to make the payment on the condition that the bankruptcy court enter a permanent injunction releasing the non-debtor and enjoining any lawsuits against the non-debtor relating to the underlying transaction or occurrence.

In effect, this "channeling injunction" creates a limited fund against which all plaintiffs with claims against the debtor and settling non-debtor must proceed. It also provides a bankruptcy-like protection to non-debtors, who have not formally invoked the bankruptcy process. The source of authority for issuing such an injunction is uncertain. In support of channeling injunctions, courts sitting in bankruptcy have invoked the broad injunctive powers of 11 U.S.C. § 105, arguing that the payment from the non-debtor (which was given only on the condition of receiving a channeling injunction)

---

550 *See* Celotex Corp. v. Edwards, 514 U.S. 300 (1995) (discussing *Pacor* with approval and noting that "related to" jurisdiction "cannot be limitless").

551 86 F.3d 482 (6th Cir. 1996).

was vital to the reorganization efforts of the debtor. But channeling injunctions seem to conflict with the terms of 11 U.S.C. § 524(e), which states that, with one exception not relevant here, "discharge of a debt of the debtor does not affect the liability of any other entity on, or the property of any other entity for, such debt."

In balancing the general terms of § 105 against the specific language of § 524(e), most courts have refused to permit channeling injunctions. In mass-tort bankruptcies, however, some courts have blessed an injunction and non-debtor release as long as the release was necessary for the reorganization to proceed and was given in return for fair consideration.[552] In one specific context—asbestos bankruptcies that have created a trust for the payment of future claims—the Bankruptcy Code now permits channeling injunctions as long as the trust complies with certain statutory conditions.[553]

iii. Resolving the Claims of "Future Future" Plaintiffs

The potential for bankruptcy to discharge "future future" claims—a power that no other aggregation tool possesses—is the power that makes bankruptcy compelling. Obviously, "future future" claims cannot be litigated; the number of claims, their seriousness, and even the identity of the claimants all remain unknown. The only avenue for their present resolution is a global settlement. As we have seen, achieving a global settlement of "future future" plaintiffs through the class-action device has thus far not panned out;[554] and no other aggregation device can address the "future future" situation. A reorganization plan that sets aside money for "future future" claimants, in return for a discharge of liability from those claims, would provide a perfect vehicle for resolution of a defendant's future liability for mass injury.

But these global settlements run into immediate trouble. As a rule, a bankruptcy discharge operates only against claims that could have been allowed in the bankruptcy case. To be allowed, a claim must mature by the date on which claims must be filed against the bankruptcy estate. Any claim that has not matured by this date is not discharged and may be asserted against the reorganized corporation. By definition, "future future" claims have not matured by the filing date. Therefore, "future future" claims seem beyond the reach of a bankruptcy discharge.

---

552 *See In re* Continental Airlines, 203 F.3d 203 (3d Cir. 2000) (collecting cases); *In re* Millennium Holdings II, LLC, 242 F. Supp. 2d 322 (D. Del. 2017) (discussing the questions left open in *Continental Airlines*).

553 *See* 11 U.S.C. § 524(g); *In re* Combustion Eng'g, Inc., 391 F.3d 190 (3d Cir. 2004) (vacating a channeling injunction when defendants had not met the terms of § 524(g)).

554 *See supra* notes 483–490 and accompanying text.

Once again, some courts have stepped into the breach. In a modest expansion of bankruptcy powers, *Grady v. A.H. Robins Co.*[555] held that the automatic stay of § 362 could extend to a "present future" claimant whose claim first matured after the filing of the bankruptcy petition, as long as the defendant's action that gave rise to the claim occurred before the filing. A somewhat larger incursion arose from *Epstein v. Official Committee of Unsecured Creditors, of the Estate of Piper Aircraft Corp.*[556] *Epstein* involved the bankruptcy of a small aircraft manufacturer that wished to obtain a discharge from any future tort liability for alleged defects in its planes. By expanding the definition of a "claim" subject to discharge, the court of appeals made future claims dischargeable as long as (1) some relationship (for instance, contact with or exposure to the product) existed between the claimant and the debtor before the reorganization plan's confirmation and (2) the basis for the debtor's liability was its pre-petition actions in designing or manufacturing an allegedly defective product. This "*Piper* test" has been criticized, in part because of due-process concerns that arise from the discharge of claims without adequate notice to future claimants who cannot yet know of the existence of their claims.[557] But even this test does not end a debtor's possible liability to "future future" claimants who have yet to be exposed to the debtor's product at the time of the bankruptcy.

A final tactic, which we addressed briefly in the last subsection, is to use a channeling injunction, entered pursuant to 11 U.S.C. § 105, that orders any future claimants to file claims against a fund established in the reorganization proceeding for the payment of such claims. The channeling injunction thus prohibits lawsuits directly against the reorganized entity, although it does require that the reorganization plan set aside money for such claims. This approach creates concerns, including the adequacy of the fund and the adequacy of the representation of future claimants (who are by definition unknown) in the reorganization proceeding. The two problems are usually handled through the bankruptcy court's appointment of a guardian or representative of future claimants, who then bargains with other creditors to obtain a proper share of the debtor's estate.

As we mentioned, in the context of asbestos litigation Congress has endorsed channeling injunctions, as long as an asbestos debtor has established a trust that complies with the terms of § 524(g).

---

[555] 839 F.2d 198 (4th Cir. 1988).

[556] 58 F.3d 1573 (11th Cir. 1995).

[557] *See* Jones v. Chemetron Corp., 212 F.3d 199 (3d Cir. 2000) (holding that a dischargeable tort claim arises only when it accrues under state law and that the claim of a future plaintiff cannot be discharged).

Congress patterned § 524(g) on existing practice; beginning with the Johns Manville bankruptcy in the 1980s, courts had fashioned injunctions channeling future claimants to asbestos trust funds through a broad interpretation of § 105 and other bankruptcy powers. The legality of such injunctions under bankruptcy law has never been definitively resolved, Due-process concerns of adequate notice and adequate representation have always loomed over the practice, both with § 524(g) injunctions (which are limited to the asbestos context) and junctions fashioned from a bankruptcy court's § 105 equitable powers.[558] In 2009, the Supreme Court cast a jaundiced eye on the practice in a case enjoining suits by future plaintiffs against Johns Manville's insurers, but it ultimately confined its holding to avoid "resolv[ing] whether a bankruptcy court, in 1986 or today, could properly enjoin claims against nondebtor insurers that are not derivative of the debtor's wrongdoing" and whether the plaintiffs had been "given constitutionally sufficient notice of the 1986 Orders."[559]

Bankruptcy's handling of future claimants has not always had a happy ending. A casualty of unrealistic assumptions and excessive payouts, the Manville Trust, which was supposed to compensate generations of future asbestos claimants, became insolvent within a few years. Judge Weinstein pushed through substantial modifications to the Trust, with the reorganized Manville Corporation contributing more assets.[560] The Manville Trust was not an isolated example. An academic study of future claimants in bankruptcy laid some of the blame for these failures on the system of designating a representative for future claimants. Unaccountable to actual clients but accountable to the court, the representatives proved ineffective at obtaining adequate compensation for future claimants while present claimants and equity holders in the corporation sought to maximize payouts for themselves.[561]

A common feature of reorganization plans establishing a trust to compensate future victims is funding the trust's ongoing operations through a percentage of the reorganized company's profits. As a result, lawyers who represent plaintiffs' interests often obtain seats on the reorganized company's board of directors. As a means of ensuring that the company honors its obligations to future

---

558 *See* Kane v. Johns-Manville Corp., 843 F.2d 636 (2d Cir. 1988) (noting but not resolving the issue of a channeling injunction's legality as a means of precluding future claims); *but see In re* UNR Indus., Inc., 20 F.3d 766 (7th Cir. 1994) (dismissing constitutional concerns).

559 *See* Travelers Indem. Co. v. Bailey, 557 U.S. 137 (2009).

560 *See In re* Joint E. & S. Dists. Asbestos Litig., 929 F. Supp. 1 (E. & S.D.N.Y. 1996).

561 *See* Thomas A. Smith, *A Capital Markets Approach to Mass Tort Bankruptcy*, 104 YALE L.J. 367 (1994).

claimants, these arrangements make sense, but they also decrease a company's willingness to seek reorganization.

d. Summary

Bankruptcy law possesses nearly all the tools necessary for single-forum aggregation: broad federal jurisdiction, removal and transfer authority, preclusive power to force related litigation into the federal forum, and anti-suit injunctions. Although its joinder provisions are a weak point, class actions have sometimes been used in conjunction with bankruptcy to good effect. In any event, the other powers more than compensate for the lack of joinder devices in the bankruptcy proceeding itself.

At the same time, bankruptcy is not perfect. Its reach does not extend far beyond the case of the debtor, thus complicating the resolution of multi-defendant litigation. It does not solve the thorny issue of ensuring adequate representation for victims of mass injury. Resolving the claims of future plaintiffs remains especially problematic, as it does for other forms of complex litigation. And, above all, the defendant must be willing to go through the bankruptcy process, which can be expensive and result in a loss of control over the company.

Therefore, bankruptcy is best regarded as one aggregation tool that, alone or in conjunction with other mechanisms, can advance the cause of single-forum resolution of large-scale disputes. It is no panacea.

2. *Parens Patriae* Actions

Translated literally as "parent of the nation," *parens patriae* refers to litigation that a government brings to protect one or more of its citizens. In the context of mass injury, a government may seek redress for injuries that its citizens suffer at the hands of a defendant that has allegedly violated one of the government's laws. For instance, if New York consumers are injured by a company's deceptive practices, the New York Attorney General may file a *parens patriae* action under New York's consumer-protection statutes to recoup the losses suffered by New Yorkers.

You will note immediately the connections between a *parens patriae* action and a class action. A single person (here, the state) brings an action on behalf of others. Such a mechanism can be especially useful in the context of negative-value claims, in which citizens have little incentive to file individually. A *parens patriae* action can deliver deterrence on a broad scope in a single forum.

Thus far, however, *parens patriae* actions have had only a modest impact on the shape of complex litigation. One problem is convincing attorney generals' offices in the relevant jurisdictions of the need to file such lawsuits, given both the limited resources of these offices and the American tradition of relying primarily on private litigation to regulate non-criminal behavior. Some attorneys general are more willing than others to flex their muscle when market failures (such as negative-value claims) make private litigation unrealistic. Because the attorney general in most states is an elected office, there is also a risk of capture: the political goal of protecting certain corporate interests may clash with the social goal of protecting citizens.

The concern with capture leads to other familiar problems like adequacy of representation and agency costs. An attorney general may have political interests (including the attorney general's own political advancement) that clash with the best interests of the state's citizens. *Parens patriae* actions do not contain a requirement that the attorney general single-mindedly pursue the interests of its citizens, nor are they dismissable because citizens within the group have conflicts of interest with each other.[562] The well-worn problem of agency costs also encounters a new twist, because the principal (the citizenry) has virtually no capacity to remove the agent (the attorney general) even when monitoring reveals clear deficiencies in the representation. The agency-cost problem is exacerbated because overstretched attorneys general's offices often refer *parens patriae* actions to private lawyers. Some referrals smack of patronage and may involve fee structures that do not work to the advantage of the citizens.[563]

To some degree, these last criticisms of *parens patriae* actions assume that a *parens patriae* action binds the citizens to the outcome that the attorney general achieves. Although some cases have so held, they are few in number and have generally made the claim only in passing. If *parens patriae* actions have no preclusive effect on citizens' private claims—and this seems the better assumption to make—concerns for adequate representation and agency costs diminish. But they do not disappear entirely.

Parens patriae actions also raise other difficulties. Any recovery achieved in an action goes to the government, which may distribute the money back to victims but may instead put the money into the public coffers to be used for other programs. And attorneys general

---

562 *See* Margaret H. Lemos, *Aggregate Litigation Goes Public: Representative Suits by State Attorneys General*, 126 HARV. L. REV. 486 (2012) (arguing that courts should either impose an adequate-representation requirement on attorneys general or prevent *parens patriae* actions from having preclusive effects).

563 *See* Paul Harzen Beach, *The* Parens Patriae *Settlement Auction*, 52 GONZAGA L. REV. 455 (2016/2017) (describing various fee structures and proposing an auction at the time of settlement to avoid some agency-cost problems).

may be more interested in obtaining injunctive relief that prevents repetition of the defendant's behavior than seeking compensation for present victims. Thus, the compensatory function of *parens patriae* actions can lag in comparison to private litigation. Moreover, each attorney general decides whether to bring an action for violating that government's law; if the violation is based on state law, fifty different attorneys general must decide whether to sue. Victims in some states may receive no representation, while victims in neighboring states do, for the defendant's identical conduct.

Parens patriae actions also raise aggregation difficulties. Attorneys general who decide to sue usually file suit in the courts of their own state. These state lawsuits are not subject to removal jurisdiction. Diversity-of-citizenship jurisdiction is not triggered when a state is the sole plaintiff; nor does a *parens patriae* action invoke the class-action or mass-action provisions of the Class Action Fairness Act (CAFA).[564] Thus, *parens patriae* actions are likely to remain dispersed across the country. Indeed, the availability of *parens patriae* actions can sometimes get in the way of other forms of aggregation. For instance, some courts have denied certification of a class seeking monetary recovery under Rule 23(b)(3) on the theory that a pending *parens patriae* action is a superior means to resolve the dispute.[565]

The most significant use of *parens patriae* actions involved suits brought against the tobacco industry in the late 1990s. Individual plaintiffs had found it difficult to proceed against these companies, which employed "scorched earth" litigation tactics that made it impossible to fund (and therefore win) individual cases. The courts had also shut down the use of class actions, holding that individual issues of causation and defenses predominated over common issues of liability. Enter the *parens patriae* action. Sometimes employing private plaintiffs' lawyers to represent them, forty-six states acted in concert to file suit both to recover their own losses (incurred in paying for medical care for smokers) and to obtain compensation for their citizens. The tobacco companies settled for $200 billion, payable over twenty-five years, while also agreeing to change their advertising practices. The uses to which states put their funds varied widely, with some states setting aside money to handle future claimants and others not doing so.[566]

---

564 *See* Mississippi *ex rel.* Hood v. AU Optronics Corp., 571 U.S. 161 (2014) (holding that a *parens patriae* action was not a "mass action" under CAFA); Purdue Pharma L.P. v. Kentucky, 704 F.3d 208 (2d Cir. 2013) (holding that a *parens patriae* action is not a class action under CAFA).

565 *See* 5 JAMES WM. MOORE ET AL., MOORE'S FEDERAL PRACTICE § 23.46[2][c] (3d ed. 2017).

566 For one discussion of this litigation and the development of the *parens patriae* theory, see Richard P. Ieyoub & Theodore Eisenberg, *State Attorney General*

As the tobacco litigation shows, one advantage of a *parens patriae* action is its ability to address the problem of future plaintiffs as well as present ones. Whether a *parens patriae* action can do so effectively, however, turns on the unresolved question of the preclusive effect of a *parens latriae* judgment on the cases of future claimants. Moreover, the tobacco-litigation experience, the comparable experience with future representatives in bankruptcy, and the political reality of satisfying present constituencies create concerns about the vigor with which an attorney general may press the interests of future claimants.

Nonetheless, in a world in which other aggregation mechanisms are foreclosed, the *parens patriae* lawsuit may provide some benefit. Like many of the aggregation mechanisms we have studied, *parens patriae* actions are only a partial solution, and they are not perfect. But in the right circumstances, they are one more arrow in the aggregation quiver.

3. Criminal and Civil-Enforcement Proceedings

Related in some ways to the *parens patriae* action, an emerging approach to the problem of mass injury is prosecution in criminal or civil-enforcement proceedings. In a number of recent high-profile cases, prosecutions have resulted in plea agreements in which a corporate defendant agrees to corporate restructuring and the restitution of large sums of money. In turn, prosecutors sometimes distribute a portion of the restitution to victims. For example, after a pharmaceutical company reached a $1.2 billion settlement with 30,000 plaintiffs who suffered side effects from one of its prescription drugs, federal prosecutors brought criminal charges for promoting the drug for unapproved uses. The defendant pleaded guilty to a misdemeanor and agreed to pay an additional $1.415 billion. Of that amount, $515 million was assessed as a criminal fine, while most of the remainder went to resolve civil lawsuits filed on behalf of the federal and state governments.

Use of the criminal-justice or civil-enforcement systems in this manner is unusual. A defendant must have acted in a way that invokes criminal or civil-enforcement responsibility. Because criminal law is concerned with retribution and deterrence, not victim compensation, the fit between the criminal process and aggregation of plaintiffs' claims in a civil proceeding, in which deterrence and compensation are the critical concerns, is imperfect. The same is generally true of civil enforcement. Moreover, the problems that we have seen throughout the material on aggregation remain. Leading the list is the problem of adequate representation. A prosecutor

---

Actions, the Tobacco Litigation, and the Doctrine of Parens Patriae, 74 TUL. L. REV. 1859 (2000).

represents the government, whose interests may diverge significantly from those of victims. Victims may also have interests that conflict with those of other victims. In particular, although the interests of future victims may be relevant, the claims of the presently injured are likely to loom larger in a prosecutor's mind when plea discussions occur. Moreover, criminal proceedings cannot be consolidated with civil cases, creating coordination problems. Nor does the government usually have mechanisms to hear victims' claims, determine proper levels of compensation, and distribute awards. And judgments arising from criminal or civil-enforcement plea agreements do not preclude individual civil suits.

Some of these difficulties could be overcome through rules that required prosecutors to seek input from victims or to better coordinate federal civil and criminal proceedings.[567] Governmental enforcement is already a principal mechanism to redress mass harm in other countries around the world. Should it continue to emerge as an alternative in this country, establishing parameters on the relationship between victims' suits and those of their government makes sense. In the meantime, enforcement proceedings remain yet another mechanism that might aid the resolution of some mass disputes in some circumstances.

B. Administrative Processes

The same observation can be made about administrative processes that have been used to resolve, or at least help to resolve, some mass disputes. The mechanisms vary. In some cases, administrative agencies, as part of their quasi-adjudicatory power over claims submitted to them, have employed class actions or class-like devices to resolve large numbers of similarly situated claims. In other cases, regulatory agencies, as part of their enforcement authority, enter into agreements with potential wrongdoers that look very much like the criminal plea agreements discussed in the last section. And in rare cases the President has invoked an authority to settle private claims against foreign entities when the national-security or foreign-policy interests of the United States so demand.

Professor Zimmerman and his co-authors have documented these processes in a series of articles. They demonstrate that victims' private enforcement of their rights through the judicial system is far

---

[567] *See* MANUAL, *supra* note 206, § 20.2 (generally recommending assignment of related criminal and civil proceedings to one federal judge when possible); *see generally* Adam S. Zimmerman & David M. Jaros, *The Criminal Class Action*, 159 U. PA. L. REV. 1385 (2011) (suggesting that criminal prosecutions function in many ways as an equivalent to class-action litigation and making recommendations to balance victim redress with prosecutorial discretion).

from the only game in the American legal system.[568] This conclusion is surprising to many people, who often think of litigation as the only means to redress mass injury.

At the same time, such processes raise all the concerns that we have detailed at length: fear of inadequacy of representation due to conflicting interests, lack of tools to assure single-forum aggregation, lack of preclusive effect of agency decisions, difficulty of distributing relief, difficulty of addressing the circumstances of future plaintiffs, and so on. Some of these problems are exacerbated because of the administrative context. For example, there is no mechanism available to consolidate judicial and administrative proceedings in a single forum. Similarly, capture of an agency by certain political interests raises new concerns not usually present with life-tenured Article III judges.

In a few *sui generis* matters, a government has stepped into the role of compensating victims injured by private conduct. Early examples include the "black lung" compensation program administered by the Department of Labor on behalf of coal miners disabled by pneumoconiosis and the childhood vaccine program that compensates children for injuries suffered as a result of drug manufacturers' vaccines. A more recent example is the September 11th victim compensation fund, in which those injured or survivors of those killed in the September 11th attacks could elect compensation from the fund rather than file suit in court.[569] Other efforts to establish similar no-fault compensation schemes have faltered. For instance, congressional bills to create a "black lung"-like system for asbestos victims and halt the crush of asbestos litigation never mustered sufficient political support.

Strong regulatory responses to mass injury are more common in other countries. Once again, however, American lawyers either advocating for victims or representing defendants must be aware of

---

[568] *See* Michael Sant'Ambrogio & Adam S. Zimmerman, *Inside the Agency Class Action*, 126 YALE L.J. 1634 (2017) (describing a recent trend among federal agencies to use procedures akin to Rule 23 to resolve the backlog of administrative claims and avoid inconsistencies in rulings); Adam S. Zimmerman, *Presidential Settlements*, 163 U. PA. L. REV. 1392 (2015) (discussing uses of presidential settlement authority); Michael Sant'Ambrogio & Adam S. Zimmerman, *The Agency Class Action*, 112 COLUM. L. REV. 1992 (2012) (arguing for greater use of aggregative procedures in administrative agencies); Adam S. Zimmerman, *Distributing Justice*, 86 N.Y.U. L. REV. 500 (2011) (describing the recent use of administrative enforcement proceedings to collect billions of dollars on behalf of victims of mass fraud and other wrongdoing).

[569] A hybrid judicial-administrative process is also possible. For instance, when a deadly outbreak of swine flu was predicted in 1976, vaccine manufacturers were reluctant to make the vaccine due to liability concerns. As a result, Congress substituted the United States for the vaccine manufacturers as defendant. Victims needed to present their claims to the Department of Justice. If no settlement was reached, a victim could then sue the United States in federal court; many of these cases were then subject to the multidistrict-litigation process.

the ways in which administrative agencies may take an interest in a mass dispute and of the ways in which agencies can help, or hinder, the ultimate resolution of the dispute.

C. Private Processes

Disputes can be, and often are, resolved privately, without the intervention of courts or government agencies. As a rule, private dispute-resolute mechanisms (settlement, mediation, arbitration, and the like) are not well positioned to deal with the demands of massive numbers of victims. In this section we examine two private processes, one of which (corporate settlement systems) has proven to have some, albeit controversial, success in resolving mass disputes and one of which (arbitration) is proving to be one of the greatest barriers to single-forum aggregation of related disputes.

1. Corporate Settlements

In a few high-profile cases, corporations facing claims of wrongdoing have sought to get ahead of bad publicity and inevitable litigation by establishing a private dispute-resolution process that victims can access without filing suit. For example, in 2015 General Motors announced a compensation system when its efforts to suppress the deadly defects of its ignition systems came to light. Similarly, in perhaps the best-known and largest corporate-settlement process, British Petroleum established a compensation system for those whose property or livelihood was damaged as a result of the 2010 Deepwater Horizon oil spill in the Gulf of Mexico.

In some senses, these compensation schemes act much like settlement class actions: they lay out schedules of compensation based on certain criteria and seek to funnel all future individual claims into a quasi-administrative process. Because such compensation systems require voluntary compliance from potential plaintiffs and because the corporation seeks to avoid the drumbeat of negative publicity, the compensation schedules provide awards in the general range of awards that victims would receive in litigation—without incurring the costs of litigation. To assure victims that they are not receiving low-ball awards, these schemes often employ "mass disaster" specialists—lawyers or insurance companies with strong reputations for compensating victims on fair terms—to establish and administer the systems.

Corporate settlement processes are far from the norm. A company that is uncertain about the amount of litigation that it will face is unlikely to establish such a system. Moreover, corporations that set up these systems are also, in a sense, negotiating against themselves: the compensation schedule now becomes the opening bid in any settlement discussions with victims who choose to litigate their disputes. British Petroleum's experience in the Deepwater Horizon disaster has also dulled the appetite for such processes. In that case, the company was forced to pay restitution so far beyond the bounds of what it had thought that it had agreed to that it took out advertisements attacking the compensation system that it had originally established.[570]

Despite their drawbacks, these processes can deliver certain benefits. They eliminate significant litigation costs, so more of the award ends up in the victim's pocket. They treat like victims alike. They offer compensation to those who cannot access a lawyer.

On the negative side are concerns whether such processes are fair to victims. By accepting immediate awards, plaintiffs forego the chance to use the discovery process to determine if the defendant's wrongdoing is even more extensive than it initially appears—and thus forego a chance to seek punitive damages or at least a higher settlement that reflects the possibility of a punitive award. Because the systems are designed by defendants to serve their interests, adequate representation is, as ever, a concern. And these schemes lack transparency or any judicial or administrative oversight that might inspire confidence in the program's fairness.[571]

Corporate settlement processes often fold into other methods for resolving disputes. The Deepwater Horizon compensation program paid out more than $6 billion, but eventually folded into a larger dispute-resolution process that included a settlement class action, White House involvement, and administrative fines—as a result of which British Petroleum paid $20.4 billion in a settlement approved in 2016.

2. Arbitration

Arbitration privatizes dispute resolution. The parties agree not to litigate a case, but instead to have the matter determined by an arbitrator, who may be a lawyer but may also be a lay person with relevant industry experience. Arbitration often involves little to no discovery, no jury, and streamlined procedures. Its proponents argue that arbitration provides expertise and lower dispute-resolution costs.

One of arbitration's catches is the requirement of an agreement; although parties may agree that arbitration is mutually advantageous and agree to it after a dispute arises, for the most part

---

570 For some of the background, see *In re* Deepwater Horizon, 732 F.3d 326 (5th Cir. 2013).

571 For a critical appraisal of the benefits and drawbacks of corporate-compensation systems, see Dama Remus & Adam S. Zimmerman, *The Corporate Settlement Mill*, 101 VA. L. REV. 129 (2015).

arbitration occurs when the parties have a pre-existing contractual relationship and agree to arbitrate on a pre-dispute basis. Arbitration's critics argue that arbitration therefore reinforces unequal bargaining power; when the more powerful party believes that arbitration is to its advantage, it can force the weaker party to accept an arbitration clause that may not be in its best interest. Other criticisms of arbitration include its expense (the parties must pay the arbitrator's fee), its lack of transparency (most arbitrations are held in secret), the lack of significant judicial oversight or appeal (courts must enforce arbitral judgments in all but rare circumstances[572]), and, related, arbitration's inability to produce legal norms that guide future behavior.

For most of its history, arbitration was seen as a one-on-one process. As such, it had little direct influence in most complex cases. But two events expanded the relevance of arbitration. First, in 2003 the Supreme Court upheld an arbitral award that provided class-wide relief; in a shift from the traditional thinking about the nature of arbitration, the Supreme Court stated that arbitrators could employ class actions to resolve disputes as long as the arbitration agreements did not preclude such actions.[573] That decision sent the major arbitration organizations scrambling for the rest of the decade, as they established class-action rules and began to develop expertise in resolving claims on a class-wide basis. As it turned out, class arbitration was a short-lived phenomenon. In *Stolt-Nielsen S.A. v. AnimalFeeds International Corp.*,[574] the Court held that an arbitration agreement must explicitly permit class actions before an arbitrator may certify a class. The Court noted that, in view of the "fundamental changes brought about by the shift from bilateral arbitration to class-action arbitration," arbitrators cannot compel parties to submit to class arbitration. Nor could an arbitrator infer from the mere fact that the parties agreed to arbitrate that they consented to class arbitration; more was required. As a practical matter, *Stolt-Nielsen* sounded the death knell of class-wide arbitration. Rarely do arbitration agreements expressly authorize class actions, and today, out of an abundance of caution, many arbitration agreements that implicate mass injury specifically exclude class arbitration.

The second event that brought the mass-injury and arbitration worlds together developed out of these limitations on class treatment. In the past fifteen years, many corporations began to insert arbitration clauses into their contracts with consumers. Whether you

---

[572] *See* 9 U.S.C. § 10 (listing limited grounds, such as corruption, fraud, evident partiality, and misconduct, on which a court may refuse to enforce an arbitral award).

[573] Green Tree Fin. Corp. v. Bazzle, 539 U.S. 444 (2003).

[574] 559 U.S. 63 (2010).

know it or not, you have undoubtedly signed such a clause; virtually every cell-phone service provider inserts such clauses in their click-and-sign agreements, and so do most credit-card companies, banks, internet retailers, and other institutions with which consumers regularly interact. The usual argument for these clauses is that arbitration is cheaper and faster, thus giving consumers products and services at a lower price. Consumer advocates, however, point out that consumers rarely assert claims in arbitration due to their negative value and that, in any event, the corporation often controls these processes, making a neutral decision impossible.

Consumer-arbitration clauses almost always exclude class arbitration. In response, some courts held arbitration clauses preventing consumers in negative-value cases from obtaining effective relief through class actions or other collective redress were unconscionable. With the class-action ban struck, consumer class actions proceeded either in arbitration or in court. But these rulings also raised a problem. Under the Federal Arbitration Act (FAA),[575] courts may refuse to enforce an arbitration clause (and thus to permit litigation to proceed) only on very narrow grounds. Although one of those grounds is unconscionability, the rulings striking arbitration clauses focused specifically on the unconscionability of the arbitration clause (as opposed to the general terms of the contract). By refusing to enforce the arbitration clause, courts were arguably avoiding the FAA's fundamental command.

In a 5–4 decision, *AT&T Mobility LLC v. Concepcion,*[576] the Supreme Court resolved the issue in favor of arbitration, holding that the FAA's purpose would be thwarted if arbitration clauses themselves could be stricken as unconscionable. If the doctrine of unconscionability were to be crafted in a manner that disfavored individualized arbitration and required class-wide solutions, then a court could similarly strike as unconscionable arbitration clauses when arbitration failed to provide other procedural opportunities (such as discovery). According to the majority, this result would frustrate the purpose of the FAA.

Concepcion involved an individual-arbitration system with many bells and whistles—including payment of a consumer's attorney's fees and a minimum award in the event that the consumer prevailed—that made individual arbitration a positive-value situation. The majority opinion stressed these features. After *Concepcion*, therefore, the argument shifted to whether an arbitration clause's ban on class-wide arbitration might be stricken

---

[575] 9 U.S.C. §§ 1–16.

[576] 563 U.S. 333 (2011).

if the consumers' arbitration claims were of negative value—meaning that the promise of individual arbitration was illusory.

In *American Express Co. v. Italian Colors Restaurant*,[577] the Court held no. *Italian Colors* involved antitrust claims by businesses against a major credit-card company. The arbitration clause contained none of the bells and whistles of the clause in *Concepcion*, so the claims were far too expensive to bring in individual arbitration. The case was also distinguishable from *Concepcion* because the no-class-arbitration clause arguably violated federal antitrust law, not state unconscionability law. The Court held that neither distinction mattered. Individual arbitration still permitted individual businesses to pursue their claims; even if the claims were prohibitively expensive to pursue through individual litigation, the arbitration clause did not cause this unfortunate economic reality.

After these cases, the Consumer Financial Protection Bureau proposed a regulation banning class-action waivers in arbitrations involving certain financial institutions. Shortly before this book went to press, Congress passed legislation to block the regulation. The issue remains a political football, with much of the game yet to be played.

Insofar as it affects complex mass disputes, the upshot is that arbitration is not a realistic option for the single-forum resolution of widespread consumer disputes. Nor are litigated class actions, which seem tailor-made for such negative-value claims, an option. Indeed, insofar as single-forum resolution is concerned, arbitration clauses have had a pernicious effect, both driving many negative-value consumer cases out of courts that could provide effective class-action or aggregate relief and into an individual-arbitration system too expensive for consumers to employ. And insofar as providing access to justice is an important social value, the increasing use of these agreements is driving more and more consumer complaints into the legal wilderness to die.

The lack of effective redress, either judicially or in arbitration, can be defended as a means of keeping down the cost of consumer goods and services. It can also be seen as a shield against meritless claims that settle for excessive sums only because of the *in terrorem* effect of class litigation. But it also allows large corporations to pocket millions of dollars for wrongs that are small in the individual instance but large in the aggregate. The only solution at present is to rely on *parens patriae* or other governmental enforcement actions to protect consumers. For the most part, however, such actions have been slow to develop.

---

[577] 577 U.S. ___, 136 S. Ct. 463 (2015).

"Sorry, you're out of luck" may not be an appealing alternative to complex litigation, but it is the alternative that many consumers face.

D. Conclusion

This is the unsatisfying note on which we leave the problem of structural complexity. No magic bullet of aggregation presently exists; no Holy Grail awaits us in the following chapters. Our solutions are imperfect and incomplete. The conflicting pulls of our system's aspirations run deep, and perhaps have no ultimate reconciliation.

Chapter 8

CONFLICT OF LAWS

Every lawsuit is determined under the law of a particular jurisdiction. When more than one jurisdiction has a legitimate interest in applying its law, courts must choose which law to adopt. For instance, if a car accident involving citizens of Montana and Utah occurs in Yellowstone National Park in Wyoming, at least four juridical entities (the three states plus the United States) have an argument that their law should decide the dispute.

The field of *conflict of laws* explores the question of which jurisdiction's law applies. Although some constitutional constraints exist, the field has for the most part developed through a common-law approach, so it is not surprising that different courts apply different principles. Because the court in which a case is filed uses the choice-of-law principles of that jurisdiction, the existence of different principles in different courts means that different law might apply to the case depending on the court in which a plaintiff files the case. Such choice-of-law considerations are often a primary factor in the plaintiff's selection of a forum.

Even a simple dispute like a car accident can invoke hard choice-of-law questions. In complex litigation, choice-of-law issues inject complications at two levels. First, the fact of varying choice-of-law principles, when combined with varying substantive law in different jurisdictions, is a cause of geographical dispersion of related claims. It is not the only cause, of course, but one way to aid single-forum aggregation of related cases is to apply a single law to all related controversies, thus removing one incentive for plaintiffs to disperse cases among courts that will choose favorable law. Indeed, some courts and commentators have suggested the creation of a unique set of choice-of-law principles for complex cases.

Second, as long as our choice-of-law principles remain as they are and the laws of different jurisdictions might apply in cases spread across the country, aggregating these cases in a single forum creates a serious management problem. An aggregated proceeding could become a legal Tower of Babel, with different facts and different discovery applicable to different claims and defenses under different law. Much of the efficiency of an aggregated proceeding would disappear, and aggregation might not even be desirable or possible. We had a small window into this problem in Chapter Six, where we saw that the application of varying state laws was a ground on which courts denied certification of a (b)(3) class.[578] More broadly, unless some way exists to reduce the number of laws that apply in an aggregated proceeding, aggregation on a broad scale may be impossible or at a minimum inefficient; cases can be organized only in smaller chunks of claims arising under the same or similar laws.

This Chapter begins with an overview of the conflict-of-laws field, with a particular emphasis on doctrines and principles that have an impact on aggregation and case management. It then examines a series of "solutions" that have been used or suggested to reduce the number of laws that might apply to a complex dispute. None of these proposals is without drawbacks and some are more theoretical than real. Lawyers who practice in the complex-litigation area must be highly sensitive to the ways in which choice-of-law concerns can advance or derail their clients' positions.

A. A Primer on Conflict of Laws

In the American federal system, choice-of-law issues arise in two ways. The first is often referred to as the "horizontal" choice-of-law question: among co-equal state sovereigns (say, Montana, Utah, and Wyoming), which state's law should apply? This question breaks into two subparts: which state's *substantive* law should apply, and which state's *procedural* law should apply? Both subparts have a common-law and a constitutional component. Second, a "vertical" choice-of-law question arises between federal and state sovereigns. Choosing federal or the applicable state's law also breaks into substantive and procedural subparts, and also involves both common-law and constitutional components.

This section briefly outlines the answers that courts have given to these questions. It is not a full treatment of a subject rich and complex in its own right. Rather, the focus is on ways in which the doctrines create difficulties for the aggregation and management of complex litigation.

1. Horizontal Choice-of-Law Principles

Because the applicable law is a preliminary question, endless examination of the question "Whose law applies?" can bog down litigation. Moreover, by the time that the issue arises during litigation, courts know how one law or another is likely to affect the outcome of the case. Picking the law may also pick the winner—thus generating unique concerns for the neutral application of choice-of-law principles, as well as concerns that the parties will shop for the best forum. Courts therefore strive to create conflict-of-laws principles that provide clear guidance, are easy to administer, are

---

[578] *See supra* note 427 and accompanying text.

fair to the litigants, and limit undesirable forum shopping. The challenge has always been to get the balance right.

Two rules of general application bear mention. First, when making a choice-of-law inquiry, a court in a state will, in almost all instances, choose that state's choice-of-law rule. In some instances under some choice-of-law methodologies, a court may use a doctrine known as *renvoi* to select the choice-of-law rule of another state. But such a move is rare. In almost all instances, the law of the forum state supplies the relevant choice-of-law principles—a fact that makes the selection of the proper forum state critical.

Assume that Wyoming law is best for a plaintiff. That fact does not necessarily mean that the lawyer should file the case in a Wyoming court: it means that the lawyer should file the case in the court of a state whose choice-of-law rules will result in the application of Wyoming law. If a Wyoming court will apply Wyoming law, then it is fine to file in Wyoming. But if a Wyoming court will apply Utah law, while a Montana court's choice-of-law principles dictate the use of Wyoming law, the lawyer should (all else being equal) file the case in Montana.

Second, parties are generally able to choose the law that will determine the case, as long as the chosen law bears some relationship to the litigation. Thus, parties can specify in their contract that the law of New York will govern all disputes arising under the contract. The following discussion assumes that the parties have not entered into such an agreement.

a. Substantive Law

With respect to the substantive law that governs a dispute, courts and scholars have proposed different methodologies to choose the law of the state that will resolve the controversy. The oldest method is usually referred to as the *lex loci* ("law of the place") approach. The approach involves a series of more or less hard and fast rules, where the law of the place in which a particular event occurred is chosen. For example, in a tort case, the rule is *lex loci delicti* ("law of the place of the wrong"). In most instances, the place of the wrong is the state in which the injury occurred. Similar rules govern contract claims (law of the place of forming the contract for issues regarding the formation or meaning of the contract and law of the place of performance for issues regarding performance), property claims (law of the place in which the property is located, as a rule), and so on.

The high point of this approach was the first *Restatement of Conflict of Laws*, which ran to hundreds of sections that specified the appropriate law for dozens of different claims and permutations on those claims. The approach was often criticized for its rigidity and for its choice of the law of a state that sometimes had only a glancing or fortuitous relationship to a dispute. (Think, for example, of a transcontinental flight that crashes in Kansas. Why should Kansas law apply, when none of the plaintiffs or defendants had any connection to Kansas?) *Lex loci* rules also raised problems of *characterization*. For example, if a party breached a contract made in Illinois to sell real property in Florida, was the dispute best characterized as a contract matter (hence, Illinois law applied) or a property matter (hence, Florida law applied)? The *lex loci* approach also contained various exceptions to avoid the rigidity of the rules. Those exceptions, including an exception that allowed a court to ignore the choice that *lex loci* rules dictated when the chosen law contravened the public policy of the forum state, increased the sense that the entire system was manipulable rather than principled.

As a result, the middle of the twentieth century saw a number of proposals to replace *lex loci* rules. One was *interest analysis*. The fundamental idea of interest analysis was to ensure that courts chose the law of a state which had an interest in the application of its law. If it turned out that one state had no interest in the application of its substantive law (for instance, what is the interest of Kansas in applying its tort law to the airplane crash when none of the parties and none of the allegedly negligent conduct causing the crash occurred there?), then a "false conflict" existed and the law of that state should not be chosen.

This insight seems correct and has been deeply influential. But interest analysis also raised difficulties. A principal problem was how to handle cases of "true conflict"—cases in which more than one state had an interest in the application of its law. Various solutions were assayed, including a "comparative impairment" approach, in which the law of the state whose interests would be more impaired if its law were not chosen would be chosen, and a "law of the forum" approach, in which a true conflict resulted in the forum court's choice of its own law (assuming that it was one of the states that had an interest in the dispute). A related difficulty was the ability of courts to manipulate the interests of the relevant states in order to create (or dispense with) a true conflict. It would be a poor excuse for a lawyer who could not argue that a particular state had *some* interest in a dispute: even Kansas has an interest in protecting its citizens from objects falling out of the sky. Interest analysis also made the process of choosing the substantive law more complex, because the law of one state might apply on one issue but the relevant interests might dictate that the law of another state should apply on another issue.

A third approach, reflected in the *Restatement (Second) of Conflict of Laws*, was a "center of gravity" or "most significant relationship" approach. The insight was to choose the law of the state that had the strongest connection to a dispute. In considering which state had the most significant contacts, a court could consider anything: the relevant interests of each state, where the relevant conduct occurred, where the relevant injury occurred, and so on. The *Restatement (Second)* distilled these factors into presumptive rules that mostly mirrored the old *lex loci* rules, but the presumptions were just that, and different courts gave more or less weight to the presumptions as opposed to the underlying factors.

Like most balancing tests, the "most significant relationship" approach is costly (due to high information demands) and uncertain (due to lack of clear rules). As a result, it too could be manipulated. As with all the choice-of-law approaches, at the time that the dispute arises, the court well knows how the law of one state might favor one party or the other. Judges are human beings, and it can be difficult for them to ignore the impulse to make the case come out "right" by choosing the "better" law. One advantage of the *lex loci* approach was its creation of *ex ante* rules that in theory took this impulse away, but the characterization problem and the exceptions meant that in practice the difficulty of choosing a neutral rule remained. Moreover, *ex ante* rules can sometimes be unfair to the parties or disrespectful to the interests of co-equal sovereign states, which is why *lex loci* proved unpopular with many judges and commentators.

A number of other approaches have also been suggested, but for the most part, the *lex loci*, interest-analysis, and most-significant-relationship approaches cover the present American waterfront.[579] Roughly a quarter of the states retain (or returned to) *lex loci* rules for one or more substantive areas. The problems that ultimately arose with interest analysis led a number of states that had adopted it to drop it, so that only California and the District of Columbia still profess allegiance to this approach—although a number of states use interest analysis to look for false conflicts and exclude states lacking any interest in the application of their law. Nearly every remaining state falls under the "most significant relationship" umbrella, although the ways in which states weigh different considerations and presumptions create a range of approaches rather than a single methodology.

In complex litigation, each of these approaches can aid or hinder aggregation and management. No approach is necessarily "best" across the range of complex cases. For instance, *lex loci* rules might work well if the question is one of interpretation of a consumer

[579] As of this writing, the American Law Institute is drafting a new *Restatement* on conflict of laws. The approach taken in the early drafts suggests something of a return to more traditional, *lex loci* rules, although the rules are more nuanced and incorporate insights from modern choice-of-law methods.

contract and if the contracts are formed in one state. The same is true of a single-event mass tort, like an airplane crash. But *lex loci* rules tend to point to differing laws in other cases: as an example, a geographically dispersed mass tort might result in the application of the laws of many states.

A most-significant-relationship approach is sometimes useful when *lex loci* rules would require the choice of disparate laws but one state is the true center of gravity in a dispute. For instance, in a geographically dispersed mass tort, the injury-causing conduct might have occurred in only one state, and it is possible that a court might choose the law of that state as the one with the greatest connection to the dispute. But the breadth of factors that weigh into a most-significant-relationship analysis makes it unlikely that every court in every state will weigh the factors to achieve a single-law result. Even when only one court—for instance, a court seeking to resolve a class-certification motion, in which the manageability and superiority of the class hinges on the application of a single law—is analyzing the issue, a court faithfully applying the most-significant-contacts approach of the relevant jurisdiction may be unable to conclude that the contacts in a single state are so dominant that the law of that state must be chosen for every claim.

The same problem infects interest analysis. In a multi-plaintiff, multi-defendant, geographically dispersed dispute, the interests of affected states are unlikely to lay out in a way that a single state's interests will always dominate and lead to the choice of that state's law for all claims.

Let us make three final observations about the choice of substantive law. First, after studying the problems that choice of law poses for complex (and even routine) disputes, you might wonder why the law of one jurisdiction must "win" and the law of all others must "lose." A more rational system might be to meld the interests of the various jurisdictions into a "gestalt" law that applies to the entire controversy. This impulse relies in part on the basic insight of interest analysis: to examine the interests of states in the application of their law and to choose the law based on those interests. But "gestalt" law is a step beyond traditional interest analysis. It turns courts into legislators, crafting a law that no jurisdiction adopted. Although the approach has some academic supporters, it has not commanded a significant following.

Second, the existence of different choice-of-law methodologies does not necessarily mean that different substantive laws will apply. A major impediment to the aggregation and management of complex litigation is the use of multiple substantive laws, *not* multiple choice-of-law rules. Assume that a dispute has connections to California,

Georgia, and Montana. The three states may use different methodologies, but if each methodology points to the application of one law (say, Montana), then most aggregation and management problems are averted. Thus, in considering solutions to the choice-of-law conundrum, do not get too hung up on the existence of multiple choice-of-law methodologies.

Third, and despite the important caution in the last paragraph, the existence of different choice-of-law methodologies undoubtedly contributes to the geographical dispersion of related litigation. A skilled plaintiff's lawyer will always take choice-of-law factors into account in selecting the forum for suit. It might well be that Georgia has the best law for a claim. If the litigation were filed in Georgia, a Georgia court might apply its law to Case A but Montana law to Case B. On the other hand, a Montana court might apply Georgia law to Case B. A lawyer handling both cases should therefore file Case A in Georgia and Case B in Montana, thus securing Georgia law for both clients. Our adversarial system entrusts plaintiffs' lawyers with the decision about where to file; in a federal system, one likely consequence of this choice that our conflict-of-laws regime creates is to send related cases into separate courts.

In this last hypothetical, you might think that the ideal solution is to consolidate the Georgia and Montana cases in one court and then to apply a single law (Georgia) to both cases. But recall that state courts have no interstate transfer mechanism to accomplish this result.[580] On the other hand, transfer can occur among federal courts. We will sort out the choice-of-law difficulties presented by federal courts shortly, but at least in this context we again see the advantage of federal courts as a forum for aggregation.

b. *Procedural Law*

The rules regarding procedural law tend to be much simpler: a forum court can apply its own procedural rules to determine a dispute. Thus, even if a court in Montana determines that California law must provide the substantive basis for the suit, Montana procedural law will decide the case. Many states recognize a few exceptions to this rule, typically with respect to procedural rules (like the burden of proof) that are closely tied to substantive rights. In these instances, the law that determines the substance of the claim also determines the procedure.

The basis for choosing the procedural law of the forum is not difficult to discern. The rule developed in the *lex loci* days and is a form of the *lex loci* rule (*lex loci fori*, or "law of the place of the forum"). It also accords with modern sensibilities. A forum state always has

---

[580] *See supra* note 114 and accompanying text.

an interest in applying its own court's procedural rules, and the state with the most significant relationship to the courtroom procedures employed is usually the forum state.

But this near-automatic rule also raises concerns. One is the problem common to all *lex loci* approaches: characterization. Although the lines are often clear, it can be difficult at the margins to tell whether an issue is one of procedure or one of substance. Thus, parties can seek to characterize a rule one way or the other to obtain a litigation advantage.

Second, as you should realize by this point in the book, procedure can affect substance. Moreover, a state's substantive law is often shaped against a background of that state's procedural rights. Thus, deciding a dispute under California substantive law but Montana procedural law creates a creature that does not exist in nature. A type of "gestalt" law is what we create when we blend one state's substantive law with another state's procedural law.

This concoction of the courts is tolerable because, for the most part, procedural effects are minimal. If pleadings in California courts need to be formatted in one way and Montana courts require a different formatting, following the Montana form is unlikely to have much impact on the parties' rights under California substantive law. But procedural rules of consequence to the resolution of mass disputes—for instance, a class-action rule—can have a significant effect on the determination of the case. Thus, applying one state's law to substantive rights and another state's law to procedural rights can create a dispute that is neither fish nor fowl.

As with advantageous substantive rights, advantageous procedural rights can induce a plaintiff to choose one forum over another. If those rights are helpful enough, a plaintiff may file in a particular court even when the substantive law that this court would choose is less helpful. The certainty that State X will apply State X's advantageous procedural law can lead plaintiffs from different jurisdictions to consider filing their cases in State X. That fact may aid single-forum aggregation, but keep in mind that, as long as State X applies the substantive law of different states to the controversy, management problems with an aggregated proceeding remain. The procedural advantages of State X may also not be sufficient to induce some plaintiffs to file in that state if State X will choose disadvantageous substantive law. Finally, unless State X has minimum contacts with each defendant, personal-jurisdiction considerations limit the ability of a court in State X to entertain the cases of some defendants.[581]

---

[581] There are significant, and often underappreciated, links between the issues of adjudicatory (i.e., personal jurisdiction) and legislative (i.e., choice of law) authority.

c. Constitutional Constraints on Horizontal Choice of Law

One idea that the prior section may have planted in your brain is that a court should adopt the *lex loci fori* approach used for procedural issues and apply its own law to all issues—both procedural and substantive—in every dispute. But that approach would not necessarily help in many complex cases; different plaintiffs who saw advantages in California law and Montana law would have reason to file their cases in, respectively, California and Montana. Such an approach might also run afoul of the constitutional constraints on choice of law—constraints that can sometimes frustrate the ability to reduce the number of laws that apply to a mass dispute.

The constitutional constraints arise from two sources: the Full Faith and Credit Clause of Article IV of the United States Constitution and the Due Process Clause of the Fourteenth Amendment. The former is an aspect of our federal structure; the latter concerns itself with, among other things, the fair treatment of litigants. For a long period, these two constraints operated independently, but *Allstate Insurance Co. v. Hague*[582] more or less merged them into a single test. *Allstate* held that, "[i]n deciding constitutional choice-of-law questions, whether under the Due Process Clause or the Full Faith and Credit Clause, this Court has traditionally examined the contacts of the State, whose law was applied, with the parties and with the occurrence or transaction giving rise to the litigation. In order to ensure that the choice of law is neither arbitrary nor fundamentally unfair, the Court has invalidated the choice of law of a State which has had no significant contact or significant aggregation of contacts, creating state interests, with the parties and the occurrence or transaction." *Allstate* was a plurality decision, but the Court applied the "significant contact or significant aggregation of contacts" test in a majority opinion in *Phillips Petroleum Co. v. Shutts*.[583]

We already examined the impact of *Shutts* on a different question: the ability of a court to exercise jurisdiction over class members who lack minimum contacts with the forum state.[584] *Shutts* also contained a second holding—on choice of law—that is also of great import. *Shutts* involved oil companies' failure to pay interest that was allegedly due on certain royalty payments to landowners. The land on which the companies drilled was located in Kansas,

---

For a classic exploration of the relationship, see James Martin, *Personal Jurisdiction and Choice of Law*, 78 MICH. L. REV. 872 (1980).

582 449 U.S. 302 (1981).

583 472 U.S. 797 (1985).

584 *See supra* notes 438–448 and accompanying text.

Oklahoma, Texas, and Louisiana. In terms of calculating the prejudgment interest due, Kansas law was most favorable. Therefore, a class representative filed a class action on behalf of all royalty owners in Kansas state court. The Kansas court determined that, under its choice-of-law principles, Kansas law applied to the calculation of interest for all class members.

The United States Supreme Court reversed. Only a small percentage of the land subject to royalty payments was in Kansas, and most of the class members had no contacts with the state. Even though the Court had held that the Kansas court could exercise personal jurisdiction over the out-of-state class members as long as the members were afforded an opt-out right, it held that Kansas courts could not apply Kansas law to determine the claims of class members who lacked a "significant contact or significant aggregation of contacts" with Kansas.

Shutts led to a sequel, *Sun Oil Co. v. Wortman*,[585] which is also instructive. After remand in *Shutts*, the Kansas courts made two determinations. First, although the statutes of limitation in Oklahoma, Texas, and Louisiana were shorter, it applied its five-year statute of limitations to all claims, including those of the class members with no connection to Kansas. Second, the Kansas courts construed the laws in Oklahoma, Texas, and Louisiana regarding liability for interest and the rate of interest in such a fashion that they would reach the same result as Kansas: that the companies were liable for prejudgment interest and that the applicable rate of interest was the rate contained in federal regulations—even though that rate exceeded the rate that these states usually assessed for prejudgment interest.

On the statute-of-limitations issue, the Court affirmed Kansas courts' use of Kansas's longer statute of limitations. Under choice-of-law principles dating back to *lex loci* days, statutes of limitation were characterized as procedural rather than substantive, so that a forum court could apply its own statute of limitations. That view came under attack as courts applying modern methodologies often held that the state whose law determined the substance of the dispute should also supply the statute of limitations. The Supreme Court held that the historical pedigree of *lex loci fori* for statutes of limitation rendered use of this approach immune to attack on either full-faith-and-credit or due-process grounds. The Court noted that the need for each state to be able to enact restrictions on access to its courts gave it an interest in applying its own statute of limitations to claims even when it could not apply its own substantive law. Although the modern trend was away from the *lex loci fori* approach,

---

585 486 U.S. 717 (1988).

the Court stated that it was disinclined to constitutionalize a particular approach to choice of law.

On the prejudgment-interest issue, the Court recognized that the Kansas court's interpretation of the laws of Oklahoma, Texas, and Louisiana were debatable. But an arguable misconstruction was insufficient to create a constitutional issue. "To constitute a violation of the Full Faith and Credit Clause or the Due Process Clause, it is not enough that a state court misconstrue the law of another State. Rather, our cases make plain that the misconstruction must contradict law of the other State that is clearly established and that has been brought to the court's attention." Because the laws of the other three states was not so clear as to foreclose the interpretation given them by the Kansas court, the Court affirmed both the availability of prejudgment interest and the higher rate of prejudgment for all class members. To be clear, it did not do so as a matter of Kansas law (*Shutts* having previously held that Kansas law could not govern the cases of those class members without Kansas connections), but rather as a matter of interpreting the laws of the other states in a manner that made these laws reach the same result as Kansas law.

This second holding is not directly a question of choice of law, which deals only with the selection of the proper law to resolve a dispute. Once the Kansas court chose Oklahoma law to apply to the claims of the owners of Oklahoma land, Texas law to Texas land, and Louisiana law to Louisiana land, the choice-of-law inquiry was done. Determining the content of the chosen law is a second and distinct analytical step, albeit one on which the Full Faith and Credit Clause and the Due Process Clause also impose constraints. At this point, you can probably appreciate what the Kansas court did in executing this second step: it effectively brought the laws of the various jurisdictions into harmony, so that a single set of legal principles applied to the claims of all class members—thus increasing the desirability and efficiency of a class proceeding. And *Sun Oil* did not prevent the Kansas court from doing so, at least in the absence of clear contrary authority in the law of the other states.

Shutts imposes a substantial constitutional barrier in choosing a single state's law to govern an aggregated proceeding involving the claims of geographically dispersed plaintiffs and defendants. *Sun Oil* softens but does not obliterate this barrier. Although state courts are on safe constitutional ground in applying their own procedural rules to determine claims decided under another state's substantive law, clear limits prevent courts from characterizing all issues as procedural. When the laws of multiple states must be applied, Kansas showed willingness to interpret those laws creatively to bring them into unison, but that type of creativity is not possible when the law is clear. Nor will every state court engage in such an enterprise. In short, although constitutional principles lie in the background of most choice-of-law determinations, they pose an important limit in complex litigation.

2. Choice of Law in a Federal System

Until now, we have discussed conflict-of-laws principles in the "horizontal" context of state-to-state choices of applicable law. In our federal system, the "vertical" context—the proper substantive and procedural law to apply to cases based on federal law or filed in federal court—presents a second challenge to the aggregation and management of complex litigation. As with the horizontal question, the analysis breaks into substantive and procedural components. Because constitutional concerns are embedded in the analysis, we blend the discussion of constitutional influences on choice of law directly into the discussion of substantive and procedural conflicts.

a. Substantive Law

When federal law is applicable, the Supremacy Clause of Article VI of the United States Constitution demands that state courts apply it. But that statement is far less helpful than it seems. First, although theoretically uniform, federal law can vary from circuit to circuit until the United States Supreme Court resolves the conflict. Courts must choose which interpretation of federal law to adopt, especially to cases that are transferred by MDL or other mechanisms from a court whose circuit adopts one view of federal law to another circuit with a different view.

Second, even when federal law applies, state law may provide supplemental claims.[586] For instance, many states have employment-discrimination laws that parallel or expand on federal obligations, so the same conduct may bring both state and federal law into play. A federal court usually has federal-question jurisdiction over the federal claim and supplemental jurisdiction over the state-law claim. State courts typically have jurisdiction over both claims as well. Thus, a court (state or federal) handling both federal and state claims must determine which state's law applies when more than one state has a connection to the dispute.

Third, federal courts also have jurisdiction over diversity cases. A federal court must choose the law to apply, whether it be the law of one of the states interested in the dispute or some "gestalt" law of its own concoction; and if it chooses the law of a particular state, the

[586] Only rarely does federal law preempt state law from applying to the dispute. Preemption doctrine is complex and evolving. For cases describing and applying the doctrine, see *Hughes v. Talen Energy Mktg., LLC*, 578 U.S. ___, 136 S. Ct. 1288 (2016), and *Wyeth v. Levine*, 555 U.S. 555 (2009).

federal court must determine the choice-of-law principle that governs the selection.

To begin with the third issue, at one point federal courts sitting in diversity claimed the power to apply "general common law" to most disputes not governed by state legislation.[587] Assume that, had the federal case instead been filed in New York state court, the New York choice-of-law regime would have dictated the use of New York law. When the actual case was filed in federal court, however, the federal court was not bound to apply New York law to the controversy, but instead could decide for itself what the best law was. This federal general common law gave plaintiffs an incentive to forum shop between state and federal court and could generatedifferent results that depended on the fortuity of the parties' citizenship.

This approach came to a screeching halt in one of the modern cornerstones of American federalism, *Erie Railroad Co. v. Tompkins*.[588] *Erie* famously declared that "[t]here is no federal general common law." Rather, federal courts in diversity cases must apply the same law as a court in the state in which the case was filed. The Court reasoned that this result was commanded by a federal statute, the Rules of Decision Act[589]; by policy concerns to preventforum shopping and inequitable treatment of like cases; and by the United States Constitution (although *Erie* was opaque about the exact provision of the Constitution that "federal general common law" offended). As critics of *Erie* have pointed out, *Erie* may have reduced one form of forum shopping (the vertical kind), but it enhanced another (the horizontal kind).

Erie left open some important questions about conflict of laws. One was how a federal court was to proceed when more than one state had a connection to the case. Was a federal court required to apply the substantive law of the forum state, the choice-of-law rule of the forum state (a rule that might choose the law of some other state), or a choice-of-law rule of the federal court's own making to choose which state's law applied? Of the three choices, the middle seemed the most logical, at least if the goal was to reduce federal-state forum shopping and to ensure like treatment of state and federal cases. The Supreme Court so held in *Klaxon Co. v. Stentor Elec. Mfg. Co.*[590] *Klaxon* relied for its holding only on *Erie*'s policy of

---

[587] *See* Swift v. Tyson, 41 U.S. (16 Pet.) 1 (1842).

[588] 304 U.S. 64 (1938).

[589] The Rules of Decision Act had originally been enacted in 1789. The modern, and little-changed, version is found at 28 U.S.C. § 1652.

[590] 315 U.S. 487 (1941) ("We are of opinion that the prohibition declared in *Erie Railroad v. Tompkins* against such independent determinations by the federal courts extends to the field of conflict of laws. The conflict of laws rules to be applied by the

uniformity, and virtually all scholars believe that the result in *Klaxon*, unlike the result in *Erie*, is not constitutionally compelled. If it so wished, Congress could enact a conflict-of-laws rule for federal courts; or, in theory, the Court itself could depart from *Klaxon* if other policies outweighed *Erie*'s concern for uniform treatment between state and federal courts.

For now, however, the law is clear. Federal courts must apply the law of the state in which they sit, including that state's choice-of-law principle, when they determine a claim under state law. Thus, filing a claim in federal court does not lessen the aggregation or management challenges that the various horizontal choice-of-law methodologies pose for complex litigation.

Because the principal transfer authorities (28 U.S.C. §§ 1404 and 1407) were enacted after *Erie*, *Erie* did not address the question of the law that should apply when a federal court sitting in diversity transfers a case to another district. For instance, suppose that a plaintiff filed a diversity case in federal court in Montana, and that Montana conflict-of-laws provisions point to Utah law. The case is then transferred to a federal court in Utah. Had the case been filed in Utah as an initial matter, however, Utah's conflict-of-laws rule would have dictated the use of Montana law. When the federal court in Montana transfers a case to a federal court in Utah, should the transferee court use Montana's conflict-of-laws rule to choose Utah law (in other words, acting as if it were still the Montana federal court) or should it use Utah's conflict-of-laws rule to choose Montana law (in other words, acting as if the case had been filed in Utah federal court originally).

In *Van Dusen v. Barrack*, the Supreme Court combined *Erie*'s anti-forum-shopping argument with the plaintiff's privilege to select the forum and the language of § 1404 to hold that a § 1404 transfer did not authorize a change in applicable choice-of-law rule.[591] Therefore, the transferee Utah court must apply the same conflict-of-laws rule as the transferor Montana court would apply. Although the Supreme Court has not addressed the issue, the Judicial Panel on Multidistrict Litigation and MDL courts have long believed that the same rule applies to MDL consolidations.[592]

---

federal court in Delaware must conform to those prevailing in Delaware's state courts.") (citation omitted).

[591] 376 U.S. 612 (1964). The rule applies regardless of whether the plaintiff or the defendant seeks a transfer. *See* Ferens v. John Deere Co., 494 U.S. 516 (1990).

[592] *See* Chang v. Baxter Healthcare Corp., 599 F.3d 728 (7th Cir. 2010) ("When a diversity case is transferred by the multidistrict litigation panel, the law applied is that of the jurisdiction from which the case was transferred . . . ."); *In re* Gen. Motors Class E Stock Buyout Sec. Litig., 696 F. Supp. 1546 (J.P.M.L. 1988) (stating that "it is

The breadth of *Erie*'s holding also answers the second question posed above: what law applies when state and federal claims are blended in a single case? Although *Erie* was a decision only about the scope of federal-court power in diversity cases, the universal assumption is that *Erie* also applies to cases invoking supplemental jurisdiction. Therefore, a federal court must apply the same law to a claim within supplemental jurisdiction as a state court in the state in which the case was filed—including the choice-of-law rule.

The first question—which interpretation of federal law should a court adopt when circuits have different interpretations and a case is transferred from a circuit with one view to a circuit with another view?—is the *Van Dusen* problem carried over to claims arising under federal law. You might logically think that the resolution of the issue would be the same, and the transferor court's view of federal law would carry forward after transfer. But you would be mistaken, at least in the eyes of most courts.

The seminal case is *In re Korean Air Lines Disaster of September 1, 1983*.[593] *Korean Air Lines* arose when a Soviet Union fighter jet shot down a commercial airplane that allegedly strayed into Soviet air space. The Warsaw Convention limited liability for damages occurring on an international flight, but the airline had failed to place the limitation in the font size required by the Convention. Under the law of the Second Circuit, that failure abrogated the limitation; the law in other circuits was unclear.

After cases were filed in district courts in the First, Second, Sixth, and District of Columbia Circuits, the Judicial Panel on Multidistrict Litigation ordered consolidated in the district court for the District of Columbia. The district court first held that, under its interpretation of federal law, the technical failure did not abrogate the damages limitation. That ruling conflicted with the Second Circuit's interpretation, thus setting up the central question: did the cases transferred from the Second Circuit carry their contrary interpretation of federal law forward with them? The district court held no, and an interlocutory appeal followed.

In an opinion by then-Judge Ruth Bader Ginsberg, the court of appeals affirmed. Acknowledging that the rule of *Van Dusen v. Barrack* required the application of the law of the transferor forum on questions of state law, the court argued that the rule should be different for transfers arising under federal law. In theory, federal law is uniform among the circuits, and the economy of multidistrict

---

not the business of the Panel to consider what law the transferee court might apply"; citing *Van Dusen*).

[593] 829 F.2d 1171 (D.C. Cir. 1987), *aff'd on other grounds* sub nom. Chan v. Korean Air Lines, 490 U.S. 122 (1989).

proceedings would be thwarted if a judge needed to juggle multiple versions of federal law. Recognizing that the transfer provisions of §§ 1404 and 1407 were silent on the matter, the court called for a definitive resolution from Congress or the Supreme Court.

The Supreme Court granted certiorari, but it resolved the underlying issue of federal law (affirming the view of the D.C. Circuit) without addressing the choice-of-law issue presented.

For the most part, courts after *Korean Air Lines* have followed the approach of the D.C. Circuit and applied the transferee circuit's law after a § 1404 or § 1407 transfer.[594] One MDL court created an exception for motions for class certification, applying the transferor circuit's interpretation of Rule 23 to state-law claims.[595] It reasoned that the cases would return to their transferor circuits for trial after completion of the MDL proceedings and the issues of class certification were so intertwined with issues of state substantive law that the transferor circuit's interpretation of Rule 23 carried forward under *Van Dusen* to the transferee court.

Korean Air Lines heightens the stakes over the transferee forum to which the Judicial Panel on Multidistrict Litigation will transfer the case, at least in cases with federal claims on which different circuits have adopted different views. You might think that the law of the transferee circuit shouldn't matter because an MDL is for pretrial proceedings, and the cases return to their transferor forums (with the transferor forums' law) before trial. As we have seen, however, many cases end in the transferee forum, either with a settlement or a dismissal on summary judgment. The transferor circuit's law can have a great deal to say about the terms of a settlement or dismissal. In addition, once the transferee MDL court rules on the federal issue (perhaps in a motion for summary judgment), that decision becomes the "law of the case."[596] In dicta, *Korean Air Lines* stated that any cases transferred back to the Second Circuit would be bound by the law of the D.C. Circuit on the applicability of the Warsaw Convention.[597]

---

[594] The American Law Institute has also endorsed the *Korean Air Lines* approach. *See* COMPLEX LITIGATION, *supra* note 101, § 6.08.

[595] *See In re* Methyl Tertiary Butyl Ether (MTBE) Prods. Liab. Litig., 241 F.R.D. 435 (S.D.N.Y. 2007).

[596] For a discussion of the "law of the case" doctrine, see Christianson v. Colt Indus. Operating Co., 486 U.S. 800 (1988) (noting that the doctrine is applied to "decisions of a coordinate court in the same case as to a court's own decisions").

[597] In one MDL proceeding, the transferee judge applied the law of the transferee circuit to enter judgment against certain federal claims. After remand of remaining claims to the transferor courts, plaintiffs sought to appeal the judgments under the more generous view of federal law adopted in the transferor circuits. The court of appeals in the transferee circuit took the extraordinary (and legally uncertain) step of issuing a writ of mandamus to the Judicial Panel to require it to re-transfer the

Despite the evident importance of the issue to the parties, the Panel professes agnosticism about how a transfer might affect the outcome of the case. But the parties do not wear such blinders, and typically argue for the selection of transferee courts with better law (though they usually mask this blatant forum shopping with neutral arguments about why one forum or judge is well suited to handle a case).

Korean Air Lines was a § 1407 case, but its principle has been applied as well to § 1404 transfers.[598] The differing approaches to transfer for diversity and federal-question claims demonstrated that no vertical choice-of-law regime can avoid issues of forum shopping: the *Van Dusen* approach encourages forum shopping when filing a case, while the *Korean Air Lines* approach encourages forum shopping when transferring a case. From the viewpoint of facilitating aggregation, it is not evident which approach is better, although the one-law approach of *Korean Air Lines* makes class certification easier to accomplish. From the viewpoint of case management, the one-law approach is also superior.

b. *Procedural Law*

State procedural law can vary from federal procedural law, and different procedures can sometimes matter to the outcome of case. Thus, as in the horizontal context, the choice of procedural law can matter a great deal.

Having a federal court apply federal procedural law to federal claims is evident. When state-law claims are involved, however, things become more complicated. In some instances, a federal statute directs the choice of procedural law. As long as the statute is constitutional, a court must follow this direction. For instance, a federal court sitting in diversity must apply § 1404 even if a state court would not transfer a case under like circumstances.[599] Conversely, Federal Rule of Evidence 501 commands federal courts to use state law of privilege when deciding a claim or defense based on state law.

Most federal procedural rules, however, are contained in the Federal Rules of Civil Procedure, in the local rules of each district, and in common-law principles. These rules contain no choice-of-law command. The Supreme Court has long recognized that *Erie* has something to say about the choice of federal or state procedural law;

---

dismissed claims to the transferee circuit, so that the appeals would occur in the transferee circuit. *See In re* Food Lion, Inc., Fair Labor Standards Act "Effective Scheduling" Litig., 73 F.3d 528 (4th Cir. 1996). For further discussion and cases, see *supra* note 131 and accompanying text.

[598] *See* Murphy v. FDIC, 208 F.3d 959 (11th Cir. 2000).

[599] *See* Stewart Org. v. Ricoh Corp., 487 U.S. 22 (1988).

after all, a party can shop for a federal forum as much for procedural as for substantive differences. The problem is that the Court's path in exploring the choice between federal and state procedural rules has been a meandering one.

Some basic propositions are generally accepted. First, when the federal and state procedural rules are the same, then conceptually the choice may matter but pragmatically it does not. The first step in any conflict-of-laws situation is to find a conflict; if there is none, a court can apply that rule and reserve the hard question to other cases in which federal and state rules diverge.

Second, the Federal Rules of Civil Procedure are promulgated pursuant to a federal statute, the Rules Enabling Act. The Enabling Act imposes two conditions on the Federal Rules: they must be "general rules of practice and procedure and rules of evidence," and they must not "abridge, enlarge or modify any substantive right."[600] Whether correctly or not (and the point has engendered a lot of scholarly and some judicial criticism), the Supreme Court has collapsed the two requirements into one; as long as a Federal Rule "really regulates procedure,—the judicial process for enforcing rights and duties recognized by substantive law and for justly administering remedy and redress for disregard or infraction of them," then it passes muster under the Enabling Act.[601] Therefore, as long as a Federal Rule is constitutional and regulates procedure, a federal court must apply it.[602] It would probably not surprise you to find out that the Supreme Court has never invalidated a Federal Rule under this test,[603] so when a Federal Rule covers a matter, a federal court will apply it.

Third, when no Federal Rule of Civil Procedure covers a situation, the choice between a federal or a varying state procedural rule requires a different analysis. At one point, the Supreme Court suggested that, given *Erie*, a federal court should conform itself to the procedures of the relevant state court to the greatest extent possible:any difference in procedure that could be "outcome determinative" required the use of the state procedural rule.[604] The Court later refined this test, indicating that a federal court must adopt the state rule of procedure only when the choice of the federal

---

600 *See* 28 U.S.C. § 2072(a)–(b).

601 *See* Subbach v. Wilson & Co., 312 U.S. 1 (1941).

602 *See* Hanna v. Plumer, 380 U.S. 460 (1965).

603 That is not to say that the Rules Enabling Act is entirely toothless. In some of its most notable class-action decisions, the Supreme Court has interpreted Rule 23 narrowly to avoid arguable collisions with the Enabling Act. *See* Wal-Mart Stores, Inc. v. Dukes, 564 U.S. 338 (2011); Ortiz v. Fibreboard Corp., 527 U.S. 815 (1999); Amchem Prods., Inc. v. Windsor, 521 U.S. 591 (1997).

604 *See* Ragan v. Merch. Transfer & Warehouse Co., 337 U.S. 530 (1949); Guaranty Trust Co. of N.Y. v. York, 326 U.S. 99 (1945).

procedural rule would implicate the "twin aims of the *Erie* rule: discouragement of forum-shopping and avoidance of inequitable administration of the laws."[605]

The clear (and possibly case-decisive) difference in the tests for applying a Federal Rule and a common-law federal procedural rule brings to the fore an interpretive question: is a Federal Rule broad enough to cover the court's action? On some occasions, the Court has construed a Federal Rule narrowly, so that the Federal Rule did not control the matter. With the Federal Rule sidelined, the Court then turned to the "twin aims" of *Erie* to determine if a state rule of procedure or a federal common-law rule applied.[606] In interpreting the breadth of the Federal Rule, the Court has examined the policies and concerns for federalism that animated *Erie*, thus turning the question of interpretation and the question of choosing the law on a similar set of questions.

The Supreme Court has never intimated, however, that a federal court's choice of a state rule of procedure is constitutionally compelled. As we saw with the horizontal choice-of-law issue, a court always has an interest in applying its own rules of procedure to determine a dispute; likewise, a federal court has an interest in applying federal procedural rules to determine federal cases. Thus, the choice of a state rather than a federal rule of procedure is driven by policy considerations.

Although these basic propositions are clear enough, the Court has sometimes had difficulty applying them to concrete situations; and this difficulty has created uncertainty in the "procedural *Erie*" doctrine. Perhaps one of the best places to test the slipperiness of the analysis is Rule 23, which dwells closer to the procedure-substance border than any other Federal Rule. Nearly every state also has a class-action rule.[607] Many of these rules differ from Rule 23, either in their language or in the interpretation that state courts have given to comparable requirements.[608] When a plaintiff asserts in federal court class-wide claims based on state law, and the state rule of procedure would generate a different result on the class-certification

[605] *See Hanna*, 380 U.S. at 468. In *Walker v. Armco Steel Corp.*, 446 U.S. 740 (1980), the Court held that the state rule of procedure applied when only the second of these twin policies was implicated.

[606] *See* Gasperini v. Ctr. for Humanities, Inc., 518 U.S. 415 (1996); *Walker*, 446 U.S. 740.

[607] *See supra* note 286.

[608] *Cf.* N.Y. C.P.L.R. 901(a) (listing five requirements for a class action that vary somewhat from Rule 23); Smith v. Bayer Corp., 564 U.S. 299 (2011) (noting that, although West Virginia's Rule 23(b)(3) contained the same language as Federal Rule 23(b)(3), the West Virginia Supreme Court had disapproved of federal courts' interpretation of the predominance requirement).

question than Rule 23 does, must a federal court adopt the state rule regarding class certification?

The Supreme Court addressed this issue in *Shady Grove Orthopedic Associates, P.A. v. Allstate Insurance Co.*[609] The plaintiffs filed the case in federal court in New York, alleging that the defendant insurance company failed to pay the required interest on late payments. This failure allegedly violated New York law, which specified $500 in statutory minimum damages for the violation. The plaintiffs brought the case as a class action under Rule 23. Because $500 per class member far exceeded the actual damages that they suffered, the class action threatened to impose significant liability on the defendant. Had the case been filed in a New York state court, no class action could have been certified; New York's class-action provision prohibited certification of a class in cases seeking to recover a penalty or statutory minimum.

That clear difference (no class action in New York state court, possible class action in New York federal court) teed up the question for the Supreme Court. In a badly fractured opinion, which was a majority for some portions, a plurality of four for others, and a plurality of three for the remainder, the Court found that Rule 23, and not New York state law, should control the issue of class certification. The central reasoning, which commanded four votes, was that Rule 23 was a rule of procedure under *Sibbach*'s "really regulates procedure" test. Because Rule 23 was valid under the Rules Enabling Act, a federal court was required to employ it. Even though, as a matter of state law, the New York limitation on class actions might be regarded as substantive, the critical question was how Rule 23 should be characterized under the Enabling Act.

Justice Stevens concurred in the result, ultimately finding that New York's restriction on statutory-minimum class actions was not so bound up in the "substantive rights and remedies" allegedly violated that Rule 23 became inapplicable. His concurrence rejected a simplistic application of *Sibbach*, and sought to breathe life into the "abridge, enlarge or modify" restriction in the Enabling Act. Justice Ginsburg's dissent for four Justices argued for a narrow interpretation of Rule 23, whose general terms did not address the Rule's specific application in cases seeking a statutory-minimum award or a penalty. Because no conflict between federal and state law existed and because the twin aims of *Erie* pointed toward the application of state law, the dissent argued that no class action could be certified.

The lack of a majority on the question of Rule 23's applicability makes *Shady Grove* an unstable opinion. Justice Stevens' opinion is

---

[609] 559 U.S. 393 (2010).

the narrowest ground explaining the result, and under traditional principles for interpreting Supreme Court opinions, it would ordinarily be regarded as controlling. But no Supreme Court Justice ever suggested the analysis that he adopted, and Justice Stevens is no longer a member of the Court. For the time being, lower courts are treating the issue as settled, and are applying Rule 23 to diversity claims even when the courts of the forum state adopt a contrary view on the certification of a class action.[610] With changes in Supreme Court personnel, however, the last word on the issue has probably not yet been written.

The "procedural *Erie*" problem applies only to state-law claims adjudicated in federal court. There is also a "reverse *Erie*" issue, so that state courts in rare instances must adopt a federal procedural rule for a federal claim heard in state court.[611]

For state-law claims heard in state court or federal-law claims heard in federal court, the answer is clear. State courts apply state procedural rules (usually, as we have seen, the procedural rules of the forum state) to resolve state-law claims, and federal courts apply federal procedural rules to resolve federal-law claims.[612]

B. Solving Choice-of-Law Issues in Complex Litigation

The prior section demonstrated some of the ways in which choice-of-law considerations can fracture the legal facets of a case and thus frustrate the single-forum aggregation and management of complex litigation. This section considers a series of techniques that can mitigate or eliminate choice-of-law difficulties. For the most part, these techniques attempt to solve the horizontal choice-of-law problem that arises when multiple state laws are in play. But some can also address the issue of overlapping state and federal claims. Their common goal is to create a single, uniform law; but as we will see, these techniques raise their own concerns.

1. Manipulating Choice-of-Law Principles

As we have seen, all choice-of-law principles are capable of manipulation. One way to achieve a single, uniform law is to ensure

---

[610] *See. e.g.*, Lisk v. Lumber One Wood Preserving, LLC, 792 F.3d 1331 (11th Cir. 2015) (holding that Rule 23 applied even when a state restriction on class actions was a part of the legislation creating a substantive right).

[611] *See* Dice v. Akron, Canton & Youngstown R.R., 342 U.S. 359 (1952) (requiring state courts hearing FELA claims to provide a statutorily required jury trial for a factual matter usually resolved by the judge under state procedural rules). *Cf.* Howlett v. Rose, 496 U.S. 356 (1990) (holding that state courts cannot adopt procedural rules that bar the prosecution of federal claims in state court when they remain open to adjudicating similar state-law claims).

[612] *See* West v. Conrail, 481 U.S. 35 (1987).

that the forum's choice-of-law rule is used in a manner that one law is chosen to govern the dispute. By "one law," we do not necessarily mean the law of one state (although that is a possibility). Both Iowa and Minnesota may have the same legal doctrine on the relevant matter, while Indiana and Kentucky have a different doctrine. As long as the forum's conflicts rule chooses Iowa law for some claimants and Minnesota law for others, a uniform law applies to all the cases.

Lex loci rules tend to be less subject to manipulation, although issues of characterization and the *lex loci* exceptions create wiggle room. Interest analysis and the balancing approach of the "most significant relationship" test are even more malleable if a judge's goal is to obtain a single law applicable to all cases.

Of course, an important question is whether such a result-oriented approach to choosing law is proper or rather makes a mockery of the principles that undergird the conflicts field. One well-known case put this question into stark relief.[613] An airplane with 273 people aboard crashed on takeoff at O'Hare Airport in Illinois. Cases were filed in federal courts in Illinois, California, New York, Michigan, Hawaii, and Puerto Rico. The decedents were residents of California, Connecticut, Hawaii, Illinois, Indiana, Massachusetts, Michigan, New Jersey, New York, Vermont, Puerto Rico, Japan, the Netherlands, and Saudi Arabia. The defendants were the manufacturer of the airplane, which was incorporated in Maryland with its principal place of business in Missouri, and the airline, which was incorporated in Delaware with its principal place of business in New York (or possibly Texas—the issue was in dispute). The airplane was designed and built (negligently, according to the complaint) in California. It was maintained (also negligently, according to the complaint) in Oklahoma.

The Judicial Panel on Multidistrict Litigation consolidated the cases in the Northern District of Illinois. A critical issue in the case was whether punitive damages were available. As the court of appeals described the situation, "[t]he law of the place of the disaster, the law of the place of manufacture of the airplane, and the law of the primary place of business of the airline do not allow punitive damages; but, the law of the primary place of business of the manufacturer of the airplane and the law of the place of maintenance of the airline do allow punitive damages." Given that state law provided the rule of decision, the choice-of-law rules of each transferor forum applied. The MDL court dutifully analyzed the transferor forum's choice-of-law rules for each case, concluding that, with one exception, each transferor forum would choose the

---

613 *See In re* Air Crash Disaster Near Chicago, Ill. on May 25, 1979, 644 F.2d 594 (7th Cir. 1981).

substantive law of a state that permitted punitive damages against the manufacturer but no transferor forum would choose the law of a state that permitted punitive damages against the airline.

Conducting the same choice-of-law analysis in an exhaustive 100-page opinion, the court of appeals determined that the MDL court had correctly determined that the airline was not subject to punitive damages, but had erred with respect to the application of the choice-of-law principles to the airplane's manufacturer. The court of appeals re-analyzed the state choice-of-law approaches of each of the six transferor forums—two of which used a "most significant contacts" approach, one of which used interest analysis, one of which used *lex loci delicti*, one of which had used *lex loci delicti* but was in a state of flux, and one of which had chosen no choice-of-law approach. The court concluded that each transferor forum would have chosen the law of a state that did not permit punitive damages against the manufacturer. As a result, neither the airline nor the manufacturer was subject to punitive damages.

The miracle by which the different choice-of-law rules all pointed to the same substantive result for both defendants was roundly criticized by scholars, who thought that the court unfairly downplayed the interests of some of the relevant jurisdictions in its desire to achieve a single law that made the multidistrict litigation manageable.[614] The American Law Institute cited *Air Crash Disaster* as an example of what is wrong with the traditional choice-of-law approach in complex litigation, noting that the Seventh Circuit's result "underscores the lack of predictability in the choice of law regime as it is applied today."[615]

The same effort to shape the choice-of-law analysis to obtain a single law can arise when all the related claims are initially brought in a single forum. For instance, in *Ysbrand v. DaimlerChrysler Corp.*,[616] the defendant manufactured minivans with allegedly defective airbags. In Oklahoma state court, the plaintiffs brought a class action on behalf of consumers in every state. Because the class excluded people who had suffered physical injuries, the claims sought recovery only for the economic loss that the class members had

---

[614] *See* Larry Kramer, *Choice of Law in Complex Litigation*, 71 N.Y.U. L. REV. 547 (1996) (calling *Air Crash Disaster* "a virtual 'how-to' manual of ways to manipulate choice-of-law analysis" and arguing that its misreading of some of the transferor forums' choice-of-law regimes was a "grotesque distortion"); Andreas Lowenfeld, *Mass Torts and the Conflict of Laws: The Airline Disaster*, 1989 U. ILL. L. REV. 157 (stating that "the airplane cases in the 1970s and 1980s seem to have made a parody not only of the conflict of laws but of the law of torts in general").

[615] *See* COMPLEX LITIGATION, *supra* note 101, at 307.

[616] 81 P.3d 618 (Okla. 2003).

suffered. The case alleged breach of warranty as well as fraud and deceit.

Class certification hinged on manageability concerns, in particular on whether a single, uniform law could be applied to all the claims. Oklahoma had adopted the "most significant relationship" test for the warranty, fraud, and deceit claims. On the warranty claims, the Oklahoma Supreme Court weighed the relevant factors, a number of which pointed toward the use of the law of the state in which each consumer purchased the minivan, and concluded that the interests of the state of manufacture (here, Michigan) should control all the warranty claims. The court specifically stated that one of the factors that led to the choice of Michigan law was the interstate system's need for "predictability and uniformity of result."

On the fraud and deceit claims, the court reacted differently. Here the balance of factors in the "most significant relationship" test tipped toward the law of the state in which each consumer received the misrepresentation (which, assuming that they bought their minivans where they lived, was their home states). The application of so many different laws, the Oklahoma Supreme Court held, created an "overwhelming burden which would make the class unmanageable." Thus, the court upheld class certification on the warranty claims but not on the deceit or fraud claims.

Of course, the Oklahoma Supreme Court could have held that the center of gravity for the fraud and deceit claims was the state in which the statements were made: Michigan. Thus, *Ysbrand* could have resulted in one law for the entire case and class certification on all claims. Whether a court should bend the choice-of-law rules law to meet the needs of a complex case is a hard question. If it does not, some (or all) of the claims of a large group of victims may

Problem 1

An arthritis drug that had been prescribed more than 100 million times was alleged to have increased the risk for heart attacks and strokes. Thousands of personal-injury suits, some of which were filed as class actions, ensued. The Judicial Panel on Multidistrict Litigation consolidated the federal cases. In deciding whether a class action originally filed in New Jersey was manageable, the MDL court conducted a choice-of-law analysis. New Jersey's regime was a blend of interest analysis and "most significant relationship" approaches. The plaintiffs argued that the law of New Jersey should apply to all claims because it was the state in which the corporate decisions that led to the injury-causing conduct occurred. Seeking to defeat class certification, the defendants argued that the law of the plaintiff's domicile (which was also presumably the place of the plaintiff's injury in most cases) was the center of gravity. What result? *See In re* Vioxx Prods. Liab. Litig., 239 F.R.D. 450 (E.D. La. 2006).

never be pursued and justice never achieved. If it does, the result seems like outcome-oriented jurisprudence rather than the neutral and objective application of legal principles. A tough choice indeed.

Accepting the reality that choice-of-law rules are likely to thwart nationwide class aggregation, some plaintiffs concoct class definitions that include members only from certain states.[617] These collections of states have little to do with each other—save for one thing. They all employ the same relevant substantive law, and the choice-of-law rule of the forum state would apply that substantive law to the class members' claims. Unless another approach to overcome the choice-of-law hurdle exists, this piecemeal strategy is often the best aggregation option available.

2. Using Federal Law

A second approach to address the existence of nonuniform state laws is to adopt federal law in place of state law. As we saw, federal law can also lack uniformity among circuits, but the federal courts have tended to solve this problem by adopting the law of the circuit in which the case is located. In order for this approach to work well, federal law would need to preempt state law; otherwise, federal law merely piles another law on top of a cacophony of state laws.

There are two possible sources of federal law. One is legislation. For instance, Congress has contemplated passing a products-liability statute that would supplant the products-liability laws of the states. If a single, uniform products-liability regime existed, more nationwide mass-tort class actions might be certified.[618] The problem with this approach is getting Congress to act. Congress is understandably reluctant to override state law, especially on matters traditionally reserved to state regulation. For example, despite repeated importuning from the likes of the United States Supreme Court and President George W. Bush, Congress never enacted legislation to resolve the biggest aggregation nightmare in American history: the asbestos-litigation crisis.

A second source is federal common law. Despite *Erie*'s admonition that there is no "federal general common law," federal common law still exists in certain enclaves. Federal common law is generally thought to be preemptive of state law to the contrary, and as federal law the Supremacy Clause demands that it be applied in

---

[617] *See, e.g.*, Briseno v. ConAgra Foods, Inc., 844 F.3d 1121 (9th Cir. 2017) (creating a class of plaintiffs from California, Colorado, Florida, Illinois, Indiana, Nebraska, New York, Ohio, Oregon, South Dakota, and Texas).

[618] To be sure, a national products-liability statute would not guarantee class certification. Individual factual issues such as causation, damages, and contributory negligence might defeat certification even if liability were uniform.

both state and federal courts. Thus, federal common law creates a single, uniform law to resolve any dispute to which it applies.

The catch is the phrase "to which it applies." The enclaves of federal common law are few in number and restricted in scope. Federal common law provides the rule of decision for cases involving the United States, boundary or water disputes between states, admiralty claims, disputes involving international relations, and a couple of other matters.[619] None of these enclaves is a breeding ground for complex litigation.

The issue, therefore, is whether federal common law could expand in scope to provide the rule of decision for the types of claims that are the grist for the complex-litigation mill. Could, for instance, courts create a federal common law of products liability or a federal common law of consumer protection?

As desirable as this approach might seem when viewed through the lens of aggregating and managing complex litigation, its problems are manifest. One is the source of a court's power to create federal common law. Most of the present enclaves of federal common law are tied closely to a jurisdictional grant in Article III (for instance, Article III gives federal courts subject-matter jurisdiction over admiralty claims, claims involving ambassadors and consuls, and controversies against the United States); at a minimum, the enclaves involve situations in which nonuniform state laws create a significant conflict with unique federal interests.[620] A second concern is the friction that federal common law generates with principles such as separation of powers (by overtaking Congress's capacity to legislate) and federalism (by claiming the states' authority to regulate behavior).

The difficulty of creating federal common law to govern a complex dispute is well illustrated by *In re "Agent Orange" Product Liability Litigation*.[621] The *Agent Orange* litigation evolved into a class action of 2.4 million veterans of the Vietnam War suing the manufacturers of herbicides used to defoliate the jungle. The herbicides allegedly caused various injuries years later. The United States was an occasional third-party defendant. In attempting to establish federal-question jurisdiction over the dispute, the plaintiffs argued that the law applicable to the manufacturers was federal common law.

The court of appeals disagreed, holding that the controversy fell into none of the usual enclaves of federal common law. It is difficult,

---

[619] For a description of these enclaves, see Jay Tidmarsh & Brian J. Murray, *A Theory of Federal Common Law*, 100 NW. U. L. REV. 585 (2006).

[620] *See* Boyle v. United Tech. Corp., 487 U.S. 500 (1988).

[621] 635 F.3d 987 (2d Cir. 1980).

however, to imagine any case for which federal law would be more appropriate: a lawsuit brought by United States military personnel against military contractors regarding war materiel purchased by the United States government for use in a foreign country during an American war. Relying on Wyoming or Maine law to determine the rights and responsibilities of military personnel and military contractors seems inappropriate, especially when those rights and responsibilities might vary from state to state. A uniform law seems a better solution.

But it was not to be. There have been a few cases in which the Supreme Court or lower courts have adopted federal common law in situations that were less compelling, but they are older and are clearly contrary to the modern trend.[622] Therefore, unless a complex case falls within one of the enclaves of federal common law—and very few do—some other mechanism to create a single, uniform law must be found.

3. Creating National-Consensus Law

The *Agent Orange* litigation eventually gave rise to one such mechanism: the use of a uniform "national consensus" law. As we have seen, conflict-of-laws rules usually lead to the selection of one state's legal principles and to the rejection of other states' right to regulate the relevant conduct. Under the "national consensus" theory, however, all relevant states would recognize that their own interests in applying their law should be sublimated to the overarching interests of all states and the nation in having one law apply to the dispute. This law, called "national consensus" law, tries to respect the interests of all states to the greatest extent possible.

This approach may sound a lot like federal common law, and it is. But technically "national consensus" law is state law, in which each state gives up the right to apply its parochial law to a dispute and agrees to use, as its state law for this dispute, a law that is a compromise of the laws of all the relevant states.

---

[622] *See* Illinois v. City of Milwaukee, 406 U.S. 91 (1972) (holding that federal common law governed a case involving interstate water pollution); Kohr v. Allegheny Airlines, Inc., 504 F.2d 400 (7th Cir. 1974) (applying a federal common law of contribution and indemnity to litigation arising from an airplane crash that fortuitously occurred in one of the few states that did not recognize contribution and indemnity claims among tortfeasors). The Supreme Court walked back the use of federal common law in *Illinois v. City of Milwaukee* nine years later. *City of Milwaukee v. Illinois*, 451 U.S. 304 (1977). In recent years, the Supreme Court has likewise refused to authorize federal common law in another case with national and international dimensions: a lawsuit by eight states against major utilities charging them with responsibility for damages due to global warming. *See*. Am. Elec. Power Co. v. Connecticut, 564 U.S. 410 (2011).

Judge Weinstein adopted this approach in the *Agent Orange* litigation.[623] He argued that the contacts of any state (the place of citizenship of some of the veterans or of a defendant) were "dwarfed by the national contacts in the case. The only jurisdiction with which all elements in the litigation undoubtedly have significant contacts, and the only unifying factor, is the nation." Given the "overwhelming need for uniformity" in this unique dispute, "either federal or national consensus substantive law [is] the only workable approach."

Problem 2

In the asbestos litigation, the settlement trust for one defendant required restructuring to remain solvent. Restructuring affected the rights of third parties. The content of those rights varied from state to state. There were "large interstate and national interests," with a "multitude of federal interests intertwined in this litigation." Should national-consensus law be applied? *See In re* Joint E. & S. Dists. Asbestos Litig., 129 B.R. 710 (E. & S.D.N.Y. 1991), *vacated on other grounds*, 982 F.2d 721 (2d Cir. 1992), *modified*, 993 F.2d 7 (2d Cir. 1993). What if the lawsuit involved a mass tort against the tobacco industry? *See In re* Simon II Litig., 211 F.R.D. 86 (E.D.N.Y. 2002), *vacated and remanded on other grounds*, 407 F.3d 125 (2d Cir. 2005).

This approach is controversial, to say the least. The court of appeals in the *Agent Orange* litigation tentatively criticized the idea, although it never reversed the decision because the case settled before the law was applied.[624] Some conflict-of-laws scholars have lambasted the decision.[625] Because of the nature of this law, judges must ultimately weigh the various interests to determine the content of the law—a task for which they may not be institutionally suited. On the other hand, why should one state law "win" and other laws "lose" when a controversy is truly national is scope, and the lawsuit questions decisions made in the conduct of a foreign war?

4. Applying the Law of the Most Restrictive State

A different idea is to choose the law of the jurisdiction that is least favorable to a particular party, and then to try the case under that law. Obviously, this approach requires the consent of the affected party. For instance, assume that states have a range of rules on an issue of importance to a mass tort. Some of the rules are highly favorable to plaintiffs, some are more middle of the road, and the law of Alabama is the least favorable to plaintiffs. Assume as well that

---

[623] *In re* "Agent Orange" Prod. Liab. Litig., 580 F. Supp. 690 (E.D.N.Y. 1984).

[624] *See In re* Diamond Shamrock Chems. Co., 725 F.2d 858 (2d Cir. 1984). Indeed, Judge Weinstein never announced what the content of this national-consensus law was, and the case settled in the face of the parties' uncertainty about whether the law would be favorable or unfavorable.

[625] *See, e.g.*, Kramer, *supra* note 614, at 562–63.

Alabama has contact with every claim in the litigation (perhaps it is the principal place of business for the defendant).

In this situation, it might be rational for plaintiffs' counsel to agree to try the case under the law of Alabama. Without a single law applying to each case, a court may decline to aggregate the case and plaintiffs might not sue individually. Before agreeing to this strategy, counsel would need to be satisfied that the value added by aggregation exceeds the increased likelihood of a negative outcome.

The plaintiffs made precisely this trade-off in *In re School Asbestos Litigation*.[626] Facing an argument that the number of state laws made a class action unmanageable, the lawyers for a putative class of school districts that had expended money remediating asbestos contamination agreed to have the law of the least favorable jurisdiction applied to them on each issue in the class action. On the eve of trial, one of the defendants sought a writ of mandamus. The court of appeals began by noting that the defendant had standing to contest the matter, even though it did not seem to be harmed by the use of favorable law, because in subsequent litigation class members could possibly collaterally attack a judgment against them by arguing that class counsel's agreement to use unfavorable law constituted inadequate representation.[627]

On the issue of using the most restrictive law, the court of appeals questioned, but did not foreclose, the approach. It held that the issue was not ripe for adjudication, in part because a new judge would try the case on remand. It also intimated that *Shutts* "requires the district court to apply the law of the individual jurisdictions," even though *Shutts* had only forbidden the selection of the law of a state with no significant contacts with a controversy.[628] At a minimum, it urged the district court on remand "to examine *Shutts* carefully before submitting the case to the jury according to the law of a hypothetical strictest jurisdiction, even if the class plaintiffs once agreed to that approach."

Using the law of the most restrictive jurisdiction faces obstacles. To begin, the disadvantaged party must be willing to consent to the use of unfavorable law. Next, that law must have some connection with each plaintiff's claim. Finally, if the case is a class action, problems with inadequate representation must be addressed. These inadequate-representation concerns are not insuperable. The

---

[626] 977 F.2d 764 (3d Cir. 1992).

[627] Under present views of the scope of collateral attack, it is not clear that the court of appeals' concern for a successful collateral attack was warranted. *See supra* Chapter 6.E.3.

[628] *See* Phillips Petroleum Co. v. Shutts, 472 U.S. 797 (1985) (discussed *supra* notes 583–584 and accompanying text).

benefits of aggregation may indeed be so great that it is in the interests of each class member to proceed under the least favorable law. But the circumstances in which the benefits of a most-restrictive-law approach outweigh the risks are limited, making this approach unappealing in most instances.

5. Choosing a Single Law with a Right to Opt Out

A related approach is to adopt a single law to govern a dispute—presumably a law that is unfavorable to the plaintiffs but one with significant contacts to the suit—and then give each plaintiff the ability to opt out of the trial conducted under that law. This approach is unlikely to resolve all claims under a single, uniform law, but it reduces the scope of litigation to an extent.

The approach has never been popular, in part because of a famous instance in which it was used: *In re Bendectin Litigation.*[629] *Bendectin* was a multidistrict proceeding with more than 2,300 plaintiffs claiming injuries due to a prescription drug. It was consolidated in Ohio, the home state of the defendant. After pretrial dispositions of some claims, the MDL judge proposed a joint trial of remaining claims under Ohio law. For the plaintiffs who had filed suit in Ohio, the trial was mandatory. For cases filed elsewhere, the judge gave the plaintiffs the option of participating in the MDL trial or obtaining a remand to their original forum.

Although Ohio law on the critical question of causation was not as favorable to plaintiffs as the law in some states, 261 out-of-state plaintiffs opted to remain in the case with 557 Ohio-filing plaintiffs. The judge then tried the case using a controversial process that we will study later.[630] The plaintiffs lost.

On appeal, the plaintiffs made a number of unsuccessful arguments. One of these arguments was the unfairness of applying Ohio law to the plaintiffs who had filed elsewhere. The court of appeals dismissed the point, noting that the plaintiffs had consented to this method of proceeding.

As a practical matter, the outcome in *Bendectin* has soured plaintiffs on the opt-out approach to creating a single law. Each side is likely to want law favorable to its positions, and neither is likely to opt into a trial using unfavorable law.

6. Developing a Unique Choice-of-Law Principle

A final strategy is to adopt a single choice-of-law principle. This approach does not directly establish the single, uniform law that is

---

[629] *See* 857 F.2d 290 (6th Cir. 1988).

[630] *See infra* notes 886–887 and accompanying text.

desirable from the viewpoint of aggregation and case management. But in many large aggregations, it makes less complicated the first step of the inquiry, which is to determine which choice-of-law rules apply to each of the claims. If the choice-of-law principle is then applied with some sensitivity to the objective of adopting a single substantive law, such a principle could make inroads on the choice-of-law problem.

Both the American Bar Association and the American Law Institute proposed that judges in mass torts should be able to adopt a choice-of-law principle tailored to the needs of complex litigation, regardless of the choice-of-law principles that the forum state generally adopted in tort cases.[631] The ALI's principles were crafted to funnel the judge toward the choice of a single substantive law where possible.

To adopt a unique choice-of-law provision, a court needs a source of authority. Because the subject of conflict of laws has developed largely on a common-law basis, a forum court could presumably modify its traditional principles to accommodate the needs of complex litigation. In effect, this is what Judge Weinstein did when he advocated for a national-consensus approach. But the instances in which a court has invoked its common-lawmaking powers to adopt this approach are few and very far between.[632]

Both the ABA and ALI contemplated that the choice-of-law rule applicable to mass actions would be given effect through an act of Congress. Although bills introduced in Congress have contemplated creating a unique choice-of-law rule for some mass torts, none has been in serious jeopardy of becoming law.

With no legislative or judicial momentum for adopting a single choice-of-law rule, this approach remains more theoretical than real. And some scholars have pointed out that creating a specialized choice-of-law rule presumes that aggregation is a desirable good and that choice-of-law principles should be manipulated to achieve that good.[633] If you are more agnostic about aggregation or believe that choice-of-law rules serve institutional and jurisprudential purposes larger than facilitating the resolution of mass disputes, developing

---

[631] *See* COMM'N ON MASS TORT, REPORT TO THE HOUSE OF DELEGATES 44 (AM. BAR ASS'N 1989); COMPLEX LITIGATION, *supra* note 101, § 6.01. The ALI also proposed choice-of-law rules for complex contract disputes and for choosing the applicable statute of limitations and the law concerning compensatory and punitive damages.

[632] For a case rejecting traditional choice-of-law principles in favor of a *lex fori* approach in when the forum had a significant connection to the litigation, see *Gruber v. Price Waterhouse*, 117 F.R.D. 75 (E.D. Pa. 1987).

[633] *See* Linda Silberman, *The Role of Choice of Law in National Class Actions*, 156 U. PA. L. REV. 2001 (2008) ("To use the class action as the justification for altering choice of law rules would be to put the cart before the horse and to misunderstand the role of both class actions and choice of law.").

unique choice-of-law rules for complex cases is less attractive. Indeed, in its most recent work on aggregate litigation, the ALI has walked away from the idea of specialized choice-of-law provisions for complex cases.[634]

C. Conclusion

To some extent, the choice-of-law issue in complex litigation is an aggregation problem, so we place it here at the end of the materials on aggregation. But the prospect of multiple applicable laws is also a management problem during pretrial and trial—a cause of complexity in gathering facts, winnowing issues for adjudication, and resolving the dispute. If good techniques exist to deal with a multiple-law dispute, the need to solve the choice-of-law problem diminishes. On the other hand, if no good techniques exist, then the only workable solution in many cases is to limit the scope of aggregation to claims arising under a single law. In this environment, the felt need to solve the choice-of-law problem intensifies, with smaller, single-law aggregations the likely result if no solution emerges.

Thus, this choice-of-law material bridges the aggregation materials in the first part of the book and the pretrial and trial-management materials to which we turn in the next two parts of the book.

---

[634] *See* PRINCIPLES OF AGGREGATE LITIGATION, *supra* note 437, § 2.05 Reporters' Notes & cmt. *a* (noting that choice of law is "a dimension of the larger inquiry into the constraints imposed by substantive law on aggregation" and that the ALI's project on aggregate litigation "contemplates no change in the body of choice-of-law principles that govern the court's selection of applicable substantive law").

Part 2

THE PRETRIAL PROCESS

This Part examines the issues that arise during the pretrial phase of a complex case. In the modern American system, a good pretrial process should gather the information necessary for the trial and narrow the issues, so that the trial is both efficiently conducted and determines the merits of the case. Both the gathering function and the narrowing function are made difficult when a case contains a plethora of factual material and a wealth of legal issues.

Pretrial complexity is often the result of mass aggregation; with aggregation comes a host of legal and factual issues, and these issues often vary from case to case. But the pretrial process can be challenging even in a two-party case. The *United States v. AT&T* antitrust litigation in the 1970s and the *United States v. Microsoft* antitrust litigation in the 1990s posed significant pretrial hurdles that the parties needed to overcome.

To try to wrestle these cases to the ground, courts have employed various *case-management* powers either to streamline the gathering of information or to narrow disputes. These two functions are interrelated, and have a chicken-and-egg quality. It is risky to narrow issues before the facts are known, because important—even winning—issues might be overlooked. But if we begin by gathering evidence, the issues are likely to proliferate rather than narrow. Some case-management powers are clearly oriented toward either streamlining evidence-gathering or narrowing issues; some do a bit of both. Some powers seek to accomplish streamlining or narrowing directly; some do so more indirectly.

A smorgasbord of case-management techniques is generally available to judges, who must pick and choose the ones that seem best for the case at hand. One of the central themes of this material, however, is the way in which different techniques can influence the outcome of the litigation. Another theme is the source of a judge's power to adopt some of the techniques; while the Federal Rules of Civil Procedure or statutes authorize the use of some techniques, other powers seem to arise from the inherent common-law authority of the court. The combination of broad inherent authority and a broad array of techniques to resolve litigation creates the risk that justice will vary substantially from courtroom to courtroom.

This Part begins by completing the story of how courts structure an aggregated proceeding. As we have seen, Part I detailed ways in which a court can define the party structure. Also important to the successful management of a complex case are the attorney structure and judicial structure. Like different party structures, however, different attorney and judicial structures can influence the outcome of a case.

Chapter Nine examines the basic issues concerning case management, as well as the types of judicial structures that a court can establish to manage a case successfully. Chapter Ten explores perhaps the most significant case-management power of the judge: the ability to establish the attorney structure to resolve a case. Chapter Eleven turns to case-management techniques that can narrow the issues in advance of trial, and Chapter Twelve examines case-management techniques that can increase the efficiency of collecting evidence.

Chapter 9

CASE MANAGEMENT AND JUDICIAL STRUCTURE

The judge of the adversarial model is neutral and passive. Because the judge must enter the trial with no predispositions about the case, maintaining the judge's distance is especially crucial during the pretrial phase. Critical pretrial tasks such as defining the issues and gathering evidence must therefore be left to the parties' lawyers.

In complex cases with myriad issues and vast amounts of information, however, leaving these tasks in the lawyers' hands risks a lengthy, expensive, and cumbersome pretrial process that might delay or even deny the delivery of justice. Replacing the traditional judge of adversarial theory seems essential for the swift, efficient, and fair resolution of controversies. From this realization emerged the concept of case management, which demands the early, active, and ongoing involvement of the judge in pretrial matters. Case management stands the traditional adversarial approach to litigation on its head.

There is no single menu of case-management techniques that judges must always employ; rather, different techniques can accomplish in different ways the narrowing of issues and the streamlining of evidence gathering. In its array of techniques, case management has thus far emphasized judicial discretion: judges have broad and only lightly reviewable powers to shape the pretrial phase of the lawsuit. As a consequence, case management threatens the judge's neutrality, as the judge becomes invested, on less than complete information about the nature of the case, with selecting particular methods for narrowing issues and streamlining the gathering of information. Effective case management can also take a significant amount of a judge's time, thus putting pressure on the rest of the cases on a judge's docket.

This Chapter first examines the nature of case management, and then explores ways in which a judge can rely on other judges or judicial adjuncts to make management more effective. Later chapters examine specific case-management powers.

A. The Rise of Case Management

The practice of case management began in a series of complex antitrust cases after World War II. Resolving these seemingly intractable cases with the hands-off, adversarial approach to judging proved difficult. A 1951 report (usually called the Prettyman Report) urged judges in these types of cases to abandon the passivity of the adversarial model, and to exercise "rigid control from the time the complaint is filed."[635] This more activist approach resulted in some successes in resolving complex cases. Over the next twenty years, judicial committees created a series of reports recommending specific techniques that should or could be used in complex cases. These reports culminated in the original *Manual for Complex and Multidistrict Litigation*, published in 1970. Now in its fourth edition (with the shortened title *Manual for Complex Litigation*, or even just "the *Manual*"), this treatise remains the go-to source for ideas about how to manage complex lawsuits.

The present *Manual* lists the qualities of good case management: it is "active," "substantive," "timely," "continuing," "firm, but fair," and "careful."[636] The goals are to involve the judge at the earliest stages of the case and to keep the judge involved. The centerpiece of case management is the conference: the judge meets with the parties at regular intervals to assess the progress of the case, resolve roadblocks, see if existing case-management measures are working, and implement new measures as appropriate. Some conference topics concern the scheduling of major litigation events (like deadlines for amending pleadings and filing motions).[637] The *scheduling orders* that emerge from the conferences can be "modified only for good cause and with the judge's consent." Conferences can and usually do explore a range of other topics, including methods to narrow or eliminate issues, avoid unnecessary proof, or create "special procedures for managing potentially difficult or protracted actions."[638]

Almost every conference results in the issuance of an order "reciting the action taken"; this "order controls the course of the action unless the court modifies it."[639] Each order is referred to as a *case management order* ("CMO") or *pretrial conference order* ("PTO"). Complex cases typically have dozens of scheduling orders and CMOs; some have well over a hundred.

The remaining chapters in Part II examine some of the specific actions that a court can take during scheduling and other case-management conferences. For now, two observations are in order. First, judges thought case management so successful in large cases that they began to import the idea into more routine litigation. Today the basic case-management rule, Rule 16, is one of the longest and

---

635 *Report of the Judicial Conference of the United States on Procedure in Anti-Trust and Other Protracted Cases* (1951), *reprinted in* 13 F.R.D. 62 (1953).

636 *See* MANUAL, *supra* note 206, § 10.13.

637 FED. R. CIV. P. 16(b).

638 FED. R. CIV. P. 16(c). The language quoted in the text is from Rule 16(c)(2)(L).

639 FED. R. CIV. P. 16(d).

most significant of the Federal Rules of Civil Procedure. Nearly every case undergoes some form of case management, although typically on a much smaller scale than the management employed in complex cases. Replacing the judge of traditional adversarial theory, the managerial judge is the new norm in the federal courts and in many state courts as well.

Second, this move to case management has not been without controversy. Critics have worried that the early and ongoing involvement required for effective case management will deprive the judge of the essential neutrality on which the adversarial approach to litigation is premised, turning the judge instead into an active participant with a particular stake in how the case should be shaped and resolved. They worry that judges have too much power to influence the direction of a lawsuit—power that is for most practical purposes unreviewable in other courts. Judges can use this power to force litigants to accept procedures and even settlements that are not in their best interests but seem fair to the judge. More broadly, this power is inconsistent with a restrained view of the scope of American judicial authority. Finally, critics argue that case management is itself costly, as judges must devote more hours managing each case.[640]

Proponents respond that case management can reduce delay and expense. They paint a picture of an adversarial system, when left to its own devices, run amok: abusive pleading and discovery practices, long delays, exorbitant expense, and truth-bending or obfuscatory examinations of witnesses. Case management is a necessary and beneficial corrective. Costs associated with more case management are more than outweighed by savings in time and money when case-management techniques reduce discovery disputes or obviate the need to try a case.[641]

To some extent, empirical evidence could settle the debate between proponents and opponents of case management. Some studies measuring the effectiveness of certain case-management techniques have occurred; the studies have measured variables such as cost, time to resolution, and attorney or client satisfaction in cases that did or did not employ these techniques. A fair characterization of these studies is that case management is largely a wash. One technique (the early, firm trial date[642]) has been shown to reduce delay without increasing cost or decreasing attorney or client

---

[640] For the classic article critiquing modern case management, see Judith Resnik, *Managerial Judges*, 96 HARV. L. REV. 374 (1982).

[641] For a strong defense of case management, see William W Schwarzer, *The Federal Rules, the Adversary Process, and Discovery Reform*, 50 U. PITT. L. REV. 703 (1989).

[642] We discuss this technique in detail *infra* Chapter 12.B.2.a.

satisfaction. But virtually all other techniques are neutral. In cases where they succeed, case-management techniques reduce cost and delay; but in cases where they fail, they add more expense and more delay. As a general matter, case management increases attorney hours but shortens the time to disposition; although early case management accompanied by discovery planning cut attorney hours while speeding up the resolution of the case.[643]

None of the empirical studies regarding case management has focused on the costs or benefits of case management or particular case-management techniques in complex litigation. Indeed, most specific case-management techniques have never been studied at all. Studies to date have selected only a few techniques for in-depth evaluation. Empirical studies also cannot evaluate other concerns—such as the loss of adversarial culture or the rise of judicial power—because these concerns are not as easily quantifiable as metrics such as cost, time to disposition, or attorney and client satisfaction.

Even though the jury remains out on case management as a theoretical and empirical matter, the train has left the station as a practical matter. The judiciary is committed to the process of case management, in cases both large and small. In complex litigation in particular, case management will occur.

The extensiveness of the judicial involvement required to manage a case raises a final concern: how can a single judge find time to manage a mass dispute while also attending to other cases on the docket? The following section explores some of the judicial structures that judges can create to manage more effectively. As we see, these structures are not without their own controversies.

B. Establishing a Judicial Structure

Traditionally a single district judge sees a case through from start to conclusion. As judges engage is more case management, however, expecting one judge to perform every judicial pretrial task in a complex case is unrealistic. There may be hundreds of disputes over discovery or dozens of motions to resolve; and many of these matters require immediate resolution to keep the case on track.

In complex cases, courts have crafted three different judicial structures to resolve the welter of legal and factual issues that can arise during the pretrial process. First, the district judge can bring in additional judges to handle certain aspects of the pretrial process.

---

643 For summaries of the most comprehensive empirical analyses of case-management techniques, see JAMES S. KAKALIK, AN EVALUATION OF JUDICIAL CASE MANAGEMENT UNDER THE CIVIL JUSTICE REFORM ACT (1996) [hereinafter KAKALIK, CASE MANAGEMENT]; James S. Kakalik et al., *Discovery Management: Further Analysis of the Civil Justice Reform Act Evaluation Data*, 39 B.C. L. REV. 613 (1998) [hereinafter Kakalik, *Discovery*].

Second, magistrate judges—who are appointed for a term of years to perform a range of tasks delegated to them by the district court—can be harnessed to the task of managing a complex case.[644] Third, special masters—who are usually appointed on an ad hoc basis to help out in a specific matter—can be employed.[645] An additional judge, a magistrate judge, or a special master all have a common benefit: they preserve the district judge's neutrality with respect to the merits of case. Beyond that advantage, however, the three approaches present different advantages and drawbacks.

To begin with using additional Article III judges, the drawbacks are usually disabling. If the point of employing judicial adjuncts is to free up judicial time to engage in managerial oversight of the case, the substitution of one judge for another results in no overall savings of judicial resources. Therefore, although other judges have been successfully employed for discrete tasks (such as mediating a settlement conference or ruling on a time-intensive motion), the use of a second judge to assist in case management is a relatively rare phenomenon.[646]

Designating a magistrate judge to handle pretrial tasks is far more common. Like district judges, magistrate judges are usually fully engaged by a range of other matters, such as arraignments, misdemeanor trials, referrals of discovery and pretrial motions from the district judge, and handling their own docket of civil cases in which the parties have consented to a trial by magistrate. Like district judges, magistrate judges do not necessarily bring expertise in complex cases to the courtroom. Moreover, in many districts a magistrate judge does not work exclusively for a single judge, so it is difficult for the magistrate judge to focus single-mindedly on one judge's big case. Magistrate judges can also add an additional layer of cost and expense; parties can file an objection to a magistrate judge's rulings and seek a different ruling from the district judge.[647]

---

644 For the general pretrial powers and duties of a magistrate judge, see 28 U.S.C. § 636.

645 For the general pretrial powers and duties of a special master, see FED. R. CIV. P. 53(a)(1)(C).

646 On the use of multiple judges, see MANUAL, *supra* note 206, § 10.122. A well-known instance of using multiple judges involved the settlement class action ultimately overturned in *Amchem*. Judge Weiner had been designated as the MDL transferee over all federal asbestos claims. When the *Amchem* settlement emerged out of this MDL, Judge Weiner asked another federal judge, Judge Reed, to determine whether class certification was proper and to preside over the fairness hearing, which involved extensive discovery and five weeks of testimony. *See* Georgine v. Amchem Prods., Inc., 157 F.R.D. 246 (E.D. Pa. 1994), *rev'd*, 83 F.3d 610 (3d Cir. 1996), *aff'd sub nom.* Amchem Prods., Inc. v. Windsor, 521 U.S. 591 (1997).

647 When the magistrate judge rules on a non-dispositive motion, such as a motion to compel discovery, the district judge may reconsider the magistrate judge's ruling only when it is "clearly erroneous or contrary to law." 28 U.S.C. § 636(b)(1)(A).

Obviously, the district judge does not wish to encourage objections as a regular practice (otherwise the appointment of the magistrate judge will serve no purpose); but rubber-stamping the work of the magistrate judge on every matter to discourage objections cedes case-management control of the case to the magistrate judge.

The *Manual for Complex Litigation* suggests that a range of factors—including the experience and qualifications of the available magistrate judges, the relationships among the attorneys, the need for direct assertion of the district judge's authority, and the district judge's available time and personal preferences—should dictate whether, and to what extent, a district judge should involve a magistrate judge in the litigation.[648] Overall, it is fair to say that magistrate judges have proven to be an important component in managing complex litigation, but they have not proven to be the cure-all for increased judicial involvement.

That leaves the third solution: ad hoc judicial officers. Long before the phenomenon of complex litigation, the English chancellors used court functionaries called "masters" to assist in the many tasks involved in resolving suits in equity. Though changed, this tradition has survived in this country, where suits in equity (and occasionally actions at law) used "special masters"—usually private lawyers with specialized knowledge in the relevant field—to preside at trial or determine the remedy in particularly difficult cases.

The appointment of a special master in a complex case promises some benefits. If the master is a private attorney,[649] the judge does not tax other judicial resources. If the master has expertise in the area, the efficiency or accuracy of decision-making can increase. Because the master is focused only on one matter, the speed of resolving pretrial matters should also increase. Moreover, because a special master can act informally, he or she can do some things—like having ex parte communications with the parties or the court—that judges cannot.[650] Special masters insulate the judge from pretrial contacts that might compromise the judge's neutrality.

On the other hand, masters rarely work for free, and one (or both) parties must pay the master's fee (usually hundreds of dollars per hour). When one party is less well off, the appointment of a special master can sap resources; and in all cases, the considerable

---

For a dispositive motion, such as a motion for summary judgment, the district judge's review after an objection is de novo. 28 U.S.C. § 636(b)(1)(C).

648 *See* MANUAL, *supra* note 206, § 10.14.

649 Magistrate judges can also be appointed as a special master. 28 U.S.C. § 636(b)(2).

650 *See* FED. R. CIV. P. 53(b)(2)(B) (requiring a court to state in the order of appointment the circumstances under which a master can speak ex parte with parties or the court).

expense of a special master creates an appearance of parties paying for a special form of justice.[651] Special masters also can create the same delays as a magistrate judge when a party objects to master's report.[652]

Federal Rule of Civil Procedure 53 controls the appointment of special masters in both jury-tried and bench-tried cases. Prior to an extensive revision of Rule 53 in 2003, the authority to appoint a master for pretrial tasks was less certain, but courts teased an authority out of the Rule's language or the court's inherent power to control litigation. After 2003, however, a pretrial master can be appointed when necessary to "address pretrial . . . matters that cannot be effectively and timely addressed by an available district judge or magistrate judge of the district."[653]

A major stumbling block to the appointment of special masters in complex litigation is *La Buy v. Howes Leather Co.*,[654] whose dicta has exercised enormous influence. In *La Buy*, a judge confronting a six-week antitrust trial and a crowded docket referred the trial to a special master, who was a local practitioner with a background in antitrust. The Supreme Court held that this reference so exceeded the district judge's authority under Rule 53 that a writ of mandamus should issue against the reference. According to the Court, the reference constituted "an abdication of the judicial function depriving the parties of a trial before the court on the basic issues involved in the litigation." Contrary to the district judge's argument, the "unusual complexity" of the case was not a reason to refer the case; it was "an impelling reason for trial before a regular, experienced trial judge rather than before a temporary substitute appointed on an ad hoc basis . . . ."

La Buy can be distinguished, for it dealt with a trial reference rather than a pretrial reference. But its basic points—federal judges must not abdicate their judicial responsibilities and complexity alone is not an adequate reason for a reference—sound a cautionary note about extensive reliance on special masters to handle pretrial tasks. If case management is a critical judicial function, foisting the task

---

651 *Cf. In re* Welding Rod Prods. Liab. Litig., No. 1:03–CV–17000, 2004 WL 3711622 (N.D. Ohio 2004) (compensating a special master at the rate of $300 per hour, authorizing as much as 1,000 of work by the master, and ordering the parties to remit a $45,000 retainer (split equally) to the court to cover the special master's initial fees and expenses). Often the true beneficiaries of a special master are litigants in other cases, who can now count on more of the judge's time.

652 Both factual findings and legal conclusions in a special master's report are reviewed de novo, although factual findings can be reviewed on a clear-error standard if the parties so stipulate. FED. R. CIV. P. 53(f)(3)–(4).

653 FED. R. CIV. P. 53(a)(1)(C).

654 352 U.S. 249 (1957).

onto someone who enjoys none of the authority, stature, experience, or life tenure of an Article III judge is problematic.

This abdication of judicial authority may be especially problematic if the master is appointed because of his or her expertise in the same type of litigation as the present case. With expertise can come bias: the special master may have clients with an interest in the case's outcome. If the master shapes the case differently than the judge would have done, the appointment of a master can create a different outcome for the litigants. In exercising the powers delegated by the district judge, the master's is also aware that his or her job depends on the satisfaction of the court and the parties; the master does not enjoy the life tenure that ameliorates such pressures for federal judges.

These reservations do not mean that references to masters should never occur. When they are delegated routine or ministerial tasks (such as examining documents to determine if they should be disclosed) under clearly delineated authority,[655] special masters can keep the judge focused on the larger picture of shaping the factual and legal development of the case. They can design and implement time-intensive, creative programs to narrow issues.

The cases reflect the same ambivalence about masters that these policy arguments do. In big cases, district courts appoint masters—perhaps not routinely, but with some frequency.[656] As a rule, the courts of appeal take a more jaundiced view of masters, especially blanket references of all pretrial matters.[657] The cases reflect that efficiency alone is an inadequate basis for a reference to a master. What constitutes an adequate basis is less clearly stated. Often concerns about the breadth of a master's authority are pretermitted by the parties' consent to the reference.[658]

---

[655] *Cf.* FED. R. CIV. P. 53(b)(2)(A), (D) (requiring an order appointing a special master to specify "the master's duties, including any investigation or enforcement duties, and any limits on the master's authority," as well as "the time limits, method of filing the record, other procedures, and standards for reviewing the master's orders, findings, and recommendations").

[656] For a case giving a master virtually plenary authority in pretrial matters, see *In re* "Agent Orange" Prod. Liab. Litig., 94 F.R.D. 173 (E.D.N.Y. 1982). *But see* MANUAL, *supra* note 206, § 10.14 (stating that referral of pretrial management to a master is "not advisable," but suggesting that a referral "for limited purposes requiring special expertise may sometimes be appropriate").

[657] *See, e.g.*, Prudential Ins. Co. of Am. v. U.S. Gypsum Co., 991 F.2d 1080 (3d Cir. 1993); *In re* Bituminous Coal Operators' Assn., Inc., 949 F.2d 1165 (D.C. Cir. 1991); *In re* United States, 816 F.2d 1083 (6th Cir. 1987). Many of the most critical cases predate the 2003 amendment to Rule 53

[658] *See In re* K-Dur Antitrust Litig., 686 F.3d 197 (3d Cir. 2012), *vacated and remanded on other grounds sub nom.* Merck & Co. v. La. Wholesale Drug Co., 570 U.S. 913 (2013).

C. Ethical Responsibilities of Judicial Officers

Ideal qualities for a judge in an adversarial model are neutrality, objectivity, and passivity. The ethical rules applicable to judges were formed with these ideals in mind. But passivity is not an ideal quality in the judge who actively manages litigation; and greater activity lessens a judge's ability to remain neutral and dispassionate. The extent to which the needs of complex litigation require an adjustment of judicial ethical norms is a critical question, for ultimately no judge can be a more creative case manager than ethical principles allow.

The limits of a judge's proper departure from traditional ethical norms in complex litigation are usually explored through a party's motion to recuse a judge. Recusal is the judicial equivalent of a lawyer's disqualification: A judge is disqualified ("recused") from a case because of some actual or apparent impropriety. The purposes of recusal are to remove a judicial officer who is unduly prejudiced against a particular party or proceeding and to ensure public confidence in the integrity of the administration of justice.[659]

Three sources provide the rules and standards of judicial conduct. The first is the Due Process Clause (and, for state judges, similar provisions of the state constitution).[660] Second, statutes may establish standards for recusal; in the federal system, the statutes are 28 U.S.C. §§ 144 and 455. Third, the applicable judicial code of conduct establishes ethical norms whose violation might require recusal. In federal court, the determinative sources are usually §§ 144 and 455, which closely track judicial codes of conduct.

Under § 144, a judge must not proceed with a case once a party in good faith claims that the judge "has a personal bias or prejudice either against him or in favor of any adverse party." Only one such claim can be made at the start of a case, and overcoming the presumption of impartiality is difficult. Under § 455(b), a judge must disqualify himself or herself in certain situations, such as personal knowledge or bias about a case, a spouse or close relative as a party, or a prior representation that touched on the case. Under § 455(a), recusal is required whenever a judge's impartiality "might reasonably be questioned." The test for recusal is an objective one: "whether a reasonable person, with knowledge of all the facts, would conclude that the judge's impartiality might reasonably be questioned."[661] Because a party moving for disqualification under § 455(a) need not show actual bias and because judges know enough

---

[659] *See* Liteky v. United States, 510 U.S. 540 (1994); Liljeberg v. Health Servs. Acquisition Corp., 486 U.S. 847 (1988).

[660] See Caperton v. A.T. Massey Coal Co., 556 U.S. 868 (2009).

[661] *In re* Kensington Int'l Ltd., 368 F.3d 289 (3d Cir. 2004).

to step aside when a *per se* situation under § 455(b) occurs, most litigation regarding recusal arises under § 455(a).[662]

A number of judges managing complex litigation have run afoul of these limits. For instance, one district judge presiding over an asbestos bankruptcy appointed advisors to engage in various case-management tasks.[663] To accomplish these tasks effectively, the advisors were empowered to speak ex parte with litigants. The judge also engaged in ex parte communications with litigants, as well as ex parte communications with the advisors. It later developed that some advisors had a conflict of interest because their responsibilities in other asbestos litigation gave them a particular viewpoint in the bankruptcy. The court of appeals held that the conflicts of interest were magnified by the ex parte discussions, and issued a writ of mandamus disqualifying the judge.

> *Question*
>
> "To decide when a judge may not sit is to define what a judge is. To define what a judge is is to decide what a system of adjudication is all about." John Leubsdorf, *Theories of Judging and Judicial Disqualification*, 62 N.Y.U. L. REV. 237, 237 (1987). Is the adversarial approach to litigation, including the passive and neutral judge of adversarial theory, an essential component of American litigation? If so, can a judge ethically act as a case manager?

Successful recusal motions based on the overly activist nature of a judge's case management are rare.[664] The fundamental question is whether judges' ethical standards should be adjusted to accommodate their more active role in complex litigation. One way to answer this question is to consider the nature of adjudication. We can never allow judges to act in a way that jeopardizes their essential role, but we might compromise on the desirable features of an ideal judge when adequate cause exists. For example, if reasoned judgment is

---

[662] It is usually understood that these statutes apply to Article III judges, magistrate judges, and judges' staff, including law clerks. The extent to which they apply to special masters and other comparable temporary judicial adjuncts is far less certain; indeed, the ethical flexibility of action that masters enjoy is sometimes cited as one of their advantages. At the same time, it seems unlikely that a reviewing court would permit such appointments if a judge were abusing the appointments process as a means to avoid the judge's ethical responsibilities.

[663] *See In re Kensington*, 368 F.3d at 294.

[664] *Compare In re* Allied-Signal, Inc., 891 F.2d 967 (1st Cir. 1989) (refusing to order recusal, in part because the "need for judicial management by the district court counsels caution prior to intervention by an appellate court" in "large, complex, and time consuming" cases), *with In re* School Asbestos Litig., 977 F.2d 764 (3d Cir. 1992) (ordering recusal of a judge who attended an all-expenses-paid seminar on asbestos litigation that was largely funded by plaintiffs' lawyers appearing in the case). *See also* Haines v. Liggett Grp. Inc., 975 F.2d 81 (3d Cir. 1992) (using the supervisory powers of 28 U.S.C. § 2106 to re-assign a case to a new judge on remand when the original judge called the defendant's industry "the king of concealment").

an essential component of adjudication, and if an adversarial approach is a desirable means to assure reasoned judgment, we would never allow a judge to decide a case if the judge is or reasonably appears to be biased to such an extent that his or her ability to decide a matter rationally might be questioned; but when the needs of a case are compelling and maintaining the judge's neutrality is not the best way to obtain a reasonable determination of the case, we might allow the judge to engage in conduct inconsistent with the judge's adversarial role. On the other hand, if adversarial process is an essential aspect of adjudication, conduct inconsistent with this approach to judging can never be tolerated.

D. Conclusion

Case management re-invents the relationship between the judge and the body politic. Restructuring the judiciary to meet the demands of complex litigation does not directly narrow the legal and factual issues for trial or streamline the process of gathering information. But creating a larger judicial structure—"Judge and Company"—allows the judge to be more active and creative in employing the issue-narrowing and information-streamlining case-management tools that we now examine in greater detail.

Chapter 10

SELECTING COUNSEL

Party control of the pretrial process is an integral—and arguably a defining—characteristic of the adversarial system. Party control strongly advances personal freedom and individual autonomy, two concepts on which the system is based. One of the hallmarks of party control is the parties' right to select their own lawyers, who then bear primary responsibility for developing and narrowing factual and legal issues. Any move away from party control over selection of their counsel is also a step away from the adversarial underpinnings of our procedural system.[665]

On the other hand, allowing each person in an aggregated proceeding to retain his or her own lawyer makes aggregation a near impossibility. Every deposition and every hearing could go on interminably, as the unique arguments and perspectives of each client are pressed. And each client would pay for work that added only marginal value to the court's determination.

Having a single counsel represent a group of litigants also streamlines the pretrial process, because it limits the number and variety of arguments that this group can present to the court. Fewer issues will be presented, and less information gathered—albeit at the cost of a court's understanding of the fine-grain detail of the individual cases of each member in the group.

If a single lawyer is to work on behalf of a group, a number of issues arise. First, who should choose the lawyers who will represent the group? Second, how can the lawyer ethically represent the interests of a group whose interests may diverge? Third, under what circumstances may the selected lawyer(s) withdraw from the representation? And last, how do we justify creating a world of legal representation in complex litigation that varies so dramatically from the world of ordinary litigation?

This Chapter explores these issues.

A. Establishing the Counsel Structure

In a large two-party suit, such as *United States v. Microsoft*, the basic adversarial model can continue to operate. When hundreds of

---

[665] *Cf.* Richardson-Merrell, Inc. v. Koller, 472 U.S. 424 (1985) (Brennan, J., concurring) ("A fundamental premise of the adversary system is that individuals have the right to retain the attorney of their choice to represent their interests in judicial proceedings."); *id.* at 442 (Stevens, J., concurring) ("Everyone must agree that the litigant's freedom to choose his own lawyer in a civil case is a fundamental right.").

cases are aggregated, however, the difficulty of allowing each litigant the right to his or her own counsel is evident. We have already seen, in class-action litigation, that a court appoints counsel to represent the interests of the class.[666] Rule 23(g) specifically provides this appointment power. In other forms of aggregation, however, no comparable rule or statute gives the court a power to appoint counsel for a group of plaintiffs or defendants.

One response for non-class settings is to leave the question of creating a legal structure to market forces. Especially in low-value cases with high start-up costs, the number of firms likely to be interested in prosecuting the litigation is small, and they can coordinate their efforts. Even in high-value cases, a few firms tend to handle most of the litigation; "feeder firms" do the intake and client-servicing work, while referring the cases for litigation matters. The firms handling the cases can then divvy up litigation tasks among themselves. Such an approach is consistent with the goal of letting the litigants establish their own representational structure, although it is unlikely that the lawyers handling the litigation know much about the clients on whose behalf they work or have much contact with their clients.[667]

Experience with the market-based approach for organizing counsel has exposed numerous flaws. One is the natural rivalry among different law firms, each of which is jockeying for the largest share of the litigation (and the fees that attend such a share). This rivalry makes long-term cooperation difficult. Another problem involves backroom deals, where firms trade plum pretrial jobs and promise favorable fee sharing in return for other firms' support as lead counsel.[668] This horse-trading causes a classic agency-cost concern, as firms who traded support for work ran up the tab on the portions of the case doled out to them.[669]

---

666 *See supra* Chapter 6.B.2.

667 To be fair, and lest you hold too idyllic a view of litigation conducted in accordance with the adversarial model, contact between lawyer and client occurs less often in traditional litigation than the model presumes. *See* Deborah R. Hensler, *Resolving Mass Toxic Torts: Myths and Realities*, 1989 U. ILL. L. REV. 89.

668 *See* John C. Coffee, Jr., *The Regulation of Entrepreneurial Litigation: Balancing Fairness and Efficiency in the Large Class Action*, 54 U. CHI. L. REV. 877 (1987) (likening consensual counsel arrangements to political conventions in which access to work is traded for votes).

669 *See In re* Fine Paper Antitrust Litig., 98 F.R.D. 48 (E.D. Pa. 1983) (finding that an initial group of plaintiffs' lawyers had planned "the distribution of patronage," and that the committee structure "generate[d] wasted hours on useless tasks, propagate[d] duplication, and mask[ed] outright padding"), *aff'd in part, rev'd in part, and remanded*, 751 F.2d 562 (3d Cir. 1984).

The other major alternative is to give the judge the authority to appoint counsel.[670] This approach has issues as well. One is the source of the judge's power to appoint counsel outside of the class-action context. Another is the standard that a judge should apply in selecting counsel. A third is the possible compromising of the judge's neutrality, as the judge may subconsciously favor appointed counsel to prove that the judge made a wise choice. Fourth, judicial appointment may create a repeat-player phenomenon in which judges return to the same lawyers, who garner appointments because they conduct themselves as the judge wishes rather than as their clients' best interests dictate. Fifth, the selection of counsel is potentially outcome-determinative of the case. Different counsel will approach the same litigation in different ways, so that any choice of counsel will cast the dye for the case's resolution—without the agreement of the parties bound by the choice. A final concern is the lack of procedural protection. In class actions, the Due Process Clause guarantees class members adequate representation. No comparable guarantee accompanies other judicial appointments of counsel.

Although both are imperfect solutions, courts have in more recent years tended to appoint counsel rather than to leave the matter to the market. The first case to acknowledge that a judge had the discretion to appoint counsel for groups of litigants was *MacAlister v. Guterma*.[671] In *MacAlister*, however, the judge refused to do so, and his decision was upheld on appeal. The prevailing judicial attitude until the mid-1970s was to let the litigants determine for themselves their counsel structure, albeit with encouragement from the court.[672]

Since then, the pendulum has swung toward the judicial appointment of counsel. A number of influential cases upheld orders that designated counsel structures for complex cases.[673] Within a very short period, a sea change in traditional adversarial theory had been effected. Today, as one of their case-management powers, district courts routinely, and without the clients' consent, structure the attorney-client relationship to meet the needs of the big case.[674]

---

670 A third possibility is to allow the litigant with the most at stake choose the counsel, on the theory that this person has the greatest incentive to monitor counsel's behavior. Congress employed this solution in the Private Securities Litigation Reform Act of 1995, which makes the shareholder with the largest claim the presumptive class representative. The chosen representative enjoys the statutory power to select counsel. *See* 15 U.S.C. § 78u–4.

671 263 F.2d 65 (2d Cir. 1958).

672 *See* MANUAL FOR COMPLEX AND MULTIDISTRICT LITIGATION § 1.92 (1972).

673 *See, e.g.*, Katz v. Realty Equities Corp., 521 F.2d 1354 (2d Cir. 1975); Vincent v. Hughes Air W., Inc., 557 F.2d 759 (9th Cir. 1977).

674 *See* MANUAL, *supra* note 206, § 10.22.

MacAlister had opined that the authority for restructuring the parties' relationship to their lawyers was the court's "inherent powers" to control litigation. Later courts have accepted that judgment.[675] Throughout the following chapters, we encounter other instances of courts that claim such inherent or common-law authority to manage litigation in the absence of a clear textual command. One theme of this Part is whether the needs of efficient resolution justify such powers.[676]

Although the Supreme Court has never decided whether inherent power to appoint counsel exists, courts have exercised the power to establish a variety of counsel relationships:

- *Liaison Counsel.* In this arrangement, each party is still represented by counsel of his or her choice. The court, however, designates one counsel to act as the liaison between the court and all other lawyers with similar interests. The liaison counsel provides notice to other counsel of actions taken by the court or the opposing side, and possibly coordinates the filing of co-counsel's papers with the court. This arrangement is not a marked departure from the adversarial system—but also one is increasingly unnecessary in a world of electronic docketing.

- *Committee of Counsel.* A court might create a committee of lawyers (often referred to as a "steering committee") to handle pretrial tasks. The court will often select as members of the committee lawyers who have the most individual clients, but other considerations also enter the picture. Committee members may have been especially adept in handling pretrial aspects of similar prior litigation, may be in a position to help finance the litigation, or may represent the interests of specific subgroups of litigants. Committees may be constituted by function, with some

---

675 A power to create a counsel structure arguably finds a home in capacious case-management language of Rule 16(c)(2)(L), which allows a court to "take appropriate action" by "adopting special procedures for managing potentially difficult or protracted actions that may involve complex issues, multiple parties, difficult legal questions, or unusual proof problems." This language is so broad, however, that interpreting it to include such a power essentially amounts to common-law rulemaking. In any event, the predecessor to Rule 16(c)(2)(L) came into existence in 1983, well after courts like *MacAlister* claimed the power to appoint counsel.

676 On the general scope of a court's inherent power in civil litigation, see *Dietz v. Bouldin*, 579 U.S. ___, 136 S. Ct. 1885 (2016) (holding that a court's inherent power must be a "reasonable response to the problems and needs confronting the court's fair administration of justice" and "cannot be contrary to any express grant of or limitation on the district court's power contained in a rule or statute") (internal quotation marks omitted).

members handling depositions, others covering motions and briefs, others conducting settlement negotiations, and so on. A well-selected steering committee ensures that diverse views are represented and diverse skills (such as conducting discovery and writing briefs) are available.

- *Lead Counsel.* A court can also appoint a single lawyer, firm, or small group of firms to represent the interests of a group and handle all the tasks during the pretrial process.

As the options progress from liaison counsel through committees to a single lead counsel, the control of individual litigants over their counsel decreases.

A court is not required to adopt any of these structures, nor is it bound to adopt only one approach if it restructures the counsel relationship. It may, for instance, appoint a lead counsel to handle discovery, and a committee to conduct settlement negotiations. The use of one attorney structure during pretrial does not require that the court adopt the same structure at trial—altghough that is often the case.[677] It is highly unusual for a court to do more than appoint liaison counsel for a group of defendants,[678] and equally unusual for a court to appoint only liaison counsel for a group of plaintiffs.

> *Question 1*
>
> Can you justify the different treatment of plaintiffs and defendants in the establishment of a counsel structure? (Hint: Are the due-process rights or the conflicts of interest different in the two contexts?)

The criteria under which a court selects counsel tend to mirror those that accompany appointment of class counsel. Competence, experience, responsibility, lack of conflicts of interest, and a reasonable fee structure all go into the calculus.[679] In order to spur competition, drive down the cost of the fees, and control agency costs, some courts have put the position of lead counsel up for auction, ultimately selecting the bid that seemed to provide the best deal for the plaintiffs.[680] You might think that all the bids were similar, but the creativity of lawyers is great. Some bids proposed a fee for a flat

---

677 As we discuss *infra* Chapter 13.A, courts often appoint a lead counsel (called trial counsel) to try a case on behalf of a group of plaintiffs. Our present focus, however, is on the courts' powers to appoint counsel for pretrial proceedings.

678 As the exception that proves the rule, see Active Prods. Corp. v. A.H. Choitz & Co., 163 F.R.D. 274 (N.D. Ind. 1995) (appointing a steering committee of defense counsel).

679 *See* MANUAL, *supra* note 206, § 10.22.

680 The seminal case was *In re* Oracle Sec. Litig., 132 F.R.D. 538 (N.D. Cal. 1990).

percentage, some proposed to graduate the fee based on the amount of the recovery, and some proposed calibrating the fee to the length of the litigation or the stage at which the case settled. In essence, in selecting a particular counsel, the court was also determining, to some extent, how the case would proceed, when it would conclude, and for how much it would settle. If the information about the bids was made public (sometimes they remained sealed, which created concerns from defendants about ex parte communications with the judge), the defendant also had a clear roadmap about the plaintiffs' counsel's strategy.

Nearly all of the cases using auctions were securities-fraud claims. The use of auctions in this area was for all intents and purposes shut down by *In re Cendant Corp. Litigation*,[681] in which the court held that, under the Private Securities Litigation Reform Act, the lead plaintiff had the statutory responsibility to select lead counsel for the class.[682] *Cendant* left open the possibility of the judicial selection of counsel (whether by auction or otherwise) only when the lead plaintiff selected inadequate counsel.[683] Although auctions in theory remain available in other forms of class or non-class litigation as a means to select lead counsel, they have never proven popular beyond the securities-fraud context.

An even more radical auction proposal designed to deal with the agency costs of appointing a lead counsel is to auction off the group's claim to the highest bidder.[684] The auction proceeds are distributed to the plaintiffs, and the winning bidder is then free to pursue the claim against the defendant. The winning bidder has the incentive to monitor the actions of his or her attorney closely, thus limiting agency costs. The auction also reduces to the case to the classic two-party form of adversarial theory. Thus far, this academic darling remains on the drawing board, but it highlights the logical endpoint of the auction process—and brings into focus the limits of a court's power to ensure faithful representation.

Only rarely is an appointment challenged because counsel is allegedly ignoring individual clients' interests, and even more rarely is such a challenge successful.[685]

---

681 264 F.3d 201 (3d Cir. 2001).

682 For further discussion of the Act's method for selecting counsel, see *supra* note 670.

683 *Cf. In re* Cavanaugh, 306 F.3d 726 (9th Cir. 2002) (replacing the presumptive lead plaintiff with another lead plaintiff because the presumptive lead plaintiff selected a counsel whose fee terms were not favorable to the class).

684 *See* Macey & Miller, *supra* note 12.

685 *See, e.g.*, Koehler v. Brody, 483 F.3d 590 (8th Cir. 2007) (affirming dismissal of claims by a class representative against class counsel who supported an allegedly inadequate settlement); Farber v. Riker-Maxson Corp., 442 F.2d 457 (2d Cir. 1971)

B. Ethical Issues in Group Representation

In examining the adequacy of class counsel, we have already explored the ethical difficulties faced by lawyers who represent groups of litigants. Representing a group poses challenges in a legal system whose ethical norms were established in a day of two-party, adversarial litigation. In such a system, the lawyer's duty is to represent the client zealously and competently within the bounds of the law. Corollaries of this expectation of loyalty are that the lawyer must have no conflicts of interest that might impinge on this loyalty and that all information obtained from the client must be held in confidence. At the same time, as an officer of the court, the lawyer has a duty to ensure that justice is done.

Meeting these dual expectations is especially difficult in large-scale litigation. The representation of multiple clients threatens to divide the attorney's loyalty among the welter of clients' interests. It also raises the danger that the lawyer will disclose information obtained from one client to advance the interests of another client.

Moreover, lead counsel often has a financial stake that far exceeds that of any individual client. The dichotomy between the client's and the lawyer's financial interests arises even in ordinary litigation, but the size of the lawyer's stake (both in absolute dollars and in relation to that of any client's stake) creates peculiar temptations for the lawyers in large aggregated proceedings.

Ethical issues are perhaps best sorted out in the context of a class on Professional Responsibility, but a few principles that shape the work of counsel bear mention here. First, in state-court litigation, the code of ethics promulgated by the state's Supreme Court or bar association applies.[686] In federal court, the ethical standards are a matter of federal law.[687] Federal courts usually adopt the code of ethics used in state court, although some courts promulgate their own standards.[688]

Second, some conflict-of-interest issues arise because of the structure of modern law firms. For instance, a partner in one office

---

(rejecting argument that an order appointing lead counsel "den[ied] appellants an appropriate opportunity to participate in the litigation").

686 *See, e.g.*, *In re* Complex Asbestos Litig., 283 Cal. Rptr. 732 (Cal. Ct. App. 1991).

687 *See, e.g.*, *In re* Am. Airlines, Inc., 972 F.2d 605 (5th Cir. 1992); MANUAL, *supra* note 206, § 10.23 n.70.

688 *Compare, e.g.*, *In re* Congoleum Corp., 426 F.3d 675 (3d Cir. 2005) (adopting state standards), *with* Dondi Props. Corp. v. Commerce Sav. & Loan Ass'n, 121 F.R.D. 284 (N.D. Tex. 1988) (applying court's own standards). *See also In re* Zyprexa Prods. Liab. Litig., 424 F. Supp. 2d 488, 492 (E.D.N.Y. 2006) ("The judiciary has well-established authority to exercise ethical supervision of the bar in both individual and mass actions," including the authority to review contingency-fee agreements).

of a multi-branch firm might represent one client, and a partner in another office might represent a second client whose interests conflict with those of the first client. The risk of conflicts increases when firms merge, or when a partner, associate, paralegal, or secretary moves firms. Traditional rules of ethics view the entire firm, and all the lawyers and staff within it, as a monolithic entity—one big "lawyer" that must never represent conflicting interests.[689] Thus, in the following discussion of the lawyer's ethical duties, "lawyer" refers to the entire law firm and its staff.

Third, most claims of ethical impropriety involve one of three scenarios: (1) the simultaneous representation of inconsistent interests (in other words, a conflict of interest within the group); (2) a prior representation that might compromise the lawyer's ability to advocate vigorously for present clients; or (3) a conflict of interest between the represented group and the lawyer.

Representing multiple clients whose interests may conflict can be an ethical thicket. Some rules are clear and usually easy to apply. A lawyer (a) can never simultaneously represent persons on opposite sides of a case; (b) cannot as a rule represent one client suing a person whom the lawyer is representing on an unrelated matter; or (c) cannot as a rule represent a client suing a person who belongs to an association that the lawyer also represents.[690] Beyond these clear cases, conflicts internal to the group are rife in aggregate litigation. Different members of a group may prefer different litigation strategies, and their different factual circumstances may invoke different legal principles or require different relief. As we saw with class actions, no magic formula determines when such conflicts rise to the level that the lawyer can no longer represent the group, and no magic potion resolves conflicts when they arise.[691]

---

689 *See, e.g.*, Fund of Funds, Ltd. v. Arthur Andersen & Co., 567 F.2d 225 (2d Cir. 1977) (conflict-of-interest analysis applied to local counsel associated with conflicted law firm); Lamb v. Pralex Corp., 333 F. Supp. 2d 361 (D. V.I. 2004) (conflict-of-interest rules apply when another firm hired a paralegal exposed to confidential information).

690 *See* GSI Commerce Sols., Inc. v. BabyCenter, L.L.C., 618 F.3d 204 (2d Cir. 2010) (disqualifying a law firm that represented a party in a suit against a corporate affiliate of another client); Westinghouse Elec. Corp. v. Kerr-McGee Corp., 580 F.2d 1311 (7th Cir. 1978) (disqualifying a law firm that represented both a party and an association of which the opposing party was a member); Cinema 5, Ltd. v. Cinerama, Inc., 528 F.2d 1384 (2d Cir. 1976) (representing a party is "prima facie improper" when the lawyer represented the opposing party on an unrelated matter). A lawyer can rebut the prima facie case by showing that the parties consented to or waived the conflict, or by showing the lack of "a significant risk of trial taint." Glueck v. Jonathan Logan, Inc., 653 F.2d 746 (2d Cir. 1981).

691 Law firms sometimes erect "Chinese walls" to prevent the lawyers who represent one set of interests from interacting with the lawyers who represent another set of interests on matters relevant to the representations. These internal devices are often essential when lawyers move laterally or law firms merge, but they are not

The second situation—a present representation that puts a lawyer at odds with a client from a prior representation—does not raise as starkly the problem of undivided loyalty, but concerns for disclosure of the former client's confidences remain. Because the policy concerns against multiple representation are less acute, courts have sometimes taken a more flexible approach to the question of sequential representation of conflicting interests. The usual approach is to ask whether a "substantial relationship" between the representations exists, with a relationship being regarded as "substantial" only when the information developed in the prior representation might be useful in the present case.[692] Once a relationship is deemed substantial, a presumption arises that confidential information from the first representation would be used impermissibly in the second representation, although some courts allow the lawyer to rebut the presumption. The strongest ground for overcoming the presumption is the consent of the prior and the present clients to the representation.

The third situation—a conflict of interest between the group as a whole and the lawyer—raises agency-cost concerns: the lawyer's incentives diverge from the interests of the group so greatly that the lawyer's ability to represent the interests of the group vigorously are called into question. Collusion between the lawyer and the opposing side is the paradigmatic conflict, but other conflicts, usually arising in connection with the size of the attorney's fee in relation to the value of a settlement to the group, are more common. Again, no clear line demarcates the problematic settlements that reflect inadequate representation from those that reward attorneys handsomely but appropriately for their efforts.

Even when a conflict exists, disqualification of the lawyer is not automatic. Some courts balance the ethical conflict against the harm that disqualification would cause. One formulation of the balance asks whether "the likelihood of public suspicion or obloquy outweighs the social interests which will be served by a lawyer's continued participation in a particular case."[693] One factor that sometimes

---

always deemed a sufficient remedy to override a conflict. *See* Cheng v. GAF Corp., 631 F.2d 1052 (2d Cir. 1980), *vacated on other grounds*, 450 U.S. 903 (1981).

692 *See In re* "Agent Orange" Prod. Liab. Litig., 800 F.2d 14 (2d Cir. 1986); Bennett Silvershein Assocs. v. Furman, 776 F. Supp. 800 (S.D.N.Y. 1991) (collecting cases on "substantial relationship"); *but see* Gov't of India v. Cook Indus., Inc., 569 F.2d 737 (2d Cir. 1978) (holding that a substantial relationship exists only if relationship between two representations is "patently clear," or actions are "identical" or "essentially the same"). *Cf. In re* Fine Paper Antitrust Litig., 617 F.2d 22 (3d Cir. 1980) (stating that counsel can sue a former client who was an unnamed member of a class action with whom counsel had no contact).

693 Woods v. Covington Cty. Bank, 537 F.2d 804 (5th Cir. 1976); *see Agent Orange*, 800 F.2d 14 (balancing "the interests of the various groups of class members and of the interest of the public and the court in achieving a just and expeditious

influences a court's decision is the potential for tactical abuse. An adversary will often seek to disqualify an opposing counsel on ethical grounds in order to obtain a tactical advantage (either replacing a well-qualified firm with a less qualified firm, delaying the litigation, or distracting the firm). This use (and abuse) has been often noted by judges.[694]

Perhaps the only long-term solution to this problem is to craft a set of ethical norms to govern large-scale litigation.[695] Shy of that solution, we can expect ongoing difficulties as lawyers must operate under a system of adversarial ethics not designed with complex litigation in mind. On the other hand, tailored ethical norms raise concerns that ethical standards vary with circumstance, and are defined ad hoc by courts. At its heart, questions about the ethical responsibilities of counsel devolve to the question of how we want lawyers in complex cases to behave. Ethical questions lie at the center of complex litigation, and no proposed solution for complex litigation is adequate unless the solution works out its ethical implications.

> *Question 2*
>
> You represent a class of victims in a federal lawsuit. Another class action pending in state court involves largely the same group. A lawyer for the defendant approaches you and tells you that the lawyers in the state case have agreed to a settlement of $10 million, but the lawyer would settle with you instead if you would settle the case for $8 million. Both settlement amounts are fair. If you decline to settle, you will receive no fees and no reimbursement for your expenses, which presently amount to $1.5 million. How would you respond to this "reverse auction" gambit by the defendant? (As an aside, if you were defense counsel, would you try this gambit?)

C. Withdrawal from Group Representation

Ethical issues surround not only the lawyer's representation of clients, but also the lawyer's decision to withdraw from that representation. Rules of professional conduct specify the circumstances in which counsel can withdraw. Although some courts express sympathy for overburdened counsel and permit

---

resolution of the dispute"). *But see* Young v. Achenbauch, 136 So.3d 575 (Fla. 2014) (rejecting the federal balancing approach and disqualifying lawyers who sought to represent as individual clients class members whose interests were adverse to other class members that the lawyers had represented).

694 *See, e.g.,* Richardson-Merrell, Inc. v. Koller, 472 U.S. 424, 441 (1985) (Brennan, J., concurring) (stating that "the tactical use of attorney-misconduct disqualification motions is a deeply disturbing phenomenon in modern civil litigation").

695 For perhaps the most thorough effort, see JACK B. WEINSTEIN, INDIVIDUAL JUSTICE IN MASS TORT LITIGATION (1995) (calling for use of a communitarian or "communicatarian" ethics).

withdrawal,[696] others are reluctant to permit counsel in a complex case to withdraw, even in the face of ruinous financial obligations.[697] The ability of counsel to sustain a representation through thick and thin is an important factor in the court's initial selection of counsel.

D. Conclusion

Just as it re-invented that relationship between judges and the public, case management re-invents the relationships between lawyer and client and between lawyer and judge. Appointing counsel is perhaps the most important case-management power possessed by judges. In many cases, it is a necessary prerequisite to successful use of issue-narrowing and evidence-gathering tools to manage the litigation. But make no mistake—no case-management power is more likely to affect the outcome of a case than appointment of counsel.

---

[696] *See In re* "Agent Orange" Prod. Liab. Litig., 571 F. Supp. 481 (E.D.N.Y. 1983).

[697] Haines v. Liggett Grp., Inc., 814 F. Supp. 414 (D.N.J. 1993).

Chapter 11

NARROWING ISSUES

The pretrial process comprises pleading, discovery, and pretrial motions. The traditional function of the process is to ready the case for trial: in other words, to identify the disputed issues and to gather the evidence relevant to those issues, so that the trial can be conducted without undue tactical surprises. The ultimate goal, of which the pretrial process is an integral part, is to resolve cases on their merits, rather than on procedural technicalities.

Toward that end, the pleading phase of the modern American lawsuit was designed to be short and simple, with just enough said in the complaint and answer to give opponents notice of the nature of the claims or defenses and the grounds on which they rest. This "notice pleading" approach contrasted with prior approaches in common-law actions; previously pleadings were designed to narrow the issues (common-law pleading) or provide a basic sense of the essential facts (code pleading). These prior pleading regimes operated without a system of discovery: pleadings were expected to do all the work of readying the case for trial.[698]

With the advent of the discovery system in the 1938 Federal Rules of Civil Procedure, the functions of narrowing issues and determining the relevant facts passed from pleading to pretrial. Although both issue narrowing and factual development are central tasks, every pretrial system must set the orientation one way or another: toward factual development (in which case the factual and legal issues tend to proliferate rather than narrow) or toward narrowing disputed issues (in which case lines of factual inquiry tend to be cut off rather than pursued). The procedural system created by the Federal Rules is oriented strongly toward factual development. The discovery devices are the most numerous and capacious in the history of the world; and control over seeking information is left largely in the hands of the parties. It is difficult to imagine any existing fact of relevance to a case that some method of discovery could not dislodge. In contrast, the issue-narrowing techniques—in

[698] Discovery sometimes occurred through a supplemental proceeding in equity. In addition to permitting a modicum of discovery, equity employed more liberal pleading rules—somewhat akin to modern notice pleading—although these rules eventually descended toward the technical rigidity of common-law pleading. In the federal system, equity recaptured its more liberal spirit in the early twentieth century. The 1912 Equity Rules, which used notice pleading and discovery, became the model for the Federal Rules of Civil Procedure, which were promulgated in 1938.

the main, motions to dismiss, requests for admission, and motions for summary judgment—are weak.

Whether or not this imbalance is appropriate for ordinary cases, it has created challenges in complex ones. Allowing the parties unfettered control over discovery in cases with vast quantities of information may give parties a way to impose significant costs on opponents—especially in asymmetrical situations in which one party has substantially more information in its possession than another. Some parties may settle cases lacking substantial merits precisely to avoid huge discovery costs. Even without such "impositional discovery" (the existence of which is hotly debated), large amounts of information tend to generate more legal and factual issues. Rather than narrowing disputes, discovery explodes them. And the time that it takes to complete the discovery of all this information, especially if the lawyers are left to their own devices, may take years.

Case management has stepped into the void, trying to balance the needs of issue narrowing and factual development by giving judges more control over both halves of this process. Of the two, issue narrowing is the main focus of case management; the managerial judge is always looking to remove issues from the case.

At the same time, case management has reshaped the goal of the pretrial process. Readying cases for trial is no longer the critical function of pretrial. Instead, the goal is to ready them for settlement or, if necessary, a decision on a case-dispositive motion. Case management is increasingly oriented to accomplishing non-trial resolutions of claims in cases both small and large.

We have already seen one of the most significant of these powers: the power to appoint counsel to represent a group. In this Chapter, we examine a number of other techniques (some traditional, some more modern and controversial). We begin with pleading, and then move to post-pleading methods.

A. Pleading Issues in a Complex Case

Pleading kicks off the lawsuit, giving opponents a sense of a party's claims or defenses. It can also serve as a means of narrowing issues or developing the facts. The notice-pleading regime of the Federal Rules generally eschews the latter two functions. In this section, we examine whether and how the demands of the big case affect the role of pleadings.

1. Heightened Pleading in Complex Cases

A plaintiff commences a case by filing a complaint.[699] Under Rule 12(b), a defendant can move to dismiss the case or any claim in the case immediately—and thus end or limit the dispute immediately. A defendant can seek dismissal for a number of reasons, including lack of subject-matter jurisdiction (Rule12(b)(1)), lack of territorial jurisdiction (Rule12(b)(2)), lack of venue (Rule12(b)(3)), insufficiency of process or service of process (Rules12(b)(4) and (b)(5)), and failure to join an indispensable party (Rule12(b)(7)). Most of these motions involve gatekeeping matters, do not require much discovery, and are unrelated to the merits of the dispute.[700] These gatekeeping motions tend not to end the litigation; the plaintiff can often cure the defect and file the case again in the same or a different forum. They do little to assist in the issue-narrowing process.

Only one motion to dismiss—the Rule 12(b)(6) motion to dismiss for failure to state a claim—is focused on the merits of the case. A complaint cannot be dismissed unless it fails to meet the Rule 8(a)'s three requirements, the principal one of which is "a short and plain statement of the claim." Traditionally the standard for dismissal is high and contained two components: first, "a complaint should not be dismissed for failure to state a claim unless it appears beyond doubt that the plaintiff can prove no set of facts in support of his claim which would entitle him to relief"; and second, the complaint needs only to "give the defendant fair notice of what the plaintiff's claim is and the grounds upon which it rests."[701]

The Supreme Court has recently amended these principles, "retiring" the first component and providing a new analysis for the second. Today a motion to dismiss requires a two-step approach. First, the judge must ignore all legal conclusions from the complaint. Second, the judge must ask whether, assuming the remaining factual allegations to be true, the complaint "plausibly" pleads a claim for relief. "Plausible" means more than "conceivable" but less than "probable." In making this determination, the judge should use his or her "judicial experience and common sense."[702]

---

[699] FED. R. CIV. P. 3.

[700] With the exception of subject-matter jurisdiction, failure to state a claim, and failure to join indispensable parties, Rule 12(b) motions are waived if not carefully preserved. *See* FED. R. CIV. P. 12(g)–(h). This waiver approach is consistent with a system that prefers adjudications on the merits rather than on gatekeeping technicalities.

[701] Conley v. Gibson, 355 U.S. 41 (1957).

[702] The two cases describing this new standard are *Bell Atlantic Corp. v. Twombly*, 550 U.S. 544 (2007), and *Ashcroft v. Iqbal*, 556 U.S. 662 (2009).

The two cases developing this new pleading standard—usually known as *Twombly* and *Iqbal*, or sometimes by the combined title *Twiqbal*—have set off a debate. At one time, the Supreme Court rejected the view that the motion to dismiss was an issue-narrowing device. Rather, the "simplified notice pleading standard relies on liberal discovery rules and summary judgment motions to define disputed facts and issues and to dispose of unmeritorious claims."[703] *Twombly* sounded a more dubious note about the capacity of discovery and summary judgment to accomplish these tasks. In adopting the new plausibility analysis, the Court noted that "proceeding to antitrust discovery can be expensive":

> It is no answer to say that a claim just shy of a plausible entitlement to relief can, if groundless, be weeded out early in the discovery process through "careful case management," given the common lament that the success of judicial supervision in checking discovery abuse has been on the modest side. And it is self-evident that the problem of discovery abuse cannot be solved by "careful scrutiny of evidence at the summary judgment stage," much less "lucid instructions to juries"; the threat of discovery expense will push cost-conscious defendants to settle even anemic cases before reaching those proceedings. Probably, then, it is only by taking care to require allegations that reach the level suggesting conspiracy that we can hope to avoid the potentially enormous expense of discovery . . . .[704]

Some scholars believe that plausibility pleading has resulted in more dismissals, while others believe that it merely confirmed existing practice and that, after allowing for the opportunity to amend pleadings, plausibility pleading has had little measurable impact on the success of a complaint.[705] To the extent that the cases have had an impact, they have likely driven litigation into state court. Many (though not all) states have declined to follow the Supreme Court's lead and retained their more liberal pleading standard. Fracturing litigation in this fashion creates aggregation problems, as we have seen.

At the same time, the Court has always resisted efforts to create "heightened pleading" requirements for particular types of cases,

---

[703] Swierkiewicz v. Sorema N. A., 534 U.S. 506 (2002).

[704] *Twombly*, 550 U.S. at 559–60 (citations omitted). Note that the same legalized-blackmail argument which has been used to narrow the scope of Rule 23, *see supra* notes 6–7, 429 and accompanying text, makes its appearance here, as a reason to insist on plausibility in pleading.

[705] For a summary of some of the leading articles and reports, see THOMAS D. ROWE, JR., ET AL., CIVIL PROCEDURE (4th ed. 2016).

including cases that are complex in nature.[706] *Twombly* was a complex case—a class action seeking recovery on behalf of consumers who alleged a vast anti-competitive conspiracy by major telecommunications carriers. After *Twombly* some lawyers and commentators tried to limit its holding to complex cases with massive discovery. But the Court rejected this effort in *Iqbal*, stating that the plausibility standard applied in all types of cases. Although some lower courts have tried on occasion to ratchet up pleading requirements for complex cases as a means of narrowing issues, the Supreme Court's consistent message has been that differential pleading standards should not arise from judicial fiat.[707]

Nonetheless, heightened pleading exists in a few enclaves of relevance to complex litigation. By rule, heightened pleading is appropriate for certain allegations, such as fraud, that may arise in complex cases.[708] By statute, heightened pleading is also required for certain elements of a securities-fraud cases brought under the Private Securities Litigation Reform Act.[709]

Finally, the Rule 12(b)(6) motion to dismiss can be used only against an entire claim or defense; it cannot excise certain issues from the case unless an entire claim or defense would collapse without the presence of that issue. For all these reasons, the motion to dismiss is a poor vehicle to narrow issues in most complex cases.

2. The Consolidated (or Master) Complaint

When parties file separate cases, the number of complaints in an aggregated proceeding can be voluminous, and judges may have a difficult time sorting out which rulings apply to which cases. To simplify the pleading phase, judges have sometimes turned to the use of a consolidated complaint. Often after appointment of counsel for the plaintiffs, the court requires the filing of a single complaint that

---

[706] *See Swierkiewicz*, 534 U.S. 506 (age discrimination and race discrimination); Leatherman v. Tarrant Cty. Narcotics Intelligence & Coordination Unit, 507 U.S. 163 (1993) (civil rights).

[707] For an opinion that was written by the person who drafted the notice-pleading requirements of Rule 8 and that argued why complex cases should rather be judged under the generous standard applicable to ordinary cases rather than a heightened pleading standard, see Nagler v. Admiral Corp., 248 F.2d 319 (2d Cir. 1957).

[708] FED. R. CIV. P. 9(b) (also noting that other allegations often common in complex litigation, such as "[m]alice, intent, knowledge, and other conditions of a person's mind[,] may be alleged generally"); *see* Hopper v. Solvay Pharms., Inc., 588 F.3d 1318 (11th Cir. 2009) (stating that the heightened pleading of Rule 9(b) requires the pleader "to assert the 'who,' 'what,' 'where,' 'when,' and 'how' of fraud[ ]").

[709] *See* 15 U.S.C. § 78u–4(b)(1)(B), –(b)(2); Tellabs, Inc. v. Makor Issues & Rights, Ltd., 551 U.S. 308 (2007) (requiring a plaintiff to plead facts rendering inference of scienter at least as likely as any plausible opposing inference).

covers all plaintiffs; this amended complaint then supersedes the prior individual complaints.

Consolidated complaints are often easier, tidier, and more economical for the court and the parties. The evident drawback is that plaintiffs are no longer "masters of their complaints"; they lose control of the proofs and arguments that they wish to make. In prior chapters, we saw that parties may be joined in a forum not of their choosing and may be represented by counsel not of their choosing. When they also lose the ability to control who to sue and on what theories to sue, the assault on the traditional adversarial model is nearly complete.[710]

For a time after the Supreme Court's decision in *Johnson v. Manhattan Railway Co.*,[711] it was believed that a federal court could not order consolidated pleadings. In 1975, however, *Katz v. Realty Equities Corp. of New York*,[712] held that a district court's order "requiring the filing and service of a single consolidated complaint for pretrial purposes upon defendants in a number of related securities cases . . . was a proper exercise of the trial judge's authority in the management of complex multiparty litigation." *Katz* upheld this power over the objection of two peripheral defendants who had been sued by only two of the twenty-one plaintiffs. Due to the consolidated pleadings that the district court ordered, these two defendants now found themselves defending against the claims of twenty-one plaintiffs and the crossclaims of thirty-nine defendants. *Katz* emphasized that the consolidation was for pretrial purposes only. The cases remained distinct; despite the increased burden to the two peripheral defendants, "[d]irecting discovery to one complaint, rather than to seventeen complaints, avoids the possible confusion and the possible problems stemming from the situation where each plaintiff pursues his individual complaint." Deciding whether to order a consolidated complaint requires a court to consider "whether the anticipated benefits of a consolidated complaint outweigh potential prejudice to the parties."

In certain aggregated proceedings, such as MDL actions, consolidated, or "master," complaints are extremely common. Curiously, the present *Manual for Complex Litigation* makes little mention of them. Consolidated pleadings have some drawbacks. As

---

[710] *Cf.* Joan Steinman, *The Effects of Case Consolidation on the Procedural Rights of Litigants: What They Are, What They Might Be Part II: Non-Jurisdictional Matters*, 42 UCLA L. REV. 967 (1995) ("The forces that isolate parties from the lawyers handling their claims, which may first be manifest in connection with pleadings, continue to operate throughout the litigation.").

[711] 289 U.S. 479 (1933) (stating that the consolidation of cases "does not merge the suits into a single cause, or change the rights of the parties, or make those who are parties in one suit parties in another").

[712] 521 F.2d 1354 (2d Cir. 1975).

you might expect, and as the defendants in *Katz* found out, one issue is their kitchen-sink nature: they tend to include all possible allegations from all complaints, thus expanding rather than narrowing the issues at the pleading stage while subsuming the individual within the collective. Another issue is the source of the court's power to order consolidation. *Katz* suggested that courts had the inherent power to enhance judicial economy in complex cases. Today, the power could be extrapolated from Rules 16(c)(2)(A), –(B), and –(L), which had not been promulgated at the time of *Katz*.[713]

Consolidated pleadings have also touched off choice-of-law issues. When cases arising under state law are transferred to an MDL forum, they bring their own choice-of-law rules with them.[714] As we saw, sorting through the multiple choice-of-law approaches, and then through the different laws to which these approaches point, is daunting. One solution to this problem was to adopt a single choice-of-law rule. Because the consolidated pleading is filed in the transferee forum, the court can arguably apply the choice-of-law rule only of the forum, thus obviating the need for a potentially complex choice-of-law analysis for the transferred suits.

One court adopted this approach,[715] but others have resisted it.[716] One concern is the powerful effect that a consolidated complaint, intended only to achieve greater efficiency, would have on the rights of litigants if the forum's choice-of-law rule applied to all consolidated cases. Another is the administrative confusion that would result if the cases are remanded to their original fora at the conclusion of the MDL proceedings: transferor courts would face the problem of deciding whether to conduct the choice-of-law analysis under the original complaint or the master complaint. As a result, "the master complaint should not be given the same effect as an ordinary complaint. Instead, it should be considered as only an administrative device to aid efficiency and economy."[717]

Courts have married the idea of consolidated pleadings to technology to enhance efficiency. Some courts have established electronic "master long-form complaints," listing all jurisdictional bases and claims that can be asserted. Plaintiffs can then

---

713 Some courts have found the authority for requiring a master complaint in Rule 42(a), which allows courts to consolidate actions and to "issue any other orders to avoid unnecessary cost or delay"; but this text is also ambiguous.

714 *See supra* note 592 and accompanying text.

715 *See In re* Bridgestone/Firestone, Inc. Tires Prods. Liab. Litig., 155 F. Supp. 2d 1069 (S.D. Ind. 2001)

716 *See In re* Propulsid Prods. Liab. Litig., 208 F.R.D. 133 (E.D. La. 2002). *See also In re* Conagra Peanut Butter Prods. Liab. Litig., 251 F.R.D. 689 (N.D. Ga. 2008) (analyzing the approaches and refusing to apply the choice-of-law rules of the MDL forum state to a class-action master complaint filed in the MDL forum).

717 *Propulsid*, 208 F.R.D. at 142.

electronically check the boxes that correspond to the jurisdictional bases and claims that they wish to bring. The defendant is deemed to have denied all the allegations.[718] Other courts have allowed plaintiffs to sign a form adopting the master complaint in lieu of filing a separate pleading.[719] Courts have sometimes allowed the lawyers for plaintiffs "to disavow the inclusion of their clients' claims within the amended consolidated complaint,"[720] but this approach is exceeding rare.

B. Post-Pleading Issue-Narrowing Devices

The Federal Rules contain two traditional post-pleading issue-narrowing devices: the Rule 36 request for admission and the Rule 56 motion for summary judgment. The former is of limited utility, and the latter, though powerful, also contains limits. Into this void has stepped case management, with a number of ad hoc issue-narrowing devices.[721] We begin with the traditional devices to establish the backdrop for modern case-management techniques.

1. Traditional Devices

Rule 36 allows a party to ask any other party to admit or deny any matter of consequence to the litigation. The responding party can admit the request, deny the request, or avoid it by claiming insufficient knowledge or information. An admitted request conclusively determines that issue for the litigation, although it has no effect on other litigation. A denied request can also be useful, for the requesting party can engage in follow-up discovery to determine the precise facts on which the denial was based.

The sole sanction for a responding party that refuses to admit a matter is payment of the requesting party's costs of proving the matter at trial. But sanctions do not arise when the admission lacks "substantial importance" or the responding party has "reasonable ground to believe" that he or she might prevail on the merits of the subject matter of the admission.[722] These exceptions weaken this value of requests for admission as an issue-narrowing tool.

The request for admission has not been an especially effective issue-narrowing tool, whether in complex or in ordinary litigation, for other reasons as well. Early in the pretrial process, when

---

[718] *See In re* Diet Drugs (Phentermine/Fenfluramine/Dexfenfluramine) Prods. Liab. Litig., MDL Docket No. 1203, 2009 WL 1924441 (E.D. Pa. June 30, 2009).

[719] *See In re* Guidant Corp. Implantable Defibrillators Prods. Liab. Litig., MDL No. 05–1708 (DWF/AJB), 2008 WL 682174 (D. Minn. Mar. 7, 2008).

[720] *See In re* Storage Tech. Corp. Sec. Litig., 630 F. Supp. 1072 (D. Colo. 1986)

[721] *See* Elliott, *supra* note 141 (tracing the rise of case management to the failure of the Federal Rules to provide adequate issue-narrowing techniques).

[722] FED. R. CIV. P. 37(c)(2).

admissions would be most effective, a responding party can almost always plead insufficient information. Moreover, the big issues in the case—"Is asbestos a defective product?" or "Did the defendant conspire to fix prices?"—are usually so hotly contested that a party can deny them without fear of sanctions. Furthermore, a truly determined adversary can deny even truthful assertions if he or she is willing to pay for the recalcitrance. To make Rule 36 even less useful, many districts have local rules that presumptively limit the number of requests that a party can propound.

The Rule 56 motion for summary judgment is another matter. Rule 56 permits a court to dismiss a claim or defense, thus providing a significant issue-narrowing capacity. A "court shall grant summary judgment" when the moving party "shows that there is no genuine dispute as to any material fact and the moving party is entitled to judgment as a matter of law."[723] Although a court typically considers summary judgment only on a party's motion, judges enjoy a *sua sponte* power to enter summary judgment, thus enhancing its usefulness as an issue-narrowing technique.[724]

When the only disputes are legal, summary judgment seems an ideal vehicle for resolving a case. When factual disputes exist, however, summary judgment's usefulness diminishes. One reason is that, unlike Rule 12(b)(6), Rule 56 examines the evidentiary merits of a claim or defense, rather than the allegations in the pleadings. For this process to be meaningful, the parties must have an opportunity to conduct discovery and gather information. As a rule, summary judgment is inappropriate until there has been "an adequate time for discovery."[725] An ideal issue-narrowing device obviates the need for discovery; here, the cost of discovery must be incurred before the motion can be entertained.

A second hurdle is the inapplicability of summary judgment as long as the material factual disputes are "genuine."[726] The line between a genuine and a non-genuine factual dispute requires us to consider the Seventh Amendment's right to civil jury trial. It is a simple matter of constitutional logic that a judge cannot decide

---

[723] FED. R. CIV. P. 56(a).

[724] *See* FED. R. CIV. P. 56(f)(3) (permitting a court to "consider summary judgment on its own after identifying for the parties material facts that may not be genuinely disputed").

[725] *See* Celotex Corp. v. Catrett, 477 U.S. 317 (1986).

[726] A fact is "material" when it is relevant to the ground on which summary judgment is sought. *See* Anderson v. Liberty Lobby, Inc., 477 U.S. 242 (1986). For instance, if there is no dispute that the defendant owed no duty to the plaintiff, but genuine disputes exist about the amount of damage that the plaintiff suffered, any disputes regarding damages are not material to a summary-judgment motion based on the lack of duty. If the motion is based on the plaintiff's lack of damages, however, summary judgment would be inappropriate.

factual issues during pretrial that a jury must decide at trial; otherwise, the Seventh Amendment's jury-trial guarantee would be hollow indeed.[727] Thus, a factual dispute is usually said to be "genuine" when a judge lacks the power to take the dispute away from a jury at trial. Rule 50(a) describes the scope of that power: a judge may enter judgment as a matter of law against a party at trial when "a reasonable jury would not have a legally sufficient evidentiary basis to find for [the non-moving] party on that issue." The unspoken obverse of Rule 50 is that, as long as credible evidence lies on both sides of a factual issue, a judge may not take the issue away from the jury under Rule 50. A priori, a court may not determine such a factual issue under Rule 56.[728]

A number of guidelines aid in determining whether a dispute must be left to a jury or instead can be resolved by a judge. First, a court must examine the entire record, not just the portions favoring the non-moving party. Next, the court must draw all reasonable inferences in favor of the non-moving party. Third, the judge must not make credibility determinations regarding witnesses; those determinations are quintessentially the jury's province. Hence, if one witness says "red" and the other "green," and the issue of color is material to the legal dispute, the court must leave the case to the jury. Finally, the only evidence of the moving party that a judge should credit is evidence "that is

Problem 1

An MDL court to which seventy cases have been transferred has worked diligently for nineteen months to resolve motions to dismiss, coordinate with judges in state cases, establish discovery orders, and set a discovery and briefing schedule for a class-certification motion. Numerous case-management conferences have been held. No discovery on the merits of the dispute has yet occurred. Without advising the court of its intention, and while discovery on class certification is ongoing, one defendant files a motion for summary judgment on the merits of the dispute. If you were managing this case as the MDL judge, what would you do? *See In re* New Motor Vehicles Canadian Export Antitrust Litig., 229 F.R.D. 35 (D. Me. 2005).

727 Of course, this logic does not require summary judgment to go as far as the constitutional line, but only that it not go farther. Nonetheless, the Supreme Court has pushed "genuineness" to its constitutional maximum. *See id.*

728 The case equating the Rule 50 and Rule 56 standards is *Anderson*, 477 U. S. 242. In cases tried to the bench, Rule 56's "genuine dispute" standard need not be the same; because the judge is the factfinder at trial, the judge can resolve factual disputes—presumably even genuine ones—during pretrial. But judges have tended to employ the standard that is used for jury trials, thus leaving factual disputes for the bench trial itself. *See generally* Jack Achiezer Guggenheim, *In Summary It Makes Sense: A Proposal to Substantially Expand the Role of Summary Judgment in Nonjury Cases*, 43 SAN DIEGO L. REV. 319 (2006) (proposing "to dramatically expand the role of summary judgment in bench trial cases where the record is sufficiently complete to allow judges to draw their own inferences and to resolve factual disputes").

uncontradicted and unimpeached, at least to the extent that that evidence comes from disinterested witnesses."[729]

These guidelines, derived from the immovable constraints of the Seventh Amendment, evidently limit Rule 56's power to narrow issues before trial.

A third possible limit on the utility of Rule 56 is the requirement that a motion is proper only when a judgment on an entire claim or defense is possible. Unlike Rule 36, Rule 56 does not appear to have the capacity to remove issues surgically from a case. When a court declines to grant summary judgment, it can enter an order establishing as true any material fact that was not genuinely disputed.[730] Some commentators have suggested that this power allows courts to engage in surgical decision-making and decide facts of consequence to a case; the Advisory Committee's note to the 2010 amendment to Rule 56 also hints in this direction. There have been academic proposals, including one that made it to the drafting stage before the Advisory Committee, to turn Rule 56 as a "summary issue narrowing" device. But the Supreme Court has not to date blessed this use of summary judgment—unless the determination of an issue leads to judgment on all or part of a claim or defense.

One issue that has attracted attention is whether the complex nature of a dispute affects the standard of Rule 56. *Poller v. Columbia Broadcasting System*[731] reversed a summary judgment in an antitrust case that appeared to present no difficult factual issues. In the course of its ruling, the Court made the following observation: "[S]ummary procedures should be used sparingly in complex antitrust litigation where motive and intent play leading roles, the proof is largely in the hands of the alleged conspirators, and hostile witnesses thicken the plot."[732]

For many years, this comment was read to mean that summary judgment was a disfavored device for complex cases. Without overruling *Poller*, however, the Court seemed to reverse course in two cases: *Celotex Corp. v. Catrett*,[733] an asbestos-exposure case in which it observed that summary judgment "is properly regarded not as a disfavored procedural shortcut, but rather as an integral part of the

---

729 *See* Reeves v. Sanderson Plumbing Prods., Inc., 530 U.S. 133 (2000) (internal quotation marks omitted).

730 FED. R. CIV. P. 56(g).

731 368 U.S. 464 (1962).

732 For a comparable sentiment, see *Kennedy v. Silas Mason Co.*, 334 U.S. 249 (1948) ("[S]ummary procedures, however salutary where issues are clear-cut and simple, present a treacherous record for deciding issues of far-flung import, on which this Court should draw inferences with caution from complicated courses of legislation, contracting, and practice.").

733 477 U.S. 317 (1986).

Federal Rules as a whole"; and more specifically in *Matsushita Electric Industrial Co. v. Zenith Radio Corp.*,[734] one of the most massive antitrust cases ever litigated. The factual theory in *Matsushita* was that Japanese manufacturers of electronic equipment had engaged in predatory pricing over several decades. The district court had granted summary judgment after years of pretrial activity, but the court of appeals reversed, believing that sufficient indirect evidence existed for a jury to infer such a conspiracy. The Supreme Court upheld the district court's grant of summary judgment. No direct evidence of predation existed, and the majority believed that the inferential indirect evidence was too thin for jury trial because such long-lasting predatory behavior defied economic common sense. The Court analyzed the defendants' conduct according to the standard of a rational economic actor, and determined the case on that basis—a move that seems analytically inconsistent with the dicta in *Poller*.

After *Celotex* and *Matsushita*, some courts began to suggest that the "genuineness" standard for summary judgment was easier to satisfy in complex cases than in ordinary ones.[735] Most courts, however, have nominally rejected this view. Some courts continue to express *Poller*'s reluctance to use summary judgment in complex litigation.[736] Most hold that the same standard applies in ordinary and complex litigation.[737]

Also relevant to this question is *Eastman Kodak Co. v. Image Technical Services, Inc.*,[738] which the Court described as "yet another case that concerns the standard for summary judgment in an antitrust controversy." *Eastman Kodak* emphasized that antitrust determinations are not to be made on the basis of presumptions and

---

734 475 U.S. 574 (1986).

735 *See* Collins v. Associated Pathologists, Ltd., 844 F.2d 473 (7th Cir. 1988) ("Contrary to the emphasis of some prior precedent, the use of summary judgment is not only permitted by *Matsushita* but encouraged . . . in antitrust cases.").

736 *See* Int'l Healthcare Mgmt. v. Haw. Coalition for Health, 332 F.3d 600, 604 (9th Cir. 2003) ("Summary judgment is only disfavored in complex antitrust litigation where motive and intent are important, proof is largely in the hands of the alleged conspirators, and relevant information is controlled by hostile witnesses.") (internal quotation marks omitted); MANUAL, *supra* note 206, § 11.34 (stating that, although "the standard for deciding a summary judgment motion is the same in all cases," the need for discovery on complicated issues may make complex cases "not as susceptible to resolution as issues in more familiar settings").

737 *See* B.F. Goodrich v. Betkoski, 99 F.3d 505 (2d Cir. 1996) (stating that, in environmental cases, summary judgment is a "powerful legal tool" that can "avoid lengthy and perhaps needless litigation," but that the "showing required to survive summary judgment also remains the same"); Thompson Everett, Inc. v. Nat'l Cable Advert., L.P., 57 F.3d 1317 (4th Cir. 1995) (noting that, although "Rule 56 is to be applied to antitrust cases no differently from how it is applied to other cases," Rule 56 is "particularly well-suited" for sorting out "the unusual entanglement of legal and factual issues frequently presented in antitrust cases").

738 504 U.S. 451 (1992).

legal fictions, but rather on the realities of market power. The district judge in *Eastman Kodak* had granted summary judgment after limited discovery; the defendant had filed the motion prior to discovery, after which the judge "permitted respondents to file one set of interrogatories and one set of requests for production of documents and to take six depositions." Although its decision to reverse the entry of summary judgment did not hinge on the fact, the Court was troubled by the thin factual record.

As is so often the case, the real issue is not the nominal standard for summary judgment; it is the application of that standard in practice. Empirical evidence suggests that motions for summary judgment are granted, in whole or in part, with some frequency in antitrust cases.[739] But the swing of the pendulum from *Poller* to *Celotex* and *Matsushita* has not been an overly dramatic one. There are ultimate constraints on how far judicial interpretation can shift the Federal Rules—among them the Seventh Amendment, our philosophy to reach decisions on the merits, our commitments to adversarial and trans-substantive process, and the potential for the parties' strategic misuse of issue-narrowing devices. If issue narrowing is to occur on a large scale, the case manager needs more weapons in the arsenal.

2. Modern Case-Management Devices

Among the case-management devices that can narrow issues, some do so directly, and others do so indirectly. The following discussion is not intended to be an exhaustive list of issue-narrowing strategies. They represent, however, an array of common strategies. Judges can mix and match strategies Many of the devices have potential outcome-determining effects, although the effects are often little understood.

a. Establishing Early, Firm Dates

One of the strong tenets of case management is the court's need to establish early, firm deadlines to complete pretrial tasks and for trial. In traditional adversarial theory, the lawyers develop the case largely according to their own timetable. This attitude, however, can create problems in large-scale cases, when lawyers, left to their own devices, may have difficulty completing pretrial tasks in a timely way.

Having the court establish deadlines seems a very modest intrusion on traditional theory. The catch, however, lies in the words "early" and "firm." By giving only limited time and refusing to relent

---

739 *See* Stephen Calkins, *Summary Judgment, Motions to Dismiss, and Other Examples of Equilibrating Tendencies in the Antitrust System*, 74 GEO. L.J. 1065 (1986).

on the deadlines, this technique is designed to focus the lawyers' attention on the crux of their cases and prevent inquiries into peripheral matters. So used, early, firm deadlines are an indirect method to narrow issues; they force the lawyers to strip the case to its essentials.

Early, firm deadlines have been used in complex litigation for some time. A seminal case upholding their use is *In re Fine Paper Antitrust Litigation.*[740] In *Fine Paper*, the district court imposed a both a discovery deadline and a trial date. Although the case was a large antitrust matter, the trial was set only ten months in the future. This date was ultimately moved back an additional nine months, with one set of plaintiffs scheduled for trial in September and another in October. The latter set of plaintiffs apparently had relied on the first set to do much of the work, or at least expected the first trial to continue past their own trial setting; in any event, they did little pretrial preparation. When the first set of plaintiffs settled shortly before the scheduled September trial, the second set was woefully unprepared to begin trial in October. The district judge refused to relent on the October trial date. The trial went so poorly for the second group of plaintiffs that the district court entered judgment against them during the trial. On appeal, the Third Circuit upheld the trial judge's discretion to establish and then firmly adhere to the trial deadline.

Fine Paper sent lawyers a message about the risk of treating pretrial and trial deadlines cavalierly. Whether justice was done was another matter. Moreover, at the time the source of the judge's power to enter these deadlines was uncertain. As part of the 1983 case-management revisions to Rule 16, however, Rule 16(b) was amended to require courts to impose deadlines for joining parties, making motions, and completing discovery. Rule 16(b) also suggests that the court establish a deadline for the trial. Rule 16(b) permits modification of these deadlines only upon a showing of good cause, thus sending the message about the firmness of deadlines. Rule 16(b) says nothing about setting deadlines "early," but the length of the deadlines remains in the trial judge's discretion.

The empirical and anecdotal data on early, firm deadlines appear impressive. One study during the early 1990s examined the efficacy of a number of case-management measures to reduce cost and delay.[741] With respect to early, firm deadlines, the study found that an early trial date was the most effective case-management tool for reducing the time to disposition. The entry of discovery deadlines also reduced the time to disposition. Both deadlines reduced attorney

---

740 685 F.2d 810 (3d Cir. 1982).

741 *See* KAKALIK ET AL., CASE MANAGEMENT, *supra* note 643.

hours spent on a case, though the reduction was statistically insignificant when only a discovery cutoff was issued. The imposition of deadlines had little effect on lawyer satisfaction or litigants' perception of fairness.

These statistics suggest that early, firm deadlines are nothing to fear. But the study did not focus specifically on complex cases, in which greater problems with the firm enforcement of deadlines might be anticipated. Moreover, the study measured primarily the variables of cost and delay, and secondarily the satisfaction of litigants, lawyers, and judges with the process. The issue that concerns us is a different one: Can early, firm deadlines narrow issues in a way that avoids needless factual development? The study does not provide an answer.

More generally, short deadlines have the potential to favor better-financed parties and those parties with greater access to information. In most big cases, shorter deadlines do not necessarily mean less discovery; they mean bigger litigation teams on each side of a case—with all the inefficiencies that more administration entails. A well-financed party is better able to assemble a large team and to endure its inefficiencies. Likewise, to the extent that shorter deadlines limit the number of issues that can be explored, the party with greater access to information (and thus less need of discovery) stands in better stead. Resolving cases on their merits becomes more difficult when information goes undiscovered due to the press of time.[742]

Finally, setting deadlines that are short but not too short (i.e., giving the lawyers adequate time to develop the hearts of their cases but inadequate time to dally on the fine points) requires the judge to have a strong intuitive feel for the litigation. How the judge obtains this feel, and how often the judge will make errors by establishing ill-fitting deadlines, remain open questions.

We do not know how serious these drawbacks are in complex litigation, for, thus far, no studies have been done to test these concerns. Because cost and delay can be measured, those data now drive the debate over case management generally and the use of early, firm deadlines particularly.

Despite these misgivings, the path is clear. Early, firm deadlines, which were first used in complex litigation, have now become a principal case-management tool for cases large and small.

---

[742] *See* MANUAL, *supra* note 206, § 21.422; WILLIAM W SCHWARZER, MANAGING ANTITRUST AND OTHER COMPLEX LITIGATION § 4–1 (1982).

b. *Bifurcation*

A direct method to narrow issues is to split the pretrial process into discrete parts, thus focusing on a small number of issues or claims at a time. Dividing a case into parts is often referred to as "bifurcation." Technically, bifurcation concerns only the division of a case into two parts. Pretrial proceedings may be split into three parts (trifurcation) or more (polyfurcation), but the term bifurcation is used loosely to describe them all.

Pretrial bifurcation should be distinguished from trial bifurcation, which we consider in Chapter Fourteen.[743] There is no necessary relationship between the decision to bifurcate the pretrial proceedings and the decision to bifurcate the trial. Nonetheless, it is likely that, once a court has split a case in a particular fashion during pretrial, the same (or similar division) will occur at trial. As we will see, trial bifurcation in jury-tried cases requires care, lest the division run afoul of the Seventh Amendment's Reexamination Clause: no facts found by one jury may be reexamined by another jury in a later trial. If the judge intends to pattern the trial bifurcation on the pretrial bifurcation, pretrial bifurcation must be done with care. The Reexamination Clause points out another concern with bifurcation: if the cases is divided in such a way that later stages will need to depose the same witnesses or examine the same evidence, bifurcation may create inefficiencies that outweigh the gains of narrowing the case into smaller bits.

For bifurcation to work well as an issue-narrowing technique, the issues or claims considered in the first level of bifurcation ideally should possess certain characteristics: the information to decide the issue is readily available; the issues selected hold a reasonable prospect of disposing of the entire case; and the evidence necessary to decide the first issues is self-contained and will not be explored again if the determination on the first issue does not end the litigation. A classic example of such an issue is the statute of limitations.

Unfortunately, such a perfect issue or claim rarely presents itself in complex cases. Usually the easy matters are not case-dispositive; and the case-dispositive matters are not easy. Therefore in deciding whether to bifurcate, a judge must compromise, balancing the likelihood that an early focus on one issue or claim will dispose of the case against considerations of cost and delay if the case is not

---

743 *See infra* Chapter 14.A.

disposed of. A judge may decide that the cost and delay of bifurcation are likely to exceed its benefits.[744]

A common form of bifurcation is to carve off liability issues from damages issues, and to handle only liability issues in the first phase of the litigation. If damages are individualized and it turns out that the defendant is not liable, bifurcation avoids extensive, plaintiff-by-plaintiff discovery. Moreover, liability and damages issues are usually distinct, so little discovery will be replicated if the case moves to a damages phase.[745]

Other forms are also possible. Bifurcation can occur for a single issue within the liability case, for a defense, or for a claim whose resolution might guide the disposition of other claims. One form of bifurcation that is exceptionally common in class-action litigation is separating discovery on class-certification issues from discovery on merits issues, with class-certification issues being handled first.[746] This approach acknowledges the substantial effect that certification will have for the management of the case; indeed, in negative-value litigation, the case may disappear if class certification fails.

The goal is clear: break up the case to expedite the resolution of the dispute. Whether and how issues are split are questions specific to each lawsuit.

As with many case-management tools, one concern with bifurcation is the source of the judge's power to bifurcate a case during pretrial. Courts often assume that the authority derives from Rule 42(b), but the express terms of the rule authorize a court, "[f]or convenience, to avoid prejudice, or to expedite and economize," only to "order a separate trial of one or more separate issues, claims, crossclaims, counterclaims, or third-party claims." The power to order pretrial bifurcation arguably lies in the interstices of one or more of the clauses of the ubiquitous Rule 16(c),[747] but no express

---

[744] *See, e.g.,* Kos Pharms., Inc. v. Barr Labs., Inc., 218 F.R.D. 387 (S.D.N.Y. 2003) ("Extending the adjudication into two or more proceedings necessarily implicates additional discovery; more pretrial disputes and motion practice; empaneling another jury or imposing more on the jurors who decide the earlier phase of the litigation; deposing or recalling some of the same witnesses; and potentially engendering new rounds of trial and post-trial motions and appeals.").

[745] *See, e.g.,* Ocean Atl. Woodland Corp. v. DRH Cambridge Homes, Inc., No. 02 C 2523, 2004 WL 609326 (N.D. Ill. Mar. 23, 2004) (noting that "the defendant would expend substantial amounts of time and resources responding to discovery requests on damages").

[746] *See, e.g.,* Harris v. Option One Mortg. Corp., 261 F.R.D. 98 (D.S.C. 2009); *but see In re* Rail Freight Fuel Surcharge Antitrust Litig., 258 F.R.D. 167 (D.D.C. 2009) (declining to bifurcate class and merits discovery because they were interwoven).

[747] Among the possibly relevant sources of authority are the powers to take action regarding: (1) "formulating and simplifying the issues, and eliminating frivolous claims or defenses," FED. R. CIV. P. 16(c)(2)(A); (2) "adopting special procedures for managing potentially difficult or protracted actions that may involve

language to that effect exists. A likelier source is Rule 26(f)(2), read in conjunction with Rule 26(c)(2),[748] but again the source of judicial power to order bifurcation, in the absence of mutual consent, is not certain.

Yet another concern with pretrial bifurcation is its potentially outcome-determinative effect. Although no studies have been done on the effect of pretrial bifurcation, studies on trial bifurcation suggest two effects: a marked pro-defendant effect in individual cases and a likely increase in litigation in the aggregate.[749] The usual explanation for this effect is that bifurcation, especially if it is done on liability issues, eliminates sympathy from the factfinder's calculus. Whether that fact is good or bad is to some extent beside the point. The reality is that a procedural choice creates a significant risk of a different outcome. A judge less inclined to buy the plaintiffs' story of liability may be more inclined to bifurcate, and the choice of procedure then helps to confirm the judge's predetermination. A judge more inclined to believe the plaintiffs' story may eschew bifurcation in favor of other techniques that have a less pro-defendant caste; the choice of those techniques may also confirm that judge's beliefs.[750]

Although plaintiffs generally argue against bifurcation, especially of the liability-damages variety, sometimes it is to their benefit. If a court is disinclined to certify a class or otherwise aggregate related litigation due to the pretrial management problems that the aggregation poses, and if no other case-management devices seem appropriate, the plaintiffs' lawyer may agree to bifurcation as the price of obtaining aggregation. Such a decision is not irrational; the plaintiffs may be even worse off if they are forced to go it alone—especially in negative-value cases.[751]

---

complex issues, multiple parties, difficult legal questions, or unusual proof problems," FED. R. CIV. P. 16(c)(2)(L); (3) "ordering a separate trial under Rule 42(b) of a claim, counterclaim, crossclaim, third-party claim, or particular issue," FED. R. CIV. P. 16(c)(2)(M); and (4) "ordering the presentation of evidence early in the trial on a manageable issue that might, on the evidence, be the basis for a judgment as a matter of law under Rule 50(a) or a judgment on partial findings under Rule 52(c)," FED. R. CIV. P. 16(c)(2)(N). None is a perfect fit.

[748] FED. R. CIV. P. 26 (f)(2) (ordering parties to consider in creating a discovery plan "whether discovery should be conducted in phases or be limited to or focused on particular issues"); (c)(1)(B) (allowing court to issue a protective order "specifying terms, including time and place or the allocation of expenses, for the disclosure or discovery").

[749] For a discussion of these studies, see *infra* notes 884–885 and accompanying text.

[750] Perhaps for these concerns or others, the *Manual for Complex Litigation* makes barely a mention of bifurcation as a case-management technique. For fleeting references, see MANUAL, *supra* note 206, §§ 11.211, 11.421.

[751] Of course, there is also the possibility that the lawyer is willing to accede to bifurcation because an aggregate proceeding holds out a chance of a higher fee than

Pretrial bifurcation also raises issues of equity and fairness for plaintiffs whose cases are bifurcated in relation to plaintiffs whose cases are not. Bifurcation also raises a grand-theory concern. As a matter of procedural design, the division of cases into a series of discrete parts is a procedural method associated most often with the discontinuous-trial method of continental or inquisitorial systems of justice, including our equity tradition. Pretrial bifurcation does not shift complex litigation entirely in that direction, but it shortens the distance. Whether increased use of bifurcation portends the demise of our tradition of common-law trial is a question that arises with virtually every case-management technique, but bifurcation raises the question most starkly.

c. Lone Pine *and Similar Orders*

Arguably a form of bifurcation, one technique for dividing up issues in a complex case deserves special mention. In mass-tort, RICO, and similar cases, courts sometimes issue orders that require plaintiffs to provide substantial information about their individual claims before the case may proceed. In a mass-tort case, for example, the court may require each plaintiff to provide evidence of the time, frequency, and duration of exposure to the toxic substance; a medical diagnosis of their injuries; and an expert opinion that exposure in the specified amount can cause the injuries claimed. In a RICO case, the plaintiffs may be required to provide detailed evidence (including exact times, locations, and witnesses or documents) concerning each wrongful predicate act; the nature of and participants in the allegedly unlawful enterprise; and, if the acts are fraudulent, the exact manner and scope of each plaintiff's reliance on the defendant's statements. In mass-tort cases, such a requirement is usually referred to as a "*Lone Pine* order," so named after the 1986 New Jersey state-court decision that first adopted this technique. In RICO cases, the requirement is usually known as a "RICO case statement." Some courts refer to the plaintiffs' required submission as a "Fact Sheet."[752]

The purpose of such an order is to ensure at the outset that each plaintiff has a bona fide claim—or, put differently, to winnow out the meritless claims without forcing the defendant to expend significant

individual litigation—even though the clients would be better off with individualized litigation. This fact shows that concerns for adequacy of counsel and agency costs travel into the case-management phase of the litigation as well.

[752] At the time of writing, a bill that has passed the House of Representatives would impose a comparable requirement in all MDL proceedings involving claims of personal injury. Within forty-five days of consolidation, the plaintiffs would be required to submit "evidentiary support (including but not limited to medical records) for the factual contentions in plaintiff's complaint regarding the alleged injury, the exposure to the risk that allegedly caused the injury, and the alleged cause of the injury." Prospects for passage in the Senate are uncertain.

resources. Proponents of the method point out that, under Rule 11, a lawyer must never file a case lacking evidentiary support, so the order merely seeks disclosure of information that should be in the lawyer's possession. To the extent that the order winnows out meritless cases, it can substantially narrow the scope of the litigation.

The leading case authorizing *Lone Pine* orders is *Acuna v. Brown & Root Inc.*[753] Two lawsuits containing 1,600 local residents alleged maladies due to the nearby uranium-processing activities of nearly one hundred defendants. The cases were brought in state court, but removed to federal court. A magistrate judge entered a pre-discovery scheduling order requiring the lawyer to file detailed information regarding exposure history, disease history, and causal connection. In response, the lawyer filed more than one thousand form affidavits from a medical expert. The expert identified various illnesses that uranium exposure can cause and asserted, after review of each plaintiff's medical data, that the plaintiff's exposure was clinically significant. The affidavits did not specify the exact manner of exposure (ingestion, inhalation, and so on) for each plaintiff. The magistrate judge held that the affidavits did not comply with the order, and after plaintiffs submitted new affidavits that did not fundamentally address the magistrate judge's concerns for most plaintiffs, the magistrate judge recommended dismissal of the cases. The district court did so.

The court of appeals affirmed the dismissal. The court began by noting the broad discretion that district judges have to manage complex litigation, especially given "the complex issues and potential burdens on defendants and the court in mass tort litigation." The plaintiffs' broad-brush complaints failed to provide defendants with any sense of how many people suffered from which illnesses. Refusing to allow the case to proceed "without better definition of plaintiffs' claims" was a decision within the trial court's managerial discretion.[754]

Other courts have been hesitant to adopt *Lone Pine* or similar orders. Some have pointed out that such an order, at least when issued as a scheduling order at the outset of the case, is inconsistent with the liberal notice-pleading requirements of Rule 8(a). Discovery and summary judgment, together with sanctions, are the means to test the validity of claims—especially when some of the information (such as exposure history) might lie in the defendants' control. Using the devices provided in the Federal Rules provides greater

---

753 200 F.3d 335 (5th Cir. 2000).

754 For another case affirming the use of a *Lone Pine* order, see Avila v. Willits Envtl. Remediation Tr., 633 F.3d 828 (9th Cir. 2011).

"consistency and safeguards"; *Lone Pine* orders should be employed only "where existing procedural devices explicitly at the disposal of the parties by statute and federal rule have been exhausted or where they cannot accommodate the unique issues of this litigation."[755] Furthermore, some critics argue that these orders should be used only when a substantial number of plaintiffs exist; they are unnecessary when the number of plaintiffs is small.[756]

Adinolfe v. United Technologies Corp.[757] particularly stressed the timing point. Although refusing to dismiss the use of *Lone Pine* orders entirely, the court held that it was not "legally appropriate (or for that matter wise) for a district court to issue a *Lone Pine* order requiring factual support for the plaintiffs' claims before it has determined that those claims survive a motion to dismiss under *Twombly*." Nor should such an order "be used as (or become) the platforms for pseudo-summary judgment motions at a time when the case is not at issue and the parties have not engaged in reciprocal discovery." To do so, *Adinolfe* argued, would create a heightened-pleading regime on which the Supreme Court has frowned. Although the concern for "expensive and time-consuming discovery without the plaintiffs first demonstrating some factual support for their claims" is valid, "it cannot be allayed by use of a scheduling order that runs counter to the adversarial process envisioned by and detailed in the Federal Rules of Civil Procedure."

A common concern with *Lone Pine* orders is, once again, the source of the court's power to adopt this case-management approach. Some parts of Rule 16(c) could be stretched to encompass such a power, but (sound familiar?) no clear authority exists.[758]

Another concern, once again, is the *Lone Pine* order's potential outcome-determining effect. Plaintiffs in cases adopting a *Lone Pine* order often have their cases dismissed before discovery commences. Plaintiffs in cases not adopting this order often proceed to discovery and settlement. To make the outcome of litigation hinge so clearly on a discretionary decision of a trial judge—one that some judges

---

755 *See In re* Digitek® Prod. Liab. Litig., 264 F.R.D. 249 (S.D. W. Va. 2010).

756 *See* Antero Res. Corp. v. Strudley, 347 P.3d 149 (Colo. 2015).

757 768 F.3d 1161 (11th Cir. 2014).

758 The two most relevant sources are Rule 16(c)(2)(A) (authorizing a court to take appropriate action regarding "formulating and simplifying the issues, and eliminating frivolous claims or defenses,") and Rule 16(c)(2)(L) (authorizing a court to take appropriate action regarding "adopting special procedures for managing potentially difficult or protracted actions that may involve complex issues, multiple parties, difficult legal questions, or unusual proof problems"). *See Avila*, 633 F.3d 828 (locating the authority in Rule 16(c)(2)(L)). *But see Antero*, 347 P.3d 149 (holding that the Colorado Rule of Civil Procedure 16, which differed somewhat from Federal Rule 16, did not authorize *Lone Pine* orders).

employ with regularity and other judges shy away from—highlights the rewards and risks ad hoc, individualized case management.

For the most part, courts have raised far fewer questions about the use of RICO case statements, even though they pose much the same set of concerns.[759]

Whatever the general merits of *Lone Pine* orders, RICO case statements, and similar orders, the process was used to undeniable effect in the asbestos MDL process. Recall that the Judicial Panel on Multidistrict Litigation finally consolidated the federal asbestos cases in the Eastern District of Pennsylvania in 1991.[760] After much of the 1990s was taken up determining if the cases could be resolved on a global basis (with the Supreme Court's 1997 decision in *Amchem*[761] and 1999 decision in *Ortiz*[762] finally determining that the answer was no), the asbestos MDL docket bloated to well over 100,000 cases, with no resolution in sight. Finally, in 2009 a new MDL judge issued an administrative order requiring all asbestos plaintiffs to submit a "fact sheet" providing a medical diagnosis or opinion demonstrating an asbestos-related injury with respect to each defendant sued. The order spurred some plaintiffs to settle with defendants, and the MDL judge dismissed all remaining cases (containing approximately 500,000 claims) that did not comply with the order.[763] The process cleared up almost the entire backlog of cases. The court of appeals affirmed the dismissals.[764]

Using fact sheets in the asbestos MDL did not raise many of the standard concerns with *Lone Pine* orders. Scientific studies about the relationship between asbestos and various disease processes were plentiful, and discovery, both in the MDL and elsewhere, had gone on for many years. Thus, the timing concerns that infect many *Lone*

---

759 *See* MANUAL, *supra* note 206, § 35.31 (describing frequent use and contents of RICO case statements, but also acknowledging that "[t]he authority of a court to order a RICO case statement has not been definitively established").

760 *See supra* note 143 and accompanying text.

761 Amchem Prods., Inc. v. Windsor, 521 U.S. 591 (1997) (discussed *supra* notes 355–361, 415–416, 487 and accompanying text).

762 Ortiz v. Fibreboard Corp., 527 U.S. 815 (1999) (discussed *supra* notes 396–401, 441, 488–490 and accompanying text).

763 The MDL judge also determined that certain physicians who were commonly used as plaintiffs' experts were not qualified to render an opinion on causation. For descriptions of the processes used in the asbestos MDL, see Eduardo C. Robreno, *The Federal Asbestos Products Liability Multidistrict Litigation (MDL-875): Black Hole or New Paradigm*, 23 WIDENER L. REV. 97 (2013); Mark A. Behrens, *Asbestos Litigation Screening Challenges: An Update*, 26 THOMAS M. COOLEY L. REV. 721 (2009).

764 *See In re* Asbestos Prods. Liab. Litig. (No. VI), 718 F.3d 236 (3d Cir. 2013); *In re* Asbestos Prods. Liab. Litig. (No. VI), 543 F. App'x 202 (3d Cir. 2013). For another MDL proceeding imposing a requirement plaintiffs whose cases were not moved onto a settlement track to submit a fact sheet, see Dzik v. Bayer Corp., 846 F.3d 211 (7th Cir. 2017) (affirming the dismissal of the claim of a plaintiff who failed to submit a fact sheet).

Pine orders did not exist. Moreover, most other case-management techniques had been tried and failed.

d. Expert Panels

Virtually all complex litigation involves expert testimony. One of the judge's great challenges is dealing with this testimony. As you might expect, plaintiffs will put forward experts who hold opinions favorable to the plaintiffs' version of the case, and defendants will use experts who hold the opposite opinions. Both sides may try to strike the expert testimony of their opponent; without such testimony, the opponent's case may well fall apart. Under the principles established in *Daubert v. Merrell Dow Pharmaceuticals, Inc.*[765] and Federal Rule of Evidence 702 (which codified *Daubert*), a federal court has an important gatekeeping role with respect to expert testimony, and must not allow the admission of expert opinions that are unreliable.

Striking an expert opinion can narrow the issues in a case dramatically. But the judge is often handicapped. Although *Daubert* gives judges some latitude, the judge must allow admission of expert testimony if it is grounded in proper scientific methodology and has sufficient support in the facts or data; a judge cannot strike an opinion just because the judge dislikes the opinion or finds the opponent's opinion better. And a judge, who rarely has training in the relevant scientific field, often has difficulty discerning valid methodologies, data, and opinions from inadmissible "junk science."

To aid in the task of evaluating and screening expert opinions, judges have on occasion turned to panels of expert witnesses. These panels can serve different functions. One is provide advice to the judge about the reliability of opinions: whether the parties' experts are relying on recognized methodologies and data. Under this approach, experts act as technical advisors to the judge.[766] A different way to use experts is to appoint them as experts who can themselves give testimony alongside the testimony of the parties' experts.[767] Of course, a judge may not know who the best experts are, so a judge may appoint experts to advise the judge about which experts the judge should appoint to provide testimony.[768]

---

[765] 509 U.S. 579 (1993).

[766] For a case using an expert panel in this fashion, see *Hall v. Baxter Healthcare Corp.*, 947 F. Supp. 1387 (D. Or. 1996). Technical advisors are not unlike special masters, although masters are typically lawyers. For additional discussion of technical advisors, see *infra* notes 878–880 and accompanying text.

[767] *See* FED. R. EVID. 706 (permitting a court to appoint its own experts).

[768] For an example of this approach, see Order No. 31, *In re* Silicone Gel Breast Implant Prods. Liab. Litig. (MDL 926), No. CV 92–P–10000–S (N.D. Ala. May 30, 1996).

The idea of using panels of experts is discussed more in the literature than it is employed in practice.[769] The *Manual for Complex Litigation* discusses both the benefits (including "reducing adversariness and potentially clarifying and narrowing issues") and the costs (including expense, delay, undue influence, and lack of neutrality) in using experts or panels of experts.[770]

The source of the authority to use experts or expert panels depends on the nature of the appointment. Federal Rule of Evidence 706 authorizes the appointment of experts to provide trial testimony. For experts that act as technical advisors, the source of authority is, again, the court's inherent power.[771]

e. Encouraging Pretrial Stipulations

Another tool for narrowing issues is to attempt to force the parties to make pretrial stipulations. This process is akin to requests for admission, but it involves the court's serious and sustained involvement.[772] Perhaps the most famous use of pretrial stipulations occurred in the mammoth *United States v. AT&T* antitrust litigation in the 1970s. The United States alleged that AT&T had maintained a monopoly for decades by means of scores of illegal practices and actions. Early in the litigation, the government identified eighty-two distinct episodes of monopolistic behavior, many of which would have been full-fledged antitrust cases in their own right.

To get control of the vast number of legal and factual issues, the district court ordered the parties to engage in a series of exchanges. They first presented their contentions and supporting information for each of the eighty-two episodes. Next, they winnowed down actual disagreements through three rounds of increasingly detailed statements, in which each side was to identify each issue that it claimed was disputed and its evidence regarding that issue. The other side was then to admit or deny each issue and state its view on the admissibility of the supporting evidence.[773]

As initially designed, this system did not work well. It bogged down as the parties expanded rather than narrowed their

---

[769] *See In re* Dow Corning Corp., 211 B.R. 545 (Bankr. E.D. Mich. 1997) (declining to appoint a panel of experts to assist in the estimation process of a mass-tort bankruptcy case, in part because the Bankruptcy Rules gave bankruptcy judges no authority to appoint special masters).

[770] *See* MANUAL, *supra* note 206, § 11.51.

[771] *See* Reilly v. United States, 863 F.2d 149 (1st Cir. 1988).

[772] The process is also akin to the preparation of a Rule 16(e) final pretrial order, which usually requires the parties to stipulate to non-controverted facts and admissibility of evidence. As useful as the final pretrial order might be for streamlining the trial, it fails as a device to narrow the issues and streamline the discovery and pretrial process.

[773] *See* United States v. Am. Tel. & Tel. Co., 461 F. Supp. 1314 (D.D.C. 1978).

disagreements in the second round of statements. The statements were roughly 2,000 pages per side, and tended to obfuscate and avoid, rather than clarify, the issues and evidence. Consequently, in a larger departure from the adversarial ideal, the judge handed over the stipulation process to a pair of special masters, who spent thirteen intensive months negotiating with nineteen teams of lawyers for each side. The process led to the government's abandonment of fourteen episodes. According to the masters, the parties also stipulated to 80 to 85 percent of the disputed facts.[774]

Several other antitrust actions subsequently employed a similar stipulation process.[775] The success of the process in these cases was not reported. The process appears not to have been widely employed in other types of complex litigation. Critics have expressed concern that this process is too expensive and cumbersome to attempt in any but the most massive cases, and they have further worried that a process of forced stipulations might change the traditional form of adversarial trial.

Whatever its merits, the source of the judge's authority to develop a stipulation process is likely grounded in the Rule 16(c)(2)(A)'s grant of authority to "consider and take appropriate action on . . . formulating and simplifying the issues, and eliminating frivolous claims or defenses" and in Rule 16(c)(2)(C)'s grant to "consider and take appropriate action on . . . obtaining admissions and stipulations about facts and documents to avoid unnecessary proof."

f. Promoting Settlement

Although case management began as an approach to narrow issues in complex cases, it has evolved into a doctrine to encourage settlement.[776] Obviously settlement "narrows" the issues into nothingness; once a case settles, it goes away. Judges enjoy numerous powers that push the parties toward settlement. For instance, they can require the parties to participate in settlement conferences. In addition, all federal courts must maintain a plan for alternative dispute resolution (ADR),[777] so the court can implement the plan or even design an ADR mechanism specifically for the case. Among these mechanisms are court-sponsored arbitration,

---

[774] For the story of this process, as told from the masters' viewpoint, see Geoffrey C. Hazard, Jr. & Paul R. Rice, *Judicial Management of the Pretrial Process in Massive Litigation: Special Masters as Case Managers*, *in* WAYNE D. BRAZIL ET AL., MANAGING COMPLEX LITIGATION 103 (1983).

[775] *See, e.g.,* Greater Rockford Energy & Tech. Corp. v. Shell Oil Co., 790 F. Supp. 804 (C.D. Ill. 1992); Ralph C. Wilson Indus., Inc. v. Am. Broad. Co., 598 F. Supp. 694 (N.D. Cal. 1984).

[776] *See* Elliott, *supra* note 141.

[777] 28 U.S.C. §§ 651–58.

mediation, and summary jury trial.[778] Other case-management strategies that we have explored can also facilitate settlement. For instance, a court can appoint settlement counsel as well as a magistrate or master specifically to conduct settlement negotiations. Bifurcating the pretrial to handle an issue that might be a sticking point for settlement is also possible.

An enduring question is how hard a judge should push the parties to settle. Judges often wield "an iron fist in a velvet glove"; judges have tremendous discretion to manage pretrial issues and can make the life of a party unwilling to settle difficult. So a judge has tools to set the case on a path toward settlement. At the same time, it seems unlikely that a judge can force sophisticated parties to settle a case that they were otherwise unwilling to settle.

The legitimacy and effectiveness judges' efforts to encourage settlement are open to debate. The most extensive studies to date show that ADR provides no to very weak benefits in terms of reducing cost and delay. ADR saves time and expenses in those cases in which it works, but adds time and expense in those cases in which it does not.[779] But the studies did not look specifically at the costs and benefits of ADR in complex cases, in which ADR's benefit-to-cost ratio might be different. Even if there were savings in time or expense, some critics object that the push toward settlement weakens the rule of law and favors the party with the superior bargaining power.[780] Advocating strongly for settlement also removes the judge from the judge's traditional, neutral adversarial role, and creates risks of bias or prejudgment of a case's merits. These concerns are especially weighty in complex litigation.

Aside from more formal case-management powers, an often overlooked way in which judges foster settlement is to give or withhold non-authoritative judicial "advice." In complex litigation, the parties often need to know the judge's views on certain legal, evidentiary, or factual issues to make strategic decisions, including the decision to settle. At the same time, as we have seen, an authoritative ruling by means of a motion to dismiss or a motion for summary judgment may not be possible.

---

778 *See* FED. R. CIV. P. 16(a)(5) (stating that one purpose of pretrial conferences is to "facilitat[e] settlement"); MANUAL, *supra* note 206, § 13.1–.24. For an overview of ADR mechanisms, see FED. JUD. CTR., GUIDE TO JUDICIAL MANAGEMENT OF CASES IN ADR (2001).

779 *See* KAKALIK ET AL., CASE MANAGEMENT, *supra* note 643; JAMES S. KAKALIK ET AL., AN EVALUATION OF MEDIATION AND EARLY NEUTRAL EVALUATION UNDER THE CIVIL JUSTICE REFORM ACT (1996).

780 The classic article is Owen M. Fiss, *Against Settlement*, 93 YALE L.J. 1073 (1984); *see also* Rex R. Perschbacher & Debra Lyn Bassett, *The End of Law*, 84 B.U. L. REV. 1 (2004) (arguing that ADR weakens the clarity and force of legal rules).

When such a sticky issue divides the parties, a judge can provide the parties with a preliminary, non-authoritative read-out of his or thinking. During pretrial conferences, this informal judicial guidance occurs all the time, as the judge expresses encouragement or skepticism about particular arguments or litigation strategies. On only a few occasions does one of these advisory opinions emerge into the limelight.[781] But these opinions can guide parties toward a resolution.

Conversely, on some occasions the best judicial response is to keep the parties in the dark. Uncertainty can foster settlements among parties who prefer clarity to risk. Generating uncertainty can therefore be a case-management tool.[782]

> *Problem 2*
>
> You are the MDL judge to whom 5,000 prescription-drug products liability cases have been transferred. An equal number of tag-along actions is expected in the next two years. The most difficult legal issues are likely to be the defendant's knowledge of the drug's dangers and individual causation. What case-management strategies would you employ?

The case-management literature rarely mentions—much less legitimates—the practice of refusing to rule. Indeed, basic principles of case management—just, speedy, and inexpensive resolution of disputes; prompt, firm, and fair judicial management; and the need to define and narrow factual and legal issues as soon as possible—point in the opposite direction.[783] The best-known case discussing the "failure to judge" issue took a dim view of the practice.[784]

Settlement does not end all of a case's complications. The judge may then be required to approve the settlement or to deal with difficult issues of distributing the award. Chapters Sixteen and Seventeen consider some of the issues that arise when the parties

---

781 *See, e.g., In re* "Agent Orange" Prod. Liab. Litig., 580 F. Supp. 690 (E.D.N.Y. 1984) (issuing a "preliminary memorandum" on choice-of-law matters).

782 Mark A. Peterson & Molly Selvin, *Mass Justice: The Limited and Unlimited Power of Courts*, 54 LAW & CONTEMP. PROBS. 227 (Summer 1991) ("[S]ome trial courts have successfully attempted to promote settlement of mass tort claims by withholding decisions on these crucial questions in order to maintain a high level of uncertainty and, consequently, risk—for both sides of the litigation.").

783 *See* MANUAL, *supra* note 206, § 10.13 ("The judge decides disputes promptly, particularly those that may substantially affect the course or extent of further proceedings.").

784 *See In re* Sch. Asbestos Litig., 977 F.2d 764 (3d Cir. 1992) (denying a writ of mandamus requiring a judge to rule on a motion for summary judgment on the facts of the case, but noting that "a district court's failure to consider the merits of a summary judgment motion is a failure to exercise its authority when it has the duty to do so").

and court jump out of the pretrial frying pan and into the remedial fire.

C. Conclusion

The original design of the Federal Rules limited the ability of the parties and the court to narrow the issues during pretrial. Begun as a response to the deficiencies that complex litigation exposed in this design, case management has now reoriented our pretrial system to some degree. But the limits on issue narrowing are still strong—sometimes unavoidably, because of Seventh Amendment constraints, and sometimes prudentially, because of other assumptions and aims of our procedural system.

At its best, the ad hoc approach of case management allows judges to tailor the techniques to the circumstances of each case, thus enhancing the efficient and fair resolution of the dispute. At its worst, it places in the hands of an increasingly powerful player in the pretrial enterprise weapons—often of uncertain provenance and unproven effectiveness—with the potential to determine the outcome of the case.

Chapter 12

STREAMLINING DISCLOSURE AND DISCOVERY

The pretrial process allows parties to discover the factual bases for disputed issues. The devices available to parties are capacious. The drafters of the 1938 Federal Rules had hoped that, once the tools of discovery shone a light on the evidence regarding a dispute, the parties would abandon weak claims and settle the rest. Discovery has not turned out quite as it was envisioned. One reason has been the proliferation of new issues that access to more information has generated—a problem that is not especially significant in a simple car accident but becomes pressing in large-scale litigation. Another reason is cost: discovery can be costly, and parties can potentially exploit that cost either to wear down a less well-off party in a war of attrition or to extract a settlement for a meritless claim that is cheaper to buy off than to litigate.

One of the principal themes of procedural reform in the past thirty-plus years has been the effort to contain discovery in order to make American litigation run more efficiently. As one aspect of these reforms, parties in most cases were required to disclose certain information without a formal discovery request. Over the same period, technology has created means to harness vast quantities of information but also has generated vast quantities of information subject to disclosure and discovery.

In complex cases that involve great amounts of information, control over the disclosure-and-discovery process is critical to the achieving an efficient and fair resolution of the controversy. This Chapter examines a number of ways in which judges in complex cases have sought to make the process run more efficiently. We begin with a description of the traditional controls on discovery, and then examine the case-management techniques that judges can employ to harness the discovery process. As with issue-narrowing techniques, these case-management strategies are often mix and match, depending on the needs of a particular case. Although in a more muted fashion, this ad hoc approach raises the ever-present concerns about the scope of judicial power and the outcome-determinative potential of these devices.

A. Traditional Discovery

Federal Rule of Civil Procedure 26 states the breadth of information that parties can obtain through discovery. There are four limits on discovery's scope: the information sought to be discovered must be relevant; it must be proportional; it must not be privileged; and it must not be protected by the work-product doctrine. Some of the information fitting within this scope is subject to automatic disclosure; thus, parties must automatically provide the identity of witnesses and documents supporting their claims or defenses to other parties.[785] The methods by which parties can obtain discovery of information are interrogatories to a party (Rule 33); written or oral depositions of any potential witness, whether a party or not (Rules 30–32); production of documents or inspection of premises from a party or subpoena of documents from a nonparty (Rules 34 and 45); and physical or mental examinations of a party or a person in the control of a party (Rule 35).[786] Although there are a few gaps (for instance, interrogatories cannot be sent to nonparties), these methods are broad enough that virtually any information within the scope of discovery can be obtained through one mechanism or another.[787]

As originally drafted in 1938, the discovery rules required court approval of certain discovery requests. In stages, however, the Rules extricated the court from this role, and by 1970 discovery was an entirely party-controlled affair. Since 1983, however, the trend has been back in the direction of tighter judicial control.

The effort to cabin the discovery process for the past thirty-plus year has proceeded along two paths. The first has been to limit the scope of discovery; the second has been to expand the case-management powers of the judge over discovery. With respect to limiting the scope of discovery, the most critical changes have been to shrink the concept of relevance, to add the concept of proportionality, and to limit the frequency and duration of discovery. With respect to the shrinking meaning of "relevance," the original

---

785 FED. R. CIV. P. 26(a)(1). Also required to be disclosed are a computation of damages and any insurance policies covering the dispute. These initial mandatory disclosures occur at the outset of the case, typically a week before the initial scheduling conference. *See* FED. R. CIV. P. 26(a)(1)(C), –(f). Further disclosures, first of testifying expert witnesses and then of the witnesses and evidence to be used at trial, are due later in the pretrial process. FED. R. CIV. P. 26(a)(2)–3. This disclosure process was first adopted in 1993, and tweaked in later amendments. As a matter of convenience, the remainder of this Chapter refers to the "discovery process," rather than the longer but more accurate "disclosure-and-discovery process." The limits on disclosure and the techniques to streamline the disclosure process are generally the same as for the discovery process.

786 Requests for admission (Rule 36) are also sometimes described as a discovery device. As we have seen, they are actually an issue-narrowing device. *See supra* note 722 and accompanying text. But the denial of a request for admission can generate discovery into the factual basis for the denial, so requests for admission are an adjunct to the discovery system.

787 For ease of description, we will usually refer to both the disclosure process and the discovery process for obtaining information as "discovery."

Federal Rules allowed parties to obtain discovery on any matter relevant to "the subject matter involved in the pending action." In the 2000 amendments, however, discovery was limited to information relevant to "the claim or defense of any party"; discovery could also be had "of any matter relevant to the subject matter involved in the action" on a showing of "good cause." In 2016, "subject matter" discovery was entirely eliminated; discovery must now be relevant to "any party's claim or defense."

With respect to the rise of proportionality, the idea that discovery should be proportional to the needs of the case first emerged in the 1983 amendments to Rule 26(b). "Proportionality" requires consideration of "the importance of the issues at stake in the action, the amount in controversy, the parties' relative access to relevant information, the parties' resources, the importance of the discovery in resolving the issues, and whether the burden or expense of the proposed discovery outweighs its likely benefit."[788] Discovery amendments since 1983 have tried in various ways to highlight the proportionality inquiry, although courts have found it difficult to apply the standard in practice. For example, to rule on the final element—whether the cost of the discovery outweighs its likely benefits—the court would need to know what the requested information is, how much it will affect the likely outcome of the case, and what the cost of production will be. Of those factors, only the last is easily quantifiable.

> *Problem 1*
>
> The plaintiff, a high-profile trader at a major securities house, files a gender-discrimination case when her employer failed to promote and then ultimately fired her. Discovery to date reveals that e-mails on defendant's servers mention the plaintiff or her job performance. The plaintiff requests every e-mail mentioning her. Many of these e-mails are contained in formats, such as back-up tapes, that are difficult to search. The best estimate is that the process of retrieving the information will cost $250,000, with another $100,000 in document-review costs for the defendant. If you are the judge, do you order the discovery, and if so, under what conditions? *See* Zubulake v. UBS Warburg, LLC, 217 F.R.D. 309 (S.D.N.Y. 2003) & 216 F.R.D. 280 (S.D.N.Y. 2003).

A separate proportionality rule pertains for the discovery of electronically stored information ("ESI"). A party need not produce ESI when it claims that the ESI is "not reasonably accessible due to undue burden or cost."[789] The requesting party, can still obtain the

[788] In addition, a court can limit discovery that is cumulative, that can be obtained more easily elsewhere, or that a party failed to obtain through discovery despite ample opportunity to do so. FED. R. CIV. P. 26(b)(2)(C)(i)–(ii).

[789] *See* FED. R. CIV. P. 26(b)(2)(B).

information on a showing of "good cause," although the court can order the requesting party to share in the cost of production. Both the "good cause" inquiry and the cost-sharing provision tend to be answered through application of seven-factor proportionality-based tests that are roughly comparable.[790]

With respect to limiting the amount of discovery, depositions are now limited to ten per side, each lasting no more than seven hours,[791] and interrogatories are limited to twenty-five per side.[792] The court can increase these numbers as appropriate.

These limits do not constrain complex litigation in a substantial way. Information relevant only to claims or defenses is already voluminous. The amounts at stake in most complex cases make it unlikely that most discovery will be seen as disproportional to the needs of the case; at best, proportionality concerns will trim a bit of discovery at the margins. The same is true of ESI. Nor do the presumptive limits on depositions and interrogatories significantly constrain the parties. Such a paltry number of depositions and interrogatories would frustrate the resolution of a mass dispute on its merits, so judges are likely to expand the limits readily.

The second development in the effort to constrain discovery has been the expansion of judges' case-management powers. The 1983 amendments added to the trial judge's Rule 16 arsenal the power to take appropriate action to avoid "unnecessary proof" and "cumulative evidence."[793] In 1993, Rule 16(c) was further expanded to give the court powers to control and schedule discovery, and Rule 26(f) was amended to require the parties to conduct a discovery-planning conference before the scheduling conference or order.

The result of these changes is a discovery system with mixed commitments. There are efforts to achieve greater efficiency and there is some movement away from adversarial practices, but the orientation still tilts toward broad, party-controlled discovery. The judge establishes parameters for an effective discovery process, but usually intervenes thereafter only to tweak the process or to resolve disputes claiming either that the requesting party has asked for too much or that the responding party has given too little discovery. At best, case management has filed off some sharp edges, but the adversarial shape of the discovery system is still alive and kicking.

---

790 *See* United States *ex rel.* Guardiola v. Renown Health, No. 3:12–CV–00295–LRH–VPC, 2015 WL 5056726 (D. Nev. Aug. 25, 2015) (applying seven factors to determine good cause and cost shifting).

791 FED. R. CIV. P. 30(a)(2)(A), –(d)(2).

792 FED. R. CIV. P. 33(a)(1).

793 For the present versions of these powers, see FED. R. CIV. P. 16(c)(2)(D).

In the main, surveys of lawyers and clients reflect a fair degree of satisfaction with the way that the discovery system works: it is not too costly and it yields the right amount of information. But there is also a broadly held view that the system works poorly in a small subset of cases—the ones that contain a lot of discoverable information.[794] In these cases, it is difficult or impossible for the lawyer to perform adequately the adversarial task of marshaling evidence to narrow issues and prepare for trial or other resolution. A single case may involve millions of documents, thousands of emails, and hundreds of witnesses. With every passing day, documents are destroyed or lost, and witnesses' memories fade. In addition, the sheer volume of discovery virtually guarantees that discovery will be costly. With cost comes the opportunity for parties to use discovery to attain tactical advantages for their clients.

Therefore, in complex cases some counterbalance to the adversarial gathering of evidence seems necessary. The following section details specific ways in which judges have employed case-management powers to streamline the discovery process.

B. Techniques to Make Discovery More Effective

This section divides case-management techniques used in the discovery process into two types: those intended to streamline the discovery process itself, and those intended to make the process of resolving discovery disputes run more efficiently. Prior chapters have already considered some of the possible techniques, such as referring discovery disputes to a magistrate judge or special master.[795] Similarly, issue-narrowing techniques like bifurcation can indirectly help to streamline discovery.

Case-management devices designed to enhance the efficiency of the discovery process can be used in different combinations. No single set of techniques applies in all cases. Moreover, just as some issue-narrowing techniques indirectly can streamline discovery, some devices designed to make discovery more effective can indirectly aid issue narrowing. Like issue-narrowing devices, devices to streamline discovery and the discovery-dispute processes can also raise the concerns about both the source of the judge's power to amend the traditional processes and the potential to alter the outcome of the litigation.

---

794 See Thomas E. Willging et al., *An Empirical Study of Discovery and Disclosure Practices Under the 1993 Federal Rule Amendments*, 39 B.C. L. REV. 525 (1998).

795 *See supra* Chapter 9.B.

1. Making Discovery Run More Smoothly

a. *The Discovery Plan*

One of the inventions of case management is discovery planning. Three weeks before the scheduling conference or order, the parties are required to confer about such matters as settling the case, arranging for initial mandatory disclosure, and creating a joint discovery plan to submit to the court. The plan is to consider a range of matters, including:

- When to complete discovery;
- Whether to break up discovery into phases;
- Whether to limit or focus discovery on specific issues;
- Whether unique issues about disclosure, discovery, and ESI will arise;
- How to address claims of privilege or work product;
- Whether the court should impose protective orders under Rule 26(c) or case-management orders under Rule 16(c).[796]

Researchers have found that discovery planning, when accompanied by case management, reduces time to disposition without increasing attorney work hours.[797]

The *Manual for Complex Litigation* strongly urges the parties to engage in discovery planning, and to consider specifically whether information might be obtained more effectively by means other than formal, and often expensive, discovery. The *Manual* regards as a "principal purpose" of the initial scheduling conference the adoption of a discovery plan.[798] But the *Manual* also cautions the judge not to accept the parties' plan or "joint recommendations uncritically. . . . [E]ven with limited familiarity with the case, the judge must retain responsibility for control of discovery."[799] That control requires "[r]egular contact with counsel through periodic conferences . . . to monitor the progress of the plan, ensure that it is operating fairly and effectively, and adjust it as needed."

The issue, of course, is what specific options counsel and the judge should adopt (or avoid) in planning discovery. The remainder of the Chapter considers these options.

---

796 FED. R. CIV. P. 26(f)(3).

797 See Kakalik et al., *Discovery*, *supra* note 643, at 652–57. The study was not targeted specifically at complex cases.

798 *See* MANUAL, *supra* note 206, § 11.421.

799 *See id.* § 11.42.

b. The Document Preservation Order

Large entities often generate more information than they can save or store. Documents in file cabinets and ESI on servers are regularly purged. Some purging is haphazard; for instance, an employee might decide one day to clean up her cubicle or delete the backlog of old e-mails. Some is routine; many companies have document-retention policies requiring the destruction of hard copies of records more than a few months old, and software is set to delete electronic records after a specified period.

Some of this information may be relevant to a lawsuit. Hence, one of the very first tasks that a lawyer must undertake is to obtain a judicial order stopping the destruction of physical and electronic information. Such an order is often called a "document preservation order" or a "litigation hold."[800] In complex litigation this order is almost *de rigueur*; one or more parties may even ask for entry of the order even before the initial scheduling conference.

> *Problem 2*
>
> A court has entered an order requiring preservation of "all documents and other records which could be potentially relevant to" the lawsuit, which claimed that the defendant was targeting minors with its marketing campaigns. For a period of thirty months, employees of the defendant failed to comply with the order. After learning of this fact, the defendant continued its monthly purging of physical and electronic records for two more months, and then waited two more months to call the court's attention to the issue. One of the defendant's experts was among the persons failing to comply. If you were the judge, what sanctions, if any, would you impose? *See* United States v. Philip Morris USA, Inc., 327 F. Supp. 2d 21 (D.D.C. 2004).

You might think that counsel who represents a party with a substantial amount of documentary or electronic information might oppose such an order, in the hope that negative information might never see the light of day. But that view is short-sighted. In the first place, positive as well as negative information might be destroyed. More important, courts are increasingly recognizing the duty to preserve information relevant to litigation.[801] An array of sanctions, as well as the tort of

---

[800] For a sample order, see *id.* § 40.25.

[801] *See* Silvestri v. Gen. Motors Corp., 271 F.3d 583 (2d Cir. 2001) ("The duty to preserve material evidence arises not only during litigation but also extends to that period before the litigation when a party reasonably should know that the evidence may be relevant to anticipated litigation."); Victor Stanley, Inc. v. Creative Pipe, Inc., 269 F.R.D. 497 (D. Md. 2010) (noting that there is "no general duty to preserve documents," but that a duty may arise from "statutes, regulations, ethical rules court orders, or the common law . . ., a contract, or other special circumstances") (internal quotation marks omitted). *Cf.* Chin v. Port Auth. of N.Y. & N.J., 685 F.3d 135 (2d Cir. 2012) (declining to hold that the failure to institute a litigation hold for six years after notification of plaintiffs' claims "constitutes gross negligence *per se*" requiring

spoliation of evidence, awaits parties who violate this duty. A preservation order protects these clients by fixing the duty and by providing counsel with the legal authority to stop further destruction.

A preservation order requires the parties and the judge to know something about the nature of the relevant information storage and data management, as well as the costs and technical feasibility of options to retain information and data. It also requires the parties and the judge to have a sense about the scope of discovery, the information necessary to prosecute or defend the case, and the existence of other sources of the information—all so that the order can be crafted as narrowly but as effectively as possible.

In a large entity, getting out the word about a preservation order and actually stopping the destruction can take a bit of time. Modest slippage in complying with the order can be expected. But sometimes the slippage is more than modest, and sometimes the ongoing destruction of documents or ESI is intentional. Because the preservation order is a judicial decree, courts have the power to sanction noncompliance. With respect to ESI, the 2015 amendment to Rule 37(e) permits a court to enter a sanction "no greater than necessary to cure the prejudice" when the destruction is unintentional. When the destruction is intentional, the court may presume that the information was unfavorable and even dismiss an action. Similar sanctions arise when documents are destroyed.

Preservation orders do not directly streamline the evidence-gathering process. If anything, they increase the amount of information that the parties must wade through. They can also be costly to implement, and non-compliance can generate satellite litigation. Nonetheless, they avoid a major source of friction in the discovery process, as well as litigation over sanctions or spoliation.

c. *Identifying and Depositing Documents*

Once parties begin to exchange documents and ESI, the process must be handled as efficiently as possible. In a case with many physical documents, it might make sense to store documents in a single location that is jointly operated and paid for by all the parties. With the rise of digital technology, another option is to send all documents to a single scanning facility, which then distributes electronic copies to the parties. However the process of collection and distribution is accomplished, it is imperative for the parties to agree on a common method of identifying documents. The classic form of identification was the Bates stamp; scanning technology can put an

---

sanctions, although this conduct could be a factor in deciding whether to impose a sanction).

equivalent marking on each page of each document. Having a single identifier for each document makes depositions and motions a much smoother process.

Therefore, another subject for an early case-management conference is establishing a process for identifying documents. Parties typically have a mutual incentive to agree on an identification method, although a court can impose a common method if they do not.[802] The need for a central depository or clearinghouse can be more controversial; the case may not justify the cost, and establishing protocols for how documents are deposited and distributed can add layers of complication. When a depository is necessary, courts are usually believed to possess the case-management power to assess an appropriate share of the cost of the depository against the parties—even against those who object to the depository because they believe that a different method for handling the litigation is better.[803]

d. *Umbrella Protective Orders*

A party may file a motion for a protective order that either to stop discovery or to impose limits on its production.[804] In complex cases, however, protective orders often have a second function: to streamline the discovery process by limiting the dissemination of sensitive information.

For instance, suppose that a plaintiff in an antitrust case sues a competitor for allegedly anti-competitive behavior. Appropriate discovery in the case might require the defendant to reveal information about marketing strategies, pricing structures, and trade secrets—all of which the plaintiff would dearly love to possess for business purposes. You might expect that the defendant would fight tooth and nail to prevent this discovery. But if the disclosure of this information could be limited to the plaintiff's lawyers on the understanding that the plaintiff or others would not have access to it, then the defendant would be less inclined to resist.

The *umbrella protective order*—which is sometimes called an *umbrella confidentiality order*, a *blanket protective order*, or a *blanket confidentiality order*—fills this role. It restricts the dissemination of information only to those permitted to see or use it. Often levels of restriction apply, depending on the sensitivity of the information: some highly sensitive information may be for the eyes of attorneys only, other less sensitive information may be shared with experts or

---

[802] *See* MANUAL, *supra* note 206, § 11.441.

[803] *See In re* Three Additional Appeals Arising out of the San Juan Dupont Plaza Hotel Fire Litig., 93 F.3d 1 (1st Cir. 1996).

[804] FED. R. CIV. P. 26(c).

certain employees of an opposing party. The parties often negotiate the terms of the umbrella protective order and present it to the court.

The order may also deal with the inadvertent disclosure of discovery, allowing the parties to continue to assert privileges or work-product protection rather than face a claim of possible waiver due to disclosure.[805] Protective orders often contain other terms, such as how to challenge a party's decision to classify information as confidential, whether disclosed information may be used in related litigation, and how the parties may use designated information in depositions or motions.[806]

The hope of the umbrella order is to reduce friction during discovery. Of one hundred confidential documents, perhaps only one or two will ultimately bear on the resolution of the case. With an umbrella order, the parties can exchange information and then focus their arguments about the evidentiary propriety of using the information on the few documents that end up mattering. So focused, the court can often make a better determination about the admissibility of the information. Thus, umbrella orders can save a great deal of headache in thrashing out the bounds of discovery.

At the same time, they can be controversial. Usually the parties negotiate the terms of an umbrella order with little input from the court; courts tend to rubber-stamp the orders because they know so little about the content of the possible discovery or the nature of the parties' relationship. To gain protection for information that is not ordinarily protectable, parties may engage in the indiscriminate designation of documents as confidential. Judges rarely become involved in checking the parties' designation, thus allowing the

---

805 We examine more about the problem of the inadvertent disclosure of privileged or work-product-protected information *infra* notes 843–845 and accompanying text. But the problem suggests one limit of umbrella orders. Parties are not going to agree to hand over attorney-client or work-product information to their opponents even with an umbrella order. As a result, such an order tends to permit protected disclosure only of trade secrets or other sensitive business data. Umbrella orders may address how to handle a situation in which attorney-client or work-product disputes will be resolved in the event that this information is inadvertently disclosed, *see infra* notes 843–844 and accompanying text, but the court will still face disputes over the discovery of privileged information and work product.

806 For a sample umbrella protective order, see MANUAL, *supra* note 206, § 40.27. With respect to using disclosed information in related litigation, other courts may give effect to an umbrella protective order as a matter of comity, but are not required to do so. *Compare* Keene Corp. v. Caldwell, 840 S.W.2d 715 (Tex. App. 1992) (notions of comity and the Full Faith and Credit Clause required a state court to defer to the protective order of a federal court), *with* Baker v. Gen. Motors Corp., 522 U.S. 222 (1998) (holding that full-faith-and-credit principles did not require a federal court in a different state to defer to a state-court injunction prohibiting the testimony of a witness).

parties to abuse the process.[807] When a case has a public-interest mien, as many complex cases do, these orders can frustrate the media's ability to report on the litigation and the public's ability to understand the litigation.[808]

Umbrella orders usually have a termination date, and like all pretrial orders, they are subject to revision. Some of the most noteworthy cases describing the limits of the process have arisen when news organizations or interested parties sought access to information filed under seal due to a confidential designation in the protective order. Courts can examine documents at that point to determine if they were properly classified, and can even lift the order protecting the information if the benefit of disclosure exceeds the harm of the parties' reliance on the order.[809] Making provisions for modification and termination of an umbrella order is critical.

e. *Using Discovery from Prior Litigation*

One way to reduce the cost of discovery is to rely on evidence collected in related cases. One party (often a plaintiff) might ask an opposing party (often a defendant) to produce all discovery from a prior case, or might seek to obtain that information from a party in the prior case. The court might then permit additional discovery in the second case only on matters unique to that case, in essence requiring the parties to litigate the common aspects of the dispute on the record produced in the prior case.[810] This approach drops the cost of discovery in the second case dramatically.

---

[807] For a case well describing the benefits and costs of protective orders, see Citizens First Nat'l Bank of Princeton v. Cincinnati Ins. Co. 178 F.3d 943 (7th Cir. 1999).

[808] The public has no constitutional right to access discovery in civil litigation. *See* Seattle Times Co. v. Rhinehart, 467 U.S. 20 (1984). Therefore, granting access lies in the discretion of the trial judge. *See* Chi. Tribune Co. v. Bridgestone/Firestone, Inc., 263 F.3d 1304 (11th Cir. 2001).

[809] Perhaps the most famous cautionary tale about modification arose in connection with the $180 million *Agent Orange* settlement, in which the defendants settled subject to a provision that information it had disclosed in confidence during discovery would be returned and remain out of public view forever. After the settlement was approved, the district court ordered the material to be unsealed and the public to be provided access. The judge further rejected the defendants' effort to renege on the settlement. The court of appeals affirmed. *See In re* "Agent Orange" Prod. Liab. Litig., 821 F.2d 139 (2d Cir. 1987). For another case finding both that the parties' abuse of the classification system required a modification to an umbrella order and that some media access to documents protected under an umbrella order and filed under seal might need to occur, see *In re* Se. Milk Antitrust Litig., 666 F. Supp. 2d 908 (E.D. Tenn. 2009) (candidly admitting that "the Court has likely failed at this point in assuring that all sealing was fully justified and that the public's right of access was guaranteed").

[810] *See In re* Temporomandibular Joint (TMJ) Implants Prods. Liab. Litig., 113 F.3d 1484 (8th Cir. 1997) (noting that district court had ordered the parties to use a document depository created in related litigation, and had permitted additional discovery only upon leave of court).

Relying on prior discovery poses a number of difficulties. One is the competence and thoroughness of the lawyers in the prior case. Another is that obtaining discovery is a bit like peeling layers from an onion. Because each lawyer has a unique take on a case, each case reveals a few more documents that might bear on the outcome; therefore, reliance on prior litigation risks overlooking relevant information—unless the litigation is truly mature and nothing remains to be discovered. The material from the prior litigation might also be protected by an umbrella protective order, or it might be subject to other confidentiality concerns. In particular, the responding party might have failed to persuade the judge in the prior case that certain information was confidential and may want to relitigate the matter before the new judge.

A well-funded party might also resist this discovery purely to force a new opponent to spend substantial sums on litigation (although the party is likely to hide behind other reasons).

The issue of using prior discovery was perhaps most thoroughly vetted in the massive antitrust litigation against AT&T. The government filed one suit. Fledgling competitors to AT&T brought separate cases. The private plaintiffs had waded through twelve million documents that AT&T produced, and culled the number of relevant documents to 2.5 million. The United States asked AT&T to produce only this subset. AT&T objected on the ground that some documents might not be relevant to the government's case, but the court found that the discovery "will ease the government's discovery burden and speed the litigation along." AT&T "had no legal interest in making the government's accumulation of proof more difficult or in delaying a trial on the merits."[811] To the extent that privileges applied to specific documents, the court agreed to establish a process to evaluate privilege claims.

The most common context in which this problem arises—attempts to discover information obtained by a grand jury investigating a party also being sued civilly—raises unique concerns due to the guarantee of grand-jury secrecy over "matters occurring before the grand jury."[812] The Supreme Court has held that, when

[811] *See* United States v. Am. Tel. & Tel. Co., 461 F. Supp. 1314 (D.D.C. 1978). AT&T continued to resist discovery by arguing in the private parties' lawsuit that an umbrella protective order should not be modified, thus denying to the government some of the discovery it sought. The court thought otherwise, and modified the order. Its decision was affirmed on appeal. *See* Am. Tel. & Tel. Co. v. Grady, 594 F.2d 594 (7th Cir. 1978) ("We are impressed with the wastefulness of requiring government counsel to duplicate the analyses and discovery already made.").

[812] FED. R. CRIM. P. 6(e)(2)(B) (stating that grand jurors, prosecutors, and staff "must not disclose a matter occurring before the grand jury"). A law-enforcement privilege may also block discovery of information from the grand jury or from government investigators assisting the grand jury. *See* Black v. Sheraton Corp. Of Am., 564 F.2d 531 (D.C. Cir. 1977).

private lawyers or civil lawyers for the government seek access to grand-jury material, disclosure is permitted only when, among other conditions, there exists a "particularized need" for the information.[813] This rule pertains to witness testimony and other information prepared for the grand jury. Whether the requirement of particularized need extends to information prepared outside of the grand jury but produced to the grand jury is a matter of some dispute among the lower courts.[814]

Often networks of lawyers working on the same type of litigation share documents produced by common opponents. In other instances, reliance on others' work creates free-rider problems. Presumably a court has the power to condition the production of discovery from a prior case on payment to the prior counsel of a fair proportion of the costs of obtaining the discovery.[815]

f. Handling Electronically Stored Information

The advent of ESI has been a boon to many industries, but a bane to many litigation departments. Technology has exploded the amount of information available—and thus the amount of information available for discovery. To take a tiny example, every time that you save a document, you have two documents (the old and the new versions) that could be relevant to a lawsuit some day; and when you overwrite the old version, you are destroying (or at least making highly inaccessible) possibly relevant information. Moreover, the constant upgrading of technologies and software for data storage means that data stored fifteen years ago in a state-of-the-art format may no longer be retrievable (think floppy disk—how would you retrieve information stored on one?).

Someday, perhaps, technology will solve the problem of collecting ESI and determining with accuracy whether it is responsive to discovery requests; such efforts are already underway. In the meantime, lawyers struggle with the volume of potentially relevant information stored in electronic formats and the expense of foraging through this information to determine whether it is

---

813 *See* United States v. John Doe, Inc. I, 481 U.S. 102 (1987); United States v. Baggot, 463 U.S. 476 (1983); Douglas Oil Co. of Cal. v. Petrol Stops Nw., 441 U.S. 211 (1979).

814 For a survey of positions, see *In re* Grand Jury Proceedings, 851 F.2d 860 (6th Cir. 1988).

815 FED. R. CIV. P. 26(c)(1)(B) (giving a court the power to enter a protective order "specifying terms, including time and place or the allocation of expenses, for the disclosure or discovery"); *cf.* Johnson v. Bryco Arms, 222 F.R.D. 48 (E.D.N.Y. 2004) ("This court has the power to require that the parties to a civil action reimburse a third party for its expenses in producing subpoenaed data.").

relevant, not privileged, and not otherwise protected from discovery.[816]

Because complex litigation often involves large quantities of ESI, lawyers and judges know that they must get ahead of the curve to prevent a discovery morass. ESI issues must be front and center in case-management conferences. Among the relevant topics will be:

- Whether to grant opposing parties access to ESI metadata (which can reflect prior versions of a document and other useful data) and system data about a computer;[817]
- Whether opposing counsel can "image" (or copy) ESI contained on the opponent's computers or servers to create a version that a party can search at will;[818]
- What search terms or methods of technology-assisted review should be used to find responsive ESI documents;[819]

---

[816] As we saw, the prevalence of ESI led to the creation of a specific ESI rule, which switched the default for certain ESI from discoverable to non-discoverable. But a showing of "good cause" readily overcomes this default rule in many instances. *See supra* notes 789–790 and accompanying text.

[817] *See* Dahl v. Bain Capital Partners, LLC, 655 F. Supp. 2d 146 (D. Mass. 2009) (denying request for metadata due to "the general uneasiness that courts hold over metadata's contribution in assuring prudent and efficient litigation"); Aguilar v. Immigration & Customs Enforcement Div., 255 F.R.D. 350 (S.D.N.Y. 2008) (discussing forms of metadata; denying discovery of most metadata after the relevant documents had already been provided in non-metadata format); *cf.* Chapman v. Gen. Bd. of Pension Benefits of the United Methodist Church, Inc., No. 09–CV–3474, 2010 WL 11408178 (N.D. Ill. July 6, 2010) (holding that a party has no obligation to produce documents in their native format, which would reveal metadata, unless the request for production so specifies). State ethics boards have begun to weigh in on the ethics of attorneys mining electronic discovery for metadata. For instance, one state allows an attorney to view inadvertently disclosed metadata when an "unscrubbed" document (i.e., a document containing metadata) is disclosed, but the lawyer may not use a program to uncover metadata the sender has tried to scrub. *See* Wash. State Bar Ass'n Rules of Prof'l Conduct Comm., Informal Op. 2216 (2012).

[818] *See* John B. v. Goetz, 531 F.3d 448 (6th Cir. 2008) (denying request to image a state agency's hard drives, despite evidence of defendant's ongoing destruction of ESI, when the data was highly confidential and raised privacy concerns as well as comity and federalism concerns).

[819] On the need for using appropriate search terms, see William A. Gross Constr. Assocs., Inc. v. Am. Mfrs. Mut. Ins. Co., 256 F.R.D. 134 (S.D.N.Y. 2009). On the use of predictive coding or other techniques of technology-assisted review to search databases for responsive discovery, see Rio Tinto PLC v. Vale S.A., 306 F.R.D. 125 (S.D.N.Y. 2015); Shannon Brown, *Peeking Inside the Black Box: A Preliminary Survey of Technology Assisted Review (TAR) and Predictive Coding Algorithms for eDiscovery*, 21 SUFFOLK J. TRIAL & APP. ADVOC. 221 (2016).

- How much "human intelligence" should be used to check the work of the "artificial intelligence" when the latter nominates documents as discoverable;[820]
- How to handle data contained in "legacy formats," on back-up tapes or other inaccessible forms, and how to exchange it among incompatible computer systems;[821]
- Whether sampling subsets of ESI might be a useful way to decide whether discovery of an entire set is cost-effective;[822]
- Whether some or all of the cost of producing ESI should be shifted to the requesting party;[823] and
- Whether the initial disclosure or discovery of ESI should be postponed until issues are narrowed.[824]

In determining how to address these and other questions, parties and the court rely significantly on information-technology experts and best practices that have developed over time. The most expensive component in the process is human time—the costs of designing an appropriate search strategy for ESI and of surveying the results of such searches to avoid inadvertent disclosure of privileged or protected information. An umbrella protective order can avoid some of these issues by "re-privileging" or treating as confidential inadvertently disclosed information subject to legal protection. But the best strategy is not to give such information away in the first place. For now, combing through ESI to find relevant information while screening out protected information remains a very expensive task.

Despite these concerns, the production of information in electronic form is also a benefit in many instances. Searching

---

820 *See* FED. R. EVID. 502(b)(2) (requiring, among other elements, that a party take "reasonable steps to prevent disclosure" of inadvertently disclosed attorney-client or work-product information in order to avoid waiving the protection); Victor Stanley, Inc. v. Creative Pipe, Inc., 250 F.R.D. 251 (D. Md. 2008) (holding that the failure to design a keyword search with care or to put a lawyer's eyes on at least a sample of the documents produced by the search resulted in a waiver of the privileges and protections for those documents).

821 *See* Zubulake v. UBS Warburg LLC, 217 F.R.D. 309 (S.D.N.Y. 2003) (discussing formats for storage of ESI and their accessibility).

822 *See id.* (ordering a sampling of data on tapes that were not reasonably accessible).

823 FED. R. CIV. P. 26(b)(2)(B) (permitting a court to "specify conditions for the discovery"), 26(c)(1)(B) (permitting a court to "allocat[e] expenses" of discovery); *see* Universal Del., Inc. v. Comdata Corp., No. 07–1078, 2010 WL 1381225 (E.D. Pa. Mar. 31, 2010) (ordering parties to share costs of creating a database of relevant documents, but producing party to bear the full costs of conducting a privilege review of the documents).

824 *See* MANUAL, *supra* note 206, § 11.13.

information in electronic form can be much faster, and copying and distributing it much cheaper. The judge's goal is often to get the parties, and especially their information-technology people, on the same page, thus avoiding many problems with searching and retrieval before they arise. The trick, which is far easier said than done, is for the judge to maximize the benefits of technology while minimizing problems with cost, incompatibility, "intrusiveness, data integrity, and information overload."[825]

g. Limiting the Quantity of Information

The Federal Rules limit the number of interrogatories and the number and duration of depositions. They also authorize courts to create local rules limiting requests for admission. The proportionality doctrine can also bar certain categories of discovery or specific requests. As we saw, none of these limits is likely to bear up in a complex case, in which the evidence necessary to decide the case cannot be reasonably obtained within such straitjackets.

More creative ways to restrict discovery are needed. Aside from hortatory advice about limiting both discovery in general and depositions in particular, however, the *Manual for Complex Litigation* is thin on particulars. A few courts have assayed some techniques that may work in specific cases. For instance, in a 1,500-plaintiff opt-in collective action, the plaintiffs suggested limiting discovery to a random sample of ninety plaintiffs. The defendant wanted more: written discovery from all plaintiffs and depositions from ten percent (or 150). The court thought that sampling made good sense, and ordered the parties' statistical experts to confer on a proper methodology.[826] Whether a sampling approach during discovery would survive the Supreme Court's subsequent treatment of statistical evidence at trial is uncertain.[827]

Relatedly, a common limit in class actions is to restrict discovery only to the named representatives, rather than to allow discovery of each class member.[828] One court has approved a different method: a survey of class members to determine whether elements of commonality and typicality have been met.[829]

---

825 *See id.* § 11.446.

826 *See* Smith v. Lowe's Home Centers, Inc., 236 F.R.D. 354 (S.D. Ohio 2006).

827 *See infra* Chapter 14.B.

828 The seminal case is *Brennan v. Midwestern United Life Insurance Co.*, 450 F.2d 999 (7th Cir. 1991), which allowed discovery against class members on matters relevant to a defense when the court was satisfied that the discovery was not a ruse to dismiss non-responding class members from the case. Most courts are more restrictive on discovery from class members. *See* Cox v. Am. Cast Iron Pipe Co., 784 F.2d 1546 (11th Cir. 1986) (holding that dismissing class members who failed to respond to discovery impermissibly turned Rule 23 into an opt-in device).

829 *See* Marlo v. United Parcel Serv., Inc., 639 F.3d 942 (9th Cir. 2011).

The *Manual* suggests another sampling technique: sampling as yet undiscovered information to determine if already produced evidence "fairly represent[s] what unrestricted discovery would have produced."[830] If the answer is yes, then the court can curtail further discovery. The *Manual* cites no cases that have attempted this approach; parties sometimes conduct surveys or sampling to generate evidence to prove a substantive element of a claim,[831] but to our knowledge not to pretermit further discovery.

> *Problem 3*
>
> In a class action alleging fraud in the marketing of cigarettes to consumers, the plaintiffs proposed to survey the class to determine the damages suffered. This survey was then to be used to set a maximum amount of the recovery for punitive damages. If you were the judge, would you order the use of surveys? *See In re* Simon II Litig., 211 F.R.D. 86 (E.D.N.Y. 2002), *vacated and remanded*, 407 F.3d 125 (2d Cir. 2005).

The *Manual* also suggests using non-traditional discovery techniques such as interviews, as well as stipulations in which parties agree that the depositions of some witnesses represent the testimony of all.[832]

Finally, although this limit relates more to trial than discovery, some MDL judges have restricted the expert witnesses who may testify at trial just to those deposed in the MDL proceeding.[833] This restriction avoids additional discovery from new witnesses after the remand of MDL cases to their transferor forums. Because many MDL cases are resolved before remand, the utility of this approach is limited. Whether MDL judges possess the authority to so bind transferor judges is also uncertain.

Beyond these techniques—and they are not an impressive lot—a court's case-management power to limit the quantity of discovery is modest.

h. Staging Discovery

A more realistic way to address the substantial discovery of a complex case is to stage discovery in such a manner that discovery proceeds efficiently. With some luck and planning, staging discovery also may provide enough information early in the case for the parties to settle the dispute.

---

830 *See* MANUAL, *supra* note 206, § 11.422.

831 *See id.* § 11.493 (discussing the use of surveys or samples to generate evidence about consumer opinions and the like).

832 *See id.* § 11.452.

833 *See, e.g.*, *In re* Factor VIII or IX Concentrate Blood Prods. Litig., 169 F.R.D. 632 (N.D. Ill. 1996).

In the early days of complex litigation, the idea of discovery *sequenced according to form* was all the rage. The idea was to require the parties to propound interrogatories first, then to request documents, and finally to take depositions. Imposing this order was thought to be one way to keep discovery from running amok. While this approach may still work in some cases, it proved far too rigid as an iron law for all complex litigation. In some cases, for instance, it makes sense to take some depositions before completing other forms of discovery.

Another approach is *targeted discovery*. A cousin of pretrial bifurcation,[834] targeted discovery trains the discovery process on a limited number of the issues in the case. Like bifurcation, targeted discovery hopes that this focus will lead to an early dismissal, withdrawal, or settlement of the case. As with bifurcation, targeting discovery works best when a discrete legal issue involving limited discovery might have a critical impact. One common form of targeted discovery is to handle the issue of class certification before addressing discovery related to the merits.

A third method is *phased discovery*. Phasing discovery breaks discovery into smaller segments. In this sense, targeted discovery is one form of phased discovery, but other divisions are also possible. Discovery can focus first on certain events, time periods, or geographical locations. It can do a quick and dirty harvesting of basic information to determine if more discovery on a matter is worthwhile or to guide further case-management or discovery planning. However discovery is phased, the early waves should be planned in such a way that later waves may become unnecessary.

The parties and judge can mix these techniques together. Perhaps a court might order the targeting of discovery just to class certification, and as part of that process order the parties to promulgate interrogatories before requesting document production.

In *Klein v. King*,[835] shareholders in a company that merged with another company brought a case alleging securities fraud. The magistrate judge, a well-known advocate of case management, designed a discovery plan that began by targeting discovery for ninety days on class certification. It rejected the defendant's "creative" suggestion to phase discovery concerning the merits of the case by the time periods that were relevant to the litigation, with discovery regarding each time period limited to ninety days. Instead, the court ordered limited discovery designed to bring about an early settlement. In "Stage One" of merits discovery, the parties were principally to disclose documents; only limited interrogatories and a

834 *See supra* Chapter 11.B.2.b.

835 132 F.R.D. 525 (N.D. Cal. 1990).

few depositions were allowed (thus sequencing discovery according to form). Settlement discussions were to follow. No motions to dismiss or for summary judgment were allowed. If the settlement discussions proved unfruitful, then "Stage Two" discovery would be targeted just to issues that proved to be the hang-up to settling the case; another round of settlement talks would follow, and dispositive motions would be considered. If the case still remained unresolved, then "Final Stage" discovery to ready the case for trial would commence. The plan included deadlines for completing each stage.

Methods for staging discovery carry risks. One is inefficiency: if the early foray into discovery does not terminate the case, it may be necessary to conduct deeper discovery of the same witnesses or entities. For instance, in *Klein* the staging process would work well if the case gsettles early, but it probably drags the case out if it does not. When the evidence regarding various issues is intertwined, trying to divide discovery on Issue A from discovery on Issue B inevitably generates borderland disputes about whether discovery that might bear on both issues should be permitted.[836] Staging also carries all the risks we discussed with bifurcation: in particular, the potential to affect the outcome of the litigation if issues are split up in a manner that addresses the stronger issues for one party first. In *Klein*, for instance, the magistrate judge clearly determined at the outset that the case should settle, and he designed a structure to make that outcome more likely.

> *Question*
>
> No study of the outcome-influencing effects of the various forms of staging discovery has ever been done. Would this fact make you cautious about employing one of the staging methods if you were managing a case?

With the exception of targeting discovery to class certification, our anecdotal impression is that a court order staging discovery by form, by targets, or by phases is unusual. Courts tend to leave the process of how best to order discovery in the hands of the lawyers. In cases of exceptional size, lawyers may informally "stage" discovery by dividing a case into "discovery tracks." Thus, one team of lawyers may focus on one set of issues while another team focuses on another set of issues. Some courts appear to have ordered, or at least acquiesced in, the use of discovery tracks.[837] This approach is often a

---

[836] *See In re* Rail Freight Fuel Surcharge Antitrust Litig., 258 F.R.D. 167 (D.D.C. 2009) (refusing to require parties to do class-certification discovery before discovery on the merits of the claim).

[837] *See In re* Multi-Piece Rim Prods. Liab. Litig., 464 F. Supp. 969 (J.P.M.L. 1979) (noting that an MDL judge "has the authority to group the pretrial proceedings on different discovery tracks according to the common factual issues or according to each defendant if necessary for the just and efficient conduct of the litigation, and to

response to a discovery deadline that is early and firm. It can create inefficiency if information relevant to the tracks overlap, and it is a possible burden to a party that is less well financed.

2. Resolving Discovery Disputes Efficiently

With the enormity of the discovery undertaking, disputes about the obligations of parties and nonparties to provide discovery are inevitable. A person who wishes to resist discovery can move for a protective order that bars or limits discovery.[838] A nonparty can also move to quash a subpoena on numerous grounds, including privilege or undue burden.[839] Comparably, a responding party may object to providing certain discovery, thus requiring the party seeking discovery to move to compel its production.[840] The advance design of a process to resolve discovery disputes can streamline discovery.

In cases that involve substantial claims of privilege, for instance, a court might get ahead of the game by writing an opinion specifying exactly what the parameters of the relevant privilege(s) are and then creating a process for parties to submit any disputed documents to the judge, a magistrate judge, or a special master for *in camera* review.[841] When appropriate, the court can order the redaction of privileged or protected information, while permitting the remainder of the document to be disclosed.[842]

Given the volume of information disclosed and the high cost of screening all information prior to disclosure, the inadvertent disclosure of privileged or work-product information is a common problem. The traditional, and very harsh, rule was that any disclosure of privileged or protected information constituted a waiver of the privilege or protection not only for that document but for all other material that was similarly privileged or protected. Some courts, however, softened this requirement in the case of inadvertent disclosures. Congress stepped into the fray in 2009 by enacting Federal Rule of Evidence 502. Rule 502 retained the traditional rule that a waiver extended to all related attorney-client or work-product

---

schedule any discovery unique to particular parties, actions or claims to proceed in separate discovery tracks concurrently with the common discovery, thus enhancing the efficient processing of all aspects of the litigation"); *cf. In re* MGM Grand Hotel Fire Litig., 660 F. Supp. 522 (D. Nev. 1987) (mentioning the use of eleven discovery tracks to take 1,400 depositions).

838 FED. R. CIV. P. 26(c).

839 FED. R. CIV. P. 45(d)(3).

840 FED. R. CIV. P. 37.

841 *See In re* "Agent Orange" Prod. Liab. Litig., 97 F.R.D. 427 (E.D.N.Y. 1983); MANUAL, *supra* note 206, § 11.431.

842 *See* EEOC v. Univ. of Notre Dame du Lac, 715 F.2d 331 (7th Cir. 1983) (ordering a redaction that was "reasonably necessary" to protect the identity of certain individuals).

information if the waiver was intentional and all the information should in fairness be considered together. If the information was inadvertent, however, then no waiver occurred as long as the "holder of the privilege took reasonable steps to prevent disclosure" and "reasonable steps to rectify the error" when the disclosure was discovered.[843]

One way to address the issues of inadvertent disclosure is to provide in an umbrella protective order for how such disclosures will be handled.[844]

Another issue involving the intentional disclosure of privileged or protected information regards sharing information with others. Sharing is usually intentional, and therefore constitutes a waiver unless an exception authorizes the disclosure. For instance, disclosure of attorney-client or work-product information to a consultant is not a waiver if the consultant possesses expertise that helps the lawyer to provide advice to the client.[845] Likewise, once a lawyer designates a consultant as a testifying expert, opposing parties are not entitled to know the content of the communications between the attorney and the expert—although they are entitled to review the information with which the expert was provided.[846]

A common source of litigation is whether one party can share information that would be regarded as work product with a co-party. Many courts recognize a *common-interest doctrine* or *joint-defense privilege* when co-parties with a common legal position share work product concerning that common position.[847] Some courts limit the doctrine to the situation in which information is shared by parties

---

[843] FED. R. EVID. 502(b); *see* Coburn Grp., LLC v. Whitecap Advisors LLC, 640 F. Supp. 2d 1032 (N.D. Ill. 2009) (analyzing Rule 502). The Rule also makes provision for information disclosed in state court—refusing to deem such disclosure a waiver in federal court as long as the disclosure meets the terms of Rule 502(b)—and for the continuing effect of an order of non-waiver in future federal or state litigation. FED. R. EVID. 502(c)–(d). Numerous state courts, including Florida and Texas, have adopted their own waiver rules. Some follow the Rule 502 model; others build in different protections.

[844] *See* Victor Stanley, Inc. v. Creative Pipe, Inc., 250 F.R.D. 251 (D. Md. 2008) (noting that conduct resulting in a waiver of privilege for 165 documents could have been avoided if the offending party had chosen not to abandon its request for a court-approved non-waiver agreement).

[845] *See* United States v. Kovel, 296 F.2d 918 (2d Cir. 1961) (attorney-client privilege); *In re* Tri-State Outdoor Media Group, Inc., 283 B.R. 358 (Bankr. M.D. Ga. 2002) (work-product protection).

[846] FED. R. CIV. P. 26(b)(4)(C); Republic of Ecuador v. Hinchee, 741 F.3d 1185 (11th Cir. 2013).

[847] *See, e.g.*, Lugosch v. Congel, 219 F.R.D. 220 (N.D.N.Y. 2003). State courts may also recognize this protection. *See* Tobaccoville USA, Inc. v. McMaster, 692 S.E.2d 526 (S.C. 2010) (holding that information exchanged among attorneys general of various states prosecuting tobacco companies was not protected by the attorney-client privilege or work-product protection, but they were protected by the common-interest doctrine).

represented by the same lawyer; other courts use the doctrine whenever the parties have a common interest in a joint defense; and still other courts arguably permit the doctrine to be invoked when the parties have not a common legal strategy but a "community of interests."[848] The parties should obtain a clear understanding of the judge's attitude toward the scope of this doctrine before sharing information with others.

A final issue involves the destruction of documents under a party's document-retention policy. When parties fail to preserve documents, sanctions litigation for destroying evidence is common; the imposition of sanctions and their severity often depend on whether the conduct was intentional or grossly negligent on the one hand, or merely negligent on the other.[849] As we have described, obtaining a document-preservation order can clarify the parties' obligations regarding document preservation and can also obviate sanctions litigation.[850]

C. Conclusion

The capacity of courts to shrink the discovery process to a manageable scope is limited. This fact is unsurprising. A broad commitment to discovery has come to define the modern American civil-litigation system. Given the costliness of discovery and the potential for its abuse, some cutbacks around the edges of that commitment can be anticipated in complex cases. But wholesale abandonment of this approach would require the design of an entirely new pretrial system—something that, understandably, no court has been willing to undertake without rulemaking authority. Our commitment to using a single set of rules to determine all types of disputes—the trans-substantive assumption of American procedure—makes the creation of one-off discovery processes especially problematic. Unless the system of discovery changes for all cases or developments in technology make discovery less expensive and time-consuming, courts in complex litigation are likely to be left with a very limited array of tools to bring discovery in complex cases under control. Of course, that result is not necessarily a bad thing for those committed to resolving major social disputes on their merits.

---

848 *See* Bank Brussels Lambert v. Credit Lyonnais (Suisse) S.A., 160 F.R.D. 437 (S.D.N.Y. 1995) (adopting middle position); Richard L. Marcus, *The Perils of Privilege: Waiver and the Litigator*, 84 MICH. L. REV. 1605 (1986).

849 *See* Victor Stanley, Inc. v. Creative Pipe, Inc., 269 F.R.D. 497 (D. Md. 2010).

850 *See supra* Chapter 12.B.1.b.

Part 3

THE TRIAL PROCESS

An implicit assumption in the first two Parts of this book was that, after aggregation and pretrial management, the trial process could rationally resolve all the claims of all the claimants. Now we put that assumption to the test. The following chapters explore issues that surround the trial of complex cases.

You might wonder whether this material is important. In American litigation, few cases come to trial. Complex cases are no exception to this rule; the amounts at stake and the difficulty of trying large cases create pressures that make non-trial resolutions attractive for lawyers and judges. Nonetheless, trial issues are significant for three reasons. First, trial is the default option when other dispute-resolution methods fail. Predicting whether a case will go to trial is nearly impossible, so every case must be prepared as if it were going to be tried. Second, the form of trial influences the pretrial preparation in which the parties will engage. For instance, if the trial employs a jury to resolve all the issues, the pretrial process needs to develop all the issues. On the other hand, if the trial involves a judge as factfinder, the judge might be able to divide the trial into a series of discrete hearings, thus dictating a different pretrial process.

Third, the manageability of a case at trial is a significant factor in a judge's decision to aggregate cases or claims. For instance, in many Rule 23(b)(3) class actions, the lawyers seeking certification must submit a trial plan describing how the case will be tried; if the case cannot be tried, the judge is likely to find the class action is unmanageable and deny certification. Hence, even if a case is unlikely to be tried, lawyers must have an idea about how to try the case effectively in order to attain aggregation. In short, trial issues are vital to the aggregation and pretrial issues that arise in all cases.

If the pretrial process has done its job well, it is possible that the trial itself will not be complex: the issues will be clearly defined, few in number, and limited in terms of evidence. Odds are, however, that a case complex during pretrial will be complex during trial. But complexity in a pretrial sense is not exactly the same as complexity at trial. To understand trial complexity, consider the roles that the adversarial system assigns to players at trial. As with pretrial, the lawyers' role is central: They define the issues in dispute, present the evidence, and make the arguments. As with pretrial, the parties do little. Unlike pretrial, however, the adversarial system gives the decision-maker(s) important responsibilities during trial. They must rule on the admissibility of evidence, find the facts, declare the law, apply the law to the facts, and, if necessary, declare a remedy. These functions can be accomplished by one person or it can be divided among various persons or groups.

Cases are "complex" in the trial sense when either the lawyers or the decision-maker(s) are incapable of performing adequately their expected functions. Among the circumstances that make the lawyers and decision-maker(s) unable to perform their tasks are:

- The information that the lawyer must marshal makes it impossible for the lawyer to formulate adequate proofs and arguments. For instance, the information may be wide-ranging and extensive, costly to obtain, or, due to time lags, no longer in existence.
- Lawyers who represent the same or similar interests may be unable to frame the facts and the issues in a way that clarifies the case for the decision-maker(s).
- The factfinder may be unable to use reasoned judgment to resolve the case. This incapacity can arise from different sources. The factfinder may lack the ability to understand the evidence because it is esoteric, technical, or overwhelmingly voluminous. The factfinder may be unable to understand the law. Or the length of trial may put demands on the factfinder's ability to deliberate.

The first two concerns are comparable to two of the concerns that define pretrial complexity. The third issue is new, because it involves the factfinder.

Chapter Thirteen begins the exploration of these issues by examining the ability of the judge to change the counsel structure or to replace the factfinder (whether a jury or even the judge) in order to ensure the rational resolution of the dispute. Chapter Fourteen examines non-traditional trial techniques that a judge might adopt to narrow the trial, enabling a more rational adjudication by limiting the amount of information presented at one time. Chapter Fifteen examines techniques to increase the factfinder's comprehension of evidence, likewise with a goal of enhancing reasoned decision-making. The issues of who fills particular roles and what techniques can be used to make evidence more comprehensible are integrally related; for instance, the use of some trial techniques (a Chapter Fourteen issue) might allow us to preserve the right to jury trial (a Chapter Thirteen issue).

Chapter 13

SELECTING THE COUNSEL AND ADJUDICATORS FOR TRIAL

The trial accomplishes tasks central to adjudication. First, it determines the law that applies to a particular disputes. Second, it decides the facts relevant to determining whether a legal violation occurred. Third, when appropriate, it declares the remedy.

In the adversarial model, the lawyers' role in accomplishing these tasks is critical. The lawyer determines which legal issues to argue and which evidence to use to prove those arguments. But also critical to adjudication at trial is the nature of the decision-maker(s) who must determine what the law is, what the facts are, and what the remedy should be.

Traditionally the trial structure and decision-maker depended on whether the case arose at common law or in equity. With the common-law trial, witnesses testified live and were subject to cross-examination; a lay jury determined factual disputes (and in some jurisdictions legal ones); the jury declared the remedy; and all claims and issues were definitively resolved in a culminating trial event. With equity, decision-making was different. "Trials" were only a series of hearings that resolved issues in an order established by the chancellor; evidence was presented in written form; and a chancellor rather than a jury made legal, factual, and remedial determinations. By the nineteenth century, however, the judge's power to determine the law in all cases was well-established; the jury's role in actions at law was relegated to finding the facts and declaring the remedy. The jury's functions were also subject to judicial controls such as the ability to order a new trial, to direct the jury's verdict, or to enter judgment notwithstanding the verdict.

The Federal Rules of Civil Procedure abolished any formal distinctions between law and equity. In the main, the trial process in the merged system ran like the common law: live witnesses, cross-examination, a single culminating trial event. But the Federal Rules also borrowed certain features from equity. For example, it allowed a case to be broken up into separate trials to further convenience, achieve greater economy, or avoid prejudice.[851]

Nonetheless, driven in part by the Seventh Amendment's jury-trial guarantees for actions at law, the old distinctions between law and equity remain relevant. A jury, not a judge, determines the facts

[851] FED. R. CIV. P. 42(b).

and, in most instances, declares the remedy in actions at law. Jury controls (the modern-day order for a new trial[852] or judgment as a matter of law[853]) are tightly circumscribed to respect the right to jury trial, and have no counterpart in suits decided without a jury. Similarly, a Rule 42 order for a separate trial "must preserve any federal right to a jury trial."

Nothing in the Federal Rules of Civil Procedure or the Federal Rules of Evidence has changed the essentially adversarial flavor of trial. In some complex cases, the standard model threatens to produce an outcome that is insufficiently grounded in reason: either the lawyer struggles to perform the task of marshaling the evidence needed to present effective arguments or the factfinder struggles to make a reasoned decision based of myriad amount of often technical information delivered over the course of weeks or months of trial. In either event, reasoned decision-making is threatened, and with it the accuracy and acceptability of the judgment itself.

In this Chapter we examine the court's ability to alter either the counsel structure or the decision-making structure to overcome these difficulties.

A. Restructuring the Counsel Relationship

By placing the lawyer firmly in charge of presenting the client's proofs and arguments to a passive jury and judge, the adversarial system guarantees the autonomy of each party to present the evidence and arguments as he or she sees fit. In the heyday of common-law pleading, in which claim joinder and party joinder were highly restricted, this guarantee of one lawyer for one client rarely caused problems. In a modern case governed by the transactional assumption of claim and party joinder, the presentation of individualized evidence and arguments for each party threatens both to create information overload and to extend trials beyond the capacity of lay factfinders to recall evidence.

As with pretrial complexity, therefore, the first question is whether to restructure the relationship between attorney and client. While any restructuring might move trials in complex cases away from our commitment (grounded in due process) to individual autonomy, it might be necessary to ensure our commitment (also grounded in due process) to reasoned adjudication.

---

852 FED. R. CIV. P. 59(a)(1).

853 The motion for judgment as a matter of law corresponds to the old motion for a directed verdict during trial. FED. R. CIV. P. 50(a). The renewal of the motion for judgment as a matter of law after trial corresponds to the old motion for a judgment notwithstanding the verdict. FED. R. CIV. P. 50(b).

In Chapter Ten, we saw that courts claimed an inherent power to appoint lead counsel or committees of counsel to work on a group's behalf during the pretrial process.[854] The next shoe to fall is the power to appoint counsel for a group at trial. In class actions certified under Rule 23, the appointment of class counsel carries with it the power to represent the class at trial. In other aggregate proceedings, judges do not enjoy a comparable source of authority in rule or statute to appoint trial counsel.

Whatever the theoretical propriety of appointing trial counsel, courts claim the inherent power to do so, and they use the power with frequency.[855] For the most part, the parties acquiesce in the power; it is difficult to find cases challenging an appointment. The most noteworthy case is *In re Air Crash Disaster at Detroit Metropolitan Airport on August 16, 1987*,[856] in which one plaintiff argued that the appointment of a lead counsel for trial "abridged her right to representation by the counsel of her choice." Relying on prior cases appointing lead counsel (most of which involved pretrial appointments), the court rejected the argument out of hand.

In making an appointment, judges will likely consider the competence of counsel and the potential conflicts of interest that might arise. Unlike Rule 23, there is no formal guarantee that the appointed counsel will adequately represent the group.

As with pretrial appointments, judges appoint lead trial counsel only for groups of plaintiffs. Defendants are generally able to retain counsel of their choice—a distinction that recognizes the conflicts of interest that might arise from the representation of co-defendants.

The pros and cons of the power to appoint trial counsel for groups of plaintiffs are largely the same as those that were discussed for pretrial appointments. On the positive side, the appointment of a single trial counsel for a group eliminates the inefficiency and confusion of a hundred lawyers presenting evidence and cross-examining witnesses on behalf of clients with similar interests. On the negative side, the lack of statutory or regulatory authority (except in class actions) to make an appointment raises concerns about the scope of judicial power to affect outcomes. In addition, the incursion on the autonomy of each plaintiff to present the case in that plaintiff's best interests is as great during trial as during pretrial—if not more so. Finally, the fine-grain strengths and weaknesses of each case disappear when a single lawyer blends multiple cases into a smooth bland consistency.

---

[854] *See supra* note 675 and accompanying text.

[855] For a general criticism, see Roger H. Trangsrud, *Mass Trials in Mass Tort Cases: A Dissent*, 1989 U. ILL. L. REV. 69.

[856] 737 F. Supp. 396 (E.D. Mich. 1989).

B. Restructuring the Adjudicator

The adjudicator's role at trial encompasses law-giving, factfinding, and remedy-declaring. The law-giving function belongs to the judge, while the factfinding and remedy-declaring functions are typically split between the judges and juries: judges retain these functions in cases tried without juries, while juries exercise these functions, subject to judicial oversight, in jury-tried cases. Both judges and juries possess limitations: they may not be expert in the technical matters raised at trial, and they have limited time and resources to devote to trial. Nonetheless, given the nature of jury trial, which must typically resolve all issues at one time and limits the ability of the jury to question witnesses or deliberate at leisure, the difficulties of rational adjudication may be more strongly felt in jury-tried cases.

This section examines the ability of the court to alter the usual structure of factfinding and law-giving due to the informational or comprehension demands of a complex case.

1. Changing the Factfinder

Unlike the restructuring of counsel relationships, the idea of restructuring of the factfinder is new. The issues are somewhat different in the context of jury-tried and bench-tried cases.

a. Replacing the Jury

Discussion of substituting for the jury a different factfinder more capable of reasoned decision-making must begin with the Seventh Amendment, which provides in full:

> In Suits at common law, where the value in controversy shall exceed twenty dollars, the right of trial by jury shall be preserved, and no fact tried by a jury, shall be otherwise re-examined in any Court of the United States, than according to the rules of the common law.

The first clause, which guarantees the right to jury trial in common-law cases, is our immediate focus. (The second clause, known as the Reexamination Clause, imposes limits that we explore in Chapter Fourteen.) The scope of the jury-trial right establishes the initial boundary around a federal judge's power to replace the jury when the needs of a complex case demand.[857] A second boundary is the power

---

[857] The Seventh Amendment applies only to cases filed in federal court; it has never been incorporated through to the Fourteenth Amendment and applied to the states. *See* González-Oyarzun v. Caribbean City Builders, Inc., 798 F.3d 26 (1st Cir. 2015) ("The Supreme Court has consistently held that states are not constitutionally required to provide a jury trial in civil cases."). Incorporation of the Seventh Amendment has never been a burning issue, because forty-eight states (Louisiana and Wyoming being the exceptions) have comparable jury trial guarantees in their

of Congress to specify by statute that a claim be tried to a jury even when the Seventh Amendment does not so demand. This power is a one-way ratchet: Congress can authorize jury trials in cases that otherwise would be tried to judges, but it cannot, consistent with the Seventh Amendment, transfer factfinding from the jury to a judge.[858] A third boundary arises from the merger of law and equity. When claims that would formerly have been tried in equity are joined with claims that would formerly have been tried at law, the jury must first determine facts relevant to both the equitable and the legal claims.[859]

The scope of the Seventh Amendment is therefore the starting point for analysis about a federal court's ability to substitute a different factfinder for a jury. In *Ross v. Bernhard*,[860] the Supreme Court described three factors that determine the Seventh Amendment right: "first, the pre-merger custom with reference to such questions; second, the remedy sought; and third, the practical abilities and limitations of juries." The first factor refers to the practices of law and equity in 1791, when the Seventh Amendment was ratified. The second factor hinges on whether damages (the usual relief at law) or an injunction (the usual relief in equity) is sought. The Supreme Court has noted that, of the first two issues, "the second stage is more important than the first"[861]—although, without retracting this statement, its later Seventh Amendment cases put a greater premium on historical practices in 1791 than on the remedy sought.[862]

Some judges and commentators have appealed to historical practices to argue that, given the limits of the common law in 1791, equity would have interceded in complex cases (had they existed in 1791), thus providing the historical warrant for judges to replace the jury as factfinder. Other judges and commentators have seized on the third prong of *Ross v. Bernhard*—"the practical abilities and limitations of juries—reach the same result.

Indeed, one of the hottest legal debates of the 1970s, for which more trees gave their lives than nearly any other, was whether the Seventh Amendment contains a "complexity exception" that allows a

---

constitutions. *See* Robert Wilson, *Free Speech v. Trial by Jury: The Role of the Jury in the Application of the Pickering Test*, 18 GEO. MASON U. CIV. RIGHTS L.J. 389 (2008).

858 There is an exception to this rule in "public rights" cases. *See* Granfinanciera, S.A. v. Nordberg, 492 U.S. 33 (1989).

859 *See* Beacon Theatres Inc. v. Westover, 359 U.S. 500 (1959) ("[O]nly under the most imperative circumstances, circumstances which in view of the flexible procedures of the Federal Rules we cannot now anticipate, can the right to a jury trial of legal issues be lost through prior determination of equitable claims.").

860 396 U.S. 531 (1970).

861 *Granfinanciera*, 492 U.S. at 42.

862 *See* City of Monterey v. Del Monte Dunes at Monterey, Ltd., 526 U.S. 687 (1999); Feltner v. Columbia Pictures Television, Inc., 523 U.S. 340 (1998).

judge in a complex case to strike the jury and determine the facts on his or her own. A few courts found such an exception.[863] Other cases did not,[864] although one of them found an exception under the Due Process Clause instead.[865] The many commentators divided on the question.[866]

The Supreme Court never entered the fray directly, but in a decision at the end of the 1980s, as the debate about the meaning of *Ross v. Bernhard* still simmered, it confined the scope of the "practical abilities and limitations" factor. The Court held that the phrase referred only to "public rights" cases, in which Congress can by statute delegate factfinding to an administrative-law judge or an Article III judge rather than a jury.[867] These "public rights" cases, which almost always involve the government as a party, are few in number. This reading of the "practical abilities and limitations" factor essentially closed down efforts to read a "complexity exception" into the third *Ross v. Bernhard* factor. The historical and due-process arguments, neither of which is strong in most instances, remain as the only possible mechanisms to strike a jury in a complex case.[868]

---

[863] *See* ILC Peripherals Leasing Corp. v. Int'l Bus. Machs. Corp., 458 F. Supp. 423 (N.D. Cal. 1978); Bernstein v. Universal Pictures, Inc., 79 F.R.D. 59 (S.D.N.Y. 1978); *In re* Boise Cascade Sec. Litig., 420 F. Supp. 99 (W.D. Wash. 1976).

[864] *See, e.g., In re* U.S. Fin. Sec. Litig., 609 F.2d 411 (9th Cir. 1979).

[865] *See In re* Japanese Elec. Prods. Antitrust Litig., 631 F.2d 1069 (3d Cir. 1980) ([W]e find the most reasonable accommodation between the requirements of the fifth and seventh amendments to be a denial of jury trial when a jury will not be able to perform its task of rational decisionmaking with a reasonable understanding of the evidence and the relevant legal standards."). The due-process argument requires a number of steps: (a) The Due Process Clause of the Fifth Amendment guarantees litigants that a decision-maker will use reason to arrive at an outcome; (b) in some cases, juries are incapable of coming to a rational decision; and (c) in the battle between the commands of the Fifth and Seventh Amendments, the Fifth wins. None of these premises is ineluctably true.

[866] For a very small sampling of authorities providing different perspectives, see Patrick Devlin, *Jury Trial of Complex Cases: English Practice at the Time of the Seventh Amendment*, 80 COLUM. L. REV. 43 (1980); Morris S. Arnold, *A Historical Inquiry into the Right to Trial by Jury in Complex Litigation*, 128 U. PA. L. REV. 829 (1980); Richard O. Lempert, *Civil Juries and Complex Cases: Let's Not Rush to Judgment*, 80 MICH. L. REV. 68 (1981); Montgomery Kersten, Note, *Preserving the Right to Jury Trial in Complex Civil Cases*, 32 STAN. L. REV. 99 (1979); Note, *The Right to a Jury Trial in Complex Civil Litigation*, 92 HARV. L. REV. 898 (1979).

[867] *See Granfinanciera*, 492 U.S. at 42 n.4.

[868] In a separate line of cases, the court has held that certain factual issues within a jury-tried case are to be determined by the judge. *See* Markman v. Westview Instruments, Inc., 517 U.S. 370 (1996) (holding that the issue of construing a patent claim is to be decided by a judge; noting that historical practice, "the relative interpretive skills of judges and juries," and "statutory policies that ought to be furthered by the allocation" of the factfinding function bear on the decision whether a particular issue is tried to a jury). Thus far, outside of the patent context, the *Markman* analysis has not carved any arguably complex issues away from the jury; but *Markman* remains a possible route to reduce a jury's factfinding in a complex case.

Perhaps the greatest flaws in arguments to strike juries are its assumptions that (1) a jury is not capable of rationally deciding certain cases, and (2) a judge is more capable than a jury. On the first point, empirical, anecdotal, and psychological evidence suggests that, contrary to the legal culture's myth, juries generally do quite well at determining facts and even have certain abilities (such as the benefit of multiple perspectives—twelve heads can be better than one) that a judge does not. Juries have trouble processing jury instructions, but that fact is an argument for clearer instructions, not the denial of a constitutional right.

On the second assumption, judges possess some factfinding advantages: notably, years of factfinding experience, the ability to deliberate at a thoughtful pace, law clerks, and the power to re-open the case and take more evidence when necessary. But the judge's years of experience do not necessarily make her a better factfinder, nor is the judge's experience more valuable than those of jury members. Some studies report that judge-jury agreement across a broad array of cases is about eighty percent;[869] another study put agreement at sixty-three percent in civil and criminal cases that were regarded as complex.[870] Other studies show that judges and juries have similar problems in assessing difficult technical evidence.[871] No studies have examined whether increased contact by the judge during pretrial case management might skew the factfinding of the judge, but that risk remains. And many litigators and judges say that the discipline and enforced simplicity of a jury trial makes it run smoother in the long run than a bench trial.

A different tack—one that retains the jury but provides a better guarantee of reasoned judgment—is to choose jury members with expertise in the subject matter of the dispute—a so-called "special," "blue ribbon," or "struck" jury. At common law, juries of experts were impaneled on rare occasion; and a party's right to obtain a special

---

[869] *See* Harry Kalven, Jr., *The Dignity of the Civil Jury*, 50 VA. L. REV. 1055 (1964); R. Perry Sentell, Jr., *The Georgia Jury and Negligence: The View from the Bench*, 26 GA. L. REV. 85 (1991); Kevin M. Clermont & Theodore Eisenberg, *Trial by Jury or Judge: Transcending Empiricism*, 77 CORNELL L. REV. 1124 (1992); AUDREY CHIN & MARK A. PETERSON, DEEP POCKETS, EMPTY POCKETS (1985).

[870] *See* Larry Heuer & Steven Penrod, *Trial Complexity: A Field Investigation of Its Meaning and Its Effects*, 18 LAW & HUM. BEHAV. 29 (1994) (noting that "our data do not support the proposition that judges and juries decide cases differently [or] that complexity influences the rationality of jury decision making").

[871] *See* Gary Wells, *Naked Statistical Evidence of Liability: Is Subjective Probability Enough?*, 62 J. PERSONALITY & SOC. PSYCHOL. 739 (1992) (stating that judges demonstrate same fallacious statistical reasoning as juries), and Richard Lempert, *Civil Juries and Complex Cases: Taking Stock after Twelve Years*, in VERDICT 181 (Robert E. Litan ed. 1993) (describing anecdotal evidence and inferences from data suggest that judges and juries have equal difficulty assessing scientific evidence).

jury on payment of its expenses was well established before 1791.[872] A few states use special juries. The power to do so at the federal level, however, is constrained by the Jury Selection and Service Act of 1968. The Act states the modest qualifications necessary for jury service; expertise is not among them.[873]

b. Replacing or Aiding the Judge as Factfinder

In non-jury cases, as well as in jury-triable cases in which the parties do not demand a jury, the judge is the factfinder. A judge may be incapable of performing this function well because of the technical nature of the evidence or the limits on the judge's time. In such cases, may a judge either appoint a better factfinder or seek assistance from experts with the requisite competence?

The option of appointing an expert to adjudicate technical facts is generally out of bounds. The essence of federal adjudication in a bench trial is an Article III judge as decision-maker. Any effort to undermine this authority violates the Constitution. In *La Buy v. Howes Leather Co.*,[874] a trial judge was facing a six-week bench trial in an antitrust case. Relying on Rule 53, the judge referred the trial to a special master, who was to recommend findings of fact and conclusions of law. The judge's reasons for the reference were docket congestion, as well as the complexity and length of the trial. The court of appeals issued of a writ of mandamus against the reference, and the Supreme Court affirmed. The Court stated that the reference amounted to "an abdication of the judicial function." It emphasized that the district court had become familiar with the litigation during pretrial and that the complexity of the case was a reason to have a skilled and experienced Article III factfinder, not a reason to appoint a surrogate factfinder.

La Buy's language is strong, but its scope is uncertain. In particular, the decision is unclear whether the reference violated Article III or Rule 53.[875] If the former, trial references to special masters will be very rare, if permissible at all. If the latter, references may still be possible. The present Rule 53 does not permit trial references in jury-tried issues unless the parties consent. But it permits a court to appoint a special master at trial to "hold proceedings and make or recommend findings of fact on issues to be

---

[872] See James B. Thayer, *The Jury and Its Development (Part II)*, 5 HARV. L. REV. 295 (1892); Note, *The Case for Special Juries in Complex Cases*, 89 YALE L.J. 1155 (1980).

[873] 28 U.S.C. § 1861–78.

[874] 352 U.S. 249 (1957).

[875] Lower courts tend to treat *La Buy* as a Rule 53 case, albeit one with Article III underpinnings. *See In re* Bituminous Coal Operators' Ass'n, 949 F.2d 1165 (D.C. Cir. 1991); *but see* Stauble v. Warrob, Inc., 977 F.2d 690 (1st Cir. 1992) (analyzing Article III constraints inherent in Rule 53).

decided without a jury" when warranted by "some exceptional condition" or by "the need to perform an accounting or a difficult computation of damages."[876] *La Buy* holds that complexity and time constraints are not in themselves "exceptional conditions," but other conditions might allow a court to make a trial reference.[877]

A judge may also have the inherent power to appoint a "technical advisor" or "expert consultant" with whom to confer on difficult factual matters, as long as the responsibility for factfinding rests ultimately on the judge's shoulders. For instance, in *Reilly v. United States*,[878] the district court appointed an economist as a technical advisor in a nonjury case when the defendant had failed to provide adequate evidence to help the court assess the costs of future medical care. The court of appeals rejected the defendant's belated objection to this procedure.

Question

In *La Buy*, Judge La Buy had appointed an attorney as master—not an economist or business person who might have had technical knowledge of the markets or industry involved. Might a referral to an expert have met the requirement of an "exceptional condition" if the trial centered on technical issues?

The source of a court's power to appoint a technical advisor is uncertain. *Reilly* rejected the argument that the appointment fell within the court's power to appoint expert witnesses under Federal Rule of Evidence 706 because the technical advisor did not testify. It also rejected resort to Rule 53, which suggests a different trial role for a master. Instead, relying on a Justice Brandeis opinion often invoked to justify trial innovations, the court of appeals cited the district court's inherent power.[879] *Reilly*'s standard for the exercise of this power—that such appointments are the "exception and not the rule," reserved for "truly extraordinary cases where the introduction of outside skills and expertise, not possessed by the judge, will hasten the just adjudication of a dispute without dislodging the delicate balance of the juristic role"—sounds not unlike the standard for a Rule 53 reference to a master.

Reilly recognized that the use of a technical advisor, whose conversations with the judge are neither subject to examination nor

[876] FED. R. CIV. P. 53(a)(1)(B).

[877] A few post-*LaBuy* cases authorize a trial reference in a non-jury case. *See, e.g.,* United States v. Suquamish Indian Tribe, 901 F.2d 772 (9th Cir. 1990) (arguably a reference for remedial matters); Loral Corp. v. McDonnell Douglas Corp., 558 F.2d 1130 (2d Cir 1977); Rogers v. Societe Internationale Pour Participations Industrielles et Commerciales, S.A., 278 F.2d 268 (D.C. Cir. 1960).

[878] 863 F.2d 149 (1st Cir. 1988).

[879] *See Ex parte* Peterson 253 U.S. 300 (1920) ("Courts have (at least in the absence of legislation to the contrary) inherent power to provide themselves with appropriate instruments for the performance of their duties.").

open to the parties, requires procedural safeguards. Among them are notice to the parties of the advisor's identity, an opportunity to object to the proposed appointment, a requirement that the advisor file a written report, a "job description" for the advisor, and an affidavit from the advisor stating compliance with this description. Although most of the safeguards were missing in *Reilly*, the court of appeals held that the defendant had waived its right to object.[880]

The Supreme Court has never decided whether the use of technical advisors is the type of "abdication of judicial function" that infected *La Buy*. The use of advisors certainly suggests a very different role for the judge—and for the lawyers, who now lose the adversarial right to control the presentation of evidence and arguments to the factfinder. Whether technical advisors remain the "way out" for judges who are unable to master technical matters necessary for rational adjudication, or whether the court must simply insist on better adversarial presentations or court-appointed expert witnesses under Rule 706, remains to be seen.

Beyond the particular concerns with technical advisors, the concerns that inhered in the use of special masters during pretrial arise with the use of special masters and technical advisors during trial. Among them are expense, delay, partiality, abuse of power, and loss of trans-substantivity. Those costs must be balanced against gains in speed, reduced trial expense, and accuracy.

2. Restructuring the Law-Giver

In our adversarial system, the judge declares the law to which the facts must be applied. Sometimes cases are legally as well as factually complex. When a case presents complex issues of law, can the law-giving function be restructured, so that a legal expert decides the law?

The answer is no. *Reed v. Cleveland Board of Education*[881] pushed the envelope on this issue to its breaking point. In *Reed*, a school-desegregation case, the district judge appointed a

---

[880] The appointment of technical advisors is rare. For a handful of cases appointing advisors, see Renaud v. Martin Marietta Corp., 972 F.2d 304, 308 n.8 (10th Cir. 1992) (toxic exposure); Burton v. Sheheen, 793 F. Supp. 1329, 1339 (D.S.C. 1992) (redistricting); Hemstreet v. Burroughs Corp., 666 F. Supp. 1096 (N.D. Ill. 1987) (patent); *cf.* Concilio de Salud Integral de Loiza, Inc. v. Perez-Perdomo, 551 F.3d 10 (1st Cir. 2008) (suggesting that the court might appoint a technical advisor in a complex Medicaid action); *In re* Joint E. & S. Dists. Asbestos Litig., 151 F.R.D. 540 (E. & S.D.N.Y. 1993) (recognizing the inherent power to appoint an advisor, but choosing to treat a consultant as a court-appointed expert witness). One proposal that would inject expertise into the federal bench without the need for technical advisors is to confirm some Article III judges with specific technical expertise. *See* Edward V. Di Lello, Note, *Fighting Fire with Firefighters: A Proposal for Expert Judges at the Trial Level*, 93 COLUM. L. REV. 473 (1993). That idea has gone nowhere in Congress.

[881] 607 F.2d 737 (6th Cir. 1979).

constitutional-law professor to help handle thorny legal questions. The professor's communications were ex parte, and consisted of drafting orders and consulting with the judge, his law clerks, and a special master. As in *Reilly*, the defendant never filed a timely objection to the appointment. Unlike *Reilly*, however, the court of appeals thought that the appointment of an advisor exceeded the court's authority. Because the defendant had not objected, the court of appeals affirmed the award of fees to the professor for the time spent consulting with the master. With regard to advice given to the judge or his clerks, no award was permitted; in conjunction with the briefing by the parties and amicus curiae, the court of appeals reasoned, the district court was capable of handling legal issues on its own. To consult with an advisor ex parte amounted to "a partial abdication of his role. . . . [T]he adversary system as it has developed in this country precludes the court from receiving out-of-court advice on legal issues in a case."

The few other cases considering the issue have flatly rejected the use of legal advisors.[882]

C. Conclusion

The courts' inherent power to restructure the lawyers' roles in complex litigation is an accepted fact. In contrast, restructuring the judge's law-giving and the jury's factfinding roles may be impossible to accomplish. In limited circumstances, the judge's factfinding role in bench trials can be changed.

That reality affects all that comes before trial. If trial could be handled by a judge, and if the judge could break the case down into a series of discrete hearings, the pretrial process would look very different, and judges might not be as reluctant to aggregate related claims into a single whole. But when trial is to a jury, and all the issues in a case must be determined at one time, the pretrial process is necessarily extensive, and aggregation is less appealing.

Making the trial run more smoothly is not simply a matter of reforming the traditional roles of lawyers, judges, and juries. The following two chapters describe other techniques either to narrow the number of issues that the factfinder must consider at one time and to help a factfinder better comprehend the evidence presented at trial. After we examine these techniques, you might profitably ask whether we need to restructure the relationships among lawyers, judges, and juries in complex trials.

---

[882] *See Reilly*, 863 F.2d 149; Young v. Pierce, 640 F. Supp. 1476 (E.D. Tex. 1986); *cf.* Madrigal Audio Labs., Inc. v. Cello, Ltd., 799 F.2d 814 (2d Cir. 1986) ("[T]he fact that 'the case involves complex issues of law or fact is no justification for reference to a Master, but rather a [com]pelling reason for trial before an experienced judge.' ").

Chapter 14

NARROWING ISSUES AT TRIAL

Vast quantities of information at trial present a challenge both for the lawyers, who must present the arguments and evidence in a manner that aids the adjudicator, and the adjudicator(s), who must digest the information to render a judgment. As we discussed in the last chapter, one important technique to simplify the presentation of arguments and evidence is to appoint a single trial counsel for a group of litigants. Courts can also employ other devices that either narrow the number of issues that the adjudicator must decide or streamline the presentation of arguments and evidence for the issues that are tried. This Chapter examines issue-narrowing techniques at trial; the next chapter examines techniques to streamline the trial and aid comprehension.

A. Bifurcation

The most obvious way to narrow the issues that the factfinder must determine is to split the case up into a series of discrete trials or hearings, in the mode of equity or the continental systems of procedure. This method limits the amount of information the lawyers must present and the factfinder must consider at any given trial. Moreover, if the issue is chosen well, the determination on that issue might eliminate the need for further proceedings.

This division of the trial into parts is called "bifurcation." (More accurately, "bifurcation" occurs when the trial is split into two parts, "trifurcation" when it is split into three parts, and "polyfurcation" when it is split into four or more parts; but the term "bifurcation" is typically used to describe them all.) Unlike its pretrial counterpart that we discussed earlier,[883] trial bifurcation has clear support in the text of the Federal Rules. Rule 42 permits a separate trial of any issue or claim "[f]or convenience, to avoid prejudice, or to expedite and economize." The sole limitation is that separate trials "must preserve any federal right to a jury trial."

Trial bifurcation suffers from many of the difficulties of pretrial bifurcation, plus the new problem of respecting jury-trial rights. Often there is no dispositive issue that is easy to try. And if the first trial does not dispose of the case, the lawsuit will drag on, and witnesses who must testify a second time will be doubly inconvenienced. Other problems include the possibility of inconsistent verdicts, the inability of a single jury to get a complete

---

[883] *See supra* Chapter 11.B.2.b.

picture of the case, the unfairness to parties who must reveal their legal strategy in the first case, the ability of a party to use two inconsistent theories in the two trials, and the mismatch between the best case-management strategy and a bifurcated trial.

Trial bifurcation also has the potential to skew a case's outcome. The available data on bifurcated trials show that, when a case is bifurcated between liability issues and damages issues with liability tried first, the chances for a defense verdict rise substantially.[884] Looking at bifurcation through a broader lens, an economic analysis of bifurcation concluded that this technique increases the incentive of plaintiffs to sue, increases the number of lawsuits, and reduces the likelihood of an out-of-court settlement—the net effect of which is possibly "to increase the aggregate cost of litigation even though it lowers the expected cost of litigating (as opposed to settling) a particular dispute."[885]

The data about the outcome-skewing effect of separate trials is backed up by the anecdotal evidence of many lawyers. Perhaps the most famous example is *In re Bendectin Litigation*.[886] In *Bendectin*, more than 2,300 federal cases were multidistricted. After giving out-of-state plaintiffs the opportunity to opt out and return to their transferor forums for trial, the district court ordered the trial of the remaining cases trifurcated. The issue of Bendectin's capacity to cause birth defects was tried first; if plaintiffs prevailed, subsequent trials on defendant's liability and individual issues of causation and damages were to be held.

The effect of trifurcation was to exclude from the first jury evidence of the defendant's alleged wrongdoing in the marketing of Bendectin, as well as the horrendous injuries that the plaintiffs had suffered. To use the plaintiffs' famous catchphrase, the trial became a "sterile or laboratory atmosphere" concerning Bendectin's health effects. After a three-week trial the jury returned a verdict for the

---

[884] The best-known study demonstrating this effect is Hans Zeisel & Thomas Callahan, *Split Trials and Time Saving: A Statistical Analysis*, 76 HARV. L. REV. 1606 (1963). Zeisel and Callahan examined real-world bifurcation between liability and damages in cases that were not complex, They found that plaintiffs received a favorable verdict in 76% of the cases tried to verdict in an all-issues trial and 44% of the cases tried to verdict in a liability-only trial—a stark drop in the rate of success. An experimental study tried a complex toxic tort case in two ways: an all-issues trial and a causation-only trial. Plaintiffs won the mock case 87.5% of the time with an all-issues trial, but only 25% of the cases bifurcated on the issue of causation. Offsetting this dramatic effect to some extent, the plaintiffs who won in the causation-only condition received significantly higher damage awards than those who had won in the all-issues condition. *See* Irwin A. Horowitz & Kenneth S. Bordens, *An Experimental Investigation of Procedural Issues in Complex Tort Trials*, 14 L. & HUM. BEHAV. 269 (1990).

[885] *See* William M. Landes, *Sequential Versus Unitary Trials: An Economic Analysis*, 22 J. LEGAL STUD. 99 (1993).

[886] 857 F.2d 290 (6th Cir. 1988).

defendant, finding that Bendectin did not cause birth defects. As a result, 844 cases—cases that would otherwise have taken 182 judge-years to try—were terminated after fifteen days of trial. Finding no injustice to the plaintiffs but significant overall economy in this procedure, the court of appeals upheld, on an abuse-of-discretion standard, the district court's decision to trifurcate.

Whether the *Bendectin* story troubles you might depend on your perception of the purpose and nature of factfinding processes. In one sense, the *Bendectin* trifurcation worked exactly as it should have. In another sense, the outcome for some of the 844 cases might have been different had the jury heard damning evidence of Merrell Dow's behavior and sympathetic evidence of the injuries to deformed children. Many *Bendectin* plaintiffs who opted out of the trifurcated trial received single all-issue trials in the transferor districts, as did most of the plaintiffs in state court. In a few of these individually tried cases, plaintiffs prevailed.[887] In thinking about *Bendectin*, another consideration is that this potentially outcome-determinative procedure was applied just to these cases, not to other product-liability or mass-tort cases.

Courts have sought to soften the concerns about bifurcation in various ways. One approach popular in asbestos cases was to "reverse bifurcate"—to try damages before liability. Another idea, which works when a group of plaintiffs are aggregated, is to bifurcate the cases of the plaintiffs on one or more liability issues but permit an all-issues trial for a small number of chosen plaintiffs. This hybrid technique gives the factfinder some flavor of the full case while (if the jury finds for the defendant) avoiding a trial of all the individual issues for each plaintiff's claim. The downsides of trying liability and damages issues together for some plaintiffs are a more extensive pretrial process and a lengthier trial.

Even if the practical and policy problems of bifurcation can be resolved, the jury-trial issue looms large. The concern revolves around the Seventh Amendment's Reexamination Clause.[888] The Clause has been interpreted to preclude a second jury from

---

[887] Because the scientific evidence linking Bendectin to birth defects was thin, the defendant also prevailed in many individual trials. Indeed, the Supreme Court's path-breaking decision giving federal judges greater gatekeeping responsibility over expert testimony arose from a Bendectin case in which the defendant challenged the scientific and medical opinions of the plaintiff's experts on the issue of causation. *See* Daubert v. Merrell Dow Pharms., Inc., 509 U.S. 579 (1993).

[888] For the full text of the Seventh Amendment see *supra* Chapter 13.B.1.a. The Reexamination Clause affects only cases tried to a jury; bench trials are not subject to its terms, allowing judges in such cases more freedom to separate claims or issues for trial.

reexamining the facts found by a prior jury.[889] Therefore, any facts determined in the first bifurcated trial must be distinct from the facts that a second jury might determine. In *Bendectin*, the court of appeals held that juries in the later liability and damages trials issue would not have reexamined the potential of Bendectin to cause birth defects; hence, trifurcation created no Seventh Amendment problem. As a general rule, bifurcation between liability and damages also passes muster. Avoidance of this constitutional issue is one reason that liability-damages bifurcation is common.

Although *Bendectin* shows that splitting liability issues into separate trials is possible, such bifurcation can pose challenges. For example, carving up a case between wrongdoing and proximate causation may require a second jury to revisit facts found by the first jury in order to determine the scope of the risk for a proximate-causation finding. The same concern might arise if proximate causation and comparative negligence are separated, due to the way in which the plaintiff's causal contribution to the injury might factor into both issues. In *In re Rhone-Poulenc-Rorer Inc.*,[890] a trial court certified a class of persons with hemophilia who became HIV-positive as a result of exposure to tainted blood products. One of the defendants' arguments against certification was that the trial of more than 5,000 plaintiffs would be unmanageable. Not so, said the district judge; the general issue of defendants' negligence could be bifurcated and tried first, with follow-up individual trials on issues of causation and comparative negligence. The court of appeals issued a writ of mandamus against the certification, in part because it thought that the district court's trial plan violated the Seventh Amendment. The trial plan would have required subsequent juries to look again at the first jury's determination of the defendants' liability, either to see whether plaintiffs' injuries flowed naturally from the wrongdoing (proximate cause) or to measure the relative culpability of each plaintiff and the defendants (comparative negligence).

Rhone-Poulenc can be criticized for an unduly broad view of the subsequent juries' tasks. Under the district court's plan, the first jury would have determined the defendants' negligence *simpliciter*. No subsequent jury would have reexamined that finding. To determine whether the defendants' fault was proximately related to each plaintiff's injury, or to weigh the defendant's fault against the plaintiff's, may require the second jury to hear some of the same

---

[889] *See* Gasoline Prods. Co. v. Champlin Refining Co., 283 U.S. 494 (1931) (permitting a retrial limited to damages issues when only the jury instructions regarding damages were erroneous).

[890] 51 F.3d 1293 (7th Cir. 1995).

evidence about the defendant's misconduct, but would not require it to re-determine the fact of defendants' liability.[891]

As *Rhone-Poulenc* shows, the inability to carve up a trial in certain ways can significantly hamper the ability of courts to aggregate cases. Without a viable way to try an aggregated proceeding, a court is unlikely to permit aggregation.

B. Trial by Formula

Imagine a case with 1,000 plaintiffs in which individual issues such as cause in fact, proximate causation, defenses, and damages will take about three days per plaintiff to try. Even if the judge can bifurcate liability issues into a separate trial, the trials on the individual issues will take 3,000 days—or about 12 full-time years of a judge's (and a jury's) time. Outcomes among comparably situated plaintiffs will inevitably vary; maintaining consistency over 1,000 cases and 12 years is impossible. Is there any way for the judge to avoid such a daunting prospect?

Enter the concept of "trial by formula" (or "trial by statistics"). The essence of trial by formula is to try a sample of the plaintiffs' cases and then to extrapolate the results of those trials to the group as a whole. As a result, the trial process is greatly shortened, and the entire group receives comparable treatment. Sampling can also attain the right level of deterrence and even enhance accuracy over the variability of individual trials at a fraction of the cost of individual trials. When no other trial method is possible, it can also deliver compensation in negative-value cases; without trial by formula, aggregation would be impossible due to a lack of any realistic trial option.

On the other hand, trial by formula frustrates the traditional, one-on-one ideal of American adjudication, depriving plaintiffs of their day in court and defendants of the right to face their accusers head on. It may also provide an accurate recovery in a global sense, but an inaccurate award—whether overcompensatory or undercompensatory—for nearly every person to whom the average award is extrapolated.

The first use of trial by formula occurred in the *Cimino* asbestos class action in the Eastern District of Texas. The class contained about 2,300 members. The district court proposed to bifurcate the trial, with liability and common defenses decided first. A second trial

---

[891] Another way to work around the problem is to retain the first jury for subsequent trials, so that one jury hears all the evidence. *See In re* Air Crash Disaster at Detroit Metro. Airport on Aug. 16, 1987, 737 F. Supp. 391 (E.D. Mich. 1989). It is not clear whether this solution meets the concerns of the Reexamination Clause, and in any event it is an impractical option in massive cases in which years might lapse between trials.

of 41 class members (15 chosen by plaintiffs, 15 chosen by defendant, and 11 chosen at random) was to follow. This second trial was to include testimony from a special master who had surveyed the class. The master would have summarized for the jury the demography, injuries, and other characteristics of the class. The jury was then to award a lump sum to the class as damages.

The defendant successfully sought a writ of mandamus against the trial plan.[892] It argued that the plan violated the Due Process Clause, the Seventh Amendment, and *Erie*.[893] Reserving judgment on the first two arguments, the court of appeals held that the substantive law of Texas, which applied to the case, required an individualized assessment of proximate causation. The attempt to assess damages on behalf of the class as a whole was inconsistent with Texas law, and thus precluded under *Erie*.

The district court went back to the drawing board. The court conducted 160 trials of randomly selected plaintiffs who suffered from each of the five diseases associated with asbestos.[894] At the end of these trials, the court averaged the verdicts for each disease type, and proposed to apply that average award to each plaintiff suffering from that disease. The plaintiffs consented to this procedure. Expert evidence showed that, to a 99% degree of confidence, the average award in each disease category represented the likely average award of individual trials. The trial court therefore overruled the defendants' objection to the procedure, and proposed entering judgment for each "extrapolation" plaintiff in the amount of the average award. Those plaintiffs whose cases were tried, on the other hand, received their actual award. In a further extrapolation, each defendant's share of damages in both the tried and extrapolated was determined not by whether any given plaintiff had been exposed to that defendant's asbestos, but rather according to the defendant's share of asbestos in the relevant worksites.[895]

Defendants appealed. The Fifth Circuit held that the plan violated the defendants' Seventh Amendment right to jury trial. With regard to the cases that had been tried, the jury had never determined, as Texas law and the Seventh Amendment required, that any given defendant's products had caused any given plaintiff's injuries. With regard to the thousands of "extrapolation" cases, the

---

892 *See In re* Fibreboard Corp., 893 F.2d 706 (5th Cir. 1990).

893 Erie R.R. v. Tompkins, 304 U.S. 64 (1938).

894 The district judge brought other judges and magistrate judges into the process, so the trial process was completed in less than one year.

895 *See* Cimino v. Raymark Indus., Inc., 751 F. Supp. 649 (E.D. Tex. 1990), *rev'd*, 151 F.3d 297 (5th Cir. 1998).

Seventh Amendment required a jury to determine the actual damages suffered by each and every plaintiff.[896]

Cimino shows how a trial-by-formula concept could work, as well as the legal obstacles in its path. The only case successfully to adopt a similar plan was *Hilao v. Estate of Marcos*,[897] in which the Ninth Circuit, prior to the Fifth Circuit's *Cimino* decision, affirmed a trial plan that was loosely based on the *Cimino* plan. The case involved approximately 10,000 victims of the repressive regime of Ferdinand Marcos. The district court randomly chose 137 cases, in which the parties conducted full discovery. A special master examined the discovery and made recommendations to the jury concerning the viability of the 137 claims and the damages due for each viable claim. He also recommended that the jury extrapolate from these damages calculation, and award the remaining 9,800 plaintiffs the average award for the type of injury from which they or their decedent suffered.[898] The jury heard additional evidence that the average award in the 137 cases would, to a 95% degree of confidence, match the average award in the remaining cases. The jury returned a verdict generally following the master's recommendations.

On appeal, the defendant did not assert a Seventh Amendment argument, but strongly contended that trial by formula violated its due-process rights. Finding that the plaintiffs, who were the ones standing to lose from this process, had consented and that the costs of the individualized trials outweighed any arguable gains in the accuracy of the outcome from the defendant's perspective, the court of appeals found no violation of due process.

The trial-by-formula process went dormant until the Ninth Circuit again blessed the process in the *Dukes v. Wal-Mart* gender-discrimination litigation. The case, which we examined in detail in Chapter Six,[899] involved approximately 1.5 million women presently or formerly employed by Wal-Mart. The Ninth Circuit permitted the case to proceed under Rule 23(b)(2) with respect to backpay awardable to class members. Because the amount of backpay varied considerably from woman to woman, the plaintiffs, in order to gain class certification, needed to propose a realistic method to determine backpay for 1.5 million class members. The Ninth Circuit relied on

---

[896] *See* Cimino v. Raymark Indus., Inc. 151 F.3d 297 (5th Cir. 1998).

[897] 103 F.3d 767 (9th Cir. 1996). The plaintiffs' attempt to collect on the judgment in *Hilao* formed the predicate for the Supreme Court's later Rule 19 decision in *Republic of the Philippines v. Pimentel*, 553 U.S. 851 (2008) (discussed *supra* note 73 and accompanying text).

[898] For those plaintiffs whose claims were found not to viable, their verdicts (valued at $0) were added into total judgment before dividing the total amount by the number of claimants in a particular category to arrive at the average verdict. In this way, the risk of loss was factored into each plaintiff's award.

[899] *See supra* 308, 332–334, 408–412, 442 and accompanying text.

its prior *Hilao* decision, stating that the district court could sample the claims, determine the average value of the backpay awards, and award the average amount to all class members.

The Supreme Court reversed the class certification on two grounds. It first held that the class action did not meet the commonality requirement on Rule 23(a)(2). It then held that Rule 23(b)(2) could not be used to award money, including the backpay awards of the class members.[900] At the end of the (b)(2) discussion, the Court offered the following observation:

> The Court of Appeals believed that it was possible to replace [individual determinations of affirmative defenses that would justify a particular employment decision in a particular class member's case] with Trial by Formula. A sample set of the class members would be selected, as to whom liability for sex discrimination and the backpay owing as a result would be determined in depositions supervised by a master. The percentage of claims determined to be valid would then be applied to the entire remaining class, and the number of (presumptively) valid claims thus derived would be multiplied by the average backpay award in the sample set to arrive at the entire class recovery—without further individualized proceedings. We disapprove that novel project. Because the Rules Enabling Act forbids interpreting Rule 23 to "abridge, enlarge or modify any substantive right," 28 U.S.C. § 2072(b) . . ., a class cannot be certified on the premise that Wal-Mart will not be entitled to litigate its statutory defenses to individual claims.

Wal-Mart's dicta seemed to sound the death knell for a process that was always more popular in the academic literature than in the real world.[901] But the Court's decision in *Tyson Foods, Inc. v. Bouaphakeo*[902] suggests that this assessment may be premature. In *Tyson* plaintiffs had allegedly been underpaid for their time donning and doffing their work clothes and gear; the company paid a set amount of time for donning and doffing, but the actual time took longer. In some but not all instances, the underpayment resulted in a denial of overtime wages, which federal and state law required

---

900 Wal-Mart Stores, Inc. v. Dukes, 564 U.S. 338 (2011). The first holding was a 5–4 decision, but the second holding, regarding "trial by formula," was unanimous.

901 For articles arguing for statistical extrapolation, see Edward K. Cheng, *When 10 Trials Are Better than 10,000: An Evidentiary Perspective on Trial Sampling*, 160 U. PA. L. REV. 955 (2012); Michael J. Saks and Peter David Blanck, *Justice Improved: The Unrecognized Benefits of Aggregation and Sampling in the Trial of Mass Torts*, 44 STAN. L. REV. 815 (1992).

902 577 U.S. ___, 136 S. Ct. 1036 (2016).

when workers hit a forty-hour work week. The company kept no records of donning and doffing times, so it became impossible to know exactly who had been deprived of overtime—and of how much overtime.

The plaintiffs proposed to solve the problem through the use of experts who observed workers donning and doffing. The experts averaged the times for different categories of workers using different gear, and then added the average time (less the time that the company had credited) to each worker's weekly hours-worked total. The experts determined that some workers were not eligible for overtime, but others were. Because the defendant had successfully argued that the case should not be bifurcated but rather that the damage award should be rendered on a lump-sum basis for the entire class, the plaintiffs' experts then extrapolated from the statistical evidence to a lump-sum $6.7 million award for the class. The jury found for the plaintiffs, but only in the amount of $2.9 million. The defendant appealed before the judge had decided how to distribute this award to class members.

The company argued that this method of calculating damages was the forbidden trial-by-formula approach. The Supreme Court disagreed. An old Supreme Court case had approved a similar method for determining the amount of overtime when the defendant had failed to keep records; in that case, the Court had pointed out that the defendant should not benefit from its wrong, and using observations and averaging was a reasonable way to calculate the loss. In *Tyson* the Court pointed out that, because an individual could use this type of evidence, there was no need to deny it to class members. Put differently, *Wal-Mart* forbade the use of statistical sampling in lieu of individualized proof in order to make a class action viable; in *Tyson* statistical sampling was viable even in an individual case, and the class-action process did nothing to change the evidence appropriately used to prove damages. Of course, as the Court noted, the ability to use statistical sampling made the argument for using a class action stronger; the proof applicable to each case was applicable to all, thus generating commonalities.

Tyson also emphasized that *Wal-Mart* did not ban all uses of statistical evidence in class actions. Statistics have long been used to prove issues in discrimination, antitrust, and securities trials. When the relevant substantive law allows such evidence to prove elements of a claim, nothing in *Wal-Mart* prevents class plaintiffs from relying on the same evidence. As a result, *Tyson* refused to adopt a *per se* rule on statistical evidence in class-action trials: "In a case where representative evidence is relevant in proving a plaintiff's individual claim, that evidence cannot be deemed improper merely because the claim is brought on behalf of a class."

Tyson sounded one cautionary note: the problem of distributing damages to class members. Given that the jury awarded a lump sum of less than half of the amount calculated by the expert, the judge faced substantial, and perhaps insurmountable, problems determining how to allocate the award among class members.

Tyson noted other limits on its decision: the company had consented to (and in fact argued for) the lump-sum damages process and had not challenged the qualifications of the experts who created the plaintiffs' damages model. Future defendants are unlikely to make either mistake. Whether *Tyson* goes further and *sub silentio* overrules *Wal-Mart*'s disapproval of trial by formula remains an open question, on which the final word has yet to be written.[903]

To the extent that statistical sampling is permitted, a host of issues surround the process. Sampling generally works best when the sampled group is homogenous and when there are large numbers. Because most judges and juries will not understand sampling methodologies and may be overly swayed by such evidence, the need to ensure the validity of the methods and results is especially critical.

Lower courts have also considered using aggregate proof in other contexts. In a class action composed of smokers who claimed that they were defrauded by misstatements about "light" cigarettes, the Second Circuit disapproved of sampling evidence to determine reliance, causation, and injury—as well as damages.[904] On each of these elements, the claim of each class member was likely to vary; the court of appeals thought that the sampling plan violated both the Rules Enabling Act and the Due Process Clause. On the other hand, the First Circuit affirmed a trial plan in an antitrust case that did not permit inquiry into individual reliance; the plan also called for calculating damages based on two variables—the amount of overcharge per unit and the number of units sold—without the defendant's ability to

Questions

Is the one-on-one adversarial presentation of claims and defenses the essence of adjudication; or is it a costly relic that must be jettisoned in mass disputes? Is the autonomy implicit in case-by-case adjudication the irreducible minimum of jury trial; or in Justice Brandeis's words, may the "new device" of trial by formula be adapted to preserve the "ancient institution" of jury trial for modern times? Is the precisely tailoring of a remedy to individual circumstance the bedrock of American adjudication; or is forcing the defendant to fully internalize the harm done to a group the bedrock?

---

[903] *See* Robert G. Bone, Tyson Foods *and the Future of Statistical Adjudication*, 95 N. CAR. L. REV. 607 (2017) (arguing that *Tyson* permits at least some statistical adjudication seemingly prohibited by *Wal-Mart*).

[904] *See* McLaughlin v. Am. Tobacco Co., 522 F.3d 215 (2d Cir. 2008).

explore the injury suffered by each class member.[905] The defendants were allowed to depose fifty class members. Because the amount of reliance did not vary substantially among them, the court held that banning inquiry into each class member's level of reliance did not raise "concerns of a constitutional dimension." As for the method of calculating damages, the court held that "[t]he use of aggregate damages calculations is well established in federal court."

Whatever the fate of trial by formula at the federal level, states also need to determine whether to adopt this method—and whether it comports with the constitutional *grundnorm* of due process. Like several of the issues we have seen in this book, trial by formula places the traditional and the progressive into stark contrast. The stakes of this debate are greater than the structure of trial, which remains a rare event. If trial by formula is ultimately validated, it will also provide a powerful impetus for aggregating related cases. One of the reasons that courts are reluctant to aggregate cases is the unmanageability of the resulting suit. In some cases, especially mass torts, trial by formula will reduce that unmanageability.

The jury, so to speak, remains out on trial by formula. Its fate bears watching.

C. Bellwether Trials

The technique that is the present darling of trial planning is the bellwether trial. The idea is to choose a limited number of cases and to try them to conclusion. The information obtained from those trials can then be used by both sides to assess whether and how to structure a settlement to resolve the remaining cases. This process conforms the cases to the traditional one-on-one, all-issues trial of the American adversarial system, thus avoiding the outcome-skewing potential of bifurcation. At the same time, it holds out the potential to avoid the expense of trial for most of the cases in the aggregate proceeding and to achieve a settlement that may treat like claimants roughly alike.[906]

The bellwether trial is a device akin to trial by formula, in the sense that the results in a limited number of cases is extrapolated to the larger whole. Because the goal is to establish a settlement to which all parties consent, however, it does not have the same due-process, jury-trial, Rules Enabling Act, and *Erie* concerns as trial by formula; the results of the bellwether cases do not bind the parties in

---

905 *See In re* Pharm. Indus. Average Wholesale Price Litig., 582 F.3d 156 (1st Cir. 2009).

906 *See also* Alexandra D. Lahav, *Bellwether Trials*, 76 GEO. WASH. L. REV. 576 (2008) (describing the pros and cons of bellwether trials and arguing that they enhance collective justice based on democratic participation values).

the untried cases or require that the average judgment be the amount awarded to each plaintiff in the settlement.

Bellwether trials have enjoyed notable successes in some MDL proceedings, in which transferee judges hold onto the remainder of the MDL cases in the hopes of forging a global settlement after the bellwether trials end.[907]

To be successful, the bellwether plaintiffs must be chosen with care. The choice need not be random; perhaps the lawyers need information about a particular matter to forge a settlement, so it makes sense to oversample cases presenting that issue. But as a general matter, random selection of cases is the best approach. Otherwise one side or the other will regard the information obtained from the bellwether trials as unreliable.

One case, *In re Chevron U.S.A., Inc.*,[908] held that, in order for a court to use the results of bellwether trials "for a purpose that extends beyond the individual cases tried," the cases chosen for trial must be randomly sampled and sufficient in number to generate statistically meaningful results. That statement seems overdrawn: parties can unquestionably use information from prior trials (even trials that were not randomly sampled) as the basis for settlement. Although it was a bit slippery on the point, the majority opinion seemed to have in mind that the judge might be able to use bellwether results preclusively, so that the results of the bellwether trials would determine the settlement amounts that the plaintiffs would receive in the untried cases. The concurrence read the majority as making such a proposal. If so, *Chevron* was blessing a trial-by-formula plan in the guise of settling the litigation. After *Wal-Mart* it is unlikely that such preclusive bellwether trials could pass muster.

D. Time Limits

Like their pretrial counterpart—early, firm deadlines—time limits at trial indirectly narrow issues. With only a certain amount of time within which to present a case, a skilled advocate will go for the jugular and ditch the extraneous. Of course, a skilled advocate will do this without time limits, so a fair question is why time limits are necessary. One answer is that, as the profession has evolved from trial lawyers into pretrial litigators, the experience and competence

---

907 *Vioxx* is perhaps the best-known MDL using bellwether trials to hammer out a settlement—even though the defendant had insisted for years that it would never settle a single case. *See In re* Vioxx Prods. Liab. Litig., 574 F. Supp. 2d 606 (E.D. La. 2008). For a description of the process co-authored by the transferee judge, see Eldon E. Fallon et al., *Bellwether Trials in Multidistrict Litigation*, 82 TUL. L. REV. 2323 (2008).

908 109 F.3d 1016 (5th Cir. 1997).

of the average member of the bar to try a lawsuit has declined. Time limits may compensate for that decline in skill.

Time limits can be imposed in different ways, each with certain advantages and disadvantages. One method is to give each side a certain number of hours or days to present its case in chief.[909] The problem with this approach is that the opposing party has an incentive to drag out cross-examinations to steal time from the opponent's case. To counteract this, another approach is to give each side a number of hours that it may spend as it wishes—on direct or cross-examination, on arguments, or on objections; when the time runs out, even in mid-question, that side's case is concluded.[910] A third approach is to allocate time on a witness-by-witness basis.[911] The second and third approaches also pose administrative problems, including how to set an appropriate number of hours, how to allocate those hours fairly among the parties (equal time is not always best, especially if one side's case is more complicated), and how to time each side accurately.

All systems of time limits have common problems. When the evidence is too voluminous or technical for the lawyer to adequately present or for the factfinder to adequately comprehend, time limits may exacerbate the difficulty in achieving reasoned decisions and raise due-process concerns.[912] In addition, using time limits in some, but not all, cases raises the usual criticism of ad hoc procedure: inequitable treatment of like cases and potential effects on outcome. Another question is the source of the court's authority to impose time limits. Inherent power is one possible source.[913] Specific provisions—such as Federal Rules of Evidence 403 and 611 or Federal Rule of Civil Procedure 16(c)(2)(O)—are sometimes invoked. The latter, which allows a court to take appropriate action with respect to "establishing a reasonable limit on the time allowed to present evidence," seems a sufficient basis of authority.

---

909 *See* MCI Commc'ns Corp. v. Am. Tel. & Tel. Co., 708 F.2d 1081 (7th Cir. 1983) (permitting twenty-six days of trial time for each side).

910 *Cf.* Flaminio v. Honda Motor Co., 733 F.2d 463 (7th Cir. 1984) ("disapprov[ing] of the practice of placing rigid hour limits on a trial" but affirming the judgment when the time limits were sufficient).

911 *See* Rohrbaugh v. Owens-Corning Fiberglas Corp., 965 F.2d 844 (11th Cir. 1992) (permitting thirty minute for directs and forty-five minutes for crosses of experts).

912 *Cf.* Newton Commonwealth Prop., N.V. v. G + H Montage GmbH, 404 S.E.2d 551 (Ga. 1991) (limiting trial time in a complex case was erroneous when the limit had "the effect of prejudicing the parties and preventing a full and meaningful presentation of the merits of the case").

913 *See* United States v. DeCologero, 364 F.3d 12 (1st Cir. 2004) (invoking inherent power in a criminal case).

E. Narrative or Summary Evidence

Another method to limit trial information is to require that evidence be submitted in condensed or summary form. For example, depositions lend themselves to summary presentation. The traditional practice for presenting deposition testimony has been for the lawyer (often assisted by another reader) to read the questions and answers to the jury. Unless Tom Cruise and Jack Nicholson are playing the two roles, transcript reading is tedious. Today the problem is often solved by using videotaped depositions in which the most salient aspects of the deposition are played back. But this approach does not always shorten the trial or the amount of information the factfinder hears; it simply shifts the tedium from the stand to the computer monitor. To speed up this process and reduce distraction, courts in some cases have required that the parties prepare a short written summary of the deposition testimony to be presented in lieu of the testimony.[914]

Some courts have gone further, and required parties to provide a short written narrative of the testimony of witnesses who appear in court. The attorney reads the statement and asks the witness if he or she would like to supplement it. After that, the witness is passed to the opponent for cross-examination.[915]

The most notable example of this "trial by affidavit" technique occurred in the *United States v. AT&T* antitrust litigation, in which the direct testimony of almost all of the 350 witnesses called to testify was submitted in writing. No background or preliminary questioning was allowed.[916] As a result, the largest antitrust trial in history "took less than a year. That's not bad."[917]

Of course, the perfunctory nature of the direct examination may deprive the judge and the jury of the opportunity to hear a story in the witness's own words and thus to form judgments about the credibility of the witness. That concern can be channeled into constitutional arguments (deprivation of the offering party's due-process rights and right to jury trial) as well as an argument (again!) about the source of the judge's power to order a narrative summary. Courts have not generally given the constitutional arguments much

---

[914] *See* Oostendorp v. Khanna, 937 F.2d 1177 (7th Cir. 1991); Kuntz v. Sea Eagle Diving Adventures Corp., 199 F.R.D. 665 (D. Haw. 2001).

[915] *See* Saverson v. Levitt, 162 F.R.D. 407 (D.D.C. 1995) (ordering use of narrative direct testimony and citing cases). *In re* Air Crash Disaster at Stapleton Int'l Airport, Denver, Colo., on Nov. 15, 1987, 720 F. Supp. 1493 (D. Colo. 1989) ("Development of techniques for the summary presentation of evidence is recommended in complex litigation.").

[916] *See* United States v. Am. Tel. & Tel. Co., 83 F.R.D. 323 (D.D.C. 1979).

[917] *See* Hazard & Rice, *supra* note 774, at 107–08.

shrift.[918] Indeed, insofar as the constitutional arguments hinge on a negative effect of summaries on rational adjudication, some experimental literature suggests that narrative summaries actually increase comprehension.[919]

The source of authority for this technique is usually said to be Federal Rule of Evidence 611(a), which allows a court to "exercise reasonable control over the mode and order of examining witnesses and presenting evidence" in order to "make those procedures effective for determining truth" and "avoid wasting time." If the power is not located in this non-specific language (and the Advisory Committee's note to Rule 611(a) raises some doubts that it should be), the inherent power of the court may again fill in the void.[920]

Courts may also require parties to submit summaries of voluminous documentary evidence, either by redacting the documents or summarizing their contents (in, hopefully, a visually compelling way).[921]

F. Other Techniques

Plaintiffs have sometimes proposed trials in which the first jury would decide the "background" issues that would establish the factual framework for later discovery and trials. Other plaintiffs have suggested "blueprint" trials, in which the first jury would leave to later triers of fact only ministerial questions of fact. For instance, in a toxic-tort case, the first jury might decide not only whether the chemical could cause the injuries alleged by a group of plaintiffs, but also what dosage or exposure level would be required to trigger the injuries. Later juries would then need to decide would be whether a specific plaintiff had an injury that the first jury correlated with the chemical, whether the plaintiff was exposed to the chemical, and

---

918 *See Oostendorp*, 937 F.2d 1177; *Stapleton International*, 720 F. Supp. 1493. *Compare In re* Burg, 103 B.R. 222 (9th Cir. BAP 1989) ("[E]ssential [due process] rights of the parties may be jeopardized by a [narrative direct testimony] procedure where the oral presentation of evidence is not allowed, where the bankruptcy court's ability to gauge the credibility of a witness or evidence is questionable and where rulings on objections to the admissibility of all direct evidence, may be unclear"), *with In re* Adair, 965 F.2d 777 (9th Cir. 1992) ("We disagree with the *Burg* panel that [a trial by affidavit] procedure raises significant due process concerns").

919 *See* Lynne Forsterlee et al., *The Cognitive Effects of Jury Aids on Decision-Making in Complex Civil Litigation*, 19 APPLIED COGNITIVE PSYCHOL. 867 (2005) (finding that summary statements, when combined with juror notetaking, enhanced mock jurors' cognition).

920 See Walker v. Action Indus., Inc., 802 F.2d 703 (4th Cir. 1986); *cf.* Edward R. Becker & Aviva Orenstein, *The Federal Rules of Evidence after Sixteen Years—The Effect of "Plain Meaning" Jurisprudence, The Need for an Advisory Committee on the Rules of Evidence, and Suggestions for Selective Revision of the Rules*, 60 GEO. WASH. L. REV. 857 (1992) (since "neither [Rule 611] nor the accompanying Advisory Committee notes encourages [narrative] statements," the Federal Rules of Evidence should be amended to permit them).

921 *See* MANUAL, *supra* note 206, §§ 11.492, 12.32.

what the level of exposure was. Thus far, courts have not been receptive to either background or blueprint trials.[922]

G. Conclusion

Many of the techniques that we have discussed can be employed in combination with other techniques: for instance, a bellwether trial could employ both time limits and narrative summaries. As courts pile novel procedure on novel procedure, a fundamental question arises: how much of the historical form of common-law trial is constitutionally enshrined in the Due Process Clause and the Seventh Amendment? Beyond the constitutional issue, there also lies concerns for fairness and equitable treatment.

Justice Brandeis once remarked that "[n]ew devices may be used to adapt the ancient institution [of jury trial] to present needs and to make of it an efficient instrument in the administration of justice. Indeed, such changes are essential to the preservation of the right."[923] Courts and scholars often cite that call to innovation when proposing new issue-narrowing devices at trial. Others are less enthusiastic about too must creative zeal. As one of us has remarked, "Our civil justice system owes a twelve-year-old girl born with foreshortened limbs after her mother took [Bendectin] the same due process that . . . we routinely afford the victims of many automobile accidents that are tried every year."[924]

---

[922] *See* United States v. Am. Tel. & Tel. Co., 83 F.R.D. 323, 335–36 (D.D.C. 1979) (declining to adopt a background trial, in part because the parties could not agree on what was a background, and what was a central, issue); Payton v. Abbott Labs, 83 F.R.D. 382, 395 (D. Mass. 1979) (holding that a blueprint trial would lead to "confusion and uncertainty, which would amount to a denial of a fair trial"); *but see* Union Carbide & Carbon Corp. v. Nisley, 300 F.2d 561, 589 (10th Cir. 1961) (approving antitrust trial plan in which the first jury established the formula for damages recovery for class members).

[923] *See Ex parte* Peterson, 253 U.S. 300 (1920).

[924] *See* Trangsrud, *supra*, at 87–88.

Chapter 15

ENHANCING FACTFINDER COMPREHENSION

In the American adversarial trial, presentation of the evidence proceeds from plaintiff to defendant, followed by the plaintiff's rebuttal. Evidence is presented in the form of exhibits or the testimony of witnesses, who are subject to direct examination, then cross-examination, then (possibly) re-direct and re-cross. Lawyers make an opening statement before presenting evidence and a closing argument after all the evidence has been presented. If a jury is involved, the jury sits passively, asks no questions, and takes no notes. The judge rules on evidentiary issues and instructs the jury, but rarely comments on the evidence or asks a question. Presenting proofs and arguments is the lawyer's job, so comments or questions might unduly influence the jury. In a bench trial, this form is less strictly followed. Briefs often take the place of opening statements and closing arguments. Even in bench trials, however, lawyers have the primary task of presenting proofs and arguments.

In complex cases, this form of trial creates a risk that the factfinder cannot comprehend the information sufficiently to reach a rational decision. The most common problems are the technical difficulty of the information presented, the volume of the evidence and (relatedly) the length of the trial, and the capacity to understand the legalese that is rife in jury instructions.

In response, courts have developed a host of comprehension-aiding techniques. Some are common-sense adaptations to the traditional form of trial. Other techniques make greater changes in the form of trial. It is common for parties and the court to employ more than one technique in a single complex trial. For many of the techniques, empirical or experimental data on their efficacy in increasing comprehension and their potential to affect outcomes is lacking.

A. Amending the Usual Order and Structure of Trial

Federal Rule of Evidence 611(a) allows a court to amend this traditional "mode and order of examining witnesses and presenting evidence." In complex cases, courts have used a number of techniques to make the trial more comprehensible. The *Manual for Complex Litigation* mentions the following alterations:[925]

- *Presenting evidence issue by issue*. Rather than the usual order, in which the plaintiff presents all evidence on all issues, followed by the defendant doing the same, this method requires the parties to present all their evidence on one issue (say, defendant's liability), followed by the defendant's evidence on the same subject. Then the parties move on to the next issue (say, causation) and do the same. There may be separate opening statements before each segment of evidence. This approach is akin to bifurcation, but the factfinder does not stop to determine the facts at the end of each segment. The idea is that, by clustering evidence issue by issue, the factfinder better comprehends each matter. One risk is that the same witnesses may need to return for different parts of the trial. The nature of the evidence may also make this approach impractical.

- *Presenting arguments by issue*. Even if the trial cannot be arranged issue by issue, the court can require the parties to present their closing arguments issue by issue. Adopting this approach can concentrate the factfinder on one issue at a time. Once again, however, evidence does not always lay out so neatly for both parties; if it did, good lawyers would likely adopt this method even without formal encouragement from the court.

- *Using sequential verdicts*. A court can focus the jury's factfinding by requiring that the jury render a verdict on one issue before rendering a verdict on another issue. This focus on a single issue may discourage jurors from getting sloppy in their reasoning and ensure that they work through each issue in a case. It can also lengthen deliberations and make more difficult the jury's ability to give and take on the various issues during deliberations—a prospect that may lead to more hung juries.

- *Making interim statements and arguments*. A judge may allow the lawyers to make interim statements or arguments as a means of reinforcing what the factfinder has just heard or providing a roadmap of what is about to occur. Downsides to this approach are

[925] *See* MANUAL, *supra* note 206, § 12.34.

the possibility that the factfinder will begin to lock into a view of the case before all the evidence is introduced and the lawyers' efforts to use interim statements to bias the jury.

In one fashion or another, all the techniques group the evidence to ensure that a factfinder can sort through massive quantities of information. Although they stop short of a formal division of issues like bifurcation, the techniques share a common impulse with bifurcation. As a result, the concerns that bifurcation presents, including the potential to affect the outcome of the litigation, could also taint these methods. We say "could," because no empirical or experimental studies have explored whether (or how) these methods might skew outcomes in comparison to a traditional or bifurcated trial. Some experimental evidence suggests that the order of the trial matters; for instance, if the evidence on plaintiff's damages is heard before evidence on liability, the plaintiff's damages award is likely to be higher.[926]

B. Using Technology

Seeing is believing. A single diagram, model, or computer animation sometimes can communicate a point more clearly than a week of testimony. Time lines, charts, glossaries, data compilations, and photographic enlargements have been around for a long time. Good advocates use them at trial all the time to convey information in a manner likely to stick with the factfinder. These cognitive aids are especially helpful in complex cases.[927]

Might it also be time to take advantage of technology to create aids that help jurors to comprehend the evidence? The question is not specific to complex civil litigation; it applies as well to criminal cases and routine civil litigation. Because cutting-edge technology is expensive, however, it makes no sense to employ it in small-stakes cases; a lawyer isn't going to spend $50,000 to produce a computer-animated reenactment in a $60,000 car-crash case, even if it dramatically increases the chance of winning. With their high stakes, however, complex cases are prime candidates for expensive illustrative aids.

But technology that enhances comprehension also creates problems. First, slick presentations might mislead rather than inform. Unsurprisingly, experimental studies show that computer-animated reconstructions of an accident influence a jury. If the

---

[926] *See* Horowitz & Bordens, *supra* note 884; *see also* WALTER F. ABBOTT ET AL., JURY RESEARCH (1993) (creating a bibliography of studies regarding the effect of the order of presentation on jury decisions).

[927] *See* MANUAL, *supra* note 206, § 12.3.

reconstruction is accurate, it increases the chances that a jury will render a verdict consistent with the physical evidence (which is good); but if the reconstruction is inaccurate, it increases the chances that a jury will render a verdict that is inconsistent with the physical evidence (which is bad).[928]

Reducing an event to a computer animation is likely to distort reality to some extent, due to the technological limitations of animation as well as to biases or errors from human input into the production process.[929] So how much distortion is too much? Courts have wrestled with this problem principally by applying traditional principles of evidence law. For instance, Federal Rules of Evidence 401, 402, and 403 permit the admission of exhibits only when they are both relevant and a probative value that is not substantially outweighed by the exhibits' unduly prejudicial impact. In addition, any data on which evidence is based must itself be admissible (which means, among other things, that the data must overcome any hearsay objection) or must be the type of data on which a testifying expert relies.[930] If the exhibit is not itself evidence, but merely an aid to illustrate a witness's testimony, the requirements for use are looser, but still demand that the aid be substantially similar to the actual event or fact that the witness testifies to.[931]

A second concern with technology is expense, especially in cases in which one party has more resources than the other. The fear is that parties who can afford visually compelling testimony will prevail because of better financing rather than better arguments. The rules of evidence are geared mostly toward prevention of misleading uses of technology; unequal finances is a matter that the law of evidence has difficulty addressing. Better financed parties have always been able to afford better lawyers, dig up more evidence, and create slicker trial exhibits. In this sense, the lopsided capacity to afford powerful

---

[928] *See* Saul M. Kassin & Meghan A. Dunn, *Computer-Animated Displays and the Jury: Facilitative and Prejudicial Effects*, 21 LAW & HUM. BEHAV. 269 (1997).

[929] *See* Betsy S. Fiedler, Note, *Are Your Eyes Deceiving You?: The Evidentiary Crisis Regarding the Admissibility of Computer Generated Evidence*, 48 N.Y.L. SCH. L. REV. 295, 311–12 (2003–04) (describing the ways in which computer animations can distort reality).

[930] The Federal Rules of Evidence describe the conditions for the admissibility of both expert testimony and hearsay. *See* FED. R. EVID. 701–06, 801–07. A party using technology must also lay a foundation for the data or information that the technology presents and for the reliability of the program that creates the presentation. *Cf.* Bledsoe v. Salt River Valley Water Users' Ass'n, 880 P.2d 689 (Ariz. Ct. App. 1994) (counsel could not use computer animation in closing argument when it had never been used during trial, no foundation had been laid for admissibility, and no opportunity for cross-examination existed). *See generally* Steven Goode, *The Admissibility of Electronic Evidence*, 29 REV. LITIG. 1 (2009) (analyzing admissibility of computer animations and simulations).

[931] *See* Hinkle v. City of Clarksburg, 81 F.3d 416 (4th Cir. 1996).

outcome-influencing technology to saw a factfinder is just new clothing on an old skeleton.

In another sense, however, this issue is different. A third concern is technology's potential to disrupt our very notion of trial. Imagine a world in which trials became public screenings of each party's three-hour, movie-quality blend of witnesses, exhibits, graphics, and animation, all streamed onto Netflix. People could watch the parties' presentations of how the relevant incidents unfolded and afterwards deliberate in chat rooms about the right result. The verdict will be by majority vote. The great lawyers of the day will be Steven Spielberg and J.J. Abrams. Unless we are willing to embrace this brave new world, we might be leery about the extensive use of expensive technology, especially when one side cannot afford to match the other side's ability to peddle its story.[932]

A final roadblock to the use of technology is courtroom capability; fancy technology won't work if the courtroom is a double-wide trailer.[933] Courtrooms are being built or retrofitted to facilitate the use of the technology that may, in some distant day, make the trial of complex cases a more comprehensible affair.

For the time being, technology is a two-edged sword, with great potential to aid comprehension and great potential to hinder it.

C. Aiding the Jury

Although judges are limited in their ability to comprehend the evidence presented in complex cases, lay juries raise particular concerns. In a number of ways, however, the traditional form of trial can be tweaked to make the jury's job of comprehending and rationally deliberating on complex evidence an easier one.

1. Questions by Judge and Jury

The model of adversarial trial presumes that the jury remains passive and that the judge intervenes only to make evidentiary rulings. The real world is a tad messier. Judges have long had the

---

[932] For a critique of such a prospect, see Richard L. Marcus, *E-Discovery and Beyond: Toward* Brave New World *or* 1984?, 236 F.R.D. 598 (2006) (stating that "[t]he face-to-face interaction of jurors in reaching such human decisions seems an important aspect of the decisionmaking process"). *See also* Van Houten-Maynard v. ANR Pipeline Co., No. 89 C 0377, 1995 WL 317056 (N.D. Ill. May 23, 1995), at *12 (excluding a computer animation in part because of undue prejudice under Federal Rule of Evidence 403; noting that "we believe that computer animation evidence, by reasons of its being in a format that represents the latest rage and wrinkle in video communications and entertainment, may well have an undue detrimental effect on other more reliable and trustworthy direct-type evidence.").

[933] This is not said entirely tongue in cheek. One of the authors is aware of a rural county courthouse that, even in 2017, matches this description.

power to ask questions of witnesses.[934] Jurors have also been permitted to ask a question of a witness on rare occasions, but only with strong judicial oversight of the process.

One way to increase comprehension is to allow jurors a freer hand in asking questions. Proponents of more juror questioning point out that such questions can clear up juror confusion of which the lawyers and judge may be unaware. It can also give the lawyers some insight into the jury's thought process, so that they can tailor the information at trial to the jury's concerns.

There are also risks to juror questioning. It can slow down the trial, and may turn jurors into advocates for certain positions rather than neutral factfinders. They can ask irrelevant questions, or raise issues that both parties prefer to stay away from. Logistical issues can be tricky: jurors probably shouldn't be allowed to blurt out questions, so the questions might need to be written down and vetted with the lawyers, who then need to calculate whether to object (and risk alienating the jurors) or let the questions stand.[935]

The empirical evidence on the effectiveness of jury questioning suggests that the process is no panacea for the ills of jury confusion, but does no harm either.[936] Juror questioning does not slow down the trial, but it also does not uncover vital issues left out by the lawyers' questions. It does not upset lawyers' strategies, turn jurors into advocates, or prove a logistical nightmare; and it helps to clarify specific points or issues in jurors' minds. At the same time, it does not increase juror satisfaction with the process.

The *Manual for Complex Litigation* cautiously favors the use of juror questioning, but its support is tepid at best.[937] Some states permit juror questioning by statute or rule.

---

934 *See* FED. R. EVID. 614(b) ("The court may examine a witness regardless of who calls the witness.").

935 *Cf.* DeBenedetto v. Goodyear Tire & Rubber Co., 754 F.2d 512 (4th Cir. 1985) (affirming decision to permit juror questioning but explaining in detail why "juror questioning is a course fraught with peril"); United States v. Johnson, 892 F.2d 707 (8th Cir. 1989) (en banc) (Lay, C.J., concurring) ("When the jury becomes an advocate or inquisitor in the process, it forsakes its role of arbiter between the government and its citizens.").

936 *See* Shari Seidman Diamond et al., *Juror Questions During Trial: A Window into Juror Thinking*, 59 VAND. L. REV. 1927 (2006); Larry Heuer & Steven Penrod, *Increasing Jurors' Participation in Trials: A Field Experiment with Jury Notetaking and Question Asking*, 12 LAW & HUM. BEHAV. 231 (1988); Nicole Mott, *The Current Debate on Juror Questions: "To Ask or Not to Ask, That is the Question,"* 78 CHI.-KENT L. REV. 1099 (2003).

937 *See* MANUAL, *supra* note 206, § 12.423. Cases reflect the same attitude. *Compare, e.g.*, United States v. Cassiere, 4 F.3d 1006 (1st Cir. 1993) (allowing questions but warning that "the practice should be reserved for exceptional situations, and should not become the routine, even in complex cases"), *with* SEC v. Koenig, 557

2. Commentary on the Evidence

A judge's commentary on the evidence can also guide a jury's comprehension. In Britain, judges have a long tradition of commenting on the evidence to the jury, although in the United States the practice has been generally frowned on as an impingement on the jury's role.[938] Judicial commentary requires a judge to have a good grasp of the evidence, and is typically most effective at the end of the case rather than as a running commentary as evidence is admitted. Judges must also guard against becoming an advocate for one side—or of creating that perception in the jury's mind.

Empirical evidence suggests that juries often decide cases in line with the judge's commentary.[939] An experimental study found that judicial commentary on and summaries of the evidence were unhelpful, and that "judges' efforts were least helpful when the evidence was particularly complex."[940]

Despite an occasional suggestion in the literature, there is little momentum to permit jurors to comment on the evidence. Permitting juror commentary could give the lawyers a window into jurors' thought process, and help the lawyers to clear up misconceptions before they affect jury deliberation. Under the traditional view of trial, jurors are never to comment on evidence until their begin deliberations. This prohibition protects the factfinding process from external influence and premature judgment. Juror commentary during trial would buck this tradition.[941]

3. Jury Notetaking

One aid to comprehension that has swept the nation's courtrooms, in cases both routine and complex, is to permit jurors to take notes. The traditional view was that notetaking might distract jurors and lead them to miss important testimony; moreover, jurors' notes, which could be inaccurate, might assume an outsized

---

F.3d 736 (7th Cir. 2009) ("Now that several studies have concluded that the benefits exceed the costs, there is no reason to disfavor the practice.").

938 *Cf.* Quercia v. United States, 289 U.S. 466 (1933) (reversing a conviction when a trial judge commented that a witness's demeanor meant that nearly everything the witness said "was a lie" because the judge "may analyze and dissect the evidence, but he may not either distort or add to it").

939 *See* HARRY KALVEN, JR. & HANS ZEISEL, THE AMERICAN JURY 417–27 (1966) (noting that judges' disagreement with jury verdicts in cases without judicial commentary ranged from 4% to 26%, but that disagreement was less than 1% in cases with judicial commentary, an indication that "the jury's revolt [against the law] is never enough to carry the jury beyond both the evidence and the judge").

940 *See* Heuer & Penrod, *supra* note 870, at 50.

941 *See* Paula Hannaford et al., *Permitting Jury Discussions During Trial: Impact of the Arizona Reform*, 24 LAW & HUM. BEHAV. 359 (2000) (describing a state-court adoption of a process that allowed juries to discuss the evidence on an interim basis).

importance in jury deliberations. Notetaking might also begin to fix certain views in jurors' minds in advance of deliberations. Rather, the traditional view held, jurors' memory of the testimony and exhibits should control.

In a world of near-universal literacy and weeks-long trials, however, notetaking makes sense. Jurors' memories can be faulty, and notetaking can help people to focus on complicated testimony. Think about how well prepared you would feel for the final exam in a law-school class if your professor barred you from taking even one note during the three months of class.

The empirical evidence on jury notetaking is weakly positive: few of the potential problems with notetaking have materialized, but benefits are on the modest side as well. One study of complex federal cases reported that jurors who took notes counterintuitively felt less well informed and had a harder time reaching a verdict.[942] A study of a simulated complex tort case found that jurors who took notes were better able to discern strong from weak cases and awarded more appropriate levels of compensation.[943]

The *Manual for Complex Litigation* supports the use of juror notetaking, albeit with certain controls.[944] Some states permit juror notetaking by statute.

4. Better Jury Instructions

One fact on which nearly all researchers agree is that jurors have a hard time understanding jury instructions.[945] Long and technical oral instructions, usually sprinkled with a fair amount of legalese, are bad enough, but then jurors are expected to recall the instructions perfectly when they retire to deliberate. And deliberation often does not clear up the jurors' confusion; a persuasive jury member can sometimes swing other jurors who held a correct view of the instructions around to an incorrect view.

To aid jury recall of instructions, some judges have overridden the traditional taboo against providing written instructions to

---

942 *See* Heuer & Penrod, *supra* note 870.

943 *See* Irwin A. Horowitz and Lynne Forsterlee, *The Effects of Notetaking and Trial Transcript Access on Mock Jury Decisions in a Complex Trial*, 25 LAW & HUM. BEHAV. 373 (2001) (finding that notetaking was more efficacious than providing access to the trial transcript as a means of enhancing mock jurors' comprehension).

944 *See* MANUAL, *supra* note 206, § 12.421. Some federal cases are more cautious about endorsing the procedure. *See* United States v. Darden, 70 F.3d 1507, 1536 (8th Cir. 1995) (holding that the trial judge properly let jury take notes on exhibits, but not on testimony; further stating that notetaking is "not a favored procedure").

945 For a good discussion of the literature, see Nancy S. Marder, *Bringing Jury Instructions into the Twenty-First Century*, 81 NOTRE DAME L. REV. 449 (2006).

jurors.[946] One study suggested that access to instructions during deliberations did not appear to help juries, but also did no harm.[947]

On the larger problem of crafting comprehensible instructions, there has been less movement. Unsurprisingly, research shoes that clearer instructions lead to better jury performance. But judges are reluctant to alter standard or pattern jury instructions, even when the instructions are opaque. If a judge's tailored instructions misstate the law on any matter, an appealable issue, carrying the risk of the retrial of a massive case, emerges. Reversal is not fanciful. One study of criminal jury instructions found that clearer instructions resulted in more convictions, suggesting that changes to jury instructions can be an outcome-influencing event.[948]

Although there is broad academic and practical support for more comprehensible instructions, the difficult work of crafting clearer instructions has not yet been undertaken.

5. Changing the Deliberation Process

The usual description of jury deliberations is that it is a "black box." The trial feeds evidence to the jury; the counsel's statements and arguments and the judge's instructions put a structure on that evidence. But when the jury retires to deliberate, we have no idea what juries do with all this information. No one is allowed inside the jury room. Perhaps juries flip a coin and then spend the rest of their time arguing about who will win the big game on Sunday. All we know is that they emerge to declare the winner and, if the plaintiff wins, what the amount of compensation is. In legal parlance, they deliver a *general verdict*.

Judges possess some tools to try to focus the jury on each issue in the case. These tools can provide some assurance that juries are evaluating the evidence in light of relevant legal principles. For instance, a judge can permit a jury to return a general verdict, but also ask the jury to answer written questions about one or more of the issues of fact that the jury must resolve.[949] The judge can then

---

946 *See* United States v. Quilty, 541 F.2d 172 (7th Cir. 1976) (holding that the decision to use written instructions rests in the trial judge's sound discretion); *see also* MANUAL, *supra* note 206, § 12.434 ("Most judges give jurors copies of the instructions to use during deliberations."). Other judges have allowed jurors to take notes on the instructions or to deliver the instructions in a more interactive, informative way.

947 *See* Larry Heuer & Steven D. Penrod, *Instructing Jurors: A Field Experiment with Written and Preliminary Instructions*, 13 LAW & HUM. BEHAV. 409 (1989).

948 *See* Jane Goodman & Edith Greene, *The Use of Paraphrase Analysis in the Simplification of Jury Instructions*, 4 J. SOC. BEHAV. & PERSONALITY 237 (1989) (suggesting that clarification of jury instructions may raise conviction rates); *see also* Stephen A. Saltzburg, *Improving the Quality of Jury Decisionmaking*, *in* VERDICT 341 (Robert E. Litan ed. 1993) (describing objections to simplified instructions).

949 FED. R. CIV. P. 49(b).

compare the verdict with the answers to make sure that the jury's verdict is justified.[950] In a similar strategy, a judge can order the jury to return a *special verdict*, in which the jury renders its findings on the factual issues in the case; the judge then enters judgment in accordance with the jury's findings.[951]

Both devices are an attempt to structure the jury's factfinding process. There is little empirical evidence about their effectiveness,[952] and there are both benefits and drawbacks to their use.[953] The *Manual for Complex Litigation* endorses the use of special verdicts or general verdicts with answers to written questions,[954] but they remain little used in complex trials.

D. Court-Appointed Experts and Masters

Nearly all complex cases involve scientific and technical issues that lie beyond the knowledge of lay factfinders. The usual approach to redress this knowledge gap is to allow each side to call expert witnesses to render opinions that assist the factfinder. In an adversarial system, some built-in incentives can lead to abuse of the expert-witness system. One side might have a reason to cloud the scientific or technical issues rather than to clarify them, and to use flim-flam experts to peddle junk science. Relatedly, some "hired gun" experts will arrive at whatever opinion the holder of the checkbook desires. Furthermore, a wealthy party might be able to buy up the best experts in the field.

These problems arise in all cases, but the risks are magnified in complex litigation, in which the stakes are high and the jury's capacity to comprehend difficult material is already weak. If the judge can ensure experts present clear, trustworthy testimony, a huge roadblock to rational factfinding will be cleared.

One avenue has been to restrict the parties' use of experts whose opinions lack reliability. Since the Supreme Court's decision in *Daubert v. Merrell Dow Pharmaceuticals, Inc.*,[955] courts have been more vigilant about screening experts to ensure that they employ

---

950 If the answers and verdict disagree, the judge has a range of options: enter judgment in accordance with the answers, direct the jury to deliberate further, or order a new trial. FED. R. CIV. P. 49(b)(3).

951 FED. R. CIV. P. 49(a).

952 *See* Heuer & Penrod, *supra* note (reporting on a field experiment in which special verdicts were found most useful in complex cases with large quantities of information).

953 For a balanced portrayal of all three devices, including their benefits and drawbacks, see Jonathan D. Casper, *Restructuring the Traditional Civil Jury: The Effects of Changes in Composition and Procedures*, *in* VERDICT, *supra* note 948, at 414.

954 *See* MANUAL, *supra* note 206, § 12.451.

955 509 U.S. 579 (1993).

sufficient data and that their methods and conclusions enjoy support in the relevant scientific or technical community.

A less utilized approach is for the court to appoint an expert or special master. Judges have the power to appoint an expert under Federal Rule of Evidence 706 or refer a matter to a trial master under Federal Rule of Civil Procedure 53(a). A court may appoint an expert by showing "cause." This loose standard conceals the real reasons that judges typically appoint an expert. One is the failure of a party to shape an issue properly for the jury's resolution. Another is the judge's belief that a "neutral" expert will aid the jury in its decision-making process. When appropriate, a judge may appoint a panel of experts rather than a single individual.[956] Unless the parties consent, masters may not perform trial tasks in jury-tried cases. In bench trials, references are possible only in "exceptional circumstances" or when a difficult computation of damages is involved.[957]

As you might expect, appointing an expert or master can have an outcome-determining influence on a case. One study showed that the court-appointed expert "dominated the proceedings" and that "the final outcome on the disputed issue was almost always consistent with the testimony of the appointed expert."[958] The study showed that judges appointed experts with greater frequency than had been thought, but that such appointments remain fairly rare.[959]

E. Conclusion

If you were underwhelmed by the techniques available to aid jury comprehension, you have reason to be. If excellent techniques existed, we would worry less about limiting information at trial or controlling discovery during pretrial. One of the overarching themes of the techniques described in this Chapter is the way in which they change the fundamental structure of adversarial trial. Another theme is whether juries will rationally address the scientific or technical issues so common in complex litigation. If the techniques do not enhance jury comprehension, the argument for abandoning

---

[956] *See* Gates v. United States, 707 F.2d 1141 (10th Cir. 1983).

[957] FED. R. CIV. P. 53(a)(1)(B).

[958] *See* Joe S. Cecil & Thomas Willging, *Accepting* Daubert*'s Invitation: Defining a Role for Court-Appointed Experts in Assessing Scientific Validity*, 43 EMORY L.J. 995 (1994).

[959] *Compare In re* Joint E. & S. Dists. Asbestos Litig., 830 F. Supp. 686 (E.& S.D.N.Y. 1993) (noting that appointment "is not commonplace," but that the "work of such experts is especially critical in dealing with complex mass tort problems such as" complex and interdependent scientific issues, thousands of parties, equitable treatment, and strong and conflicting interests in character of relevant data), *with* Kian v. Mirro Aluminum Co., 88 F.R.D. 351 (E.D. Mich. 1980) (rejecting the use of "a court-sponsored witness, who would most certainly create a strong, if not overwhelming, impression of 'impartiality' and 'objectivity,' could potentially transform a trial by jury into a trial by witness").

juries in complex cases, which we explored in Chapter Thirteen, strengthens.[960] If we cannot strike juries or do much to aid their comprehension, the argument for alternatives to trial—such as arbitration before an expert adjudicator or resolution in an administrative agency—also strengthens. Conversely, the argument for aggregating mass disputes weakens.

As we leave the material on the trial phase of a complex dispute, you should reflect back on the aggregation and pretrial phases of a complex dispute. If no realistic methods exist to ensure that a trial in a complex case will produce a rational, acceptable judgment, then we must rethink our commitment to adversarial adjudication to resolve such disputes, mustn't we? A procedural system's trial method can dictate logically antecedent choices, like the party structure of a lawsuit and the structure of the pretrial process. And those structures determine whether and to what extent various substantive rights can be enforced, even when the case is not tried. This Chapter starkly raises one of the hardest questions in complex litigation: to what extent are we willing to make compromises with our procedural traditions to keep alive our aspirations of jury trial and rational dispute resolution?

---

[960] *See supra* Chapter 13.B.1.a.

Part 4
THE REMEDIAL PHASE

In the study of complex litigation, the issue of remedies often receives short shrift. Structuring a case is intellectually challenging, crafting pretrial strategies is creative and intense, and trial is exciting. Remedies, on the other hand, seem mundane. In the real world, nothing is further from the truth. A wonderfully executed campaign of aggregation, pretrial, and trial means nothing if the remedy that the lawyer seeks is impossible or excessively costly to obtain. Lawyers must keep their eyes firmly on the prize.

Many cases that are complex in the aggregation, pretrial, or trial phases of a case are also complex in the remedial phase. But not always. Some cases that are difficult to aggregate or to push through pretrial and trial present no significant issues of remedies. Conversely, cases that present few challenges in the aggregation, pretrial, or trial phases generate enormous difficulties at the remedial stage. An excellent example is *Brown v. Board of Education*, in which the liability phase essentially ended in three years but the remedial phase carried on for nearly forty more.[961]

At first blush, remedial complexity seems to have little to do with the other forms of complexity. Few rules concerning remedies are found in the Federal Rules of Civil Procedure. The issue of the quantum of the remedy is separate from the issue of the procedures that should be used to arrive at a remedy. Put differently, the fields of remedies and civil procedure are distinct.

Real cases, however, care little about the niceties of academic pigeonholing. As we shall see, many of the same themes that we have considered throughout this book find new voice in the field of remedies. The principal issues are two: declaring an appropriate remedy after a trial or at the settlement, and implementing the remedy that is declared. Chapter Sixteen explores the first issue, and Chapter Seventeen explores the second. Once each chapter lays out the central problems of declaration or implementation, it then examines whether judicial adjuncts can aid in the resolution of the problems.

---

[961] 347 U.S. 483 (1954) (liability decision); 349 U.S. 294 (1955) (remedial decision). Linda Brown Smith, who had been the lead plaintiff in *Brown v. Board of Education* as a schoolgirl, returned to court in 1979 on behalf of her own children, claiming that Topeka's school system retained vestiges of illegal discrimination—an allegation that was upheld after years of additional litigation. *See* Brown v. Board of Educ., 978 F.2d 585 (10th Cir. 1992).

Finally, Chapter Eighteen takes a short look at an important question that, at a practical level, often drives complex litigation and influences the behavior of lawyers: attorney's fees. Although attorney's fees are not strictly a remedial question, a court often awards the fees for plaintiff's lawyers during, and as part of, the remedial phase.

Chapter 16

DETERMINING A REMEDY AFTER JUDGMENT OR AT SETTLEMENT

The fundamental question of remedial law is what "a court . . . will do—simultaneously—*for* the victim, *through* the wrongdoer."[962] In American remedial law, the "rightful position" principle is the traditional answer to this question.[963] This principle holds that a wrongdoer must restore the victim to the position that the victim would have enjoyed if no wrong had occurred, or maintain the victim in the present position if no harm from the wrong has yet occurred. In some cases, when the wrong and its harmful effects have been irreversibly suffered, the only way to give this principle effect is to award the plaintiff an amount of money that compensates the victim for the harm. In other cases, when the wrong has not yet occurred or some of the effects of the wrong might yet be avoided, an injunction (or sometimes a declaration) might be an appropriate remedy. "Might be" is the appropriate tense; for a number of reasons, a court can decline to issue an equitable remedy (the injunction) and leave the plaintiff to an after-the-injury legal remedy (damages).

When a case comes to trial, the factfinder typically declares the remedy. Because the judge finds the facts in equitable proceedings, a judge determines the scope of the injunction. Because juries find the facts in legal proceedings, the jury determines the amount of damages (subject to judicial controls such as the grant of a new trial for grossly excessive or inadequate awards).

In some complex cases, declaring the proper remedy at trial poses difficulties for the relevant factfinder. The first section of this Chapter examines this issue.

But most cases, including most complex cases, settle before trial. Because the parties agree on the terms, you might think that determining the remedy in a complex settlement poses no problems. Sometimes, however, determining a proper remedy at settlement is no easier for the parties than it is for a factfinder. Moreover, in some

---

[962] Doug Rendleman, *Remedies—The Law School Course*, 39 BRANDEIS L.J. 532 (2001).

[963] This is Professor Douglas Laycock's term. An older phrase is the "original position" principle. Principles other than the rightful position can sometimes apply. For instance, in some circumstances a remedy can be calculated in terms of the defendant's gain rather than the plaintiff's loss—in other words, a restitutionary remedy. Likewise, in some cases the law permits punitive damages as punishment for intentional wrongdoing or wrongdoing that was deliberate indifference to the rights of victims.

cases, a court must approve the settlement before it takes effect; thus, the difficulty of determining whether a remedy is proper falls on the judge. In other cases, a few parties who refuse to consent to the settlement threaten to hold up the deal for all. The second section of this Chapter explores these issues.

In some instances, a judge may be able to call on special masters or other judicial adjuncts to aid the process of determining remedies. The final section of this Chapter examines this power, which once again raises concerns about the use of ad hoc judicial officers to perform important adjudicatory tasks.

A. Remedies in a Judgment

Determining the proper remedy in the injunctive context raises issues that are distinct from those raised in the damages context. Hence, we treat the remedial issues regarding injunctions and damages separately. Before we explore these issues, however, a word on the division between common law and equity.

As a general matter, the common law provided monetary compensation for past harms. Equity generally issued orders to prevent harm or to prevent the future consequences of a past harm. That distinction in remedy, which developed over time, was never absolute; sometimes law gave remedies that looked like injunctions, and sometimes equity ordered the payment of money. Nonetheless, the division between law and equity, with its division in available remedies, became one of the hallmarks of the unique system of English justice. The long historical struggle between law and equity resulted in the development of certain principles that preserved the independence of the common law against the encroachments of the Chancellor. The principles can be hardened into a pair of adages: equity will not provide a remedy when there is an "adequate remedy at law," and equity steps in only when the injury is "irreparable" (i.e., cannot be repaired by an action at law).

The inadequacy of a legal remedy and the irreparability of injury are two ways of saying the same thing. Because the line between which injuries were irreparable and which were not was always moving over time, the precise boundary between common law and equity was more a historical matter than a logical one.

Carried into modern times, the "irreparable injury" rule means that, in some cases, a court will not provide an equitable remedy even when an injunction best achieves the rightful position. For instance, due to the burdens on a court in shaping and policing an injunction, the court may decide that it is better to let the harm occur and compensate with damages. The reasons that a plaintiff must accept a second-best damages remedy vary.[964]

The basic point is that certain principles constrain a court's choice of remedy. We do not further examine these reasons here, but instead proceed on the assumption that a court has determined that either injunctive relief or a damages remedy is appropriate.

1. Injunctive Relief

With the rightful position as the guiding principle, the process of declaring an injunctive remedy appears to be simple: determine the position that the victim would occupy but for the threatened unlawful conduct and award either a *preventive injunction* that maintains the victim in that position (if no harm has yet occurred as a result of the conduct) or a *reparative injunction* that restores the victim to that position by preventing further harm (if the harm has already begun to cause harm). The injunction commands the defendant to engage no longer in the unlawful practice—an easy order to make!

In the real world, things are never so easy. Injunctions that repeat existing legal standards or order a defendant to "obey the law" are rarely useful; an injunction must specify the precise conduct that a defendant must perform or refrain from performing. In other words, an injunction must particularize the law's general commands to the unique circumstances of the parties. The challenge of tailoring an injunction to the wrong increases substantially when an injunction requires a governmental or private institution to conform its behavior to legal requirements that it has violated over long periods of time. And the challenge is further compounded when the defendant's unlawful conduct has already occurred: a reparative injunction can, at best, prevent the additional harmful effects of an accomplished wrong.

Take, for example, the school-desegregation cases that followed in the wake of *Brown v. Board of Education*. You might think that a simple injunction—"Admit all African-American children to school on a non-discriminatory basis"—would do the job. But many school systems had for years maintained two separate sets of schools, one for white children and one for black children, and the schools were not equal. School teachers were also often segregated by race. And segregated schools often generated segregated living patterns. As a judge, would you re-draw the boundaries for attendance at each school, and what would you do if boundaries (reflecting segregated

---

[964] For examination of the circumstances when an injunctive remedy is inferior, and of the circumstances when a court will decline to award the injunctive remedy even though it is superior, see DOUGLAS LAYCOCK, MODERN AMERICAN REMEDIES ch. 5 (4th ed. 2010).

living patterns) still resulted in essentially segregated schools? What would you do about unequal facilities? What would you do about white and black school teachers—especially white teachers who disliked teaching black children and treated them badly? What would you do if white families fled into suburban enclaves, leaving the school system almost entirely filled with black children and frustrating your ability to achieve integration? Would you order the families to move back to their old neighborhoods? If so, how do you distinguish between families who moved out of racial animus from those who moved to be closer to job opportunities? What do you do about the disparities in wealth and opportunity that fifty or more years of inferior education had created? In short, is it really possible to undo the harms from segregation by means of an injunction?

These questions are the tip of an iceberg. Precisely tailoring the remedy to the wrong is often challenging, and sometimes impossible, in "institutional reform" or "structural injunction" cases. Crafting an injunction becomes even more difficult when different groups of litigants in an aggregated proceeding stand in different positions with regard to the wrongdoer. The remedy that makes sense for a senior in high school might be very different from the remedy that makes sense for a kindergartner, even though both have been exposed to the same unlawful segregation.

It would be understandable if judges threw up their hands and ordered the school system just to do a bunch of good stuff to make the education better for all children. This "do good" approach to declaring an injunctive remedy is an alternative to the rightful position. Over the years, some cases have abandoned the rightful position in favor of an injunctive remedy designed to further the policies of the law that the defendant violated.[965]

At stake in the seemingly academic debate between the rightful-position and do-good approaches is a vision about the nature of the judiciary. Is it intended only to remedy precisely the wrongs brought before it? Or is it a policy-making institution empowered to fashion a better world once wrongdoing occurs? In choosing between these visions, separation-of-powers questions loom large. When a federal judge seeks to hold a state institution accountable, so do concerns for federalism. Also added into the mix are issues for judicial competence. Judges are lawyers, typically without degrees in finance or educational policy. They may lack the talent and know-how to reform complex corporate or government entities.

---

[965] *See, e.g.*, Bailey v. Proctor, 160 FF.2d 78 (1st Cir. 1947) (ordering the dissolution of an investment trust whose corporate structure was subsequently made illegal but which continued to exist under a grandfather clause at the time that it engaged in unlawful activities).

Perhaps the most famous case straddling the line between the rightful-position and do-good approaches is *Swann v. Charlotte-Mecklenburg Board of Education*,[966] in which the Supreme Court upheld the district court's decision to bus school children to achieve greater racial balance in the school district. *Swann* contains language tipping its hat toward the rightful position, stating that "[a]s with any equity case, the nature of the violation determines the scope of the remedy." At the same time, *Swann* states that "the scope of a district court's equitable powers to remedy past wrongs is broad, for breadth and flexibility are inherent in equitable remedies" and that "[t]he remedy for such segregation may be administratively awkward, inconvenient, and even bizarre in some situations."[967]

In subsequent cases, the Supreme Court sided decisively with the rightful-position principle as the basis for remedying constitutional violations.[968] It has even indicated that courts might not be able to go as far as the rightful position due to separation-of-powers and federalism concerns.[969]

A rightful-position injunction is even more difficult to craft when third parties must cooperate to achieve meaningful injunctive relief. In the Detroit school-desegregation litigation, white flight into surrounding suburbs had emptied the Detroit school system of nearly all white school children. To make a desegregation remedy meaningful, the district court approved a plan that encompassed the suburban school districts. In a closely divided opinion, the Supreme Court held that, because the suburban school districts had not violated the Constitution through unlawful segregation, they could not be included in the remedial plan.[970]

That holding left the district judge with the near-impossible task of crafting an order that created any effective remedy for the Detroit children who were the victims of unlawful segregation. The district

---

966 402 U.S. 1 (1971).

967 Other cases express similar sentiments about the breadth of equitable power. *See, e.g.*, Brown v. Plata, 563 U.S. 493 (2011); Hutto v. Finney, 437 U.S. 678 (1978).

968 *See, e.g.*, Milliken v. Bradley, 418 U.S. 717 (1974) ("[T]he remedy is necessarily designed, as all remedies are, to restore the victims of discriminatory conduct to the position they would have occupied in the absence of such conduct."); Dayton Bd. of Educ. v. Brinkman, 433 U.S. 406 (1977) (holding that a desegregation order should correct only the "incremental segregative effect" of illegal discrimination).

969 *See* Milliken v. Bradley, 433 U.S. 267 (1977) (stating that, in addition to the requirements of the rightful position, "the federal courts in devising a remedy must take into account the interests of state and local authorities in managing their own affairs, consistent with the Constitution"); *accord* Missouri v. Jenkins, 515 U.S. 70 (1995).

970 *See Milliken*, 418 U.S. at 745 ("[W]ithout an interdistrict violation and interdistrict effect, there is no constitutional wrong calling for an interdistrict remedy.").

court essentially threw in the towel, but the court of appeals reversed.[971] It recognized the "extremely difficult (if not impossible) assignment . . . of formulating a decree which would eliminate the unconstitutional segregation found to exist in the Detroit public schools, without transgressing the limits established by the Supreme Court." But it ordered the judge to keep trying.

Faced with such constraints, some courts have worked with school districts to create magnet programs or other educational enhancements designed to lure children from private or suburban public schools. When measured against the rightful position, however, these approaches sometimes cross a bridge too far. Had there been no unlawful segregation, school districts would almost certainly not have created these enhancements, so tying these programs to the wrong of racial segregation is difficult. While courts enjoy some flexibility in creating enhancements as a means of trying to achieve racial balance, that flexibility is not infinite.[972]

Further complicating the remedial picture is the modification of structural-reform injunctions. Again using school desegregation as an example, the ongoing incremental effects of past segregation eventually wane. Must a school district be required to bus or keep open magnet schools for the next century? Federal Rule of Civil Procedure 60(b) describes six general conditions under which a judgment can be modified. The circumstance typically applicable to modifications of permanent injunctions is Rule 60(b)(5), which permits relief from a final judgment when, among other things, "applying it prospectively is no longer equitable." This open-textured provision had traditionally been read to emphasize the finality of the judgment and permit modification of an injunction only on proof of "grievous wrong."[973] But the Supreme Court more recently has injected flexibility in the standard, allowing modifications when "a significant change in facts or law warrants revision of the decree and . . . the proposed modification is suitably tailored to the changed circumstance."[974]

This subsection has focused on the remedial problems in school-desegregation cases to give you a sense of the difficulties in declaring an injunctive remedy. Comparable problems exist in other institutional-reform cases that require the restructuring of a major

---

971 *See* Bradley v. Milliken, 540 F.2d 229 (6th Cir. 1976), *aff'd*, 433 U.S. 267 (1977).

972 *See Jenkins*, 515 U.S. 70 (rejecting an effort to provide a school system with state-of-the-art facilities and programs that were not tied to erasing the incremental segregative effect that the system's unlawful practices had created).

973 *See* United States v. Swift & Co., 286 U.S. 106 (1932).

974 *See* Rufo v. Inmates of the Suffolk Cty. Jail, 502 U.S. 367 (1992); *accord* Horne v. Flores, 557 U.S. 433 (2009).

corporation or government entity with long-settled practices. Think, for instance, of a company with a corporate culture that countenances sexual harassment and discrimination. Changing the company's practices is likely to encounter deep-seated hostility and resistance from stakeholders who benefit from the existing system.

In a sense, moving an institution toward compliance is a problem of implementing the remedy, which the next chapter discusses. But many judges are skilled political actors who do not want to be seen as ineffective. They might tailor a remedy to what is achievable rather than to what the law demands, thus limiting the scope of the remedy to something less than the rightful position.[975] In other words, problems in implementing a remedy can feed back to affect the scope of the remedy.

Accommodating the various concerns while remaining faithful to the rightful-position principle can put a judge between a rock and a hard place. In one of the most famous articles ever written, Abram Chayes argued that in "public law litigation"—a phrase he coined—the rightful position's close association of right with remedy, as well as the rightful position's worldview of litigation as a private dispute-resolution process, had collapsed in favor of a new paradigm.[976] Among the types of cases that Professor Chayes mentioned as emblematic of this "public law" paradigm were institutional reform cases concerning desegregation, prison conditions, and antitrust violations. In the new paradigm, the violation of a right did not necessarily determine the scope of the remedy. The remedy was often the subject of negotiation, rather than an *a priori* outgrowth of the violation. In defining the remedy, the judge played a large role that was antithetical to traditional adversarial theory.

Professor Chayes had a point. In some instances, the inadequacy of the rightful-position principle to redress large-scale wrongs is patent. As Chayes documented, courts were not reluctant to abandon the principle to achieve a fair and appropriate outcome. Although Chayes did not use the phrase, he was documenting a judicial shift toward a do-good approach in complex litigation.

But Chayes wrote forty years ago, when courts were more willing to jettison the rightful-position principle to craft a fair, if not perfectly tailored, response to wrongdoing. There is much to be said for this "public law litigation" approach. We have seen similar judicial responses to complexity in its other forms: judges casting aside traditional limits on judicial power to ensure that adjudication's basic functions (declaring the law, finding the facts,

---

[975] For the classic expression of this concern, see Owen M. Fiss, *Foreword: The Forms of Justice*, 93 HARV. L. REV. 1 (1978).

[976] *See* Chayes, *supra* note 3.

and determining the remedy) are carried out effectively in large-scale litigation.

As we have seen, however, traditional principles sometimes prove too strong for a judge in a complex case to overcome. The re-emergence of the rightful-position principle as the dominant approach to providing injunctive relief is yet another example. Today judges must typically obey the rightful-position principle. Foreclosing the do-good avenue hobbles judges in the important adjudicatory function of providing an injunctive remedy that both redresses the wrong and provides relief to the victims.

Limits on injunctive relief are not the end of the story. Even when equity could not or would not provide a remedy, a party could go to law and obtain damages. Determining the right amount of money to compensate for a widespread wrong, however, carries its own difficulties.

2. Monetary Relief

Imagine that a judge determines that injunctive relief for the school children of Detroit is impossible. Could the judge instead award each child an amount of money to compensate for an education in a segregated environment? You can immediately see the difficulties involved. With the rightful position as guide, the judge must determine the exact amount of harm that a segregated environment caused each child. How can a judge know which child would have been a venture capitalist and which a construction worker, and how can the judge tie loss in opportunity to the fact that the school was segregated?

In some cases, determining the right monetary remedy is no easier than determining the right injunctive relief. First, valuing losses can be difficult. Part of the problem is assigning a value to certain types of injury. For instance, if a child is educated in an illegally segregated school, what is the value of the violated constitutional right?[977] Even when an objective measure of damages is available, a large number of victims with variable awards makes the determination of each award difficult—especially when the amounts of the individual awards are small enough that the cost of determining the award wipes out its value. Second, a jury may have difficulty keeping different victims distinct. It is also difficult to expect that jurors will give up years of their lives to hear the evidence

---

[977] The Supreme Court has tended to solve this issue by awarding nominal damages for violations of constitutional rights unless the violation caused an "actual injury." In cases of actual injury, traditional tort damages such as lost wages or earning capacity, medical expenses, pain, suffering, and mental anguish are available. *See* Carey v. Piphus, 435 U.S. 247 (1978).

of individualized damages for thousands of plaintiffs. Third, victims may be unknowable, at least through reasonable means.

These problems can overlap in a single case. For instance, in *Democratic Central Committee of the District of Columbia v. Washington Metropolitan Area Transit Commission*,[978] the transit authority overcharged bus riders in the 1960s. When the case settled two decades later, the amount of the overcharge was easy to calculate. But determining who had ridden on buses, how many trips they had taken, and how to deliver a remedy of a few pennies for infrequent riders without the cost of the remedy eating up the award were enormous roadblocks.

A similar problem of victim identification can arise in employment-discrimination cases. Take *Dougherty v. Barry*.[979] The local fire department engaged in racial discrimination in promoting two African-American firefighters. Eight white firefighters sued. Five of the eight were ultimately deemed to have valid claims. It was impossible to know which two would have been promoted had no discrimination occurred. The amount of the wrong was easy to calculate: it was the difference between the wages and benefits that the two deserving firefighters would have made after the promotion and the wages and benefits they earned in their present jobs. But which two firefighters deserved the money? The universe of possible victims was well defined, but the actual victims were unknowable.

These problems derive from the demands of the rightful-position principle. It is not enough to force the defendant to disgorge an amount equivalent to the plaintiffs' loss; these damages, in their individually correct amounts, must also go to the victims. Deterrence alone is insufficient; compensation is also necessary.

As with injunctive relief, the issue is whether the rightful-position principle can bend to the needs of the big case. When the amount of wrong is known but the universe and identity of the victims is unknowable (as in *Democratic Central Committee*), a judge could distribute damages pro rata among victims who submit claims (even if that results in overcompensation because fewer than all the victims submitted claims). Or the judge can limit the awards for those who submitted valid claims to actual damages, and then find another use for excess funds. Among the possible uses are: (1) return the excess funds to the defendant, on the theory that the plaintiffs have not proven greater injury; (2) escheat the funds to the government; (3) create a trust fund that must spend the money in ways that advances the interests of those who are similarly situated to the victims—a "next best" class of victims, so to speak; or (4) give

---

978 84 F.3d 451 (D.C. Cir. 1996).

979 869 F.2d 605 (D.C. Cir. 1989).

the excess funds to a charitable organization whose mission generally aligns with the objective of the lawsuit—a remedy that has become known as *cy pres* relief.[980] *Democratic Central Committee* chose the option of allowing the defendant to purchase better equipment for present-day bus riders, delivering the remedy to a next-best class that somewhat overlapped with the true victims.

When the amount of the wrong and the universe of possible victims are known but the identity of the actual victims is unknown (as in *Dougherty*), choices such as escheat, trust funds, or *cy pres* seem unnecessary. The choices are essentially three: (1) pay nothing to anyone, on the theory that the plaintiffs failed to prove their damages; (2) pay each plaintiff the full amount, on the theory that the defendant should not profit when the lack of certainty results from a wrong of its own making; or (3) divvy up the award among all the victims on an equal basis. *Dougherty* held that, if the victims could not be identified, the damages should be split equally among the five firefighters with eligible claims. This approach gets the level of deterrence right, but it overcompensate the three plaintiffs who would not have been promoted and undercompensates the deserving two.[981]

You should recognize in the *Dougherty* remedy overtones of the "trial by formula" problem we discussed above.[982] Because the defendant's liability has been adjudicated, it tends toward the permitted *Tyson Foods*[983] rather than the impermissible *Wal-Mart*[984] end of the spectrum, but *Tyson Foods* relied on Fair Labor Standard Act precedents that are not necessarily applicable beyond that context.

Cy pres relief is a more common response to implementation issues than declaration issues. For that reason, we defer further consideration of the issue to the following chapter.[985]

These problems do not affect every case. Sometimes technology can be used to identify victims and to determine the amount of their losses. In *Smilow v. Southwestern Bell Mobile Systems, Inc.*,[986] the

---

[980] Originally, *cy pres* was a doctrine from the law of trusts. When it became impossible for a charitable trust to meet its purposes (perhaps the trust was to maintain a church, and the church burned beyond repair), the Chancellor could redirect the trust assets to a similar purpose (perhaps the support of the church that parishioners now attended).

[981] For a case choosing to award each victim of discrimination the full remedy if the defendant could not prove which discrimination victim was entitled to the promotion, see Kyriazi v. W. Elec. Co., 465 F. Supp. 1141 (D.N.J. 1979).

[982] *See supra* Chapter 14.B.

[983] Tyson Foods, Inc. v. Bouaphakeo, 577 U.S. ___, 136 S. Ct. 1036 (2016).

[984] Wal-Mart Stores, Inc. v. Dukes, 564 U.S. 338 (2011).

[985] *See infra* notes 1064–1073 and accompanying text.

[986] 323 F.3d 32 (1st Cir. 2003).

defendant allegedly overcharged for cell-phone minutes. The court of appeals held that a class could be certified, based in part on assurances from the plaintiffs' expert that he could fashion a computer program that would identify the victims of the overcharge and credit their accounts in the amount of the overcharge.

When available, the rightful-position principle remains the gold standard for determining monetary remedies. Departures from that standard are controversial. The genius of the rightful-position principle is its capacity to deter the wrongdoer and compensates the victim in exact and equal measure. Alternatives to this principle risk over- or under-deterrence of the defendant, as well as under- or over-compensation of victims. Alternatives that treat both victim and wrongdoer fairly are difficult to find, and may be impermissible if we insist on the individualized tailoring of damages. If courts are unwilling to bend the principle, however, then trials in aggregated cases (whether a class action or otherwise) become impossible.

We have seen how difficulties in trying aggregated proceedings dispose many courts not to aggregate cases. Therefore, insisting on compliance with the rightful position has effects far beyond determining the remedy. Depending on your view about the value of individualized justice in a mass-injury world, the rightful position may be either a cornerstone of or a roadblock to the fair and equitable resolution of complex litigation.

B. Remedies in a Settlement

Most cases settle. The reality is no different for complex cases. The rightful position may guide a settlement's terms, but it does not strictly dictate the remedy. Thus, parties enjoy more creativity in specifying a remedy. That leeway may be something that a judge disposed to aggregate cases may rely on: even when the judge knows that determining a remedy at trial would be difficult or impossible, the judge may calculate that the case will settle by means of a mechanism that the judge or jury could not impose.

One example is *In re Combustion, Inc.*[987] The defendants had allegedly exposed their workers to dangerous chemicals and polluted the surrounding neighborhood. The extent to which the contamination had injured the 10,000 plaintiffs was hotly debated. The parties ultimately settled for a lump sum of $20 million, leaving the court to determine the proper distribution. The court turned to a special master, who devised a point-based system that accounted for medical problems, duration of exposure, and proximity to the facility. Other criteria disqualified claimants. The master created four categories with maximum and minimum amounts set for each

987 978 F. Supp. 673 (W.D. La. 1997).

category, thus allowing some tailoring of awards to individual circumstances. This system, which simplified the award of damages by using limited objective criteria, may not have led to the precise rightful-position award for each plaintiff, but it saved a jury from the numbing task of calculating 10,000 individual awards.

Despite the flexibility of settlement, difficult issues arise in settling injunctive and monetary claims. Consent and approval are perhaps the most important. In ordinary litigation, a lawyer's ethical responsibilities require that the lawyer obtain from the client fully informed consent. Consent implies actual notice of the settlement's terms and an explanation of relevant considerations. If the client refuses to consent, the claim does not settle. On the other hand, if the client consents to the settlement, the court has no role in approving (or disapproving) the settlement. The settlement is a private contractual matter.

This model of client control and judicial non-involvement is consonant with the ethos of individual autonomy that undergirds the adversarial system. But this model grates against the demands of complex litigation. The ways in which our system has responded to concerns about consent and approval depend on the nature of the proceeding: class action or non-class aggregation.

1. Consent and Approval in Class Actions

Class actions stretch traditional litigation and professional-responsibility paradigms in many ways. The point of settlement is no different. When a class action settles, a court must enter an order approving or disapproving the settlement. If the court approves the settlement, this judgment binds class members to the terms of the settlement. Class members enjoy no individual right to accept or reject the settlement.

Class members receive protections in return for this loss of autonomy. First, class representatives and class counsel must adequately represent members' interests throughout the litigation, including at the time of settlement.[988] Thus, at least one class representative must consent to the settlement after full disclosure of the settlement's terms.[989] Second, class members must receive reasonable notice of the settlement.[990] If class members are known,

---

[988] *See* FED. R. CIV. P. 23(a)(4). On the broader meaning of adequate representation, see *supra* notes 286–293, 331–380 and accompanying text.

[989] *Cf.* Parker v. Anderson, 667 F.2d 1204 (10th Cir. 1982) (affirming a district court's approval of a settlement even though nine of the eleven class representatives opposed the settlement and ten of the eleven eventually fired class counsel).

[990] *See* FED. R. CIV. P. 23(e)(1) ("The court must direct notice in a reasonable manner to all class members who would be bound by the proposal."). For reasonably identifiable members, the Supreme Court required notice through first-class mail, *see* Eisen v. Carlisle & Jacquelin, 417 U.S. 156 (1974), but the case was decided before the

notice must take the form of first-class mail, e-mail, or other means that will reach them. For unknown class members, substituted notice—such as newspaper, television, and radio ads or social-media posts—must be employed.

Third, any class member can object to the settlement.[991] These *objectors* can challenge the adequacy of the class representation as well as other class-action requirements, or they can attack the substance of the settlement. If their objections are overruled, they can appeal the decision.[992] This ability to object, while critical to ensuring that the settlement considers the interests of all class members, raises certain problems that we will consider shortly.

Fourth, if the class action was previously certified as an opt-out (b)(3) class action, a court has discretion to provide class members with a second opt-out opportunity at the time of settlement.[993] A second opt-out opportunity provides class members who believe that the settlement is a bad deal an opportunity to continue to press their claims. In this sense, it is an alternative to objecting: a class member can either, through an objection, try to improve the deal or, through opting out, leave the class. Class counsel, whose fees may go down, and the defendant, who faces the prospect of continuing litigation, often oppose a second opt-out opportunity. The same concern for continued litigation makes some judges reluctant to permit a round of opt-outs at the time of settlement.

If the case comes to the judge as a (b)(3) settlement class action, in which class certification and settlement approval are sought simultaneously,[994] then the judge has no discretion: class members enjoy an absolute right to opt out at the time of settlement.

Fifth, when a class-action settlement is proposed in federal court, the defendant must notify the appropriate state official (usually the state's attorney general) and the appropriate federal official (usually the United States Attorney General) of the terms of the settlement and certain other matters. The appropriate officials

---

development of e-mail or other means of communication with lower costs and comparable reliability in reaching class members.

[991] *See* FED. R. CIV. P. 23(e)(5) ("Any class member may object to the [settlement] proposal if it requires approval . . . .").

[992] *See* Devlin v. Scardelletti, 536 U.S. 1 (2002) (holding that an objector who timely challenged the settlement at the fairness hearing may appeal without needing to intervene in the litigation).

[993] FED. R. CIV. P. 23(e)(4). The judge's decision to permit or deny a second opt-out opportunity is measured under an abuse-of-discretion standard on appeal. *See* FED. R. CIV. P. 23(e)(3) advisory committee note to 2003 amendment (stating that the decision under Rule 23(e)(4) "is confided to the court's discretion"); Denney v. Deutsche Bank AG, 443 F.3d 253 (2d Cir. 2006) (applying an abuse-of-discretion standard).

[994] For discussion of settlement class actions, see *supra* Chapter 6.D.

then have ninety days within which to examine the settlement and file any objections on behalf of their citizens.[995]

The final, and perhaps most significant, protection is judicial approval when the settlement would bind the class members (as it almost always does). The standard for approving the settlement is "fair, reasonable, and adequate."[996] As we examine shortly, a great deal of law lies behind these few words.

This suite of protections acts as a substitute for the individual consent required in ordinary litigation. These protections are a mix of the loyalty, voice, and exit strategies that, as we described in Chapter Six, Rule 23 employs to ensure that class representatives and class counsel pursue the interests of class members.[997] The adequacy requirement and judicial approval assure loyalty; notice and a right to object provide voice; and notice and an (admittedly not always available) opportunity to opt out permit exit.

The protections come together in the *fairness hearing*, at which the trial judge hears evidence and arguments about the settlement's fairness.

Often the settlement first exposes the fault lines and conflicting interests within a class. Class counsel and the settling defendant have no incentive to reveal these problems at the fairness hearing because they have a mutual interest in obtaining approval. Thus, the judge lacks the adversarial presentation of views that the American system relies on to surface contrary arguments.

Objectors fill this gap. A significant number of opt-outs can also signal to the judge that class members perceive problems with the settlement. Because most certified class actions involve negative-value or small-value claims, however, significant opt-out activity is unlikely.[998] Objectors are usually the better source of information about potential defects in the settlement.

---

995 28 U.S.C. § 1715. This notification provision was added as a part of the Class Action Fairness Act of 2005.

996 FED. R. CIV. P. 23(e)(2) ("If the proposal would bind class members, the court may approve it only after a hearing and on finding that it is fair, reasonable, and adequate.").

997 *See supra* note 361 and accompanying text.

998 According to one study of class actions in four federal courts, at least some opt-out activity occurred in 9% to 21% of all class actions, and in 36% to 58% of class actions that provided an opt-out opportunity at settlement. The total number of opt-outs was small, ranging from 0.1% to 0.2% of all class members. *See* WILLGING ET AL., *supra* note 381, at 52–53. *See also* Theodore Eisenberg & Geoffrey Miller, *The Role of Opt-Outs and Objectors in Class Action Litigation: Theoretical and Empirical Issues*, 57 VAND. L. REV. 1529 (2004) (finding an opt-out rate of less than one tenth of one percent in products-liability actions).

But objectors are not always white knights trying to rescue a horrible settlement from the clutches of greedy and collusive class counsel. Some objectors, and their lawyers, act strategically. They know that even an unsuccessful objection can slow down the process of settlement approval, so they file objections purely to extract a side payment from class counsel (or perhaps the defendant) to make them withdraw the objections. Class counsel or the defendant may be happy to buy off the objector when a quick settlement is in their interest. For instance, if an objection would delay the award of a $10 million attorney's fee for two years while the settlement works its way through the trial and appellate courts, class counsel might rationally decide to pay the objector $5,000 and the objector's lawyer $75,000 to go away. So-called "bad objectors" exploit this reality to extort payments that do not improve the quality of the settlement for class members.

Some lawyers and scholars regard bad objectors and their lawyers as a major problem in present class-action practice.[999] Rule 23(e)(5) presently addresses the issue by requiring judicial approval before an objection is withdrawn, but the judge, who has an incentive to move a big case off the docket, does not always want to peer deeply into the side settlement. A number of proposals have been floated to address the issue. As of this writing, a proposed amendment to Rule 23(e)(5), which requires objectors to state the reasons for their objections and further requires judicial approval of payments to objectors, is likely to become effective in December 2018.

The concern with bad-faith objections should not obscure the good faith of many objectors. These objections point out weaknesses in the representation or the settlement that can lead the judge to withhold approval.[1000] In many instances, objections spur the parties to renegotiate the settlement and provide better relief to class members. When a judge believes that an objector made a positive contribution to the ultimate settlement, the judge may award the objector's counsel fees to be paid from the overall fee award given to counsel.[1001] Of course, not all objections—even those made in good

---

[999] *See, e.g.*, Edward Brunet, *Class Action Objectors: Extortionist Free Riders or Fairness Guarantors*, 2003 U. CHI. LEGAL F. 403 (2005); Brian T. Fitzpatrick, *The End of Objector Blackmail?*, 62 VAND. L. REV. 1623, 1631 (2009); John E. Lopatka & D. Brooks Smith, *Class Action Professional Objectors: What to Do About Them?*, 39 FLA. ST. U. L. REV. 865 (2012).

[1000] For example, objectors carried the day and led to rejection of the settlements in two of the Supreme Court's most significant class-action decisions, *Amchem Products, Inc. v. Windsor*, 521 U.S. 591 (2997), and *Ortiz v. Fibreboard Corp.*, 527 U.S. 815 (1999).

[1001] A fee award to objectors' counsel is not required and is especially unlikely when the objections lack substantial merit or do little to improve the settlement. *See In re* UnitedHealth Group Inc. PSLRA Litig., 643 F. Supp. 2d 1107 (D. Minn. 2009) ("Objectors' Counsel is entitled to an award equal to their contribution . . . nothing.").

faith—have merit, and a judge may reject objectors' arguments and approve the settlement as it is.

Whether there are objections or not,[1002] a district court must assess the settlement under the "fair, reasonable, and adequate" standard. Courts have tended to expand on this language through a set of factors that frame the inquiry. At present, the factors are not uniform among the circuits; some circuits have as few as four factors, while others list seven to nine factors with perhaps an additional fifteen factors that also might influence the fairness inquiry.[1003] Despite the variability in the stated standard, the basic inquiry is the same everywhere. At the core, the court must decide "whether the interests of the class are better served by the settlement than by further litigation."[1004] Courts usually employ a two-step process. The first step looks for "procedural" indicators of a defective settlement, such as inadequate representation, lack of inquiry into the case's merits, or lack of arm's-length, tough negotiation. The second step checks the settlement for "substantive" defects—in particular, whether the settlement fund is too small in relation to the expected value of the case (calculated as the full value of the case less discounts for the risks and expenses of continued litigation).

Both sets of checks are critical. The central question is whether the settlement is a good value for the class. It is often difficult for a judge, who knows little about the evidence and theories in the case, to calculate accurately the case's full value or the risks and costs of

---

[1002] A four-district study found that at least one objection was filed in about half of class settlements, with complaints about the size of class counsel's fee being the most common ground and the insufficiency of the award to class members being the second most common. *See* WILLGING ET AL., *supra* note 381, at 56–57. *See also* Theodore Eisenberg & Geoffrey Miller, *The Role of Opt-Outs and Objectors in Class Action Litigation: Theoretical and Empirical Issues*, 57 VAND. L. REV. 1529, 1532–33 (2004) (reporting that on average, less than five percent of the class objected to a settlement in civil rights cases, and objections in securities and consumer cases were lower); *id.* ("The overall impression across the range of cases in the study is that . . . objections are extremely uncommon.").

[1003] The best known and most widely used constellation of factors are the *Grinnell* factors, named after the case that first adopted them. *See* City of Detroit v. Grinnell Corp., 495 U.S. 448 (2d Cir. 1974), *abrogated on other grounds*, Goldberger v. Integrated Res., Inc., 209 F.3d 43 (2d Cir. 2000). There are nine factors in total; they include the "complexity, expense and likely duration of the case," "the reaction of the class to the settlement," "the stage of the proceedings and the amount of discovery completed," the risks of continuing litigation, and the reasonableness of the settlement fund in light of "the best possible recovery" and "all attendant risks of litigation." *See* Wal-Mart Stores, Inc. v. Visa U.S.A., Inc., 396 F.3d 96 (2d Cir. 2005). In the Third Circuit, these factors are known as the *Girsh* factors, named after the case that adopted the *Grinnell* factors. *See* Girsh v. Jepson, 521 F.2d 153 (3d Cir. 1977); *see also In re* Prudential Ins. Co. Sales Practices Litig., 148 F.3d 283 (3d Cir. 1999) (applying the *Girsh* factors). The present *Manual for Complex Litigation* lists fifteen factors, plus an additional thirteen considerations that can aid a court in determining the proper weight to give to each factor. *See* MANUAL, *supra* note 206, § 21.62.

[1004] *See* MANUAL, *supra* note 206, § 21.61.

continued litigation. This problem is exacerbated because the parties have an incentive to withhold information because they do not want to let the opposing party or non-settling parties know the strengths and weaknesses of their cases, especially given that the settlement might fail.[1005] An indirect way to check on substantive fairness is to examine the procedural inputs into the settlement. Aside from ensuring that the constitutional demand of adequate representation, focusing on the quality of the representation and the negotiating process provides important clues about the settlement's substantive merits.[1006]

The same rulemaking process that resulted in proposed changes to Rule 23(e)(4) also generated an amendment to Rule 23(e)(2). The amendment, which is also on track to become effective in December 2018, retains the "fair, reasonable, and adequate" standard. But it also establishes four factors, with the third factor further broken into four subfactors, that a court must consider in determining a class settlement's fairness. The factors are:

- whether "the class representatives and class counsel have adequately represented the class";
- whether "the proposal was negotiated at arm's length";
- whether "the relief provided for the class is adequate, taking into account:
    - "the costs, risks, and delay of trial and appeal;
    - "the effectiveness of any proposed method of distributing relief to the class, including the method of processing class-member claims, if required;
    - "the terms of any proposed award of attorney's fees, including timing of payment; and"
    - any side agreements between the parties and counsel made in connection with the settlement; and
- whether the proposal treats class members "equitably relative to each other."

The first two factors focus on procedural considerations and the second two factors focus on substantive considerations.

Although the pending amendment provides new language to which courts must conform their approval decisions, the amendment

1005 *See* MANUAL, *supra* note 206, § 21.641.

1006 *See* William B. Rubenstein, *The Fairness Hearing: Adversarial and Regulatory Approaches*, 53 UCLA L. REV. 1435 (2006).

is unlikely to change significantly the process of approving class settlements. For the most part, the factors that the amendment proposes map onto the factors that courts already apply. True, some factors that courts examine at present, such as the reaction of class members to the settlement and the amount of discovery completed, go unmentioned, but these considerations can be easily shoehorned into the pending amendment's explicit factors. Conversely, the amendment's express focus on attorney's fees and on the equitable treatment of class members is new, but both considerations are implicit in the adequate-representation inquiry of most present multi-factor tests.

Behind the factors lies a large body of precedent that shapes the district court's "fair, reasonable, and adequate" inquiry. Here too the pending amendment is unlikely to change existing law. Rather, existing law should swallow the pending amendment and produce the same results—albeit now clothed in Rule 23(e)(2)'s new language.

Although an exhaustive analysis of the precedent is not possible in this short treatise, a few basic propositions should provide a good idea of the main points of the courts' inquiry into the fairness of a settlement. First, some courts create a presumption of fairness when "a class settlement [is] reached in arm's-length negotiations between experienced, capable counsel after meaningful discovery."[1007] In effect, compliance with the procedural considerations puts a thumb on the scale in favor of the strength of the settlement. This presumption accords with the often-expressed view that "[t[he compromise of complex litigation is encouraged by the courts and favored by public policy."[1008] Because settlement class actions have not yet been tested in the crucible of litigation, the presumption is less applicable in these cases.[1009]

Second, a court must consider whether the settlement's value is roughly comparable to the expected value of the class's claims. Although assessing the expected value of a class's claims is difficult, courts must at least engage in an effort to make the calculation. For example, in *Reynolds v. Beneficial National Bank*,[1010] the district court approved a $25 million settlement in a consumer-finance class action, but made no finding that the settlement was a reasonable

---

1007 *Wal-Mart*, 396 F.3d at 116 (quoting MANUAL FOR COMPLEX LITIGATION, THIRD § 30.41 (1995)). The present iteration of the *Manual* does not include this language or frame the issue in this fashion, but the presumption had already worked its way into the cases by then.

1008 *Id.* at 117 (internal quotation marks omitted).

1009 *See* D'Amato v. Deutsche Bank, 236 F.3d 78 (2d Cir. 2001) ("When a settlement is negotiated prior to class certification, . . . it is subject to a higher degree of scrutiny in assessing its fairness.").

1010 288 F.3d 277 (7th Cir. 2002).

compromise in light of the risks and costs of continued litigation. The court of appeals reversed. The court acknowledged that "[a] high degree of precision cannot be expected in valuing a litigation, especially regarding the estimation of the probability of particular outcomes." Moreover, the fairness hearing should not be turned "into a trial on the merits." Nonetheless, when the trial judge "made no effort to translate his intuitions about the strength of the plaintiffs' case, the range of possible damages, and the likely duration of the litigation if it was not settled," the settlement could not stand: "some approximate range of percentages, reflecting the probability of obtaining each of these outcomes in a trial (more likely a series of trials), might be estimated, and so a ballpark valuation derived."

To aid the judge in this process of valuing a settlement, parties often call expert witnesses to discuss the merits of the class members' cases, as well as accountants, actuaries, or statisticians to help calculate a net expected value for the class's claims. Because both sides have an interest in settling the case, the judge must guard against opinions inflating the value of a settlement.[1011]

Judges are especially attuned to relief of illusory value. A classic example is the "coupon settlement," in which a class of consumers receives coupons that allow the members to purchase future products from the defendant at a discount. A classic example is *In re General Motors Corp. Pick-Up Truck Fuel Tank Products Liability Litigation*.[1012] An allegedly defective design of the fuel tanks made the defendant's trucks susceptible to explosion under certain collisions. The defendant sold about 5.7 million trucks with the defect. The case settled, with the defendant agreeing to give customers a $1,000 coupon good toward the purchase of another of the defendant's trucks or a transferable $500 coupon for the purchase of certain top-of-the-line trucks. Redemption of the coupons was required within fifteen months. Class counsel received $9.5 million in attorney's fees.

The district court valued the settlement at about $2 billion, but the court of appeals found that most of this paper value was illusory. Even with coupons, few customers would be able to afford a new vehicle, which cost between $20,000 and $33,000, within the redemption period. The court of appeals regarded the coupons as more of a sales promotion for the defendant than a thing of value for the class members, who might feel beholden to buy another vehicle

---

[1011] *See* Eubank v. Pella Corp., 753 F.3d 718 (7th Cir. 2014) (reversing a settlement approval when, among other reasons, the court did not estimate the likely value of the claims at trial and the $90 million estimate of the class's expert accountant appeared to be inflated by a factor of ten in relation to the actual claims that class members filed against the settlement fund).

[1012] 55 F.3d 768 (3d Cir. 1995).

that they did not need or want. The failure to provide for other options, such as retrofitting a new tank on the truck, further lent to the sense that the coupons lacked real value for the class.

Coupon settlements like *GM Pick-Up Truck* are something of an urban legend. Although they occurred on rare occasion, they were never a mainstay of class settlements. Nonetheless, opponents of class actions seized on the poor value that coupon settlements returned to class members as one of the outrages emblematic of the corruption at the heart of the American class action: class counsel who walked away with millions while class members got next to nothing. The unfairness of coupon settlements, especially in state court, became one of the foundational arguments for the Class Action Fairness Act of 2005 (CAFA). CAFA's proponents argued that expanded federal jurisdiction over class actions was necessary because federal judges would better police coupon settlements than state judges. CAFA also included a specific provision to tamp down coupon settlements: the amount of class counsel's fees was to be based on the value of the coupons that were actually redeemed.[1013]

Coupons are not the only relief that is potentially illusory. Injunctive relief can also create problems. For instance, in *In re Subway Footlong Sandwich Marketing and Sales Practices Litigation*,[1014] the plaintiffs claimed that some of the defendant's loaves used to make a footlong sandwich were actually less than a foot long. The amount of dough that the defendant used was identical in each loaf; the variability of the baking process, however, led some of the bread to come up a bit short. Plaintiffs settled for an injunction in which the defendant undertook certain practices to ensure that loaves were a foot long. The defendant also agreed to pay $520,000 in attorney's fees. The court held that the injunctive provisions, which added nothing to the amount of dough used in any loaf, "do not benefit the class in any meaningful way." Indeed, "[a] class settlement that results in fees for class counsel but yields no meaningful relief for the class 'is no better than a racket.' . . . No class action settlement that yields zero benefits for the class should be approved, and a class action that seeks only worthless benefits for the class should be dismissed out of hand."[1015]

1013 *See* 28 U.S.C. § 1712. This provision also requires the court to find in writing, after a hearing, that a coupon settlement is fair, reasonable, and adequate, and to consider awarding any unredeemed coupons to charitable or governmental organizations. *Id.* § 1712(e). *Cf. In re* Sw. Airlines Voucher Litig., 799 F.3d 701 (7th Cir. 2015) (holding that § 1712 does not require a court to award fees based on a percentage of the redeemed coupons, but permits the use of a lodestar (i.e., hourly rate) to compensate class counsel).

1014 869 F.3d 551 (7th Cir. 2017).

1015 *Id.* at 556 (quoting *In re* Walgreen Co. Stockholder Litig., 832 F.3d 716 (7th Cir. 2016)). *Walgreen* similarly rejected a settlement in which a stockholder class

Another form of illusory relief arises when the process for class members to submit claims is so onerous that few class members will go to the trouble of doing so.[1016] This problem is particularly acute for negative-value claims. The need for a simple claims process is one reason why settlements often provide modest relief to claimants with minimal proof of loss. But doing so creates a Catch-22. As we have seen, when a simplified claims process does nothing to weed out false claims, a court may refuse to certify a class on ascertainability grounds.[1017]

Illusory relief is also an issue when the defendant is already sponsoring a voluntary compensation program, and the class settlement merely incorporates that program into the settlement. In such cases, it is not clear that class counsel has achieved anything of real value for class members.[1018]

A third concern in many settlements is an equitable distribution of the proceeds among class members. "Equitable" does not mean equal; as the Supreme Court noted in *Ortiz v. Fibreboard Corp.*,[1019] the distribution must not treat claims of different strength equally. Rather, the settlement should provide relief that roughly reflects the relative strength of various claims in relation to each other. As the failure to provide any recovery for valid consortium claims in *Amchem*[1020] showed, this obligation precludes zeroing out the valuable claims of some class members just to throw more money toward the claims of other class members. Conversely, class members whose claims are of roughly the same strength should obtain settlement proceeds of roughly equivalent amounts. We have used the word "roughly" a lot in this paragraph. In a class settlement, a court is not expecting precise tailoring of the relief to the facts of each class member's claim, and some lumping of dissimilar claims into a

---

action settled for an injunction requiring the defendant to provide additional disclosures in advance of a stockholders' meeting that were "largely or even entirely worthless to the shareholders," but class counsel received $370,000. *See also Eubank*, 753 F.3d 718 (rejecting a settlement in part because the defendant previously established a warranty-extension program that was incorporated into the settlement and claimed by class counsel as part of the value conferred by the settlement).

[1016] *See* Gascho v. Global Fitness Holdings, LLC, 822 F.3d 269 (6th Cir. 2016) (noting a "concern about settlement structures that are contrived to discourage claims," including onerous proof-of-purchase requirements and confusing websites or claims forms).

[1017] *See* Carrera v. Bayer Corp., 727 F.3d 300 (3d Cir. 2013); *see also supra* Chapter 6.B.1.a (discussing the ascertainability requirement).

[1018] *Cf. In re* Hyundai & Kia Fuel Econ. Litig., 881 F.3d 679 (9th Cir. 2018) (remanding settlement class action in part because the district court failed to consider the value that the settlement added to the defendant's voluntary reimbursement program and set attorney's fees accordingly).

[1019] 527 U.S. 815 (1999).

[1020] Amchem Prods., Inc. v. Windsor, 521 U.S. 591 (1997).

single payment category may be necessary to make the distribution of settlement proceeds run efficiently.

A settlement may permissibly use factors other than strength of claim without running afoul of the concern for equitable treatment. For instance, monetary class settlements often create tiers of compensation based on the amount of evidence that a class member must supply to prove entitlement to recovery. A settlement may grant a modest (nuisance-value) payment to class members who provide no proof of loss, a greater payment when some proof of loss is provided, and an even greater payment when the class member provides full information demonstrating to the claims administrator the claim's validity.

Although some variability between the expected value of a class member's claim at trial and the value of settlement award can therefore be anticipated, the unjustified dissimilar treatment of similar claims and the unjustified similar treatment of dissimilar claims raise concerns. One concern is adequate representation: as *Amchem* held, a settlement that creates winners and losers is often reflective of (or creates) internal conflicts of interest that make the representation inadequate. Another is the substantive unfairness of the settlement.

A common problem regarding fair distribution is the differential treatment of class representatives. Class settlements often provide "incentive payments," or an extra monetary award, to the class representatives. In theory, these payments induce class representatives to step forward and compensate them for the work they perform on behalf of the class, including consultations with class counsel, time in depositions, and the like. But the risk of these payments is that they overbear the class representative, who becomes more interested in achieving a large personal payoff than in ensuring that the settlement is a good deal for the class members who receive much less. A class representative would be hard pressed to say no to a deal that pays her $100,000 even though it provides pennies to the remainder of the class.

As we briefly explored,[1021] courts are sensitive to the dangers of incentive payments. These payments may rise a level that the court deems the class representative inadequate. Or the payment may be so in excess of actual work performed that the court questions the overall fairness of the settlement. Courts sometimes require that documentation of the tasks performed and hours spent by class representatives accompany the request for an incentive award.[1022]

[1021] *See supra* note 354 and accompanying text.

[1022] *See* Shane Grp., Inc. v. Blue Cross Blue Shield of Mich., 825 F.3d 299 (6th Cir. 2016); *see also In re* Southwest Airlines Voucher Litig., 799 F.3d 701 (7th Cir.

Another difficult issue occurs when the case settles for a lump sum, rather than providing for an open-ended settlement in which each class member receives a defined benefit. Distributing a limited fund among class members creates the potential for a conflict of interest unless structural protections to ensure equitable treatment are built into the settlement.[1023]

A final common concern for the fairness of the settlement is the size of the attorney's fee. The class settlement often—although not always—specifies a particular amount for attorney's fees. In other cases, counsel submits a fee request. In either event, unless a fee-shifting statute is available, the class settlement will include a pot of money sufficient to pay the fees or an agreement from the defendant to pay the fee that the court orders. The court is not bound by any fee agreements of the parties or by any request for fees. Rather, it must determine for itself a reasonable fee, and it can reduce the fee request to an appropriate amount.[1024] The amount of the attorney's fees is usually included in the notice sent to the class. As we mentioned, an allegedly excessive award is one of the most common objections lodged against a settlement.

As with incentive payments to class representatives, excessively large attorney's fees can overbear the ability of class counsel to work in the best interests of the class. This agency-cost problem has been with us throughout this book and bears significantly on the decision whether to aggregate related cases.

It is the moment of settlement at which this concern emerges most starkly. Almost surely, the fees that class counsel receives will exceed the amount that any class member has at stake in the litigation. That fact has led class-action critics to complain that class actions are run for the benefit of class counsel, not class members. This critique is overblown. True, in many small-stakes cases counsel receives more than any class member, but the aggregate compensation to the class and the deterrence value of the settlement are still considerable. Comparing the dollar-amount recovery of a

---

2015) (denying an incentive payment of $15,000 to a class representative who failed to disclose a potential conflict of interest with class counsel, even though the conflict did not harm the class; further reducing the fee awarded to class counsel by the same amount).

[1023] *Cf. In re* Nat'l Football League Players Concussion Injury Litig., 821 F.3d 410 (3d Cir. 2016) (affirming a settlement approval when the settlement included structural protections such as uncapped awards, subclasses, and a special master to avoid internal conflicts of interest).

[1024] *See* FED. R. CIV. P. 23(h). Under this Rule, whether in the settlement or afterwards, class counsel must move for an attorney's fee award. Notice of the motion must be directed toward class members, who have a right to object. A judge may hold a hearing, and must make findings regarding the award. To avoid additional notices and hearings, the court usually rolls the issue of the attorney's fee into the fairness hearing.

single class member to the fee of counsel is rarely helpful. The issue is whether the class action enriches counsel while doing next to nothing for class members.

Chapter Eighteen explores the calculation of attorney's fees in greater detail. For now, it is enough to know that the court will usually examine the issue of counsel's fee as part of the settlement. A "large" fee sounds an alarm. A fee can be large in either of two ways: it can be large in an absolute sense, so that the amount of the fee seems disproportionate to the amount of work that counsel performed; or it can be large relative to the recovery that the class receives. For instance, a $100 million fee in a $1 billion class settlement is not a large percentage of the recovery, but if counsel achieved the settlement after only 1,000 hours of work (i.e., an effective hourly rate of $100,000), a court would almost surely lower the request for this award. Conversely, an attorney's fee of $500,000 for a class action in which counsel worked 2,000 hours (i.e., an effective hourly rate of $250) is not large in an absolute sense, but if the settlement provides class members with only $25,000, the ratio of fee to class recovery might lead a court to question if the settlement was designed to benefit counsel or the class.

On the question of the absolute size of the award, courts often cross-check counsel's fee award against the hours worked to make sure that the award is not excessive. Studies also show that, at the median, attorney's fees tend to run between twenty and thirty percent of the benefit received by the class; and as the size of the award increases, the percentage of the recovery decreases.[1025] Cases in which the fee award rises to an alarming level in comparison to class benefits are not the norm.

One court of appeals has established a presumption that a fee award that exceeds the benefit to the class (i.e., more than half of the settlement's proceeds go to counsel) should be disapproved.[1026] Other

---

[1025] *See* THOMAS E. WLLGING ET AL., EMPIRICAL STUDY OF CLASS ACTIONS IN FOUR FEDERAL DISTRICT COURTS (1996) (reporting median rates for attorneys' fees of 27 to 30 percent in a sample of sixty-eight class settlements); Theodore Eisenberg & Geoffrey P. Miller, *Attorney Fees and Expenses in Class Action Settlements: 1993–2008*, 7 J. EMPIRICAL LEGAL STUD. 248 (2010) (reporting mean fee awards from 11 to 27 percent of the recovery and medians from nineteen to twenty-five percent in a sample of 689 class settlements between 1993 and 2008); Brian T. Fitzpatrick, *An Empirical Study of Class Action Settlements and Their Fee Awards*, 7 J. EMPIRICAL LEGAL STUD. 811 (2010) (reporting a mean and median between 25 and 30 percent in a sample of 444 class settlements in 2006 and 2007).

[1026] *See* Pearson v. NBTY, Inc., 772 F.3d 778 (7th Cir. 2014) ("[T]he presumption should we suggest be that attorneys' fees awarded to class counsel should not exceed a third or at most a half of the total amount of money going to class members and their counsel."). *See also Eubank*, 753 F.2d 718 (overturning an order approving a settlement when, among other problems, the settlement returned a likely benefit of $8.5 million to the class and counsel received $11 million in fees).

courts have declined to be so rigid.[1027] But fees that approach or exceed half of the settlement are likely to be subject to objector attack, judicial scrutiny, and reduction—and even risk an outright rejection of the settlement. This reality feeds back on a prior problem: counsel may inflate the purported value of the settlement both to make the settlement look more attractive and to reduce the percentage of the settlement seemingly going to counsel. As one check on the problem, courts may award a portion of the attorney's fee to counsel for objectors when the objections improve the settlement in ways that benefit the class.

One red flag for courts is a "clear sailing" agreement in the class settlement. Under such an agreement, the defendant agrees not to oppose the amount of the fees requested by class counsel. You might think that the defendant has little reason to oppose a fee request. In some cases, however, the settlement calls for the defendant to pay the fees of class counsel in the amount that the court awards; in other words, the fee does not come directly out of the class recovery. In other cases, the defendant might worry that an excessive fee award gives ground for a collateral attack on the settlement due to inadequate class representation. Thus, a clear-sailing provision can remove one player (the defendant) with an incentive object to the size of the fee award.

A clear-sailing agreement does not automatically disqualify a settlement for approval, but it should raise the antennae of judges and lead them to look harder at the relative benefits of the settlement for class and counsel.[1028]

[1027] *See Gascho*, 822 F.3d 269 (6th Cir. 2016) (rejecting the presumption as "an inflexible, categorical rule" that fails to account for the social and law-enforcement value that negative-value consumer class actions provide); *accord In re* Motor Fuel Temperature Sales Practices Litig., 872 F.3d 1094 (10th Cir. 2017). For an argument that the worries over the size of the class counsel's fees are often misplaced given that the principal value of small-stakes class actions is deterrence, see Brian T. Fitzpatrick, *Do Class Action Lawyers Make Too Little?*, 158 U. PA. L. REV. 2043 (2010) (arguing that in small-stakes class actions, "it is hard to see, as a theoretical matter, why the lawyers should not receive everything and leave nothing for class members at all").

[1028] *Compare National Football League Players*, 821 F.3d at 447 ("We join our sister circuits in declining to hold that clear sailing provisions are *per se* bars to settlement approval while nonetheless emphasizing that they deserve careful scrutiny in any class action settlement."), *with In re* Bluetooth Headset Prods. Liab. Litig., 654 F.3d 935 (9th Cir. 2011) (reversing approval of a settlement with a "clear sailing" clause and a "kicker" clause that any amounts in the fund set aside for attorney's fees that was not awarded to counsel was to be returned to the defendant; noting that "the kicker makes it less likely that the settlement can be approved if the district court determines the clear sailing provision authorizes unreasonably high attorneys' fees").

> **Problem**
>
> A class action alleged that the defendant's diapers caused excessive diaper rash. The case settled, with defendant agreeing to certain labeling and website changes as well as a one-box refund of diapers for class members who had not taken advantage of a prior refund offer and who still had their original receipts and UPC codes from the diaper box. The class representatives received $1,000 per diaper-using child in their household. Class counsel received $2.73 million. As district-court judge, would you approve the settlement? *See In re* Dry Max Pampers Litig., 724 F.3d 713 (6th Cir. 2013).

The *Manual for Complex Litigation* lists a series of additional checks on the settlement, most of which fall into one of these four categories of a tough negotiation process, an adequate settlement value in relation to the strength of the claims, equitable treatment of class members, and reasonable attorney's fees.[1029]

Solely or in combination, these concerns can lead a judge to question the value of a class settlement. In such cases, the decision whether to approve the settlement is not binary. The judge can work with the parties and objectors—and often does so—to craft a settlement that addresses the concerns that the judge has identified. The judge may become an active participant in the second round of negotiations that ultimately deliver a remedy to the class.

2. Consent and Approval in Non-Class Aggregation

Non-class aggregations, such as MDLs, are a different kettle of fish. Traditionally the law has viewed such aggregations as individual cases writ large, so all the usual rules of settlement apply: each client must consent, the lawyer must abide the client's wishes, and the court has no role in approving or disapproving the deal. Clients who refuse to accept the settlement can continue to pursue their claims.

In aggregate litigation, gaining consent from all affected clients can be difficult, especially when the numbers are great. When the interests of some plaintiffs diverge from those of others, universal consent may be impossible. But an agreement that settles fewer than all the cases is usually unattractive to the defendants, who prefer global peace.

One tactic used to induce client consent is a provision in the settlement agreement requiring plaintiffs' counsel to recommend the settlement to all clients and obligating counsel to move to withdraw from the representation of any client who refuses to enter the settlement. Defendants want such a provision because it provides

---

[1029] *See* MANUAL, *supra* note 206, § 21.62.

assurance that plaintiffs' counsel does not settle the weak cases while holding out the strong cases for further litigation. It also fosters global resolution of the claims. On the other hand, such a side agreement may put too much pressure on clients to accept the deal, for finding new counsel to step into a massive case will be very difficult. Most legal ethicists are critical of such provisions.[1030]

A related tactic is to include in the settlement agreement a provision that reserves to the defendant the right to walk away from the deal if a specified number or percent of the plaintiffs refuse to accept the settlement. Reserving the right to walk away puts pressure on plaintiffs' counsel, who garners a substantial fee only if the settlement goes through. In some cases, the number of refusals is set at zero: if any plaintiffs reject the settlement, the entire deal collapses. In other cases, the settlement accommodates some dissents; in the *Vioxx* litigation, for example, the deal was voidable only if more than fifteen percent of the MDL plaintiffs declined to accept the deal. But *Vioxx* also involved other "sweeteners"—including the threat of plaintiffs' counsel withdrawal—that aimed to keep the plaintiffs in line.

Two other approaches of uncertain legality have emerged to address the problem of client consent. One involves changing the retainer agreement, so that each client agrees to accept the settlement as long as a pre-defined percentage of the lawyer's other clients in the same matter accept the deal. This approach raises ethical concerns—specifically, a potential conflict with Model Rule of Professional Conduct 1.8(g), which has been adopted in most American jurisdictions. Rule 1.8(g) provides: "A lawyer who represents two or more clients shall not participate in making an aggregate settlement of the claims of . . . the clients . . . unless each client gives informed consent, in a writing signed by the client."

In *The Tax Authority, Inc. v. Jackson Hewitt, Inc.*,[1031] a lawyer representing 154 franchisees in a suit against the franchisor entered into a retainer agreement in which each client agreed to be bound by the vote of a weighted majority of the franchisees (i.e., a vote in which each client's vote was weighted according to the value of the client's claims) with respect to the settlement. The agreement also provided that any settlement would be apportioned according to the same weighed formula.

The lawyer entered an aggregate settlement, with all but eighteen franchisees supporting the settlement. The eighteen who

[1030] *See* Howard M. Erichson, *The Trouble with All-or-Nothing Settlements*, 58 KAN. L. REV. 979 (2010).

[1031] 898 A.2d 512 (N.J. 2006).

refused to consent were not a weighted majority. On the defendant's motion, the trial court enforced the settlement against the holdouts.

On appeal, the New Jersey Supreme Court held that Rule 1.8(g) forbade the retainer agreement. It stated that an agreement that "violates the ethical rules governing the attorney-client relationship may be declared unenforceable." The Court thought that the language of Rule 1.8(g) was clear and that an ex ante retainer agreement could not substitute for the requisite consent. It noted that individual consent lay at the heart of the attorney-client relationship and that a majority-vote rule might create conflicts of interest for the lawyer. Nonetheless, because it had not previously interpreted Rule 1.8(g), the New Jersey Supreme Court applied the ruling only prospectively and enforced the settlement against the holdout franchisee who had appealed.

The American Law Institute has proposed softening Rule 1.8(g). It has recommended enforcing aggregate settlements when a "substantial-majority vote" of claimants supports the settlement and when certain procedural prerequisites (including clear disclosure of the substantial-majority provision in the retainer agreement) are observed.[1032] But focusing only on this provision misses an important point. The change to voting in lieu of consent was part of a larger package of reforms for aggregate litigation. Other reforms included an adequate-representation requirement for counsel and judicial approval of "substantial-majority vote" settlements. Unless some procedural and substantive guarantees of a settlement's fairness exist as a substitute for individual consent, the potential for a majority of claimants and counsel to overbear the conflicting interests of a discrete minority of claimants makes a majority-vote provision unattractive.[1033]

A second approach to sidestep the requirement of client consent is judicial approval of mass settlements. Although the ALI recommended judicial approval as part of its substantial-majority-vote concept,[1034] it did not recommend any role for judicial approval in other aggregate-litigation settlements; here, client consent remained a sufficient check on a settlement's fairness. A number of MDL courts, however, have reviewed aggregate settlements for their fairness. For instance, in the MDL proceeding involving injuries to

---

[1032] *See* PRINCIPLES OF AGGREGATE LITIGATION, *supra* note 437, § 3.17(b).

[1033] For a strong critique of the ALI's proposed substantial-majority-voting rule, see Howard M. Erichson & Benjamin C. Zipursky, *Consent Versus Closure*, 96 CORNELL L. REV. 265 (2011) ("[The ALI's] advance consent proposal presents a client-client conflict of interest that is nonconsentable.").

[1034] For the terms of how judicial approval operates in the ALI's proposal, see PRINCIPLES OF AGGREGATE LITIGATION, *supra* note 437, § 3.18.

workers who responded to the 9/11 attacks, the MDL judge rejected a proposed settlement as inadequate.

The authority for judges to review aggregate settlements—to say nothing of their power to reject a seemingly inadequate settlement—is controversial. Judicial review and approval are required in a few contexts (principally, class actions and some antitrust and environmental litigation) and are possible when parties request it (perhaps as a part of a consent decree that the court will need to enforce). Otherwise, judges must rely on some notion of inherent power to review aggregate settlements. As we have seen repeatedly, however, claiming a power does not justify it. That reality is especially true when the power interferes with the core freedom of litigants to control critical decisions regarding the disposition of their claims.[1035]

The effort to build into aggregate settlements some of the protections of class actions is understandable, particularly because aggregate settlements are susceptible to the agency-cost problems of all mass litigation. But class-action protections are designed to compensate class members for the loss of control over their claims. In non-class aggregate litigation, litigants nominally retain that control, including the right to refuse to accept a settlement. For some observers, adding protections on top of this right smacks of paternalism. For others, protections are necessary to correct the power asymmetry between counsel and client. The final word on striking the right balance between consent and fairness has yet to be written.

3. Scope of the Release

In return for a settlement payment, the defendant usually extracts a release from the plaintiff. The release defines the claims that the plaintiff is "selling" to the defendant in return for a settlement payment. As a general rule, a release is worded broadly, so that the plaintiff gives up not only the claims that were litigated but also all claims arising from the same transaction that could have been asserted. Such a release is the equivalent of a judgment entitled to claim-preclusive effect.[1036] The difference is that claim preclusion, which requires a judgment, derives its authority from the law of judgments, while a release, which requires a settlement, derives its power from the law of contract.

[1035] For a trenchant criticism of such claims of power, see Jeremy T. Grabill, *Judicial Review of Private Mass Settlements*, 42 SETON HALL L. REV. 123 (2012) ("[N]othwithstanding charges of collusion and coercion, there is no need or justification for judicial review of private mass tort settlements because such settlements bind only those plaintiffs who affirmatively opt in to them.").

[1036] For a discussion of the breadth of claim preclusion, see *supra* Chapter 5.A.

In non-class aggregate litigation, the plaintiffs can release any claims they wish. A valid release requires full disclosure of the release's terms to the client, the client's consent, and no other grounds under the law of contract to void the release. Assuming these prerequisites, any claims, related or unrelated to the lawsuit, can be settled.

In class actions, class members do not individually consent to the settlement. Nonetheless, a class settlement usually releases the claims that were actually litigated. The defendant can also obtain a release of claims that were not presented if "the released conduct arises out of the identical factual predicate as the settled conduct."[1037] This rule encourages settlement and aids the efficient and comprehensive resolution of large numbers of claims.[1038] For the release to be effective, however, the class members must have received adequate representation on the released claims. Claims that could not have been certified for class treatment thus lie beyond the scope of the release.

Several issues regarding the alleged overbreadth of class-action releases recur with frequency. First, a release is enforceable even when it includes claims that could not have been asserted due to jurisdictional or other defects.[1039] Second, the settlement must provide appropriate value for all released claims, including those that were never filed. In *Kaufman v. American Express Travel Related Services Co.*,[1040] the court noted that certain claims that were not litigated received no compensation in the settlement but were subject to release. The district court and the court of appeals were both troubled by the breadth of the release, but the court of appeals affirmed the settlement, on an abuse-of-discretion standard, because no evidence had been presented to prove that the non-litigated claims had value. In the process, the court of appeals reiterated a district court's obligation "to scrutinize what claims the class is giving up and what the class is receiving in exchange."

Third, some class actions have sought to release class members' future claims against the defendant. There is no absolute barrier to releasing future claims, although the "identical factual predicate" requirement for releasing non-litigated claims acts as an important limit on such releases. In addition, courts will scrutinize such a

---

[1037] *See* Wal-Mart Stores, Inc. v. Visa U.S.A., Inc., 396 F.3d 96 (2d Cir. 2005) (internal quotation marks omitted).

[1038] *See* Halley v. Honeywell Int'l, Inc., 861 F.3d 461 (3d Cir. 2017).

[1039] *See* Matsushita Electric Industrial Co. v. Epstein, 516 U.S. 367 (1996) (holding that a state-court judgment approving a settlement that released claims over which federal courts had exclusive jurisdiction was entitled to preclusive effect in federal court under the Full Faith and Credit Act).

[1040] 877 F.3d 276 (7th Cir. 2017).

settlement provision closely to ensure adequate representation on, and fair value for, the released future claims.[1041] A release of future claims arising from ongoing conduct is likelier to pass muster than a release of claims regarding conduct in which the defendant has not yet, but may, engage.

Finally, settlements that provide a release of liability for future conduct have come under attack as illegal under the Rules Enabling Act, which requires that no Federal Rule of Civil Procedure "abridge, enlarge, or modify any substantive right."[1042] The argument is that settlement approvals under Rule 23(e) effectively alter the future rights of the parties. Because settlements do not result in an adjudication of the controversy but arise from the voluntary agreement of the parties, no court of appeals has yet accepted the argument, which, if ever successful, could dramatically change the ability to settle injunctive claims.[1043]

C. Using Masters and Adjuncts in Determining a Remedy

As we will see in the following chapter, courts often use judicial adjuncts, such as special masters appointed under Rule 53, to implement and enforce the terms of a judgment or settlement. Courts can also employ masters during the process of determining the remedy. Rule 53(a)(1)(B)(ii) specifically permits a reference to a master when there exists "the need to perform an accounting or resolve a difficult computation of damages."

In addition, courts sometimes appoint masters or other adjuncts to act as mediators to achieve a settlement. When a case settles for a lump sum, a master can also be employed to determine the amount of the remedy to which individual class members or claimants are entitled.[1044] Special masters or other judicial officers can provide structural protection to prevent or mitigate conflicts of interest

---

[1041] *Compare Halley*, 861 F.3d 461 (holding that the district court did not abuse its discretion is approving a settlement that released "unknown" and "unforeseen" claims), *with In re* Payment Card Interchange Fee & Merch. Discount Antitrust Litig., 827 F.3d 223 (2d Cir. 2017) (holding that the release of future claims for certain members who could not opt out and who received no benefit from the settlement of present claims in return for giving up future claims of potential value was improper because "the benefits of litigation peace do not outweigh class members' due process rights to adequate representation").

[1042] 28 U.S.C. § 2072(b).

[1043] *See In re* Motor Fuel Temperature Sales Practices Litig., 872 F.3d 1094 (10th Cir. 2017); *see also* Sullivan v. DB Invs., Inc., 667 F.3d 273 (3d Cir. 2011) (rejecting Rules Enabling Act and federalism challenges to a settlement releasing claims that were allegedly invalid under state law).

[1044] *See* Balander v. Hermes Consolidated, Inc., 295 F. App'x 902 (10th Cir. 2008).

within class-action or aggregate litigation.[1045] A court can also use a master or other adjunct to assist in determining the amount of attorney's fees.[1046]

D. Conclusion

The tale of determining remedies in complex litigation is a familiar one. Traditional doctrines that reinforce the adversarial orientation of our procedural system—for instance, the rightful-position principle and client consent—ill fit the needs of large-scale litigation. The issue again is how much tradition should bend (or, put differently, how much additional power judges should enjoy) to meet the needs of complex litigation. The answer again depends on the source of the traditional rules. Constitutional norms, like the due-process guarantee of adequate representation, bend not at all, although they can sometimes be interpreted sympathetically to the needs of a complex case. Rules of quasi-constitutional stature, such as the rightful position, are also difficult to sidestep. But other rules, such as the right of every litigant to consent to a settlement of his or her claim, can be altered when the policy arguments against them are strong enough, as they sometimes are.

Alterations in the rules determining remedies usually result in the accretion of power to the judge, who steps in when the parties cannot easily meet their obligations. Increasing judicial power when the realities of complex litigation make it difficult for other players to fulfill their traditional roles has been a theme throughout this book. As you near the book's conclusion, you should be forming a clearer opinion about the wisdom of expanded judicial authority. Is the model of an empowered judge a positive development—one in which complex litigation has blazed the trail for the litigation of the future? Is it a necessary evil that should be tolerated only when necessary to ensure that victims of mass injury receive an effective and just remedy? Or is the empowered judge a wrong turn that should be resisted in every facet of a complex case?

[1045] *See In re* Nat'l Football League Players Concussion Injury Litig., 821 F.3d 410 (3d Cir. 2016). *See also* PRINCIPLES OF AGGREGATE LITIGATION, *supra* note 437, § 3.09 (suggesting that a "special officer" could be appointed to represent the interests of the victims in the settlement, a "neutral or special master" could be appointed as a "neutral advisor" on the fairness of the settlement, or an expert could be appointed "to analyze technical or scientific aspects of a proposed settlement" when the "anticipated benefits" of an appointment outweigh the "likely cost and delay").

[1046] *See* FED. R. CIV. P. 23(h)(4) ("The court may refer issues related to the amount of [class counsel's fee] award to a special master or magistrate judge . . . ."); Pearson v. NBYT, Inc., 772 F.3d 778 (7th Cir. 2014) (suggesting an "independent auditor," appointed under the authority of Federal Rule of Evidence 706, to "estimate the reasonableness of class counsel's billing rates").

Chapter 17

IMPLEMENTING THE REMEDY

Once a court determines the remedy, the court and the lawyers must implement it. This issue of implementing a remedy is not always distinct from the problem of declaring a remedy. If a case of 10,000 plaintiffs settles for a lump sum of $20 million, distributing the money to individual victims can be seen, through one lens, as a problem of determining the proper remedy for each individual; or the distribution can be seen, through another lens, as a problem of implementing the agreed remedy of $20 million. Moreover, the relationship between determining and implementing remedies is somewhat dependent: for example, judges are unlikely to order an injunctive remedy if it cannot be implemented.[1047]

Although little of substance turns on the distinction between determining and implementing remedies, the distinction can help the parties to focus better on exactly what the remedial problem is and how best to respond to it. For ease of exposition, therefore, this Chapter explores a set of issues that generally fall on the side of implementing remedies. Once again, we divide the discussion between injunctive and monetary relief.

A. Implementing Injunctive Remedies

In some complex cases, remedial implementation is a difficult enterprise. First, implementation may require years of incremental adjustments that re-orient an institution's internal culture or create an infrastructure to support the reforms that an injunction aims to establish. Second, the judge is usually ill-equipped, in terms of both experience and resources, to engage in the day-to-day administration or oversight of prisons, school systems, or other institutions operating under a structural decree. Finally, remedial implementation often hinges on the compliance of third persons (such as legislators who hold the purse strings or middle managers who make employment decisions), and that compliance may be difficult to achieve when the nonparties oppose the remedy and garner power from that opposition.

Courts have developed a number of mechanisms to deal with these problems.

[1047] *See supra* note 975 and accompanying text.

1. Removing Impediments to Implementation

When a party claims that a legal obstacle bars the full implementation of the remedy, the court may be able to enjoin enforcement of the obstacle. Perhaps the strongest, and most controversial, example of this power is *Missouri v. Jenkins*.[1048] In *Jenkins* a school district under an order to integrate its schools wished to establish magnet programs and improve its facilities as a way to draw white students back into the district. An obstacle to funding the improvements was a Missouri constitutional amendment that capped the local property taxes that could be used to fund educational enhancements. The district court nonetheless imposed a tax increase. The court of appeals, and ultimately the Supreme Court, held that the district court did not enjoy the power to raise taxes directly, but that it did have the authority to enjoin the operation of any state laws, including the state constitution, which prevented the school district from adequately funding the remedy. The five-member majority in *Jenkins* sounded supportive of the district court's ultimate power to raise taxes, but it held that a court should not use such a power until all lesser means to implement the remedy—like suspending the tax cap—had failed. A vigorous dissent of four Justices, who formed the core of a subsequent *Jenkins* opinion limiting the scope of the district court's power to order educational enhancements, argued that the district court did not have the power to enjoin the enforcement of the state constitution; rather, such a power offended both federalism and separation-of-powers principles, including the "no taxation without representation" cornerstone on which the Republic was founded.[1049]

Although *Jenkins* is an extreme example, a court's equitable and constitutional authority to remove legal impediments to implementing a remedy is broad. In many cases, however, the impediments are practical rather than legal. Here too judges have considerable room to use a range of tactics to build support among the parties or the public for the remedy, and thus to sweep away potential obstacles to implementation.

For instance, in many structural-injunction cases, the judge tasks the defendant with creating the first draft of the decree. That proposal becomes the basis for negotiations between the parties about the shape of the decree. In bringing the defendant into the process of creating a remedy, the court creates more buy-in from the

---

1048 495 U.S. 33 (1990).

1049 The Court's subsequent opinion, which held that some of the remedial measures that the district ordered were impermissible, did not overrule, but can certainly be read to limit, the scope of the holding in the first *Missouri v. Jenkins* case. *See* Missouri v. Jenkins, 515 U.S. 70 (1995) (discussed *supra* notes 969, 972 and accompanying text).

defendant. This approach can be applauded as a pragmatic attempt to use less rather than more judicial power to find a workable solution in an intractable situation that could otherwise bring the court's efficacy into question. But it can also be criticized for employing half measures to remedy a wrong rather than the full measures that victims deserve. If the initial proposal ultimately proves inadequate, starting with the defendant also delays the effective delivery of a remedy.

Judges can also seek to drum up support for a structural injunction by holding public hearings to garner input or explain changes. They may meet with key legislators, administrators, or experts in the field to get a better sense of what is possible. They may also appoint judicial adjuncts to perform these tasks. These departures from the traditional role of the judge in adversarial litigation have been subject to criticism, but most courts and scholars agree that broad authority exists.[1050]

A traditional power that judges can employ to deal with party intransigence in implementing a remedy is contempt, which can be either criminal or civil in nature.[1051] In order to get an institution to act, the contempt sanction must often be draconian to be successful. For instance, in *Spallone v. United States*,[1052] the City of Yonkers agreed to settle a housing discrimination lawsuit. The consent decree was politically unpopular, and a majority of the city council, which had initially voted to approve the consent decree, refused to pass the legislation necessary to implement the relief. The district judge applied direct pressure on the city by levying a $100 fine that doubled for each day that the city refused to comply, as well as a non-increasing $500-per-day fine against each council member who refused to vote to implement the consent decree. After twenty-five days, the fine against the city would have reached more than $1 billion per day, but the court of appeals suspended the fines after seven days, when they amounted to $12,800 per day. The court of

---

1050 *See, e.g.*, Bradley v. Milliken, 620 F.2d 1143 (6th Cir. 1980) (refusing to order the recusal of a judge who commissioned officers and appeared at public forums in a desegregation case, but expressing concern about the judge's conduct). For a small sampling of the wealth of literature—ranging from the anecdotal to the highly theoretical—on the scope of judicial authority to implement structural decrees, see OWEN M. FISS & DOUG RENDLEMAN, INJUNCTIONS (2d ed. 1984); OWEN M. FISS, THE CIVIL RIGHTS INJUNCTION (1978); DONALD L. HOROWITZ, THE COURTS AND SOCIAL POLICY (1977); Barry Friedman, *When Rights Encounter Reality: Enforcing Federal Remedies*, 65 S. CAL. L. REV. 735 (1992); Susan P. Sturm, *A Normative Theory of Public Law Remedies*, 79 GEO. L.J. 1355 (1991); Special Project, *The Remedial Process in Institutional Reform Litigation*, 78 COLUM. L. REV. 784 (1978); Note, *Implementation Problems in Institutional Reform Litigation*, 91 HARV. L. REV. 428 (1977).

1051 *See* Int'l Union, United Mine Workers of Am. v. Bagwell, 512 U.S. 821 (1994) (describing the three forms of criminal contempt, civil coercive contempt, and civil compensatory contempt, as well as the procedures that attach to each form).

1052 493 U.S. 265 (1990).

appeals affirmed the contempt sanctions several weeks later, although it capped the city's fine at $1 million per day. Within a short time, Yonkers had essentially become bankrupt, with plans for vital services such as garbage pickup to be suspended and most city workers to be laid off.

After about two weeks, two council members switched their votes. The city and council members still continued to challenge the contempt orders in the Supreme Court. The Supreme Court declined to review the contempt sanction against the city, but the Court's language seemed strongly supportive of them. With regard to the contempt sanction against the council members, however, the Court noted that sanctions against the recalcitrant council members created separation-of-powers, federalism, and free-speech concerns. Given "the reasonable probability that sanctions against the city would accomplish the desired result" (which it did), the Court thought that the contempt sanction against the legislators was premature and impermissible. "Only if [the contempt sanction against the city] failed to produce compliance within a reasonable time should the question of imposing contempt sanctions against petitioners even have been considered."

Using the contempt power to ratchet up pressure slowly is consistent with the usual approach to implementing structural injunctions: try to cajole rather than coerce compliance. For this reason, judges are typically reluctant to reach into the judicial tool box to pull out contempt until it is absolutely necessary. The judge has no stronger medicine to bring a recalcitrant party into compliance with an injunction than contempt, and if that does not work, the available options are very few. Perhaps a court can close a company down or put a city into receivership as an ultimate form of contempt,[1053] but that act could have far-flung repercussions for workers or communities and may be excessively punitive in light of the nature of the underlying wrong.

2. Overseeing the Implementation of the Remedy

Even when a large institution supports the implementation of the injunction, hiccups can arise. Mid-level people on whom the remedy ultimately depends may not be on board, the general terms of the injunction may need to be particularized to specific contexts, or the original plans may prove ineffective. To address these issues, a judge often must exercise ongoing monitoring and oversight to

[1053] *See* Newman v. Alabama, 466 F. Supp. 628 (M.D. Ala. 1979) (naming the Governor the receiver for a state prison system after noting that "[f]urther injunctions or contempt proceedings will not accomplish the task of compliance; such remedies promise only confrontation and delay. When the usual remedies are inadequate, a court is justified in resorting to a receivership, particularly when it acts in aid of an outstanding injunction.").

ensure that the remedy is effectively implemented and is adjusted as circumstances warrant.

Oversight issues often require patience, pragmatism, and, on occasion, hard-heartedness. Because it is often impossible for the judge to oversee every aspect of the reorganization of a large, complex institution and inappropriate for the judge to assume the responsibility of actually running the institution, the judge again must rely on a host of judicial adjuncts, including special masters and monitors with the organization.[1054] In rare instances a judge may appoint a receiver to run a truly recalcitrant institution.[1055] These adjuncts often receive broad powers from the court.

As with other uses of judicial adjuncts, however, certain concerns arise: the unconventional and often ex parte nature of the adjuncts' operations, the creation of a bureaucracy with greater affinity to the administrative than the judicial process, cost, ineffectiveness, overly broad mandates, separation-of-powers and federalism concerns, and abdication of the traditional judicial function are the most frequently mentioned.[1056]

3. Dealing with Third-Party Intransigence

As the *Spallone* saga reveals, implementing a remedy often requires the cooperation of third parties. Legislators must vote necessary funds; executives must put into place programmatic reforms; the public must accept the legitimacy of the court and remedy. Unless key players buy into the injunction, the remedy is unlikely to be effective. Many judges are skilled political actors, and, as we have seen, they may meet and negotiate with key figures to create acceptance of the ordered remedy. But these efforts will not always be successful, especially when the key players derive their political or social power from the very fact that they are "sticking it to the man" and resisting the court.

[1054] *See, e.g.*, Ruiz v. Estelle, 679 F.2d 1115 (5th Cir. 1982), *amended in part and vacated in part on other grounds*, 688 F.2d 266 (5th Cir. 1982) (approving the use of a special master appointed under Rule 53 to ensure that a prison-reform decree was properly implemented, as well as several monitors). On the use of monitors to ensure corporate compliance after criminal or civil proceedings have been resolved, see Veronica Root, *The Monitor-"Client" Relationship*, 100 VA. L. REV. 523 (2014).

[1055] *See, e.g.*, Morgan v. McDonough, 540 F.2d 527 (1st Cir. 1976) (affirming the appointment of the school district superintendent as receiver of South Boston High School).

[1056] *See* Newman v. Alabama, 559 F.2d 283 (5th Cir. 1977) (rejecting a 39-member "Human Rights Committee" to monitor compliance in a prison-reform case when committee members did not have monitoring expertise, size made the committee unwieldy, the committee's mandate was too broad, and the committee functionally had taken over the administration of the prison). *See also* Women Prisoners of the D.C. Dep't of Corr. v. Dist. of Columbia, 93 F.3d 910 (D.C. Cir. 1996) (reversing order that authorized monitors to "perform the functions of local authorities" and therefore "effectively usurp[ed] the executive functions of the District").

The problem of third-party intransigence returns us, in a sense, to where this book began: how do we include all interested parties in a single case? As we learned, a court can usually issue binding orders only against parties to a case. Hence, in some situations, the best response is to join the recalcitrant person, thus establishing judicial power over the person. But this is rarely an effective solution. For one thing, joinder after establishing liability usually cannot bind the third party to rulings that occurred before joinder. For another, many third parties do not have the type of legal interest that permits their joinder. Suppose that an influential local pastor tells his parishioners to disobey a desegregation plan or to move to a white suburb. Under what theory can the pastor be joined as a party? The pastor has committed no legal wrong. Should the pastor wish to intervene in the case, Rule 24 could arguably be interpreted expansively enough to allow the pastor to join.[1057] But if the pastor prefers to remain on the outside of the lawsuit throwing rocks at the remedy, his forced joinder seems unlikely.

Spallone, which refused to authorize the contempt power against legislators who were blocking implementation of a remedy, shows the difficulty of bringing the court's power home to third parties. But *Spallone* is an unusual case with highly charged facts, as well as separation-of-powers, federalism, and free-speech overtones. The classic case of a judicial response to nonparty intransigence is *United States v. Hall*,[1058] in which the district court was struggling to enforce an unpopular desegregation decree. Hall was an African-American community activist who vehemently opposed the plan. Eventually the district court issues an ex parte order preventing the parties, or anyone else with actual notice of the order, from entering onto school grounds except in limited situations. After having been specifically served with a copy of the order, Hall entered onto school property to protest the court's orders and was held in contempt by the district court.

The court of appeals upheld the contempt sanction. According to *Hall*, a court has an inherent power "to protect its ability to render a binding judgment." That power extended not only to the parties to the dispute, but also to those nonparties with actual knowledge of the order, when the activities of the nonparties might "disturb[ ] in any way the adjudication of the rights and obligations as between the original plaintiffs and defendants." The court of appeals was also unpersuaded that the ex parte nature of the order was, under the circumstances, inappropriate.

1057 *See supra* Chapter 2.B.3.

1058 472 F.2d 261 (5th Cir. 1972).

Hall's extension of an injunction to a nonparty is not justified by the Federal Rules of Civil Procedure. Rule 65(d)(2) limits the binding effect of an injunction to three categories of persons: "the parties"; "the parties' officers, agents, servants, employees, and attorneys"; and "other persons who are in active concert or participation with" these individuals. Hall fell into none of these categories. His contempt sanction can be justified, if at all, only through the inherent power of a federal court to enforce its orders.

In dicta, the Supreme Court has signaled apparent approval of *Hall*'s use of contempt against a nonparty.[1059] Even in *Spallone*, the Court broadly hinted that, had the sanctions against the city proven ineffective, the court would have been able to hold the legislators in contempt. This acquiescence is difficult to square with the Court's usual insistence that nonparties cannot be bound by a judgment—even when they are aware of the judgment and even when their absence threatens to undo the effect of the judgment.[1060] A possible reconciliation is that Hall threatened to compromise the efficacy of judgment by doing something that he had no right to do (enter the school grounds), while nonparties who insist on the exercise of their legal rights cannot be forced to sacrifice them just to make the remedy more effective.

> *Question*
>
> *Hall*'s argument that courts have an inherent power to protect their judgments sounds a bit like the proposition that the All-Writs Act, 28 U.S.C. § 1651, incorporates the Anti-Injunction Act's exception allowing a federal court to issue injunctions to stay state court proceedings when necessary "to protect or effectuate its judgments." As we have seen (*see supra* notes 230–250 and accompanying text), in recent years the Supreme Court has tended to limit the scope of the All-Writs Act and the Anti-Injunction Act. Do those limits affect the holding in *Hall*?

B. Implementing Monetary Remedies

Related but different problems arise in implementing an award of monetary relief. Distributing the award to victims is the principal difficulty. A secondary issue is, once again, third-party intransigence, albeit in a different form. Some defendants may refuse to settle a case as long as they remain exposed to claims from other parties, including co-defendants. Whether courts can sweep away these

---

[1059] *See* Washington v. Wash. State Commercial Passenger Fishing Vessel Ass'n, 443 U.S. 658 (1979); Golden State Bottling Co. v. NLRB, 414 U.S. 169 (1973).

[1060] *See* S. Cent. Bell Tel. Co. v. Alabama, 526 U.S. 160 (1999); Richards v. Jefferson Cty., 517 U.S. 793 (1996); Martin v. Wilks, 490 U.S. 755 (1989); *see generally supra* notes 261–265 (describing the circumstances in which nonparty preclusion may arise).

claims to implement a settlement again raises the question of a court's power to alter nonparty's rights to bring a complex case to a conclusion.

1. Distributing Money

As we have described, one difficulty in distributing monetary relief arises when a case involves a lump-sum judgment or settlement. When claims and damages vary, figuring out how much each victim deserves from this lump sum can be difficult. Other problems in distributing an award arise when many of the victims are unknown or when the cost of determining the appropriate amount of individual recoveries is so high that most or all of the awards will be consumed in the process of providing a remedy. Weeding out opportunistic claimants from true victims is another issue. Yet another problem may involve getting the victims to file a claim in the first place, especially when the recovery is so small that many people may not regard the effort as worthwhile.

These distributional concerns have a common question at their core: how important is it to compensate victims precisely (as the rightful position demands) as opposed to deter defendants? From a compensation perspective, the important thing is to give each victim his or her due. From a deterrence perspective, the important thing is to take the money from the defendant; whether it goes to the victims is irrelevant. As a deterrence matter, the only reason to pay the victim is to provide an incentive to the victim to bring suit.[1061] In a mass dispute, however, that incentive is typically unnecessary: the size of the attorney's fees is likely to attract interest in the lawsuit. So compensation is unnecessary to provide deterrence. But is compensation a *sine qua non* of the private litigation process, so that the inability to deliver the correct amount of compensation to each victim defeats the lawsuit in the end?

Courts in judgments, as well as settlings parties in their agreements, have tried to address some of these issues by creating schedules that key compensation to simple, objective criteria such as proximity to and duration of exposure, medical condition, and extent of proof of injury. Developing these criteria often poses difficulties for the lawyers who represent the victims, for they must make tradeoffs among different groups of claimants with different injuries.[1062] To make the process run more smoothly, courts and parties can employ special masters, panels of physicians, and insurance companies to

---

[1061] *See* RICHARD A. POSNER, ECONOMIC ANALYSIS OF LAW §§ 6.10, 21.11 (7th ed. 2007).

[1062] *See* Silver & Baker, *supra* note 357, at 1468 ("Conflicts of interest and associated tradeoffs among plaintiffs are an unavoidable part of all group lawsuits and all group settlements.").

establish eligibility criteria, assess claims, and distribute proceeds from a judgment or settlement.[1063]

In addition, courts may limit attorney's fees to a percentage of the amount of claims actually asserted against a fund, rather than the full value of the fund, as a means of encouraging counsel to make their best efforts to recruit victims to file claims for compensation.

Perhaps the thorniest issue, and one that concentrates the debate about compensation versus deterrence on a single point, is what to do when some of the compensation fund goes unclaimed. Should those who filed claims get more, even if they end up being overcompensated? Should the unclaimed funds revert to the defendant? Or can the court direct the funds to another, likely charitable, purpose?

This set of questions involves the doctrine of *cy pres*.[1064] *Cy pres* originally was (and still is) a doctrine of trust law developed to deal with a charitable trust that could no longer meet its intended purpose: perhaps, for instance, a trust was established to maintain a church, but the church burned down and was not rebuilt. Courts needed to determine whether the trust funds should be given back to the grantor (or the grantor's heirs), should escheat to the government, or should be directed to a similar charitable purpose (perhaps the maintenance of a nearby church). *Cy pres* (from the law French "*cy pres comme possible*," or "as near as possible") was the principle invoked when the funds were rededicated to another charitable purpose.

You can see how the basic problem of *cy pres* resembles the problem of distributing relief in complex cases. Money that has been designated for a purpose (compensating victims) fails to achieve that purpose fully, typically due to a low claiming rate by victims. Relying on the *cy pres* analogy, some courts began to distribute unclaimed funds to charitable purposes. Often the charity was loosely associated with purpose of the lawsuit: for instance, the judge might give the excess proceeds from a toxic-tort case to an environmental organization or a college's biology department. But sometimes judges gave the money to a favorite local charity.

[1063] For a description of some common features of claims-resolution facilities, see Mark A. Peterson, *Giving Away Money: Comparative Comments on Claims Resolution Facilities*, 53 LAW & CONTEMP. PROBS. 113 (Autumn 1990).

[1064] Some courts have used the label "fluid recovery," rather than "*cy pres*," to describe the issue. *See* Mirfasihi v. Fleet Mortg. Corp., 356 F.3d 781 (7th Cir. 2004) (noting that "*cy pres*" is "badly misnamed, but the alternative—'fluid recovery'—is no less misleading"). Both labels discuss the same phenomenon, so the exact label is unimportant. In recent years, courts have tended to use "*cy pres*" rather than "fluid recovery."

Cy pres became controversial as it turned into a vehicle that avoided the obligation to provide individual compensation to the victims of mass wrongdoing. Defendants argued that unclaimed funds should be returned to them.[1065] Objectors claimed that unclaimed funds proved that counsel was more concerned with generating an award from which they could claim a large fee than with adequately representing victims. Defenders of *cy pres* made three arguments. First, without *cy pres* either the claiming plaintiffs or the defendants would receive a windfall: giving the unclaimed funds to plaintiffs who already received an award would overcompensate those plaintiffs, while returning the unclaimed funds to the defendant would underdeter the defendant. Second, the cost of determining who was owed the unclaimed funds—including the costs of notice and distribution—might exceed the size of the fund, so that attempts to distribute the money was wasteful. Third, returning the money to the defendant resulted in insufficient deterrence. These arguments concluded with the proposition that giving the money to a charity that worked to advance interests aligned with the purpose of the lawsuit created a benefit for victims who received no monetary award.

These arguments suggest different stopping points for *cy pres* relief. Under one approach, *cy pres* is possible even when distribution of unclaimed funds is economically feasible. Under the other, *cy pres* is available only when further distribution of funds is infeasible.

The American Law Institute essentially adopted the latter approach to *cy pres* relief, recommending that any unclaimed funds from a settlement be presumptively distributed to victims who were already participating in the settlement and that *cy pres* distributions be allowed only when "the amounts involved are too small to make individual distributions economically viable."[1066] But the ALI also carved out a small additional exception that allowed *cy pres* when "other specific reasons exist that would make further distributions impossible or unfair." When *cy pres* was permissible, the ALI specified that the recipient of the *cy pres* award must be someone "involving the same subject matter as the lawsuit that reasonably approximates the interests being pursued by the class."

In recent years, courts have been unwilling to permit a *cy pres* remedy unless awarding individual remedies proves infeasible. In some instances, however, the infeasibility requirement may lead to

---

[1065] This argument is unavailing in settlements in which the parties agree that unclaimed funds will be put to a *cy pres* use. Plaintiffs often press for a *cy pres* clause to prevent reversion; and while defendants would generally prefer a reversion of unclaimed funds, they are willing to cave on the issue as long as the settlement places a cap on their liability.

[1066] *See* PRINCIPLES OF AGGREGATE LITIGATION, *supra* note 437, § 3.07.

cy pres on a broad scale. For example, in *In re Google Referrer Header Privacy Litigation*,[1067] a class action alleged that Google violated the privacy of the users of its search engines by disclosing the users' search terms to owners of other websites. The case settled for $8.5 million—$3.2 million in attorney's fees and $5.3 million set aside for six organizations that agreed to promote awareness or support research regarding privacy protection on the Internet. After a hearing in which the district court vetted the proposals from the organizations, it approved the settlement. Objectors, who argued that a *cy pres*-only settlement was impermissible, appealed.

The court of appeals affirmed the approval of the settlement and the fee award. Regarding the settlement, the court of appeals noted that none of the objectors had proven that they suffered any monetary injury from the defendant's actions, nor did they contest that the settlement had value to the class and themselves. It then stated that none of its prior cases had "imposed a categorical ban on a settlement that does not include direct payments to class members."[1068] As reasons for permitting a *cy pres*-only settlement, it pointed to the weakness of the claims and the fact that each class member would receive four cents from the settlement. Distributing a remedy of such small amount was infeasible.

The objectors proposed that funds be distributed to a few class members by lottery or to award class members who filed claims $5 or $10 apiece, on the theory that such an amount might induce a sufficient number of class members to file claims against the $5.3 million fund. Both alternatives were feasible and would have assured that the settlement found its way into the hands of class members, although those who received money would have been vastly overcompensated. The court of appeals did not reject either method, but it also did not believe that the district court abused its discretion in finding that the settlement as negotiated was fair and free of

---

[1067] 869 F.3d 737 (9th Cir. 2017), *petition for cert. granted sub nom.* Frank v. Gaos, 2018 WL 324121 (U.S. Apr. 30, 2018) (No. 17–961). Certiorari in *Frank* was granted just as this book went to press. Its ultimate result is likely to have great influence in the *cy pres* field.

[1068] The court of appeals for the Ninth Circuit, which decided *Google Referrer*, had been active in setting boundaries around *cy pres* settlements. *See, e.g.*, Lane v. Facebook, Inc., 696 F.3d 811 (9th Cir. 2012); Nachshin v. AOL, LLC, 663 F.3d 1034 (9th Cir. 2011).

collusion. Super-compensatory remedies to some victims were not necessarily better than a *cy pres*-only remedy.

Other courts have exhibited a more doubtful attitude toward *cy pres* relief. In *Klier v. Elf Autochem North America, Inc.*,[1069] the settlement agreement in a toxic-exposure case provided for different lump-sum awards to three subclasses. Members of one subclass did not submit enough claims to exhaust their fund. The settlement agreement did not provide a process for distributing unclaimed funds. The district court distributed the excess funds on a *cy pres* basis to a scholarship program, two museums, and a charity nominated by the court (a local history and genealogy library). The Fifth Circuit held that the *cy pres* distribution was an abuse of discretion, and the court should instead have directed the unused funds to the benefit of one of the other subclasses. The court thought that this approach best comported with the language of the settlement agreement, thus defeating the defendant's argument that any unclaimed funds reverted to it. But the court also stated that this result was dictated by law: direct distributions to class members are preferable because "[t]he settlement-fund proceeds, having been generated by the value of the class members' claims," are "the property of the class."[1070] A concurring opinion went even further, arguing that, had the settlement agreement not waived the defendant's right to seek reversion, unclaimed settlement funds were required to be returned to the defendant. Put differently, *cy pres* relief, additional compensation to class members, and an escheat to the government were all illegitimate. The dissent concluded with the

> *Problem*
>
> A class action alleging that a defendant sold customer information to telemarketers settled. Within the class were 1.4 million people who bought nothing from the telemarketers and 190,000 people who bought deceptively marketed financial services that they did not need. The settlement provided that the defendant would disgorge the $243,000 in profits it made from selling the information. In addition, the defendant established a fund of $2.4 million to make payments ranging from $10 to $135 to the 190,000 victims of the telemarketing scams, and $750,000 in attorney's fees. Because the $243,000 fund amounted to less than twenty cents per class member, the settlement added this amount to the $2.4 million available to the telemarketing victims. The defendant retained a reversionary interest in any unclaimed funds. The parties justified the transfer as a form of *cy pres* relief necessitated by the infeasibility of providing individual relief. Should the settlement be approved? *See* Mirfasihi v. Fleet Mortg. Corp., 356 F.3d 781 (7th Cir. 2004).

1069 658 F.3d 468 (5th Cir. 2011).

1070 *See* Klier v. Elf Autochem N. Am., Inc., 658 F.3d 468 (5th Cir. 2011).

observation that "[o]ur adversarial system should not effectuate transfers of funds from defendants beyond what they owe *to the parties* in judgments or settlements."[1071]

Some hints about the Supreme Court's views on *cy pres* cropped up in a denial of certiorari.[1072] When a class of Facebook users sued the company for violating their privacy rights, the company settled for $9.5 million, with $3 million going to class counsel for fees and costs and to the class representatives for incentive payments. The remaining $6.5 million went into *cy pres* relief, on the familiar theory that individual awards to Facebook users would be so small that the distribution would not be worthwhile. The foundation to which the *cy pres* award was made was newly constituted, and included on its board of directors a senior employee of the defendant. To make matters more nettlesome, the settlement agreement also released future claims of class members.

Although the Supreme Court denied certiorari, Chief Justice Roberts took the unusual step of issuing a statement respecting the denial of certiorari. The Chief Justice agreed that the case did not warrant Supreme Court review because the objections focused on features peculiar to the settlement, so that "[g]ranting review of this case might not have afforded the Court an opportunity to address more fundamental concerns surrounding the use of such remedies in class action litigation." Those issues included "when, if ever, such relief should be considered; how to assess its fairness as a general matter; whether new entities may be established as part of such relief; if not, how existing entities should be selected; what the respective roles of the judge and parties are in shaping a *cy pres* remedy; [and] how closely the goals of any enlisted organization must correspond to the interests of the class."

2. Dealing with Third-Party Intransigence

In contrast to injunctive relief, monetary relief does not usually depend on the good will or the actions of third parties. The defendant pays the money and that's that. In some cases, however, third parties make settlement difficult. Defendants prefer global peace. Among the claims that can thwart global peace are contribution and indemnity claims from co-defendants. A defendant usually does not wish to settle with the plaintiffs when it remains potentially liable on these third-party actions.

[1071] *Id.* at 482 (Jones, Ch. J., concurring).

[1072] Marek v. Lane, 571 U.S. 1003 (2013). The Ninth Circuit's opinion is *Lane*, 696 F.3d 811. Before petitioning for a writ of certiorari, objectors sought en banc review in the court of appeals. Although en banc rehearing was denied, six members of the court of appeals dissented from that decision. *See* Lane v. Facebook, Inc., 709 F.3d 791 (9th Cir. 2013).

In response, some courts have entered "settlement bar orders" that extinguish all claims from co-defendants that are related to the litigation and that are asserted against a settling defendant. In effect, the bar order gives the settling defendant global peace in return for its settlement with the plaintiffs.

Courts that have authorized bar orders often do so on the theory that public policy favors settlement, especially in complex litigation.[1073] Because bar orders usually reach the claims of co-defendants, they do not suffer directly from the prohibition that a court's orders cannot bind nonparties, but it is evident that due process requires, at a minimum, that the co-parties subject to a bar order receive notice and an opportunity to be heard. Courts that have approved bar orders have split over whether the order can reach only contribution claims, both contribution and indemnity claims, or all claims that are related to the underlying suit (whether contribution, indemnity, or independent in nature).[1074]

The source of authority to issue bar orders is uncertain and their legality is less than clear.[1075] When a court enters a bar order, it must often ensure that the amount of the settlement is deducted from any damages that the non-settling defendants ultimately owe to the plaintiffs, lest the plaintiffs gain a windfall recovery.[1076]

The settlement-bar doctrine raises, as had the power of a court to make its injunction effective against nonparties, the breadth of a court's power to bind others to its decisions as a means of bringing a complex dispute to a satisfactory close. The same tension that has recurred throughout this book—each person's adversarial right to a day in court versus the need to resolve mass litigation in an efficacious manner—emerges again as a central issue.

[1073] *See In re* U.S. Oil & Gas Litig., 967 F.2d 489 (11th Cir. 1992) ("[B]ar orders play an integral role in facilitating settlement.").

[1074] *Compare U.S. Oil & Gas*, 967 F.3d 489 (barring all claims), *with In re* Heritage Bond Litig., 546 F.3d 667 (9th Cir. 2008) (overturning a bar order that sought to release claims other than contribution and indemnity claims); AAL High Yield Bond Fund v. Deloitte & Touche, LLP, 361 F.3d 1305 (11th Cir. 2004) (limiting *U.S. Oil & Gas* to claims for contribution and indemnity, not independent claims); Gerber v. MTC Elec. Techs. Co., 329 F.3d 297 (2d Cir. 2003) (same).

[1075] *See* TBG, Inc. v. Bendis, 36 F.3d 916 (10th Cir. 1994) (rejecting the proposition "that the interest in settlement can give courts the power to bar statutory contribution claims," but suggesting that the All Writs Act may provide a source of authority to enter bar orders over contribution claims in appropriate cases); *id.* (suggesting that, for state-law claims, the issue of a court's capacity to bar a claim is ultimately a question of state law).

[1076] *See In re* Jiffy Lube Sec. Litig., 927 F.3d 155 (4th Cir. 1991) (reversing a bar order that failed to provide a proper setoff method to protect the non-settling defendants from compensating plaintiffs for losses for which the settling defendants had already paid).

C. Conclusion

Remedial complexity poses different issues than the other forms of complexity. Gone, at least directly, are procedural concerns—like transactionalism, trans-substantivity, and jury trial—that constrain judicial authority in other phases of litigation. Still, important connections to other forms of complexity remain. Adversarialism remains an important theme, both as a buttress for the rightful-position principle and as a limit on a court's ability to implement remedies. The problem of agency costs and inadequate representation often become most acute in the remedial phase, especially as a remedy is implemented or distributed. Finally, the scope of judicial power to overcome the barriers that complex litigation places in the way of efficient and fair resolutions of mass disputes remains a constant theme.

Chapter 18

ATTORNEY'S FEES

Our final topic is attorney's fees. The subject may strike you as a matter of grubby practicality that does not belong in a book devoted to how complex cases should be resolved. Grubby or not, the subject of fees is one of enormous importance to complex litigation. At a practical level, without money to be made, the field of complex litigation would not exist. Lawyers would devote their talents to other legal endeavors that paid better. At a theoretical level, we have seen repeatedly how concerns for agency costs, collusion, and inadequate representation have shaped doctrine. In one way or another, these concerns all arise because of the temptations of money—money principally in the form of attorney's fees. Furthermore, as a matter of policy, the old prosecutorial adage "follow the money" applies no less in complex litigation. If we are going to understand how the players in the complex-litigation enterprise act, and if we are going to propose reforms that might make them act in a more socially beneficial manner, we need to understand lawyers' present incentive structure.

The starting point for any discussion about attorney's fees in American litigation is the "American rule." The American rule requires each side to bear its own attorney's fees and costs.[1077] It is distinguishable from the "loser-pays" rule (sometimes called the "English rule"), which requires the losing party to bear the fees and expenses for both parties. The American rule creates an incentive to bring cases of less certain merit than the loser-pays rule, although it also can help to keep down the costs of litigation: under the loser-pays rule, parties believing that they have an excellent chance of winning have little reason to hold down litigation costs. Although the American rule is the default approach in virtually every American jurisdiction,[1078] there are many exceptions: at the federal level, for example, approximately two hundred statutes provide for fee shifting in favor of the prevailing party.[1079]

1077 *See* Alyeska Pipeline Serv. Co. v. Wilderness Soc'y, 421 U.S. 240 (1975).

1078 Only Alaska adopts a loser-pays rule as a general matter. *See* ALASKA STAT. § 09.60.010 (2012). *See also* TEX. CIV. PRAC. & REM. CODE ANN. § 38.001 (West 2005) (permitting fee shifting in a range of civil matters); Stephen B. Burbank et al., *Private Enforcement*, 17 LEWIS & CLARK L. REV. 637 (2013) (discussing the general use of the American rule in state courts).

1079 *See* HENRY COHEN, CONG. RESEARCH SERV., AWARDS OF ATTORNEYS' FEES BY FEDERAL COURTS AND FEDERAL AGENCIES (2008) (listing fee-shifting statutes, as well as fee-shifting provisions at common law and under the Federal Rules of Civil Procedure). A number of these statutes are imbalanced, in the sense that the standard

Usually discussions about attorney's fees in complex litigation center on the fees of plaintiffs' lawyers. Scant attention is paid to fees of defense counsel. To some extent, this lack of emphasis is understandable. Defense counsel do not bring lawsuits, so if we are trying to foster an environment with a socially optimal level of litigation, focusing on the incentives that fee structures create for plaintiffs' lawyers makes more sense. Moreover, the fee paid to defense counsel is a boring subject. Ethical proscriptions prevent defense lawyers from being paid on a contingency basis. While some defense lawyers work on a salary or a retainer, almost all earn their fees by charging their clients by the hour.

Although charging by the hour may seem uninteresting, the effect of hourly rates on defense counsel's litigation behavior is well known: they "prefer to leave no stone unturned, provided, of course, they can charge by the stone."[1080] Some plaintiffs' lawyers contend that restrictive doctrines for which defense counsel in complex litigation advocate (sometimes successfully) arise from counsel's incentive to drag out proceedings rather than from the desire to represent defendants effectively.[1081] Defense counsel, of course, do not accept this characterization of their motivations. Whatever the truth—and it likely varies somewhat from case to case and law firm to law firm—it is important to understand that discussion about the impact of attorney's fees on complex litigation should not be entirely about the fees of plaintiffs' lawyers.

That said, the rest of this Chapter focuses on the fees of plaintiffs' lawyers.

Plaintiffs' lawyers can use a number of methods to charge for their services. Like defense counsel, they can be a salaried employee of the plaintiff. They can work on a retainer. They can charge by the hour. But plaintiffs' lawyers also have another option: they can employ a contingency fee, under which they obtain a percentage of the recovery if—and only if—the case results in a recovery for the client. Ethical rules in every jurisdiction limit the percentage to a reasonable amount. Traditionally, a one-third contingency fee was

---

for fee shifting in favor of a plaintiff is different from, and usually less onerous than, the standard for fee shifting in favor of a defendant. *See* Fox v. Vice, 563 U.S. 826 (2011) (noting that 42 U.S.C. § 1988 "ordinarily" permits a prevailing plaintiff in certain civil-rights actions to obtain a fee, but it limits fees to prevailing defendants under "a different standard" that requires a showing that the plaintiff's claim was "frivolous, unreasonable, or without foundation") (internal quotation marks omitted).

[1080] *See* Deborah L. Rhode, *Ethical Perspectives on Legal Practice*, 37 STAN. L. REV. 589 (1985).

[1081] *Cf.* Samuel Issacharoff et al., *Bargaining Impediments and Settlement Behavior*, *in* DISPUTE RESOLUTION: BRIDGING THE SETTLEMENT GAP 51 (David A. Anderson ed. 1996) ("[L]awyers foment controversy and prolong litigation because they make money by doing so.").

the norm, although lawyers in some jurisdictions may now charge forty percent (with the fee rising to fifty percent if there is an appeal). The client also remains responsible for paying the costs of litigation. In theory, this fee contains two components: an amount that compensates the lawyer for his or her time and an amount that compensates the lawyer for the risk that the lawyer will earn no fee. This latter component is, in essence, a subsidy from successful clients to unsuccessful clients.

A contingent fee allows people who cannot otherwise afford a lawyer (that is, cannot afford a lawyer's hourly rate) to have access to legal representation. For that reason, it is despised by many defendants because it enables litigation that they otherwise would not face. Because the contingent fee is rarely useful in cases seeking injunctive relief (how can a lawyer receive a percentage of an injunction?), the cases that contingent fees especially enable are claims seeking money. In cases involving an injunction, a lawyer must be compensated in a different way—usually on an hourly basis if the lawyer works directly for the client but perhaps on a salaried basis if the lawyer works for a public-interest group that agrees to represent a plaintiff.

As a general matter, the fee is a private matter between lawyer and client, as long as the fee stays within the ethical guideline of reasonableness. The court has no role in setting or policing the fee. The same *laissez faire* attitude prevails in aggregate litigation. As we have seen, non-class aggregate litigation has traditionally been viewed as just a bunch of individual cases stuck together, so that the rules that applied to individual litigation pertain to aggregate litigation as well. As a result, the fees that counsel earn for representing a group is none of the court's business. This hands-off attitude means that the lawyers can—and sometimes do—walk away with a third to forty percent of some very large aggregate recoveries, even though the level of risk or the level of additional work on any individual case would not seem to justify such a fee. Because courts regulate the fees awarded in a class action, the largely unregulated nature of fees in non-class aggregate litigation can factor into a lawyer's decision about the form in which aggregation occurs.[1082]

[1082] One of the arguments that the objectors made in the *Amchem* settlement was that class counsel held their 14,000 existing clients' cases out of the class settlement and struck a side deal with the defendants. In some instances, the lawyers obtained compensation for individual clients even though the class settlement provided nothing for similarly situated class members. As a result, the lawyers stood to gain a larger fee from the individual cases than the fee they would have earned from those cases had they been folded into the class action. The district court did not accept the argument that this split of the cases amounted to unethical behavior or created a conflict of interest. Although the smell of the issue hung in the air on appeal, neither the Third Circuit nor the Supreme Court ultimately held that counsel's representation of the class was therefore inadequate. *See* Georgine v. Amchem Prods., Inc, 157 F.R.D.

In three situations, however, judges have the power to award fees. First, in class actions, Rule 23(h) permits the judge "to award reasonable attorney's fees and nontaxable costs that are authorized by law or by the parties' agreement." Second, a court may award fees when a fee-shifting statute or rule authorizes an award. Finally, a court may award a fee to an attorney whose work creates a "common benefit" or "common fund" for a group of litigants.

In class actions, the somewhat open-ended and permissive language of Rule 23(h) has crystalized into a fairly clear rule: courts will in almost every instance determine the appropriate award and will not leave the amount of the award to be set by the parties' agreement. Because they tend to ignore the fee established in the retainer agreement between class counsel and the class representatives, the court must adopt another method to determine a reasonable fee for class counsel.

Courts tend to employ one of two methods. Under the first, known as the "lodestar method," the fee is determined by multiplying the hours worked by the hourly rate commensurate with a lawyer's experience, talent, and locality. Once the hourly fee is determined, a court then retains the discretion to raise or lower this fee by means of a "multiplier." This multiplier can reflect such factors as the risk that the lawyer took on, the degree of success obtained, the quality of the lawyer's performance, and other factors.[1083] For instance, in *In re Sears, Roebuck & Co. Front-Loading Washer Products Liability Litigation*,[1084] the plaintiff classes settled for $900,000. In the settlement, the defendant also agreed to pay the fees of class counsel, who agreed to seek no more than $6 million for their representation in a novel and difficult case. Class counsel produced billing records that showed that their fees had been $3.25 million, and they asked the district for a multiplier of 1.85 to bring the fees up to $6 million.

The district court limited the fees to $2.7 million and the multiplier to 1.75, for a total fee of $4.77 million. The defendant appealed, and the court of appeals reversed. It noted that the average multiplier in the circuit was 1.85, but it also cited a study showing

---

246 (E.D. Pa. 1994), *rev'd*, 83 F.3d 610 (3d Cir. 1996), *aff'd* sub nom. Amchem Prods., Inc. v. Windsor, 521 U.S. 591 (1997). For an impassioned argument—made by one of the ethics experts whose opinion the district court rejected—that this arrangement was unethical, see Koniak, *supra* note 378, at 1055 ("[The defendants] paid class counsel on the side, by which I mean outside the class action proceeding through the client settlements, for agreeing to support the class settlement. Or to put it even more bluntly, [the defendants] bought off the class lawyers.").

[1083] *See* Perdue v. Kenny A. *ex rel.* Winn, 559 U.S. 542 (2010) (stating that, under one fee-shifting statute (42 U.S.C. § 1988), the use of a multiplier should be "a rare circumstance" and that a case's complexity is reflected in the hours worked and therefore should not ordinarily be used as a separate consideration).

[1084] 867 F.3d 791 (7th Cir. 2017).

that the nationwide multiplier for cases in which the recovery was less than $1.1 million was only .88.[1085] Although the circuit had adopted a presumption that attorney's fees should not exceed the benefit to the class,[1086] the court thought that the difficulty of the case, the "powerful corporation" that was the opponent, and the effort of counsel merited a somewhat greater award: $2.7 million, the amount of fees with no multiplier.

The second approach to awarding fees is the percentage-of-the-fund method. As the name suggests, the award operates on the usual contingency-fee principle and gives a percentage of the class's recovery to counsel. This method is more difficult to apply in the context of injunctive relief, although it is often possible to value injunctive relief by determining the benefit of the relief to class members or the cost of compliance to the defendant. As we described above, class counsel's fees under this method usually range from twenty to thirty percent of the total value of the judgment or settlement, with the percentage generally falling to less than twenty percent as the size of the award to the class increases.[1087] In determining the appropriate percentage, the court considers the same factors that influence a decision regarding the size of a multiplier: risk, success, complexity, and the like.

In recent years, the percentage-of-the-fund approach has tended to dominate.[1088] But it is important not to read too much into that fact. Whatever the approach used by the court, the judge often checks the result against the other approach, just to make sure that the fee award is not badly out of line.[1089] Moreover, the choice in federal court may be dictated by state law when the claim is based on diversity jurisdiction.[1090]

[1085] The cited study was Eisenberg & Miller, *supra* note 1025.

[1086] *See supra* note 1026 and accompanying text.

[1087] *See* sources cited *supra* note 1025.

[1088] *See, e.g., In re* Baby Prods. Antitrust Litig., 708 F.3d 163 (3d Cir. 2013) (noting that the percentage-of-the-fund approach "is 'generally favored in cases involving a common fund' ") (quoting *In re* Prudential Ins. Co. of Am. Sales Practice Litig., 148 F.3d 283, 333 (3d Cir. 1998))); Wal-Mart Stores, Inc. v. Visa U.S.A., Inc., 396 F.3d 96 (2d Cir. 2005) ("The trend in this Circuit is toward the percentage method . . . ."); Swedish Hosp. Corp. v. Shalala, 1 F.3d 1261 (D.C. Cir. 1993) ("[A] percentage-of-the-fund method is the appropriate mechanism for determining the attorney fees award in common fund cases"). *But see* McDaniel v. Cty. of Schenectady, 595 F.3d 411 (2d Cir. 2010) (noting the trend toward the percentage-of-the-fund approach, but upholding the use of a lodestar approach).

[1089] *See Baby Products*, 708 F.3d 177–78; *In re* Hyundai & Kia Fuel Econ. Litig., 881 F.3d 679 (9th Cir. 2018) (encouraging courts to cross-check their fee awards by a second method as a means of avoiding "unreasonable results").

[1090] *See* Chieftain Royalty Co. v. Enervest Energy Institutional Fund XIII-A, L.P., 861 F.3d 1181 (10th Cir. 2017) (stating that *Erie* requires a federal court to adopt the method for calculating fees employed in state court and setting aside a fee award

The oft-stated reason for preferring the percentage-of-the-fund method is that it "directly aligns the interests of the class and its counsel and provides a powerful incentive for the efficient prosecution and early resolution of litigation. In contrast, the lodestar creates an unanticipated disincentive to early settlements, tempts lawyers to run up their hours, and compels district courts to engage in a gimlet-eyed review of line-item fee audits."[1091] But the percentage-of-the-recovery approach suffers from the flaws common to all contingency fees, including the incentive to cut a quick deal rather that to fight for every dollar that the class deserves.

One method avoids the problems of both the lodestar and the percentage-of-the-fund approach: calculate class counsel's fee by paying the lawyer the appropriate hourly fee and then add to that amount a percentage of the total recovery that reflects the risk that the lawyer took on. This blend of lodestar and contingency fee aligns the interests of class and counsel perfectly: counsel has an incentive to litigate until another dollar's work of work will not yield another dollar's worth of benefit to the class, but no further.[1092] As yet, however, no court has adopted this approach.

When fee-shifting statutes or rules require a court to award fees, the same two methods also apply. Perhaps because of some early Supreme Court precedent in civil-rights cases in which the recoveries were not large or injunctive relief was at issue, the general practice has been for courts to use the lodestar method (including a multiplier) to calculate fees.[1093]

Finally, as the Court described in *Boeing Co. v. Van Gemert*, "a litigant or a lawyer who recovers a common fund for the benefit of persons other than himself or his client is entitled to a reasonable attorney's fee from the fund as a whole."[1094] This common-fund

---

under Rule 23(h) that adopted the percentage-of-the-fund approach because Oklahoma state courts used the lodestar approach).

[1091] *See Wal-Mart*, 396 F.3d at 121 (internal quotation marks, bracketing, and citations omitted).

[1092] For a proof of this proposition, see Kevin M. Clermont & John D. Currivan, *Improving on the Contingency Fee*, 63 CORNELL L. REV. 529 (1978). The authors created this fee structure for individual litigation, but recognized its applicability to class actions. For tweaks to the proposal to better align the incentives of class and counsel, see Jay Tidmarsh, Cy Pres *and the Optimal Class Action*, 82 GEO. WASH. L. REV. 767 (2014).

[1093] *See* Blum v. Stenson, 465 U.S. 886 (1984) (holding that " 'reasonable fees' under § 1988 are to be calculated according to the prevailing market rates in the relevant community"; further recognizing that an upward or downward adjustment of the fee is permissible when an hourly-rate method "results in a fee that is either unreasonable low or unreasonably high"); Hensley v. Eckerhart, 461 U.S. 424 (1983) ("The most useful starting point for determining the amount of a reasonable fee is the number of hours reasonably expended on the litigation multiplied by a reasonable hourly rate.").

[1094] *See* Boeing Co. v. Van Gemert, 444 U.S. 472 (1980).

doctrine, which "is designed to prevent freeloading" by litigants who benefit from a lawyer's work,[1095] originated in equity as an exception to the American rule. The source of a court's power to award fees was said to be its jurisdiction over the fund that the lawyer's work created.

Traditionally, the common-fund doctrine applied only when the beneficiaries of the lawyer's work were few in number and easily identified, when the benefits could be traced with accuracy, and when the cost could be shifted with some exactitude.[1096] In *Van Gemert*, the Court held that these criteria applied to class actions, thus paving the way for judicial oversight of the fees of class counsel in the days before the adoption of Rule 23(h). Although it is most often applied in that context, the common-fund doctrine has also been applied to cases outside of class actions, including insurance-subrogation litigation, bankruptcy or receivership proceedings, stockholder derivative actions, and a few others.[1097] The scope of the doctrine varies from state to state. As with other areas, judges calculate the proper attorney's fee either through an hourly-rate or a percentage-of-the-fund method.

Beyond these three circumstances, however, judges have not traditionally enjoyed much power to regulate or set attorney's fees. This hands-off approach has come under increasing attack in aggregate litigation. Without judicial control over fees, the concern that aggregate litigation will be run principally for the benefit of plaintiffs' lawyers increases—especially because, as we have seen, aggregate litigation does not have the checks on attorney behavior, such as an adequate-representation requirement or judicial approval of settlements, that class actions enjoy. On the other hand, the source of a judge's authority to control fees is uncertain, and there is also the fear that policing fees in aggregate litigation will be the camel's nose that leads to judicial regulation of every fee agreement in every lawsuit.

Despite these concerns, judges in some multidistrict litigation have begun to regulate the fees of the MDL's steering committee or lead counsel. The tool they have used to do so is the common-fund doctrine: the work of the MDL counsel creates a defined benefit for an identifiable group, and the means for calculating the lawyers' fees with some exactitude (hourly rates or a percentage of the fund)

[1095] *See* U.S. Airways, Inc. v. McCutchen, 569 U.S. 88 (2013).

[1096] *See* Alyeska Pipeline Serv. Co. v. Wilderness Soc'y, 421 U.S. 240 (1975).

[1097] *See* Morris B. Chapman & Assoc., Ltd. v. Kizman, 739 N.E.2d 1263 (Ill. 2000) (ordering the payment of fees to an attorney who prosecuted a wrongful-death action that benefited the decedent's heirs).

exist.[1098] Although MDLs are not class actions, the analogy to class actions is evident.

When an MDL case settles in the MDL forum, the settlement fund lies within the control of the MDL judge, and the analogy to a class action is clear. But when cases are remanded to their transferor fora and plaintiffs settle or prevail at trial thereafter, the source of the judge's power to require that the MDL plaintiffs' original lawyers, who have picked up the case again, contribute a portion of their fee is trickier. MDL judges have relied on the common-fund doctrine, on principles of equity and ethics, on contract and restitution law, and on their inherent case-management authority to justify orders that original counsel pay MDL counsel a share of any proceeds ultimately obtained.

Increasingly, judges require fee-transfer agreements, in which the original lawyers agree at the outset of an MDL proceeding to pay an assessment set by the court (usually 2% to 6% of the amounts ultimately recovered) into an interest-bearing fund to compensate and reimburse MDL counsel. The agreement is often enforced through a pretrial order obligating the defendants to withhold the assessed amount from any settlement or judgment and to pay this amount into the fund. These fee-transfer agreements can even reach into state-court litigation, for the pretrial order often forbids any lawyer who refuses to contribute to the fund to use any work product generated in the MDL.

Fee-transfer agreements have created problems. When a case settles during the MDL process, the MDL lawyers sometimes seek to increase the fees set forth in the original agreement and require plaintiffs to waive any objections if they wish to participate in the settlement. The defendant is perfectly happy to withhold a higher percentage: doing so does not require the defendant to pay any more, and it gives defendants some control over the fees MDL counsel earn. By agreeing to pay MDL counsel more handsomely, defendants also "buy" the acquiescence of MDL counsel to the settlement, and they can trade the prospect of higher fees to obtain more favorable terms on other matters. In short, this system creates a serious risk of collusion and conflict of interest.[1099]

Regulating the fee that the MDL counsel receives is only a part of the issue. Any amounts that the MDL counsel earns comes out of

---

[1098] For a discussion of some of the high-profile cases in which MDL judges have employed the common-fund approach to create a pool of money to compensate MDL counsel, see Elizabeth Chamblee Burch, *Judging Multidistrict Litigation*, 90 N.Y.U. L. REV. 71 (2015).

[1099] *See* Charles Silver & Geoffrey P. Miller, *The Quasi-Class Action Method of Managing Multi-District Litigations: Problems and a Proposal*, 63 VAND L. REV. 107 (2010).

the fee that the original lawyer agreed to charge the client in the retainer agreement. Nothing prohibits the original lawyer from taking the remainder of the attorney's fee. Suppose that a lawyer enters into a contingency arrangement with a client for a one-third fee. The case is sent to an MDL proceeding, where lead counsel engineers a settlement that will pay the client $300,000. The settlement requires that ten percent ($30,000) be given to the lead MDL counsel. The client's original lawyer can still charge the client $70,000 (the original one-third fee of $100,000 less the $30,000 paid to MDL lead counsel), even though the lawyer may have done little work to resolve the case.[1100]

Some courts have responded to this issue by capping the contingent fees that the originally retained lawyers can earn from an MDL case.[1101] The usual basis for doing so is the "quasi-class action" nature of the MDL proceeding, coupled with the common-fund rationale applied to class actions.[1102] Other sources of power, such as ethical rules, the court's inherent authority, and the need to protect the interests of impaired victims, are also sometimes cited. Critics point out that privately retained counsel often do important work, such as collecting cases and funneling them into the MDL, addressing client questions while the MDL is ongoing, and helping clients navigate the claims-administration process when the MDL proceeding results in a settlement. Limiting the fees of the original counsel also discourages lawyers from filing these claims and disregards the autonomy of lawyers and clients to reach their own arrangements regarding fees.[1103]

This debate provides one final window into a critical but unresolved issues in complex litigation: the nature of the MDL process. On the one hand, if we view the MDL process as a "quasi-class action," it makes sense to import the protections that class actions have established for class members, including adequate representation, settlement approval, and control of attorney's fees. On the other hand, if the MDL is an amalgam of individual lawsuits

---

[1100] Other methods have also been employed to determine the amount of the original lawyer's residual fee. We choose this method for simplicity of exposition.

[1101] *See, e.g.*, *In re* Zyprexa Prods. Liab. Litig., 424 F. Supp. 2d 488 (E.D.N.Y. 2006) (limiting the maximum fee chargeable by privately retained lawyers to thirty-five percent, although giving a special master authority to adjust that amount slightly upward or downward).

[1102] *See id.*; *In re* Vioxx Prods. Liab. Litig., 650 F. Supp. 2d 549 (E.D. La. 2009) (noting that court supervision of the conflict between the original and MDL counsel, both of whom wish to maximize their fee, is necessary).

[1103] *See* Burch, *supra* note 1099, at 109–16; *see also* Morris A. Ratner, *Achieving Procedural Goals Through Indirection: The Use of Ethics Doctrine to Justify Contingency Fee Caps in MDL Aggregate Settlements*, 26 GEO. J. LEGAL ETHICS 59 (2013) (questioning the use of ethical rules to justify caps on attorney's fees in MDL cases).

joined together only for convenience, it makes sense to rely on the protections against collusion and excessive agency costs that clients enjoy in individual litigation: client monitoring, informed consent, and the lawyer's ethical obligations. The two visions of the multidistrict-litigation process, which competes with the class action as the most effective aggregation device available in the present American litigation landscape, have run side by side throughout this book. It is little surprise that the tension remains as we examine the important end-of-litigation issue of attorney's fees.

More generally, the issue of attorney's fees represents one of the fulcrum points in complex litigation. If there were no money to be made in complex litigation—for lawyers on both sides—there would be no complex litigation. Money, in the form of attorney's fees, creates problems, such as the ever-present risk of collusion and other agency costs, which haunt the field. Money, in the form of attorney's fees, also provides an opportunity to shape behavior and to establish a better system for handling complex disputes that reach court. But that opportunity also requires handing over to judges more power to regulate the relationship between attorney and client, as well as faith that judges can discern the optimal structures for resolving mass disputes.

EPILOGUE

At the start of this book we posed a question: what exactly is complex litigation? We suggested then that the best way to think about an answer to the question was to see the ways in which doctrines, ideas, policies, statutes, and constitutional provisions interacted over the course of complex cases, and then to find common threads or themes among them.

At this point, you could probably supply a pretty good working definition of complex litigation: cases in which the ordinary rules of procedural and remedial law do not work well. You also now know why they do not work well. Modern American procedure is built on a welter of foundational assumptions that cannot all be fully realized. The adversarial system, with its many incentives for strategic behavior by both litigants and lawyers, is not designed to achieve socially optimal levels of aggregation, to ensure socially optimal disclosure of information or definition of issues, or to establish a workable trial format for vast numbers of parties, claims, and evidence. Processes that might do so can create outcome-affecting inequities among cases. Other foundational concerns, such as individual autonomy, efficiency, equality of opportunity, and limited government (especially limited judicial power), cannot all peacefully co-exist.

There is no lexical ordering of these foundational principles; all are incommensurable goods. Over the range of the many doctrines we have explored, each of these ideas has had its day in the sun. Sometimes one principle seems to win out, sometimes another, and sometimes a compromise emerges. The field is ever evolving and endlessly inventive. But there are also strong pressures to keep litigation in traditional channels. The field is pulled in so many different directions that some rather hard-hearted pragmatism seems to be the only way to make sense of it all—in which case there really is no definition of "complex litigation" at all.

We believe, however, that a functional characterization of complex litigation is possible. Our understanding of complex litigation begins with the adversarial system—a system that we will not defend here as better than any other method for organizing proofs and arguments. It is, however, the system that we have received through tradition. Like any adjudicatory system, the adversarial system assigns to various players in the litigation enterprise—lawyer, judge, jury, and party—certain roles and responsibilities. Lawyers have the primary responsibility for structuring the case, developing the issues and evidence, and presenting the proofs and arguments at trial. The judge is passive and detached from these tasks, partly in order to maintain neutrality and partly in order to assure the individual autonomy and limited governmental authority implicit in an adversarial system. The judge's role is only to rule on disputes brought before the court, to determine the law applicable to the dispute, and in some cases to determine the facts as well. Juries are also passive and neutral, resolving factual disputes by using the evidence that the lawyers provide them. The parties decide whether to litigate, choose their lawyers, supply information during pretrial and trial, and implement the declared remedy.

A theme unifying the doctrines we have examined is the breakdown in these adversarial roles due to the realities of large-scale disputes. The breakdown can occur in any aspect of litigation—from structuring the case to pretrial to trial to remedies—and can affect the roles of multiple players involved in that aspect of the case. Sometimes the breakdown results from the structural, procedural, or remedial limits of our adjudicatory system; sometimes it results from strategic, non-optimal behavior by lawyers or parties.

A second theme unifying the doctrines we have examined is non-traditional nature of the response to the breakdown: judges assert greater powers than traditional adversarial theory allows. The source of the judge's authority to do so has been a constant and nagging question throughout this book. Sometimes a clear grant of authority exists, as with some of the case-management powers that Federal Rule of Civil Procedure 16 describes. Sometimes a judge relies on a source of authority of ambiguous and uncertain scope, such as the All Writs Act. Often the judge invokes the court's "inherent authority" to engage in a practice that no statute or rule authorizes. Whatever the exact source of authority and whatever the exact nature of the judicial response—and these vary with the nature of the breakdown—the judge is not the passive, neutral, umpireal judge of old.

Judges are not, however, all-powerful. Constitutional, statutory, code-based, common-law, institutional, and practical boundaries constrain them. When these constraints hold sway, the breakdowns that massive disputes cause may be unfixable. When we ease traditional constraints, though, other intractable problems arise. Procedure affects outcome. The exceptional uses of judicial power in complex litigation affects the outcomes of those cases in relation to cases in which judges employ different powers or do not exercise these powers at all.

For some, our system is ultimately better off by respecting traditional judicial boundaries, even if the cost of that adherence is the inability to resolve complex disputes. For others, empowering judges to resolve large social disputes in a tailored and effective manner is worthwhile, even if the cost of judicial creativity is the inequity that arises because different procedures create different outcomes for different groups of litigants.

We can summarize these concerns in the following definition. Complex litigation involves those cases in which (1) the rules, doctrines, or circumstances make it impossible for the relevant player to perform a task that our adversarial process has assigned to the player in a manner that assures the rational, fair, and efficient adjudication of the entire dispute, (2) rational, fair, and efficient adjudication can be attained with the curative application of a judicial power that is inconsistent with traditional limits on judicial behavior; and (3) if it is applied, this non-traditional judicial power results in the use of different, potentially outcome-determinative procedures or rules for similarly situated cases.

This definition contains no happy ending. When constitutional, statutory, or other constraints prevent judges from using greater power, the adversarial system must slog along with no guarantee that rational, fair, and efficient adjudication will occur for all persons involved in the dispute. When greater power is permissible and is applied, differential outcomes among like cases gnaw at our sense of fairness and equity. Nor would a shift to some other procedural system solve the problem, for every system contains parameters that, in some subset of cases, make it impossible for the players to perform the tasks necessary to achieve rational, fair, and efficient adjudication for all.

This is the story of complex litigation. Lawyers, judges, and parties strive for justice, but they cannot perfectly attain it.

TABLE OF CASES

INDEX

References are to Pages